T0295446

GMAT® FOCUS
PREMIUM PREP

The Staff of The Princeton Review

PrincetonReview.com

Penguin
Random
House

The Princeton Review
110 East 42nd St, 7th Floor
New York, NY 10017

Published in the United States by Penguin Random House, LLC, New York.

ISBN: 978-0-593-51780-2
eBook: 978-0-593-51781-9
ISSN: 2997-285X

Editor: Patricia Murphy
Production Artist: Jason Ullmeyer
Production Editor: Kathy Carter and Heidi Torres

Printed in the United States of America.

10 9 8 7 6 5 4 3 2 1

The Princeton Review Publishing Team
Rob Franek, Editor-in-Chief
David Soto, Senior Director, Data Operations
Stephen Koch, Senior Manager, Data Operations
Deborah Weber, Director of Production
Jason Ullmeyer, Production Design Manager
Jennifer Chapman, Senior Production Artist
Selena Coppock, Director of Editorial
Orion McBean, Senior Editor
Aaron Riccio, Senior Editor
Meave Shelton, Senior Editor
Chris Chimera, Editor
Patricia Murphy, Editor
Laura Rose, Editor
Isabelle Appleton, Editorial Assistant

Penguin Random House Publishing Team
Tom Russell, VP, Publisher
Alison Stoltzfus, Senior Director, Publishing
Emily Hoffman, Associate Managing Editor
Patty Collins, Executive Director of Production
Mary Ellen Owens, Assistant Director of Production
Alice Rahaeuser, Associate Production Manager
Maggie Gibson, Associate Production Manager
Suzanne Lee, Senior Designer
Eugenia Lo, Publishing Assistant

For customer service, please contact **editorialsupport@review.com**, and be sure to include:

- full title of the book

- ISBN

- page number

Acknowledgments

Our GMAT course is much more than clever techniques and powerful computer score reports; the reason our results are great is that our teachers care so much about their students. Thanks to all the teachers who have made the GMAT course so successful, but in particular the core group of teachers and development people who helped get it off the ground: Alicia Ernst, Tom Meltzer, Paul Foglino, John Sheehan, Mark Sawula, Nell Goddin, Teresa Connelly, Phillip Yee, Kimberly Beth Hollingsworth, Bobby Hood, Chris Chimera, Chris Hinkle, Peter Hanink, Cathy Evins, and Doug Scripture.

Special thanks to John Fulmer and Kyle Fox for their valuable contributions to GMAT Focus Premium Prep.

Special thanks to Adam Robinson, who conceived of and perfected the Joe Bloggs approach to standardized tests and many of the other successful techniques used by The Princeton Review.

We are also, as always, very appreciative of the time and attention given to each page by Emma Parker, Heidi Torres, and Jason Ullmeyer.

Contents

Get More (Free) Content
at **PrincetonReview.com/prep**

As easy as 1·2·3

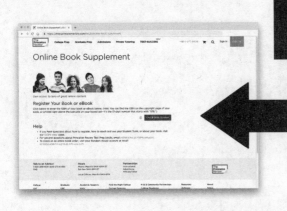

1 Go to PrincetonReview.com/prep or scan the **QR code** and enter the following ISBN to register your book: **9780593517802**

2 Answer a few simple questions to set up an exclusive Princeton Review account. *(If you already have one, you can just log in.)*

3 Enjoy access to your **FREE** content!

Once you've registered, you can...

- Take 3 full-length practice GMAT Focus exams

- Access the GMAT Focus Question Bank

- Get our take on any recent updates to the GMAT

- Research admission rates and average test scores for dozens of popular business schools

- Access our guide to financial aid, admissions, writing winning application essays, MBA job prospects, and more

- Check to see if there have been any corrections or updates to this edition

Need to report a potential **content** issue?

Contact **EditorialSupport@review.com** and include:

- full title of the book
- ISBN
- page number

Need to report a **technical** issue?

Contact **TPRStudentTech@review.com** and provide:

- your full name
- email address used to register the book
- full book title and ISBN
- Operating system (Mac/PC) and browser (Chrome, Firefox, Safari, etc.)

Look For These Icons Throughout The Book

 PREMIUM PORTAL

 ONLINE VIDEO TUTORIALS

 ONLINE ARTICLES

 ONLINE PRACTICE DRILLS

 ONLINE PRACTICE TESTS

 PROVEN TECHNIQUES

 APPLIED STRATEGIES

 TIME-SAVING TIP

 OTHER REFERENCES

 WATCH OUT

Dear Test-Taker,

There is a lot of content that could be tested on GMAT Focus.

Virtually all that content is covered in this book.

Therefore, this book is very long.

We set out to create a book with a simple goal in mind: we want you to achieve the GMAT score of your dreams. We've loaded this book with enough practice questions, tests, and discussion about the GMAT that nothing you see on test day is going to be a surprise to you. Before you even see a single question, you are going to be provided with information and details to give you confidence that the GMAT is the right test for you to take to help achieve your career goals.

Over the years, The Princeton Review has learned a lot of important lessons about preparing to take standardized tests. Many of those lessons that pertain to the GMAT are in the pages of this book.

But we've also learned a lot of lessons about students such as yourself. And central to those lessons is that no two students follow the same path to success. Some of you are going to thoroughly comb through every page, take every practice test, send questions to our editorial team, and think about nearly nothing else until test day. If this sounds like you, then you're going to love this book. You might even give it a permanent spot on your mantle.

Others of you want a book that helps you triage how to spend your time. You have only so many hours a day or week to devote to your studies. You're going to see a book this big, that feels this heavy, and know you are unlikely to see every page and work through every question. If this sounds like you, then we have good news. You are also going to love this book. The opening diagnostic test is going to give you a good sense of where you are with each question type. The closing diagnostic test is going to let you know just how far you've come and what you still may need to brush up on to maximize your score.

In short, we created a book that you can use to maximize your time in order to maximize your score. We think you'll love it. But don't take our word for it. See for yourself.

Happy studying,

The Princeton Review

Part I
Orientation

Chapter 1
Introduction

Congratulations on your decision to attend business school, and welcome to *GMAT Focus, Premium Prep*! Preparing for the GMAT is an important part of the process, so let's get started. This chapter will provide you with a strategic plan for acing the GMAT Focus, as well as an overview of the test itself, including question formats and information on how the test is scored.

WHAT TO EXPECT FROM THIS BOOK: A STRATEGIC PLAN FOR ACING THE NEW GMAT

The Graduate Management Admission Test (GMAT) is changing. Technically, we should probably say the GMAT is changing *again*. In fact, by the time you read this sentence, it's possible the GMAT will have already changed. After introducing the Integrated Reasoning section in 2012, the Graduate Management Admission Council (GMAC) has decided to make further adjustments to the test by rolling out the GMAT Focus Edition. The updates to the GMAT are another shift in the long history of tweaks the GMAC has rolled out over the years, all done ostensibly to better parrot the skills required to succeed in modern industry.

Alas, we'll (mercifully) spare you any further history lessons. After all, you came here to learn about how to succeed at the new GMAT, not to trace the steps of how we got here. So, let's get cracking.

WHAT YOU WILL LEARN IN THIS BOOK

1. Learn the Famed Princeton Review Test-Taking Strategies

In the next few chapters, you'll find the strategies that have given our GMAT students the edge for more than 20 years.

2. Learn the Specific Skills You'll Need

Our courses include an extremely thorough review of the skills our students need to ace the GMAT, and this book will give you that same review.

3. Periodically Take Simulated GMATs to Measure Your Progress

As you work through the book, you'll want to take our online practice tests to see how you're doing. Our practice tests can be found at PrincetonReview.com. In addition, we actively encourage students to use the *GMAT Official Guide 2023–2024,* which is published by the GMAC. It contains actual test questions from previous administrations of the GMAT. You should also take at least one of the real practice tests available through the GMAT website, www.mba.com.

4. Hone Your Skills

Using the detailed score reports from your practice exams and the diagnostic tests, you'll be able to zero in on problem areas and quickly achieve proficiency through additional practice. And as your score rises on the adaptive sections, this book is ready with more difficult question bins to keep you on track for the score you need.

5. Keep Track of the Application Process

Throughout the book, you will find informative sidebars explaining how and when to register for the test, how and when to apply to business school, the advantages and disadvantages of applying early, and much more. Plus, at PrincetonReview.com, you'll be able to take advantage of our powerful web-based tools to match yourself with schools that meet your needs and preferences.

WHAT IS THE GRADUATE MANAGEMENT ADMISSION TEST?

The Graduate Management Admission Test (GMAT) is a standardized test that business schools use as a tool to help decide whom they are going to accept into their MBA programs.

Where Does the GMAT Come From?

The GMAT is published and administered by the GMAC, a private company. We'll tell you more about them later on in this book.

What Does the Test Look Like?

The GMAT is offered on computer only at approved testing centers or by online appointment for those who wish to take the GMAT in a familiar environment, such as at home. The test contains three 45-minute sections that present multiple-choice questions.

> 1. A 21-question Quantitative Reasoning section that focuses on problem solving style math questions in algebra and arithmetic
> 2. A 23-question Verbal section that focuses on Reading Comprehension and Critical Reasoning questions
> 3. A 20-question Data Insights section that focuses on Data Sufficiency and Integrated Reasoning style questions—two question types found only on the GMAT

On average, this would give you right around two minutes for each question in each section. You must answer a question in order to get to the next question—which means that you can't skip a question and come back to it. And while you are not required to finish any of the sections, your score will be adjusted downward to reflect questions you do not complete.

On each section, approximately one-quarter of the questions you encounter will be experimental and will not count toward your score. These questions, which will be mixed in among the regular questions, are there so the test company can try out new questions for future tests. We'll have much more to say about the experimental questions later.

There is also a 10-minute optional break period that can be taken after the first or second section. If you take the break after the first section, then you will not have the option to take a break after the second section.

But Wait, There's More

One of the first options you'll encounter when taking the GMAT is the option to choose from one of six possible orders for the exam sections. You pick your preferred section order on the day of the test.

Here are the possible section orders:

You do not need to choose up front after which section you take your break. You'll be presented with the option as soon as the first section ends, no matter which section you choose.

Order #1	Order #2	Order #3
Quantitative Reasoning	Verbal Reasoning	Data Insights
Verbal Reasoning	Data Insights	Verbal Reasoning
Data Insights	Quantitative Reasoning	Quantitative Reasoning
Order #4	**Order #5**	**Order #6**
Quantitative Reasoning	Verbal Reasoning	Data Insights
Data Insights	Quantitative Reasoning	Quantitative Reasoning
Verbal Reasoning	Data Insights	Verbal Reasoning

How Do You Know What Order to Pick?

The answer to that depends on your goals for the test and your level of comfort with the different sections. Are you looking to get a high Quantitative score, but you don't care so much about the Verbal? Has your school told you they never consider the Verbal Reasoning section? Are you good at Data Insights but not so good at Quantitative?

The answers to these questions and other questions like them help to inform your section order choice.

What Information Is Tested on the GMAT?

You'll find several different types of multiple-choice questions on the GMAT.

Quantitative Reasoning (21 questions total)
- Algebra and arithmetic questions in a roughly 50%-50% split

Verbal Reasoning (23 questions total)
- Reading Comprehension (tests your ability to answer questions about a passage)—10–14 questions
- Critical Reasoning (a logic-based question type recycled from the LSAT)—approximately 9–13 questions

Data Insights (20 questions total)
- Data Sufficiency (a strange type of problem that exists on no other test in the world)—approximately 5–7 questions
- Integrated Reasoning (tests your ability to read and interpret charts, graphs, and data in 4 different question formats)—13–15 questions
   o Table Analysis—data is presented in a sortable table (like an Excel spreadsheet); each question usually has three parts.
   o Graphics Interpretation—a chart or graph is used to display data; each question usually has two parts; answers are selected from drop-down boxes.
   o Multi-Source Reasoning—information (a combination of charts, text, and tables) is presented on two or three tabs; each set of tabbed information is usually accompanied by three questions.
   o Two-Part Analysis—each question usually has five or six options of which you need to pick two.

A Note on Integrated Reasoning Style Questions

The official GMAT doctrine no longer officially refers to Integrated Reasoning (IR) questions. Instead, this specific question type is lumped in under the Data Insights section and given no particular name at all. However, there are specific approaches and strategies for working with this type of question. For the sake of clarity, we will continue to refer to Integrated Reasoning questions throughout this book to describe Graphics Interpretation, Two-Part Analysis, Table Analysis, and Multi-Source Reasoning questions in the aggregate.

How Is the GMAT Scored?

As soon as you are finished taking the GMAT, the computer will calculate and display your unofficial results. Each section will receive an individual score between 60 and 90 points in 1-point increments, as well as a percentile rank for that section. These section scores will all contribute equally to calculate your total score between 205 and 805 in 10-point increments, as well as your overall percentile rank.

Scores on the individual sections of the GMAT are based on three factors: the number of questions you answer, whether you answered the question correctly, and the parameters of the question (such as difficulty). Your score improves if you answer more questions, answer them correctly, and answer them at a higher level of difficulty.

The percentile ranking for each section is there to give you a sense of how you performed compared to other test-takers. For example, if you see a percentile of 72 next to your Data Insights score, it means that 72 percent of the people who took this test scored lower than you did on the Data Insights section.

Here are the average scores for the total and each of the sections, according to GMAC.

Section	Average Score	Standard Deviation
Total	546.01	89.08
Quantitative	77.71	6.42
Verbal	78.99	4.5
Data Insights	74.41	6.14

WHAT IS THE PRINCETON REVIEW?

The Princeton Review is a test-preparation company founded in New York City. It has branches in more than 50 cities across the country, as well as abroad. The Princeton Review's techniques are unique and powerful, and they were developed after a study of thousands of real GMAT questions. They work because they are based on the same principles that are used in writing the actual test. The Princeton Review's techniques for beating the GMAT will help you improve your scores by teaching you to:

- think like the test-writers
- take full advantage of the computer-adaptive algorithms upon which the GMAT is based
- find the answers to questions you don't understand by using Process of Elimination
- avoid the traps that test-writers have set for you (and use those traps to your advantage)

How Closely Does The Princeton Review Monitor the GMAT?

Very closely. We regularly publish a new edition of this book to reflect the subtle shifts that happen over time or any major changes to the GMAT. For the latest information on the GMAT, please visit our website PrincetonReview.com.

Is This Book Just like The Princeton Review Course?

No. You won't have the benefit of taking 10 computer-adaptive GMATs that are scored and analyzed by our computers. You won't get to sit in small classes with a small group of other highly motivated students who will spur you on. You won't get to work with our expert instructors who can assess your strengths and pinpoint your weaknesses. There is no way to put these things into a book.

What you will find in this book are some of the techniques and methods that have enabled our students to crack the system—plus a review of the essentials that you cannot afford not to know and some customized study guides to help you allocate your time to the highest priority areas.

Two Warnings

Many of our techniques for beating the GMAT may be very different from the way that you would naturally approach problems. Some methods may even seem counterintuitive. Rest assured, however, that many test-takers have used our methods to get great GMAT scores. To get the full benefit of our techniques, you must trust them. The only way to develop this trust is to practice the techniques and persuade yourself that they work.

Integrated Reasoning style questions are unlike Problem Solving and Data Sufficiency questions in that they can involve interaction with the content on your screen. For example, for many question types the answer choices are in drop-down menus, there are tables that you may want to sort, or a question may include multiple tabs that contain information you'll need to solve the problem. Needless to say, re-creating this type of interactivity is beyond the capabilities of a book. We'll outline how the content in this book differs from the test for Integrated Reasoning questions when we get to that discussion. For now, just recognize Integrated Reasoning can be a challenging question type to put in book format.

Practice with Real Questions

One reason coaching books do not use real GMAT questions is that GMAC won't let them. So far, the council has refused to let anyone (including us) license actual questions from old tests. As we mentioned above, the council has its own review book, *GMAT Official Guide 2023–2024*, which we heartily recommend that you purchase. GMAC also puts out preparation materials called GMAT Focus Official Starter Kit, which can be downloaded for free from www.mba.com. This kit includes two computer-adaptive tests plus additional practice sets, all of which feature real GMAT questions. By practicing our techniques on real GMAT items, you will be able to prove to yourself that the techniques work and increase your confidence when you actually take the test.

Additional Resources

In addition to the material in this book, we offer a number of other resources to aid you during your GMAT preparation.

Register your book at PrincetonReview.com to gain access to your Student Tools, the companion website to this book. There you will find:

- 3 GMAT Focus exams
- Our GMAT Focus Online Drills
- Business School Resources

Premium Student Tools
To gain access, follow the instructions on page viii.

Summary

o   By using a combination of The Princeton Review's study materials and published content directly from GMAC, you will be able to improve your score on the GMAT.

o   The test itself is taken on a computer. It consists of the following:

Section	Question Types	Time	Number of Questions	Score
Quantitative Reasoning	• Problem Solving	45 minutes	21 Questions	60-90
Verbal Reasoning	• Reading Comprehension • Critical Reasoning		23 Questions	
Data Insights	• Integrated Reasoning • Data Sufficiency		20 Questions	
Overall Score: 205–805				

Chapter 2
Taking the GMAT: What to Expect

This chapter will outline what to expect on and leading up to test day, the basics of the GMAT's layout, and how the computer-adaptive scoring algorithm works.

REGISTERING TO TAKE THE GMAT

To register for the GMAT, visit the website at www.mba.com.

The easiest way to register for the exam is online. You can register to take the GMAT Exam Delivered at a Test Center or the GMAT Exam Delivered Online, which can be taken at a private location, like your home. Both options allow you to schedule the time of the exam, so choose a timeslot that works best with your personal preferences.

Stay updated on the latest test changes through your Student Tools or by checking the GMAT website.

The registration fee varies depending on your location and how the test is delivered. In the United States, the fee to take the GMAT Exam Delivered at a Test Center is $275 and $300 to take the GMAT Exam Delivered Online. Those who schedule an exam in certain countries will incur taxes. Tax rate information is available at www.mba.com in the GMAT registration section. Note that checks or money orders payable in U.S. dollars must be drawn from banks located in the United States or Canada.

PRACTICING TO TAKE THE GMAT

As you prepare for the GMAT, it's important to know—in advance—what the experience of taking the test is like so that you can mimic those conditions during practice tests. When you are taking a practice test, turn off your telephone, and strictly observe all time limits and restrictions. To mimic the experience of working with scratch work resources, buy a spiral notebook filled with grid paper or a whiteboard that meets the permitted dimensions. If you know what time you will be taking the real GMAT, try to schedule your practice tests around the same time of day.

A Week Before GMAT
If you registered to take the GMAT Exam at home, make sure your personal computer meets the system requirements. More information is available at www.mba.com.

If you are the sort of person who likes to have a mental picture of what a new experience will be like, you might even consider visiting the test center ahead of time. This serves two purposes: first, you'll know how to get there on the day of the test, and second, you'll be familiar with the ambiance in advance.

The Days Before the Test

Try to keep to your regular routine. Staying up late to study the last few nights before the test is counterproductive. It's important to get regular amounts of exercise and sleep. Continue the study plan you've been on from the beginning, but taper off toward the end. You'll want to take your last practice exam no later than several days before the real test, so that you'll have time to go over the results carefully. The last day or so should be devoted to any topics that still give you trouble.

The Night Before the Test

If you are taking the GMAT at a testing center, now is the time to get together the things you will need to take with you for the test: a government-issued ID card, directions to the test center (if you haven't already been there), a mental list of the five schools you wish to receive your test scores (if you can't identify these when you take the test, you will have to pay an additional fee per school to get scores sent out later). Don't bother to take a calculator—no outside calculators are permitted on the GMAT. An onscreen calculator is provided for the Integrated Reasoning questions in the Data Insights section.

What to Take to the Test Center
1. A government-issued ID
2. A snack
3. A bottle of water

If you are taking the GMAT at home, prepare your testing space. Get together the items you will need with you for the exam: a government-issued ID card and your physical whiteboard (if you are planning to use one). Remove all prohibited items from the testing area. Use the GMAT Exam Online Pretest Checklist on www.mba.com to ensure you have taken all the required steps to prepare for the exam.

Once you have gathered everything you need, take the night off. Relax. There is no point in last-minute cramming. You are as ready as you are going to be.

Do Not Take Food or Drinks

As of 2023, individuals are no longer permitted to take food or drinks into the testing center and leave them in a locker to eat during a break.

The official GMAT language states these items are not allowed "unless expressly pre-authorized as an accommodation."

The Day of the Test

If you are taking the test in the morning, get up early enough so that you have time to eat breakfast, if that is your usual routine, and do a couple of GMAT questions you've already seen in order to get your mind working. If you are taking the test in the afternoon, make sure you get some lunch, and, again, do a few GMAT problems. You don't want to have to warm up on the test itself.

AT THE TESTING CENTER

You'll be asked to present your government-issued ID, and an employee will take your photograph and scan your palm using a palm vein scanner. Finally, you'll be led to the computer station where you will take the test. The station consists of a desk with a computer monitor, a keyboard, a mouse, the equivalent of five erasable noteboards, and a noteboard pen. The marker they will give you to write in your scratch booklet has a tendency to dry up when left uncapped—so during breaks, remember to cap it. If you need another marker or another scratch booklet during the test, simply raise your hand, and a proctor will bring it. However, the timer won't stop while the proctor brings you another scratch booklet or marker. Therefore, use your practice tests to learn to fit your scratch work into one scratch booklet. Before the test starts, make sure you're comfortable. Is there enough light? Is your desk sturdy? Don't be afraid to speak up if something is off or uncomfortable.

There will almost certainly be other people in the same room at other computer stations taking other computer-adaptive tests. You might be seated next to someone taking the licensing exam for architects, or a test for school nurses, or even a test for golf pros.

None of the people in the room will have necessarily started at the same time. The testing center employee will show you how to begin the test, but the computer itself will be your proctor from then on. It will tell you how much time you have left in a section, when your time is up, and when to go on to the next section.

The test center employees will be available if you have a question. They will also monitor the room for security purposes. Just in case their eagle eyes aren't enough, video and audio systems will record everything that happens in the room.

The process sounds less human than it really is. Our students have generally found the test center employees to be quite nice.

What Does the GMAT Measure?

The GMAT is not a test of how smart you are. Nor is it a test of your business acumen or even a predictor of your grades in business school. It's simply a test of how good you are at taking the GMAT. In fact, you will learn that by studying the very specific knowledge outlined in this book, you can substantially improve your score. The test-writers think in predictable ways. Because of this, you can improve your score by learning to think like them.

HOW THE COMPUTER ADAPTIVE GMAT SECTIONS WORK

To check out which b-schools are the "Toughest to Get Into," take a look at the Business School Ranking lists at PrincetonReview.com.

How Computer Adaptive Testing Works

To understand how to beat the GMAT, you have to understand how the test works.

Unlike paper-and-pencil standardized tests that begin with an easy question and then become progressively tougher, the GMAT typically begins by giving you a medium question. If you get it correct, the computer gives you a slightly harder question. If you get it wrong, the computer gives you a slightly easier question, and so on. The idea is that the computer will zero in on your exact level of ability very quickly, which allows you to answer fewer questions overall and allows the computer to make a more finely honed assessment of your abilities.

What You Will See on Your Screen

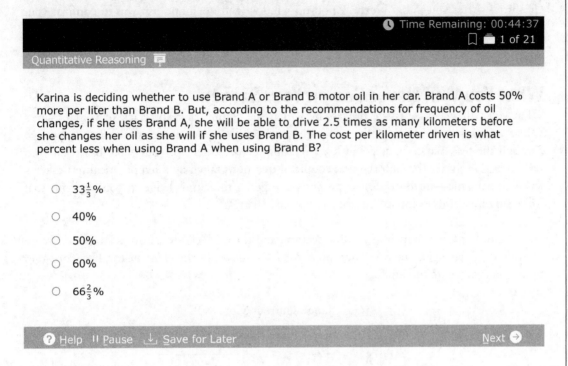

The problem you're working on at any particular moment will be near the top of the screen. Here are the main interface items you will see on the screen:

End Exam—By clicking on this button, you can end the test at any moment. We don't recommend that you do this unless you actually become ill. Even if you decide not to have your test scored (an option they will give you at the end of the exam), you might as well finish—it's great practice, and besides, GMAC has no intention of giving you a refund.

Time—The time you have left to complete the section is displayed in the upper right of the screen. You can hide the time by clicking on it, and you can make it reappear by clicking on the icon that appears in its place. During the last few minutes of the test, the time is automatically displayed and you cannot hide it.

Question Number—The number of the question that you are working on is also displayed in the upper right, and it works just like the time display: you can hide it by clicking on it or make it reappear by clicking on the icon. During the last few minutes of the test, the question number is automatically displayed and cannot be hidden.

Bookmark—Also in the upper right of the screen is a bookmark function. You can use this feature to mark questions for review and edit at the end of the section. We'll discuss this in more detail a little later on.

Help—During the test, this button provides test and section directions and information about using the software.

Next—When you've answered a question by clicking on the small bubble in front of the answer you think is correct, press this button.

Confirm—After you press "Next," a pop-up window will open and ask you to confirm your answer. Select "yes" to continue to the next question.

What You Will Never See on Your Screen

What you will *never* see is the process by which the computer keeps track of your progress. When you start each section, the computer assumes that your score is average. As you go through the test, the computer will keep revising its assessment of your score based on your responses. Let's walk through the first couple of questions taken by a hypothetical test-taker— let's call her Jane—to illustrate the point. We're going to acknowledge to you up front that we've simplified this example a bit for the sake of clarity.

Jane begins her Quantitative Reasoning section, and the GMAT test assumes an average score of around 77. Jane gets the first question correct. As shown in the chart below, her score goes up to somewhere around an 80.

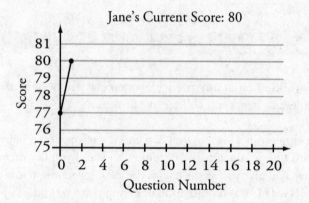

Because Jane got the first question correct, the computer selects a harder problem for her second question. Whoops! Jane makes a mistake and gets this question incorrect. As a result, her score goes down to a 78.

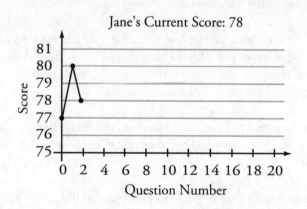

The computer now selects a slightly easier problem. Jane gets this question correct, and her score goes up to a 79.

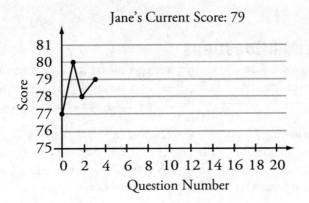

Now the computer starts to wonder if Jane got the second question wrong by mistake. But it's not going to credit Jane the benefit of the doubt. It's going to give her a slightly harder problem still, and Jane is going to have to prove it. Jane gets this question right, too, and now her score is back to an 80.

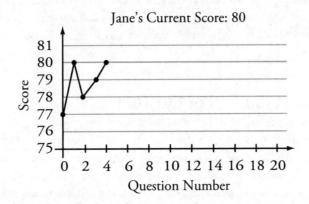

You get the idea. At the very beginning of the section, your score moves up or down in larger increments than it does at the end, when GMAC believes it is merely refining your score. The questions you will see on your test come from a huge pool of questions held in the computer in what the test-writers call "difficulty bins"—each bin with a different level of difficulty. The story of Jane's first four questions is a great example of one of the two factors that can affect your score: early questions count more than later questions. In fact, this is one of the foundational principles for cracking the GMAT that we'll discuss in a later chapter.

A World on Experimental Questions

The Experimental Questions

Roughly 3–4 of the questions in any section are experimental and won't count toward your score. The difficulty of an experimental question does not depend on your answer to the previous question. You could get a question correct and then immediately see a fairly easy experimental question.

So, if you feel you are getting a lot of questions correct and suddenly see a question that seems too easy, there are two possibilities: a) you are about to fall for a trap, or b) it's an experimental question and really is easy. That means it can be very difficult for you to judge how you are doing on the section. Your best strategy is to simply try your best on every question.

What Happens at the End of a Section

At the end of a section, test-takers can use any remaining time to interact with a review and edit screen. As you move through the section, you can bookmark any question you might like to revisit at the end of the section. On the review and edit screen, you can navigate back to any bookmarked or non-bookmarked question. You can change your answer to up to 3 questions per section.

What Happens at the End of the Test

When you finish your exam, you will be provided a Score Preview that contains four scores and percentile rankings: Quantitative Reasoning, Verbal Reasoning, Data Insights, and Total. The test will prompt you to decide if you'd like to accept your scores. You have two minutes to decide. If you say no, or you allow the two minutes to expire, the scores will be canceled, and you will not be able to send those scores to your prospective schools. If you were to take the exam again, your future official score reports would not show this test. You can reinstate previously canceled scores up to 4 years and 11 months after your exam date for a $50 fee. Before beginning your exam, you may have selected up to five schools to receive your official score report. Deciding you want the test to count will prompt the computer to provide your unofficial score report on the screen and send your official scores to the selected schools. Within 20 days, you will receive your official results online and can send them to other schools for free. If you decide to accept the scores but later decide you want to cancel them, you can do so within 72 hours for an additional fee.

What Happens If You Don't Get to Every Question in a Section?

If you run out of time without having answered all the questions in a section, the computer just moves you on to the next section. As we said earlier, the computer keeps an updated estimate of your score as you move through the section. If you don't get to answer some questions, the computer deducts points (based on an algorithm) and gives you a score based on the questions you *have* answered.

For questions that have multiple parts, you need to answer every part of the question before you move on to the next question.

If Something Weird Happens at the Test Center...

We have found that almost nothing ever goes wrong at the test centers. They are professionally run. But in the unlikely event that there is a technical glitch with your assigned computer, or if you want to complain about test center conditions or some other anomaly, it is best to start the process before you leave the test center by filing a complaint immediately after the test is over. If possible, get the test center staff to corroborate your complaint. Then, as soon as possible after the test is over, contact GMAT Customer Service by one of the following methods:

Contact Form: support.mba.com/hc/en-us/requests/new
Phone: 800-717-4628 or 408-636-0231

Summary

- Schedule your GMAT test online during a time that is convenient for you but that meets your schools' deadlines.

- To find out more about taking the GMAT Delivered Online, go to mba.com/exams/gmat-exam/plan-for-exam-day/taking-the-exam-delivered-online.

- In the days leading up to the test, make sure you are prepared for test day with all the necessary materials, paperwork, and technical requirements (if you are taking the test at home).

- The GMAT always starts you off with a medium question. If you get it correct, you get a harder question; if you get it wrong, you get an easier question. The test assigns you a score after each answer and quickly (in theory) hones in on your level of ability.

- There is a penalty for skipping questions, so make sure to get to every question in the test.

Chapter 3
Cracking
the GMAT:
Fundamental
Strategies for
Success

This chapter provides an introduction to three key axioms of maximizing your GMAT score: proper pacing, Process of Elimination, and recognizing trap answers.

KNOW THE THREE FUNDAMENTAL STRATEGIES

No matter what section or question type you are working on at any given moment, no matter what score you are hoping to achieve, there are three fundamental strategies that apply across all areas of the GMAT. Those three strategies are:

- Proper Pacing
- Process of Elimination
- Recognizing Trap Answers

PROPER PACING

Earlier in this book, we discussed two realities of the GMAT.

1. If you don't answer every question in a section, you are moved to the next section and receive a score based on the questions you *did* answer. This is a de facto penalty for leaving questions unanswered.
2. At the start of the test, your score increases or decreases by greater margins than it does at the end of the test. The scoring algorithm is working to determine broad ranges for what your score should be at the beginning of the test and is simply refining the specifics at the end of the test.

These are incredibly important concepts to appreciate because they directly influence how your score is calculated. And, they set the stage for why proper pacing is so important.

What Factors Influence How the GMAT Calculates Your Score

There are three prominent factors that influence how the GMAT calculates your score:

> Proper pacing means ensuring you have a chance to mark an answer down for every question!

- The number of questions you answered correctly (with harder questions being worth more than easier questions)
- Early questions count slightly more than later questions
- The number of questions you answer

These factors mean two things for your pacing strategy:

- Give a little more time to earlier questions than later questions
- Balance getting questions correct with ensuring you have enough time to answer each question

Give Earlier Questions a Little More Time than Later Questions

Think again about how the GMAT determines your score. Your score shifts more based on the answers to the first handful of questions than it does based on the answers to later questions. Another way to think of this is that the earlier questions set the broad score ranges you will fall into, and the later questions fine-tune your specific spot in those ranges.

> We covered how the GMAT determines your score in Chapter 2. If you don't remember (or didn't read it), check it out for a refresher.

Because earlier questions are worth more, it makes sense for you to slightly favor earlier questions over later ones. Do your best to get earlier questions correct, but not at the expense of all the other questions. While earlier questions are worth more, the difference is not profound enough to justify devoting half your time to the first 7 or so questions. Consider the following example of two fake students.

The first student begins the Quantitative Reasoning section and gets the first 11 questions correct but gets the next 10 questions wrong. The second student gets the first 10 questions wrong but gets the next 11 questions correct. Who do you think scores better?

If you answered that you think the first student scored better, you'd be correct. There's no denying that the earlier questions count more than the later ones. But, by how much do you think the first student outperformed the second?

The answer is not as much as you'd think. While the first student may get a 75 on the section, the second student might receive a 71. And while the four-point swing may be the difference between the 30th percentile and the 60th percentile, neither student is going to perform as well as the student who gets the first 5 questions wrong but gets the next 16 correct. And that student is not going to perform as well as the student who gets 5 questions wrong but spreads them randomly throughout the test.

In the end, the best strategy to maximize your score is simply to get as many questions correct as you can. To do so effectively, you need to make sure you keep enough time on the clock to give yourself a shot at answering every question.

Make Sure You Answer Every Question

The pacing chart in the next section should help keep you on track to answer each question and give yourself a fair shot at puzzling out the correct answer. It's important to remember that there is a de facto penalty for not answering a question, so make sure to see them all.

Pacing Chart

How can you ensure you're on track to answer each question while still allotting slightly more time to earlier questions? How does your current or desired score impact time allotment? These are perfectly reasonable questions. The following pacing charts should help you keep on track.

Quantitative Reasoning Pacing

Score	Questions	
	1 to 10	11 to 21
60 to 73	30 minutes	15 minutes
75 to 79	27 minutes	18 minutes
80 to 90	25 minutes	20 minutes

Verbal Reasoning Pacing

Score	Questions	
	1 to 11	12 to 23
60 to 76	30 minutes	15 minutes
77 to 81	27 minutes	18 minutes
82 to 90	25 minutes	20 minutes

Data Insights Pacing

Score	Questions	
	1 to 10	11 to 20
60 to 71	30 minutes	15 minutes
72 to 77	27 minutes	18 minutes

Pacing Advice

If you take a look at those pacing charts closely, you'll see that we encourage you to try to answer most questions in between 1 to 3 minutes.

If you answer a question in less than 1 minute, you leave yourself open to the possibility of making preventable mistakes. Even if you solve a question in less than a minute, take the time to reread the question and make sure you haven't missed anything.

When you spend more than 3 minutes on a question, it becomes more likely that you will run the risk of not being able to finish the section. If you find you've spent around 3 minutes on a question but just need a few more seconds to finish some calculations then, by all means, complete the problem. But if you are still working on how to approach the problem, it's time to apply some POE, guess, and move on.

Keeping Track of Your Pacing

Pacing is important, but it also can't be a distraction. You certainly won't benefit from obsessively checking the clock before, during, and after every question.

Instead of constantly checking the clock, apply the 5-question check in rule. Notice how the pacing charts above are broken into groups of approximately 10 questions. After the first 5 questions of the pacing group you are working through, check the clock. If you are within 1 minute in either direction of where you should be about halfway through the group, your pacing is on track. Keep it up!

If you are more than one minute behind schedule, it's time to speed up. Speeding up doesn't necessarily mean working faster. Instead, it means to not let yourself get stuck on any more questions until your pacing has caught up.

If you are more than one minute ahead of schedule, slow down! You can use that extra time to make sure you're not making any avoidable mistakes. You may even want to take 5 seconds to take a deep breath and recenter yourself before your next question.

When to Use the Review and Edit Feature

All the most carefully laid pacing plans can be laid to waste by a particularly sticky question. You may encounter a question you know you can do but it is taking longer to do it than you'd like. You know you should move on from the question and should not devote as much time as you have to it, but you feel like with a few more minutes of work you could get it right. This is when you should use the review and edit feature.

Many test-takers are intrigued by the review and edit feature as an opportunity to gain a couple of extra points at the end of the test. And while it certainly could result in some additional points earned, that's not the primary use case for the feature.

The primary use case for the review and edit feature is to prevent you from taking too much time on any one question. While taking the GMAT, you may find yourself working on a question for longer than recommended to keep on pace to ensure you get a chance to see every question. In the event you find yourself spending a long time on a single question, the best strategy is to mark the question for later review, select an answer, and move on. Once you complete the section, you can use any remaining time to go back and review that question.

Do not fall into the trap of believing the review and edit feature deserves a prominent place in your overall testing strategy. In many cases, you may not even have time left over at the end of the section to use the feature. The best strategy is simply to do your best to answer the question correctly the first time. But, if you find yourself spending longer than you should on any given question, it is nice to know there is an option to move on to another question and revisit the problematic question later.

PROCESS OF ELIMINATION

Thus far, we've established a couple of truths about the GMAT:

- While taking the GMAT, you must submit an answer for every question you see before you can see the next one.
- The Edit function allows you to return to 3 questions at the end of a section and change your answer, but you still must submit an answer to the question.
- It is a good test-taking strategy to make sure you answer every question.

So, if you have to answer the question in front of you in order to see the next one, it's strongly recommended that you make sure to answer every question, and if the GMAT algorithm is giving you questions that are relatively difficult for you, as it should and will, what do you do when you find a question you do not know how to answer?

Look for Wrong Answers Instead of Correct Ones

It seems obvious enough that, because GMAT questions are multiple choice, one of the answer choices must be correct. But what is sometimes less obvious is that you do not always have to know the correct answer in order to get a question correct. One of the answer choices has to be correct. You just have to find it.

You may not know the correct answer, but you may know enough to eliminate some of the wrong ones. Wrong answers are often easier to spot than correct answers. Sometimes they just sound weird. Other times they're logically impossible. While it is rare to be able to eliminate all four of the incorrect answer choices on the GMAT, you will almost always be able to eliminate at least one of them—and frequently two or more—by using Process of Elimination. Process of Elimination (POE for short) will enable you to answer questions that you don't have the time to figure out exactly. We will refer to POE frequently throughout this book. It is one of the most important and fundamental tools you will use to increase your score.

Here's an example of Process of Elimination in action:

Paul is driving from his apartment to his parents' house and back along the same route. If he averaged 60 miles per hour on the way to his parents' house and 80 miles per hour on the way back, what was his approximate speed for the round trip?

(A) 60
(B) 68.6
(C) 70
(D) 72.4
(E) 80

Let's say you have no idea how to work this problem and you've spent close to the time you're willing to allot to it. You know by now that you should move on to the next question because you want to make sure you have enough time to answer every question. You want to make a guess and possibly bookmark this question for editing later. But how do you pick which answer to guess?

Don't Pick Randomly

Before guessing, try to eliminate some answer choices to improve your odds of guessing the correct answer. Let's take a look at the question again and see if there are some answer choices that can be eliminated. Are any of the answer choices too easy or too obvious? Choice (C) is the average of 60 and 80, which are the speeds listed in the question, but an aggressive user of POE will be suspicious of this answer as too straightforward. Eliminate it. How about (A) and (E)? Would it make sense for the average to be 60 or 80 if we know Paul drove one leg of the trip at an average speed faster or slower than those times? No! The average has to be somewhere between 60 and 80. Eliminate (A) and (C).

> Remember, just because you bookmark the question for review using the edit feature later doesn't mean you'll actually have time to revisit it. The best strategy is to try to get the question right the first time.

In no time at all, without having to do any computation-heavy math, we used POE to successfully improve the chances of correctly guessing the answer to this question to 50%. And while it's best to solve questions outright, POE is a critical tool to help you move past some time-consuming questions and increase the chances of maximizing your score.

When to Use POE

There are many circumstances when using POE to eliminate answer choices is going to serve you well, but the three most prominent are:

- When a question is taking you a long time to complete, and you need to move on
- When you are running out of time on a section and need to ensure you answer each question
- When you've encountered a particularly difficult question you are unsure how to solve

POE is not a substitute for actually solving a question. If you know how to solve a problem, then that is what you should do. But, when you are in a pinch, knowing how to use POE effectively can increase the odds of you getting a question correct.

Scratch Work

Process of Elimination is a powerful tool, but it's powerful only if you keep track of the answer choices you've eliminated. On a computer-adaptive test, you obviously can't cross off choices on the screen—but you can cross them off on your scratch paper. Don't be afraid to use it!

You have only so many tools at your disposal, and the scratch paper the testing center provides is one of them. Many test-takers often ignore the scratch paper—especially on the Verbal side of the test. Don't be one of them! Use the scratch paper to keep track of eliminated answer choices, jot down notes about questions and passages, and keep yourself organized.

RECOGNIZING TRAP ANSWERS

It's not hard to see why GMAC favors the computer adaptive format for the GMAT. It ensures that test-takers receive questions of an appropriate difficulty level and only see harder questions if they first answer the easier questions correctly.

But, as you now know, you don't always need to know how to answer a question in order to answer it correctly. In fact, using POE, you can give yourself a pretty good chance to correctly guess the answer to a question that you otherwise have no idea how to solve.

The GMAT wouldn't be worth much if any student could routinely guess the correct answer to difficult questions by picking answer choices that seem correct. So they create incorrect answer choices that either look correct or are the result of partial calculations or improper reading. These are trap answers, and they are designed to trip up most test-takers who are going to guess on any given question.

Almost everybody gets stuck on at least a few questions when they take the GMAT. And make no mistake, some of GMAT's questions can be very hard! Sooner or later, you may run into a question you just don't know how to do. Even after applying some POE savvy, you still may have 3 or 4 possible answer choices.

The Truth About Guessing

Most people who guess on a GMAT question choose the answer that seems correct. In other words, they play a hunch. Sometimes these hunches are correct; sometimes they are not. However, the difficulty of a question is not related to how hard an average person may find the content, but is based on the number of people who get the question wrong.

The most common way people believe GMAC adjusts the difficulty level of a question is to make a complex question about a complex topic. And they certainly do this! But, they also regularly adjust the difficulty level of a question by including good trap answers based on what they believe (and their research shows) are the most common mistakes people are likely to make.

Because of this, your Process of Eliminate strategies can and should shift based on how difficult you think any given question is likely to be.

- On easy questions, the obvious answer tends to be the correct answer.
- On medium questions, the obvious answer is correct only some of the time.
- On difficult questions, the obvious answer is almost always wrong.

Of course, there is no way for you to "know" the difficulty level of a question on test day. You'll have to make educated guesses. The more questions you work through, the more likely you are to start to recognize the hallmarks of difficult GMAT questions.

To ace the GMAT, it is not enough to know how to read and to understand algebra, arithmetic, data methods, or verbal reasoning. You have to be able to dodge GMAC's traps. In this section, we'll discuss how to use the traps to your advantage and make yourself more likely to pick the right answer. First, let's understand how GMAC constructs answer choices.

Question Difficulty
GMAT questions are rated according to the number of people who get them wrong, not the question content.

Hard = 70 percent or more of people get it wrong

Medium = about 50 percent of people get it wrong

Easy = fewer than 30 percent of people get it wrong

Put Yourself in GMAC's Shoes
Imagine you are writing a multiple-choice test. Here is a problem you've written:

During a sale, a store sells $\frac{1}{5}$ of its books. The following day, the sale continues and the store sells $\frac{1}{5}$ of the remaining books. What fraction of the original books remains in the store?

Let's look at all the components of this question a student who answers it correctly would have to work through. First, a student needs to understand that the second $\frac{1}{5}$ is coming out of the books that are remaining after the first day. That is, there are $\frac{4}{5}$ of the books left after the first day, and the store sells $\frac{1}{5}$ of those books, not another $\frac{1}{5}$ of the total.

This means the store sells $\frac{1}{5}$ of $\frac{4}{5}$ of the total books on the second day, or $\frac{4}{25}$ of the total. So the store sold $\frac{1}{5}$ of the total and then another $\frac{4}{25}$ of the total, for a final total of $\frac{9}{25}$ of the original books sold. Then the student has to subtract that from 1 because the question asks what fraction *remains* in the store: the answer is $\frac{16}{25}$.

Now imagine you are the question writer. This question has a lot of elements to it already, and now you need to come up with the answer choices. You have to make one of the answer choices $\frac{16}{25}$, since that's the correct answer, but how should you come up with the other answer choices? You could make up random fractions, but if a test-taker missed a couple of steps, or did them wrong, the answer they do come up with is unlikely to be one of the random fractions you chose. If the answer the test-taker came up with is not one of the options, they now know they did something incorrectly. They can return to the question, and they might figure out the correct way to solve it or be able to make a more educated guess and get the answer right. You need a better way to come up with answer choices than random choice.

Constructing Trap Answers

You want to make sure that only the students who really know the correct answer get the question right. You only want a student who understood the question to get it right and to weed out students who could get it right if they realized they'd made a mistake.

To do that, you create answer choices based on what a student might do wrong. So let's figure out what that is.

A student might think the second $\frac{1}{5}$ was coming from the total and miss that the question is asking about how many books are left. This student adds $\frac{1}{5} + \frac{1}{5}$, which sums to $\frac{2}{5}$. That would be a good answer choice to use.

Another student might get that same part wrong but understand that the question was asking about how many books are left, so they would subtract $\frac{2}{5}$ from 1 to yield $\frac{3}{5}$. This would be another good answer to use.

A student who really doesn't understand the problem might just multiply the two fractions. $\frac{1}{5} \times \frac{1}{5} = \frac{1}{25}$. Make another answer choice $\frac{1}{25}$.

How about a student who did everything correct but misread the question? The student gets that the store sold $\frac{9}{25}$ of the books over the two days and is so excited that they didn't fall into a trap in the first couple steps that the student sees $\frac{9}{25}$ in the answer choices and goes ahead and picks it without rereading the question.

So now you've made sure that most students who don't know how to solve the problem don't get it right. Either they do it wrong but don't realize it because their answer is there, or they look at the answer choices and find one that seems like it could be correct based on the numbers in the problem. But your correct answer is disguised—it isn't obvious how to get to it because it's the result of several steps. This bumps up the difficulty level of the question because you've ensured that it would be almost impossible for a student to get the problem right without knowing exactly how to do it and carefully avoiding your traps.

Here's your finished question:

During a sale, a store sells $\frac{1}{5}$ of its books. The following day, the sale continues and the store sells $\frac{1}{5}$ of the remaining books. What fraction of the original books remains in the store?

(A) $\frac{1}{25}$

(B) $\frac{9}{25}$

(C) $\frac{2}{5}$

(D) $\frac{3}{5}$

(E) $\frac{16}{25}$

Don't Fall for the Traps

A well-developed sense of the kinds of trap answers GMAT question writers employ and a feel for the relative difficulty level of any given question are your best friends when scouting out trap answers. Knowing how the test-writers think about constructing answer choices gives you a massive advantage to work through those sticky situations for which POE is most valuable.

More Reasons to Know Trap Answers

Beyond helping out in situations that call for POE, understanding trap answer choice construction is a major ally in avoiding self-inflicted mistakes. If you arrive at an answer choice too easily or if you have a strong sense of trap answers and the choice you arrive at just feels wrong, stop! Listen to that instinct, and be sure to double-check your work and reread the question.

Finally, an increased awareness of trap answer choice construction will make you a savvier, more conscientious test-taker. The more aware you are of potential pitfalls, the less likely you are to stumble into them.

No Relief on the Verbal Portion

Let's pretend again: you still work for GMAC, and you write a reading passage. Let's use a short one, to keep it simple.

> For most of the 20th century, big companies dominated an American business scene that seemed to thrive on its own grandness of scale. The expansion westward, the growth of the railroad and steel industries, an almost limitless supply of cheap raw materials, plus a population boom that provided an ever-increasing demand for new products (although not a cheap source of labor) all coincided to encourage the growth of large companies.

Then you write a question:

> To what does the passage credit as bolstering the growth of large companies?

And you write the correct answer:

> The combination of a variety of conditions favorable to big businesses

Why did you write an answer choice like that instead of something that is explicitly stated in the passage? You only want students who have a good understanding of the passage as a whole and read the answer choices carefully to get the question correct.

Verbal Trap Answers

Next, you make some trap answers. Would you write a trap answer like, *The lack of government intervention prior to the Sherman Antitrust Act?* No, because nothing about that was mentioned in the passage, and it can be too easily eliminated by test-takers.

You want to write trap answers that sound plausible. How about:

> The high cost of labor for expanding businesses

The passage says this more or less, but it doesn't answer this particular question because high labor costs don't help businesses grow. It's a trap because students might pick it if they forget what the question is actually asking, or if they misunderstand the meaning of the word *bolster*.

You might also write:

> Large companies' ability to transport steel via railroads

> Greater demand for new products in the West than in the East

> Cheap labor as a result of a population boom

Notice that all of these are not supported by the passage but have some elements that are found within the passage. In fact, they are, respectively, examples of the common GMAT Reading Comprehension trap answer types: Recycled Language, No Such Comparison, and Reversal. We'll go into much greater detail on these later on. Your correct answer, however, is 100% supported by what is in the passage.

Summary

- ○ The three fundamental strategies for success on the GMAT are:
  - • Proper Pacing
  - • Process of Elimination
  - • Recognizing Trap Answers

- ○ The GMAT determines your score primarily based on the number of questions you answer correctly, at what point in the test you answer questions correctly, and the total number of questions you answer.

- ○ Pacing is important to maximize your score because it allows you the opportunity to answer every question while slightly favoring earlier questions over later questions and ensuring you get a chance to work through each question to try to get the correct answer.

- ○ Whenever you don't know the correct answer to a question or are pressed for time and need to move on to another question, use Process of Elimination to eliminate wrong answers and improve your odds of guessing correctly.

- ○ GMAC constructs incorrect answer choices in order to minimize the likelihood that a test-taker who did not understand the question can correctly guess the answer.

- ○ Knowing how GMAC test-writers construct trap answers can help increase your score by helping you recognize incorrect answers and treat the answer choices you do arrive at with scrutiny.

Part II
Diagnostic Test 1

Chapter 4
Diagnostic Test 1

TAKING THE DIAGNOSTIC

No matter your circumstances, before getting into the specifics of the sections, you should take the first diagnostic test found in this chapter. The goal of the diagnostic is to give you a sense of the types of questions you might see on the GMAT and to give you a baseline to evaluate your performance.

Before you dive into the diagnostic, there are a couple of things you should keep in mind. The diagnostic is separated into different content sections. There are no integrated reasoning style questions in the diagnostic. Each section has a mix of question types ranging in difficulty from easy to hard.

Once you finish the diagnostic test, score it using the diagnostic answer key found at the start of Chapter 5 and revisit the questions you got incorrect in the explanations.

While the results of this test are not an accurate representation of an actual GMAT score, it is a way for you to monitor progress and compare your performance on Diagnostic Test 1 with that on Diagnostic Test 2, found near the end of the book. Once you've made your way through the content of the book, take the second diagnostic and compare the results to the first!

Diagnostic Test 1

36 Questions

Arithmetic

1. If p is an integer such that $-8 < p < 8$, what is the product of all the possible even values of p ?

   (A) −14,746
   (B)   −2,304
   (C)   −384
   (D)   −64
   (E)   0

2. If the three children in the Yao family are all at least one year apart in age, are they all less than 11 years old?

   (1) The sum of the children's ages is less than 22
   (2) The age of the oldest child is twice that of the youngest child

   (A) Statement (1) ALONE is sufficient, but statement (2) alone is not sufficient.
   (B) Statement (2) ALONE is sufficient, but statement (1) alone is not sufficient.
   (C) BOTH statements TOGETHER are sufficient, but NEITHER statement ALONE is sufficient.
   (D) EACH statement ALONE is sufficient.
   (E) Statements (1) and (2) TOGETHER are not sufficient.

3. If x is a positive integer such that $x = \sqrt[3]{k}$, then what is the value of x ?

   (1) $200 < k < 1{,}100$
   (2) x is prime

   (A) Statement (1) ALONE is sufficient, but statement (2) alone is not sufficient.
   (B) Statement (2) ALONE is sufficient, but statement (1) alone is not sufficient.
   (C) BOTH statements TOGETHER are sufficient, but NEITHER statement ALONE is sufficient.
   (D) EACH statement ALONE is sufficient.
   (E) Statements (1) and (2) TOGETHER are not sufficient.

4. For the first month of a three-month period, Judy used 19 gallons of gas and her car averaged (arithmetic mean) 24 miles per gallon. For the second month of the three-month period, she used 31 gallons of gas and her car averaged 26 miles per gallon. At the end of the three-month period, Judy used a total of 72 gallons of gas and her car averaged 27 miles per gallon. How many miles per gallon did Judy average in the third month?

   (A) 28
   (B) 29
   (C) 30
   (D) 31
   (E) 32

GO ON TO THE NEXT PAGE.

5. Claudio wants to arrange his book collection on a bookshelf such that all books of the same genre are grouped together and the order of the genres is always fantasy, biographies, and science fiction. He has 3 fantasy novels, 2 biographies, and 4 science fiction novels. How many ways can the books on his bookshelf be arranged?

   (A)   32
   (B)   48
   (C)   124
   (D)   288
   (E)   396

6. If $xy = -1$, then what is $|x - y|$?

   (1) x is an integer
   (2) y is an integer

   (A)   Statement (1) ALONE is sufficient, but statement (2) alone is not sufficient.
   (B)   Statement (2) ALONE is sufficient, but statement (1) alone is not sufficient.
   (C)   BOTH statements TOGETHER are sufficient, but NEITHER statement ALONE is sufficient.
   (D)   EACH statement ALONE is sufficient.
   (E)   Statements (1) and (2) TOGETHER are not sufficient.

7. If $m = \dfrac{\left(\dfrac{1}{6} + \dfrac{3}{8} - \dfrac{1}{4}\right)}{\left(\dfrac{7}{3}\right)}$, then $\sqrt[3]{\dfrac{1}{m}} =$

   (A) 2

   (B) $\dfrac{1}{2}$

   (C) $2\sqrt[3]{2}$

   (D) $\dfrac{\sqrt[3]{4}}{2}$

   (E) $\dfrac{\sqrt[3]{2}}{7}$

8. 450 is what percent greater than 15 ?

   (A)   30
   (B)   290
   (C)   300
   (D)   2,900
   (E)   3,000

9. Amy, Barb, and Claire are going on an 800-mile trip in Amy's car. They agree to split the cost for gas such that Barb and Claire each pay twice the amount that Amy pays. Amy's car averages 25 miles to the gallon, and gas costs $1.25 per gallon. If Barb and Claire each pay twice the amount for gas that Amy pays, how much does Barb pay for gas?

   (A) $8
   (B) $16
   (C) $24
   (D) $32
   (E) $40

GO ON TO THE NEXT PAGE.

Algebra

1. If $7y = 4x + 1$ and $z + 3 = 3y + 2$, then what is the value of x when $z = 8$?

   (A)   1
   (B)   2
   (C)   3
   (D)   4
   (E)   5

2. Is $k \leq p$?

   (1) $k > 0$
   (2) $k^3 = p$

   (A)   Statement (1) ALONE is sufficient, but statement (2) is not sufficient.
   (B)   Statement (2) ALONE is sufficient, but statement (1) alone is not sufficient.
   (C)   BOTH statements TOGETHER are sufficient, but NEITHER statement ALONE is sufficient.
   (D)   EACH statement ALONE is sufficient.
   (E)   Statements (1) and (2) TOGETHER are not sufficient.

3. What is the value of k ?

   (1) $2k^2 + 7k + 6 = 0$
   (2) $4k^2 + 12k + 9 = 0$

   (A)   Statement (1) ALONE is sufficient, but statement (2) alone is not sufficient.
   (B)   Statement (2) ALONE is sufficient, but statement (1) alone is not sufficient.
   (C)   BOTH statements TOGETHER are sufficient, but NEITHER statement ALONE is sufficient.
   (D)   EACH statement ALONE is sufficient.
   (E)   Statements (1) and (2) TOGETHER are not sufficient.

4. If x, y, and z are consecutive negative odd integers such that $x > y > z$, is $xy > |z|$?

   (1) $z < -5$
   (2) $|x| > 1$

   (A)   Statement (1) ALONE is sufficient, but statement (2) alone is not sufficient.
   (B)   Statement (2) ALONE is sufficient, but statement (1) alone is not sufficient.
   (C)   BOTH statements TOGETHER are sufficient, but NEITHER statement ALONE is sufficient.
   (D)   EACH statement ALONE is sufficient.
   (E)   Statements (1) and (2) TOGETHER are not sufficient.

GO ON TO THE NEXT PAGE.

5. If x and y are distinct non-zero integers, is

$$x < \left(x^2 - y^2\right)^{\frac{1}{3}} ?$$

(1) $x^2 > y^2$
(2) $x^3 < y^3$

(A) Statement (1) ALONE is sufficient, but statement (2) alone is not sufficient.
(B) Statement (2) ALONE is sufficient, but statement (1) alone is not sufficient.
(C) BOTH statements TOGETHER are sufficient, but NEITHER statement ALONE is sufficient.
(D) EACH statement ALONE is sufficient.
(E) Statements (1) and (2) TOGETHER are not sufficient.

6. In the equation $ax^2 + bx + c = (3x - d)^2$, x is a non-zero variable and a, b, c, and d are constants. What is the value of d ?

(1) $c = 9$
(2) $a - x = 10$

(A) Statement (1) ALONE is sufficient, but statement (2) alone is not sufficient.
(B) Statement (2) ALONE is sufficient, but statement (1) alone is not sufficient.
(C) BOTH statements TOGETHER are sufficient, but NEITHER statement ALONE is sufficient.
(D) EACH statement ALONE is sufficient.
(E) Statements (1) and (2) TOGETHER are not sufficient.

7. What is the cube root of the square root of 128 ?

(A) $\sqrt[6]{2}$
(B) $2\sqrt[6]{2}$
(C) $2\sqrt[3]{2}$
(D) $2\sqrt{2}$
(E) 2

GO ON TO THE NEXT PAGE.

Reading Comprehension

Questions 1–3 are based on the following passage:

A mysterious new material is surprising
scientists with its ability to conduct electricity
without resistance (a measure of an object's
Line opposition to the flow of electric current) at
(5) close to room temperature, about 60 degrees
Fahrenheit. While known superconductors typically
function only in extremely frigid temperatures,
though at atmospheric pressures, the new
material only survives under very high pressures,
(10) such as those near the center of the Earth.
Still, while the compound composed of carbon,
sulfur, and hydrogen isn't immediately feasible
for use, it demonstrates the possibility of zero-
resistance materials that are functional at normal
(15) temperatures. Known technological uses for
superconductors abound and include generators
for wind turbines as well as magnetic resonance
imaging machines. But the need for temperatures
below −140 degrees Celsius for these common
(20) superconductors currently poses a significant
limitation to their usage. Previously tested
materials that demonstrated superconductivity
comprised only two elements, and the copious
research on such compounds means that they
(25) are well-understood. This three-component
compound has expanded the possibilities for
future superconductor research. Since such a
combination is unique in its superconductivity,
scientists cannot yet explain this material's
(30) properties or how it can function at such unusually
high temperatures.

1. The primary purpose of the passage is to

(A) compare technologies in one field to those
in another field
(B) determine the ideal temperature for
a material
(C) evaluate the implications of a
scientific discovery
(D) enumerate potential applications of a
new technology
(E) speculate about potential future
scientific developments

2. The author mentions the highlighted phrase
most likely in order to

(A) explain how pressures vary in different
regions of the Earth
(B) highlight a drawback of
common superconductors
(C) compare the requirements of
different superconductors
(D) describe the primary location in which
superconductors function
(E) emphasize the difficulty of achieving
extremely low temperatures

3. Each of the following is mentioned in the
passage as a characteristic of the new
material EXCEPT

(A) It is composed of three elements.
(B) It can function at temperatures
above freezing.
(C) It requires high amounts of pressure.
(D) It could lead to new and
useful technologies.
(E) It is well-understood.

GO ON TO THE NEXT PAGE.

Reading Comprehension

Questions 4–6 are based on the following passage:

Mitochondrial DNA from both ancient and modern chicken specimens may provide evidence about the origin of these birds in South America.
Line Cooper's contradiction of Storey's hypothesis
(5) that the chicken was introduced to the region by traveling Polynesians hundreds of years ago is bolstered by evidence that chickens found in the two regions are genetically distinct. Cooper also challenges Burley's contention that Polynesians
(10) must have reached the New World because they found Easter Island and share common flora, such as the bottle gourd and sweet potato, with South America. Cooper's claim that a connection between the South Pacific islands and the South
(15) American continent does not exist is based upon his team's comparison of the DNA from chicken bones collected at Polynesian archaeological sites and feathers from modern Polynesian chickens with the DNA of both ancient and modern South
(20) American chickens.

However, modern DNA has limited applicability in determining the origin of a species in one part of the world. For instance, chickens, among other animals and objects, moved around the world
(25) as people traveled; the chickens on the Pacific Islands today do not necessarily represent those that existed in the region several centuries ago. Furthermore, Cooper's belief severs the historical connection between the regions and displaces the
(30) South American plants that are generally accepted as products of Polynesian trade. Therefore, Cooper's dispute may require a broader view of the strong research supporting both sides of the chicken origin debate.

4. The author of the passage mentions plants that are common to both South America and Polynesia most likely in order to

(A) suggest that DNA evidence is mainly useful for comparing modern species
(B) point out a potential challenge to the idea that South American chickens did not originate in Polynesia
(C) suggest that animals were involved in local, as opposed to international, trade
(D) suggest that the chicken probably arrived in South America not from Polynesia but from another region
(E) provide evidence that disproves Cooper's claim about the South American chicken's origin

5. The passage suggests which of the following about Cooper's DNA evidence?

(A) It did not provide a definitive indication of whether Polynesians traded with South Americans.
(B) It demonstrated that modern chickens in Polynesia were not related to ancient South American chickens.
(C) It used primarily modern, rather than ancient, genetic material.
(D) It is consistent with the prevailing theory regarding plants that occur in Polynesia and South America.
(E) It bolstered the theory that Polynesians introduced chickens to South America.

6. According to the passage, Cooper and Burley disagree on which of the following points?

(A) Whether voyaging Polynesians traveled to South America
(B) The idea that the South American sweet potato exists in Polynesia
(C) The time period in which chickens appeared in South America
(D) How Polynesians located Easter Island
(E) The extent to which modern DNA is useful in ascertaining the regional origin of a species

GO ON TO THE NEXT PAGE.

Questions 7–10 are based on the following passage:

Over the past century, the United States population has continued to grow and so has the amount of hurricane activity along the Gulf
(Line) and Atlantic coastlines. For meteorologists, a
(5) better understanding of storm frequency and characteristics can assist in hurricane forecasts, which in turn guides infrastructure planning and even insurance rates. Unfortunately, fewer than 200 years of historical weather records exist
(10) in the U.S., and in that time only a handful of category 5 hurricanes—the most destructive tropical cyclones—have made landfall. This paucity of data presents a challenge in accurately predicting the likelihood of future devastating
(15) storms. Consequently, some researchers have turned to a relatively new field, paleotempestology, which examines geologic evidence of prehistoric hurricane landfalls to better understand the frequency with which they occur.

(20)   In one early study, Liu and Fearn extracted sediment samples from a lake in Louisiana that was isolated from the Gulf of Mexico by a narrow barrier beach: only a storm could cause water and materials to flow from the ocean to the lake.
(25) By analyzing the overwash layers, the layers of coarse beach sediment observable on the bottom of the lake, the scientists were able to produce a rough storm history for the region, dating back several thousand years. Some have questioned this
(30) method, however, as it does not conclusively verify the sediments' provenance.

Another paleotempestological strategy relies on offshore-indicative foraminifera, single-celled organisms that are similarly thought to have
(35) arrived in a body of water via storm surges. Unlike sediments, which may be of unknown origin, if a species of foraminifera is native to the sea, its presence in a body of water adjacent to a barrier beach provides more compelling evidence as to
(40) the necessity of a historic storm. Nonetheless, Hippensteel's and Martin's method, too, must be qualified: scientists disagree about precisely which taxa are considered "offshore-indicative," and dating methods used on foraminifera fossils merely
(45) demonstrate the age of the fossils, not necessarily when a hurricane might have occurred.

Although scientists have produced estimates of hurricane recurrence rates, the limitations of paleotempestological research temper the
(50) reliability of such predictions. Moreover, long-term changes in weather and climate affect the frequency of tropical storms, which further casts doubt on the field's ability to relate past storm data to the potential for future hurricanes.

7. Which of the following best describes the organization of the passage?

(A) After introducing an area of research, the author outlines its history and then casts doubt on its credibility.

(B) The author describes a problem, evaluates two approaches to the problem, and then questions the usefulness of a field of study.

(C) The author explains the origins of a scientific field and refutes potential criticisms to the field.

(D) After comparing two methodologies, the author demonstrates why one is superior to the other.

(E) After illustrating a scientific dilemma, the author explores differing perspectives on the dilemma and then reconciles the viewpoints.

8. According to the passage, which of the following is a potential drawback to the sediment analysis method mentioned in the second paragraph?

(A) Scientists' inability to easily access overwash layers deep below a lake

(B) The difficulty in proving precisely where the sediments came from

(C) Incomplete knowledge regarding what types of sediments might have oceanic origins

(D) Disagreement among researchers as to the validity of fossil evidence

(E) The lack of reliability in current methods for dating sediments

GO ON TO THE NEXT PAGE.

9. It can be inferred from the passage that the two research methods described in the passage have which of the following in common?

    (A) They involved bodies of water that were not connected to oceans.
    (B) They were conducted in Louisiana.
    (C) They did not provide useful paleotempestological data.
    (D) They used historical records in conjunction with ecological data to construct storm timelines.
    (E) Their validity has been rejected by most meteorologists.

10. Each of the following is mentioned as a potential benefit of paleotempestological research EXCEPT

    (A) the ability to predict hurricane recurrence
    (B) accurate regional insurance rates
    (C) planning of structural facilities
    (D) a greater understanding of hurricane patterns
    (E) preventing destructive hurricanes

GO ON TO THE NEXT PAGE.

Critical Reasoning

1. **Grocer:** Organic produce requires less pesticide use than conventionally grown produce. Pesticides impact the health of the ecosystem, which affects the health of consumers. Shoppers can realize health benefits by buying produce that is organically grown and can become more health-wise and prone to choose organic produce through strategic marketing. Therefore, a nationwide mailing campaign of a brochure extolling the benefits of organic produce will help the ecosystem of our entire country.

Which of the following, if true, poses the most serious challenge to the argument?

(A) The negative impact on the ecosystem from the pollution and waste generated by the national mailing campaign will meet or exceed the positive environmental impacts from more people eating organic produce.

(B) Eating a healthy diet is only one part of what it takes to lead an environmentally-friendly lifestyle.

(C) Organic produce is already available in nationwide grocery chains in every major city.

(D) The exact health benefits realized by consuming organic produce cannot be estimated for the nation as a whole.

(E) Conventional produce will make up a smaller proportion of the produce departments in grocery stores in the future.

2. The Mohs scale of mineral hardness categorizes the ability of one natural sample of mineral to make a visible scratch on another mineral. To measure the hardness of a certain mineral X on the scale, one finds the hardest mineral that mineral X can scratch, or the softest mineral that can scratch mineral X. However, at times, minerals that are classed as lower hardness on the Mohs scale can create microscopic disruptions on minerals that have a higher Mohs hardness. These microscopic disruptions can sometimes damage the structural integrity of the harder mineral.

Which of the following, if true, most helps to explain how minerals lower on the Mohs scale can still affect minerals that are higher on the Mohs scale?

(A) Microscopic disruptions are not considered "scratches" for the determination of a Mohs scale number.

(B) The Mohs scale was created in 1812 without the more complete knowledge of mineral hardness that exists today.

(C) The softer minerals' impact on the harder minerals is imperceptible to the naked eye.

(D) Such anomalies do not exist when using the Vickers scale, which is a more precise measure of mineral hardness than the Mohs scale.

(E) Minerals that are scratched often bear some residue of the mineral that inflicted the scratch.

GO ON TO THE NEXT PAGE.

3. A student response survey found that students who paid for 10 or more in-person tutoring sessions on an hour-by-hour basis missed or rescheduled a session on average once every five sessions. By contrast, those students who purchased tutoring sessions in ten-hour packages missed or rescheduled a session on average only once every ten sessions. This indicates that students are at least partly motivated by the amount of money they have invested for in-person tutoring.

Which of the following, if true, calls into question the explanation above?

(A) The price per hour was slightly more expensive for those who bought individual hours.

(B) Many students who missed or rescheduled sessions did so although they made a strong verbal commitment beforehand to be present.

(C) All students must pay a 10% fee for rescheduling any tutoring session, but if a student cancels a session entirely, the entire cost is forfeited.

(D) Upon purchase of any tutoring hours, students are required to immediately schedule all the purchased hours.

(E) Students who try to reschedule tutoring sessions without enough notice may not be able to make up the session in a timely fashion, so that it counts as a missed session.

4. **Graduate Student:** While there is no doubt that the themes in my new thesis *An Examination of Warp Protocols* echo the themes in the latest quantum physics textbook of my respected mentor, titled *Hypotheses in Hyperspace*, the accusations of plagiarism I face from the committee are invalid. Although both works take similar positions on a relatively new field, I had never read my mentor's textbook, which was published three months ago, before completing my thesis.

Which of the following, if true, provides the most support for the graduate student's position?

(A) An abstract of *Hypotheses in Hyperspace* had appeared in a widely circulated physics journal a year and a half prior to the book's publication.

(B) The themes explored in the thesis and the textbook are both founded on, and extensions of, prior research by a renowned physicist.

(C) The textbook was published by a company that devotes most of its catalogue to chemistry texts.

(D) Since the book's publication, other students who have been mentored by the author of *Hypotheses in Hyperspace* wrote papers exploring themes in that book.

(E) The author began writing *Hypotheses in Hyperspace* before the graduate student began writing *An Examination of Warp Protocols*.

GO ON TO THE NEXT PAGE.

5. **Psychologist:** Negotiators who lie regularly to cover up mistakes or to form new business alliances know that "truth adherence"—the closeness with which a story aligns to the known facts—is more likely to win a listener's trust than a completely unfamiliar story with corroboration from others. Clearly, people are more willing to trust a story that feels familiar but has a few inconsistencies than a story that is entirely new but completely verifiable.

Which of the following most seriously calls into question the psychologist's conclusion?

(A) Negotiators who are regular liars are only slightly more likely than others to use stories that have "truth adherence" to form new business alliances.

(B) Although an entirely false story would immediately put the listener on guard, negotiators who are regular liars would never use such a tactic.

(C) Most people who negotiate do lie once in a while, but only a very few do so regularly.

(D) People tend not to become negotiators unless they already have a tendency to lie on a regular basis.

(E) People are more likely to trust a negotiator if they have been referred by friends in common or trusted business acquaintances.

6. The aeronautics commission recently released a report detailing a problem with the thrusters on the newly developed XR rocket. The rocket was designed to explore the near planets in the solar system but not within the orbit of the Moon. Federal regulations require the public to be alerted about any flaw in the design of spacecraft intended primarily to traverse space within the Moon's orbit, but not further out in space. However, the aeronautics commission decided to release its report as soon as the flaw was discovered.

Which of the following, if true, most helps to explain the decision made by the aeronautics commission?

(A) Until the government decided on the current regulations, the regulatory committee considered implementing stricter regulations that would require public disclosure of problems with any sort of spacecraft.

(B) Spacecraft designed for traversing space solely within the orbit of the Moon have a greater likelihood of impacting the earth in the event of a problem.

(C) The admission of a design flaw is not enough to deter the public from supporting future developments in space exploration technology.

(D) Funding for future spacecraft might be affected if the flaws in the current rockets are made public.

(E) The aeronautics commission has recently received negative publicity for a lack of transparency regarding craft design.

GO ON TO THE NEXT PAGE.

7. Prima ballet dancers typically begin training between the ages of five and eight. Many ballet enthusiasts believe there is a distinct advantage not only in sheer years of training but also because the early exposure to dance helps shape how young muscles develop. However, even though many prima ballet dancers begin their overall training at a younger age, **they do not go on pointe any earlier than other ballet dancers, typically between the ages of 10 and 12.** Since the bones of the foot require time to mature, many ballet instructors delay pointe work until this age. Therefore, it's more likely that instead of early work shaping the ballet dancer's muscles towards expertise, **the gifted young performer naturally gravitates toward ballet classes.**

The portions in bold play which of the following roles in the argument?

(A) The first is a claim that the argument sets out to dispute, and the second is the conclusion formed on the resolution of that dispute.

(B) The first is evidence against a common belief, and the second is that common belief.

(C) The first is evidence in support of a position with which the argument disagrees, and the second is that position.

(D) The first is evidence that supports an alternative explanation for a phenomenon, and the second is the refutation of that explanation.

(E) The first offers support for a position the argument advocates, and the second is that position.

8. There are many websites that offer metrics for evaluating college-level writing. Nevertheless, professors should never allow students to use these websites to evaluate the merits of their own essays assigned in the course. While the metrics are written to allow easy comprehension, the proper application of the metrics to the specifics of the essay requires a disinterested, objective perspective.

Which of the following, if true, most strengthens the argument?

(A) The student who spent time researching and crafting an essay is usually in a better position to evaluate the merits of the essay than a professor who typically only reads the essay once.

(B) In order to evaluate an essay, one must have some knowledge of the background topic of the essay.

(C) Few students evaluate the essays that other students have written for the same assignment and so they lack a broad perspective on what makes an essay worth merit.

(D) Any essay written by a college student, when evaluated using these metrics, will demonstrate less merit than would an essay written by a professional writer.

(E) For the purposes of a college course, anonymous peer review is the best method of assessing the merits of an assigned essay.

GO ON TO THE NEXT PAGE.

9. Running shoes have to be replaced periodically since the repeated force of impact wears down the sole and collapses the insole. High-tech running shoes that incorporate memory foam and gel inserts adapt to the individual stride, last much longer, and contribute to improved running performance. However, ordinary running shoes cost much less and casual runners do not get enough use out of high-tech shoes to justify the expense of the materials. Therefore, for |most runners, high-tech running shoes do not save money.

Which of the following would be most useful to know in evaluating the argument?

(A) If there are shoe materials that increase running performance but do not cost as much as memory foam and gel inserts
(B) Whether casual runners are interested in improved running performance
(C) How the price of the materials typically used in high-tech running shoes compares to that of materials used in high-tech shoes tailored to other sports
(D) The length of time an ordinary running shoe and a high-tech running shoe can be used before needing to be replaced
(E) Whether the shoes would be used for any other sport or recreational activity aside from running

10. The election committee in the country of Jana analyzed the records of the Ostrich political party in light of new information about the opposing political party, the Prawn party. The analysis revealed that every year for the last 40 years, the Ostrich party's projections of what Prawn party political donations would be 3 years later were wrong by an average of 22%. The review also revealed that in every year for the last 40 years, the Ostrich party estimate of the Prawn party political donations for the previous year—which the Prawn party never released for public information—was only off by an average of 0.2%.

Which of the following claims is most strongly supported by the information given?

(A) Prawn party political donations fluctuated widely in the last 40 years.
(B) Prior to the new information, the Prawn party had not intentionally released data intended to mislead the Ostrich party's projections.
(C) The average percent by which the Ostrich party's projections of the Prawn party political donations were wrong increased over time.
(D) Even before the new information was released, the Ostrich party had reason to believe their projections were incorrect.
(E) The Ostrich party's projections had no impact on the country of Jana.

END OF DIAGNOSTIC TEST

Chapter 5
Diagnostic Test 1: Answers and Explanations

DIAGNOSTIC TEST 1: MULTIPLE CHOICE ANSWER KEY

Let's take a look at how you did on Diagnostic Test 1. Follow the three-step process in the answer key below and go read the explanations for any questions you got wrong, or you struggled with, but got correct.

STEP 1 ➤➤ **Check your answers and mark any correct answers with a ✔ in the appropriate column.**

Arithmetic									
Q #	Ans.	✔	Chap. #	Section	Q #	Ans.	✔	Chap. #	Section
1	E		9	Zero	6	C		18	More Ways to Plug In
2	C		18	Plugging In on Yes/No Questions	7	A		12	Fractions
3	C		12	Radicals	8	D		12	Percentages
4	D		5	Averages	9	B		14	Plugging in The Answers (PITA)
5	D		15	Permutations and Computations					

Algebra									
1	E		13	Solving Equalities	5	C		18	Plugging In on Yes/No Questions
2	E		18	Plugging In on Yes/No Questions	6	E		13	Solving Equalities
3	B		13	Quadratic Equations	7	B		12	Radicals
4	D		18	Plugging In on Yes/No Questions					

STEP 2 ➤➤ **Add the total number of correct answers for each test section. Then, divide the number correct by the number of total questions to get your percent correct.**

Test Section	Number Correct	Total Questions	Percent Correct
Arithmetic		9	
Algebra		7	

CORRECT ANSWERS

$$\frac{\boxed{}}{\boxed{}} = \boxed{}\%$$

\# TOTAL QUESTIONS   PERCENT CORRECT

STEP 3 ➤➤ **Use the results above to customize your study plan. You may want to start with, or give more attention to, the chapters with the lowest percents correct.**

STEP 1 » Check your answers and mark any correct answers with a ✔ in the appropriate column.

Reading Comprehension								
1	C		21	Primary Purpose	6	A		21	Retrieval
2	C		21	Specific Purpose	7	B		21	Structure
3	E		21	Retrieval	8	B		21	Retrieval
4	B		21	Specific Purpose	9	A		21	Inference
5	A		21	Inference	10	E		21	Retrieval

Critical Reasoning								
1	A		22	Weaken Questions	6	E		22	Resolve/Explain Questions
2	A		22	Resolve/Explain Questions	7	E		22	Identify the Reasoning Questions
3	A		22	Weaken Questions	8	E		22	Strengthen Questions
4	B		22	Strengthen Questions	9	D		22	Evaluate Questions
5	E		22	Weaken Questions	10	D		22	Strengthen Questions

**STEP 2 »** Add the total number of correct answers for each test section. Then, divide the number correct by the number of total questions to get your percent correct.

Test Section	Number Correct	Total Questions	Percent Correct
Reading Comprehension		10	
Critical Reasoning		10	

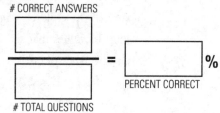

STEP 3 » Use the results above to customize your study plan. You may want to start with, or give more attention to, the chapters with the lowest percents correct.

ARITHMETIC

1.　**E**　Since p is an integer between –8 and 8, the possible even values of p are –6, –4, –2, 0, 2, 4, and 6. Since one of those integers is 0, the product of these integers is 0. The correct answer is (E).

2.　**C**　This is a Yes/No data sufficiency question, so be prepared to Plug In more than once. The known information is that the three children in the Yao family are all at least one year apart in age. The statements need to provide a way to determine the ages. Consider Statement (1). Given that the sum of the children's ages is less than 22, Plug In three values for the children that add to less than 22. If the children are 5, 6, and 7, then the sum of the ages is 18. In this case, all three children are less than 11, so the answer to the question is Yes. Now Plug In different values trying to get an answer of No. If the children are 3, 4, and 12 years old, then the sum of the ages is 19. In this case, not all of the children are less than 11 years old, so the answer is No. The statement produces both a Yes and a No answer to the question, so the statement is insufficient. Write down BCE. Now consider Statement (2). Given that the oldest child is twice as old as the youngest child, Plug In three values for the children. If the children are 5, 7, and 10, then all three children are less than 11, so the answer to the question is Yes. Now Plug In different values in an attempt to get an answer of No. If the children are 6, 8, and 12 years old, then not all of the children are less than 11 years old, so the answer is No. The statement produces both a Yes and a No answer to the question, so the statement is insufficient. Eliminate (B). Now consider both statements together. The statements combine to dictate that the sum of the children's ages is less than 22 and the oldest child is twice as old as the youngest child. Plug In values that satisfy both statements. If the youngest child is 4, the oldest 8, and the middle child 6, the sum of the ages is 18. In this case, all three children are less than 11, so the answer to the question is Yes. Now Plug In again in an attempt to get an answer of No. If the oldest child is 11, that makes the youngest child 5.5 and the middle child at least 6.5 years old. This totals 23, which violates Statement (1). All the numbers that satisfy both statements produce an answer of Yes to the question. The statements combined are sufficient. The correct answer is (C).

3.　**C**　This is a value data sufficiency question, so begin by determining what is known and what is needed to answer the question. The question states that $x = \sqrt[3]{k}$ and asks for the value of x. To answer the question, the statements need to provide a value of x or k. Consider Statement (1). If $k = 1{,}000$, then $x = \sqrt[3]{1{,}000} = 10$. However, if $k = 216$, then $x = \sqrt[3]{216} = 6$. Statement (1) produces two different answers to the question. Statement (1) is insufficient. Write down BCE. Consider Statement (2). If $x = 5$, then the answer to the question is 5. If $x = 13$, then the answer to the question is 13. So, Statement (2) is insufficient. Eliminate (B). Now consider Statements (1) and (2) together. If $x = 7$, then both Statements (1) and (2) are satisfied, and the answer to the question is 7. If $x = 5$ or if $x = 11$, then Statement (2) is satisfied, but Statement (1) is not. The only value for x that satisfies both Statements (1) and (2) is 7, which means that Statements (1) and (2) together are sufficient. The correct answer is (C).

4. **D** Begin the question by determining how many total miles Judy drove in the first two months of the three-month period and the total for the three-month period. In the first month, Judy averaged 24 miles per gallon and used 19 gallons, so she drove $24 \times 19 = 456$ miles. In the second month, she averaged 26 miles per gallon and used 31 gallons, so she drove $26 \times 31 = 806$ miles. For all three months, Judy averaged 27 miles per gallon and used 72 gallons, so she drove $27 \times 72 = 1,944$ miles. This means she drove $1,944 - 456 - 806 = 682$ miles in the third month. Judy used a total of 72 gallons of gas for the three-month period, which means she used $72 - 19 - 31 = 22$ gallons of gas in the third month. So, Judy's average miles per gallon for the third month is $\frac{682}{22} = 31$. The correct answer is (D).

5. **D** This is a permutation problem, so evaluate it one step at a time. The problem states that the novels must be grouped by genre. There are 3 fantasy novels. Determine how many different ways the fantasy novels can be arranged. There are 3 options for the first fantasy novel, 2 options for the second, and 1 option for the third, so there are $3 \times 2 \times 1 = 6$ ways to arrange the fantasy novels. Repeat this for each of the different genres. There are $2 \times 1 = 2$ ways to arrange the biographies and $4 \times 3 \times 2 \times 1 = 24$ ways to arrange the science fiction novels. The total number of ways the books can be arranged is the product of all the arrangements by genre. The total number of ways to arrange the books is $6 \times 2 \times 24 = 288$. The correct answer is (D).

6. **C** This is a value data sufficiency question, so begin by determining what is known and what is needed to answer the question. The question provides that $xy = -1$ and asks for the value of $|x - y|$. The statements need to give specific values of x and y. Because there are variables, Plug In. Consider Statement (1). If $x = 2$, then $y = -\frac{1}{2}$ and the value of $|x - y|$ is $\frac{5}{2}$. However, if $x = 3$, then $y = -\frac{1}{3}$ and the value of $|x - y|$ is $\frac{10}{3}$. The statement produces more than one value for the question, so it is insufficient. Write down BCE. Consider Statement (2). If $y = 2$, then $x = -\frac{1}{2}$ and the value of $|x - y|$ is $\frac{5}{2}$. However, if $y = 3$, then $x = -\frac{1}{3}$ and the value of $|x - y|$ is $\frac{10}{3}$. The statement produces more than one value for the question, so it is insufficient. Eliminate (B). Now work with both statements together. The only number that allows for both x and y to be integers and $xy = -1$ is if one of the values is 1 and the other is -1. No matter which variable is equal to 1 and which to -1, the result of $|x - y|$ is always 2. Because the two statements combined produce one value for the answer, the statements combined are sufficient. The correct answer is (C).

7. **A** The question states that $m = \dfrac{\left(\frac{1}{6} + \frac{3}{8} - \frac{1}{4}\right)}{\left(\frac{7}{3}\right)}$. Multiply the fraction by the reciprocal of the fraction in the denominator, which yields $m = \dfrac{3}{7}\left(\dfrac{1}{6} + \dfrac{3}{8} - \dfrac{1}{4}\right)$. Before applying the distributive property, find common denominators for all the fractions inside the parentheses, which makes $m = \dfrac{3}{7}\left(\dfrac{1}{6} + \dfrac{3}{8} - \dfrac{1}{4}\right) = \dfrac{3}{7}\left(\dfrac{4}{24} + \dfrac{9}{24} - \dfrac{6}{24}\right)$. Now add and multiply to find that $m = \dfrac{3}{7}\left(\dfrac{4}{24} + \dfrac{9}{24} - \dfrac{6}{24}\right) = \dfrac{3}{7}\left(\dfrac{7}{24}\right) = \dfrac{1}{8}$. Use this value in the expression and solve to find that $\sqrt[3]{\dfrac{1}{m}} = \sqrt[3]{\dfrac{1}{\left(\frac{1}{8}\right)}} = \sqrt[3]{8} = 2$. The correct answer is (A).

8. **D** This question asks for the percent difference between two numbers, so use the percent change formula. The percent change formula is $\dfrac{difference}{original} \times 100$. In this question, 15 is the original number, so the percent change is $\dfrac{450 - 15}{15} \times 100 = \dfrac{435}{15} \times 100 = 2{,}900$ percent. The correct answer is (D).

9. **B** Divide 800 miles by 25 miles/gallon to determine that 32 gallons of gas are needed for the trip. Multiply 32 gallons by \$1.25/gallon to find that it costs \$40 total for the gas for the trip. If Barb and Claire each pay twice what Amy pays, then Barb and Claire each pay 40% of the cost of the gas, and Amy pays 20%. Barb's cost equals $\$40 \times 40\% = \$16$. The correct answer is (B).

ALGEBRA

1. **E** If $z = 8$, then $z + 3 = 3y + 2$ becomes $8 + 3 = 3y + 2$ and $y = 3$. Use the value of y in the first equation to find that $7(3) = 4x + 1$ and $x = 5$. The correct answer is (E).

2. **E** This is a Yes/No data sufficiency question, so be prepared to Plug In more than once. The question asks if $k \le p$. Evaluate the statements individually. Consider Statement (1). The inequality $k > 0$ doesn't give any information about p, which means that Statement (1) is insufficient. Write down BCE. Consider Statement (2). Plug In. If $k = 2$ and $p = 8$, then this statement is $2^3 = 8$. In this case, Statement (2) is satisfied and the answer to the question is Yes. Plug In again in an attempt to get an answer of No to the question. If $k = \dfrac{1}{2}$ and $p = \dfrac{1}{8}$, then the statement is $\left(\dfrac{1}{2}\right)^3 = \dfrac{1}{8}$. This is true, so Statement (2) is satisfied. However, the answer to the question is now No. The statement produces

both a Yes and a No answer to the question, so the statement is insufficient. Eliminate (B). Consider Statements (1) and (2). The values used to Plug In for Statement (2) also satisfy Statement (1). This means that both statements combined can create both a Yes and No answer to the question. Both statements combined are insufficient to answer the question. The correct answer is (E).

3. **B** This is a value data sufficiency question, so determine what is known and what is needed in order to answer the question. The question asks for the value of k. There is no other information known from the question. To be sufficient, the statements need to provide a way to solve for a single value of k. Consider Statement (1). This is a quadratic. Factor $2k^2 + 7k + 6 = 0$ to get $(2k + 3)(k + 2) = 0$, which means that $k = -\frac{3}{2}$ or $k = -2$. Because there is more than one possible value of k, Statement (1) is insufficient. Write down BCE. Consider Statement (2). Factor $4k^2 + 12k + 9 = 0$ to get $(2k + 3)(2k + 3)$ and $k = \frac{3}{2}$. There is a single value of k, which means that Statement (2) is sufficient. The correct answer is (B).

4. **D** This is a Yes/No data sufficiency question, so be prepared to Plug In more than once. The question states that x, y, and z are consecutive negative odd integers such that $x > y > z$. The question asks if $xy > |z|$. Because xy are both negative and the question asks for $|z|$, both values are positive numbers. Consider Statement (1). Plug In values that satisfy the statement. If $z = -7$, then $y = -5$ and $x = -3$. In this case, the answer to the question is Yes because $15 > 7$. In fact, no matter what number is Plugged In for z, the answer to the question is always Yes because the product of xy is greater than z. Statement (1) produces a consistent Yes answer to the question, so the statement is sufficient. Write down AD. Consider Statement (2). Plug In a value for x that satisfies the statement. If $x = -3$, then $y = -5$ and $z = -7$. Like Statement (1), this produces a Yes answer to the question. Any value of x that satisfies the statement results in an answer of Yes to the question. Statement (2) produces a consistent Yes answer to the question, so the statement is sufficient. The correct answer is (D).

5. **C** This is a Yes/No data sufficiency question, so be prepared to Plug In more than once. If $x < (x^2 - y^2)^{\frac{1}{3}}$, then the question can be rewritten as asking if $x^3 < x^3 - y^2$. Consider Statement (1). If $x^2 > y^2$ and x and y are positive, then $x > y$. However, if x and y are negative, then $x < y$. Plug In $x = 3$ and $y = 2$. This satisfies Statement (1). The answer to the question is No because $27 < 9 - 4$ is false. Plug In again. If $x = -3$ and $y = 2$, then the statement is satisfied. Now the answer to the question is Yes because $-27 < 9 - 4$ is true. Because the statement produces two different answers to the question, the statement is insufficient. Eliminate (A) and (D). Consider Statement (2). Plug In $x = 2$ and $y = 3$. This satisfies Statement (2). The answer to the question is No because $8 < 4 - 9$ is false. Plug In again. If $x = -3$ and $y = 2$, then the statement is satisfied. The answer to the question is Yes because $-27 < 9 - 4$ is true. Because the statement produces two different answers to the question, the statement is insufficient. Eliminate (B). Consider Statements (1) and (2) together. Plug In $x = -3$ and $y = 2$, which satisfies Statement (1) and Statement (2). The answer to the question is Yes because $-27 < 9 - 4$ is true. Plug In again in an attempt to get a No answer to the question. If x and y are both positive, then Statement (1) is satisfied only when $x > y$. In that case, Statement (2) is not satisfied. If x and y are both negative, then Statements (1) and (2) are satisfied only when $x < y$. If x is positive and y is

negative, then Statement (2) is not satisfied. When x is negative and y is positive, Statements (1) and (2) are satisfied if $|x| > |y|$. In order to satisfy both statements, x must be negative, and y can be positive or negative. If Statement (1) is satisfied, then $x^2 - y^2$ is positive, which means that x is always less than $x^2 - y^2$, and the answer to the question is Yes. Statements (1) and (2) together are sufficient. The correct answer is (C).

6. **E** This is a value data sufficiency question, so determine what is known and what is needed in order to answer the question. If $ax^2 + bx + c = (3x - d)^2$, then $ax^2 + bc + bx + c = 9x^2 - 6dx + d^2$, which means that $a = 9$, $b = -6d$ and $c = d^2$. Subtract $9x^2 - 6dx$ from both sides, which results in $c = d^2$. The statements need to provide a way to solve for the value of d given this information. Consider Statement (1). If $c = 9$, then $9 = d^2$, and $d = 3$ or $d = -3$. Statement (1) produces two different answers to the question, so it is insufficient. Eliminate (A) and (D). Consider Statement (2). If $a - x = 10$, then $9 - (-1) = 10$ and $x = -1$. This does not provide any information regarding how to solve for d, which means that Statement (2) is insufficient. Eliminate (B). Now consider Statements (1) and (2). From Statement (1), $9 = d^2$ and Statement (2) provides no information about how to solve for d. Statements (1) and (2) together are insufficient. Eliminate (C). The correct answer is (E).

7. **B** Translate the question into an expression and solve. The expression in the question can be translated to $\sqrt[3]{\sqrt{128}}$. A root is the same thing as a fractional exponent. Therefore, the square root of 128 can be written as $128^{\frac{1}{2}}$. The cube root of this number can be written as $\left(128^{\frac{1}{2}}\right)^{\frac{1}{3}}$. Use the Power-Multiply rule of exponents to find that $\left(128^{\frac{1}{2}}\right)^{\frac{1}{3}} = 128^{\frac{1}{6}}$. All of the answer choices have a base of 2, so rewrite 128 as its prime factorization, which is 2^7. Now the expression can be written as $\left(2^7\right)^{\frac{1}{6}} = 2^{\frac{7}{6}}$. Factor out $2^{\frac{6}{6}}$ from the expression and manipulate to find that $2^{\frac{7}{6}} = \left(2^{\frac{6}{6}}\right)\left(2^{\frac{1}{6}}\right) = 2\sqrt[6]{2}$. The correct answer is (B).

READING COMPREHENSION

1. **C** The subject of the question is the passage as a whole and the task of the question is indicated by the phrase *primary purpose*, so this is a primary purpose question. The passage introduces a *mysterious new material* that is *surprising scientists with its ability to conduct electricity without resistance...at close to room temperature*. The passage then compares this substance with other *superconductors* and then states that the material *demonstrates the possibility of zero-resistance materials that are functional at normal temperatures*. The remainder of the passage discusses the different aspects of the new material and how they may impact the use of superconductors. Evaluate the answer choices individually, looking for one that reflects the primary purpose of the passage. Choice (A) is a no-such-comparison answer as the passage does not *compare technologies in one field to those in another field*. Eliminate (A). Choice (B) is a memory trap as the passage does mention *temperature* in multiple places. But temperature is not the primary

purpose of the passage. Eliminate (B). Choice (C) is a good paraphrase of the primary purpose of the passage, so keep it. Choice (D) is a reversal of the information in the passage. The passage states that *scientists cannot yet explain this material's properties or how it can function at such unusually high temperatures*. If scientists cannot yet explain how the material functions at the temperatures at which it is found, then they cannot yet discuss applications of the material. Eliminate (D). Choice (E) is a memory trap. The passage does speculate about potential impacts of the material's discovery, but this is not the primary purpose of the passage. Eliminate (E). The correct answer is (C).

2. **C** The subject of the question is the phrase *atmospheric pressures,* and the task of the question is referenced by the phrase *most likely in order to,* so this is a purpose question. Determine why the author uses the phrase *atmospheric pressures.* The sentence in question is *While known superconductors typically function only in extremely frigid temperatures, though at atmospheric pressures, the new material only survives under very high pressures, such as those near the center of the Earth.* In this sentence, the conditions in which *known superconductors typically function* are compared to the conditions in which *the new material only survives.* One of the conditions in which known superconductors function is *at atmospheric pressures,* while the new material only survives *under very high pressures, such as those near the center of the Earth.* Therefore, the passage mentions *atmospheric pressures* to compare the conditions for the function of known superconductors and the conditions for the survival of the new material. Evaluate the answer choices individually, looking for one that reflects this idea. Choice (A) is a memory trap as the passage does mention different regions of the Earth, but this is not the purpose of discussing atmospheric pressures. Eliminate (A). Choice (B) is a reversal of the information in the passage as functioning at atmospheric pressures is one of the reasons common superconductors are used. Eliminate (B). Keep (C) because it is a good paraphrase of the purpose of mentioning *atmospheric pressures.* Choice (D) is a memory trap. *Atmospheric pressures* is listed as one of the conditions in which common superconductors function, but the purpose of mentioning atmospheric pressures is not to *describe the primary location.* Eliminate (D). Choice (E) is another memory trap. The passage does mention *extremely frigid temperatures* and atmospheric pressures as conditions for common superconductors. The passage also mentions *the need for temperatures below –140 degrees Celsius* for common superconductors to function as an issue. But *atmospheric pressures* is not mentioned to *emphasize the difficulty of achieving extremely low temperatures.* Eliminate (E). The correct answer is (C).

3. **E** The subject of the question is *characteristic(s) of the new material* and the task is referenced by the phrase *mentioned in the passage,* so this is a retrieval question. Determine what the passage says about the characteristics of the new material. The passage says the new material has the *ability to conduct electricity without resistance…at close to room temperature* and *survives under very high pressures.* The material is *composed of carbon, sulfur, and hydrogen* and has *expanded the possibilities for future superconductor research* despite that scientists *cannot yet explain this material's properties or how it can function at such unusually high temperatures.* This is an EXCEPT question, so evaluate the answer choices individually, looking for the one not mentioned in the passage. Eliminate (A) because the passage says the material is *composed of carbon, sulfur, and hydrogen.* Eliminate (B) because the passage says the material can function *at close to room temperature.* Eliminate (C) because the material *survives under very high pressures.* Choice (D) can also be eliminated as the material

has *expanded the possibilities for future superconductor research.* Choice (E) is a reversal of the information in the passage that scientists *cannot yet explain this material's properties or how it can function at such unusually high temperatures.* The correct answer is (E).

4. **B**   The subject of the question is *plants that are common to both South America and Polynesia* and the task of the question is referenced by the phrase *most likely in order to*, so this is a purpose question. Determine what the passage says about these plants. The first paragraph says that Cooper *challenges Burley's contention that Polynesians must have reached the New World because they found Easter Island and share common flora, such as the bottle gourd and sweet potato, with South America.* The second paragraph states that *Cooper's belief severs the historical connection between the regions and displaces the South American plants that are generally accepted as products of Polynesian trade.* Therefore, plants are mentioned as another piece of evidence regarding the contested connection between South America and Polynesia. Evaluate the answer choices individually, looking for one that reflects this idea. Choice (A) is a memory trap from the passage, which states *modern DNA has limited applicability in determining the origin of a species in one part of the world.* This is not a reason why the passage mentions plants, so eliminate (A). Choice (B) is a good paraphrase of the information in the passage, so keep (B). Choice (C) is a reversal of the information in the passage, which states *chickens, among other animals and objects, moved around the world as people traveled.* Eliminate (C). Choice (D) is a memory trap. While the passage does mention plants to *suggest that the chicken probably arrived in South America not from Polynesia but from another region*, the passage also mentions the plants as a reason why there is a connection between South America and Polynesia. This answer choice does not address both claims about the plants in the passage. Eliminate (D). Choice (E) is also a memory trap as the plants are considered *evidence that disproves Cooper's claim about the South American chicken's origin.* But the plants are also mentioned as an argument in support of Cooper's claim. Eliminate (E). The correct answer is (B).

5. **A**   The subject of the question is *Cooper's DNA evidence* and the task of the question is referenced by the word *suggests*, so this is an inference question. Determine what the passage says about Cooper's DNA evidence. Cooper's team conducted a *comparison of the DNA from chicken bones collected at Polynesian archaeological sites and feathers from modern Polynesian chickens with the DNA of both ancient and modern South American chickens* as evidence of *Cooper's contradiction of Storey's hypothesis that the chicken was introduced to the region by traveling Polynesians hundreds of years ago.* The passage then states *modern DNA has limited applicability in determining the origin of a species in one part of the world* and that *Cooper's dispute may require a broader view of the strong research supporting both sides of the chicken origin debate.* Evaluate the answer choices, looking for one that reflects this idea. Choice (A) is a good paraphrase of the information in the passage. Keep (A). Choice (B) is a reversal of the information in the passage that says *modern DNA has limited applicability in determining the origin of a species in one part of the world.* Eliminate (B). Choice (C) is a reversal of the information in the passage that Cooper's team used *DNA of both ancient and modern South American chickens.* Eliminate (C). Choice (D) is a reversal of the information in the passage as the *prevailing theory regarding plants that occur in Polynesia and South America* is also part of the debate on the origin of chickens in South America. Eliminate (D). Choice (E) uses the recycled language *bolstered*, but this is used to state that *chickens found in the two regions are genetically distinct* and not as a boon to Cooper's DNA evidence. Eliminate (E). The correct answer is (A).

6. **A**   The subject of the question is what *Cooper and Burley disagree on*, and the task of the question is referenced by the phrase *According to the passage*. This is a retrieval question, so determine what the passage says about Cooper and Burley's disagreement. According to the passage, Cooper *challenges Burley's contention that Polynesians must have reached the New World because they found Easter Island and share common flora, such as the bottle gourd and sweet potato, with South America.* Look for an answer that reflects this idea. Choice (A) is a good paraphrase of the information in the passage. Keep (A). Choice (B) is a reversal of the information in the passage as it is not explicitly stated that Cooper believes the South American sweet potato does not exist in Polynesia. Eliminate (B). Choice (C) is a reversal of the information in the passage. Cooper and Burley disagree on *whether* chickens appeared in South America from Polynesia, not the *time period*. Eliminate (C). Choice (D) uses the recycled language *Easter Island,* but the passage does not give any indication that either disagrees that the Polynesians located the island. Eliminate (D). Choice (E) is a memory trap. One of the contentions in the passage is regarding *the extent to which modern DNA is useful in ascertaining the regional origin of a species.* However, this is not a disagreement between Cooper and Burley. Eliminate (E). The correct answer is (A).

7. **B**   The subject of the question is the passage as a whole and the task of the question is referenced by the phrase *describes the organization,* so this is a structure question. Identify the key sentences in each paragraph. The first paragraph's last two sentences are the key sentences. They state *This paucity of data presents a challenge in accurately predicting the likelihood of future devastating storms. Consequently, some researchers have turned to a relatively new field, paleotempestology, which examines geologic evidence of prehistoric hurricane landfalls to better understand the frequency with which they occur.* The second paragraph introduces *one early study* of paleotempestology that involved extracting sediment samples *from a lake in Louisiana that was isolated from the Gulf of Mexico by a narrow barrier beach.* The second paragraph's key sentence is the last, which states *Some have questioned this method, however, as it does not conclusively verify the sediments' provenance.* The third paragraph introduces *another paleotempestological strategy.* The passage mentions in the last sentence that this method is also *called into question* by scientists. The final paragraph concludes the *limitations of paleotempestological research temper the reliability of such predictions.* Evaluate the answer choices individually, looking for one that reflects the structure of the passage. Choice (A) can be eliminated because the passage does not begin by *introducing an area of research.* Choice (B) is a good outline of the organization of the passage. Keep (B). Eliminate (C) because it is a reversal of the information in the passage. The passage does not *refute potential criticisms.* Choice (D) is a no-such-comparison answer. The passage does not compare two methodologies and *demonstrate why one is superior to the other.* Eliminate (D). Choice (E) is incorrect because the passage does not reconcile different viewpoints. Eliminate (E). The correct answer is (B).

8. **B**   The subject of the question is *the sediment analysis method,* and the task is referenced by the phrase *according to the passage.* This is a retrieval question. The question asks about *a potential drawback* of the analysis, so look for the information in the second paragraph that mentions a drawback. The second paragraph states *some have questioned this method, however, as it does not conclusively verify the sediments' provenance.* The word *provenance* means place of origin, so the potential drawback is that the analysis does not indicate where the sediment came from. Evaluate the answer choices individually,

looking for one that reflects this idea. Choice (A) contains the recycled language *overwash layers*, but the claim that scientists were unable to *easily access* these layers is a reversal of the information in the passage. The passage does not give any indication of any issue accessing the overwash layers. Eliminate (A). Choice (B) is a good paraphrase of the information in the passage, so keep (B). Choice (C) contains a memory trap regarding oceans. While the paragraph does mention ocean sediment, it is not concerned with *knowledge regarding* the types of sediment. Eliminate (C). Choice (D) is a memory trap of the third paragraph. The third paragraph discusses *fossils*, and the potential drawback cited in the third paragraph is the *validity of fossil evidence*. Eliminate (D). Choice (E) is a reversal of the information in the passage, which states that from sediment *scientists were able to produce a rough storm history for the region, dating back several thousand years*. Eliminate (E). The correct answer is (B).

9. **A**   The subject of the question is *the two research methods described in the passage* and the task of the question is referenced by the word *inferred*, so this is an inference question. The question asks what the two research methods have in common, so determine what the passage says about each method. The first method involved *sediment samples from a lake in Louisiana that was isolated from the Gulf of Mexico by a narrow barrier beach* that resulted in the ability to *produce a rough storm history for the region, dating back several thousand years*. The first method also has a drawback noted in the passage. The second method involved *offshore-indicative foraminifera, single-celled organisms that are similarly thought to have arrived in a body of water via storm surges* and also contains a drawback outlined in the passage. Evaluate the answer choices individually, looking for one that describes something in common between the two methods. Choice (A) is true as both methods *involved bodies of water that were not connected to oceans*. Keep (A). Choice (B) uses the recycled language *Louisiana*. While the first method was conducted with samples from a lake in Louisiana, the second method does not mention a specific location. Eliminate (B). Choice (C) is a reversal of the information as the methods did produce useful data but there were questions about the methodology. Eliminate (C). Choice (D) is a memory trap. The first method was able to *construct storm timelines*, but the second method was only able to *demonstrate the age of the fossils, not necessarily when a hurricane might have occurred*. Eliminate (D). Eliminate (E) as well as it contains the extreme language *rejected*. The validity was not rejected by any scientists. The scientists only raised questions about the data. Eliminate (E). The correct answer is (A).

10. **E**   The subject of the question is *a potential benefit of paleotempestological research*, and the task of the question is referenced by the word *mentioned*. This is a retrieval question. Determine what the passage says about this research. The research was turned to in response to the *challenge in accurately predicting the likelihood of future devastating storms*. The passage describes the research as a *relatively new field* which *examines geologic evidence of prehistoric hurricane landfalls to better understand the frequency with which they occur*. It states that *the limitations of paleotempestological research temper the reliability of such predictions* and *long-term changes in weather and climate affect the frequency of tropical storms, which further casts doubt on the field's ability to relate past storm data to the potential for future hurricanes*. This is an EXCEPT question, so the correct answer will not be mentioned in the passage. Choice (A) is directly supported by the information in the passage. which states that *a better understanding of storm frequency and characteristics can assist in hurricane forecasts, which in turn guides infrastructure planning and even insurance rates*. Eliminate (B) and (C). Choice (D) is

a reversal of the information in the passage that states the field *examines geologic evidence of prehistoric hurricane landfalls to better understand the frequency with which they occur.* Choice (E) is not mentioned as one of the potential benefits of the research, so keep it. The correct answer is (E).

CRITICAL REASONING

1. **A** The question task is indicated by the phrase *poses the most serious challenge,* so this is a weaken question. Find the conclusion, premise, and pattern or assumption. The conclusion of the argument is *doing a nationwide mailing campaign of a brochure extolling the benefits of organic produce will help the ecosystem of our entire country.* The premise is *pesticides impact the health of the ecosystem, which affects the health of consumers.* This argument follows a Planning pattern, since the conclusion is about what course of action to take. The assumption is that there is no problem with the plan to *help the ecosystem of our entire country* with *a nationwide mailing campaign of a brochure.* The correct answer will expose a problem with the plan.

    (A) Correct. This answer reveals a problem with the plan. If the negative impact of the mailing campaign meets or exceeds the positive impact of more people eating organic produce, then the plan is not effective.

    (B) No. The impact of eating a healthy diet on how close an individual is to leading an environmentally-friendly lifestyle is out of scope.

    (C) No. This answer strengthens the argument. If *Organic produce is already available in nationwide grocery chains,* then the plan is more likely to work.

    (D) No. This answer is out of scope. This answer choice weakens the connection between organic produce and health benefits.

    (E) No. This answer strengthens the argument. If there is less conventional produce in the store, then there may be more organic produce. If there is more organic produce, then the plan is more likely to work.

    The correct answer is (A).

2. **A** The question task is referenced by the phrase *most helps to explain,* so this is a resolve/explain question. Specifically, the task is to find the answer that explains *how minerals lower on the Mohs scale can still affect minerals that are higher on the Mohs scale.* Find the conflict in the argument. The argument states *However, at times minerals that are classed as lower hardness on the Mohs scale can create microscopic disruptions on minerals that have a higher Mohs hardness.* The correct answer will explain how minerals can have a lower classification yet still damage harder minerals.

    (A) Correct. This answer explains that the damaging *microscopic disruptions* don't count as *scratches* for purposes of Mohs classification.

(B) No. This answer would make the conflict worse because it questions the validity of the Mohs scale.

(C) No. This answer choice addresses only one side of the argument. The answer confirms that the disruptions can't be seen by the *naked eye*; however, it doesn't explain whether *naked eye* is the standard for a *visible scratch* that determines the Mohs classification.

(D) No. This answer is giving an alternative to the Mohs scale, but this choice is out of the scope of the task as it does not explain *how minerals lower on the Mohs scale can still affect minerals that are higher on the Mohs scale.*

(E) No. This answer explains only one side—that softer minerals can damage the integrity of harder minerals—but this choice doesn't explain why the minerals are classed as harder and softer on the Mohs scale.

The correct answer is (A).

3. **A** The question task is referenced by the phrase *calls into question,* so this is a weaken question. Find the conclusion, premise, and assumption or pattern. The conclusion is *that students are at least partly motivated by the amount of money they have invested for in-person tutoring* and the premise is the findings of the *student response survey.* This argument follows a sampling pattern. The standard assumption of a sampling pattern is that the sample is representative. The correct answer will give new evidence that shows the sample is not representative or cannot be trusted.

(A) Correct. If those who bought individual hours paid more per hour, then they have a greater financial incentive, and yet the group with individual hours has more sessions that are missed or rescheduled.

(B) No. The *strong verbal commitment* a student made to be present is out of the scope of the argument.

(C) No. The rescheduling fee or cancellation fee for a session is out of the scope of the argument.

(D) No. This answer suggests that scheduling purchased hours one hour at a time might lead to a lower missed or rescheduled rate when compared to purchasing 10 hours all at once.

(E) No. How sessions are classified as rescheduled or missed is out of the scope of the argument.

The correct answer is (A).

4. **B** The question task is referenced by the phrase *provides the most support,* so this is a strengthen question. Find the conclusion, premise, and pattern or assumption in the argument. The conclusion is *the accusations of plagiarism I face from the committee are invalid.* The premise is *I had never read my mentor's textbook, which was published three months ago, before completing my thesis.* The graduate student is arguing against the committee's claim of plagiarism. The committee's argument follows a causality pattern. The committee assumes the cause of the *similar positions* in the two works is *plagiarism.* The standard assumption of a causality pattern is that there is no other cause and it's not a coincidence. To support the student's defense against this assumption, the correct answer

needs to weaken the committee's assumption of causality. Therefore, the correct answer will provide an alternate cause for the *similar positions* in the mentor's text and the student's thesis.

(A) No. This weakens the student's position, as it suggests there was ample time to become exposed to the ideas in the mentor's work.

(B) Correct. This indicates that both the student's and the mentor's works were influenced by a third scientist, which would support that the student has not plagiarized the mentor.

(C) No. This answer indicates that the mentor's physics book was published by a company that doesn't usually publish physics. This information is out of the scope of the question.

(D) No. This weakens the student's position. If other students had time to write papers on the mentor's book, then it is possible for this student to write a thesis based on the same work.

(E) No. This weakens the student's position. This indicates the mentor's work was started before the student's thesis, so the student might have had some exposure to the ideas before publication.

The correct answer is (B).

5. **E** The question task is referenced by the phrase *calls into question,* so this is a weaken question. Find the conclusion, premise, and patterns or assumption. The conclusion is *people are more willing to trust a story that feels familiar but has a few inconsistencies than a story that is entirely new but completely verifiable.* The premise is *"truth adherence"—the closeness with which a story aligns to the known facts—is more likely to win a listener's trust than a completely unfamiliar story with corroboration from others.* In this argument, the language shifts from people's *trust* being connected to the *closeness with which a story aligns to the known facts* to people's *trust* being connected to *a story that feels familiar but has a few inconsistencies.* The argument fits the causality pattern, as it assumes the root cause of *trust* in a story is whether it *aligns to the known facts* and therefore *feels familiar* even though it may have *a few inconsistencies.* The standard assumption of a causality pattern is that there is no other cause and it's not a coincidence. The correct answer will provide evidence to weaken this assumption by bringing up another cause of *trust* in a story.

(A) No. This answer is out of scope. This answer targets the incidence of *"truth adherence,"* which is just a part of the premise, rather than the assumption that *trust* in a story is caused by whether it *aligns to the known facts* and therefore *feels familiar.*

(B) No. This answer strengthens the premise that *negotiators who lie regularly* know that *"truth adherence"…is more likely to win a listener's trust.*

(C) No. This answer is out of scope. This answer targets the premise that there are *negotiators who lie regularly.*

(D) No. This answer introduces a new causal relationship, that people who *become negotiators* are those who already *have a tendency to lie,* which may strengthen the premise that there are *negotiators who lie regularly.*

(E) Correct. This answer provides another reason for *trust* in a story from a negotiator: the source or person who tells the story, rather than whether the story has "*truth adherence*" or *aligns to the known facts.*

The correct answer is (E).

6. E The question task is referenced by the phrase *most helps to explain,* so this is a resolve/explain question. The argument presents a contradiction. The contradiction is that *the aeronautics commission decided to release its report as soon as the flaw was discovered* despite the rocket being *designed to explore the near planets in the solar system but not within the orbit of the Moon*, even though *Federal regulations require the public to be alerted about any flaw in the design of spacecraft intended primarily to traverse space within the Moon's orbit, but not further out in space.* The correct answer will provide new information that bridges both sides and gives a reason for the commission to release the report.

(A) No. This answer gives more information about the regulations, but not why the commission decided to release a report about the flaw. This answer only explains one side of the conflict.

(B) No. This answer explains why the regulations apply only to spacecraft within the Moon's orbit, but not why the commission decided to release a report about the flaw. This answer explains only one side of the conflict.

(C) No. This answer choice is out of scope. It rules out a possible consequence of the commission's decision but doesn't explain why the commission decided to release the report about the flaw when it wasn't required.

(D) No. This answer makes the conflict worse, as it is a reason for the commission not to release the report.

(E) Correct. If the *commission has recently received negative publicity for a lack of transparency*, then the commission has another reason to release the report about the flaw.

The correct answer is (E).

7. E The task of this question is referenced by the phrase *roles in the argument,* so this is an identify the reasoning question. Identify the conclusion and premise. The conclusion is *it's more likely that instead of early work shaping the ballerina's muscles towards expertise, the gifted young performer naturally gravitates toward ballet classes.* The second bolded phrase is a part of the conclusion. The premises are *they do not go on pointe any earlier than other ballerinas, typically between the ages of 10 and 12* and *Since the bones of the foot require time to mature, many ballet instructors delay pointe work until this age.* The first bolded phrase is a premise that supports the conclusion.

(A) No. While the second bolded phrase is a conclusion, the first bolded phrase is a premise that supports the conclusion, not a claim that the argument sets out to dispute. This answer is only a partial match.

(B) No. While the first bolded phrase is evidence against the common belief *many think* in the second sentence, the conclusion containing the second bolded phrase disagrees with that common belief. This answer is only a partial match.

(C) No. This answer does not match the structure of the passage. The first phrase is a premise that supports the argument itself, not the position it disagrees with.

(D) No. While the first bolded phrase is evidence that supports the alternative explanation that *the gifted young performer naturally gravitates toward ballet classes* found in the conclusion, the second phrase is not a refutation of that explanation. This answer is only a partial match.

(E) Correct. The first phrase is a premise in support of the conclusion, and the second phrase is the explanation or position the author advocates.

The correct answer is (E).

8.　**E**　The question task is referenced by the phrase *strengthens the argument,* so this is a strengthen question. The conclusion is *professors should never allow students to use these websites to evaluate the merits of their own essays assigned in the course,* and the premise is *the proper application of the metrics to the specifics of the essay requires a disinterested, objective perspective.* Thus, the argument fits the causality pattern. The standard assumption of a causality pattern is that there is no other cause and it's not a coincidence. The argument assumes that the cause of being able to *evaluate the merits of their own essays* is a *disinterested, objective perspective,* which the students do not have. The correct answer will uphold this assumption by ruling out another cause or confirming the link between a *disinterested, objective perspective* and a student *evaluating the merits* of their own essay.

(A) No. This answer weakens the conclusion, as it states that students are better at evaluating their own essays.

(B) No. This answer weakens the conclusion, as it suggests that it is *knowledge of the background topic,* not *a disinterested, objective perspective,* that is needed to evaluate an essay.

(C) No. This answer is out of scope. The answer choice suggests that students are unskilled at evaluating essays of *other students.* However, this argument is about the assumption that they lack the requirements to *evaluate the merits of their own essays.*

(D) No. This answer is out of scope. It suggests that the student *essay will demonstrate less merit* than *an essay written by a professional.* However, this argument is about how skilled students are at evaluating their own essays, not how skilled they are at writing those essays.

(E) Correct. If *anonymous peer review is the best method of assessing the merits of an assigned essay,* then this supports the assumption that the cause of being able to *evaluate the merits* of a student essay is *a disinterested, objective perspective.*

The correct answer is (E).

9. **D** The task of the question is referenced by the phrase *useful to know in evaluating the argument,* so this is an evaluate question. Find the conclusion, premise, and assumption or pattern. The conclusion is *for most runners, high-tech running shoes do not save money,* and the premise is *ordinary running shoes cost much less and casual runners do not get enough use out of high-tech shoes to justify the expense of the materials.* The correct answer will bring up a consideration that connects the conclusion and the premise.

(A) No. Other *shoe materials that increase running performance but do not cost as much* is out of the scope of the argument.

(B) No. The interests of casual runners are out of the scope of the passage.

(C) No. This answer is out of scope as it contrasts the materials used in shoes of *other sports.*

(D) Correct. This answer ties the conclusion and the premise together. If most runners do not save money by purchasing the high-tech running shoes, then knowing the length of time a shoe lasts is integral to understanding how often a new shoe must be purchased.

(E) No. This answer is out of scope as it targets whether these shoes *would be used for any other sport.*

The correct answer is (D).

10. **D** The task of the question is referenced by the phrase *strongly supported,* so this is a strengthen question. The passage discusses the Ostrich party's projections of Prawn party political donations *for the last 40 years.* The passage states that the projections were for *3 years later* and were *wrong by an average of 22%.* The passage also states that the Ostrich party estimated *Prawn party political donations for the previous year* and these estimates were *only off by an average of 0.2%.* The correct answer will be something that is true based on the information in the passage.

(A) No. How much the *Prawn party political donations fluctuated* is out of the scope of the passage and not supported by the information given.

(B) No. This statement is weakened by the information in the passage. If the *Prawn party had not intentionally released data intended to mislead the projections of the Ostrich party,* then there must be another reason for the projections to be off by 22%.

(C) No. The *average percent* of how *wrong* the Ostrich party's projections are is out of the scope of the passage.

(D) Correct. If the Ostrich party had accurate estimates for the previous year, then they would know that their 3-year projections were wrong.

(E) No. The *impact on the country of Jana* is out of scope.

The correct answer is (D).

Part III
How to
Crack the
GMAT Math

Chapter 6
GMAT Math:
Principles and POE

An overview of what to expect from the Quantitative
Reasoning and Data Insights sections of the GMAT
and how to use POE tools to improve your score.

The Math Sections on the GMAT

Broadly defined, "math" on the GMAT comes in two primary sections: Quantitative Reasoning and Data Insights. They both test a number of concepts that all fall under the general umbrella of "math," though the content of any given question in either section can range from algebra, arithmetic, statistics, and data analysis.

What's Covered in the Quantitative Reasoning Section

The 21 questions on the Quantitative section of the GMAT appear only in the regular problem-solving style that you're almost assuredly familiar with from other standardized tests, such as the SAT. Each question asks a specific question and is followed by 5 answer choices. On the actual test, each of the answer choices has a bubble next to it that you click to select it as your answer. During the course of this book, when we discuss the answer choices for a problem-solving question, we refer to answer choices as the letters A–E.

The Quantitative section of the GMAT tests your general knowledge of two primary subjects: Arithmetic and Basic Algebra.

What's Covered in the Data Insights Section

The four Integrated Reasoning question formats are:

Multi-Source Reasoning
Table Analysis
Two-Part Analysis
Graphics Interpretation

We'll cover these in more detail in the Data Insights chapter.

The data insights section has 20 questions that appear in two different formats. About 65%–75% of the questions are what we are going to refer to as Integrated Reasoning-style questions. In prior iterations of the GMAT, this question type had its own dedicated section called "Integrated Reasoning." The question type hasn't changed at all, but GMAC decided to roll this question type into the Data Insights section and no longer officially refers to them as "Integrated Reasoning" questions. In this book we will continue to refer to these questions as Integrated Reasoning style questions in order to distinguish them from the other question types.

Integrated Reasoning-style questions can come in one of four different formats that present a chart, table, scenario, or tabs of information. A single Integrated Reasoning question can have multiple parts to it, each of which must be answered correctly in order to receive credit for a correct answer to the question.

Data Sufficiency questions come in two flavors: Value and Yes/No. Value questions ask to you determine a specific value. Yes/No questions ask you to provide a Yes or No answer to a question.

The remaining 25%–35% of the Data Insights section are Data Sufficiency questions. These questions are unlike any other question type you've likely encountered before. They present a question and two subsequent statements. To correctly answer the question, you must determine if one, either of, both combined, or neither of the statements provides enough information to definitively answer the question.

In general, the Data Insights section of the GMAT tests your knowledge of basic statistics, data fluency, and lateral reasoning.

The Princeton Review Approach

For the most part, what you'll find on the GMAT is a kind of math that you haven't had to think about in years: junior high school and high school math. Because most people who apply to business school have been out of college for several years, high school math may seem a bit like ancient history. Because it's probably been a long time since you've needed to reduce fractions or solve for the value of a variable, the first thing to do is review the information tested on the GMAT by going through our math review. Along the way, you'll learn some valuable test-taking skills that will allow you to take advantage of some of the inherent weaknesses of standardized testing.

NOW LET'S LOOK AT THE INSTRUCTIONS

During the test, you'll be able to see test instructions by clicking on the "Help" button at the bottom of the screen. However, to avoid wasting time reading these during the test, read our version of the instructions for Problem Solving questions now:

Problem Solving Directions: Solve each problem and choose the best of the answer choices provided.

Numbers: This test uses only real numbers; no imaginary numbers are used or implied.

Diagrams: All problem-solving diagrams are drawn as accurately as possible UNLESS it is specifically noted that a diagram is "not drawn to scale." All diagrams are in a plane unless stated otherwise.

No Calculators on Quant!
One form of extra help you won't be allowed during the Quantitative section of the GMAT is a calculator. All calculations for the Quant section must be done the old-fashioned way—by hand. To get used to this, you should retire your calculator (especially during practice tests) until after you have finished with your real GMAT.

POE AND GMAT MATH

In an earlier chapter,, we introduced you to Process of Elimination—a way to increase your chances of picking a correct answer by eliminating incorrect answers.

In this section, we are going to focus on what to look for when using POE on GMAT math problems.

But, first things first.

A Reminder

The strategies we're going to outline for you in this chapter are often misunderstood by students. It's not that the concepts are overly difficult or foreign. In fact, they rely mostly on straightforward logical reasoning and simply paying close attention to the problem.

However, many students believe that these strategies are a one-stop shop for GMAT success. This is emphatically not the case.

When you are confronted with a GMAT math problem, your primary goal should be to solve the problem using the math concepts and strategies covered in this book. Solving the question should be your goal every time a new math question appears on your screen. Solving the problem is plans A, B, and C. You should take an internal inventory of the question—determine the kind of math being tested, the possible steps for completing the problem, the information provided by the problem—and then you should reach into your math toolkit to pull out the appropriate tools to solve the problem.

The POE strategies we are going to discuss are not a cheat code to solving math problems. These strategies should be considered an emergency valve. They are a rip cord for you to pull when you need it the most. That usually means that you are either stuck—the solution isn't working out—or that you are running out of time.

Hard Questions

Unless you are a truly proficient mathematician, or for some reason the adaptive portion of the GMAT testing algorithm is broken that day (hint: it won't be), you are likely to run into a math problem that you don't know how to solve. What do you do? Spending a lot of time hammering away at a problem is not necessarily the best idea, as you have other problems that you need to work on that may be easier to solve. So, you decide to guess and move on. Maybe even mark the question for editing and review later, time permitting. That's a good idea!

This is yet another reminder of the importance of answering every question. Do not get too stubbornly stuck on one question that you miss the chance to see all of them, especially those that may be easier to solve!

But wait! Before you make your guess, apply some POE strategies. You may still need to guess, but your odds of guessing correctly will be greater if you've already eliminated some answer choices. This way, you have the best possible chance at answering an additional hard question correctly, which will improve your score.

Running Out Of Time

Let's say you're nearing the end of the allotted time for the Quantitative section, and you look up only to realize that you have more questions left than you have time to work on. You know it's in your best interest to click on an answer for all the questions on the test, so you decide to guess on the remaining questions.

But wait! Don't guess randomly. Try some of these POE strategies for these remaining questions. If you can eliminate some answers before you guess, great!

Let's Get to Work

Now that we've established when you should use these POE strategies, it's time to discuss the actual strategies. For the remainder of this chapter, we are going to assume that you have already tried to answer the question using math concepts and that you were unsuccessful. Or, that you are running out of time and need to make quick, educated guesses about the answers. You are ready to break the glass and use your emergency tools. But what are those tools, and how do you wield them?

Take a look at the following question. Using the knowledge you gained from Chapter 3, are there any answer choices that you can eliminate using POE?

> Twenty-two percent of the cars produced in the United States are manufactured in Michigan. If the United States produces a total of 40 million cars, how many of these cars are produced outside of Michigan?
>
> (A) 8.8 million
> (B) 18 million
> (C) 22 million
> (D) 28.2 million
> (E) 31.2 million

Ballparking

Let's see if we can eliminate any answer choices from this problem quickly and without doing any heavy lifting. The problem is asking for the number of the 40 million cars produced in the United States that are produced outside of Michigan. The problem also states that 22 percent of the cars produced in the United States are produced in Michigan, so you know that 78 percent of the cars produced in the United States are produced outside of Michigan. Are there any answer choices that could be easily eliminated using this information and some test savvy? Well, if there are 40 million cars produced in the United States and over 50% of them are produced outside of Michigan, then the number of cars produced outside of Michigan must be greater than 20 million. Using this information, you can eliminate (A) and (B) because they are less than 20 million.

This tactic is called Ballparking, which usually involves either making rough comparisons of numbers or rough estimates of the size of an answer. In this case, a sense for the relative size of the number that is the correct answer allows for two answer choices to be eliminated.

Partial Answers

Let's apply another POE tool to the same question and see if there are any other answer choices that can be eliminated.

> Twenty-two percent of the cars produced in the United States are manufactured in Michigan. If the United States produces a total of 40 million cars, how many of these cars are produced outside of Michigan?
>
> (A)   ~~8.8 million~~
> (B)   ~~18 million~~
> (C)   22 million
> (D)   28.2 million
> (E)   31.2 million

So, you've already eliminated two of the answer choices based on ballparking. If you can eliminate one more, you've got a fifty-fifty shot at getting the question correct by guessing. You read the question again and notice that the question asks about twenty-two percent of the cars produced in the United States and that one of the answer choices is, conveniently, 22 million.

Under normal circumstances, a number repeating itself from the question stem as an answer choice is not a reason to eliminate an answer. But, you're running out of time! You need to apply POE tools aggressively. Placing a choice of 22 million in the answer choices sure seems like it COULD be a trap—it's there for the student who just remembers the number from the question stem. They do a little bit of work on the question and keep seeing that number 22 show up. So, they pick it.

This is a version of a partial answer. Partial answers are answer choices that match part of a question or a portion of a calculation. They are designed to be appealing to test-takers who don't read the full question or who are in a hurry and feel comfortable with choosing a recognizable number.

How can you use this information to your advantage? When you are looking to guess on a question, it helps to think critically about the answer choices. Does a certain answer choice look too obvious or easy? If so, there's a good chance it's a partial answer and, absent doing the actual problem, would be a good candidate to be eliminated before you guess.

Many times partial answers also come in the form of answers that can be derived from one step, or answers that contain numbers or variables that are similar to those found in the problem. If you're pressed for time and looking to guess, look for these types of answer choices to eliminate.

Finally, the best way to avoid partial answers is to get into the habit of reading the question stem one more time before selecting your answer. That way, you can be sure that you are answering the question that was asked!

Putting It All Together

Congratulations! On the last question you were able to deploy POE tools on math questions to eliminate 3 of the 5 answer choices. With practice, you'll be able to do this quickly. And while these tools are no substitute for actually solving the problem, giving yourself a 1-in-2 chance of getting a question correct by guessing is better than the 1-in-5 chance you'd have if you didn't eliminate any answer choices.

Try the following problem and look for ways to eliminate answer choices using Ballparking and partial answers.

The output of a factory is increased by 10% to keep up with rising demand. To handle the holiday rush, this new output is increased by 20%. By approximately what percent would the output of the factory now have to be decreased in order to restore the original output?

(A) 20%
(B) 24%
(C) 30%
(D) 32%
(E) 70%

Here's How to Crack It

The factory raises its output by 10% and then raises it again by 20%. The problem is asking for the amount the factory will need to lower its output to return to the original level. For this example, don't worry about solving the problem. Just practice eliminating incorrect answer choices using Ballparking or partial answers.

Choice (A) is just a repeat of the numbers in the question, which is a warning sign of a partial answer, so eliminate (A). Choice (C) is the result of adding the two percentages in the question together. This is too easy and a warning sign of a partial answer, so eliminate (C). Choice (E) is significantly greater than the information in the problem would suggest. Even if it's unclear by how much the factory needs to lower its output, the amount by which the factory raised its output is not even close to 70%. Also, 70% is the result of subtracting the sum of the two percentages in the question from 100%. Eliminate (E).

The remaining answer choices, (B) and (D), are not as easily eliminated as (A), (C), and (E). Figuring out which answer to eliminate next would require solving the problem. However, if you are in a rush or do not know how to answer this question, you could have eliminated three of the five answer choices and given yourself a good chance at correctly guessing the answer to the question. Those are better odds than guessing randomly! The correct answer, by the way, is (B).

Look at another example:

A student took 6 courses last year and received an average (arithmetic mean) grade of 100 points. The year before, the student took 5 courses and received an average grade of 90 points. To the nearest tenth of a point, what was the student's average grade for the entire two-year period?

(A) 90
(B) 92.5
(C) 95
(D) 95.5
(E) 97.2

Here's How to Crack It

Again, assume you're running out of time or are unsure how to solve this problem. Can you eliminate any answer choices to improve your odds of correctly guessing the answer? The problem states that the student received average grades of 100 and 90 in a two-year period. The question wants to know the average grade of the student for the entire two-year period. If the lowest grade the student averaged is 90, it is not possible for the student's average to be 90, so (A) can be eliminated. Choice (C) has all the warning signs of a partial answer, as 95 is just the average of 100 and 90, the two numbers found in the problem, so (C) is also a good candidate to be eliminated.

The remaining answer choices are not as easy to eliminate. One of the three remaining answer choices has to be correct. If you were to guess, you'd have a 33% chance of getting the question correct.

Summary

o The Quantitative Reasoning section of the GMAT includes 21 problem-solving questions focusing primarily on arithmetic and basic algebra skills.

o The Data Insights section of the GMAT includes 20 questions that are either Integrated Reasoning or Data Sufficiency questions. Questions in this section test your knowledge of basic statistics, data fluency, and lateral reasoning.

o Process of Elimination allows you to eliminate answer choices even when you don't know how to do a problem or you are running out of time. There are two types of answer choices to look for in these situations: Ballparking and partial answers.
   - **Ballparking:** Some GMAT answer choices can easily be found to be false by using rough estimates of numbers in the problem that make the numbers easier to work with.
   - **Partial answers:** GMAC likes to include, among the answer choices, answers that are partial completions of the problem. Recognize these answer choices by looking for choices that require little or no work, or are similar to the numbers in the problem.

Chapter 7
GMAT Math: Plugging In

Possibly the single most impactful strategy for increasing your score on the Quantitative Reasoning and Data Insights sections of the GMAT. The Plugging In family of strategies can simplify even the most difficult of questions.

In this chapter, we'll show you some powerful techniques that will enable you to solve certain types of algebra problems without using traditional algebra. If you are uncomfortable with algebra, you'll find a lot of these techniques valuable as they can make some of the toughest algebra questions far easier to solve. Even if you are an algebra whiz, proficiency of these techniques can be a big timesaver for certain questions and can be a failsafe if you run into a question you're not quite sure how to solve.

NOT EXACTLY ALGEBRA: BASIC PRINCIPLES

Algebra is used to come up with general solutions to problems. For example, you might know (for whatever reason) that the price of a new pair of shoes in relation to the cost of a pair of jeans is $3j + 20$, where j is the cost of the jeans. Based on this formula, if you know that the jeans cost \$50, then you know that the shoes cost \$170. But, you also know the cost of the shoes if the jeans cost \$75.

In most algebra problems on the GMAT, you need to find an algebraic expression that matches the description of the relationship given in the problem. For the situation above, the problem might read as follows:

> At a certain store, the price of a pair of shoes is twenty
> dollars more than three times the price of a pair of jeans.
> If the price of a pair of jeans is j dollars at this store, then
> what is the price, in dollars, of a pair of shoes, in terms of j ?
>
> (A) $20 - 3j$
> (B) $3j + 20$
> (C) $3j - 20$
> (D) $3j + 60$
> (E) $20j + 3$

You might consider this question a fairly easy algebra question. To solve it, you might just start translating the phrase "the cost of a pair of shoes is twenty dollars more than three times the cost of a pair of jeans." But, anytime you start writing algebraic equations based on information in the question, you open yourself up to possible errors.

Plugging In is a great way to avoid making mistakes when you are manipulating variables.

The truth is, most people are much better doing arithmetic than they are doing algebra. So, instead of trying to come up with a general solution—the algebraic solution—let's pick a number and come up with a specific solution. Then, we'll just choose the answer that matches! That is, let's turn algebra into arithmetic.

We call this approach **Plugging In**. It is perhaps our most powerful math technique and will allow you to solve complicated problems more quickly than you might have ever thought possible. Plugging In is easy. There are three steps involved.

Plugging In

1. Pick numbers for the variables in the problem.
2. Using your numbers, find an answer to the problem. At The Princeton Review, we call this the target answer.
3. Plug your numbers into the answer choices to see which choice equals the answer you found in step 2.

Let's look at the same problem again:

---◯---

At a certain store, the price of a pair of shoes is twenty dollars more than three times the price of a pair of jeans. If the price of a pair of jeans is j dollars at this store, then what is the price, in dollars, of a pair of shoes, in terms of j ?

(A) $20 - 3j$
(B) $3j + 20$
(C) $3j - 20$
(D) $3j + 60$
(E) $20j + 3$

Here's How to Crack It

Let's pick a number for j. Let's say that the jeans cost $10. (We don't need to worry about being realistic!) Write down "$j = 10$." We've now transformed the problem from an algebra problem into an arithmetic problem.

Here's what the problem now asks:

At a certain store, the price of a pair of shoes is twenty dollars more than three times the price of a pair of jeans. If the price of a pair of jeans is **10** dollars at this store, then what is the price, in dollars, of a pair of shoes, ~~in terms of j~~?

You'll notice that we've substituted 10 for the variable j in the original problem. You'll also notice that we've crossed out the phrase "in terms of j." Once we put a number into the problem, the phrase "in terms of" has no meaning, so we can ignore it.

Using $10 for the price of the jeans, the price of the pair of shoes is $50. All we did was translate the phrase "the price of a pair of shoes is twenty dollars more than three times the price of a pair of jeans." Three times the price of the pair of jeans is $3 \times \$10 = \$30$. Twenty dollars more is just $\$30 + \$20 = \$50$. The numerical answer to our problem is $50. Write that number down on your noteboard and circle it to indicate that it is your target answer.

Now you just need to find the answer that matches $50 when you substitute 10 for *j*. You should write down A, B, C, D, E on your noteboard and work out each answer choice. Here's what that looks like:

(A) $20 - 3j = 20 - 3(10) = -10$
(B) $3j + 20 = 3(10) + 20 = 50$
(C) $3j - 20 = 3(10) - 20 = 10$
(D) $3j + 60 = 3(10) + 60 = 90$
(E) $20j + 3 = 20(10) + 3 = 203$

Choice (B) is the only answer that matches the target answer, so it is the answer to this problem. You'll note that we checked all five answer choices. We did that to be sure we were picking the correct answer.

Another Reason to Plug In

For most folks, plugging numbers into a problem is a much more natural way to think than using algebra. Has any high school coach ever told their team, "Run 6*x* sprints, where *x* equals two full lengths of the field"? The players might comply, but you can be sure they'd have to think about the instructions first. Complicate the request with *y*, the number of players on the team, and *z*, the number of meters of the field, and you've got a real headache. Essentially, Plugging In is a matter of putting numbers back into a form that you are used to working with.

Why Plug In? Because It Makes Difficult Problems Easy!

You might be thinking, "Wait a minute! It was just as easy to solve this problem algebraically. Why should I Plug In?" To see why, let's take a look at another version of the problem.

At a certain store, the price of a pair of shoes is twenty dollars more than three times the price of a pair of jeans and the price of a sweater is fifty percent more than the price of a pair of shoes. If the price of a pair of jeans is *j* dollars at this store, then what is the price, in dollars, of a pair of shoes, a sweater, and a pair of jeans, in terms of *j* ?

(A) $1.5j + 10$
(B) $3j + 20$
(C) $4.5j + 30$
(D) $5.5j + 30$
(E) $8.5j + 50$

Here's How to Crack It

This version of the problem is wordier, and that helps to make it more confusing. Let's try Plugging In. As before, we'll start by making $j = 10$. So, the jeans cost $10. Next, we know the relationship between the price of the jeans and the cost of the shoes. The price of the shoes is "twenty dollars more than three times the price of the jeans." So, the price of the shoes is $50. Finally, the sweater costs "fifty percent more than the price of the shoes." So, the sweater is $50 + $25, or $75. So, the cost of all three items is $10 + $50 + $75 = $135. Be sure to circle $135.

Now it's time to find the answer that equals 135 when $j = 10$. Choice (A) is 25, so cross it off. Choice (B) is 50, so it's wrong. Choice (C) is 75, so it's also wrong. Choice (D) is 85, so it can be eliminated. Finally, (E) is 135. Choice (E) matches the target and is the correct answer.

By the way, (D) is what you get if you misread how to calculate the cost of the sweater. If you were doing the algebra, the cost of the shoes is $3j + 20$. It would be pretty easy to think that the price of the sweater is then $1.5j + 10$, which is fifty percent of the cost of the shoes rather than fifty percent *more*. Of course, you could make this mistake while working with the numbers too. But, what's easier—to see that $25 is not more than $50 or to see that $1.5j + 10$ is not more than $3j + 20$?

To recap, there are two reasons why you'd want to Plug In even if you are pretty good at algebra.

1. Plugging In can make even the hardest algebra problems much easier to solve.
2. The test-writers have thought about all the possible ways you might mess up the algebra while working the problem. If you make one of those mistakes, your answer will be among the answer choices, and you'll most likely wind up picking the wrong answer.

Plugging In: Not Just for Quantitative Reasoning

Plugging In techniques can also be used for Data Sufficiency questions. While there can be numerous use cases, the most prominent use case for Plugging In on Data Sufficiency questions comes with Yes/No style questions.

If P is a set of integers, is the average of P equal to the median of P?

(1.) There are an equal number of integers greater than and less than the median and average of Set P.
(2.) There are an odd number of integers in Set P.

Here's How to Crack It

This is a Yes/No Data Sufficiency question, so be prepared to Plug In more than once. The question stem states that P is a set of integers, and the question asks if the average of P is equal to the median of P. For the statements to be sufficient, they need to provide information that produces a consistent Yes or No answer to the question.

Evaluate Statement (1). Statement (1) provides the detail that there are an equal number of integers greater than and less than the median and average of Set P. Plug In values for Set P that satisfy this statement. If Set P is [1, 2, 3], then there are an equal number of integers greater than and less than the median and average. In this case, the median and average are both equal to 2, which means the answer to the question is Yes, the average of P is equal to the median of P. Plug In again and try to get an answer of Yes. If P is [1, 2, 3, 5], then the average is 2.75 and the median is 2.5. There are an equal number of integers greater than and less than the median and average, so the statement is satisfied. In this case, the answer to the question is No, the average of P is not equal to the median of P. This statement does not produce a consistent Yes or No answer to the question, so Statement (1) is insufficient. The only possible remaining answer choices are (B), (C), and (E). Eliminate (A) and (D).

Now evaluate Statement (2). Statement (2) provides the detail that there are an odd number of integers in Set P. There are no further restrictions on the integers for Set P, which means Set P could be anything. For instance, Set P could be the integers [1, 2, 3] but could also be the integers [1, 2, 100, 3052, 4800]. Because there is no further information about the numbers in Set P, Statement (2) will not produce a consistent answer to the question, and it is insufficient. Eliminate (B).

<table>
<tr><td>

**Data Sufficiency
Plugging In**

We're showing you here
how to use Plugging
In for Data Sufficiency
questions. We discuss
the strategic approach
to Data Sufficiency
questions later on in
this book—for now, just
work on recognizing
opportunities to Plug
In on Data Sufficiency
questions and how to
approach them.

</td><td>

Evaluate both statements together. Plug In values for Set P that satisfy both statements. The set [1, 2, 3] satisfies both statements as the average and median are both 2, there is one value less than and one value greater than 2, and there are an odd number of integers. In this case, the answer to the question is Yes, the average of P is equal to the median of P. Plug In again and try to get an answer of Yes. Because there has to be an odd number of integers, the median value is always going to be the middle value. In order for the number of integers greater than and less than the median and average to be equal, it must also be true that the average and median are equal. If the average is greater than the median, then the number of integers greater than the average is less than the numbers greater than the median. If the average is less than the median, then the number of integers less than the average is less than the number of integers greater than the median. No matter what values are Plugged In for the values of set P, the statements combine to produce a consistent Yes answer to the question. Eliminate (E). The correct answer is (C).

</td></tr>
</table>

How Do I Know If I Can Plug In?

What are the indicators that suggest you can Plug In on a question? Any time you see a question that is based on algebra, you should think about ways to Plug In. However, the most obvious signs are when there are variables in the question stem and answer choices. When you see that, you can very likely Plug In on the question.

What Number Should I Plug In?

While you can plug in any number, you'll find that certain numbers work better than others. Ideally, you want a number that makes it easy to perform the calculations for the problem. For most problems, you can just use small, simple numbers such as 2, 5, or 10. However, you also want numbers that make sense within the context of the problem. For example, for a problem that uses percents, plugging in 100 would be a good idea. Different numbers work for different types of problems. As you practice, you'll get

better at picking good numbers—especially if you keep asking yourself "What number will make this problem easy?" You also shouldn't be afraid to change your number if the calculations start to get messy.

> ## What to Plug In
> - Numbers that make the math easy!
> - Small, simple numbers such as 2, 5, or 10
> - Percents? Try 100
> - Hours or Minutes? 30 or 120
>
> ## What NOT to Plug In
> - Avoid using 0 or 1
> - Numbers that appear in the problem or in the answer choices

Sometimes the best way to select a number is to use a little common sense. Here's an example:

> If Jim drives k miles in 50 minutes, how many minutes will it take him to drive 10 miles at the same rate?
>
> (A) $\dfrac{500}{k}$
>
> (B) $\dfrac{k}{500}$
>
> (C) $60k$
>
> (D) $10k$
>
> (E) $\dfrac{50}{k}$

Q: If 80% of a certain number x is 50% of y and y is 20% of z, then what is x, in terms of z?

A. $5z$
B. $3z$
C. $z/4$
D. $z/5$
E. $z/8$

Turn to page 91 for the answer.

Here's How to Crack It

There are variables in the question stem and answer choices, so Plug In! Any number you choose to Plug In for k will eventually yield the answer to this problem, but there are some numbers that will make your task even easier.

We need to find a good number for k. We need to discover how long it takes Jim to drive 10 miles and already know how long it will take him to drive k miles in 50 minutes. So, what if k was equal to half of 10, or $k = 5$. The question would now read:

If Jim drives 5 miles in 50 minutes, how many minutes will it take him to drive 10 miles at the same rate?

Now the problem is pretty easy! Since Jim is going to drive twice the distance, it's going to take twice the time. So the target number is 100 minutes. Now, all we need to do is find the answer that matches the target when $k = 5$. Start with (A). Divide 500 by 5 to get 100, which matches the target answer! Check the remaining answer choices, looking for any that match the target answer. Choice (B) is 1/100, so eliminate it. Choice (C) is 300, so eliminate it. Choice (D) is 500, so eliminate it. Choice (E) is 10, so eliminate it. The only answer choice that matches the target answer is (A), which is the correct answer.

Do I Need to Check All the Answers?

In the previous question, we found an answer choice that matched the target number after checking the first answer choice, (A). Nonetheless, we continued to check all the answer choices anyway. Why did we do that?

It is possible when Plugging In to get more than one answer choice that matches the target number. To make sure you are selecting the true correct answer, you need to check each answer choice individually. If you find more than one answer choice that matches the target answer, the way to determine the correct answer is simple: Plug In a different value for the answer choices that match the target answer. Keep Plugging In until one of the answer choices is eliminated.

More Times to Plug In

So far, we've been looking at questions that have explicit variables in both the problem and the answer choices. When you see variables in the problem or answer choices, that's one of the signs to Plug In.

However, sometimes GMAC expects you to use algebra to answer a question that doesn't have explicit variables. You can still Plug In on these problems. In fact, *you should consider Plugging In whenever you feel the urge to do algebra*. The urge to do algebra is the ultimate sign that the problem can be cracked using some form of Plugging In.

Let's take a look at some other ways to Plug In.

Plugging In with Hidden Variables

Some problems have a hidden variable. For these problems, all the calculations are usually based on one item, but you don't know the value of that item. There's a simple solution—just plug in a value for the item!

Let's look at an example:

A merchant reduces the original price of a coat by 20 percent for a spring sale. Finding that the coat did not sell, the merchant reduces the spring price by a further 15 percent at the start of the summer. The coat's summer price is what percent of its original price?

(A) 35%
(B) 64%
(C) 65%
(D) 68%
(E) 80%

A: The answer is (E). If you plugged in 100 for x, then you found y must equal 160. The question tells us 160 (our y) equals 20% of z. That means z equals 800. Now it should be simple to see that x equals z divided by 8.

Here's How to Crack It

You may have noticed that this problem never gave us the coat's original price. You may have felt the urge to do algebra starting to kick in as you read the problem. For example, you might have started to say to yourself, "Well, if the price of the coat is x, then the spring price is...." That's your sign that you can do this problem as a Plug In! All you need to do is pick a price for the coat.

Let's make the original price of the coat $100. *When you are solving a percent problem, 100 is a great number to plug in.* The merchant discounts the price of the coat by 20% for the spring sale. Twenty percent of $100 is $20, so the spring price is $80. For the summer, the spring price of the coat is discounted by another 15%. Fifteen percent of $80 is $12, making the summer price $68.

The question asks for the summer price as a percent of the original price. In other words, $68 is what percent of $100? 68%. The answer is (D).

Easy Eliminations

If you were running out of time, you'd need to make a guess. But you could eliminate some obviously wrong answers first. When you read the problem fast, you might be tempted to think that the overall reduction is 20% + 15% = 35%, but that's too easy. So, cross off (A). Choice (C) is just 100 − 35 = 65. Also, too easy. Finally, (E) is what you get after the first reduction. The answer is probably (B) or (D).

Another way to tell that you can probably solve a question as a Hidden Plug In is to look at the answer choices. The answer choices for Hidden Plug In questions are typically percents, fractions, or sometimes ratios.

At College P, one-fourth of the students are seniors and one-fifth of the seniors major in business. If two-fifths of all students at the college major in business, the business majors who are not seniors are what fraction of all business majors?

(A) $\dfrac{1}{20}$

(B) $\dfrac{1}{8}$

(C) $\dfrac{7}{20}$

(D) $\dfrac{7}{15}$

(E) $\dfrac{7}{8}$

It Works for Ratios, Too!

You can also Plug In when the answer choices are expressed as ratios. Here's how a similar question would be written as a ratio problem.

At College P, one-fourth of the students are seniors and one-fifth of the seniors major in business. If two-fifths of all students at the college major in business, then what is the ratio of senior business majors to non-senior business majors?

(A) 1:3
(B) 1:5
(C) 1:7
(D) 1:8
(E) 7:8

As before, just plug in 100 for the number of students. There are 5 seniors who are business majors and 35 business majors who are not seniors. The ratio is 5:35, which reduces to 1:7. The answer is (C).

Here's How to Crack It

You may have noticed that while this problem provides lots of fractions to work with, it never reveals how many students attend College P. Of course, knowing the total enrollment at the college would make solving the problem fairly straightforward. So, before you start setting up equations based on x students at College P, let's plug in a number for the total students.

An easy way to come up with a good number when the problem has fractions is to simply multiply the denominators of the fractions together. In this case, that's $4 \times 5 \times 5 = 100$. Don't worry, by the way, that some of the denominators are not distinct. Multiplying by the extra 5 may help us to avoid getting a result that leads to some fractional part of a student!

So, if there are 100 students at the college, there are 25 seniors and 75 students who are not seniors. Next, you know that one-fifth of the seniors major in business, so that's 5 seniors who are business majors. Since two-fifths of all students are business majors, the college has 40 business majors. Of those 40 business majors, $40 - 5 = 35$ of the business majors are not seniors. So, the fraction of business majors who are not seniors is $\dfrac{35}{40} = \dfrac{7}{8}$. The correct answer is (E).

Plugging In the Answers (PITA)

Some algebra questions ask for a numerical answer. GMAC expects you to write an equation, solve it, and then pick the answer. However, the person who wrote the problem had to do all of that hard work. So, rather than duplicate all of the work the question writer did, why not just test out the answers to see which one works?

We call this method of solving the problem **Plugging In the Answers** (or PITA for short). You'll find that solving problems this way can save you a lot of time and help you to avoid common algebra mistakes. There are three steps involved when you Plug In the Answers.

Proven Technique: PITA

Plugging In the Answers

1. Write down the answers, determine what they represent, and label them.
2. Start with (C) and work the steps of the problem.
3. Look for some sort of condition that must be met to make the answer correct.

Let's take a look at an example.

At a certain restaurant, the price of a sandwich is $4.00 more than the price of a cup of coffee. If the price of a sandwich and a cup of coffee is $7.35, including a sales tax of 5%, what is the price of a cup of coffee, EXCLUDING the sales tax?

(A) $1.50
(B) $3.00
(C) $4.00
(D) $5.50
(E) $7.00

Here's How to Crack It

If there were no answer choices, you'd be forced to write an equation and solve it. However, because you know the answer must be one of the five provided choices, it will be easier and faster to simply try the answers.

Start by writing down the answers and labeling them as "coffee." Now, start with (C). If the cup of coffee costs $4.00, what can you figure out? The problem states that the sandwich costs $4.00 more than the cup of coffee, so the sandwich is $8.00. Make a column for "sandwich" and write down $8.00 next to (C). You now know that the cost of the sandwich and the cup of coffee is $12.00. Based on the information in the question stem, is it possible for the price of the sandwich and the cup of coffee to be $12.00? The question states that the price of a sandwich and a cup of coffee is $7.35. Therefore, we know that $4.00 is too expensive to be the value for the cup of coffee, so eliminate (C).

Scratch Work
When you Plug In the Answers, make your scratch work look like an Excel spreadsheet. Label your columns and put your results for each column next to the answer choice you are checking. Doing so will help you to cut down on mistakes and check subsequent answer choices more quickly.

So far, your work should look like this:

Coffee	Sandwich	Total
A) $1.50		
B) $3.00		
~~C) $4.00~~	$8.00	$12.00
D) $5.50		
E) $7.00		

Now you need to determine if the next answer choice you should try is a greater or lesser price for the cup of coffee than $4.00. If $4.00 for the cup of coffee was too great, then any value greater than $4.00 will also be too great. This means you can eliminate (D) and (E).

The only remaining answer choices are (A) and (B). There is no need to debate over which one to choose next, just pick an answer choice and get started.

Try (B). If the cup of coffee costs $3.00, then the sandwich is $7.00. That would make the total cost of the coffee and sandwich $10.00. This is still greater than the information provided in the question stem. Eliminate (B).

Here's what the work should look like at this point:

Coffee	Sandwich	Total
A) $1.50		
~~B) $3.00~~	$7.00	$10.00
~~C) $4.00~~	$8.00	$12.00
~~D) $5.50~~		
~~E) $7.00~~		

There's really no need to test (A). When Plugging In the Answers, one of the answer choices has to be correct. If you've eliminated 4 of the answer choices, then whatever is left must be correct! However, if the coffee costs $1.50, then the sandwich costs $5.50. Together the two items cost $7.00. The tax on the two items is 5% of $7.00 or $0.35. So, the total with tax is $7.35, which meets the condition stated in the problem. The answer is (A).

───────────────○───────────────

Plugging In the Answers: Advanced Principles

As seen in the previous problem, when we solved via PITA for (C), we knew right away that we needed a value less than (C), so we could easily eliminate (D) and (E) as well. However, there are times when you won't be sure. Rather than wasting time trying to decide if you need a bigger or smaller number, just pick an answer choice and try it. You'll actually waste less time testing an extra answer choice or two than you will trying to decide which type of number to try next.

Jim is now twice as old as Fred, who is two years older than Sam. Four years ago, Jim was four times as old as Sam. How old is Jim now?

(A) 8
(B) 12
(C) 16
(D) 20
(E) 24

Here's How to Crack It

This question has numbers in the answers, and you probably started to think "Well, if Jim is x years old, then Fred is…." The urge to do algebra means that it's time to Plug In the Answers. Start with (C).

The answers represent possible ages for Jim. If Jim is 16 years old, then Fred is 8 because Jim is twice as old as Fred. Next, you know that Fred is two years older than Sam, so Sam is 6. Now, you need to compare Jim's age and Sam's age four years ago. Four years ago, Jim was 12 and Sam was 2. Remember that there's always a condition in the problem that must be met by the correct answer.

When to Plug In the Answers
- The question asks for a specific amount, and that amount is represented by the answer choices.
- You have the urge to set up and solve an equation.

In this case, Jim's age four years ago must be four times that of Sam. Is 12 four times 2? No. So, (C) can be eliminated.

Here's what your work should look like up to this point.

	Now			**4 years ago**	
	Jim	Fred	Sam	Jim	Sam
A)	8				
B)	12				
~~C) 16~~		8	6	12	2
D)	20				
E)	24				

Now, it's time to choose a bigger or smaller number. But, it isn't really clear which direction to go, is it? So, rather than waste a lot of time trying to figure that out, just pick an answer and try it. If Jim is 20 years old now, as in (D), then Fred is 10 and Sam is 8. Four years ago, Jim was 16 and Sam was 4.

Here's what your work should look like.

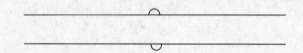

	Now			4 years ago	
	Jim	Fred	Sam	Jim	Sam
A) 8					
B) 12					
~~C) 16~~	8	6		12	2
D) 20	10	8		16	4
E) 24					

Since 4 × 4 = 16, the condition in the problem is met. Choice (D) is the correct answer.

Challenge Question

A certain game requires players to collect both blue tokens, which are worth b points each, and red tokens, which are worth r points each. If p percent of Player A's points are from blue tokens and q percent of Player A's tokens are red, which of the following is an expression for the value of p, in terms of b, r, and q ?

(A) $\dfrac{100bq}{bq + 100r - qr}$

(B) $\dfrac{10{,}000b - 100bq}{100b - bq + qr}$

(C) $\dfrac{bq + 100r - qr}{100bq}$

(D) $\dfrac{100b - bq}{100r - 100bq - qr}$

(E) $\dfrac{100b - bq + qr}{10{,}000b - 100bq}$

Here's How to Crack It

There are variables in the answer choices, so plug in values for b, r, and q. However, there is information in the question stem that should first be considered. The question asks for the value of p in terms of b, r, and q, where b and r represent the point values of blue tokens and red tokens, respectively, and q represents the number of red tokens acquired by Player A expressed as a percentage of all Player A's tokens. Had the question provided the total number of tokens acquired by Player A, then plugging in values of b, r, and q would have allowed for the calculation of p, the percentage of points earned from blue tokens. The question does not provide the number of tokens acquired by Player A, so not only is this a Plug In question, it's also a Hidden Plug In question. Let Player A acquire 10 tokens, and let $b = 5$, $r = 2$, and $q = 80$.

GMAT Focus Premium Prep

If Player A acquired 10 tokens during the game, and $q = 80\%$ of the tokens that were red, then Player A acquired 8 red tokens and 2 blue tokens. If each blue token is worth 5 points and each red token is worth 2 points, then Player A earned $2 \times 5 = 10$ points from blue tokens and $8 \times 2 = 16$ points from red tokens, for a total of $10 + 16 = 26$ points. In this case, the percentage of points that were earned from blue tokens is $p = \dfrac{10}{26} \times 100$. Circle the target answer, $\dfrac{1,000}{26}$.

Now, plug $b = 5$, $r = 2$, and $x = 80$ in for each of the answer choices, looking for the choice that equals $\dfrac{1,000}{26}$. Choice (A) is $\dfrac{100(5)(80)}{(5)(80)+100(2)-(80)(2)} = \dfrac{40,000}{440}$, which reduces to $\dfrac{4,000}{44}$, or $\dfrac{1,000}{11}$. Eliminate (A). Choice (B) is $\dfrac{10,000(5)-100(5)(80)}{100(5)-(5)(80)+(80)(2)} = \dfrac{10,000}{260}$, which reduces to $\dfrac{1,000}{26}$. Keep (B). Choice (C) is $\dfrac{(5)(80)+100(2)-(80)(2)}{100(5)(80)} = \dfrac{440}{40,000}$. Eliminate (C). Choice (D) is $\dfrac{100(5)-(5)(80)}{100(2)-100(5)(80)+(80)(2)} = \dfrac{100}{-39,640}$. Eliminate (D). Choice (E) is $\dfrac{100(5)-(5)(80)+(80)(2)}{10,000(5)-100(5)(80)} = \dfrac{260}{10,000}$. Eliminate (E). The correct answer is (B).

Plugging In the Answers Advanced Tips

1. If you're not sure whether you need a bigger or smaller number, don't waste time. Just pick another answer choice and try it.
2. You may be able to eliminate some numbers that are too big or too small before you start Plugging In. If you can, just start with the middle number that you have left.
3. If you have both easy-to-work-with numbers and messy numbers in the answer choices, try the easy-to-work-with numbers first.

Must Be

Some questions use the words "must be." For example, the question may ask which of the expressions in the answers *must be* even or *must be* divisible by 3. These questions can be solved easily by Plugging In. However, you'll probably need to Plug In at least twice to find the answer.

Here's all you need to do.

Must Be Plugging In

1. Pick numbers for the variables in the problem. Be sure to satisfy any restrictions for the variables.
2. Eliminate any answer choices that don't match what you are looking for.
3. Plug in the most different kind of number you are allowed to try. For example, if you tried an even number, try an odd number.
4. Repeat until only one answer remains.

If n is a positive integer, which of the following must be even?

(A) $(n-1)(n+1)$
(B) $(n-2)(n+1)$
(C) $(n-2)(n+4)$
(D) $(n-3)(n+1)$
(E) $(n-3)(n+5)$

Here's How to Crack It

There are variables in the question stem and answer choices, so Plug In. Start by picking a value for n. Choose a value for n that makes the calculations easy, such as $n = 2$. Evaluate each answer choice, looking for one that results in an even integer. Choice (A) equals 3, so eliminate it. For (B), the expression equals 0. Remember that 0 is an even number, so keep this answer choice. But you aren't done yet. Just because you've found one case where this answer choice is even doesn't mean it will always be even. Keep checking the answers. Choice (C) is also equal to 0, so keep it as well. Choice (D) equals –3, which is an odd integer, so eliminate it. Choice (E) equals –7 and can also be eliminated.

Next, try a new number. Since this problem is about even and odd numbers, it makes sense to try an odd number next. How about $n = 3$? You need to check only the two answers that remain. Choice (B) equals 4, which is still even. However, (C) now equals 7, so it can be eliminated. The correct answer is (B).

Here's what your work should look like once you have worked through the entire problem.

		$n = 2$	$n = 3$
A)	~~$(n-1)(n+1)$~~	3	
B)	$(n-2)(n+1)$	0	4
C)	~~$(n-2)(n+4)$~~	0	7
D)	~~$(n-3)(n+1)$~~	−3	
E)	~~$(n-3)(n+5)$~~	−7	

Which Plugging In Method Should I Use?

The problems that can be solved with the different Plugging In methods have a cadence that is unique to them. Being able to quickly identify the presence of this cadence will enable you to more easily determine which Plugging In method can be employed to solve the problem.

Below is a table that lays out these cues and the Plugging In method that is associated with them. While familiarity with this table can help you learn to identify what Plugging In method may be useful for a given problem, the only way to become more efficient at utilizing these methods is to do practice problems. Immediately following this table is a short quiz on identifying Plugging In problems and which Plugging In method to choose. At the end of the Plugging In section is a 10-question drill on Plugging In problems. Both the short quiz and the drill are excellent primers for using Plugging In, but they may not be enough. Make sure to work through the practice tests and employ the Plugging In strategies where possible.

When the problem contains...	You should consider...
variables in the question stem and answer choices	Plugging In
a missing value that the entire problem is based on, or answer choices that are percents, fractions, or ratios	Plugging In for the hidden value
numbers in the answer choices, a question that asks for a specific amount, answer choices that represent that amount, and information that makes you want to write an equation	Plugging In the Answers
the phrase *must be*	Plugging In more than once

Using the table above and the knowledge provided in the section thus far, identify which of the following questions can be solved with Plugging In methods and which Plugging In method could be used. Finding the correct solution is not the point of this drill, so no answer choices are provided. There is a 10-question Plugging In drill with full questions and answer choices later in this section.

Which Plugging In Method Should I Use? Quiz

Question	Should You Plug In?	Plugging In Method
1. If Mark's current age is three times greater than Jenny's age was 5 years ago, then, in terms of Jenny's current age, what is Mark's current age?		
2. What number is 625% of 3,420?		
3. If $x^2 > 17$ and $x^3 > -512$, then which of the following must be true of x?		
4. The original price of a shirt was increased by 25% and then decreased by 15% to a final price of $105. What was the original price of the shirt?		
5. A certain square has an area of 24 and a height that is 1.5 times its width. What is the perimeter of the square?		

DRILL 1 (Plugging In)

Work your way through the following 10-question drill and use a Plugging In method for each of the questions. Remember, for many Plugging In questions, there are multiple ways to solve the problem, and the problem can always be solved without Plugging In. The point of this drill is not to get as many questions correct as you can. The point of this drill is to practice the Plugging In techniques. So, even if you think you know a faster way to solve the problem, try to solve it using Plugging In. The answers can be found in Part V.

1. List L : 1, $\sqrt{2}$, x, x^2

   In list L, if $x > 0$ and the range of numbers is 4, then what is the value of x?

   (A) 5
   (B) 4
   (C) 2
   (D) $\sqrt{5}$
   (E) $\sqrt{4}$

2. If $r \neq s$ and $t > 0$, which of the following must be true?

    (A) $(r - s)t > 0$
    (B) $(r - s)t \neq 0$
    (C) $rt + st > 0$
    (D) $(r^2 - s^2)t > 0$
    (E) $(r - s)t > \dfrac{r - s}{t}$

3. Is $xy > 0$?

    (1) $|x| + 8|y| = 0$
    (2) $8|x| + |y| = 0$

    (A) Statement (1) ALONE is sufficient, but statement (2) alone is not sufficient.
    (B) Statement (2) ALONE is sufficient, but statement (1) alone is not sufficient.
    (C) BOTH statements TOGETHER are sufficient, but NEITHER statement ALONE is sufficient.
    (D) EACH statement ALONE is sufficient.
    (E) Statements (1) and (2) TOGETHER are not sufficient.

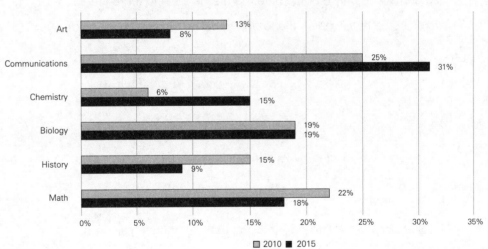

Distribution of Majors at University X, 2010 and 2015

4. In 2015, if $\dfrac{2}{6}$ of the majors in math focused on statistics, approximately what percent of all majors focused on statistics?

    (A) 3%
    (B) 6%
    (C) 9%
    (D) 12%
    (E) 15%

5. If x and y are integers such that $x^2 + y^2 < 46$ and $0 < x \le 5$, then which of the following represents all possible values of y ?

   (A) $-6 \le y \le 6$
   (B) $-6 \le y \le 5$
   (C) $-5 \le y \le 5$
   (D) $5 \le y \le 4$
   (E) $-4 < y \le 4$

6. Are the integers x, y, and z consecutive?

   (1) The average (arithmetic mean) of x, y, and z is y.
   (2) $y - x = z - y$

   (A) Statement (1) ALONE is sufficient, but statement (2) alone is not sufficient.
   (B) Statement (2) ALONE is sufficient, but statement (1) alone is not sufficient.
   (C) BOTH statements TOGETHER are sufficient, but NEITHER statement ALONE is sufficient.
   (D) EACH statement ALONE is sufficient.
   (E) Statements (1) and (2) TOGETHER are not sufficient.

7. If the probability of selecting, without replacement, 2 red marbles from a bag containing only red and blue marbles is $\dfrac{3}{55}$ and there are 3 red marbles in the bag, what is the total number of marbles in the bag?

   (A) 10
   (B) 11
   (C) 55
   (D) 110
   (E) 165

8. When integer y is divided by 2, is the remainder 1 ?

   (1) $y > 5$
   (2) y is prime

   (A) Statement (1) ALONE is sufficient, but statement (2) alone is not sufficient.
   (B) Statement (2) ALONE is sufficient, but statement (1) alone is not sufficient.
   (C) BOTH statements TOGETHER are sufficient, but NEITHER statement ALONE is sufficient.
   (D) EACH statement ALONE is sufficient.
   (E) Statements (1) and (2) TOGETHER are not sufficient.

9. One-fourth of the cars that an automobile manufacturer produces are sports cars, and the rest are sedans. If one-fifth of the cars that the manufacturer produces are red and one-third of the sports cars are red, then what fraction of the sedans is red?

(A) $\dfrac{7}{45}$

(B) $\dfrac{5}{36}$

(C) $\dfrac{1}{4}$

(D) $\dfrac{7}{20}$

(E) $\dfrac{1}{2}$

10. If Amy drove the distance from her home to the beach in less than 2 hours, was her average speed greater than 60 miles per hour?

(1) The distance that Amy drove from her home to the beach was less than 125 miles.
(2) The distance that Amy drove from her home to the beach was greater than 122 miles.

(A) Statement (1) ALONE is sufficient, but statement (2) alone is not sufficient.
(B) Statement (2) ALONE is sufficient, but statement (1) alone is not sufficient.
(C) BOTH statements TOGETHER are sufficient, but NEITHER statement ALONE is sufficient.
(D) EACH statement ALONE is sufficient.
(E) Statements (1) and (2) TOGETHER are not sufficient.

Summary

o   Most of the algebra problems on the GMAT are simpler to solve *without* algebra, using the Plugging In family of techniques.

o   Plugging In is easy. There are three steps:
   • Pick numbers for the variables in the problem.
   • Using your numbers, find an answer to the problem. (Write that answer down and circle it.)
   • Plug your numbers into the answer choices to see which choice equals the answer you found in the previous step.

o   When you Plug In, try to choose convenient numbers—those that are simple to work with and make the problem easier to manipulate.

o   When you Plug In, avoid choosing 0, 1, or a number that already appears in the problem or in the answer choices.

o   On problems with variables in the answers that contain the words "must be" or "could be," you may have to Plug In more than once to find the correct answer.

o   Plugging In the Answers is easy. There are five steps:
   • Always start with (C). Plug that number into the problem and see whether it makes the problem work.
   • If (C) is too small, try the next larger number.
   • If (C) is too big, try the next smaller number.
   • If you're not sure which way to go, don't sweat it. Just pick a direction and try it out!
   • If the question asks for the least or greatest number, start with the least or greatest answer choice.

Chapter 8
Data Insights: Fundamentals of Integrated Reasoning Style and Data Sufficiency Questions

Integrated Reasoning style questions are varied, and Data Sufficiency questions are unlike any question you've seen before. This chapter outlines what you should expect from each of these question types.

Anywhere from 25% to 35% of the questions on the Data Insights section are Data Sufficiency questions. Let's talk about POE strategies that will help make this odd question type easy.

WHAT ARE INTEGRATED REASONING STYLE QUESTIONS?

During the Data Insights section of the GMAT, you will likely encounter between 13–15 Integrated Reasoning style questions. These question types are:

- Table Analysis
- Two-Part Analysis
- Multi-Source Reasoning
- Graphics Interpretation

However, most of these questions have multiple parts that must be answered correctly in order to get credit for the question. For example, a Table Analysis question usually has three statements that you need to evaluate.

There Is a Calculator for Integrated Reasoning Style Questions

There is a calculator available for Integrated Reasoning style questions. This calculator is not available for Data Sufficiency questions.

The calculator for the Integrated Reasoning section is relatively basic. There are buttons to perform the four standard operations: addition, subtraction, multiplication, and division. In addition, buttons to take a square root, find a percent, and take a reciprocal round out the available functions. There are also buttons to store and recall a value in the calculator's memory. To use the calculator, you'll need to open it by clicking on the "calculator" button in the upper left corner of your screen. The calculator will generally open in the middle of your screen, but you can move it around so that you can see the text of the problem or the numbers on any charts or graphs that are part of the question. The calculator is available for all Integrated Reasoning questions. You can enter a number into the calculator either by clicking on the onscreen number buttons or by typing the number using the keyboard.

Here's what the calculator looks like:

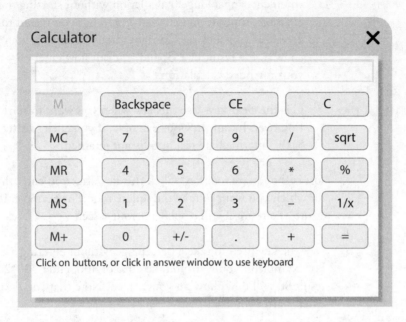

For the most part, the keys on the onscreen calculator work as you might expect. However, a few keys may not work as expected. Oddly enough, that's particularly true if you are accustomed to using a more sophisticated calculator. So here are a few tips about using some of the calculator keys:

MC MC is the memory clear key. Use this key to wipe out any values that you have stored in the calculator's memory.

MR MR is the memory recall key. Use this key to return any value that you have stored in the memory to the calculation area. For example, if you want to divide the number currently on your screen by the number in the memory, you would enter the key sequence / MR =.

MS MS is the memory store key. Use this key to store the number currently on the screen in the calculator's memory.

M+ M+ is the memory addition key. Use this key to add the current onscreen number to the number in the calculator's memory. For example, if 2 is stored in the calculator's memory and 3 is on screen, then clicking M+ will result in 5 being stored in the calculator's memory.

Backspace Backspace is used to clear the last digit entered. Use this key to correct mistakes when entering numbers without clearing the entire number. For example, if you entered 23 but meant to enter 25, click backspace and then enter 5.

Calculator Practice Tip

When you practice for the Integrated Reasoning section, use a calculator similar to the calculator provided by GMAC. If you are doing online practice, use the onscreen calculator. If you are working problems from this book, use a basic calculator rather than that fancy calculator that you might still have from your high school or college math classes.

CE

CE is the clear entry button. Use this button to correct a mistake when entering a longer calculation without starting over. For example, suppose you entered 2*3+5 but you meant to enter 2*3+9. If you click on CE right after you enter 5, your screen will show 6, the result of 2*3, and you can now enter +9= to finish your intended calculation.

C

C is the clear key. Use this key when you want to start a calculation over. In our previous example, if you click C after you enter 5, the intermediate result, 6, is not retained.

sqrt

sqrt is the square root key. Click this key after you enter the number for which you want to take the square root. For example, if you enter 4 sqrt, the result 2 will display on your screen.

%

% is the key used to take a percentage without entering a decimal. For example, if you want to take 20% of 400, enter 400*20%. The result 80 will now show on your screen. Note that you do not need to enter = after you click %.

1/x

1/x is used to take a reciprocal. Click this key after you enter the number for which you want to take the reciprocal. For example, the keystrokes 2 followed by 1/x produces the result 0.5 on your screen. Again, note that you do not need to enter = after you click 1/x.

Be sure that you thoroughly understand the way the keys for the onscreen calculator work to avoid errors and wasted time when you take your GMAT.

THE QUESTION TYPES

Let's take a more detailed look at each of the question types. In the following examples, we are not going to solve any of the problems. In some cases, we aren't even going to show you the full answer choices. We'll revisit these questions in a later chapter, where we show you strategies for answering each question type. For now, we just want you to become familiar with the different question types.

INTEGRATED REASONING STYLE QUESTIONS

Table Analysis

Table Analysis questions present data in a table. If you've ever seen a spreadsheet—and really, who hasn't?—you'll feel right at home. Most tables have 5 to 10 columns and anywhere from 6 to 25 rows. You'll be able to sort the data in the table by each column heading. The sort function is fairly basic, however. If you're used to being able to sort first by a column such as state and then a column such as city to produce an alphabetical list of cities by state, you can't do that type of sorting for these questions. You can sort only one column at a time.

Here's what a Table Analysis question looks like:

Sort By Select... ▼ **1**

National Park		Visitors			Area	
Name	State	Number	% Change	Rank	Acres	Rank
Grand Canyon	AZ	4,388,386	0.9	2	1,217,403	11
Yosemite	CA	3,901,408	4.4	3	791,266	16
Yellowstone	WY	3,640,185	10.5	4	2,219,791	8
Rocky Mtn.	CO	2,955,821	4.7	5	265,828	26
Zion	UT	2,665,972	−2.5	8	145,598	35
Acadia	ME	2,504,208	12.4	9	47,390	47
Bryce	UT	1,285,492	5.7	15	35,835	50
Arches	UT	1,014,405	1.8	19	76,519	42
Badlands	SD	977,778	4.7	22	242,756	28
Mesa Verde	CO	559,712	1.7	30	52,122	46
Canyonlands	UT	435,908	−0.1	36	337,598	23

The table above gives information for the most recent year on total visitors and total acreage for 11 US National Parks. In addition to the numbers of total visitors and total acreage for each National Park, the table also provides the percent increase or decrease over the total visitors for the year prior and the rank of the National Park for total visitors and total acreage in the most recent year. **4**

Each column of the table can be **2** sorted in ascending order by clicking on the word "Select" above the table and choosing, from the drop-down menu, the heading of the column on which you want the table to be sorted.

Consider each of the following **3** statements about these National Parks. For each statement indicate whether the statement is true or false, based on the information provided in the table.

True False **5**
- ○ ○ The park that experienced the greatest percent increase in visitors also had the least total acreage.
- ○ ○ The park with the median rank by the number of visitors is larger than only one other park by acreage.
- ○ ○ The total number of visitors at Arches in the year prior was fewer than 1,000,000.

When you take the Integrated Reasoning section, you will not see the circled numbers shown in the example above. We've added those so we can talk about different parts of a Table Analysis question. Here's what each circled number represents:

1 This is the Sort By drop-down box. When opened, you'll see all the different ways that you can sort the data in the table. In this table, for example, the possibilities are National Park Name, National Park State, Visitors Number, Visitors % Change, Visitors Rank, Area Acreage, and Area Rank. You can always sort by every column.

2 These are the standard directions for a Table Analysis question. These directions are the same for every Table Analysis question. After you've read these directions once, you don't really need to bother reading them again.

3 These lines are additional directions. These additional directions are slightly tailored to the question. However, they'll always tell you to base your answers on the information in the table. They always tell you which type of evaluation you are to make for each statement: true/false, yes/no, agree/disagree, etc. Again, you can probably get by without reading these most of the time.

4 These lines explain the table. Mostly, this information will recap the column headings from the table. Occasionally, you can learn some additional information by reading this explanatory text. For example, the explanatory text for this table states that the Visitors Number column is for the most recent year and that % Change column shows the change from the year prior to the most recent year.

5 These statements are the questions. Typically, there are three or four statements, and you need to evaluate and select an answer for each. The good news is that you can answer these in any order. However, if you try to move to the next question without selecting a response for one or more statements, a pop-up window opens to inform you that you have not selected an answer for all statements. You cannot leave any part of the question blank.

If you've read through the statements, you may have noticed that the questions asked you to do things such as calculate a percentage or find a median. That's typical for Table Analysis questions. You've probably also realized just how helpful the sorting function can be in answering some questions.

Graphics Interpretation

Graphics Interpretation questions give you one chart, graph, or image and ask you to answer two questions based on that information. The questions are statements that include one drop-down box. You select your answer from the drop-down box to complete the statement.

Here's an example of a Graphics Interpretation question:

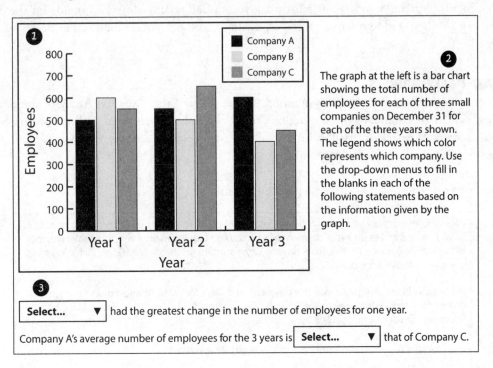

① The graph at the left is a bar chart showing the total number of employees for each of three small companies on December 31 for each of the three years shown. The legend shows which color represents which company. Use the drop-down menus to fill in the blanks in each of the following statements based on the information given by the graph.

③ [Select... ▼] had the greatest change in the number of employees for one year.

Company A's average number of employees for the 3 years is [Select... ▼] that of Company C.

As with the Table Analysis questions, we've added the circled numbers so we can point out the different things that you'll see on your screen for a Graphics Interpretation question. Here's what each circled number represents:

① The chart, graph, or image is always in the upper left of the screen. As shown here, the chart will take up a good deal of the screen. It will certainly be large enough that you can clearly extract information from it. You can expect to see a variety of different types of charts or graphs including scatterplots, bar charts, line graphs, and circle (or pie) charts. For the most part, you'll see fairly standard types of graphs, however. Be sure to check out any labels on the axes as well as any sort of included legend.

② These lines provide an explanation of the graph or chart. Mostly, you'll be told what the chart represents as well as what the individual lines, bars, or sectors may represent. Sometimes, you'll be given some additional information, such as when measurements were made. For example, here you are told that the bars show the numbers of employees for each firm on December 31 of the year in question. This information is typically extraneous to answering the questions. The explanatory information always ends with the same line about selecting your answers from the drop-down menu.

③ These are the questions. Graphics Interpretation questions typically include two statements. You don't have to answer them in order, but you must answer them both to move on to the next question. Each statement is typically a single sentence with one drop-down menu. Each drop-down menu typically includes three to five answer choices. Choose the answer choice that makes the statement true.

Graphics Interpretation questions mostly ask you to find relationships and trends for the data. You can also be asked to calculate averages, medians, and percentage increases or decreases.

Two-Part Analysis

Next up is the Two-Part Analysis question. In many ways, the Two-Part Analysis question is most similar to a standard math question. You'll typically be presented with a word problem that essentially has two variables in it. You'll need to pick an answer for each variable that makes some condition in the problem true.

Here's an example of a Two-Part Analysis question:

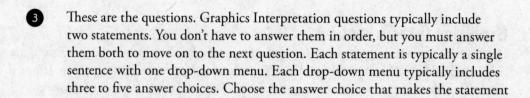

Two families buy new refrigerators using installment plans. Family A makes an initial payment of $750. Family B makes an initial payment of $1200. Both families make five additional payments to pay off the balance. Both families pay the same amount for their refrigerators including all taxes, fees, and finance charges. ①

In the table below, identify a monthly payment, in dollars, for Family A and a monthly payment, in dollars, for Family B that are consistent with the installment plan described above. Make only one selection in each column. ②

Family A	Family B	Monthly payment
○	○	$50
○	○	$80
○	○	$120 ③
○	○	$160
○	○	$250
○	○	$300

As you might have surmised, we have once again added the circled numbers so we can describe the different parts of the question. Here's what each circled number represents:

① This first block of text is the actual problem. Here, you'll find the description of the two variables in the problem. You'll also find the condition that needs to be made true. As with any word problem, make sure that you read the information carefully. For these problems, you should also make sure that you are clear about which information goes with the first variable, and which information goes with the second.

2 This part of the problem tells you how to pick your answers. Mostly, this part tells you to pick a value for column A and a value for column B based on the conditions of the problem. This part is mostly boilerplate text that varies slightly from problem to problem.

3 These are the answer choices. Two-Part Analysis questions generally have five or six answer choices. You choose only one answer choice for each column. It is possible that the same number is the answer for both columns. So if that's what your calculations indicate, go ahead and choose the same number for both columns.

Most Two-Part Analysis questions can be solved using math that is no more sophisticated than simple arithmetic. There is one exception to that, however. While most Two-Part Analysis questions are math problems, you may see one that looks like a Critical Reasoning question. For these, you'll be given an argument and you'll need to do something like pick one answer that strengthens and one answer that weakens the argument. For these questions, just use the methods from our Critical Reasoning chapter.

Multi-Source Reasoning

Finally, we come to the Multi-Source Reasoning question, which presents information on tabs. The information can be text, charts, graphs, or a combination. In other words, GMAC can put almost anything on the tabs! The layout looks a little bit like Reading Comprehension because the tabbed information is on the left side of your screen while the questions are on the right side.

Here's an example of a Multi-Source Reasoning question:

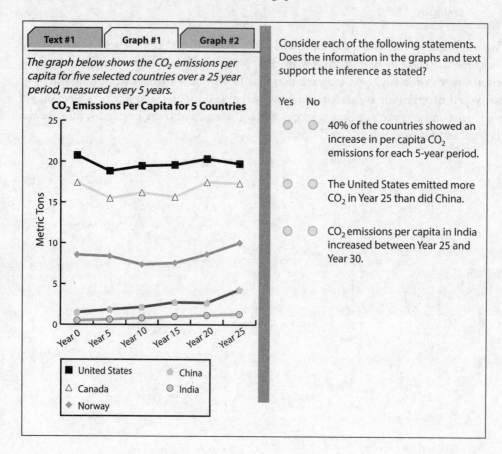

Again, we've added circled numbers to indicate the different parts of the question. Here's what each circled number represents:

 The tabs appear across the top left of the screen. Some questions have two tabs and some, as in this example, have three. The tabs typically give you some sort of indication about what's on the tab. The currently selected tab is white, while the unselected tabs are grey. GMAC can put almost anything on each tab including graphs, tables, charts, text, or some combination. It's a good idea to take a few seconds to get your bearings before attempting the questions. Make sure you know what is on each tab and how the information on one tab relates to information on the other tab or tabs.

② The information for each tab appears on the left of the screen. In this case, the information is a graph. When you see a chart or graph, be sure to check out the axes. You should also look for a legend or other information to help explain the information shown by the graph or chart. For tables, check out the column headings so as to better understand the table. Finally, don't neglect to read any supplied headings for the chart, graph, or table. Sometimes that's all you need for the chart to make sense.

③ These are the basic instructions for how to respond to the statements. These instructions help to explain how you need to evaluate each statement. Here, for example, you need to determine whether the statements are valid inferences. In other cases, you may be asked to evaluate the statements for a different choice, such as true or false.

④ These are the actual questions. You need to pick a response for each statement. If you fail to respond to one or more statements, you won't be able to advance to the next question in the section. In other words, these statements work just like the statements for the Table Analysis question type.

Multi-Source Reasoning questions usually come in sets. Each set typically consists of three separate questions. Two of those questions are typically in the statement style as shown in the previous example. It's also possible to get a standard multiple-choice question as part of the set. For a standard multiple-choice question, there are five answer choices, and you select one response.

You may need information from more than one tab to respond to a statement or multiple-choice question. Don't forget to think about the information on the other tabs while evaluating the statements. That's why it's important to take a few moments to get familiar with what's on each tab before starting work on the questions.

WHAT IS DATA SUFFICIENCY?

If you've never heard of Data Sufficiency, that's because this question type is unique to the GMAT, and these questions definitely require some getting used to. If you have already taken a GMAT practice exam, or the actual GMAT, you may have spent several minutes just trying to understand the directions for Data Sufficiency questions.

However, Data Sufficiency questions really just test the same basic foundational math skills you learned in high school, just like Problem Solving, but with a twist—a strange question format.

Here's what a Data Sufficiency question looks like on the GMAT:

What is the value of y ?

(1) y is an even integer such that $-1.5 < y < 1.5$.
(2) Integer y is not prime.

(A) Statement (1) ALONE is sufficient, but statement (2) alone is not sufficient.
(B) Statement (2) ALONE is sufficient, but statement (1) alone is not sufficient.
(C) BOTH statements TOGETHER are sufficient, but NEITHER statement ALONE is sufficient.
(D) EACH statement ALONE is sufficient.
(E) Statements (1) and (2) TOGETHER are not sufficient.

Each Data Sufficiency question consists of a question followed by two statements. There are also five possible answer choices, as shown. The answers are the same for every Data Sufficiency question, so once you learn what each means, you won't need to spend time rereading them. You'll just be able to think about them as (A), (B), (C), (D), and (E), which is how we'll refer to them.

Notice that there are two words that the answer choices keep repeating—*alone* and *sufficient*. So, it looks like we're supposed to evaluate the statements on their own—at least at first. Moreover, our task is evidently to determine whether we have sufficient information to answer the question.

That's how Data Sufficiency differs from Problem Solving. In Problem Solving questions, you are asked to give a numerical answer to the question. In fact, the inclusion of five numerical answer choices tells you that you can assume that the question can be solved. For Data Sufficiency questions, however, you're not being asked to solve the question but to decide WHETHER the question can be solved. It may, in fact, turn out that the statements do not provide sufficient information to answer the question.

Data Sufficiency Question Types

There are two types of Data Sufficiency questions.

The first and most prominent type of question is one that asks to determine a specific value. The question could ask for the value of a variable or for the value of a scenario. Your job is to determine if there is enough information in the statements to arrive at a consistent value as an answer for the question.

The second, less common, type of Data Sufficiency question is one in which the question asks a Yes or No question. Your job will be to determine if the information in the statements provides a means to arrive at a consistent Yes or No answer to the question.

Data Sufficiency Answer Choices

The answer choices for data sufficiency questions are unique enough that they warrant their own section!

Let's take a look at each answer choice individually.

Choice (A) is correct when Statement (1) ALONE is sufficient, but Statement (2) alone is not sufficient. In other words, the correct answer is (A) if the first statement contains enough information to determine a consistent answer to the question, but the second statement does NOT provide enough information to determine a consistent answer to the question.

Choice (B) is correct when Statement (2) ALONE is sufficient, but Statement (1) alone is not sufficient. This is the inverse of Choice (A). If the second statement provides enough information to determine a consistent answer to the question and the first statement does NOT, the correct answer is (B).

Choice (C) is correct when BOTH statements TOGETHER are sufficient, but NEITHER statement ALONE is sufficient. This means that when you evaluate the information in the first statement by itself you cannot get a consistent answer to the question, and when you evaluate the information in the second statement by itself you cannot get a consistent answer to the question. But, when you combine the information in the statements and consider them at the same time, you CAN arrive at a consistent answer to the question.

Choice (D) is correct when EACH statement ALONE is sufficient. You evaluate the first statement and find the information contained within that statement is enough to produce a consistent answer to the question. Then, you evaluate the second statement and find the information contained within that statement is also enough to produce a consistent answer to the question. If this scenario is true, the correct answer is (D). It's worth noting here that if you arrive at an answer to the question, the answer will work for both statements.

Finally, (E) is correct when Statements (1) and (2) TOGETHER are not sufficient. This is more-or-less the inverse of (C). Neither statement alone provides enough information to answer the question and, when you combine the information from both statements and consider them together, there is still not enough information to determine a consistent answer to the question. In this scenario, the correct answer is (E).

Now, let's revisit the earlier question and talk about how to solve it.

Data Sufficiency: How To

To watch tips and strategies on how to more easily solve complex Data Sufficiency problems, visit your Student Tools.

Here's How to Crack It

The first answer choice—(A)—indicates that we should first look at Statement (1) by itself to see if it is sufficient to answer the question.

In fact, the best way to work Data Sufficiency problems is to look at *one statement at a time*. So, ignore Statement (2). Here, we've replaced Statement (2) with question marks to indicate that we are looking only at the first statement—almost as though we had covered up the second statement.

What is the value of y ?

(1) y is an even integer such that $-1.5 < y < 1.5$.
(2) ????

Now we're ready to evaluate Statement (1) alone. There are three integers between −1.5 and 1.5: −1, 0, and 1. As we'll cover in a later chapter, 0 is an even integer. Therefore, Statement (1) provides enough information to help us determine that $y = 0$. The question stem asks for the value of y. Because Statement (1) provides enough information to determine a single value for y, it provides sufficient information to answer the question.

Look at the answer choices again. Choice (A) is the correct answer when Statement (1) ALONE is sufficient, but Statement (2) alone is not sufficient. We know that Statement (1) alone is sufficient to determine a consistent value of y, so do we know (A) is the correct answer?

Nope, not yet! We haven't evaluated Statement (2) so we do not know if the second part of (A)—that Statement (2) alone is not sufficient—is true. We need to evaluate Statement (2) alone before selecting any answer choices. In fact, that is one of the keys to Data Sufficiency questions—always evaluate both statements independently first!

So let's do it. Forget you've ever seen Statement (1) and evaluate Statement (2) alone.

We're not ready to choose the first answer—(A)—yet, however, because the second part of the answer choice states that Statement (2) alone is not sufficient. Now, forget that you have ever seen Statement (1).

What is the value of y ?

(1) ????
(2) Integer y is not prime.

The second statement tells us only that y is not prime. So, possible values for y include 1, 4, 6, 8, etc. Look at the question stem again. The question stem asks for the value of y. Do we know the value of y based on the information provided in Statement (2)? No, we don't. We know a bunch of possible values for y, but no consistent value. So, Statement (2) alone is not sufficient to answer the question.

Now we know that both parts of (A) are true because Statement (1) is sufficient and Statement (2) is not sufficient:

> (A)   Statement (1) ALONE is sufficient, but statement (2) alone is not sufficient.

Or, in other words, the correct answer is (A).

DATA SUFFICIENCY: EXAMPLES OF ANSWERS

Now that you've seen and worked a Data Sufficiency question, let's take one more quick look at the answer choices to really dig in.

By making small changes to the example you've just seen, we can provide examples of each of the answer choices. Next to each example, you'll find a graphic that provides a quick and dirty way to understand and remember each answer choice. Here's the example for (A) again:

> (A)   Statement (1) ALONE is sufficient, but statement (2) alone is not sufficient.

What is the value of y ?

> (1) y is an even integer such that $-1.5 < y < 1.5$.
>
> (2)   Integer y is not prime.

(A) ① ✗

Now, let's make some changes to the statements, to get an example of (B).

> (B)   Statement (2) ALONE is sufficient, but statement (1) alone is not sufficient.

What is the value of y ?

> (1)   Integer y is not prime.
>
> (2) y is an even integer such that $-1.5 < y < 1.5$.

(B) ✗ ②

As you can see from this example, (B) is pretty much the flip side of (A). In this case, the first statement provides no help in determining the value of y, but the second statement tells us that $y = 0$.

A few more changes produce an example of (C).

(C)   BOTH statements TOGETHER are sufficient, but NEITHER statement ALONE is sufficient.

What is the value of *y* ?

(1)   *y* is an even integer.

(2)   −1.5 < *y* < 1.5

The first statement tells us that *y* is even, but there are a lot of even integers. The second statement gives us a range of values for *y*, but, by itself, we don't know a consistent value for *y*. So, neither statement is sufficient on its own. But, when we put them together, we know that *y* is an even integer between −1.5 and 1.5, which means that *y* = 0.

Now, let's get an example of (D).

(D)   EACH statement ALONE is sufficient.

What is the value of *y* ?

(1)   *y* is an even integer such that −1.5 < *y* < 1.5.

(2)   For any integer *a* ≠ 0, *ay* = 0.

As pointed out in previous examples, the information in Statement (1) allows us to conclude that *y* = 0. The information in the second statement also tells us that *y* is 0, because the only way for the product of *ay* to equal 0 is if either *a* or *y* is 0. Since *a* can't be 0, *y* must be 0. Note how the statements independently allow us to arrive at the conclusion that *y* = 0 for (D).

Finally, let's look at an example of (E).

(E)   Statements (1) and (2) TOGETHER are not sufficient.

What is the value of *y* ?

(1)   *y* is an even integer.

(2)   Integer *y* is not prime.

For this example, there's no way to determine the value of *y*. The first statement doesn't provide a consistent answer to the question because *y* could be any even integer. The second statement also doesn't provide a consistent answer to the question because *y* can be any integer that isn't prime. When we combine the statements, we know that *y* is a not prime even integer, which describes every even integer except the number 2. Because the statements combined do not produce a consistent answer to the question, (E) is now correct.

Below, you'll find the full graphic for all of the answers. You may find it helpful to keep the graphic handy until you are completely comfortable with what each answer choice means.

Summary

- o There are four Integrated Reasoning style question types. Be sure that you familiarize yourself with these.
  - Table Analysis
  - Graphics Interpretation
  - Two-Part Analysis
  - Multi-Source Reasoning

- o There is an on-screen calculator available for Integrated Reasoning-style questions that you should understand how to work.

- o "Data Sufficiency" means just that—sufficiency. These questions are asking you if the data presented is enough to solve the problem.

- o Every Data Sufficiency problem consists of a question followed by two statements. You must decide whether the question can be answered based on the information in the two statements.

- o The best strategy for Data Sufficiency problems is to look at one statement at a time. Cover up the other statement with your hand if you need to so that you can completely focus on one statement at a time.

Chapter 9
Data Insights: Strategic Approach to Integrated Reasoning Style Questions

Integrated Reasoning style questions have their own unique quirks. As with any section on a standardized test, doing well requires a blend of content knowledge and strategy. Test-takers who approach this question type with a firm grasp of strategy will do better than those who do not.

INTEGRATED REASONING STYLE QUESTIONS

GENERAL STRATEGIES

Some strategies apply to the entire section, and you'll use these methods on almost every question. The more consistently you apply these pointers, the better you'll do, and the more efficiently you'll use your time.

Get Your Bearings

What Do the Questions Look Like?

If you aren't sure what the Integrated Reasoning style questions look like, check out the previous chapter. We introduced the four question types there.

Before you can use a chart, graph, or table to answer questions, you need to understand the information on it. So, before you evaluate any statements or answer any questions, take a few moments to review the charts, graphs, and tables.

For charts and graphs, make sure you look at the axes. Take note of what each axis measures and the units used to make the measurements. Also, read any headings or titles because those can provide valuable insight into the purpose of the graph. There may be a legend. If there is, take a moment to identify the different items that the chart or graph compares. For tables, make sure that you look at each column heading. This sort of review is essential before you start working on evaluating the statements or answering the questions that go with Table Analysis and Graphics Interpretation questions.

For Multi-Source Reasoning questions, you need to review the information that is on each tab. It's also a good idea to look for connections between the charts on one tab and those on the others. One way that you can do so is to think about what quantities you'd be able to calculate if you used the information from two charts. For example, if one chart shows the number of cars per day that several factories produce and another chart shows the number of days those factories were active in a year, you know that you could calculate the total number of cars each factory produced that year.

Read What You Need When You Need It

Both Table Analysis and Graphics Interpretation questions include a blurb of text that explains the table or chart. While GMAC includes this information to help you to understand the table or chart, you may not need to take the time to read it.

Most of the charts and tables are understandable without the explanatory text. So if your review of the chart or table doesn't turn up any unusual quantities or units that need further explanation, you're most likely ready to get to work on the actual questions. You can also be guided by the questions. If something about the question or statement isn't making sense, then you can always go back and read the explanatory information.

Valid Inferences

Both Table Analysis and Multi-Source Reasoning items can include statement style questions. In some cases, you'll be asked to decide whether the statement is true or false. In other cases, you'll be asked whether the information supplied supports the inference as stated and then respond yes or no. That's a little different from asking whether the statement is true or false. After all, there's the possibility that there is insufficient information to conclude whether the statement is true or false. If that's the case, you need to pick "no" as your answer.

It's also important to remember that a valid inference is something that you know to be true. You know something is true if you can support it with evidence. GMAC knows, however, that most people start thinking "interpret" or "read into" when they see the word "infer." So, some statements provided on Table Analysis and Multi-Source Reasoning questions attempt to get you to read too much into the information on the chart or table to come up with a conclusion. For example, there may be a clear trend on a chart showing that a company has increased its sales for every year between 2000 and 2008. The statement may try to get you to conclude that the company also increased its sales in 2009, even though 2009 is not shown on the chart. That's not a valid inference! Be careful that you don't mix up "true" and "very likely" when evaluating what can be inferred from the data.

> **What's an Inference?**
> An inference is a statement that you can prove true using supplied facts or other evidence.

IR STYLE QUESTIONS BEYOND MATH

While many of the Integrated Reasoning style questions you'll encounter during the Data Insights section of the GMAT are going to test math-related topics or look more like questions you might see on the Verbal Reasoning section of the GMAT.

Non-Math Focus

Certain questions on the Data Insights section won't ask you to do any math at all. Instead, these questions will ask you to notice a pattern or interpret a chart. For example, consider the following diagram:

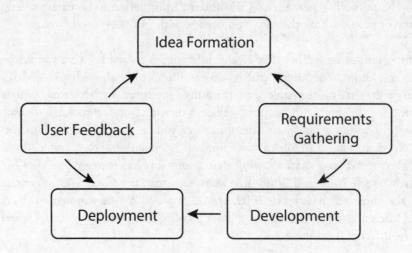

A non-math focus Data Insights question may present you a block cycle chart as shown above and provide a block of text that describes a scenario. The ensuing questions will ask you about specific details. For instance, it might ask you to determine at what stage in the process a company is in or determine what the next steps are for a product that just finished doing a certain activity.

This type of question tests your ability to reason through a chart and understand how different aspects of a chart interact with one another.

Critical Reasoning Focus

These types of questions will look a lot like critical reasoning questions found in the verbal reasoning section of the GMAT. We're not going to get into detail here about how to approach and solve these types of questions—you can find all the relevant information about that process in the Critical Reasoning chapter of this book.

But, it's worth noting that there are some differences between the Data Insights questions that look like Critical Reasoning questions and actual Critical Reasoning questions. The most prominent distinction is that Critical Reasoning questions in the Data Insights section of the GMAT will ask you to select two different statements related to the prompt. Sometimes those statements will be related to each other, and one will require the other. Other times, those statements will be independent of one another but address two different aspects of the prompt.

For example, consider the following prompt:

> According to mutual fund sales experts, a successful year for a stock fund should result not only in increased investor dollars flowing into the fund, but also in increased investor dollars flowing into other mutual stock funds offered by the same company. However, while last year the Grafton Mutual Company's "Growth Stock Fund" beat average market returns by a factor of two and recorded substantial new investment, the other stock funds offered by Grafton did not report any increase whatsoever.

If this prompt was in the verbal reasoning section, you will be presented with 5 answer choices, and the question may ask you to determine which of them is supported by the inferences in the passage.

However, in the Data Insights section you will still be presented with 5 answer choices. But, instead of selecting a single choice that is supported by the inferences in the passage, you may be asked to select one statement that strengthens the argument and one that weakens the argument. Or, you might be asked to select the cause-and-effect relationship that could explain why the other stock funds offered by Grafton did not report any increase.

The answer choices will be presented to you in the style of a Two-Part Analysis question, which we will cover in more detail later on in this chapter.

Inference Focus

This question type is similar to the Critical Reasoning style question described in the prior section, but instead of asking you to determine what supports the argument, you'll be asked to determine what is true based on the information in the argument. This is very similar to Inference style questions that are covered in great detail in the Critical Reasoning section. As before, the primary difference is the need to select two different answers instead of one, in the style of Two-Part Analysis questions.

For example, using the same example from the prior section about Grafton Mutual Company, this type of question may ask you to determine what must be true and what must be false based on the information in the argument. You can read all about the best way to attack that line of questioning in the Critical Reasoning section of this book!

Complete the Statement Focus

The last specific question focus in the Data Insights section that is not necessarily related to math can be found on both Graphics Interpretations and Two-Part Analysis questions. These are unique questions, especially for Graphics Interpretations questions which usually ask two distinct fill-in-the-blank style questions about a chart or graph. With Complete the Statement focus questions, you'll be given one statement with two blanks. Your job is to fill in the blanks that correctly correspond to the information in the chart that accurately completes the intended meaning of the statement.

A complete the statement focus question might look something like this:

> New technology now makes it feasible for computer call-in help desk services to route calls they receive to almost anywhere, theoretically allowing employees to work from home, without the need for a daily commute.
>
> The adoption of this policy would be most likely to (1) _____ productivity if employees did not (2) _____ .

There would be 5 answer choices, and you would be asked to select the appropriate answer that fills blank (1) and blank (2) that creates a consistent and accurate meaning for the statement.

TABLE ANALYSIS

Table Analysis questions always include one table to display data. You'll be asked to evaluate three or four statements. You may be asked whether the statements are true or false based on the data in the table. You may also be asked whether the statements represent valid inferences based on the table.

While you won't be called upon to provide numerical answers as part of Table Analysis questions, you may need to perform some calculations to evaluate the statements. For example, you may be asked to verify that a certain percentage of the items in the table have a certain characteristic.

The Sort Function

The sort function allows you to sort the data in the table by any column. However, the sort function will sort only one column at a time. So forget all those fancy multiple column sorts that you can do with Excel.

To see how the sort function works for Table Analysis questions, let's look at a very simple table. This table is really too simple for a GMAT question, but it will help us to illustrate how the sort function works.

When you first see the table, it is typically sorted by one key statistic from the table. All numerical sorts are always smallest to largest. This table, for example, is sorted by Median Household Income and represents the original sort for this table.

City	State	Median Household Income
Rochester	NY	$51,086
Philadelphia	PA	$62,171
Salt Lake City	UT	$62,642
New York	NY	$67,066

Now, here's what you'll see if you sort by State.

City	State	Median Household Income
Rochester	NY	$51,086
New York	NY	$67,066
Philadelphia	PA	$62,171
Salt Lake City	UT	$62,642

If you sort next by City, you might expect that Rochester and New York would exchange positions. That's particularly true if you are used to the way that Excel lets you sort by multiple columns.

However, what you'll really get is an alphabetical listing by City. Here's what the sort by City looks like.

City	State	Median Household Income
New York	NY	$67,066
Philadelphia	PA	$62,171
Rochester	NY	$51,086
Salt Lake City	UT	$62,642

Question Order
In general, you should just evaluate the statements in order for Table Analysis questions. Of course, if you get stuck on one statement, skip over it, evaluate the other statements, and come back to the one that gave you trouble.

To Sort or Not to Sort

While the sort feature can be a huge help when answering some questions, you may not need to use it to answer every question. In some cases, you may need to find only one piece of information on the table. In other cases, the table may not have that many rows. Table Analysis questions can have as few as six rows of data. It may be faster to simply scan the table for the information that you need.

On the other hand, remember that sorting the table takes only a few seconds. If you think sorting will help, do it! One thing you shouldn't do, however, is spend time trying to organize the statements so that you do as little sorting as possible. You're actually likely to waste more time trying to come up with the perfect order in which to evaluate the statements than you would if you wind up sorting the same way twice in evaluating the statements.

Let's revisit the Table Analysis question from the previous chapter and work through the questions.

Sort By [Select... ▼] **1**

National Park		Visitors			Area	
Name	State	Number	% Change	Rank	Acres	Rank
Grand Canyon	AZ	4,388,386	0.9	2	1,217,403	11
Yosemite	CA	3,901,408	4.4	3	791,266	16
Yellowstone	WY	3,640,185	10.5	4	2,219,791	8
Rocky Mtn.	CO	2,955,821	4.7	5	265,828	26
Zion	UT	2,665,972	−2.5	8	145,598	35
Acadia	ME	2,504,208	12.4	9	47,390	47
Bryce	UT	1,285,492	5.7	15	35,835	50
Arches	UT	1,014,405	1.8	19	76,519	42
Badlands	SD	977,778	4.7	22	242,756	28
Mesa Verde	CO	559,712	1.7	30	52,122	46
Canyonlands	UT	435,908	−0.1	36	337,598	23

The table above gives information for the most recent year on total visitors and total acreage for 11 US National Parks. In addition to the numbers of total visitors and total acreage for each National Park, the table also provides the percent increase or decrease over the total visitors for the year prior and the rank of the National Park for total visitors and total acreage in the most recent year. **4**

2 Each column of the table can be sorted in ascending order by clicking on the word "Select" above the table and choosing, from the drop-down menu, the heading of the column on which you want the table to be sorted.

3 Consider each of the following statements about these National Parks. For each statement indicate whether the statement is true or false, based on the information provided in the table.

True False **5**

○ ○ The park that experienced the greatest percent increase in visitors also had the least total acreage.

○ ○ The park with the median rank by the number of visitors is larger than only one other park by acreage.

○ ○ The total number of visitors at Arches in the year prior was fewer than 1,000,000.

Here's How to Crack It

As with any Table Analysis question, the first step is to make sure that you take a moment to understand the information presented by the table. While it might be tempting to jump straight to the statements, you'll be able to evaluate the statements more efficiently when you first take a moment to understand the information on the table. Looking at the column headings can also help you to decide whether you need to read the explanatory information under the table.

The first two columns of this table—National Park Name and National Park State—are self-explanatory. More importantly, however, the first column—National Park Name—tells you that this table provides information about national parks. Next, you get information about visitors to the national parks included in the table. The third column heading—Visitors Number—is pretty clear. However, you don't know the time period for the visitation numbers. The next column—Visitors % Change—shows increases or decreases from some previous time period. Again, you don't know the time period just by looking at the table. Do the time periods matter? Probably not. You'll probably learn the time period from the statements. If the statements seem to indicate that the time periods matter, you can read the explanatory text at that time.

The next column—Visitors Rank—is potentially more confusing, however. Does the rank refer to the number of visitors or the percent change? That's an important distinction for understanding the information in the table. There are two ways to figure out what's being ranked. You could scan the table looking for evidence. Of course, that could be time-consuming. Or, you could scan the explanatory text beneath the table. *If you don't understand one of the column headings shown in the table, that's when you want to read the explanatory text.* The explanation indicates that the rank refers to the total number of visitors. As a bonus, you now also know that the visitation numbers are for the most recent year.

The last two column headings—Area Acres and Area Rank—are also pretty clear. Note that the inclusion of Area Rank means that you won't need to deal with the larger number in the Area Acres column if all you need to do is compare the size of one park to another. The same is also true of the inclusion of the Visitors Rank column. The inclusion of these columns makes it much easier to make some types of comparisons about the parks in the table. That's definitely something to make note of as you finish reviewing the information presented by the chart.

We'll just evaluate the statements in order. First, we'll evaluate:

> The park that experienced the greatest percent increase in visitors from the year prior to the most recent year also had the least total acreage.

This statement is typical of the sorts of statements that you are called upon to evaluate for Table Analysis questions. Note that there are two possible sorts that you could perform to evaluate this question. First, you could sort by Visitors % Change. You could also sort by Area Acres. So, what's the best? Sort by only one of those columns? Sort by both? Sort by neither?

With 11 rows of data, you'll probably find it safer to sort by at least one of the columns. But which one? Well, note that the table provides you with ranking information for the areas of the parks. The smaller numbers used to rank the parks by area make it easier to identify the smallest park by area without sorting.

However, you might reasonably be worried about missing which park had the greatest percent increase by visitors. So, sort by Visitors % Change.

Sort It Out
Decide the best way to sort the table. For some statements, you may be able to sort in more than one way. Sort by the column with the larger numbers or more complex data.

Here's what the sorted table looks like:

National Park		Visitors			Area	
Name	State	Number	% Change	Rank	Acres	Rank
Zion	UT	2,556,972	−2.5	8	145,598	35
Canyonlands	UT	435,908	−0.1	36	337,598	23
Grand Canyon	AZ	4,388,386	0.9	2	1,217,403	11
Mesa Verde	CO	559,712	1.7	30	52,122	46
Arches	UT	1,014,405	1.8	19	76,519	42
Yosemite	CA	3,901,408	4.4	3	791,266	16
Rocky Mtn.	CO	2,955,821	4.7	5	265,828	26
Badlands	SD	977,778	4.7	22	242,756	28
Bryce	UT	1,285,492	5.7	15	35,835	50
Yellowstone	WY	3,640,185	10.5	4	2,219,791	8
Acadia	ME	2,504,208	12.4	9	47,390	47

It's clear that Acadia had the greatest percent increase in the number of visitors from the year prior to the most recent year. Acadia was ranked 47th in terms of overall acreage. You could sort the chart by Area Acres or by Area Rank at this point to finish evaluating the statement. However, since you know Acadia's rank for acreage, it's probably slightly faster to simply scan to see if any park had a higher rank for area. In this case, Bryce was ranked 50th, so this first statement is false.

Now, let's take a look at the second statement:

> The park with the median rank by the number of visitors is larger than only one other park by acreage.

Again, you may be considering several different ways to sort the chart. Start by asking yourself "What's hardest to see right now?" Remember that your chart will still be sorted as shown above, which is the sort that you did to evaluate the first statement. This sort makes it pretty hard to see which park had the median rank for visitors, so it makes sense to sort by Visitors Rank.

Here's what the sorted chart looks like:

National Park		Visitors			Area	
Name	State	Number	% Change	Rank	Acres	Rank
Grand Canyon	AZ	4,388,386	0.9	2	1,217,403	11
Yosemite	CA	3,901,408	4.4	3	791,266	16
Yellowstone	WY	3,640,185	10.5	4	2,219,791	8
Rocky Mtn.	CO	2,955,821	4.7	5	265,828	26
Zion	UT	2,665,972	−2.5	8	145,598	35
Acadia	ME	2,504,208	12.4	9	47,390	47
Bryce	UT	1,285,492	5.7	15	35,835	50
Arches	UT	1,014,405	1.8	19	76,519	42
Badlands	SD	977,778	4.7	22	242,756	28
Mesa Verde	CO	559,712	1.7	30	52,122	46
Canyonlands	UT	435,908	−0.1	36	337,598	23

With the table sorted by Visitors Rank, it's now fairly easy to find the park with the median rank. To find a median, you start by putting the items on a list into numerical order, which we just did by sorting the list. Then, you can just choose the middle number. In this case, Acadia is the park in the middle position since there are 5 parks ranked before it and 5 parks ranked after it.

Note that you could have also sorted the list by Visitors Number. Since data is always sorted from least to greatest, Canyonlands would have been the first row of the table and Grand Canyon would have been the last row. But, Acadia still would have been in the middle. We chose to sort by Visitors Rank because that term was mentioned in the question, and it's easier to work with smaller numbers.

Having identified Acadia as the park with the median rank, you now need to decide whether to sort the table again. Since the table provides ranks for the total acreage of the parks on the list, you likely don't need to sort again. Acadia is 47th by acreage. One park, Bryce, with a rank of 50, is smaller. So, Acadia, the median park by visitation, is larger than only one other park on the list. The second statement is true.

Use Your Noteboards
For more complicated statements, you may want to make a list of the items that satisfy a condition in the statement.

Note, however, that if the table had not provided ranks for the parks by total area, then you most likely would have wanted to sort by Area Acres. After all, it's a lot easier to see that only one number is greater than 47 than to see that only one number is less than 47,390. Remember that sorting takes only a few seconds, and you should sort whenever you think doing so will help you to accurately find what you need on the table.

Now it's time to finish the question by evaluating the third statement. The third statement claims:

The total number of visitors at Arches in the year prior was fewer than 1,000,000.

Calculations Required

Expect to do some calculations such as computing an average or a percent change to evaluate one or two of the statements in a Table Analysis question.

Calculator Time!

Don't forget that you can use the onscreen calculator to perform messy calculations such as dividing through by 101.8!

Because this statement involves only a single data point, you don't really need to worry about doing any sorting. Even the most involved GMAT tables will have fewer than 30 rows of data. It will never be an issue to quickly scan the table, no matter how it is currently sorted, to find one data point. Just use the current sort which has Arches in the 8th row.

Next, you need some information about Arches to evaluate the statement. The table shows that Arches had 1,014,405 visitors in the most recent year. The table also shows that the number of visitors in the most recent year was 1.8% greater than it was in the year prior. In order to answer the question, determine what number 1,014,405 is 1.8% greater than.

$$1{,}014{,}405 = \left(\frac{101.8}{100}\right)x$$

The value of x is the number of visitors to Arches in the prior year. Solve for x by multiplying both sides by 100 and then dividing both sides by 101.8 to find a value for x of 996,469 rounded to the nearest integer. Therefore, statement 3 is true.

The following is what your answers should look like just before you click next to move on to the next question.

Sort By   Select... ▼ ①

National Park		Visitors			Area	
Name	State	Number	% Change	Rank	Acres	Rank
Grand Canyon	AZ	4,388,386	0.9	2	1,217,403	11
Yosemite	CA	3,901,408	4.4	3	791,266	16
Yellowstone	WY	3,640,185	10.5	4	2,219,791	8
Rocky Mtn.	CO	2,955,821	4.7	5	265,828	26
Zion	UT	2,665,972	−2.5	8	145,598	35
Acadia	ME	2,504,208	12.4	9	47,390	47
Bryce	UT	1,285,492	5.7	15	35,835	50
Arches	UT	1,014,405	1.8	19	76,519	42
Badlands	SD	977,778	4.7	22	242,756	28
Mesa Verde	CO	559,712	1.7	30	52,122	46
Canyonlands	UT	435,908	−0.1	36	337,598	23

The table above gives information for the most recent year on total visitors and total acreage for 11 US National Parks. In addition to the numbers of total visitors and total acreage for each National Park, the table also provides the percent increase or decrease over the total visitors for the year prior and the rank of the National Park for total visitors and total acreage in the most recent year. ④

Each column of the table can be ② sorted in ascending order by clicking on the word "Select" above the table and choosing, from the drop-down menu, the heading of the column on which you want the table to be sorted.

Consider each of the following ③ statements about these National Parks. For each statement indicate whether the statement is true or false, based on the information provided in the table.

True False ⑤

○ ● The park that experienced the greatest percent increase in visitors also had the least total acreage.

● ○ The park with the median rank by the number of visitors is larger than only one other park by acreage.

● ○ The total number of visitors at Arches in the year prior was fewer than 1,000,000.

GRAPHICS INTERPRETATION

Graphics Interpretation questions provide you with one chart, graph, or image. Each chart is followed by two statements. Each statement contains one drop-down list from which you choose one answer. Your job is to pick the answer that makes the statement true. Each drop-down list typically contains between three to five answer choices.

You'll find a few sentences of explanatory text to the right of the chart or graph. As with Table Analysis questions based on how well you understand the information in the chart or graph, you may not need to read this explanatory information.

So, what should you look for when you review the chart or graph? Start by looking at any labels on the axes. Are quantities being measured in common, easily understood units? You should also look to see if the chart or graph has any titles that help to explain the data it shows. Finally, see if there's any sort of legend that helps to differentiate different types of data.

Let's revisit the Graphics Interpretation question from the previous chapter and work through the questions.

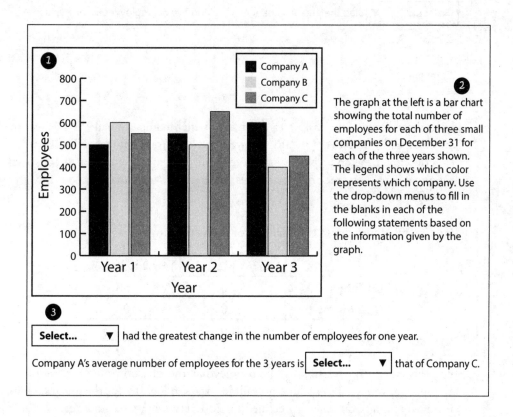

Here's How to Crack It

Before we get started discussing this question, note that we've expanded the drop-down list for the first statement. When the question first appears on the screen, none of the drop-downs are expanded. Here, we just wanted to show what the expanded drop-downs look like in the context of a question.

The first step in answering any Graphics Interpretation question is to review the chart or graph. In this case, there's a bar chart. The vertical axis shows the number of employees, which seems fairly easy to understand. The horizontal axis shows results for three years. The different colored bars are explained by the legend—there are three companies. So, this chart seems fairly straightforward. It shows the number of employees for three companies for three different years.

With everything on the chart so clearly marked, there's little reason to read the explanatory text to the right of the chart. Note that the only piece of information that the explanatory text really adds is that the number of employees for each company was tallied on December 31 of each year. That's the sort of detail that often turns out to be irrelevant in answering the questions. Remember that you can always go back to read the explanatory text if it seems like you need to know something that wasn't clearly reflected on the chart or graph.

Let's take a look at the questions. As with Table Analysis questions, it's best to just evaluate the statements in order. If one of them gives you trouble or seems particularly time consuming, you can always skip over it and evaluate the other statements first. Of course, you'll need to pick an answer for all statements before you can move to the next question.

Here's the first statement again:

| Select... ▼ | had the greatest change in the number of employees for one year.

Company A
Company B
Company C

For this statement, the task is to determine which company had the greatest overall changes in employees in any one-year period. You'll probably find it helpful to write down the changes on your noteboard. You may even want to construct a rough table to keep track of the changes. In that way, you can easily spot the largest overall change.

Here's a table that shows the changes for each company:

	Year 1 to Year 2	Year 2 to Year 3
Company A	50	50
Company B	−100	−100
Company C	100	−200

For this statement, it's important to note that the question asks for the greatest change. So, you need to include overall decreases in looking for the greatest change. Employment at Company C declined by 200 between Year 2 and Year 3. The correct answer to statement one is "Company C."

Avoid Common Errors
Be careful when you read the chart. Are you looking at the right item? It's also a good idea to write down the data before performing any calculations with the data.

Here's the second statement showing the possible answers:

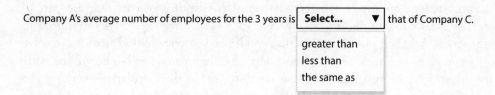

Company A's average number of employees for the 3 years is [Select...   ▼] that of Company C.

> greater than
> less than
> the same as

To evaluate this statement, you need to calculate the average number of employees for Companies A and C. Questions that ask you to perform calculations, such as finding an average, are fairly common for Graphics Interpretation questions. Just be sure to read the information from the chart carefully. Common errors for questions such as this one usually involve reading the information for the wrong company or mixing the information for two companies.

For Company A, the total number of employees for each year was 500, 550, and 600. To find the average, take the sum of the three numbers to get 1,650. Now, just divide by 3 because you want the average over three years. The average number of employees for Company A is 550.

For Company C, the total number of employees for each year was 550, 650, and 450. The average number of employees per year for Company C is also 550. So, the correct answer for the second statement is "the same as."

Here's what your answers should look like just before you click next to move on to the next question:

> **Calculator Required?**
> While using the calculator is fine, you may be able to do the calculations for some questions faster without the calculator. Make sure you need the calculator before you use it!

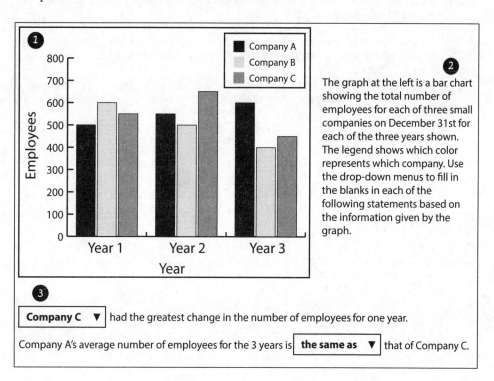

① [bar chart]

Legend:
- Company A
- Company B
- Company C

Y-axis: Employees (0 to 800)
X-axis: Year 1, Year 2, Year 3 / Year

② The graph at the left is a bar chart showing the total number of employees for each of three small companies on December 31st for each of the three years shown. The legend shows which color represents which company. Use the drop-down menus to fill in the blanks in each of the following statements based on the information given by the graph.

③ [**Company C**   ▼] had the greatest change in the number of employees for one year.

Company A's average number of employees for the 3 years is [**the same as**   ▼] that of Company C.

TWO-PART ANALYSIS

Most Two-Part Analysis questions will remind you of the word problems that are part of the Quantitative Reasoning section of the GMAT. The only difference is that you'll need to pick two answers rather than one! It's likely that you'll need to do some calculations to solve most Two-Part Analysis questions. For the most part, the math you'll need to do will be fairly straightforward arithmetic. You may find that it's faster to do the calculations without the calculator. However, remember that the calculator is available. Just don't forget to set up your calculations before entering them into the calculator.

For most Two-Part Analysis questions, the two answers that you need to pick are related or linked in some way. When that's the case, you may be able to identify one part as easier to solve than the other. If so, do the easier part first. It's also important to remember that working with the answer choices is often easier for these questions. While some Two-Part Analysis questions can be solved algebraically, it's very often faster to just test out the answer choices. In other words, you'll be able to use a form of Plugging In The Answers.

Let's relook at the Two-Part Analysis question we saw in the previous chapter.

Two families buy new refrigerators using installment plans. Family A makes an initial payment of $750. Family B makes an initial payment of $1200. Both families make five additional payments to pay off the balance. Both families pay the same amount for their refrigerators including all taxes, fees, and finance charges. **1**

In the table below, identify a monthly payment, in dollars, for Family A and a monthly payment, in dollars, for Family B that are consistent with the installment plan described above. Make only one selection in each column. **2**

Family A	Family B	Monthly payment
○	○	$50
○	○	$80
○	○	$120 **3**
○	○	$160
○	○	$250
○	○	$300

Here's How to Crack It

Begin by taking inventory of the information in the question. The question states that both families pay the same amount for their refrigerators and that both families make five additional payments to pay off the balance. Since Family B's initial payment is $450 more than that of Family A, Family A's monthly payment must be greater than that of Family B. This information can help you when you start testing answer choices but also allow you to eliminate some choices to start. If Family A's payment must be greater than Family B's, then Family A's payment cannot be the least value and Family B's payment cannot be the greatest. Eliminate $50 for Family A and $300 for Family B.

The other thing to notice in this question is that there is a crucial piece of information missing: the cost of the refrigerator. In this case, Plugging In the Answers will enable us to verify that the cost of that fridge is the same for both families. You can set the problem up just like you would a PITA question with one change. So that you can keep track of your Process of Elimination, write the answer choices down twice, leaving some space between the answers to show any quantities that you needed to calculate. Of course, you'll label your answer choices just as you would with any other PITA question. For this problem, you can label your columns of numbers as "A's payment" and "B's payment." Here's what your initial setup should look like:

A's payment		B's payment	
$50		$50	
$80		$80	
$120		$120	
$160		$160	
$250		$250	
$300		$300	

Note that we've already crossed off $50 for Family A and $300 for Family B, as discussed earlier. As with any other PITA question, it makes sense to start with a number in the middle. We'll start with $160 for Family A's payment.

The problem states that Family A makes 5 payments, so the total of those 5 payments is $800. Moreover, the problem also states that Family A made an initial payment of $750. So, if Family A made payments of $160, then the refrigerator cost $750 + $800 = $1,550. That's what goes into the next column for Family A.

What about Family B? If Family A makes payments of $160, then Family B's payments must be less than that amount. So, Family B could make payments of $50, $80, or $120. For each of those numbers, calculate how much Family B would have paid for the refrigerator. Here's what your table should look like at this step:

A's payment	A's Total	B's payment	B's Total
~~$50~~		$50	$1,450
$80		$80	$1,600
$120		$120	$1,800
$160	$1,550	$160	
$250		$250	
$300		~~$300~~	

How do you know if you've found the correct answers? Remember that the problem states that both families pay the same amount for their refrigerators. Since Family B cannot pay $1,550 for their refrigerator, you can eliminate $160 as an answer for Family A.

It's not that clear whether Family A's payment needs to be greater or less than $160. So just pick a direction and try it. Let's try $250 for Family A's payment. If Family A's payment is $250, then their refrigerator costs $750 + (5 × $250) = $2,000. For Family B, none of the answers we've already worked out make their refrigerator cost $2,000. However, we can also check what happens if Family B makes monthly payments of $160. In that case, Family B's refrigerator costs $1,200 + (5 × $160) = $2,000. So, the answers are $250 for Family A and $160 for Family B.

Here's what your completed table looks like:

A's payment	A's Total	B's payment	B's Total
~~50~~		50	$1,450
~~80~~		80	$1,600
120		120	$1,800
~~160~~	$1,550	160	$2,000
250	$2,000	250	
300		300	

Here's what your answers should look like just before you click next to move on to the next question:

Two families buy new refrigerators using installment plans. Family A makes an initial payment of $750. Family B makes an initial payment of $1200. Both families make five additional payments to pay off the balance. Both families pay the same amount for their refrigerators including all taxes, fees, and finance charges. **1**

In the table below, identify a monthly payment, in dollars, for Family A and a monthly payment, in dollars, for Family B that are consistent with the installment plan described above. Make only one selection in each column. **2**

Family A	Family B	Monthly payment
○	○	$50
○	○	$80
○	○	$120 **3**
○	●	$160
●	○	$250
○	○	$300

Check Your Answers
Always double check your answers for a Two-Part Analysis question. Flipping your answers is a very common mistake for these questions. Make sure you have the correct answer for each column.

We used a form of Plugging In the Answers (PITA) to solve the previous question. You can use that approach for most of the Two-Part Analysis questions that you see. Here's a recap of the steps.

PITA for Two-Part Analysis Questions

1. Write down the answer choices on your noteboard. Make two columns and leave some space between.

2. Decide which variable is easier to work with. For example, you might be able to eliminate some answers for one variable because those answers are too big or too small.

3. Write a label over each column of numbers. Label the first column as the easier variable to work with.

4. Starting with an answer in the middle for the first column, work the steps of the problem. For the second column, remember that you may need to test only the answers that are bigger or smaller than the number you worked with in the first column.

5. Check for a match between the first and second column that makes a condition in the problem true.

For some Two-Part Analysis questions, however, you won't be able to use PITA. For the problem we just discussed, the two monthly payments were linked because both families needed to pay the same amount for a refrigerator. For some Two-Part Analysis questions, however, the variables are either unlinked or, at least, less linked.

Let's look at an example:

Jack divides $30,000 between two investments. He invests 35% of the money in Investment A, which pays 4% simple interest annually for 5 years. He invests the remainder of the money in Investment B, which pays 2% interest compounded semiannually for 4 years.

In the table below, identify the total interest earned, in dollars, for Investment A and the total interest earned, rounded to the nearest dollar, for Investment B that are consistent with the investments described above. Make only one selection in each column.

Investment A	Investment B	Interest Earned
○	○	$392
○	○	$870
○	○	$1,560
○	○	$1,616
○	○	$2,100
○	○	$3,347

Here's How to Crack It

For this question, note that there's no common condition that needs to be satisfied. Rather, there are two independent calculations. That's how you know that you can't use PITA to solve this question.

The solution to this question starts with calculating how Jack divides the $30,000 between the two investments. Start by calculating 35% of $30,000. Remember that you can just use the onscreen calculator: $30,000 \times 0.35 = 10,500$. So, $10,500 is invested in Investment A and the rest, or $19,500, is invested in Investment B.

Next, it's time to calculate the interest earned on each investment. Investment A earns simple interest at a rate of 4% per year for 5 years. To find simple interest, you multiply the principal amount, $10,500, by the interest rate, 0.04, by the time period, 5 years. Here's what the calculation looks like:

$$\$10,500 \times 0.04 \times 5 = \$2,100$$

The onscreen calculator makes doing the calculation an easy, one-step operation. Just make sure that you use the right numbers from the problem!

For Investment B, the interest is compounded semiannually. That means that every six months the interest is added to the principal so that interest can be earned on the combined amount. There are several ways to calculate compound interest. One of the easiest is to divide the yearly interest rate by the compounding period. For this problem, the investment pays 2% per year, but the interest is compounded twice per year.

So, that's 1% every six months. In four years, there are 8 compounding periods. To find the account balance at the end of 4 years, you'd calculate the interest for the first six months by multiplying by 0.01. Then, you'd add that amount to the principal and repeat the calculation. Keep calculating until you've done all 8 compounding periods. Of course, since you are multiplying each time, there's a shorter way. Here's what the overall calculation looks like.

$$\$19{,}500 \times (1.01)^8 = \$21{,}115.71$$

To find the interest, just subtract \$19,500 from the account balance. The interest earned is \$1,616, rounded to the nearest dollar.

Here's what your answers should look like just before you click next to move on to the next question:

> Jack divides \$30,000 between two investments. He invests 35% of the money in Investment A, which pays 4% simple interest annually for 5 years. He invests the remainder of the money in Investment B, which pays 2% interest compounded semiannually for 4 years.
>
> In the table below, identify the total interest earned, in dollars, for Investment A and the total interest earned, rounded to the nearest dollar, for Investment B that are consistent with the investments described above. Make only one selection in each column.
>
> | Investment A | Investment B | Interest Earned |
> |:---:|:---:|:---:|
> | ○ | ○ | \$392 |
> | ○ | ○ | \$870 |
> | ○ | ○ | \$1,560 |
> | ○ | ● | \$1,616 |
> | ● | ○ | \$2,100 |
> | ○ | ○ | \$3,347 |

MULTI-SOURCE REASONING

For Multi-Source Reasoning questions, you'll be given a variety of information that can include text, charts, tables, and graphs. The information is arranged on 2 or 3 tabs. Multi-Source Reasoning questions typically come in sets of 2 or 3.

When a new Multi-Source question appears on your screen, you should take a minute to review the information on each tab. As usual, you should check out things like the axes on graphs and any headings for the charts. But for Multi-Source Reasoning questions, you should also determine how the information on one tab relates to the information on the other tabs.

Let's look at the example from the previous chapter. This time, we'll take a look at the information on all three tabs. We'll also discuss how to evaluate statements and answer questions.

| **Text #1** | **Graph #1** | **Graph #2** |

The population of a country affects its ability to compete in the global economy. On the one hand, a large population can be a source of inexpensive labor that can attract investment. On the other hand, large populations can also create resource allocation problems, especially for items such as food, clean water, and health care.

Increased wealth sometimes results in reduced population growth. The table below compares the population and population growth rates for the United States, Canada, Norway, India, and China in Year 25 of a 25 year long survey.

Country	Population	Rate of Growth
United States	295,753,000	0.9%
Canada	32,312,000	1.0%
Norway	4,623,000	0.7%
India	1,095,000,000	1.4%
China	1,304,000,000	0.6%

Consider each of the following statements. Does the information in the graphs and text support the inference as stated?

Yes   No

○   ○   40% of the countries showed an increase in per capita CO_2 emissions for each 5-year period.

○   ○   The United States emitted more CO_2 in 2005 than did China.

○   ○ CO_2 emissions per capita in India increased between 2005 and 2010.

Here's How to Crack It

We'll review the information one tab at a time before we start evaluating the statements. The first tab, Text #1, provides some background information about the ways in which a country's population can affect its participation in the global economy. This tab also presents a table with population and growth rates for five countries. Notice that you need to read the included information on this tab to determine that the table displays data from Year 25 of a 25-year long survey. Unlike the other question types that we've discussed, you should always read any text that's included on a tab in a Multi-Source Reasoning question.

Now, here's the information for the second tab:

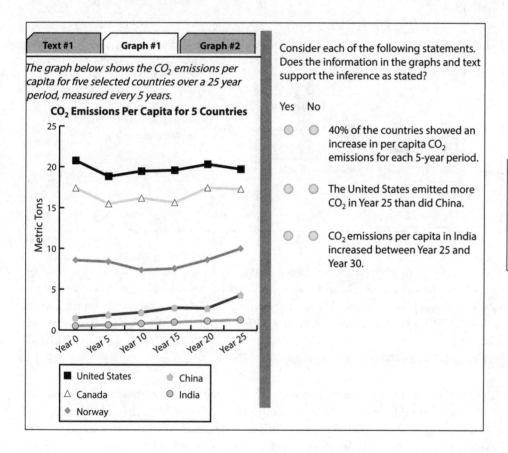

This tab shows CO_2 emissions for five countries over a 25-year period. Notice that the countries on this tab are the same as the countries on the first tab. It's also important to note that the CO_2 emissions on this tab are per capita emissions. Since the first tab provided information about populations for Year 25, it would be possible to calculate approximate total CO_2 emissions for these five countries for Year 25. While you don't necessarily need to consider all the calculations you could perform, thinking about what you could calculate is an excellent way to notice connections between the data provided on the tabs.

Next, let's take a look at the information on the third tab:

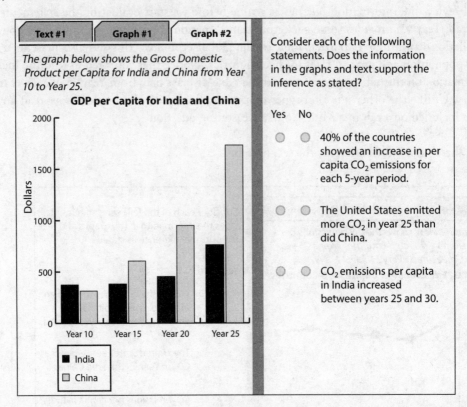

| Text #1 | Graph #1 | **Graph #2** |

The graph below shows the Gross Domestic Product per Capita for India and China from Year 10 to Year 25.

GDP per Capita for India and China

Consider each of the following statements. Does the information in the graphs and text support the inference as stated?

Yes | No

- ⊙ ⊙ 40% of the countries showed an increase in per capita CO_2 emissions for each 5-year period.

- ⊙ ⊙ The United States emitted more CO_2 in year 25 than did China.

- ⊙ ⊙ CO_2 emissions per capita in India increased between years 25 and 30.

This tab provides GDP information about two of the countries, India and China, discussed on the first two tabs. The information on this tab is provided for a subset of the timespan from the second tab. The second tab showed the 25-year range while this information is only for the 15-year timespan. The GDP information is provided as per capita information. Again, that means that the information on the first tab could be used to calculate the overall GDP for India and China. Of course, that calculation can be completed only for Year 25.

Now that we've reviewed the information on each tab, it's time to start evaluating the statements. But first, we need to consider the directions carefully. The directions state that you are supposed to consider the question "Does the information in the graphs and text support the inference as stated?" Remember our discussion of valid inferences. An inference is a statement that you know to be true because you can back it up with proof.

There are really three cases to consider when evaluating these statements. If the graphs and other information on the tabs are sufficient to show that the statement is true, answer "yes." If the graphs and other information on the tabs are sufficient to show that the statement is false, answer "no." What if there is simply insufficient information to conclusively show that the statement is either true or false? In that case, you answer "no" because the information did not support the inference. In other words, the task here is a little different from simply evaluating whether the statements are true or false. After all, GMAC could have made the answer choices True and False rather than Yes and No.

Remember, however, that most GMAC statements won't try to trick you that way. But it is important to remember that you need proof to claim that something can be inferred. You will see statements that try to get you to read into or interpret the information. Such activities do not lead to valid inferences!

Let's take a look at the first statement:

> 40% of the countries showed an increase in per capita CO_2 emissions for each 5-year period.

The first step in evaluating a statement for a Multi-Source Reasoning question is to determine which tab or tabs contain the information that you need. For this statement, the second tab contains information about per capita CO_2 emissions, so select that tab. Next, start checking out the trend lines on the graph. We've reprinted the chart from the second tab below.

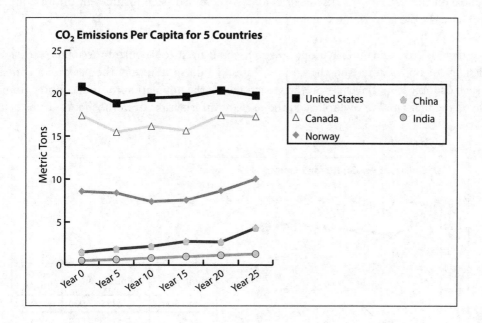

The trend lines for the United States, Canada, and Norway clearly show both increases and decreases between five-year periods, so none of those countries fit the requirements of the statement. The trend line for China needs to be examined carefully. China's CO_2 emissions per capita increase for four out of the five five-year periods shown. However, China's emissions decreased slightly between Year 15 and Year 20. So, China also does not fit the requirements of the statement. Only India's trend line shows an increase for every five-year period depicted on the graph. But that means that only 1 out of 5 or 20% of the countries showed an increase in CO_2 emissions for each five-year period. So the answer to the first statement is "no."

Next, let's take a look at the second statement:

> The United States emitted more CO_2 in Year 25 than did China.

Evaluating this statement is a little trickier than evaluating the first statement. First, be careful of the wording. The statement is about total CO_2 emissions rather than the per capita emissions that are shown by the chart on the second tab. So, while the emissions chart does show that per capita emissions for the United States were greater than those for China in Year 25, you cannot base your answer only on that piece of information. Remember that the test-writers will try to get you to make hasty conclusions, so always check out the wording of the statement carefully.

Since none of the provided charts allows you to simply look up the information for this statement, you need to determine if you have sufficient information to evaluate the statement. To go from per capita CO_2 emissions in Year 25 to total CO_2 emissions in Year 25, you need to know the populations for China and the United States in Year 25. That information is provided by the table on the first tab. As discussed before, if there had been insufficient information, you could have clicked "no" right away for your answer.

Since there is sufficient information, however, you'll need to calculate the total Year 25 CO_2 emissions for both China and the United States. To do so, multiply the per capita emissions for each country from the chart on the second tab by the population for that country from the table on the first tab. We've duplicated the relevant information from the first two tabs below.

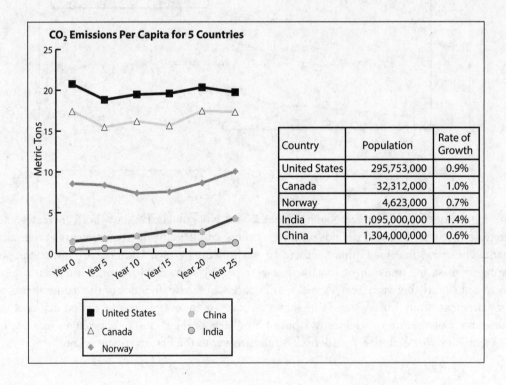

Of course, you won't be able to split the view on your computer screen this way. So you'll need to write down some of the relevant information on your noteboards. You should use your noteboards to take notes whenever you need information from two different tabs. Simply trying to remember the numbers can cause errors and waste time. For example, to evaluate this statement, you might jot down the Year 25 per capita CO_2 emissions for the United States and China. Then, go to the first tab to get the population numbers for each country.

For the United States, per capita CO_2 emissions in Year 25 were approximately 20 metric tons. The U.S. population in 2005 was 295,753,000. So, the total Year 25 CO_2 emissions for the United States was $20 \times 295,753,000 = 5,915,060,000$ metric tons. For China, the per capita CO_2 emissions are approximately 4.8 and the population was 1,304,000,000. So, China's total CO_2 emissions for Year 25 were $4.8 \times 1,304,000,000 = 6,259,200,000$, greater than those of the United States. Therefore, the answer to the second statement is "no."

It's time to tackle the third statement:

> CO_2 emissions per capita in India increased between Year 25 and Year 30.

In contrast with the second statement, evaluating this statement is certainly less time-consuming. However, as we'll see, you'll need to remember what is necessary for a valid inference. The necessary information is displayed on the graph on the second tab. Again, we've duplicated the necessary information below.

Use Your Noteboards
If the information you need is on two different tabs, use your noteboards to keep track of the information from one of the tabs.

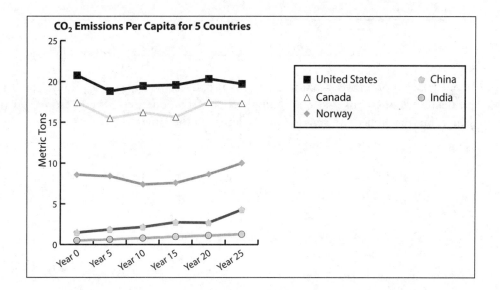

Now it's time to be careful. Notice that the chart displays data only up to Year 25. While India's per capita CO_2 emissions have shown a steady increase over the 25-year period shown on the chart, that's not sufficient for a valid inference. Since the chart does not display the actual numbers for Year 30, the answer to the third statement is "no."

Here's what your answers should look like just before you click next to move on to the next question:

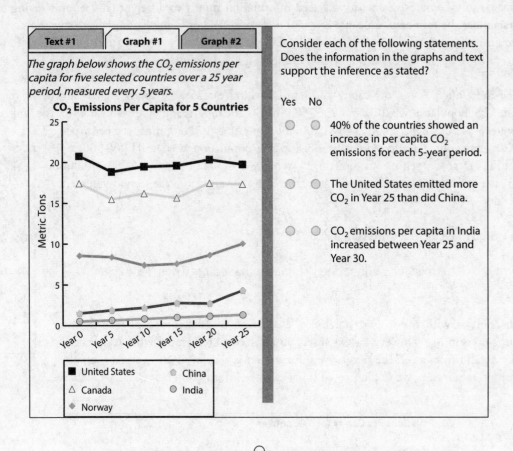

As mentioned, Multi-Source Reasoning questions usually come in sets. Typically, you'll get two statement style questions and one multiple-choice style question. The questions on the right change, but the tabbed information on the left stays the same.

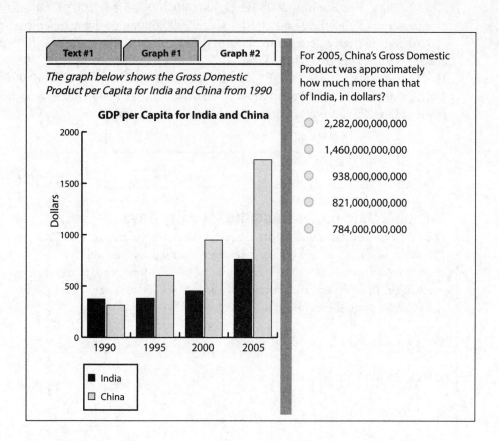

Text #1 **Graph #1** **Graph #2**

The graph below shows the Gross Domestic Product per Capita for India and China from 1990

GDP per Capita for India and China

■ India
□ China

For 2005, China's Gross Domestic Product was approximately how much more than that of India, in dollars?

○ 2,282,000,000,000

○ 1,460,000,000,000

○ 938,000,000,000

○ 821,000,000,000

○ 784,000,000,000

Here's How to Crack It

As with any other Multi-Source Reasoning question, your first step is to determine which chart or charts contain the relevant data. For this question, you certainly need the bar chart on the third tab because that chart shows information about GDP. The bar chart is shown above. However, the bar chart displays data about GDP per capita, and the question asks about overall Gross Domestic Product. So, you'll also need the 2005 population numbers from the table on tab one. We've reproduced the relevant table below.

Country	Population	Rate of Growth
United States	295,753,000	0.9%
Canada	32,312,000	1.0%
Norway	4,623,000	0.7%
India	1,095,000,000	1.4%
China	1,304,000,000	0.6%

To answer the question, you need to multiply each country's GDP per capita from 2005 by its population from 2005. Then, subtract India's GDP from that of China.

Need More Practice?
Check out the GMAT
Focus Drills on your
online Student Tools!

Based on the bar chart, China's 2005 per capita GDP was approximately $1,750. Since China's population in 2005 was 1,304,000,000, China's 2005 GDP was approximately $1,750 × 1,304,000,000 = $2,282,000,000,000. (Remember that you can use the onscreen calculator to perform the calculation.) For India, the 2005 per capita GDP was approximately $750, while India's population was 1,095,000,000. That means that India's GDP was approximately $750 × 1,095,000,000 = $821,250,000,000. Now, just subtract to find that China's 2005 GDP was approximately $1,460,750,000 more than that of India. That's closest to (B).

Complex Calculations and the Memory Keys

The problem just discussed featured several longer calculations. Your calculator at home probably has parentheses, which makes entering such a calculation a one-step operation. Is there a way to do this calculation in one-step using the onscreen GMAT calculator which doesn't have parentheses? Sure, use the memory keys!

Enter the following keystrokes:

1750 * 1304000000 = | MS |

750 * 1095000000 = | +/− | | M+ | | MR |

These keystrokes will minimize the number of times you need to enter the large numbers, which helps to avoid errors.

Summary

o   Before you jump into the Integrated Reasoning-style questions, get your bearings and peruse each tab or piece of information.

o   Integrated Reasoning style questions don't always strictly test math concepts and can include critical reasoning, inference, and complete the statement questions.

o   On Table Analysis questions, know that you can sort by only one column at a time. If you think that sorting will help, go for it. But don't waste time devising the perfect order to evaluate statements.

o   On Graphics Interpretation questions, start by looking for labels on the axes and finding the legend if there is one.

o   On Two-Part Analysis questions, do some algebra or PITA to get to the right answer. Be careful that you select the right button in the right column when answering these questions.

o   On Multi-Source Reasoning questions, take a minute to review the information on each tab before you jump in. Think about how the information on one tab relates to the information on other tabs.

Chapter 10
Data Insights: Strategic Approach and Strategies for Data Sufficiency Style Questions

Data Sufficiency style questions can be some of the most frustrating question types for test-takers. This chapter outlines the steps you need to take in order to excel on this question style.

DATA SUFFICIENCY: BASIC POE STRATEGY

Similar to every other question type on the GMAT, Data Sufficiency questions have overarching strategies for effectively applying POE.

First, however, let's restate one of the most important strategies for working any Data Sufficiency question: *Evaluate the statements one at a time before you think about combining them.* Many people mistakenly pick (C)—you need both statements together—when it would have been possible to answer the question with only the information in the first statement or the second statement. Generally, people make this mistake when they read both statements right after reading the question stem. In fact, this is the most common mistake that test-takers make when working Data Sufficiency questions.

In order to avoid making common mistakes on Data Sufficiency questions, you need to stay organized and follow a process. What should that process be? We're glad you asked.

Process of Elimination Flowchart

Here's a handy flowchart that outlines for you how to approach any Data Sufficiency style question. Through your first 10–20 attempts at Data Sufficiency questions, you should keep this chart at the ready. As you get more experienced with the question style, you may find continued use of the flowchart unnecessary. However, if you ever find yourself having trouble keeping your process organized for Data Sufficiency questions, feel free to pull this chart out again and do some more practice.

Combining the Statements

Notice how late in the process you combine the statements. Remember that one of the most common mistakes on Data Sufficiency is combining the statements before you have properly evaluated each statement on its own.

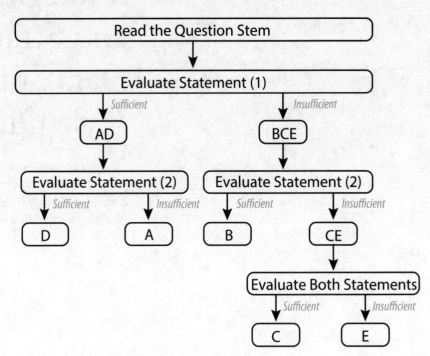

BREAKING DOWN THE FLOWCHART

Step 1: Read the Question Stem

We're going to break down the flowchart one step at a time. Why? Because it's an incredibly useful tool and one of the primary ways POE can be applied to Data Sufficiency questions!

You need to begin every Data Sufficiency question by reading the question stem. This seems a fairly obvious starting point, but for Data Sufficiency questions you're looking primarily at two elements. The first element you're looking for from the question stem is the question itself. In order to evaluate if the statements provide sufficient information to answer the question, you must first know what question you are trying to answer.

The second element you're looking for from the question stem includes any parameters, restrictions, or rules that have to be followed in order to answer the question. Consider the following question stem:

$$\text{If } y > x > 0, \text{ what is the value of } \frac{x}{y}?$$

The question in the question stem is to look for the *value of* $\frac{x}{y}$. The question stem also dictates that $y > x > 0$. Any value of x and y provided by, or derived from, the statements must meet this requirement.

Step 2: Evaluate Statement (1)

The next step in the flowchart is to evaluate Statement (1). As we talked about earlier, it is critically important that you evaluate the statements one at a time. Think about the information provided in Statement (1) and only Statement (1). If you find yourself unable to resist the urge to read and consider Statement (2) before fully evaluating Statement (1) on its own, you can even go so far as to cover up Statement (2).

When evaluating Statement (1) you are attempting to determine if the information in the statement, combined with the information or restrictions in the question stem, is enough to produce a consistent answer to the question. Consider many different possibilities for the statement. Do everything you can to be certain that the conclusion you arrived at is true—the information in Statement (1) is sufficient or insufficient to answer the question.

Step 3: AD/BCE

Now it's time for the first round of POE!

Ask yourself the question: was the information in Statement (1) sufficient or insufficient to answer the question?

If the information in Statement (1) is sufficient to answer the question, that means we can eliminate (B), (C), and (E). Why? Because these choices require that Statement (1) on its own NOT be sufficient. Choice (B) is correct only when Statement (2) is sufficient, but Statement (1) is not. Choice (C) is correct only when the information in both statements must be combined to have sufficient information to answer the question, which means that neither statement individually is sufficient on its own. Choice (E) is correct only when neither statement individually nor both statements combined is sufficient to answer the question.

> When you are finished evaluating Statement (1) you can apply POE aggressively to narrow down to the remaining answer choices:
>
> Statement (1) is sufficient: AD
> Statement (1) is insufficient: BCE

If the information in Statement (1) is insufficient, that means we can eliminate (A) and (D). Why? Because (A) and (D) require that Statement (1) on its own IS sufficient. Choice (A) is correct only when Statement (1) is sufficient, but Statement (2) is not. Choice (D) is correct only when both statements individually are sufficient.

No matter what, once you are finished evaluating Statement (1) you will be left with either 2 or 3 possible answer choices: AD or BCE.

Step 4: Evaluate Statement (2)

Up next, it's time to take a look at the information provided by Statement (2). You'll evaluate this statement the same way you evaluated Statement (1). Namely, you need to evaluate it without considering <u>any</u> of the information provided to you by Statement (1). Pretend that Statement (1) does not exist. Cover it up if you have to. You are trying to determine if the information in Statement (2), in combination with any parameters set for by the question stem, is enough to determine a consistent answer to the question.

No matter if Statement (1) was sufficient or not, you'll be able to eliminate at least one more answer choice after evaluating Statement (2). If Statement (1) was sufficient and you were left with only AD as possible answer choices, then evaluating Statement (2) is the last step you'll need to take. If Statement (2) is sufficient on its own to answer the question, then the correct answer is (D). If Statement (2) is insufficient on its own to answer the question, then the correct answer is (A).

However, if Statement (1) was insufficient to answer the question, then you have one more step to do to arrive at the correct answer. If Statement (1) was insufficient but Statement (2) is sufficient, then congratulations! There is no more work for you to do. The correct answer is (B). But, if Statement (2) is insufficient, you'll need to move on to the next step in the flowchart. Eliminate (B) and move on to step 5.

Step 5: Evaluate Both Statements

You've evaluated Statement (1) on its own and found it was insufficient to provide a consistent answer to the question. You eliminated (A) and (D) and were left with only BCE as possible correct answers. You then evaluated Statement (2) on its own and also found it was insufficient to provide a consistent answer to the question. This means you can eliminate (B). But you're still left to decide between (C) and (E).

In order to determine if the correct answer is (C) or (E), evaluate both statements combined. What this means is you consider the information from Statement (1) AND you consider the information from Statement (2), as well as any parameters from the question stem. When you consider both statements at the same time, is the information provided sufficient to determine a consistent answer to the question? If so, the correct answer is (C). If not, the correct answer is (E).

Practice Makes Perfect

At this point, you may be thinking to yourself: "5 steps to follow to answer one question? There's no way I'll get through all the questions in time!"

There's no doubt that Data Sufficiency questions can be time consuming. You'll need to make sure you keep a good sense of the time you spend on any given question so you don't throw off the timing for the whole section because of one question.

But, the more you practice Data Sufficiency using the logic laid out in the flowchart, the faster you will be able to move through the steps. Eventually, you won't have to think about the steps at all! So, keep at it and keep practicing.

Of course, there may come a situation in which you are either running low on time or are taking too long on a single question and you just need to guess and move on.

DRILL 2: (AD/BCE)

In the following drill, each question is followed by only one statement. Based on the first statement, decide if you are down to AD or BCE. The answers can be found in Part V.

1. What is the value of x ?

    (1) $y = 4$
    (2) ????

2. Is y an integer?

    (1) $2y$ is an integer.
    (2) ????

3. A certain room contains 12 boys and girls. How many more boys than girls are there?

   (1) There are three girls in the room.
   (2) ????

4. What number is x percent of 20 ?

   (1) 10 percent of x is 5.
   (2) ????

Aggressive POE for Data Sufficiency

The flowchart represents the basic approach for Data Sufficiency problems. Ideally, you'll be able to work through every step and come up with the best answer possible without hitting a single snag, difficult problem, or time constraint. Also ideally, your dream business school will call you tomorrow and tell you not to worry about the GMAT at all and tell you you've been granted a full ride solely on the basis of your charming personality.

If either of those things happens to you, let us know. We want to hear from you.

If you're like virtually everybody else, however, you will likely hit some snags or need to move quickly through some Data Sufficiency problems. If you come across this situation, there are some tricks you can use to make educated guesses in a timely manner.

Work Through Evaluating Statement (1)

If you're running low on time and need to quickly guess on a Data Sufficiency problem, one of the best things you can do to improve your odds of getting the question correct is to try to quickly evaluate Statement (1). If you can determine if Statement (1) is sufficient or insufficient, you can quickly eliminate at least 2 answer choices, which means you can improve your odds of guessing correctly from 1 in 5 to at least 1 in 3 by narrowing the answer choices down to AD or BCE.

Take Inventory

Remember, you don't need to solve the question in a Data Sufficiency problem—you just need to determine if the information provided is sufficient enough that you COULD solve the problem! One of the ways GMAC likes to make difficult Data Sufficiency questions is to make a hard to parse, complicated statement sufficient. They are hoping test-takers will confuse not being able to understand or work through the statement with the same thing as the statement being insufficient.

Instead of trying to solve the question, take inventory of what you need to know to solve it that is currently missing. Even if you can get a general idea of what you need to know, you can then scan the statements for that information or ways to derive that information. When you're in a time crunch, this can be a great way to improve your chances of correctly guessing the answer.

Now that you've worked through a drill to get acquainted with the idea of using POE to get down to AD or BCE after evaluating the first statement, let's look at a full question to see how we can apply these principles.

If $x + y = 3$, what is the value of xy ?

(1) x and y are integers.
(2) x and y are positive.

(A)   Statement (1) ALONE is sufficient, but statement (2) alone is not sufficient.
(B)   Statement (2) ALONE is sufficient, but statement (1) alone is not sufficient.
(C)   BOTH statements TOGETHER are sufficient, but NEITHER statement ALONE is sufficient.
(D)   EACH statement ALONE is sufficient.
(E)   Statements (1) and (2) TOGETHER are not sufficient.

Here's How to Crack It

The first step to working a Data Sufficiency question is to evaluate the information in the question stem. The goal of Data Sufficiency questions is to evaluate whether the statements contain enough information to produce a consistent answer to the question. To do that, you first need to know what the question is! In this case, you are looking to determine if the statements provide enough information to determine a value of xy. The question also provides some context for the values of x and y by stating that it must be true that $x + y = 3$.

Now that you know what the question is, you know how to evaluate the statements and can begin working with the statements. The next step in our flowchart is to evaluate Statement (1). Statement (1) states that x and y are integers. Stop here and think: what do you know about the potential values for x and y? You know that they have to be integers, but you also know that $x + y = 3$. What are possible values of x and y that could meet both of these parameters? The values $x = 2$, $y = 1$ satisfy the parameters. All of the statements and parameters for the question are met, so what is the answer to the question? In this case, the value of $xy = (2)(1) = 2$.

Consider other possible values of x and y that satisfy the parameters that x and y are integers and $x + y = 3$. How about $x = 3$, $y = 0$? This satisfies both parameters. What is the answer to the question now? The value of $xy = (3)(0) = 0$.

Does the information contained in Statement (1) provide a way to solve for a consistent answer to the question? No, it does not! Therefore, Statement (1) is NOT sufficient to answer the question. The flowchart says that the only possible answers are BCE, so eliminate (A) and (D).

The next step in the flowchart is to Evaluate Statement (2). Evaluate this statement in a similar way to Statement (1), making sure that the parameters in the statement and the question stem are met.

Statement (2) dictates that x and y are positive. What are possible values for x and y that meet this condition and also meet the condition that $x + y = 3$? One possible pairing of values is $x = 2$, $y = 1$. This produces an answer to the question of $xy = (2)(1) = 2$. However, another possible set of values for x and y that meet the parameters is $x = 1.6$, $y = 1.4$. In this case, the value of $xy = (1.6)(1.4) = 2.24$.

Does the information contained in Statement (2) provide a way to solve for a consistent answer to the question? Nope again! Because Statement (2) is not sufficient, the only possible remaining answer choices are CE. Eliminate (B).

The next step in the flowchart is to Evaluate Both Statements. Between both statements and the question stem, there are 3 parameters that define possible values for x and y: x and y are integers, x and y are positive, and $x + y = 3$. What are possible values for x and y that satisfy all three parameters? If $x = 2$ and $y = 1$, then all three parameters are met and $xy = 2$. Are there other values of x and y that satisfy the parameters? If $x = 1$ and $y = 2$, then the parameters are met. In this case, the answer to the question is $(1)(2) = 2$.

There are no other values of x and y that meet all three parameters. Does the combined information from both statements provide a means to determine a consistent answer to the question? Yes! Both statements combined are sufficient to answer the question. Look at the flowchart to find that the correct answer is (C).

TWO FLAVORS OF DATA SUFFICIENCY

As if working on understanding a completely unique and bedeviling question style isn't enough, Data Sufficiency questions can take two different shapes based on the expected response to the question. Consider the difference between the following two examples:

What is the difference between the mean and the median of Set A ?

Is the mean of Set A greater than the median of Set A ?

In both questions you'll be working with Set A, which is either provided to you or you'll need to determine it from the statements. In both questions, you'll need to know the mean and the median of Set A. However, in the first question the answer is a value. This is what we refer to as a Value Data Sufficiency question. In the second question the answer is "Yes" or "No." We refer to this as a Yes/No Data Sufficiency question. Each of these question types requires a slightly different approach.

VALUE DATA SUFFICIENCY APPROACH: PIECES OF THE PUZZLE

Value Data Sufficiency questions are by far the most common style of Data Sufficiency question. In this style of Data Sufficiency question, you are looking to evaluate if the information in the statements is sufficient to determine one consistent value as an answer to the question.

For this question type, follow the Pieces of the Puzzle approach. Begin by reading the question stem and ask yourself "What do I know from the information in the question?" Write down the answer to this question on your scratch paper. Anything the question stem provides you as information, make note of it. If any of the information can be quickly translated into an equation, go ahead and do so.

> Sometimes the question stem of value Data Sufficiency questions does not provide you anything! Instead, it may simply ask what the value of something is. In this case, the answer to the question "What do you know?" is nothing!

After answering the question "What do I know?", next ask "What do I need to know in order to answer the question?". It's very important that you try to do this without looking at the statements. Try to anticipate what you might need to know in order to answer the question being asked. By taking inventory of the question in this way, you know what information the statements need to provide in order to be sufficient to answer the question.

Once you determine what you know and what you need to know in order to answer the question, continue with the basic approach flowchart as usual by evaluating Statement (1).

Try out the Pieces of the Puzzle approach to Value Data Sufficiency questions on the question below:

If a comedian plays two shows and twice as many tickets are available for the evening show as for the afternoon show, what percentage of the total number of tickets available for both shows has been sold?

(1)   A total of 450 tickets is available for both shows.

(2)   Exactly $\frac{3}{5}$ of the tickets available for the afternoon show have been sold, and exactly $\frac{1}{5}$ of the tickets available for the evening show has been sold.

(A)   Statement (1) ALONE is sufficient, but statement (2) alone is not sufficient.
(B)   Statement (2) ALONE is sufficient, but statement (1) alone is not sufficient.
(C)   BOTH statements TOGETHER are sufficient, but NEITHER statement ALONE is sufficient.
(D)   EACH statement ALONE is sufficient.
(E)   Statements (1) and (2) TOGETHER are not sufficient.

Here's How to Crack It

This is a Value Data Sufficiency question, so begin by reading the question stem asking yourself "What do I know?". You know that there are 2 shows and that the evening show has twice as many available tickets as the afternoon show. You could represent the second piece of this information with the equation $E = 2A$, where E is the number of tickets available for the evening show and A is the number of tickets available for the afternoon show. Therefore, the total number of tickets available can be represented by the equation $2A + A = $ *Total Available Tickets*. There is no further information provided by the question stem.

Next, ask yourself "What do I need to know in order to answer the question?" The question asks to determine the total percentage of the total number of tickets available for both shows that has been sold. Consider what information is needed to answer this question. To determine the percentage, you need the total number of tickets that are available for both shows, and you need the total number of tickets sold for both shows. You could write an equation for that, but it may be a bit too time intensive—and remember, you don't actually need to solve the question! So long as the statements provide a way to solve for the total number of tickets available for both shows and the total number of tickets sold, you will be able to determine an answer to the question.

Look at the flowchart and follow the next step. The next step in the flowchart is to evaluate Statement (1). When evaluating Statement (1), determine if Statement (1) provides enough information to determine the total number of tickets available for both shows and the total number of tickets sold for both shows. Statement (1) states that a total of 450 tickets is available for both shows. This provides enough information to determine the total number of tickets available for both shows. When combined with the information in the question stem, Statement (1) can be used to determine the number of tickets available for each show. If $2A + A = 450$, then $A = 150$. Use this value of A to determine that $E = 2A = 2(150) = 300$. However, this statement does not provide enough information to determine the total number of tickets sold for both shows. Therefore, Statement (1) does not provide enough information to answer the question, so Statement (1) is insufficient.

Follow the flowchart and see that when Statement (1) is insufficient to answer the question, the only possible remaining answer choices are (B), (C), and (E). Eliminate (A) and (D).

The next step is to evaluate Statement (2). Statement (1) provides the fraction of tickets available for the afternoon show that have been sold and the fraction of tickets available for the evening show that have been sold. Statement (2) provides enough information to determine the number of tickets sold for each of the shows if the number of tickets available for each show is known. However, Statement (2) does not provide any information about the total number of tickets available for each show. Therefore, Statement (2) does not provide enough information to answer the question, so Statement (2) is insufficient.

Follow the flowchart and eliminate (B). The only remaining answer choices are (C) and (E).

The next step is to evaluate both statements together. Statement (1) provides enough information to determine the total number of tickets available and the total number of tickets available for each show. Statement (2) provides enough information to determine the number of tickets sold for each show so long as there is information about the total number of tickets available for each show. When considered together, statements (1) and (2) provide enough information to determine the total number of tickets available and the total number of tickets sold. This is the information we determined was needed to answer the question. Therefore, both statements combined are sufficient to answer the question. The correct answer is (C).

———————————◯———————————

Let's try another Value Data Sufficiency question.

———————————◯———————————

Automobile *A* is traveling at two-thirds the speed that Automobile *B* is traveling. At what speed is Automobile *A* traveling?

(1) If both automobiles increased their speed by 10 miles per hour, Automobile *A* would be traveling at three-quarters the speed that Automobile *B* would be traveling.
(2) Automobile *B* travels 75 miles in 95 minutes.

(A) Statement (1) ALONE is sufficient, but statement (2) alone is not sufficient.
(B) Statement (2) ALONE is sufficient, but statement (1) alone is not sufficient.
(C) BOTH statements TOGETHER are sufficient, but NEITHER statement ALONE is sufficient.
(D) EACH statement ALONE is sufficient.
(E) Statements (1) and (2) TOGETHER are not sufficient.

Here's How to Crack It

This is a Value Data Sufficiency question, so begin by reading the question stem, asking yourself "What do I know?" You know there are 2 automobiles and that Automobile *A* is traveling at two-thirds the speed of Automobile *B*. The speeds of Automobile *A* and Automobile *B* can be represented by the equation $A = \frac{2}{3}B$. There is no further information provided by the question stem.

Next, ask yourself "What do I need to know in order to answer the question?" The question asks for the speed of Automobile *A*. The speed of Automobile *A* can be determined if you know the distance Automobile *A* traveled and the time it took Automobile *A* to go that distance. Alternatively, the speed of Automobile *A* can be determined if you know the speed, or a way to calculate the speed, of Automobile *B*.

Look at the flowchart and follow the steps. The next step in the flowchart is to evaluate Statement (1). When evaluating Statement (1), determine if Statement (1) provides enough information to determine the speed of Automobile A. Statement (1) provides another equation for the relationship between the speeds of Automobiles A and B. Written out in an equation, the information in Statement (1) is $A + 10 = \frac{3}{4}(B + 10)$. Between the information in Statement (1) and the information provided in the question stem, you have two distinct equations with the same two variables. This means you can solve for both variables by stacking the equations. Remember: you don't need to solve the question; you just need to know that you have enough information to solve it. The information in Statement (1) provides a way to solve for the speed for Automobile A, so Statement (1) is sufficient.

Follow the flowchart and see that when Statement (1) is sufficient to answer the question, the only possible remaining answer choices are (A) and (D). Eliminate (B), (C), and (E).

The next step is to evaluate Statement (2). Statement (2) states that Automobile B travels 75 miles in 95 minutes. This is enough information to determine a speed for Automobile B, which can then be used with the information from the question stem to determine a speed for Automobile A. Again, you don't need to solve the question; you just need to know that you have enough information to solve it. The information in Statement (2) is sufficient to solve for the speed for Automobile A. Eliminate (A). The correct answer is (D).

DRILL 3 (Data Sufficiency Parts and Wholes)
The answers can be found in Part V.

1. If only people who paid deposits attended the Rose Seminar, how many people attended this year?

    (1) 70 people sent in deposits to attend the Rose Seminar this year.
    (2) 60% of the people who sent deposits to attend the Rose Seminar this year actually went.

    (A) Statement (1) ALONE is sufficient, but statement (2) alone is not sufficient.
    (B) Statement (2) ALONE is sufficient, but statement (1) alone is not sufficient.
    (C) BOTH statements TOGETHER are sufficient, but NEITHER statement ALONE is sufficient.
    (D) EACH statement ALONE is sufficient.
    (E) Statements (1) and (2) TOGETHER are not sufficient.

2. Luxo paint contains only alcohol and pigment. What is the ratio of alcohol to pigment in Luxo paint?

   (1) Exactly 7 ounces of pigment are contained in a 12-ounce can of Luxo paint.
   (2) Exactly 5 ounces of alcohol are contained in a 12-ounce can of Luxo paint.

   (A) Statement (1) ALONE is sufficient, but statement (2) alone is not sufficient.
   (B) Statement (2) ALONE is sufficient, but statement (1) alone is not sufficient.
   (C) BOTH statements TOGETHER are sufficient, but NEITHER statement ALONE is sufficient.
   (D) EACH statement ALONE is sufficient.
   (E) Statements (1) and (2) TOGETHER are not sufficient.

3. A car drives along a straight road from Smithville to Laredo, going through Ferristown along the way. What is the total distance by car from Smithville to Laredo?

   (1) The distance from Smithville to Ferristown is $\frac{3}{5}$ of the distance from Smithville to Laredo.
   (2) The distance from Ferristown to Laredo is 12 miles.

   (A) Statement (1) ALONE is sufficient, but statement (2) alone is not sufficient.
   (B) Statement (2) ALONE is sufficient, but statement (1) alone is not sufficient.
   (C) BOTH statements TOGETHER are sufficient, but NEITHER statement ALONE is sufficient.
   (D) EACH statement ALONE is sufficient.
   (E) Statements (1) and (2) TOGETHER are not sufficient.

4. If a store sold 30 more televisions this month than last month, by what percent has the number of televisions sold increased from last month to this month?

   (1) This month the store sold 150 televisions.
   (2) Last month the store sold 80% as many televisions as this month.

5. What is the average (arithmetic mean) of a list of 6 consecutive two-digit integers?

   (1) The remainder when the fourth integer is divided by 5 is 3.
   (2) The ratio of the largest integer to the smallest integer is 5:4.

Find the answers to all Challenge Questions in Part V!

Challenge Question #1

If Angela is twice as old as the combined ages of Bill and Charlie, then how old is Charlie?

(1) Four years from now, the sum of all three people's ages will be 108.

(2) Five years ago, the average (arithmetic mean) of all three people's ages was 27.

YES/NO DATA SUFFICIENCY: PLUGGING IN

Yes/No Data Sufficiency questions are less common than Value Data Sufficiency questions. In this style of Data Sufficiency question, the question stem will ask a Yes or No question. You are evaluating if the statements provide enough information to determine a consistent "Yes" or "No" answer to the question.

For this question type, we can usually rely on our old friend Plugging In! Typically for Yes/No Data Sufficiency questions, there will be a variable to solve for or some kind of missing information. When evaluating the statements, look for opportunities to Plug In. Not every Yes/No Data Sufficiency question is best approached via Plugging In, but many can.

But be careful! Anytime you Plug In on a Data Sufficiency question, you'll need to Plug In more than once. The first value you Plug In will yield a "Yes" or "No" answer to the question. The goal of the second (or maybe third) Plug In is to try to find a way to get the opposite answer. Try different types of numbers like fractions, extreme values, and negatives.

Sufficient Statements for Yes/No Data Sufficiency

One element that makes Yes/No Data Sufficiency questions tricky is that the only answer that matters is the response of Yes or No, and so long as that answer is consistent no matter the scenario, the statement is sufficient. Consider the following table that outlines the requirements for if a statement is sufficient:

Answer to the question	Is the statement sufficient?
Always Yes	Sufficient
Sometimes Yes, Sometimes No	Insufficient
Always No	Sufficient

For many test-takers, it is the last situation that causes unforced errors and incorrectly answered questions. Over the years, we've been conditioned to believe that answers of No are synonymous with False and incorrect answers. However, on Yes/No Data Sufficiency questions if the information in the Statement provides a consistent answer of No to the question, the statement is sufficient.

Work through the following Yes/No Data Sufficiency questions.

———————◯———————

Is x an integer?

(1) $5x$ is a positive integer.
(2) $5x = 1$

Here's How to Crack It

This is a Yes/No Data Sufficiency question, so be prepared to Plug In more than once. Start by evaluating the question stem. The question stem presents a variable, x, and the question asks if x is an integer. There is no further information provided by the question stem. Because this is a Yes/No Data Sufficiency question, the statements are sufficient if they provide a way to generate a consistent Yes or No answer to the question.

Evaluate Statement (1). Statement (1) provides information that $5x$ is an integer. This is a great opportunity to Plug In! Pick a value for x that satisfies the requirement in the statement that $5x$ is an integer. If $x = 2$, then the statement is satisfied. In this case, the answer to the question is Yes, x is an integer. Now, Plug In again a different number to try to make the answer to the question No, x is not an integer. For the answer to be No, x cannot be an integer. If $x = \frac{1}{5}$, then $5\left(\frac{1}{5}\right) = 1$. This satisfies the requirement in the statement but changes the answer to the question because now the answer is No, x is not an integer. Because the statement did not provide information that produced a consistent answer to the question, Statement (1) is insufficient. The only possible remaining answer choices are (B), (C), and (E). Eliminate (A) and (D).

The next step is to evaluate Statement (2). This statement provides the information that $5x = 1$. With this information, it is possible to solve for the value of x. There is no need to perform the calculation. The information in the question stem will produce a single value for x, so the statement is sufficient. Eliminate (C) and (E). The correct answer is (B).

Notice how we didn't bother to solve for the value of x using the information from Statement (2). It isn't necessary to solve for the value of x—all we need to know is that we could solve for it if we wanted to. In this case, not solving for x saved us from one of the more common errors that trip up test-takers in a question like this. Let's see why by solving for the value of x. If $5x = 1$, then $x = \frac{1}{5}$. What is the answer to the question in the question stem? The answer is No, x is not an integer. For many test-takers, the negative statement No is often confused as being the same thing as not sufficient. But that's not correct! All that matters is that the information in the statement provides a way to arrive at a consistent answer to the question.

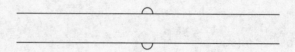

Did Candidate X receive more than half of the 30,000 votes cast in the general election?

(1) Candidate Y received 12,000 of the votes cast.
(2) Candidate X received 1.5 times the number of votes cast than did Candidate Y.

Here's How to Crack It

This is a Yes/No Data Sufficiency question, so be prepared to Plug In more than once. Start by evaluating the question stem. The question stem wants to know if Candidate X received more than half of the 30,000 votes cast in the general election. Half of 30,000 votes is 15,000, so the question is really asking if Candidate X received more than 15,000 votes. Because this is a Yes/No Data Sufficiency question, the statements are sufficient if they provide a way to generate a consistent Yes or No answer to the question.

Evaluate Statement (1). Statement (1) provides that Candidate Y received 12,000 of the votes cast. Many test-takers see a statement such as this and assume that Candidate X must have received the difference of 30,000 – 12,000 = 18,000 votes. However, neither this statement nor the question provides any insight into the number of candidates in the general election. If there are 3 candidates in the general election (X, Y, and Z) and Candidate Z received 2,000 votes, then Candidate X received 30,000 – 12,000 – 2,000 = 16,000 votes. In this case the answer to the question is Yes, Candidate X received more than half the votes in the general election. However, if Candidate Z received 16,000 votes, then Candidate X received only 2,000 votes. In this case, the answer to the question is No, Candidate X did not receive more than half the votes in the general election. Because Statement (1) does not provide a consistent Yes or No answer to the question, the statement is insufficient. Because Statement (1) is insufficient, the only possible answers to the question are (B), (C), and (E). Eliminate (A) and (D).

Now evaluate Statement (2). Statement (2) is that Candidate X received 1.5 times the number of votes cast than did Candidate Y. Similar to Statement (1), many test-takers will assume that there are only 2 candidates in the election. If there were only 2 candidates in the election, then this statement would provide enough information to determine that Candidate X received 18,000 votes and Candidate Y received 12,000 votes. In this scenario, the answer to the question is Yes, Candidate X received more than half the votes in the general election. However, if there were 3 candidates in the election, then it is possible that Candidate Y received only 2,000 votes. In this case, Candidate X would have received 3,000 votes and Candidate Z would have received 25,000. In this scenario, the answer to the question is No, Candidate X did not receive more than half the votes in the general election. Because Statement (2) does not provide a consistent Yes or No answer to the question, the statement is insufficient. Eliminate (B). The only remaining possible answer choices are (C) and (E).

The next step is to evaluate both statements together. Statement (1) provides the number of votes Candidate Y received, and Statement (2) provides the number of votes Candidate X received in relation to Candidate Y. When considering both statements together, it is possible to determine that Candidate X received 18,000 votes. The answer to the question is Yes, Candidate X received more than half the votes in the general election. Eliminate (E). The correct answer is (C).

DRILL 4 (Yes or No)

The answers can be found in Part V.

1. If x is a positive number, is $x < 1$?

   (1) $2x < 1$
   (2) $2x \leq 2$

   (A) Statement (1) ALONE is sufficient, but statement (2) alone is not sufficient.
   (B) Statement (2) ALONE is sufficient, but statement (1) alone is not sufficient.
   (C) BOTH statements TOGETHER are sufficient, but NEITHER statement ALONE is sufficient.
   (D) EACH statement ALONE is sufficient.
   (E) Statements (1) and (2) TOGETHER are not sufficient.

2. Is x positive?

   (1) $xy = 6$
   (2) $xy^2 = 12$

   (A) Statement (1) ALONE is sufficient, but statement (2) alone is not sufficient.
   (B) Statement (2) ALONE is sufficient, but statement (1) alone is not sufficient.
   (C) BOTH statements TOGETHER are sufficient, but NEITHER statement ALONE is sufficient.
   (D) EACH statement ALONE is sufficient.
   (E) Statements (1) and (2) TOGETHER are not sufficient.

3. Are x and y integers?

   (1)   The product xy is an integer.
   (2) $x + y$ is an integer.

   (A)   Statement (1) ALONE is sufficient, but statement (2) alone is not sufficient.
   (B)   Statement (2) ALONE is sufficient, but statement (1) alone is not sufficient.
   (C)   BOTH statements TOGETHER are sufficient, but NEITHER statement ALONE is sufficient.
   (D)   EACH statement ALONE is sufficient.
   (E)   Statements (1) and (2) TOGETHER are not sufficient.

4. Is $3^n > 2^k$?

   (1) $k = n + 1$
   (2) n is a positive integer.

Find the answers to all Challenge Questions in Part V!

Challenge Question #2

If a and b are positive integers, is $2\sqrt[3]{a} < \sqrt[3]{a + b}$?

(1) $7a < b$
(2) $7a < a + b$

Common Mistakes in Data Sufficiency

Over the years, our expert teachers and tutors at The Princeton Review have noticed some patterns in reasons why test-takers get Data Sufficiency questions wrong. Of course, sometimes test-takers get a question wrong because they just don't know how to work a question. But there are some common avoidable errors that test-takers make, which we hope to help you avoid.

Watch out for these common traps!

Error #1) Assuming the Statements Are Missing Information

Sometimes test-takers pick (E) because the question was designed to make it appear that the statements did not provide sufficient information. This is a useful trap for Data Sufficiency questions as it is really effective at tripping up test-takers who are moving too quickly through the steps of evaluating the statements.

Consider this example:

What is the value of $r^2 + s$?

(1) $t - u = 8$
(2) $r^2t - su + st - r^2u = 24$

Here's How to Crack It

Many test-takers who try to answer this question too quickly will be tempted by (E). There are two variables in the question stem but four variables in the statements. It is unclear what the variables t and u have to do with finding the values of r^2 and s. As a result, many test-takers will select (E). Alas, those test-takers have reached their conclusion too quickly.

Just because the statements do not appear to provide the required information, it doesn't mean that there is no way to answer the question.

Here's how this one is solved.

This is a Value Data Sufficiency question, so begin by asking "What do I know?" In this case, the question stem does not provide a lot of information, so you do not know anything.

Next, ask "What do I need to know to answer the question?" The question asks about the value of $r^2 + s$. In order for a statement to be sufficient, it must provide enough information to determine the values of r and s, or a way to calculate the value of the expression $r^2 + s$.

Evaluate Statement (1). There's no way to determine anything about r and s from information about t and u. As a result, Statement (1) is insufficient. Eliminate (A). The possible answers are (B), (C), and (E).

Now, let's work with Statement (2). The equation provided does contain the two variables in the question stem. Let's try grouping the expressions differently:

$$r^2t - su + st - r^2u = 24$$

$$(r^2t + st) - (r^2u + su) = 24$$

$$t(r^2 + s) - u(r^2 + s) = 24$$

$$(r^2 + s)(t - u) = 24$$

This statement does not provide any way to determine a consistent answer to the question. Eliminate (B). The possible answers are (C) and (E).

Now evaluate both statements together. Using the information in Statement (1), the expression $t - u$ found from Statement (2) can be replaced with 8. It is possible to determine the value of $r^2 + s$ using this information. The statements combined are sufficient. Eliminate (E). The correct answer is (C).

Error #2) Assuming Confusing Statements Are Not Sufficient

Because the GMAT test-writers know that people don't like to pick things that they don't understand, the test-writers will sometimes pair a fairly easy statement with one that is difficult to understand. The test-writers do this because they know that many test-takers will conclude that the difficult-to-understand statement is insufficient.

A certain company's financial report lists monthly expenses over the course of a calendar year for three primary categories: Real Estate, Technology, and Payroll. For the calendar year, is the company's greatest expense Payroll?

(1)   The range of monthly expenses for Payroll is three times that of Real Estate and twice that of Technology.
(2)   For every $500 in Payroll expense there was $400 in Real Estate expense, and for every $120 In Real Estate expense there was $200 in Technology expense

Here's How to Crack It

This is a Yes/No Data Sufficiency question, so be prepared to Plug In more than once. The question stem provides the information that the company's financial report contains three primary categories: Real Estate, Technology, and Payroll. The question asks if Payroll is the company's greatest expense. To provide a consistent Yes or No answer to the question, the statements need to provide a way to determine the expenses for the different categories or provide a relationship between the different categories.

Evaluate Statement (1). This statement provides information about the relationship between the ranges of the monthly expenses for each category. This information does not provide any details about the actual expense for the calendar year, only the range of expenses. This is not the information needed to answer the question, so Statement (1) is insufficient. The only remaining answer choices are (B), (C), and (E). Eliminate (A) and (D).

Evaluate Statement (2). This statement is a great example of a confusing statement that many test-takers would assume is insufficient. However, keep in mind the information needed in order to answer the question. In order to be sufficient, the statements need to provide a relationship between the different categories. This statement provides a relationship by linking all three of the categories together through their relationship to Real Estate expenses. This relationship guarantees that a single, consistent answer can be determined from the statement, which means Statement (2) is sufficient to answer the question. Eliminate (C) and (E). The correct answer is (B).

For anyone interested in how the information in Statement (2) could be used to solve the problem, create a common ratio by determining the least common multiple between the two values for Real Estate expenses, $400 and $120. The least common multiple is $1,200. To get a Real Estate expense value of $1,200 multiply the first ratio by 3 and the second ratio by 10. This results in a combined ratio for Payroll : Real Estate : Technology of $1,500 : $1,200 : $2,000. Therefore, Payroll is not the company's greatest expense, and the answer to the question is "No."

Error #3) Not Being Skeptical of Problems That Seem Too Easy

GMAT test-writers are very good at disguising hard questions as easy ones. They figure that if a problem looks easy, a test-taker will be less diligent and less careful than when a problem looks hard.

Now, put GMAC's ability to pass off hard questions as easy questions into the context of the adaptive nature of the test. If you start to do well, the computer will feed you a harder question. But if you continue to think that all of the questions are pretty easy, you could wind up getting some hard questions wrong!

What was the average (arithmetic mean) attendance for baseball games played at Memorial Stadium during the months of June and July?

(1) The average numbers of people attending baseball games at Memorial Stadium for June and July were 23,100 and 25,200, respectively.
(2) There were 20 baseball games played in June at the stadium and 22 games played in July.

Here's How to Crack It

This is a Value Data Sufficiency question, so begin by asking yourself "What do I know?" The

question stem asks to solve for the average attendance for baseball games at Memorial Stadium

during June and July. The expression for averages is $\frac{total}{number\ of\ things}$.

Next, ask yourself "What do I need to know in order to answer the question?" In order to answer the question, the statements need to provide a number of attendees at the baseball games as the total, and the number of games played as the number of things.

Evaluate Statement (1). Statement (1) provides the average number of people attending baseball games for June and July individually. This information could be used to determine the total number of people who attended games during each month if the Statement also provided the number of games played each month. However, that information is not provided by this statement. The statement is not sufficient. The remaining answer choices are (B), (C), and (E).

Next, evaluate Statement (2). Statement (2) gives the number of games played in June and July individually. This information can be used to find the number of things needed to determine the average. However, this statement does not provide any information about the total number of attendees for each month. Statement (2) is insufficient. Eliminate (B).

Now consider the statements together. The average number of attendees for June and July individually from Statement (1) can be paired with the number of games played in each month individually from Statement (2) to determine the total attendees for each month individually. These values can be added together to get the total number of attendees for both months. The information from Statement (2) can then also be used to get the number of things. The statements together provide enough information to determine the average attendance for baseball games during June and July. Eliminate (E). The correct answer is (C).

What is the common error that a test-taker could make on this question? Many test-takers see Statement (1) and incorrectly believe they can average the averages of the two months to determine the overall average. This is not only incorrect, but also far too easy. Any question that works out that easily should immediately raise skepticism. If you find yourself thinking a statement is far too easy or too obvious, slow down and reevaluate. You may just save yourself from getting an incorrect answer!

Error #4) Remembering Statement (1) When Evaluating Statement (2)

Test-takers will often, unknowingly, use the information from Statement (1) as part of their evaluation of Statement (2).

At a business dinner, people were offered coffee or tea. If all the diners had either coffee or tea, how many of the diners had tea?

(1) Of the 60 people at the dinner, 10% had tea.
(2) Fifty-four people had coffee.

Here's How to Crack It

This is a Value Data Sufficiency question, so begin by asking "What do I know?" The question stem states that all the diners had either coffee or tea. There is no other information provided by the question stem, so this is all the information you know.

Next, ask "What do I need to know in order to answer the question?" The question asks for the number of diners that had tea. In order to be sufficient, the statements must provide a way to determine the total number of diners that had tea. This means the statements could provide a way to determine the total number of diners who were at the dinner and the number of diners who had coffee as a way to reveal the number of diners who had tea.

Evaluate Statement (1). Statement (1) provides the information that there were 60 diners at the dinner and 10% of them had tea. This information provides a total for the number of diners and the percentage of those diners that had tea, so it is enough information to answer the question. Statement (1) is sufficient. The only remaining possible answers are (A) and (D). Eliminate (B), (C), and (E).

Now evaluate Statement (2). Statement (2) provides the number of diners at the dinner who had coffee. However, Statement (2) does not provide a total number of diners or a relationship between the number of diners who had coffee and the number who had tea, so there is no way to determine the number of diners who had tea. This statement is insufficient. Eliminate (D). The correct answer is (A).

How could this question trip up a test-taker? Any test-taker who does not adequately separate out the information provided in Statement (1) from the information provided in Statement (2) will read Statement (2) and believe that the number of diners is 60. They would be wrong!

Putting It All Together

The biggest reason for falling for any of these traps always boils down to going too fast. We have just run through a list of common ways that test-takers make mistakes when answering Data Sufficiency questions, and all of these ways were different. However, these errors invariably happen from thinking that it's okay to answer Data Sufficiency questions quickly. Just because you don't need to compute an answer to a Data Sufficiency question doesn't mean that you can race through the question.

Recognizing the common errors test-takers make on Data Sufficiency questions can sometimes help you guess your way to the right answer. That can be helpful if you find a question confusing or if you are running short on time close to the end of the section.

Summary

○ The instructions for Data Sufficiency questions are very complicated. Memorize them now. Here is a pared-down checklist:
- The first statement ALONE answers the question.
- The second statement ALONE answers the question.
- You need both statements TOGETHER to answer the question.
- Both statements SEPARATELY answer the question.
- Neither statement together or separately answers the question.

○ Use POE to narrow down the field. If you know that Statement (1) is sufficient, you are already down to a 50/50 guess: (A) or (D). If you know that Statement (1) is not sufficient, you are already down to a one-in-three guess: (B), (C), or (E).

○ If you are stuck on Statement (1), skip it and look at Statement (2). POE will be just as helpful.

○ If Statement (2) is sufficient, you will be down to (B) or (D). If Statement (2) is not sufficient, you will be down to (A), (C), or (E).

○ The math content of the Data Sufficiency questions is exactly the same as it is on the regular math questions.

○ As you would in the regular math problems, look for the clues that tell you how to solve Data Sufficiency problems.

○ When a problem asks a yes-or-no question, remember that the answer can be no.

○ In yes-or-no questions, a statement is sufficient if it always gives us the *same* answer: always yes or always no. If the answer is sometimes yes and sometimes no, the statement is insufficient.

o   In Data Sufficiency questions, look for opportunities to simplify or restate the question. If a question asks, "Did the foreman reject 40% of the 12,000 computers manufactured?" you could simplify that to ask, "Did the foreman reject 4,800 computers?"

o   In intermediate and difficult Data Sufficiency problems, you must be on guard against careless assumptions. Take your time and treat every question the way you would the hardest question on the test.

Chapter 11
Basic Principles of GMAT Math

In order to succeed on the Quantitative Reasoning and Data Insights sections of the GMAT, you need a solid foundation of math terms and concepts. If terms like absolute value, least common multiples, and prime numbers sound familiar, but you can't quite place them or you want to see them in the context of a GMAT question, this chapter can help.

SETTING THE STAGE

Somehow, we've managed to cover five full chapters in the math section of this book and have yet to talk in any detail about specific math concepts. What can we say—there's a lot to the GMAT!

The first five chapters are all about laying the foundation of how to succeed on the GMAT—we've discussed the logistics and details of the different sections, how to employ Process of Elimination, introduced you to the powerful Plugging In family of strategies, and completed a deep dive on the intricacies of the Data Insights section.

And now, at long last, we're going to put all that prework to the test. This is the first of the next handful of chapters that talk specifically about concepts that could be tested on the GMAT and show examples of how those concepts could be tested.

While you work through these concept-related chapters, employ the strategies and tactics we've covered thus far. Find opportunities to Plug In. Follow the steps of the flowchart for working with Data Sufficiency questions. Think about the uniqueness of Integrated Reasoning style questions and how you would approach them on test day. Apply POE aggressively. In essence, treat the concepts introduced here, and the questions associated with them, as you would questions on the actual GMAT.

Let's get started.

Integers

If you randomly polled people on the street and asked them to give you a number, chances are most of them are going to say an integer. Integers are sometimes called whole or natural numbers. They can be positive or negative, but they cannot be fractions. Some examples of positive integers are:

$$1, 2, 3, 4, 5, \text{etc.}$$

Some examples of negative integers

$$-1, -2, -3, -4, -5, \text{etc.}$$

On the GMAT, integers are unlikely to be tested explicitly. That is, you are unlikely to see any question that simply asks you to identify integers from a list. But, the concept of integers may very well be implicitly used as a parameter in a question to increase difficulty or provide some restrictions.

Here's how the concept of integers might play in the GMAT.

If p and q are integers, is $\dfrac{p+q}{2}$ an integer?

(1) $p < 17$
(2) $p = q$

(A) Statement (1) ALONE is sufficient, but statement (2) alone is not sufficient.
(B) Statement (2) ALONE is sufficient, but statement (1) alone is not sufficient.
(C) BOTH statements TOGETHER are sufficient, but NEITHER statement ALONE is sufficient.
(D) EACH statement ALONE is sufficient.
(E) Statements (1) and (2) TOGETHER are not sufficient.

This is a Yes/No Data Sufficiency question, so be prepared to Plug In more than once. The question asks if $\dfrac{p+q}{2}$ is an integer and provides the information that both p and q are integers. This question uses information about integers to qualify the values of the variables as well as a central part of the question itself. In order for the statements to be sufficient, they need to provide information that yields a consistent Yes or No answer to the question.

Evaluate Statement (1). The information about p does not restrict the value of p enough to determine a reasonable value of p and provides no information about q. For example, if $p = 16$ and $q = 2$, then the answer to the question is Yes. However, if $p = 16$ and $q = 1$, then the answer to the question is No. This statement does not provide a consistent answer to the question, so it is not sufficient. The remaining answer choices are (B), (C), and (E). Eliminate (A) and (D).

Next, evaluate Statement (2). The statement provides the information that $p = q$. Plug In values for p and q. If p and q equal 10, then the answer to the question is Yes. Plug In again and try to get an answer of No. If p and q equal 9, then the answer to the question is still Yes. In fact, no matter what number you Plug In for p and q, the sum of $p + q$ is always going to be an even integer, which means the answer to the question is always Yes. The statement is sufficient. Eliminate (C) and (E). The correct answer is (B).

a and *b* are nonzero integers such that $0.35a = 0.2b$. What is the value of *b* in terms of *a* ?

(A) $0.07a$
(B) $0.57a$
(C) $0.7a$
(D) $1.75a$
(E) $17.5a$

Here's How to Crack It

There are variables in the question stem and answer choices, so Plug In. The question stem dictates that *a* and *b* are nonzero integers, which means they could be either positive or negative integers. Plug In a value for *a* that makes the math as simple as possible. If $a = 20$, then $0.2b = 0.35(20) = 7$ and $b = 35$. This is the target number. Plug In $a = 20$ into each of the answer choices to see which results in a value of $b = 20$. When an integer is multiplied by a decimal, the value of the integer decreases. Therefore, (A), (B), and (C) will all have a product less than 20. Eliminate those answer choices. Choice (D) is $1.75(20) = 35$, which matches the target answer, so keep (D). Choice (E) is much greater than 35, so eliminate it. The correct answer is (D).

Positive and Negative

Positive numbers lie to the right of zero on the number line. Negative numbers lie to the left of zero on the number line.

Positive integers become greater as they move away from 0; negative integers become lesser. Look at this number line:

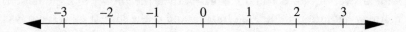

2 is greater than 1, but −2 is less than −1.

Having Trouble Memorizing?
If you have trouble memorizing rules such as positive and negative or odds and evens, don't sweat it! Just use a simple example (2 + 2, 2 x 3, −2 + −1, etc).

There are three rules regarding the multiplication of positive and negative numbers:

> positive × positive = positive
>
> positive × negative = negative
>
> negative × negative = positive

If you add a positive number and a negative number, subtract the number with the negative sign in front of it from the positive number.

$$4 + (-3) = 1$$

If you add two negative numbers, you add them as if they were positive, and then put a negative sign in front of the sum.

$$-3 + -5 = -8$$

Zero

Zero is a special little number. It is an integer, but it is neither positive nor negative. However, try to remember these facts about zero:

- 0 is even.
- 0 plus any other number is equal to that other number.
- 0 multiplied by any other number is equal to 0.
- You cannot divide by 0.

Absolute Value

The **absolute value** of a number is the distance between that number and 0 on the number line. The absolute value of 6 is expressed as $|6|$.

$$|6| = 6$$

$$|-5| = 5$$

Digits

There are ten digits:

$$0, 1, 2, 3, 4, 5, 6, 7, 8, 9$$

All integers are made up of digits. In the integer 246, there are three digits: 2, 4, and 6. Each of the digits has a different name:

> 6 is called the units (or ones) digit.
> 4 is called the tens digit.
> 2 is called the hundreds digit.

A number with decimal places is also composed of digits, although it is not an integer. In the decimal 27.63, there are four digits:

> 2 is the tens digit.
> 7 is the units digit.
> 6 is the tenths digit.
> 3 is the hundredths digit.

Let's see how the GMAT could test fairly basic concepts like zero, absolute value, positive and negative numbers, and digits:

If x is an integer, then which of the following statements about $x^2 - x - 1$ is true?

(A) It is always odd.
(B) It is always even.
(C) It is always positive.
(D) It is even when x is even and odd when x is odd.
(E) It is even when x is odd and odd when x is even.

Here's How to Crack It

This question is a great example of how GMAT tries to take fairly simple concepts such as integers, evens, odds, and positive and negative integers and make them into more complicated questions. One way to solve this question is to follow the rules of multiplying and subtracting odd and even numbers while considering any differences in output based on whether x is positive or negative.

However, there are variables in the question stem, so try Plugging In values for x. The question asks to evaluate which of the answer choices is true, so be prepared to Plug In more than once. If $x = 2$, then the value of the expression is 1. Look at the answer choices. Choices (A), (C), and (E) are all true. Plug In a different value for x and evaluate those answer choices again. If $x = 3$, then the expression evaluates to 5. In this case, (E) is no longer true, but (A) and (C) are true. Plug In again. If $x = 0$, then the expression evaluates to −1. Choice (C) is no longer true, so eliminate it. The correct answer is (A).

$$FGF$$
$$\underline{\times\ G}$$
$$HGG$$

In the multiplication problem above, *F*, *G*, and *H* represent distinct odd digits. What is the value of the three-digit number *FGF* ?

(A)   151
(B)   161
(C)   171
(D)   313
(E)   353

Here's How to Crack It

The question stem states that F, G, and H are distinct odd digits, so the only possible values for these variables are 1, 3, 5, 7, and 9. The question asks for the value of FGF. At first glance, you may believe the only way to solve this problem is to substitute every odd digit into the three variables until you stumble upon the correct answer.

However, anytime you encounter a GMAT problem that seems like the only way to solve it is just through repetitive calculations, stop and look for a pattern in the problem. Look at this problem one digit at a time. The equation states that F × G = G. No matter what number is used for G, the only way to make that equation true is if F = 1. This means you can eliminate (D) and (E).

Because F = 1, the only possible values for G and H are 3, 5, 7, and 9. Now look at the second digit, which states that G × G has a product with a units digit equal to G. The only value for G where that is possible is if G = 5. Therefore, the value of FGF is 151. The correct answer is (A).

If x and y are integers such that $5 < |y| < 9$ and $4 < |x| < 10$, which of the following represents all possible values of xy ?

(A) $-90 < xy < 20$
(B) $-36 < xy < -20$ and $36 < xy < 90$
(C) $-90 < xy < -20$ and $20 < xy < 90$
(D) $-50 < xy < 20$ and $-20 < xy < 50$
(E) $-36 < xy < -20$ and $20 < xy < 36$

Here's How to Crack It

Plug In all possible values for x and y. Because the inequalities in the question stem are absolute values, the representation of all possible values of xy has a negative range and a positive range. The least possible negative value of xy is -90 and the greatest possible negative value is -20, so it can be written that $-90 < xy < -20$. The least possible positive value of xy is 20 and the greatest possible positive value is 90, so it can be written that $20 < xy < 90$. Therefore, the possible values of xy are $-90 < xy < -20$ and $20 < xy < 90$. The correct answer is (C).

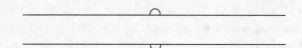

What is the units digit of $3^{22} - 2^{20}$?

(A)   3
(B)   4
(C)   6
(D)   7
(E)   9

Here's How to Crack It

The units digit of $3^{22} - 2^{20}$ is going to be equal to the difference between the units digits of 3^{22} and 2^{20}. Begin by looking for patterns in the units digits for these numbers. Start with 3^{22}. Determine the units digit of 3^x, where x is increasing values, and look for repeating values. The unit digit of 3^1 is 3, 3^2 is 9, 3^3 is 7, 3^4 is 1, 3^5 is 3. From there, the pattern repeats itself. The pattern repeats every 4 values of x, which means that the units digit of 3^{20} is 1, 3^{21} is 3, and 3^{22} is 9.

Next, determine the units digit of 2^{20} using the same method. The units digit of 2^1 is 2, 2^2 is 4, 2^3 is 8, 2^4 is 6, 2^5 is 2. The pattern has begun repeating, which means the units digit of 2^{20} is 6.

Therefore, the difference between the units digit of 3^{22} and 2^{22} is $9 - 6 = 3$. The correct answer is (A).

Remainders

If an integer cannot be divided evenly by another integer, the integer that is left over at the end of division is called the **remainder**. Thus, remainders *must* be integers.

$$2 \overline{)\, 7 \atop \displaystyle 3}$$
$$\underline{-6}$$
$$1 \qquad \leftarrow \text{remainder}$$

Odd or Even

Even numbers are integers that can be divided evenly by 2, leaving no remainder. Here are some examples:

$$-6, -4, -2, 0, 2, 4, 6, \text{ etc.}$$

Any integer, no matter how large, is even if its last digit is divisible by 2. Thus 777,772 is even.

Odd numbers are integers that cannot be divided evenly by 2. Put another way, odd integers have a remainder of 1 when they are divided by 2. Here are some examples:

$$-5, -3, -1, 1, 3, 5, \text{ etc.}$$

Any integer, no matter how large, is odd if its last digit is not divisible by 2. Thus 222,227 is odd.

There are several rules that always hold true for even and odd numbers:

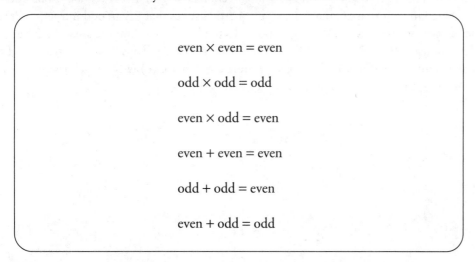

$$\text{even} \times \text{even} = \text{even}$$

$$\text{odd} \times \text{odd} = \text{odd}$$

$$\text{even} \times \text{odd} = \text{even}$$

$$\text{even} + \text{even} = \text{even}$$

$$\text{odd} + \text{odd} = \text{even}$$

$$\text{even} + \text{odd} = \text{odd}$$

It isn't necessary to memorize these, but you must know that the relationships always hold true. The individual rules can be derived in a second. If you need to know *even × even*, just try 2 × 2. The answer, in this case, is even, as *even × even* always will be.

Q: 20,179.01792
In the number above, which of the following two digits are identical?
(A) The tens digit and the hundredths digit
(B) The ones digit and the thousandths digit
(C) The hundreds digit and the tenths digit
(D) The thousands digit and the tenths digit
(E) The thousands digit and the hundredths digit

Turn to page 190 for the answer.

A: Both the thousands digit and tenths digit are 0.

Consecutive Integers

Consecutive integers are integers listed in order of increasing value without any integers missing in between. For example, −3, −2, −1, 0, 1, 2, 3 are consecutive integers. Only integers can be consecutive.

Some consecutive even integers: −2, 0, 2, 4, 6, 8, etc.

Some consecutive odd integers: −3, −1, 1, 3, 5, etc.

Distinct Numbers

If two numbers are **distinct**, they cannot be equal. For example, if x and y are distinct, then they must have different values.

Work through a couple of examples of how the GMAT may test this content.

───────────○───────────

If y is an odd integer, which of the following must be an even integer?

(A) $y + 2$
(B) $y + 6$
(C) $2y - 1$
(D) $3y$
(E) $3y + 1$

Here's How to Crack It

There are variables in the question stem and answer choices, so Plug In. This is a must be question, so be prepared to Plug In more than once. The question states that y is an odd integer, so Plug In an odd integer for y such as $y = 3$. The question asks to identify which of the answer choices must be an even integer. If $y = 3$, then (A) is 5, so eliminate it. Choice (B) is 9, so eliminate it. Choice (C) is 5, so eliminate it. Choice (D) is 9, so eliminate it. Choice (E) is 10, which is even. It is the only remaining answer choice, so the correct answer is (E).

───────────○───────────

If the remainder when a certain integer x is divided by 5 is 2, then each of the following could also be an integer, EXCEPT

(A) $\dfrac{x}{17}$

(B) $\dfrac{x}{11}$

(C) $\dfrac{x}{10}$

(D) $\dfrac{x}{6}$

(E) $\dfrac{x}{3}$

Here's How to Crack It

There are variables in the answer choices, so Plug In. To get a remainder of 2 when x is divided by 5, x must be a multiple of 5 plus 2 more. In other words, x could be 7 or 12 or 17 or 22, etc. Now, go through the answer choices, plugging in numbers for x that allow them to be integers as well. For example, if $x = 17$, then (A) is $\dfrac{17}{17}$, which is an integer. Eliminate (A).

If $x = 22$, then the result is $\dfrac{22}{11}$, which is an integer. Eliminate (B). Choice (C) is not an integer, so keep (C). Choices (D) and (E) are also not integers, so keep (D) and (E). Plug In again. If $x = 12$, then (C) is not an integer but (D) and (E) are. Eliminate (D) and (E). The correct answer is (C).

If a and b are positive integers, is ab odd?

(1) $b = 3$
(2) a and b are consecutive integers.

(A) Statement (1) ALONE is sufficient, but statement (2) alone is not sufficient.
(B) Statement (2) ALONE is sufficient, but statement (1) alone is not sufficient.
(C) BOTH statements TOGETHER are sufficient, but NEITHER statement ALONE is sufficient.
(D) EACH statement ALONE is sufficient.
(E) Statements (1) and (2) TOGETHER are not sufficient.

Here's How to Crack It

This is a Yes/No Data Sufficiency question, so be prepared to Plug In more than once. The question asks if ab is odd if a and b are positive integers. Evaluate the statements individually. Statement (1) states that $b = 3$. Plug in different values for a. If $a = 2$, then $ab = 6$ and the answer to the question is "No." If $a = 3$, then $ab = 9$ and the answer to the question is a "Yes." Statement 1 does not provide a consistent Yes or No answer to the question, so eliminate (A) and (D). The only choices that remain are (B), (C), and (E).

Statement (2) states that a and b are consecutive integers. Plug in some values for a and b. If $a = 2$ and $b = 3$, then $ab = 6$ and the answer to the question is "No." If $a = 3$ and $b = 4$, then $ab = 12$ and the answer is still "No." The product of any two consecutive integers is even, and the answer to the question is always "No." Statement (2) is sufficient. The correct answer is (B)

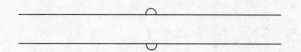

What is the remainder when positive integer n is divided by 17 ?

(1) n divided by 51 has a remainder of 36
(2) n divided by 31 has a remainder of 4

(A)   Statement (1) ALONE is sufficient, but statement (2) alone is not sufficient.
(B)   Statement (2) ALONE is sufficient, but statement (1) alone is not sufficient.
(C)   BOTH statements TOGETHER are sufficient, but NEITHER statement ALONE is sufficient.
(D)   EACH statement ALONE is sufficient.
(E)   Statements (1) and (2) TOGETHER are not sufficient.

Here's How to Crack It

This is a value data sufficiency question, so determine what is known and what is needed to answer the question. The question provides that n is a positive integer. To determine the value of the remainder when n is divided by 17, a value for n needs to be determined or a pattern needs to be revealed by the statements. Consider Statement (1), which states that n divided by 51 produces a remainder of 36. In order to determine the value of n that satisfies the statement, add 51 and 36 to produce 87. Dividing 87 by 51 gives a result of 1 with a remainder of 36, so Statement (1) is satisfied. When 87 is divided by 17, the result is 5 with a remainder of 2. When $n = 87$, the remainder is 2. Try another value of n. When $n = 138$, then the result of 138 divided by 51 is 2 with a remainder of 36. This value of n satisfies Statement (1). When 138 is divided by 17, the result is 8 with a remainder of 2. This is the same remainder as when $n = 87$. In fact, any value of n that satisfies Statement (1) produces a remainder of 2 for the question. Statement (1) is sufficient. Write down AD. Consider Statement (2). If $n = 35$, then the result of 35 divided by 31 is 1 with a remainder of 4. Statement (2) is satisfied. The result when 35 is divided by 17 is 2 with a remainder of 1. Try another value of n. If $n = 66$, then the result of 66 divided by 31 is 2 with a remainder of 4. Statement (2) is satisfied. The result when 66 is divided by 17 is 3 with a remainder of 15. The value of the remainder when n satisfies Statement (2) is at least two different values for the answer to the question. Therefore, Statement (2) is insufficient. Eliminate (D). The correct answer is (A).

Prime Numbers

A **prime number** is a positive integer that is divisible only by two numbers: itself and 1. Thus 2, 3, 5, 7, 11, and 13 are all prime numbers. The number 2 is both the least and the only even prime number. Neither 0 nor 1 is a prime number. All prime numbers are positive.

Divisibility Rules

If there is no remainder when integer x is divided by integer y, then x is said to be **divisible** by y. Put another way, divisible means you can evenly divide the greater number by the lesser number with no remainder. For example, 10 is divisible by 5.

> **Some Useful Divisibility Shortcuts:**
> - An integer is divisible by 2 if its units digit is divisible by 2. Thus, 772 is divisible by 2.
> - An integer is divisible by 3 if the sum of its digits is divisible by 3. We can instantly tell that 216 is divisible by 3 because the sum of the digits $(2 + 1 + 6)$ is divisible by 3.
> - An integer is divisible by 4 if the number formed by its last two digits is divisible by 4. The number 3,028 is divisible by 4 because 28 is divisible by 4.
> - An integer is divisible by 5 if its final digit is either 0 or 5. Thus, 60, 85, and 15 are all divisible by 5.
> - An integer is divisible by 6 if it is divisible by both 2 and 3, the factors of 6. Thus, 318 is divisible by 6 because it is even, and the sum of $3 + 1 + 8$ is divisible by 3.
> - Division by zero is undefined. The test-writers won't ever put a zero in the denominator. If you're working out a problem and you find yourself with a zero in the denominator of a fraction, you've done something wrong. By the way, a 0 in the numerator is fine. Any fraction with a 0 on the top is 0.
>
> $$\frac{0}{1} = 0$$
>
> $$\frac{0}{4} = 0$$
>
> $$\frac{4}{0} = \text{undefined}$$

Q: Which of the following numbers is prime?
0, 1, 15, 23, 33

Turn to page 195 for the answer.

Factors and Multiples

An integer, *x*, is a factor of another integer, *y*, if *y* is divisible by *x*. So, in other words, $y = nx$, where *y*, *n*, and *x* are all integers. For example, 3 is a factor of 15 because 15 = (3)(5). All the factors of 15 are 1, 3, 5, and 15.

The **multiples** of an integer, *y*, are all numbers 0, ±1*y*, ±2*y*, ±3*y*... etc. For example, 15 is a multiple of 3 (3 × 5); 12 is also a multiple of 3 (3 × 4). When you think about it, most numbers have only a few factors, but an infinite number of multiples. The memory device you may have learned in school is "factors are few; multiples are many."

Every integer greater than 1 is both its own greatest factor and least positive multiple.

Least Common Multiples

If an integer, *x*, is divisible by two integers, *n* and *m*, then *x* is a common multiple of *n* and *m*. For example, 30 is a common multiple of 5 and 6. The lowest multiple that two numbers have in common is called the **least common multiple**. For our example, 30 is also the least common multiple of 5 and 6.

> Prime numbers, divisibility rules, least common multiples, greatest common factors, and prime factorization are all central components of Number Theory. You'll see these concepts again, and in more detail, in the Number Theory chapter.

The most straightforward way to find a least common multiple is to simply start listing the positive multiples of both integers. When you find a number that is on both lists, that number is the least common multiple.

For example, here's how you find the least common multiple of 4 and 6.

Multiples of 4: 4, 8, 12, 16, 20...

Multiples of 6: 6, 12...

Since 12 is on both lists, 12 is the least common multiple of 4 and 6.

Greatest Common Factor

If two integers, *n* and *m*, are both divisible by an integer, *x*, then *x* is a common factor of *n* and *m*. For example, 6 is a common factor of both 12 and 18. The highest factor that two numbers have in common is referred to as the **greatest common factor**. For our example, 6 is also the greatest common factor of 12 and 18.

The most straightforward way to find a greatest common factor is to simply list the factors of both numbers. Then you just need to find the greatest number that is on both lists.

For example, here's how you find the greatest common factor of 12 and 18.

Factors of 12:   1, 2, 3, 4, 6, 12

Factors of 18:   1, 2, 3, 6, 9, 18

Since 6 is the greatest number on both lists, 6 is the greatest common factor of 12 and 18.

Prime Factors

If an integer, *x*, that is a factor of an integer, *y*, is also prime, then *x* is called a **prime factor** of *y*. For example, 3 and 5 are prime factors of 15.

To find the prime factors of an integer, use a factor tree:

A: 23. Remember, neither 0 nor 1 is prime.

All positive integers greater than 1 have unique prime factorizations. So, it doesn't matter which pair of factors you start with when you use the factor tree.

The prime factorization of 12 is $2 \times 2 \times 3$.

DRILL 5

The answers to these questions can be found in Part V.

1. If *x* is a positive integer, is *x* divisible by 48 ?

   (1)   *x* is divisible by 8.
   (2)   x is divisible by 6.

   (A)   Statement (1) ALONE is sufficient, but statement (2) alone is not sufficient.
   (B)   Statement (2) ALONE is sufficient, but statement (1) alone is not sufficient.
   (C)   BOTH statements TOGETHER are sufficient, but NEITHER statement ALONE is sufficient.
   (D)   EACH statement ALONE is sufficient.
   (E)   Statements (1) and (2) TOGETHER are not sufficient.

2.. If *x* is a positive integer, is the greatest common factor of 150 and *x* a prime number?

   (1)   *x* is a prime number.
   (2)   *x* < 4

   (A)   Statement (1) ALONE is sufficient, but statement (2) alone is not sufficient.
   (B)   Statement (2) ALONE is sufficient, but statement (1) alone is not sufficient.
   (C)   BOTH statements TOGETHER are sufficient, but NEITHER statement ALONE is sufficient.
   (D)   EACH statement ALONE is sufficient.
   (E)   Statements (1) and (2) TOGETHER are not sufficient.

3. If *x* and *y* are integers greater than 1, is *x* prime?

   (1)   The only factors of integer *y* are 1 and *y*
   (2)   The least common multiple of *x* and *y* is *xy*

   (A)   Statement (1) ALONE is sufficient, but statement (2) alone is not sufficient.
   (B)   Statement (2) ALONE is sufficient, but statement (1) alone is not sufficient.
   (C)   BOTH statements TOGETHER are sufficient, but NEITHER statement ALONE is sufficient.
   (D)   EACH statement ALONE is sufficient.
   (E)   Statements (1) and (2) TOGETHER are not sufficient.

4, If x, y are distinct positive integers, then which of the following must be true about $x^2 + y + 1$?

- (A)   It is odd when x is a factor of y
- (B)   It is even when x is odd and y is odd
- (C)   It is odd when y is a factor of x
- (D)   It is even when x is even and y is odd
- (E)   It is odd when x is odd and y is even

5. Is P divisible by 15 ?

- (1)   The greatest common prime factor of P and 65 is 13
- (2)   The greatest common prime factor of P and 95 is 19

- (A)   Statement (1) ALONE is sufficient, but statement (2) alone is not sufficient.
- (B)   Statement (2) ALONE is sufficient, but statement (1) alone is not sufficient.
- (C)   BOTH statements TOGETHER are sufficient, but NEITHER statement ALONE is sufficient.
- (D)   EACH statement ALONE is sufficient.
- (E)   Statements (1) and (2) TOGETHER are not sufficient.

6. What is the value of w ?

- (1) w is a factor of 51
- (2) $w > 17$

- (A)   Statement (1) ALONE is sufficient, but statement (2) alone is not sufficient.
- (B)   Statement (2) ALONE is sufficient, but statement (1) alone is not sufficient.
- (C)   BOTH statements TOGETHER are sufficient, but NEITHER statement ALONE is sufficient.
- (D)   EACH statement ALONE is sufficient.
- (E)   Statements (1) and (2) TOGETHER are not sufficient.

Challenge Question #3

Find the answers to all Challenge Questions in Part V!

x and y are integers less than 60 such that x is equal to the sum of the squares of two distinct prime numbers, and y is a multiple of 17. Which of the following could be the value of $x - y$?

- (A)   −19
- (B)   −7
- (C)   0
- (D)   4
- (E)   9

Summary

○ Without a review of the basic terms and rules of math tested on the GMAT, you won't be able to begin to do the problems.

○ Study the vocabulary and rules in the preceding chapter to get this stuff back into your head. If you find that you need extra practice, head to the Student Tools for additional online drills.

Chapter 12
Working Difficult Questions

Come test day, chances are that you're going to run into a problem you don't know how to solve. In this chapter, you're going to learn some tools to help you develop a game plan for how to handle questions you're not sure how to solve.

CRACKING HARD MATH PROBLEMS

What Is a Hard Math Problem?

Before we discuss how to crack hard math problems, we need to pause for a moment to define the term *hard math problem*. The GMAT test-writers have a very precise definition of a hard math problem. For the test-writers, question difficulty is just a measure of how many people answer the question incorrectly. If a large percentage of test-takers, such as more than 70 percent, answer a question incorrectly, the question is a hard question!

Our definition of a hard math problem is pretty simple: *A hard math problem is any math question that you don't know how to solve.*

That means that this chapter is not about content, such as probability, that is sometimes considered hard. Instead, this chapter covers a series of techniques that you can use whenever your first reaction to a problem is "I don't think I know how to solve this problem."

How Are Hard Questions Created?

One way test-writers up the difficulty of questions is by testing unfamiliar content. However, the difficulty of a question is not exclusively dependent on the content tested by the question. By including good trap answers, test-writers can significantly increase the difficulty level of a question.

In other words, there's more than one way to create a hard math problem. Sometimes the GMAT creates a hard math problem by testing less familiar content. Other times, they include good trap answers.

Let's take a look at an example of a hard question.

The original price of a new tech item is increased by 10 percent. Two months later, the new price is increased by 20 percent. The final price of the item is what percent greater than the original price?

(A) 10%
(B) 20%
(C) 22%
(D) 30%
(E) 32%

Here's How to Crack It

There are percentages in the answer choices and no starting number, so solve by Plugging In. If the original price of the tech item is $100, then the price after the 10 percent increase is $110. After the 20 percent price increase, the final price is $1.2 \times \$110 = \$132$. The original price was $100, and the final price is $132, so the final price is 32% greater. The correct answer is (E).

Mistakes vs. Hard Questions

Before we start discussing strategies for solving hard questions, we need to take a moment to remember that hard questions are not the only cause of incorrect answers. Even test-takers who get the highest possible scores see questions mostly about routine topics. While most GMAT test-takers encounter a few questions that they don't know how to answer, those questions aren't the only ones that they get wrong. So we need to distinguish mistakes from hard questions.

Everybody has had the experience of getting a question wrong because they misread something in the question or made a silly calculation error. In many cases, these sorts of errors cause more wrong answers than hard questions.

While it is important to learn how to solve hard questions, it is often easier to improve your score by working to eliminate mistakes on questions that you already know how to solve. Learning good test-taking techniques such as slowing down, reading the question more carefully, and rereading the question before submitting your answer can often add a big boost to your score.

Common Causes of Mistakes

So what are some of the most common causes of mistakes when solving GMAT math questions? And what are the remedies?

Here are some of the most common causes of mistakes:

- **Going too fast.** The GMAT is, of course, a timed test. And there certainly are problems where it feels like time has accelerated while you are doing that problem! However, you still have, on average, two minutes to solve each question. Because it's likely that you can solve some questions a little faster than two minutes, you'll have an extra minute or so to spend on a few questions. There's no need to race through questions. In fact, if you get an answer to a question very quickly and you've done little or no work, you are almost certainly about to fall for a trap answer. You definitely want to reread the question to see whether you missed anything if you get an answer too quickly.

- **Improper Pacing.** Going too fast is about individual questions. Improper pacing is about the entire section. Some test-takers spend way too much time on some questions and race through others to make up the time spent. Because there's a penalty for leaving questions blank, spending too long on even a handful of questions might damage your score if you don't finish the section. Or, you may need to guess on too many questions at the end, which can also damage your score. The remedy is to remember that 3 minutes is the maximum amount of time that you should spend on any one question. If you are at the 3-minute mark and are still trying to figure out how to do the problem, it's time to guess and move on.

- **Doing the Work in Your Head.** It's tempting to try to do the work in your head because it feels like you are saving time. It's also tempting to try to skip a lot of steps, even if you are writing down some of your work. However, both of those strategies tend to be false savings of time because they increase the likelihood of making mistakes. Use the noteboards to write down your work, and don't skip steps! It's better to take a few extra seconds to answer the question and get it right than to race through it and get it wrong.

- **Misreading the Question.** One of the most common causes of mistakes on GMAT problems actually has nothing to do with math! Many test-takers read problems too quickly and miss key information as a result. Get into the habit of rereading questions before you pick your answer. Spending time practicing GMAT questions can also help you to avoid misreading the question because it gets you familiar with the way that the GMAT constructs questions.

- **Hard Questions.** And, of course, sometimes the cause of a mistake is a hard question that you don't know how to do. In this chapter, we'll be taking a look at some strategies that you can use to solve hard questions.

What Is a Hard Math Problem (Part II)?

Earlier, we defined a hard math problem as *any math question that you don't know how to solve*. There are two behaviors that often indicate that you are dealing with a hard math question. If you pay attention to these behaviors, you'll know when to use the strategies described in this chapter.

Some hard problems leave you feeling like you've hit a brick wall. You just don't know what to do. You don't even know how to get the problem started.

Other hard problems leave you feeling like there may be too many ways to get the problem started. You may be afraid to pick an approach because you are afraid that there's a faster approach, or a better approach. Alternatively, you may be able to see the first step of the problem but aren't sure what to do next. As a result, you never really get the problem started.

No matter what the situation, it's important to remember that solving a math problem is often an experimental process. Test-takers who get very high scores often don't know all the steps to solve a problem when they get started. They just aren't afraid to try something. If it doesn't work out, they try something else.

Two Traits of Successful Test-Takers

Good standardized test-takers have two seemingly conflicting characteristics. On the one hand, these successful test-takers tend to be very consistent in how they approach questions. On the other hand, good test-takers tend to be flexible. When their preferred tool for solving a particular type of question doesn't work, they try something else.

Consistency is often key to solving math questions on a standardized test. Good standardized test-takers are good at pattern recognition. They've learned to recognize certain types of problems and to respond with a solution strategy that they know usually works on that type of problem. For example, a test-taker might respond to seeing variables in the answer choices by always Plugging In. This approach allows these test-takers to get to work faster when solving problems. Rather than worrying about whether there's a faster way or a better way to solve the problem, good test-takers just get to work solving the problem. This sort of consistent approach—trying the same tool for every problem that has certain characteristics—saves time in the section overall, even if there may be a faster approach for some problems.

However, test-takers who embrace a consistent approach are also flexible in their approach when necessary. Every so often they may discover that their preferred tool doesn't work very well on the type of problem that it usually solves. In those cases, these test-takers look for another way to approach the problem.

Both characteristics—consistency and flexibility—are important to getting a good score on the Quantitative section of the test. Consistency will get you most of the way to a good score, and most of this book is about learning consistent approaches, such as Yes-No Plugging In for Data Sufficiency. This chapter is about building some flexibility into your approach.

Six Strategies for Hard Math Problems

So, what approach can you try when your favorite, consistent approach fails?

We have developed the six strategies listed below for working on hard questions. In most cases, these strategies are designed to help you get problems started. In many cases, if you can get the problem started, you can ultimately find the solution.

Here's a list of the six strategies. In the pages that follow, we'll explain each strategy and how to use it.

1) Use the Word You Know
2) Try a Simpler Example
3) Be Methodical/Look for Patterns
4) Remember What the GMAT Tests
5) Number Savvy
6) Advanced POE for Data Sufficiency

Strategy 1: Use the Word You Know

When most people encounter a hard math problem, their brain focuses on the part of the problem that seems hard. We may worry about the math term that we aren't sure we understand. Or, we may panic about the complicated-looking expression. Or, we may focus on wording that seems confusing.

However, most of these problems also contain math terms or phrases that are far more straightforward. Sometimes the best approach is to simply start with the more understandable part of the problem.

We call that strategy Use the Word You Know. Here's how it works.

If the prime factorization of integer $x = 3^a \times 5^b \times 11^c$ and $abc \neq 0$, then which of the following could be a multiple of x?

(A)   33
(B)   45
(C)   110
(D)   330
(E)   385

Here's How to Crack It

Don't worry about the expression for x. We'll get to that. Instead, identify a math term that's easy to work with. In this case, start with the term *multiple*. Once you identify a term that you know, consider the definition or properties of that term. What makes one number a multiple of another? If integer a is a multiple of integer b, then $a = nb$, where n is an integer. Based on that definition, if a is a multiple of b, then $\frac{a}{b} = n$, where n is an integer. That's our way to work with the answer choices. If the answer choice divided by x results in an integer, then that answer choice is a multiple of x. Next, we need to pay attention to the part of the problem that states that $abc \neq 0$. That condition means that none of a, b, or c can equal zero. Hence, the minimum value of x is $3^1 \times 5^1 \times 11^1 = 165$. Since none of 33, 45, or 110 results in an integer when divided by 165, eliminate (A), (B), and (C). Next, try (D). Because $\frac{330}{165} = 2$, an integer, 330 is a multiple of x. The correct answer is (D).

The previous problem illustrates how starting with the word you know works. Start by ignoring the part of the problem that seems hard or unfamiliar. Instead, focus on the math terms that you know. Review the definitions or properties of those terms. Use those properties to map out a solution strategy. Or, at the very least, use those properties to find the first step of the solution. Work from that first step to find additional steps to solve the problem.

Here's another:

For $n > 1$, the sequence x_n, is defined by $x_n = \sqrt{x_{n-1}}$. If $x_1 > 0$, is the median of the first four even-numbered terms in the sequence greater than the median of the first four odd-numbered terms in the sequence?

(1) $x_4 > \dfrac{1}{3}$

(2) $x_2 = \dfrac{1}{9}$

Here's How to Crack It

The question presents a sequence that contains a square root, which increases the difficulty of this question. The question asks about the median of the first four even-numbered terms in the sequence and the median of the first four odd-numbered terms in the sequence. Focus on the term *median*. The median of an even-numbered list of numbers is the average of the middle two numbers in the ordered list. The first four even-numbered terms in the sequence are x_2, x_4, x_6, and x_8, so the median of the first four even-numbered terms in the sequence is found by the expression $\dfrac{x_4 + x_6}{2}$. The first four odd-numbered terms in the sequence are x_1, x_3, x_5, and x_7, so the median of the first four odd-numbered terms in the sequence is found by the expression $\dfrac{x_3 + x_5}{2}$. Therefore, the question seeks to determine if $\dfrac{x_4 + x_6}{2} > \dfrac{x_3 + x_5}{2}$.

The inclusion of the square root in this problem suggests a difficult problem. Before proceeding with the statements, consider the properties of square roots. The square root of a number greater than 1 always results in a lesser number. For instance, $\sqrt{4} = 2$. However, the square root of a number less than 1 always results in a greater number. For instance, $\sqrt{\dfrac{1}{4}} = \dfrac{1}{2}$. Because the sequence in the question involves a square root, if the first term in the sequence is greater than one, each subsequent term is less than the previous. If the first term in the sequence is less than one, each subsequent term is greater than the previous. Therefore, if $x_1 > 1$, then $x_1 > x_2 > x_3 > x_4 > x_5 > x_6$. In this case, the answer to the question is "Yes" because $\dfrac{x_4 + x_6}{2} > \dfrac{x_3 + x_5}{2}$. If $x_1 < 1$, then $x_1 < x_2 < x_3 < x_4 < x_5 < x_6$ and the answer to the question is "No" because $\dfrac{x_4 + x_6}{2} < \dfrac{x_3 + x_5}{2}$.

Evaluate Statement (1). This statement states that $x_4 > \frac{1}{3}$. Plug In a value of x_4 that satisfies this statement. If $x_4 = \frac{1}{2}$, then the value of $x_1 = \frac{1}{256}$. According to the information about square roots discussed earlier, this means the answer to the question is "No." Now Plug In again in an attempt to get an answer of "Yes." If $x_4 = 2$, then the value of $x_1 = 256$. According to the information about square roots discussed earlier, this means the answer to the question is "Yes." The statement produces two different answers to the question, so the statement is insufficient. Write down BCE.

Now evaluate Statement (2). Statement (2) provides a definitive value for x_2. The value of x_2 can be used to calculate that $x_1 = \frac{1}{81}$. Therefore, the answer to the question is "No." This statement cannot produce another answer to the question, so the statement is sufficient. The correct answer is (B).

Strategy 2: Try a Simpler Example

Sometimes the GMAT likes to test familiar concepts in unfamiliar ways. One way that the test-writers accomplish this feat is to ask you to apply standard rules of arithmetic to unusual numbers. For a simple example, consider finding a percentage of a number. It's not very hard to find 10% or 25% of a number. It's a little harder to find 2% of a number, but most test-takers can do that. But suppose you were asked to find $\frac{1}{8}$% of a number. Now, suppose the number were a fraction and that the answer choices were decimals. That's exactly the sort of situation that the GMAT might use on a harder problem.

For these types of problems, it's important to remember that the standard rules of arithmetic apply no matter how unusual the numbers. However, sometimes you need to remind yourself how the rules work. One good way to do that is to work the problem with easier numbers first. Then, apply those same steps to the harder numbers. We call that strategy Try a Simpler Example.

Here's an example of a problem that we can solve using the Try a Simpler Example strategy.

———————————————————————— ○ ————————————————————————

The value of 3^{-19} is what percent of the value of $\dfrac{3^{-16}+3^{-17}+3^{-18}+3^{-19}}{8}$?

(A) $\dfrac{1}{5}\%$

(B)   8%

(C)   20%

(D)   40%

(E)   200%

Here's How to Crack It

Start with the Use the Word You Know strategy. Rather than focusing on the weird numbers, focus on the recognizable term *percent*. Calculating a percentage involves dividing a part by a whole. While helpful, the weird numbers make it hard to know what should be divided by what. So, it's time to employ the Try a Simpler Example strategy. To use the strategy, replace the weird numbers in the problem with some simpler numbers. Suppose the problem said:

The value of 2 is what percent of the value of 10?

To solve that problem, you would divide 2 by 10 and multiply the result by 100. It's going to work the same way with the weird numbers. Start by dividing the first number by the second number and multiplying the result by 100.

The first step of the solution is:

$$\frac{\left(3^{-19}\right)}{\left(\dfrac{3^{-16}+3^{-17}+3^{-18}+3^{-19}}{8}\right)} \times 100$$

Now it's time to start working on the calculation. Once again, the intimidating numbers can make it hard to see what needs to be done. However, the numerator of the fraction (3^{-19}) is being divided by a fraction. To divide a number by a fraction, multiply the number by the reciprocal of the fraction:

$$3^{-19} \times \frac{8}{3^{-16}+3^{-17}+3^{-18}+3^{-19}} \times 100$$

Or,

$$\frac{3^{-19} \times 8}{3^{-16} + 3^{-17} + 3^{-18} + 3^{-19}} \times 100$$

There's no exponent rule that is immediately applicable, so look for ways to factor. Factoring often provides a way to use one of the three exponent rules when none of those three rules seems to apply. In this case, factor 3^{-19} out of the denominator to get:

$$\frac{3^{-19} \times 8}{3^{-19}\left(3^3 + 3^2 + 3 + 1\right)} \times 100$$

Note that factoring involves using the Multiply-Add exponent rule. For example, $3^{-19} \times 3^3$ = 3^{-16}. The 3^{-19} in the numerator can be used to cancel the 3^{-19} in the denominator. By the way, canceling numbers in the numerator and denominator is really just an application of the Divide-Subtract exponent rule.

After canceling:

$$\frac{8}{3^3 + 3^2 + 3 + 1} \times 100 =$$

$$\frac{8}{40} \times 100 =$$

$$\frac{1}{5} \times 100 = 20\%$$

The correct answer is (C).

$\circ$

Here's another problem in which the Try a Simpler Example strategy will help us to devise a solution.

For any positive integer n, the sum of the first n positive multiples of 3 equals $\dfrac{(3n)(n+1)}{2}$. What is the sum of all the multiples of 3 between 299 and 601 ?

(A)   15,150
(B)   22,275
(C)   45,000
(D)   45,450
(E)   90,900

Here's How to Crack It

The test-writers have supplied a formula, and they are hoping that you try to solve the problem using the formula. However, the provided formula doesn't exactly match the situation in the problem. The formula can be used to find the sum of the first 200 multiples of 3—600 is the 200th multiple of 3—but the problem asks for the sum of only the multiples of 3 between 299 and 601.

Let's ignore the formula and think about a simpler example. Suppose that you just needed to find the sum of 3, 6, and 9, the first three multiples of 3. That's pretty easy—the sum is 18. However, notice that the sum, 18, is also the product of the average of the three numbers, 6, and the number of numbers, 3. Moreover, because the numbers are evenly spaced, the median and the average are equal. So, to solve the problem, we just need to know how many multiples need to be summed and find the median, which is equal to the average, of those multiples.

There are 301 numbers between 300 and 600, inclusive. One-third of those numbers are multiples of 3. There are 101 numbers between 300 and 600, inclusive, that are multiples of 3.

Now we need the median of those 101 numbers. First, note that 300 is the 100th multiple of 3. We need the value of the 50th multiple of 3 after 300. That value is 300 + (3)(50) = 450.

To find the sum asked for in the problem: 101 × 450 = 45,450. The correct answer is (D).

In this problem, the formula didn't really apply to the situation, and there were too many numbers to simply add them up. By working with a simpler example first, we were able to determine that the problem was a question about averages. Time-consuming calculations or numbers that are unwieldy can often indicate that using the Try a Simpler Example strategy might be helpful in finding a better way to do the required calculation.

Use the Try a Simple Example strategy when

- Large or otherwise complicated numbers make the problem confusing
- You can only think of a very time-consuming way to work with the numbers in the problem
- You are unsure how to apply standard math rules to the problem

Strategy 3: Be Methodical/Look for Patterns

The GMAT test-writers view the Quantitative section as a test of quantitative reasoning ability. As a result, they sometimes write problems that try to determine whether you can start from a short list of facts, rules, and operations and reason how to apply those to a new situation. One key facet of mathematical reasoning is looking for patterns. Sometimes the point of a GMAT question is to see whether you can find and apply a pattern for a given situation.

Here's an example:

```
 111
 112
 113
 121
 .....
+333
```

The addition problem shown above shows five of the 27 different three-digit integers which can be formed using only the integers 1, 2, and 3. What is the sum of these 27 integers?

(A) 1,998
(B) 2,700
(C) 3,996
(D) 5,994
(E) 6,660

Here's How to Crack It

Obviously, the GMAT test-writers don't expect you to write out the 27 three-digit numbers and add them up. When confronted with a calculation that very few people could complete in two or three minutes, there's going to be a better way to work with the numbers. One method to find that better way is to look for a pattern.

In this problem, take a look at the hundreds digits of the numbers. If you were to write out the next five numbers (122, 123, 131, 132, 133), you'd see that nine of the 27 numbers have a hundreds digit of 1. That also means that nine of the numbers have a hundreds digit of 2, and nine of the numbers have a hundreds digit of 3.

This same logic applies to the tens digits. There are nine numbers with a tens digit of 1, nine with a tens digit of 2, and nine with a tens digit of 3. Of course, the same logic also applies to the units digits of the 27 numbers.

To find the sum of the 27 numbers, find the sums of hundreds, tens, and units digits.

For the hundreds digits: $9(100 + 200 + 300) = 5,400$

For the tens digits: $9(10 + 20 + 30) = 540$

For the units digits: $9(1 + 2 + 3) = 54$

The sum of the 27 numbers is $5,400 + 540 + 54 = 5,994$. The correct answer is (D).

In this problem, the key to the solution was to find the pattern so that 27 numbers could be summed in an efficient way. Without finding the pattern, it would have been difficult to find the sum in the time allotted—especially when you don't have access to a calculator. This problem also illustrates one of the most important tools for finding a pattern—write out enough of the numbers to see the pattern!

———————————○———————————

Here's another question in which the key is to find a pattern:

———————————○———————————

If $8^2 + 10^2 + 12^2 + 14^2 + 16^2 = 760$, then what is the percent increase from $8^2 + 10^2 + 12^2 + 14^2 + 16^2$ to $24^2 + 30^2 + 36^2 + 42^2 + 48^2$?

(A) 200%
(B) 300%
(C) 600%
(D) 800%
(E) 900%

Here's How to Crack It

Clearly, the test-writers don't expect you to compute the value of $24^2 + 30^2 + 36^2 + 42^2 + 48^2$ by squaring each number and finding the sum of the results. But do you notice how the brain focuses on the weird numbers in the problem? We can shift the focus away from the numbers by using the Use the Word You Know strategy. In this case, the known math term is percent increase. The formula for calculating a percent increase is $percent\ increase = \dfrac{difference}{original} \times 100$. We already know the value of the original number, $8^2 + 10^2 + 12^2 + 14^2 + 16^2$, so we need a way to find the difference between the two numbers.

Now it's time to look for a pattern. Sometimes finding a pattern means matching part of one expression to a corresponding part of another expression. Here we can compare the corresponding parts of each expression by writing the second expression beneath the first:

$$8^2 + 10^2 + 12^2 + 14^2 + 16^2$$

$$24^2 + 30^2 + 36^2 + 42^2 + 48^2$$

It's easy to see that each number in the new expression is 3 times the corresponding number in the original expression. Rewrite the new summation as

$$(3 \times 8)^2 + (3 \times 10)^2 + (3 \times 12)^2 + (3 \times 14)^2 + (3 \times 16)^2$$

$$= (9 \times 8^2) + (9 \times 10^2) + (9 \times 12^2) + (9 \times 14^2) + (9 \times 16^2)$$

$$= 9 \times (8^2 + 10^2 + 12^2 + 14^2 + 16^2)$$

$$= 9 \times 760$$

Resist the urge to do the multiplication in favor of going straight to the percent increase formula:

$$percent\ increase = \frac{\left(9 \times 760\right) - 760}{760} \times 100$$

After factoring out 760 in the numerator:

$$percent\ increase = \frac{760\left(9 - 1\right)}{760} \times 100$$

After canceling:

$$percent\ increase = 8 \times 100 = 800\%$$

The correct answer is (D).

This question illustrates that finding patterns is often about matching corresponding parts of expressions. Matching corresponding parts of expressions makes it easier to see uniform changes from one part of an expression to its corresponding part in another expression. Matching corresponding parts of expressions is also a way of working methodically, which is often an important part of finding patterns.

Use the Look for Patterns strategy when:

- You start thinking that a complicated formula is necessary to solve a problem.
- You can think of only a very time-consuming way to work with the numbers in the problem.

When looking for a pattern, work methodically. You are much more likely to find a pattern when you work in a methodical way.

Strategy 4: Remember What the GMAT Tests

Doctors have a saying: "Think horses, rather than zebras." The saying means that a patient who presents with unusual symptoms is much more likely to have a fairly common disease that just happens to be presenting in an atypical fashion than to have a rare disease.

The saying also applies to hard math questions on a test such as the GMAT. The GMAT is a standardized test. As such, it needs to routinely test the same, relatively short, list of topics. If the GMAT strayed from that list of topics too frequently, it would be impossible to compare scores from test-takers who took the test in different months or years. Therefore, if you see a question and you can't immediately classify the topic, just remember that it is far more likely that the question is testing a standard topic in an unusual way than testing an unusual topic. That's the crux of the Remember What the GMAT Tests strategy.

Here's an example:

A terminating decimal is one which has only a finite number of nonzero digits. Which of the following numbers has a reciprocal which is a terminating decimal?

(A) $\dfrac{455}{31}$

(B) $\dfrac{1,045}{43}$

(C) $\dfrac{770}{23}$

(D) $\dfrac{650}{19}$

(E) $\dfrac{800}{13}$

Here's How to Crack It

Obviously, the GMAT test-writers don't expect you to divide the numbers. The numbers are too messy to work with quickly, and the GMAT doesn't test raw calculating ability. However, knowing that the GMAT does not test raw calculating ability does provide a clue about how to proceed.

If the test-writers don't expect you to simply divide the numbers, there's likely some rule at work. So, start reviewing rules that the GMAT does test. The question stem uses the term *terminating decimal*, so start there.

Consider a few different numbers. Division by 3 always produces a non-terminating decimal unless the dividend is divisible by 3. For example, $1 \div 3 = 0.\overline{33}$ and $2 \div 3 = 0.\overline{66}$. Division by 4, on the other hand, always produces a terminating decimal. For example, $1 \div 4 = 0.25$, $2 \div 4 = 0.5$, $3 \div 4 = 0.75$, and $4 \div 4 = 1.0$. Division by 5 always produces terminating decimals. Division by 7 always produces non-terminating decimals unless the dividend is divisible by 7. Other numbers that work like 3 and 7 include 11 and 13.

Now, note that the decimal representation of $\frac{1}{6}$ is $0.1\overline{6}$, a non-terminating decimal. The prime factors of 6 are 2 and 3, so $\frac{1}{6}$ can be written as $\frac{1}{2} \times \frac{1}{3}$, or the product of a terminating decimal and a non-terminating decimal. If you try a few other examples of multiplying a terminating decimal and a non-terminating decimal, you'll see that the product is always a non-terminating decimal. It's also true that the product of two non-terminating decimals is also a non-terminating decimal.

So, now we have the rule that this problem is testing—the product of a terminating and a non-terminating decimal is a non-terminating decimal. This rule is exactly the sort of rule that the GMAT likes to test. The rule can be deduced through some elementary quantitative reasoning. Moreover, the application of the rule depends on looking at prime factors, a favorite GMAT topic.

To apply the rule, first take the reciprocal of an answer choice. Then, look at the prime factorization of the denominator. If the prime factors of the denominator include any numbers that produce non-terminating decimals when used as the divisor, that answer choice is a non-terminating decimal.

For (A), the reciprocal is $\frac{31}{455}$, so look at the prime factorization of 455. The prime factorization of 455 is $455 = 5 \times 7 \times 13$. Because division by either 7 or 13 produces a non-terminating decimal, (A) can be eliminated.

For (B), the reciprocal is $\frac{43}{1,045}$. The prime factorization of $1,045 = 5 \times 11 \times 19$. Because division by either 11 or 19 results in a non-terminating decimal, (B) can be eliminated.

For (C), the reciprocal is $\frac{23}{770}$. The prime factorization of $770 = 2 \times 5 \times 7 \times 11$. Because division by either 7 or 11 results in a non-terminating decimal, (C) can be eliminated.

For (D), the reciprocal is $\frac{19}{650}$. The prime factorization of $650 = 2 \times 5^2 \times 13$. Because division by 13 results in a non-terminating decimal, (D) can be eliminated.

For (E), the reciprocal is $\dfrac{13}{800}$. The prime factorization is $800 = 2^4 \times 5^3$. Because division by both 2 and 5 results in terminating decimals, the decimal representation of the reciprocal of this answer choice is a terminating decimal.

The correct answer is (E).

At first glance, this problem might have looked like it was simply testing whether you knew what a reciprocal was and how to divide. However, the numbers didn't divide easily, and the GMAT doesn't test raw calculating ability. That led us to consider what the problem was really testing—a rule about multiplication with decimals—a topic that the GMAT does test.

Here's another example:

Which of the following integers can be written as both the sum of 5 consecutive odd integers and 7 consecutive odd integers?

(A) 49
(B) 70
(C) 140
(D) 215
(E) 525

Here's How to Crack It

If the numbers in the answer choices were smaller, this problem might not seem as intimidating. If the answer turns out to be one of the larger numbers, it's unlikely that you'll be able to quickly find the answer by writing out lists of consecutive odd integers and finding their sums.

Let's try to determine what concept this problem tests. For most GMAT problems, it's clear from the wording which concepts are being tested. For other problems, however, the wording may not make it obvious which concepts are being tested. Remember, however, that it is far more likely that any given GMAT question is testing a regularly tested topic in an unusual way than it is testing an infrequently tested topic.

So, let's see whether we can determine what this problem is testing. Each list of numbers consists of consecutive odd integers, which means that the numbers are evenly spaced. It also means that the numbers are part of an arithmetic sequence. The GMAT does test some basic ideas about sequences, including that the sum of a (finite) arithmetic sequence can be found by multiplying the average of the numbers in the sequence by the number of numbers in the sequence. Moreover, when the numbers in a list of numbers are evenly spaced, the average of the numbers is equal to the median of the numbers.

Now we have a way to solve this problem. In a sense, the problem is just an average question in disguise. The correct answer needs to be both the product of 5 and the average (or median) of a list of 5 consecutive odd integers and the product of 7 and the average (or median) of a list of 7 consecutive odd integers. That means that all we need to do is find an answer that is divisible by both 5 and 7 and ensure that the quotient of each division is an odd integer.

Choice (A) can be eliminated because 49 is not divisible by 5. Choice (B), 70, is divisible by both 5 and 7; however, the quotient in each case is an even number. Eliminate (B). Dividing (C), 140, by 5 or 7 also results in an even quotient. Eliminate (C). Choice (D) can be eliminated because 215 is not divisible by 7. The quotient when (E), 525, is divided by 5 is 105, and the quotient when it is divided by 7 is 75. Because both quotients are odd, 525 is the sum of 5 consecutive odd integers (101 + 103 + 105 + 107 + 109) and 7 consecutive odd integers (69 + 71 + 73 + 75 + 77 + 79 + 81). The correct answer is (E).

Here's what you need to remember about the Remember What the GMAT Tests strategy:

- Just because a problem *looks* like it is testing an unusual topic, doesn't mean that it *is* testing an unusual topic.
- It's more likely that a problem is testing a routine topic in an unusual way than that it is truly testing an unusual topic.
- If you can recast the problem as a familiar topic, you can probably find a way to solve the problem.

Strategy 5: Number Savvy

The time limit is one of the biggest challenges of the GMAT. Most test-takers wish for an extra 10 or 15 minutes to work the problems. Unfortunately, the GMAT test-writers are not likely to accede to the wish any time soon!

However, it is important to remember, as we have mentioned a few times before, that the GMAT does not test raw calculating ability. Every problem on the GMAT is designed so that some percentage of test-takers can do the problem in roughly 2 minutes. The harder the problem, the smaller that percentage of test-takers might be, but the GMAT doesn't use problems that no percentage of test-takers can do in the time allotted.

The people who can do the problems that seem to include time-intensive calculations generally find smart, efficient ways to work with the numbers in the problem. We refer to those smart, efficient ways of working with numbers as Number Savvy. Number Savvy is a skill that you can develop. As you practice, be on the lookout for times that you find yourself filling up the page with calculations. You should also be on the lookout for times when you find yourself doing tedious calculations, such as division to four decimal places. There are almost always better ways to work with the numbers in those situations. If you look for those ways as you practice, you can develop your Number Savvy.

We'll take a look at some Number Savvy principles, but first, let's look at an example for which Number Savvy is important.

$$\left(\frac{1}{3}\right)^{-2}\left(\frac{1}{9}\right)^{-3}\left(\frac{1}{27}\right)^{-4} =$$

(A) $\left(\frac{1}{27}\right)^{-9}$

(B) $\left(\frac{1}{27}\right)^{-24}$

(C) $\left(\frac{1}{3}\right)^{-144}$

(D) $\left(\frac{1}{3}\right)^{-20}$

(E) $\left(\frac{1}{3}\right)^{20}$,

Here's How to Crack It

Sometimes the GMAT likes to write questions that have shock value. In this problem, the numbers were picked to try to shock you into forgetting that basic rules of arithmetic still work even when the numbers get messy! There are only three exponent rules—multiply-add, divide-subtract, power-multiply—and they work no matter how unusual or messy the numbers are. This is another case for using the Remember What the GMAT Tests strategy. The GMAT does not test raw calculating ability. The GMAT does, however, test number savvy. Here, the problem is testing whether you can work with numbers in smart and efficient ways.

First, let's dispose of the fractions. The GMAT knows that many test-takers dislike working with fractions. And, of course, applying a negative exponent to a fraction can make the problem seem all the more confusing. However, we can rewrite the fractions using negative exponents:

$$\left(\frac{1}{3}\right)^{-2}\left(\frac{1}{9}\right)^{-3}\left(\frac{1}{27}\right)^{-4}$$

$$= \left(3^{-1}\right)^{-2}\left(9^{-1}\right)^{-3}\left(27^{-1}\right)^{-4}$$

Now, notice that we are looking for the product of three numbers. The only thing keeping us from using the Multiply-Add exponent rule is that the bases are not the same. However, the GMAT tends to choose the numbers in a problem for a reason. In this case, notice that the denominators of the fractions are all powers of 3. The fractions can be rewritten so that they all use the same base:

$$\left(3^{-1}\right)^{-2}\left(9^{-1}\right)^{-3}\left(27^{-1}\right)^{-4}$$

$$=\left(3^{-1}\right)^{-2}\left(\left(3^2\right)^{-1}\right)^{-3}\left(\left(3^3\right)^{-1}\right)^{-4}$$

Now, apply the Power-Multiply rule:

$$\left(3^{-1}\right)^{-2}\left(\left(3^2\right)^{-1}\right)^{-3}\left(\left(3^3\right)^{-1}\right)^{-4}$$

$$=\left(3^{-1}\right)^{-2}\left(3^{-2}\right)^{-3}\left(3^{-3}\right)^{-4}$$

Apply the Power-Multiply rule again:

$$\left(3^{-1}\right)^{-2}\left(3^{-2}\right)^{-3}\left(3^{-3}\right)^{-4}$$

$$= (3)^2 (3)^6 (3)^{12}$$

It's time to use the Multiply-Add rule:

$$= (3)^2 (3)^6 (3)^{12} = 3^{20}$$

Of course, there's no answer that looks like 3^{20}, so we'll need to find a way to rewrite 3^{20} so that it looks like one of the answer choices. We can use the Power-Multiply rule to do that:

$$3^{20} = \left(3^{-1}\right)^{-20} = \left(\frac{1}{3}\right)^{-20}$$

The correct answer is (D).

There are other ways to work with the numbers in this problem. However, the problem does illustrate two key tenets of Number Savvy. First, basic operations and rules, such as the three exponent rules, work even when the numbers are messy. Second, finding ways to rewrite numbers is often an important part of performing a calculation in an efficient way.

Here are some other Number Savvy principles:

1) Resist the urge to multiply or divide until absolutely necessary.
2) It's often better to work with fractions than decimals because fractions give you the opportunity to cancel.
3) Look for ways to cancel or reduce numbers before multiplying or dividing.
4) Divisibility is about shared prime factors.
5) Multiplying the numerator and denominator of a fraction by the same number doesn't change the value but may give you nicer numbers to work with.
6) Look for ways to factor or distribute.

Let's look at a problem that uses some of these principles to simplify a calculation.

Jack currently invests $425 per month in a mutual fund. He would like to increase his monthly contribution to the equivalent of $110 per week for a one-year period. Rounded to the nearest $0.01, by how much does Jack need to increase his monthly investment?

(A) $15.00
(B) $33.33
(C) $36.67
(D) $51.67
(E) $76.67

Here's How to Crack It

Conceptually, the solution to this problem isn't hard. All you need to do is multiply $110 by 52 and divide the result by 12 to find the new monthly investment, then subtract $425, the current monthly investment. However, if you go about the calculation in the standard way, you'll be doing more work than is necessary and you'll probably find the calculation time-consuming.

Let's think about using some of those Number Savvy principles. First, we'll resist the urge to multiply or divide until necessary. So, rather than starting by multiplying $110 by 52, we'll just set up a fraction that shows the entire calculation that needs to be completed to find the new monthly investment:

$$\frac{110 \times 52}{12} =$$

Now look for ways to cancel—12 and 52 are both divisible by 4. Canceling results in:

$$\frac{110 \times 13}{3} =$$

That looks better, but we can rewrite the fraction and use the distributive law to make the calculation a little nicer.

$$\frac{110 \times 13}{3}$$

$$= 110\,\frac{13}{3}$$

$$= 110\left(4 + \frac{1}{3}\right)$$

Then, using the distributive law:

$$= 440 + \frac{110}{3}$$

Finally, divide 110 by 3 to get \$36.67, rounded to the nearest 0.01, and the new monthly investment is $440 + 36.67 = \$476.67$. The difference in the monthly investments is $\$476.67 - 425 = \$51.67$. The correct answer is (D).

Strategy 6: Advanced POE for Data Sufficiency

People who write standardized tests are good at two things: statistics and psychology. Test-writers study the ways that people react to certain kinds of situations that occur in problems. Then they write questions to take advantage of those behaviors.

One of the things that the GMAT test-writers know is that test-takers generally don't pick answers that they don't understand. In the context of a data sufficiency problem, that means that test-takers are likely to select (E) when they don't understand something about the question stem or when they don't understand how the information in the statements applies to the question.

You should pick (E) only when you can identify some piece of information that you needed the statements to provide and that you didn't get. Be careful that you don't fall into the trap of thinking that (E) means "I don't know."

Let's look at an example:

———————————○———————————

Is $k!$ a factor of $n!$?

(1) The greatest prime factor of $k!$ is 5.
(2) 7 is a factor of $n!$.

Here's How to Crack It

Don't be thrown by the factorials. Instead, employ the Use the Word You Know strategy to focus on the word *factor*. How do you know that one number is a factor of another? If necessary, use the Try a Simpler Example strategy. How do you know that 2 is a factor of 10? If you divide 10 by 2, you get 5, an integer.

That means this question stem can be recast as "Is $\dfrac{n!}{k!}$ an integer?" For this fraction to evaluate to an integer, every number that is part of $k!$ must also be part of $n!$. For that to happen, $n!$ must be greater than $k!$. We'll likely need the statements to provide information about the values of both k and n to answer the question.

Statement (1) provides information about $k!$. If 5 is the greatest prime factor of $k!$, then k either equals 5 or 6 as both 5! and 6! have 5 as their greatest prime factor. However, the statement provides no information about the value of n, so the statement is insufficient. Write BCE.

Statement (2) provides information about the value of $n!$. If 7 is a factor of $n!$, then $n \geq 7$. However, Statement (2) provides no information about the value of k, so it is insufficient on its own. Eliminate (B).

Combining the two statements shows that $n > k$ and hence that $n! > k!$. The answer to the question is always "Yes" when the statements are combined. The correct answer is (C).

———————————○———————————

The use of the factorials in the previous question stem and statements will confuse some test-takers who might be tempted to pick (E). However, it's a bad idea to pick (E) based on confusion about what the statements or question stem means. In that situation, it's actually better to guess an answer other than (E).

In our chapter on Data Sufficiency, we described the AD/BCE approach. One of the reasons that approach is so effective is that it reminds you to evaluate each statement independently before considering the statements together.

However, many test-takers read the question stem and both statements at the same time. The GMAT test-writers are aware of this behavior and write questions that make it look like the information can be easily combined to yield the answer to the question. It's important to remember that there are really two parts to the description of (C). While (C) does state that the information in the combined statements answers the question, it also stipulates that neither statement alone provides the answer to the question.

Let's take a look at a question for which (C) is the trap answer.

If k is the average (arithmetic mean) of prime integers x and y, is k prime?

(1) $x = 3$
(2) $y = x + 2$

Here's How to Crack It

Note that a test-taker who reads both statements at the same time might quickly conclude that the answer is (C). You can answer the question with both statements, but doesn't that just seem a little too easy? Of course, evaluating each statement on its own before evaluating the statements together can help us to avoid this trap!

Plug In to evaluate Statement (1). If $x = 3$ and $y = 7$, then $k = 5$, and the answer to the question is "Yes." However, if $x = 3$ and $y = 13$, then $k = 8$, and the answer to the question is "No." Statement (1) is insufficient. Write down BCE.

Now, Plug In to evaluate Statement (2). When plugging in for this statement, it's also a good idea to be methodical as that might help to identify a pattern. The question stem states that x and y are prime integers, so start by making $x = 3$, the least prime integer that makes y an integer. If $x = 3$, then $y = 5$ and $k = 4$, and the answer to the question is "No." Next, try $x = 5$, the next prime integer greater than 3. If $x = 5$, then $y = 7$ and $k = 6$, and the answer to the question is "No." If $x = 11$, then $x = 13$ and $k = 12$, and the answer to the question is "No." (Note that we had to skip over $x = 7$ because then y is 9, which is not prime.)

We are getting a consistent answer of "No," and we can see the pattern. The statement is producing pairs of consecutive odd numbers that are also prime. Because the values of x and y are consecutive odd numbers, their average is the even number between them. Because all even numbers, except for 2, are not prime, all numbers that satisfy Statement (2) produce an answer of "No" to the question. The correct answer is (B).

Finally, let's go back to the idea that people don't like to pick answers that they don't understand. Sometimes the GMAT will give you a data sufficiency problem in which one statement is much easier to understand than the other. In those situations, a good number of test-takers are tempted to pick the answer that states that the easier statement is sufficient but that the harder statement is insufficient. However, in these situations, it's usually a better bet to pick (D); both statements are independently sufficient.

Let's take a look at a problem in which one statement is easier to evaluate than the other.

Five different integers are selected at random from the numbers 1 to 100. Each of the selected numbers is then divided by integer n. What is the value of n?

(1) The greatest possible remainder for any selected integer is 4.
(2) For some selected integer, k, the quotient when k is divided by n is 9, the quotient when k is divided by $n + 2$ is 6, and the difference of the remainders is 3.

Here's How to Crack It

Start by evaluating Statement (1). Remainders are always less than the divisor. Use the Look For Patterns strategy by considering the possible remainders when dividing by 3.

When 3 is divided by 3, the remainder is 0.

When 4 is divided by 3, the remainder is 1.

When 5 is divided by 3, the remainder is 2.

When 6 is divided by 3, the remainder is 0 again.

The pattern starts to repeat at this point. The possible remainders when dividing by 3 are 0, 1, and 2. So the greatest possible remainder when dividing by 3 is 2. Note that 2 is one less than 3. Now we have the rule—the greatest possible remainder when dividing by integer n is $n - 1$.

Apply that rule to Statement (1). If the greatest possible remainder is 4, then the divisor is $4 + 1 = 5$. The first statement is sufficient. Write down AD.

Evaluate Statement (2). Note that Statement (2) is a lot wordier and a lot more confusing as a result. If you knew the rule, Statement (1) was easy to evaluate. Even if you didn't know the rule, it wasn't too difficult to determine that Statement (1) meant that $n = 5$. So if you're starting to think that Statement (2) can't be sufficient, it's a good time to remember that when a fairly straightforward statement is paired with a wordier, more confusing statement, the wordier, more confusing statement is also usually sufficient. The better bet for this problem is that the answer is (D). Let's see why.

We can use Statement (2) to write two equations in terms of k, the dividend, n, the divisor, and r, the remainder. The first part of Statement (2) tells us that when k is divided by n, the quotient is 9. So, k can be expressed as $k = 9n + r_1$. The second part of Statement (2) tells us that when k is divided by $n + 2$, the quotient is 6. So, k can also be expressed as $k = 6(n + 2) + r_2$. As both expressions equal k, the two expressions can be set equal:

$$9n + r_1 = 6(n + 2) + r_2$$

Next, distribute to get:

$$9n + r_1 = 6n + 12 + r_2$$

Rearrange to get:

$$3n = 12 + (r_2 - r_1)$$

Statement (2) also tells us that the difference of the remainders is 3, so $3n = 12 + 3$, and $n = 5$. The correct answer is (D).

———————————————○———————————————

Summary

o The GMAT defines a hard math question as one that most test-takers get wrong.

o The GMAT makes hard math questions by either testing less familiar content or including answer choices that are good trap answers.

o Knowing how to solve hard math questions is important, but most incorrect answers are the result of mistakes due to moving too quickly, not keeping pace, doing math in your head, and misreading the question.

o When you encounter a question you do not know how to solve, try to use one of the six strategies for solving hard math questions:
   • Use the word you know
   • Try a simpler example
   • Be methodical/look for patterns
   • Remember what the GMAT tests
   • Number savvy
   • Advanced POE for Data Sufficiency

Chapter 13
Arithmetic

A review of averages, medians, modes, rates, proportions, ratios, fractions, decimals, rate and work problems, percentages, and percent change.

Here are the specific arithmetic topics tested on the GMAT:

1. Arithmetic Operations
2. Fractions
3. Proportions
4. Decimals
5. Ratios
6. Percentages
7. Percent Change
8. Averages
9. Medians and Modes
10. Rate and Work Problems

In this chapter, we will first discuss the fundamentals of each topic and then show how the test-writers construct questions based on that topic. Typically, these types of questions will show up during the Quantitative section, but the principles can surface during Data Insights questions. In order to make sure you're well-prepared for any scenario, you'll see practice questions for multiple styles strewn throughout this section.

ARITHMETIC OPERATIONS

There are six arithmetic operations you will need for the GMAT:

1. **Addition** $(2 + 2)$ The result of addition is a sum or total.
2. **Subtraction** $(6 - 2)$ The result of subtraction is a difference.
3. **Multiplication** (2×2) The result of multiplication is a product.
4. **Division** $(8 \div 2)$ The result of division is a quotient.
5. **Raising to a power** (x^2) In the expression x^2, the little 2 is called an exponent.
6. **Finding a square root** $\left(\sqrt{4}\right)$ $\sqrt{4} = \sqrt{2 \times 2} = 2$

Which One Do I Do First?

In a problem that involves several different operations, the operations must be performed in a particular order, and occasionally GMAC likes to see whether you know what that order is. Here's an easy way to remember the order of operations:

Please **E**xcuse **M**y **D**ear **A**unt **S**ally
or
PEMDAS

The letters stand for Parentheses, Exponents, Multiplication, Division, Addition, and Subtraction. Do operations that are enclosed in parentheses first; then take care of exponents; next multiply and divide; finally add and subtract, going from left to right.

DRILL 6

Just to get you started, solve each of the following problems by performing the indicated operations in the proper order. Then, try out the basic concepts on some questions in the format of GMAT questions. The answers can be found in Part V.

1. $74 + (27 - 24) =$

2. $(8 \times 9) + 7 =$

3. $2(9 - (8 \div 2)) =$

4. $2(7 - 3) + (-4)(5 - 7) =$

5. $4(-3(3 - 5) + 10 - 17) =$
    - (A) -27
    - (B) -4
    - (C) -1
    - (D) 32
    - (E) 84

6. What is the value of x?

    (1) $x^3 = 8$
    (2) $x^2 = 4$

    - (A) Statement (1) ALONE is sufficient, but statement (2) alone is not sufficient.
    - (B) Statement (2) ALONE is sufficient, but statement (1) alone is not sufficient.
    - (C) BOTH statements TOGETHER are sufficient, but NEITHER statement ALONE is sufficient.
    - (D) EACH statement ALONE is sufficient.
    - (E) Statements (1) and (2) TOGETHER are not sufficient.

Associative and Distributive Laws

There are two operations that can be done in any order, provided they are the only operations involved: *when you are adding or multiplying a series of numbers, you can group or regroup the numbers any way you like.*

$2 + 3 + 4$ is the same as $4 + 2 + 3$
and
$4 \times 5 \times 6$ is the same as $6 \times 5 \times 4$

This is called the **Associative Law**, but the name will not be tested on the GMAT.

Another law that GMAC likes to test states that

$a(b + c) = ab + ac$ and $a(b - c) = ab - ac$.

This is called the **Distributive Law**, but again, you don't need to know that for the test. Sometimes the Distributive Law can provide you with a shortcut to the solution of a problem. If a problem gives you information in "factored form"—$a(b + c)$—you should distribute it immediately. If the information is given in distributed form—$ab + ac$—you should factor it.

DRILL 7

If the following problems are in distributed form, factor them; if they are in factored form, distribute them. Then do the indicated operations. Answers are in Part V.

1. $x^2 + x$

2. $(55 \times 12) + (55 \times 88)$

3. $a(b + c - d)$

4. $abc + xyc$

A GMAT problem might look like this:

5. If $x = 6$, what is the value of $\dfrac{2xy - xy}{y}$?
   - (A) −30
   - (B)   6
   - (C)   8
   - (D)   30
   - (E) It cannot be determined from the information given.

6. If $ax + ay + az = 15$, what is $x + y + z$?

   (1) $x = 2$
   (2) $a = 5$

   (A)   Statement (1) ALONE is sufficient, but statement (2) alone is not sufficient.
   (B)   Statement (2) ALONE is sufficient, but statement (1) alone is not sufficient.
   (C)   BOTH statements TOGETHER are sufficient, but NEITHER statement ALONE is sufficient.
   (D)   EACH statement ALONE is sufficient.
   (E)   Statements (1) and (2) TOGETHER are not sufficient.

Challenge Question #4

> Find the answers to all Challenge Questions in Part V!

A device calculates the worth of gemstones based on quality such that a gem with a quality rating of $q - 1$ is worth 5 times more than a gem with a quality rating of q, and a gem with a quality rating of $q - 4$ is worth 625 times more than a gem with a quality rating of q. According to this device, the worth of a gem with a quality rating of $p - r$ is how many times greater than that of a gem with a rating of p ?

   (A) $p^5 - r^5$
   (B) r^5
   (C) $(p - r)^5$
   (D) 5^r
   (E) $5r$

FRACTIONS

Fractions can be thought of in two ways:

> - A **fraction** is just another way of expressing division. The expression $\frac{1}{2}$ is exactly the same thing as 1 divided by 2. $\frac{x}{y}$ is nothing more than x divided by y. In the fraction $\frac{x}{y}$, x is known as the **numerator** and y is known as the **denominator**.
>
> - The other important way to think of a fraction is as $\frac{\text{part}}{\text{whole}}$. The fraction $\frac{7}{10}$ can be thought of as 7 parts out of a total of 10 parts.

Adding and Subtracting Fractions with the Same Denominator

To add two or more fractions that have the same denominator, simply add the numerators and put the sum over the common denominator. For example:

$$\frac{1}{7} + \frac{5}{7} = \frac{(1+5)}{7} = \frac{6}{7}$$

Subtraction works exactly the same way:

$$\frac{6}{7} - \frac{2}{7} = \frac{6-2}{7} = \frac{4}{7}$$

Adding and Subtracting Fractions with Different Denominators

Before you can add or subtract two or more fractions with different denominators, you must give all of them the same denominator. To do this, multiply the numerator and denominator of each fraction by a number that will give it a denominator in common with the others. If you multiplied each fraction by any old number, the fractions wouldn't have their original values, so the number you multiply by has to be equal to 1. For example, if you wanted to change $\frac{1}{2}$ into sixths, you could do the following:

$$\frac{1}{2} \times \frac{3}{3} = \frac{3}{6}$$

We haven't actually changed the value of the fraction, because $\frac{3}{3}$ equals 1.

If we wanted to add:

$$\frac{1}{2} + \frac{2}{3}$$

$$\frac{1}{2} \times \frac{3}{3} + \frac{2}{3} \times \frac{2}{2}$$

$$\frac{3}{6} + \frac{4}{6} = \frac{7}{6}$$

The Bowtie

The Bowtie method has been a staple of The Princeton Review's materials since the company began in a living room in New York City in 1981. It's been around so long because it works so simply.

To add $\dfrac{3}{5}$ and $\dfrac{4}{7}$, for example, follow these three steps:

Step One: Multiply the denominators together to form the new denominator.

$$\frac{3}{5}+\frac{4}{7}=\frac{}{5\times 7}=\frac{}{35}$$

Step Two: Multiply the first denominator by the second numerator ($5 \times 4 = 20$) and the second denominator by the first numerator ($7 \times 3 = 21$) and place these numbers above the fractions, as shown below.

See? A bowtie!

Step Three: Add the products to form the new numerator.

$$\frac{3}{5}+\frac{4}{7}=\frac{21+20}{5\times 7}=\frac{41}{35}$$

Subtraction works the same way.

Note that with subtraction, the order of the numerators is important. The new numerator is $21 - 20$, or 1. If you somehow get your numbers reversed and use $20 - 21$, your answer will be $-\dfrac{1}{35}$, which is incorrect. One way to keep your subtraction straight is to always multiply **up** from denominator to numerator when you use the Bowtie.

Multiplying Fractions

To multiply fractions, just multiply the numerators and put the product over the product of the denominators. For example:

$$\frac{2}{3} \times \frac{6}{5} = \frac{12}{15}$$

Reducing Fractions

When you add or multiply fractions, you often end up with a big fraction that is hard to work with. You can usually reduce such a fraction. To reduce a fraction, find a factor of the numerator that is also a factor of the denominator. It saves time to find the biggest factor they have in common, but this isn't critical. You may just have to repeat the process a few times. When you find a common factor, cancel it. For example, let's take the product we just found when we multiplied the fractions above:

$$\frac{12}{15} = \frac{4 \times \cancel{3}}{5 \times \cancel{3}} = \frac{4}{5}$$

Get used to reducing all fractions (if they can be reduced) *before* you do any work with them. It saves a lot of time and prevents errors in computation.

For example, in that last problem, we had to multiply two fractions together:

$$\frac{2}{3} \times \frac{6}{5}$$

Before you multiplied 2×6 and 3×5, you could have reduced $\frac{2}{3} \times \frac{6}{5} = \frac{2 \times \cancel{6}}{\cancel{3} \times 5} = \frac{2 \times 2}{5} = \frac{4}{5}$.

Dividing Fractions

To divide one fraction by another, just invert the second fraction and multiply:

$$\frac{2}{3} \div \frac{3}{4}$$

which is the same thing as...

$$\frac{2}{3} \times \frac{4}{3} = \frac{8}{9}$$

You may see this same operation written like this:

$$\frac{\dfrac{2}{3}}{\dfrac{3}{4}}$$

Again, just invert and multiply. This next example is handled the same way:

$$\frac{6}{\dfrac{2}{3}} = \frac{6}{1} \times \frac{3}{2} = \frac{18}{2} = 9$$

When you invert a fraction, the new fraction is called a **reciprocal**. $\frac{2}{3}$ is the reciprocal of $\frac{3}{2}$. The product of two reciprocals is always 1.

Converting to Fractions

An integer can be expressed as a fraction by making the integer the numerator and 1 the denominator: $16 = \frac{16}{1}$.

The GMAT sometimes gives you numbers that are mixtures of integers and fractions, for example, $3\frac{1}{2}$. It's easier to work with these numbers if you convert them into fractions. Simply multiply the denominator by the integer, then add the numerator, and place the resulting number over the original denominator.

$$3\frac{1}{2} = \frac{(3 \times 2) + 1}{2} = \frac{7}{2}$$

Comparing Fractions

In the course of a problem, you may have to compare two or more fractions and determine which is greater. This is easy to do as long as you remember that you can compare fractions directly only if they have the same denominator. Suppose you had to decide which of these three fractions is greatest:

$$\frac{1}{2}, \frac{5}{9}, \text{ or } \frac{7}{15}$$

To compare these fractions directly, you need a common denominator, but finding a common denominator that works for all three fractions would be complicated and time consuming. It makes more sense to compare these fractions two at a time. We showed you the classical way to find common denominators when we talked about adding fractions earlier.

Let's start with $\frac{1}{2}$ and $\frac{5}{9}$. An easy common denominator for these two fractions is 18 (9×2).

$$\frac{1}{2} \qquad \frac{5}{9}$$

$$\frac{1}{2} \times \frac{9}{9} \qquad \frac{5}{9} \times \frac{2}{2}$$

$$= \frac{9}{18} \qquad = \frac{10}{18}$$

Because $\frac{5}{9}$ is greater, let's compare it with $\frac{7}{15}$. Here the easiest common denominator is 45. But before we do that...

Two Shortcuts

Comparing fractions is another situation in which we can use the Bowtie. The idea is that if all you need to know is which fraction is greater, you just have to compare the new numerators. Again, simply multiply the denominator of the first fraction by the numerator of the second and the denominator of the second by the numerator of the first, as shown here.

$$9 \times 1 = 9 \quad \frac{1}{2} \diagdown\!\!\!\diagup \frac{5}{9} \quad 2 \times 5 = 10$$

$$10 > 9, \text{ therefore } \frac{5}{9} > \frac{1}{2}$$

You could also have saved yourself some time on the last problem by a little fast estimation. Again, which is greater? $\frac{1}{2}$, $\frac{5}{9}$, or $\frac{7}{15}$?

Let's think about $\frac{5}{9}$ in terms of $\frac{1}{2}$. How many ninths equal a half? To put it another way, what is half of 9? 4.5. So $\frac{4.5}{9} = \frac{1}{2}$. That means $\frac{5}{9}$ is *greater* than $\frac{1}{2}$.

Now let's think about $\frac{7}{15}$. Half of 15 is 7.5. $\frac{7.5}{15} = \frac{1}{2}$, which means that $\frac{7}{15}$ is *less* than $\frac{1}{2}$.

PROPORTIONS

A fraction can be expressed in many ways. $\frac{1}{2}$ also equals $\frac{2}{4}$ or $\frac{4}{8}$, etc. A **proportion** is just a different way of expressing a fraction. Here's an example:

If 2 boxes hold a total of 14 shirts, how many shirts are contained in 3 boxes?

Here's How to Crack It

The number of shirts per box can be expressed as a fraction. What you're asked to do is express the fraction $\frac{2}{14}$ in a different way.

$$\frac{2\,(\text{boxes})}{14\,(\text{shirts})} = \frac{3\,(\text{boxes})}{x\,(\text{shirts})}$$

To find the answer, all you need to do is find a value for x such that $\frac{2}{14} = \frac{3}{x}$. The easiest way to do this is to cross-multiply.

$2x = 42$, which means that $x = 21$. There are 21 shirts in 3 boxes.

> **Proportions and Ratios**
> Proportions are really ratios. While a proportion question asks about the number of shirts *per* box, a ratio question might ask about the number of red shirts to blue shirts in a box.

DRILL 8

The answers to these questions can be found in Part V.

1. $5\dfrac{3}{4} + \dfrac{3}{8} =$

2. Reduce $\dfrac{12}{60}$

3. Convert $9\dfrac{2}{3}$ to a fraction

4. Solve for x in $\dfrac{9}{2} = \dfrac{x}{4}$

5. $\dfrac{\left(\dfrac{\frac{4}{5}}{\frac{3}{5}}\right)\left(\dfrac{\frac{1}{8}}{\frac{2}{3}}\right)}{\dfrac{3}{4}} =$

   (A) $\dfrac{3}{100}$

   (B) $\dfrac{3}{16}$

   (C) $\dfrac{1}{3}$

   (D) 1

   (E) $\dfrac{7}{16}$

6. If $x = \dfrac{\dfrac{5}{9}+\dfrac{15}{27}+\dfrac{45}{81}}{3}$, then $\sqrt{1-x} =$

(A) $\dfrac{\sqrt{5}}{9}$

(B) $\dfrac{5}{9}$

(C) $\dfrac{2}{3}$

(D) $\dfrac{\sqrt{5}}{3}$

(E) $\dfrac{15}{9}$

7. If $\dfrac{1}{y} = 2\dfrac{2}{3}$, then $\left(\dfrac{1}{y+1}\right)^2 =$

(A) $\dfrac{9}{64}$

(B) $\dfrac{3}{8}$

(C) $\dfrac{64}{121}$

(D) $\dfrac{121}{64}$

(E) $\dfrac{64}{9}$

Fractions: Advanced Principles

Now that you've been reacquainted with the basics of fractions, let's go a little further. More complicated fraction problems usually involve all of the rules we've just mentioned, with the addition of two concepts: $\dfrac{\text{part}}{\text{whole}}$ and the rest.

Q: There are only roses, tulips, and peonies in a certain garden. There are three roses to every four tulips and every five peonies in the garden. Expressed as a fraction, what part of the flowers in the garden are tulips?
Turn to page 241 for the answer.

A cement mixture is composed of 3 elements. By weight, $\frac{1}{3}$ of the mixture is sand, $\frac{3}{5}$ of the mixture is water, and the remaining 12 pounds of the mixture is gravel. What is the weight of the entire mixture in pounds?

(A)   4
(B)   8
(C)   36
(D)   60
(E)   180

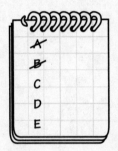

Easy Eliminations

Before we even start doing serious math, let's use some common sense. The weight of the gravel alone is 12 pounds. Because we know that sand and water make up the bulk of the mixture—sand $\frac{1}{3}$, water $\frac{3}{5}$ (which is a bit more than half)—the entire mixture must weigh a great deal more than 12 pounds. Choices (A) and (B) are out of the question. Eliminate them.

Here's How to Crack It

The difficulty in solving this problem is that sand and water are expressed as fractions, while gravel is expressed in pounds. At first there seems to be no way of knowing what fractional part of the mixture the 12 pounds of gravel represent, nor do we know how many pounds of sand and water there are.

The first step is to add up the fractional parts that we do have:

$$\frac{1}{3}+\frac{3}{5}=\frac{1}{3}\left(\frac{5}{5}\right)+\frac{3}{5}\left(\frac{3}{3}\right)=\frac{14}{15}$$

Sand and water make up 14 parts out of the whole of 15. This means that gravel makes up what is left over—the rest: 1 part out of the whole of 15. Now the problem is simple. Set up a proportion between parts and weights.

$$\frac{1}{15}=\frac{12}{x} \quad \begin{matrix}\text{pounds (of gravel)} \\ \text{pounds (total pounds)}\end{matrix}$$

Cross-multiply: $x = 180$. The answer is (E).

Andre has already saved $\frac{3}{7}$ of the cost of a new car, and he has calculated that he will be able to save $\frac{2}{5}$ of the remaining amount before the end of the summer. What fraction of the cost of the new car will he still need to save after the end of the summer?

(A) $\frac{6}{35}$

(B) $\frac{8}{35}$

(C) $\frac{12}{35}$

(D) $\frac{23}{35}$

(E) $\frac{29}{35}$

Here's How to Crack It

Because there are fractions in the answer choices, and they're fractions of an unspecified amount, the quickest way to solve this problem is to Plug In. Make the price of Andre's dream car $35—the denominators of the fractions in the problem are 7 and 5 (both factors of 35) and, moreover, 35 is in the denominator of *all* of the answer choices.

If the car costs $35, and Andre has already saved $\frac{3}{7}$ of that, or $15, he currently has $20 left to save. Before the end of the summer, he'll be able to save $\frac{2}{5}$ of that remaining $20, or $8. That will give him a total of $23 saved toward his car, leaving him $12 to go. Expressed as a fraction of the cost of the car, that's $\frac{12}{35}$, and the correct answer is (C).

As always, watch those trap answers. Choice (D) is the fraction of the cost that Andre will have saved by the end of the summer. Choice (A) is what you'd get if you calculated Andre's summer earnings as two-fifths of the total cost of the car instead of two-fifths of what Andre has left to save. Choice (E) is what you'd get if you made both mistakes.

A: The relationship between roses, tulips, and peonies was expressed as a ratio. To find the fractional part, first find the *whole*. We know the parts are 3 roses, 4 tulips, and 5 peonies. $3 + 4 + 5 = 12 =$ the whole. What fractional part of the flowers are tulips? 4 out of a total of 12, otherwise known as $\frac{4}{12}$ or $\frac{1}{3}$.

On Monday, an animal shelter housed 55 cats and dogs, and by Friday exactly $\frac{1}{5}$ of the cats and $\frac{1}{4}$ of the dogs had been adopted. If no new cats or dogs were brought to the shelter during this period, what is the greatest possible number of pets that could have been adopted from the animal shelter between Monday and Friday?

(A) 11
(B) 12
(C) 13
(D) 14
(E) 20

Here's How to Crack It

The question asks you for the greatest number of animals that could have been adopted from the shelter within the parameters of the problem. Because a greater proportion of dogs than cats was adopted, you should seek a scenario that maximizes the number of dogs adopted. You must also satisfy the other conditions of the problem, however; the number of cats, for example, must be a multiple of 5, because that is the only way that $\frac{1}{5}$ of the cats can be adopted.

Because you want to maximize the number of dogs in the shelter, start by assuming the minimum possible number of cats, 5. This would leave 50 dogs in the shelter. This solution, unfortunately, is impossible; because 50 is not evenly divisible by 4, there cannot be 50 dogs in the shelter. Could there be 10 cats at the shelter? No, because this would leave 45 dogs, again making it impossible for exactly $\frac{1}{4}$ of the dogs to be adopted. 15 cats is the magic number, as it means there are 40 dogs. $\left(\frac{1}{5} \times 15\right) + \left(\frac{1}{4} \times 40\right) = 3 + 10 = 13$ animals. The correct answer is (C).

| For more free content, visit PrincetonReview.com

At a college football game, $\frac{4}{5}$ of the seats in the lower deck of the stadium were sold. If $\frac{1}{4}$ of all the seats in the stadium are located in the lower deck, and if $\frac{2}{3}$ of all the seats in the stadium were sold, what fraction of the unsold seats in the stadium are in the lower deck?

(A) $\frac{3}{20}$

(B) $\frac{1}{6}$

(C) $\frac{1}{5}$

(D) $\frac{1}{3}$

(E) $\frac{7}{15}$

Here's How to Crack It

Solve this one using Plugging In. First, plug in a number of seats for the entire stadium. Choose a number that divides easily by 3, 4, and 5. For the purposes of this explanation, let's say the stadium seats 60,000 people. The problem states that $\frac{2}{3}$ of all the seating in the stadium was sold, meaning that 40,000 of the 60,000 seats were sold. It also states that $\frac{1}{4}$ of the seating is located in the lower deck. Because $\frac{1}{4}$ of 60,000 is 15,000, that means the stadium has 15,000 seats in the lower deck. Of those 15,000 seats, according to the problem, $\frac{4}{5}$, or 12,000, were sold. The question asks what fraction of the unsold seats in the stadium were in the lower deck. Because 40,000 seats were sold in the entire stadium, a total of 20,000 were unsold; of the 20,000 unsold seats, 15,000 − 12,000 = 3,000 were in the lower deck. The fraction $\frac{3,000}{20,000}$ reduces to $\frac{3}{20}$, so the correct answer is (A).

DECIMALS ARE REALLY FRACTIONS

A decimal can be expressed as a fraction, and a fraction can be expressed as a decimal.

Decimals or Fractions

Whether you prefer decimals or fractions, you must be able to work with both. The ability to work comfortably and confidently with decimals and fractions is vital to GMAT success.

$$0.6 = \frac{6}{10}, \text{ which can be reduced to } \frac{3}{5}$$

$$\frac{3}{5} \text{ is the same thing as } 3 \div 5$$

Which would you rather figure out—the square of $\frac{1}{4}$ or the square of 0.25? There may be a few of you out there who've had so much practice with decimals in your work that you prefer decimals to fractions, but for the rest of us, fractions are infinitely easier to deal with.

Occasionally, you will have to work with decimals. Whenever possible, however, convert decimals to fractions. It will save time and eliminate careless mistakes. In fact, it makes sense to memorize the fractional equivalent of some commonly used decimals:

$$0.2 = \frac{1}{5} \qquad\qquad 0.6 = \frac{3}{5}$$

$$0.25 = \frac{1}{4} \qquad\qquad 0.\overline{66} = \frac{2}{3}$$

$$0.\overline{33} = \frac{1}{3} \qquad\qquad 0.75 = \frac{3}{4}$$

$$0.4 = \frac{2}{5} \qquad\qquad 0.8 = \frac{4}{5}$$

$$0.5 = \frac{1}{2}$$

Adding and Subtracting Decimals

To add or subtract decimals, just line up the decimal points and proceed as usual. Adding 6, 2.5, and 0.3 looks like this:

$$
\begin{array}{r}
6.0 \\
2.5 \\
+\ 0.3 \\
\hline
8.8
\end{array}
$$

Multiplying Decimals

To multiply decimals, simply ignore the decimal points and multiply the two numbers. When you've finished, count all the digits that were to the right of the decimal points in the original numbers you multiplied. Now place the decimal point in your answer so that there are the same number of digits to the right of it. Here are two examples:

$$\begin{array}{r} 0.3 \\ \times\ 0.7 \\ \hline 0.21 \end{array}$$

There are a total of two digits to the right of the decimal point in the original numbers, so you place the decimal so that there are two digits to the right in the answer.

$$\begin{array}{r} 14.3 \\ \times\ 0.232 \\ \hline 3.3176 \end{array}$$

There are a total of four digits to the right of the decimal point in the original numbers, so you place the decimal such that there are four digits to the right in the answer.

Dividing Decimals

The best way to divide one decimal by another is to convert the number you are dividing by (in mathematical terminology, the **divisor**) into a whole number. You do this by simply moving the decimal point as many places as necessary. This works as long as you remember to move the decimal point in the number that you are *dividing* (in mathematical terminology, the **dividend**) the same number of spaces.

For example, to divide 12 by 0.6, set it up the way you would an ordinary division problem:

$$0.6\overline{)12.}$$

To make 0.6 (the divisor) a whole number, you simply move the decimal point over one place to the right. You must also move the decimal one place to the right in the dividend. Now the operation looks like this:

$$0.6\overline{)12.}$$
$$6\overline{)120}$$
$$\underline{20}$$
$$6\overline{)120}$$

Rounding

To round a decimal, look at the digit to the right of the digits place you are rounding to. If that number is 0–4, there is no change. If that number is 5–9, round up.

Rounding Decimals

9.4 rounded to the nearest whole number is 9.
9.5 rounded to the nearest whole number is 10.

When GMAC asks you to give an approximate answer on an easy question, it is safe to round numbers. But you should be leery about rounding numbers on a difficult question. If you're scoring in a high percentile, rounding off numbers will be useful to eliminate answer choices that are out of the ballpark, but not to decide between two close answer choices.

DRILL 9

The answers to these questions can be found in Part V.

1. $\begin{array}{r} 34.26 \\ -\ 0.96 \\ \hline \end{array}$

2. $\begin{array}{r} 27.3 \\ \times\ 9.75 \\ \hline \end{array}$

3. $\dfrac{19.6}{3.2} =$

4. $\dfrac{\frac{4}{0.25}}{\frac{1}{50}} =$

On the GMAT, there might be questions that mix decimals and fractions:

5. $\dfrac{\frac{3}{10} \times 4 \times 0.8}{0.32}$

    (A)   0.96
    (B)   0.333
    (C)   3.0
    (D)   30.0
    (E)   96.0

6. If *x* and *y* are reciprocals, what is the value of *x* + *y* rounded to the nearest hundredth?

(1) $x = 0.2$
(2) $y = 5$

(A) Statement (1) ALONE is sufficient, but statement (2) alone is not sufficient.
(B) Statement (2) ALONE is sufficient, but statement (1) alone is not sufficient.
(C) BOTH statements TOGETHER are sufficient, but NEITHER statement ALONE is sufficient.
(D) EACH statement ALONE is sufficient.
(E) Statements (1) and (2) TOGETHER are not sufficient.

First Things First
On *all* questions, before you do any serious calculations, take a moment to see whether the answer choices make sense. Eliminate trap answer choices. Do this first because those "trap" choices usually reflect the result of a common (but incorrect) approach to the problem. Eliminate first and you won't think (falsely), "Aha, I've got it." Instead, you'll know you took a misstep somewhere.

RATIOS

Ratios are close relatives of fractions. A ratio can be expressed as a fraction and vice versa. The ratio 3 to 4 can be written as $\frac{3}{4}$ as well as in standard ratio format: 3:4.

There Is Only One Difference Between a Ratio and a Fraction

A fraction compares a part-to-whole relationship. A ratio compares a part-to-part relationship. It's that simple. Check out the box below for a handy visual representation.

Fraction:
$$\frac{\text{part: 3 women}}{\text{whole: 7 people}}$$

Ratio:
$$\frac{\text{part: 3 women}}{\text{part: 4 men}}$$

(The whole is 7.)

Aside from That, All the Rules of Fractions Apply to Ratios

A ratio can be converted to a percentage or a decimal. It can be cross-multiplied, reduced, or expanded—just like a fraction. The ratio of 1 to 3 can be expressed as:

$$\frac{1}{3}$$

$$1{:}3$$

$$\frac{2}{6}$$

$$\frac{3}{9}$$

Check out the following two examples of Ratio problems formatted like a GMAT question.

The ratio of men to women in a room is 3 to 4. If there are 20 women, what is the number of men in the room?

Here's How to Crack It

No matter how many people are actually in the room, the ratio of men to women will always stay the same: 3 to 4. What you're asked to do is find the numerator of a fraction whose denominator is 20, and which can be reduced to $\frac{3}{4}$. Just set one fraction equal to another and cross-multiply:

$$\frac{3}{4} = \frac{x}{20} \qquad 60 = 4x \qquad x = 15$$

The answer to the question is 15 men. Note that $\frac{15}{20}$ reduces to $\frac{3}{4}$.

> The ratio of women to men in a room is 3 to 4. If there are a total of 28 people in the room, how many are women?

This problem is more difficult because, while we are given the ratio of women to men, we are not given a specific value for either the women or the men. If we tried to set up this problem as we did the previous one, it would look like this:

$$\frac{3}{4} = \frac{x}{y}$$

Of course, you can't solve an equation that has two variables.

Here's How to Crack It

You need a way to see how the total number of people in the room, which you know is 28, can be broken down into groups of 3 women and 4 men.

A good way to solve the problem is to use a Ratio Box. Here's what that looks like for the information provided by the problem:

	Women	Men	Total
Ratio	3	4	
Multiplier			
Actual Number			28

To use a Ratio Box, you need a ratio and an actual number. Now, remember that ratios compare parts to parts. So, if you add up the parts, you get a group (or total) of 7 people.

Next, the key idea of a ratio is the multiplier, which allows you to make the group greater or lesser while keeping everything in the same ratio. For this problem, you don't want a group of 7 people. You want a group of 28. So, you multiply $7 \times 4 = 28$.

To keep everything in the same ratio, you just need to remember that whatever you do to one part, you need to do to every part. So, multiply the ratio numbers for both the women and men by 4.

Here's what the box looks like when it is completed:

	Women	Men	Total
Ratio	3	4	7
Multiplier	4	4	4
Actual Number	$12 = (3 \times 4)$	$16 = (4 \times 4)$	$28 = (7 \times 4)$

There are 12 women in the room.

DRILL 10

The answers to these questions can be found in Part V.

1. Over the course of a soccer season, 30 percent of the players on a team scored goals. What is the ratio of players on the team who scored goals to those who did not?

   (A) 3 to 10
   (B) 1 to 3
   (C) 3 to 7
   (D) 1 to 1
   (E) 3 to 1

2. The Binary Ice Cream Shoppe sells two flavors of cones: vanilla and chocolate. On Friday, the ratio of vanilla cones sold to chocolate cones sold was 2 to 3. If the store sold 4 more vanilla cones, the ratio of vanilla cones sold to chocolate cones sold would have been 3 to 4. How many vanilla cones did the store sell on Friday?

   (A) 32
   (B) 35
   (C) 42
   (D) 48
   (E) 54

3. An automobile dealership sells only sedans and coupes. It sells each in only two colors: red and blue. Last year, the dealership sold 9,000 vehicles, half of which were red. How many coupes did the dealership sell last year?

    (1)   The dealership sold three times as many blue coupes as red sedans last year.
    (2)   The dealership sold half as many blue sedans as blue coupes last year.

    (A)   Statement (1) ALONE is sufficient, but statement (2) alone is not sufficient.
    (B)   Statement (2) ALONE is sufficient, but statement (1) alone is not sufficient.
    (C)   BOTH statements TOGETHER are sufficient, but NEITHER statement ALONE is sufficient.
    (D)   EACH statement ALONE is sufficient.
    (E)   Statements (1) and (2) TOGETHER are not sufficient.

PERCENTAGES

A **percentage** is just a fraction in which the denominator is always equal to 100. Fifty percent means 50 parts out of a whole of 100. Like any fraction, a percentage can be reduced, expanded, cross-multiplied, converted to a decimal, or converted to another fraction: $50\% = \dfrac{1}{2} = 0.5$.

An Easy Percent Problem

5 is what percent of 20 ?

Q: What is $\dfrac{1}{4}$ % of 40?

Turn to page 253 for the answer.

Here's How to Crack It

Whenever you see a percent problem, you should be thinking $\dfrac{\text{part}}{\text{whole}}$. In this case, the question asks you to expand $\dfrac{5}{20}$ into another fraction in which the denominator is 100.

$$\frac{\text{part}}{\text{whole}} = \frac{5}{20} = \frac{x}{100}$$

$$500 = 20x$$

$$x = 25$$

$$\frac{25}{100} = 25\%$$

Percent Shortcuts

In the last problem, reducing $\frac{5}{20}$ to $\frac{1}{4}$ would have saved you time if you knew that $\frac{1}{4} = 25\%$. Here are some fractions and decimals whose percent equivalents you should know:

$$\frac{1}{4} = 0.25 = 25\%$$

$$\frac{1}{2} = 0.50 = 50\%$$

$$\frac{1}{3} = 0.333\ldots \text{ (a repeating decimal)} = 33\frac{1}{3}\%$$

$$\frac{1}{5} = 0.20 = 20\%$$

Some percentages simply involve moving a decimal point. To get 10 percent of any number, simply move the decimal point of that number over one place to the left:

10% of 6 = 0.6
10% of 60 = 6
10% of 600 = 60

- To get 1 percent of any number, just move the decimal point of that number over two places to the left:
1% of 600 = 6
1% of 60 = 0.6
1% of 6 = 0.06

- To find a more complicated percentage, break the percentage down into easy-to-find chunks:

20% of 60:	10% of 60 = 6; 20% of 60 is double 10%, so the answer is 2×6, or 12.
30% of 60:	10% of 60 = 6; 30% of 60 is three times 10%, so the answer is 3×6, or 18.
3% of 200:	1% of 200 = 2; 3% of 200 is just three times 1%, so the answer is 3×2, or 6.
23% of 400:	10% of 400 = 40. Therefore, 20% equals 2×40, or 80. 1% of 400 = 4. Therefore, 3% equals 3×4, or 12. Putting it all together, 23% of 400 equals $80 + 12$, or 92.

A store sells a six-pack of soda for $2.70. If this represents a savings of 10 percent of the individual price of cans of soda, then what is the price of a single can of soda?

(A) $ 0.35
(B) $ 0.40
(C) $ 0.45
(D) $ 0.50
(E) $ 0.55

A: There are a number of ways to calculate the answer, but the simplest is to first calculate 1% of 40 by moving the decimal point two places to the left. This gives 0.4 as a result. Dividing this result by 4 gives us 0.1—the answer.

Here's How to Crack It

If a six-pack sells for $2.70, then each would cost 45 cents when purchased together. When purchased individually, the price is higher than 45 cents, so cross off (A), (B), and (C). Let's plug in (D). Choice (D) says the price of an individual can is 50 cents. 10% of 50 cents is 5 cents, so the price per can of a six-pack would be 50 – 5 = 45 cents. Therefore, (D) is correct.

A Medium Percent Problem

Like medium and difficult fraction problems, medium and difficult percent problems often involve remembering the principles of $\frac{\text{part}}{\text{whole}}$ and the rest.

A motor pool has 300 vehicles, of which 30 percent are trucks. 20 percent of all the vehicles in the motor pool are diesel, including 15 trucks. What percent of the motor pool is composed of vehicles that are neither trucks nor diesel?

(A) 95%
(B) 90%
(C) 65%
(D) 55%
(E) 10%

There's a handy formula for calculating mixed groups. It isn't a priority for you to memorize (you just saw the problem calculated without it), but the formula can be helpful on some questions. Here it is: **Group 1 + Group 2 – both + neither = total.** Here's what that looks like using the numbers from the vehicle problem. 90 trucks + 60 diesel – 15 diesel trucks + x = 300. 135 + x = 300. x = 165, or 55% of 300.

Here's How to Crack It

Do this problem one sentence at a time.

1. A motor pool has 300 vehicles, of which 30% are trucks. Thirty percent of 300 = 90 trucks, which means that 210 (the rest) are *not* trucks.
2. Twenty percent of all the vehicles are diesel, including 15 trucks. Twenty percent of 300 = 60 diesel vehicles, 15 of which are trucks, which means there are 45 diesel vehicles that are *not* trucks.

3. What percent of the motor pool is composed of vehicles that are neither truck nor diesel? We know from sentence number 1 that there are 210 nontrucks. We know from sentence number 2 that of these 210 nontrucks, 45 are diesel. Therefore, 210 − 45, or 165, are neither diesel nor truck.

The question asks what percent of the entire motor pool these 165 nondiesel nontrucks are.

$$\frac{165}{300} = \frac{x}{100} \qquad 300x = 16{,}500$$

$x = 55$, so the answer is (D).

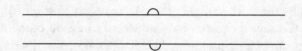

At apartment complex Z, 30 percent of the residents are men over the age of 18, and 40 percent are women over the age of 18. If there are 24 children living in the complex, how many total residents live in apartment complex Z ?

(A)   32
(B)   80
(C)   94
(D)   112
(E)   124

Here's How to Crack It

All together, the percentages of men and women add up to 70%, so that means 30% of the residents at this complex are children. Just set up an equation:

$$\frac{30}{100} = \frac{24}{Z}$$

Solving for Z, the total number of residents is 80. The answer is (B).

You could also Plug In the Answers. Choice (C) seems difficult, so why not start with (B), which has an easy number to work with? 30% of 80 = 24, and 40% of 80 = 32. So there is a total of 24 + 32 = 56 adults. If (B) is correct, there should be 24 kids. And guess what? That's just what the problem says.

Percent Increase or Decrease

Another type of percent problem you may see on the GMAT has to do with *percent increase* or *percent decrease*. In these problems, the trick is always to put the increase or decrease in terms of the *original* amount. See the following example:

The cost of a one-family home was $120,000 in 1980. In 1988, the price had increased to $180,000. What was the percent increase in the cost of the home?

(A)   60%
(B)   55%
(C)   50%
(D)   40%
(E)   33.3%

Here's How to Crack It

The actual increase was $60,000. To find the percent increase, set up the following equation:

$$\frac{\text{amount of increase}}{\text{original amount}} = \frac{x}{100}$$

In this case, $\dfrac{\$60,000}{\$120,000} = \dfrac{x}{100}$. So, $x = 50$ and the answer is (C).

To solve a percent *decrease* problem, simply put the amount of the decrease over the original amount.

What's the Original Amount?

GMAT test-writers like to see if they can trick you into mistaking which number was the original amount. On percent decrease problems (sometimes called "percent less" problems), the original is the larger number; on percent increase problems (sometimes called "percent greater" problems), the original is the smaller number.

DRILL 11
The answers to these questions can be found in Part V.

1. What is the quotient when 0.25% of 600 is divided by 0.25 of 600 ?

   (A)   10
   (B)   1
   (C)   0.1
   (D)   0.01
   (E)   0.001

2. A department store receives a shipment of 1,000 shirts, for which it pays $9,000. The store sells the shirts at a price 80 percent above cost for one month, after which it reduces the price of the shirts to 20 percent above cost. The store sells 75 percent of the shirts during the first month and 50 percent of the remaining shirts afterward. How much gross income did sales of the shirts generate?

   (A) $10,000
   (B) $10,800
   (C) $12,150
   (D) $13,500
   (E) $16,200

3. A certain gas station discounts the price per gallon of all gasoline purchased after the first 10 gallons by 10 percent. The total per gallon discount for 25 gallons of gas purchased at this station is what percent of the total per gallon discount for 20 gallons of gas?

   (A)   80%
   (B)   100%
   (C)   116.7%
   (D)   120%
   (E)   140%

4. If 70 percent of the female and 90 percent of the male students in the senior class at a certain school are going on the senior trip and the senior class is 60 percent female, what percent of the senior class is going on the senior trip?

   (A)   82%
   (B)   80%
   (C)   78%
   (D)   76%
   (E)   72%

5. If 75 percent of all Americans own an automobile, 15 percent of all Americans own a bicycle, and 20 percent of all Americans own neither an automobile nor a bicycle, then what percent of Americans own *both* an automobile and a bicycle?

    (A)   0%
    (B)   1.33%
    (C)   3.75%
    (D)   5%
    (E)   10%

Compound Interest

Another type of percent problem involves **compound interest**. If you kept $1,000 in the bank for a year at 6% simple interest, you would get $60 in interest at the end of the year. Compound interest would pay you slightly more. Let's look at a compound-interest problem:

Ms. Lopez deposits $100 in an account that pays 20% interest, compounded semiannually. How much money will there be in the account at the end of one year?

    (A) $118.00
    (B) $120.00
    (C) $121.00
    (D) $122.00
    (E) $140.00

Easy Process of Elimination

How would you work this problem if you were running out of time, or not sure how to find compound interest? Look for answer choices that can be eliminated via POE. The question asks for compound interest but (B) is the calculation of simple interest. Because finding simple interest is how to start a compound interest problem, (B) is a partial answer and can be eliminated. If you know that compound interest is always a *little bit* more than simple interest, you can eliminate (A) and (E) via Ballparking. Solving this problem from here requires knowledge of calculating compound interest. But, if you were having difficulty with this problem or were running out of time, POE can make this a fifty-fifty guess!

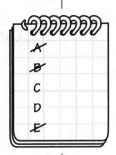

Here's How to Crack It

To find compound interest, divide the interest into as many parts as are being compounded. For example, if you're compounding interest semiannually, you divide the interest into two equal parts. If you're compounding quarterly, you divide the interest into four equal parts.

When Ms. Lopez deposited $100 into her account at a rate of 20% compounded semiannually, the bank divided the interest into two equal parts. Halfway through the year, the bank put the first half of the interest into her account. In this case, because the full rate was 20% compounded semiannually, the bank deposited 10% of $100 (10% of $100 = $10). Halfway through the year, Ms. Lopez had $110.

For the second half of the year, the bank paid 10% interest on the $110 (10% of $110 = $11). At the end of the year, Ms. Lopez had $121.00 in her account. She earned $1 more than she would have earned if the account had paid only simple interest. The answer is (C).

―――――――――○―――――――――

AVERAGES

To find the **average** of a list of n numbers, simply add the numbers and divide by n. For example:

Reminder!
Averaging problems often have easy eliminations, so be sure to look for them—*before* you solve.

$$\text{The average of 10, 3, and 5 is } \frac{10+3+5}{3} = 6.$$

A good way to handle average problems is to set them up in the same way every time. Whenever you see the word *average*, you should think:

$$\frac{\text{total sum of the items}}{\text{total number of the items}} = \text{average}$$

A One-Step Average Problem

In a simple problem, GMAC will give you two parts of this equation, and it will be up to you to figure out the third. Let's warm up those old average skills.

―――――――――○―――――――――

What is the average (arithmetic mean) of the numbers 3, 4, 5, and 8 ?

Here's How to Crack It

In this case, they've given us the actual numbers, which means we know the total sum (3 + 4 + 5 + 8 = 20) and the total number of items (there are four numbers). What we're missing is the average.

$$\frac{\text{total sum of the items}}{\text{total number of the items}} = \text{average} \qquad \frac{20}{4} = x \qquad x = 5$$

―――――――――○―――――――――

Here's another one:

_____◯_____

If the average (arithmetic mean) of 7 numbers is 5, what is the sum of the numbers?

Here's How to Crack It

In this case we know the total number of items and the average, but not the total sum of the numbers.

$$\frac{\text{total sum of the items}}{\text{total number of the items}} = \text{average} \qquad \frac{x}{7} = 5 \qquad x = 35$$

_____◯_____

A Two-Step Average Problem

This is the same problem you just did, made a little more difficult:

_____◯_____

The average (arithmetic mean) of 7 numbers is 5. If two of the numbers are 11 and 14, what is the average of the remaining numbers?

Here's How to Crack It

Always set up an average problem the way we showed you above. With more complicated average problems, take things one sentence at a time. The first sentence yields:

$$\frac{\text{total sum of the items}}{\text{total number of the items}} = \text{average} \qquad \frac{x}{7} = 5 \qquad x = 35$$

> ### The Average Test-Taker
>
> A common mistake by the average test-taker is thinking they can take the average of two averages. Take a look at the following question:
>
> > If Fred's average score on his first two tests was 70, and his average score on his next three tests was 80, what was his average score on all the tests?
>
> The average test-taker wants to say the answer is 75, which is just the average of 70 and 80. This test-taker either forgets, ignores, or misses the information that the first average was based on two tests, while the second average was based on three tests. Therefore, the average score is not 75, and the average test-taker would get this question wrong.
>
> Avoid this mistake by slowing down and reading the full question!

The sum of *all* the numbers is 35. If two of those numbers are 11 and 14, then the sum of the remaining numbers is 35 − (11 + 14), or 10. The question asks, "What is the average of the remaining numbers?" Again, let's set this up properly:

$$\frac{\text{total sum of the remaining numbers}}{\text{total number of the remaining numbers}} = \text{average} \qquad \frac{10}{5} = y \qquad y = 2$$

Why did we divide the total sum of the remaining numbers by 5? There were only 5 remaining numbers!

Medians and Modes

Calculating the average of a list of numbers is one way to find the "middle" of these numbers, but there are two other ways that yield slightly different results. To find the **median** of a list of n numbers, just reorder the numbers from least to greatest, and pick the middle number.

If n is odd, this is a piece of cake:

The median of 4, 7, 12, 14, 20 = 12.

If n is even, it's still easy—just add the two middle numbers together and divide by 2:

The median of 4, 12, 14, 20 $= \dfrac{12 + 14}{2} = 13$.

To find the **mode** of a list of n numbers, just pick the number that occurs most frequently…

The mode of 5, 6, 3, 9, 3, 28, 3, 5 = 3.

…but remember that a list of numbers *can* have more than one mode:

The modes of 3, 3, 3, 4, 5, 5, 5 = both 3 and 5.

Here's a relatively easy problem:

> **Mean**
> When a question refers to an average, the words "arithmetic mean" will often follow in parentheses. This is not just to make the problem sound scarier. **Arithmetic mean** is the precise term for the process of finding an average that we've illustrated in the problems above.

4, 6, 3, y

If the mode of the list of numbers above is 3, then what is the average (arithmetic mean) of the list?

(A) 7
(B) 3
(C) 4
(D) 9
(E) 12

Here's How to Crack It

The mode of the list of numbers is 3, which means that y must also equal 3 (because the mode is the number that occurs most frequently in the list). So now all we have to do is find the average of 4, 6, 3, and 3. The correct answer is (C).

RANGE

To find the range of a list of n numbers, take the least number and subtract it from the greatest number. This measures how widely the numbers are dispersed.

The range of 4, 3, 8, 12, 23, 37 = 37 − 3 = 34.

DRILL 12

The answers to these questions can be found in Part V.

$$\{1, 4, 6, y\}$$

1. If the average (arithmetic mean) of the set of numbers above is 6, then what is the median?

    (A)   5
    (B)   6
    (C)   7
    (D)   13
    (E)   24

2. Steven has run a certain number of laps around a track at an average (arithmetic mean) time per lap of 51 seconds. If he runs one additional lap in 39 seconds and reduces his average time per lap to 49 seconds, how many laps did he run at an average time per lap of 51 seconds?

    (A)   2
    (B)   5
    (C)   6
    (D)   10
    (E)   12

3. A certain seafood restaurant gets a delivery of fresh seafood every day of the week. If the delivery company charges d dollars per delivery and c cents per delivered item and the restaurant has an average (arithmetic mean) of x items delivered per day, then which of the following is an expression for the total cost, in dollars, of one week's deliveries?

    (A) $\dfrac{7cdx}{100}$

    (B) $d + \dfrac{7cx}{100}$

    (C) $7d + \dfrac{xc}{100}$

    (D) $7d + \dfrac{7xc}{100}$

    (E) $7cdx$

4. If Set X contains 10 consecutive integers and the sum of the 5 least members of the set is 265, then what is the sum of the 5 greatest members of the set?

(A) 290
(B) 285
(C) 280
(D) 275
(E) 270

$$\{3, 5, 9, 13, y\}$$

5. If the average (arithmetic mean) and the median of the set of numbers shown above are equal, then what is the value of y ?

(A) 7
(B) 8
(C) 10
(D) 15
(E) 17

6. During a five-day period, Monday through Friday, the average (arithmetic mean) high temperature was 86 degrees Fahrenheit. What was the high temperature on Friday?

(1) The average high temperature for Monday through Thursday was 87 degrees Fahrenheit.
(2) The high temperature on Friday reduced the average high temperature for the five-day period by 1 degree Fahrenheit.

(A) Statement (1) ALONE is sufficient, but statement (2) alone is not sufficient.
(B) Statement (2) ALONE is sufficient, but statement (1) alone is not sufficient.
(C) BOTH statements TOGETHER are sufficient, but NEITHER statement ALONE is sufficient.
(D) EACH statement ALONE is sufficient.
(E) Statements (1) and (2) TOGETHER are not sufficient.

7. The average (arithmetic mean) of integers r, s, t, u, and v is 100. Are exactly two of the integers greater than 100 ?

(1) Three of the integers are less than 50.
(2) None of the integers is equal to 100.

(A) Statement (1) ALONE is sufficient, but statement (2) alone is not sufficient.
(B) Statement (2) ALONE is sufficient, but statement (1) alone is not sufficient.
(C) BOTH statements TOGETHER are sufficient, but NEITHER statement ALONE is sufficient.
(D) EACH statement ALONE is sufficient.
(E) Statements (1) and (2) TOGETHER are not sufficient.

8. At Company R, the average (arithmetic mean) age of executive employees is 54 years old and the average age of non-executive employees is 34 years old. What is the average age of all the employees at Company R ?

   (1) There are 10 executive employees at Company R.
   (2) The number of non-executive employees at Company R is four times the number of executive employees at Company R.

   (A) Statement (1) ALONE is sufficient, but statement (2) alone is not sufficient.
   (B) Statement (2) ALONE is sufficient, but statement (1) alone is not sufficient.
   (C) BOTH statements TOGETHER are sufficient, but NEITHER statement ALONE is sufficient.
   (D) EACH statement ALONE is sufficient.
   (E) Statements (1) and (2) TOGETHER are not sufficient.

9. The new recruits of a military organization who score more than 2 standard deviations below the mean of their physical conditioning test are required to retest. If the test scores are normally distributed and have an arithmetic mean of 72, what is the score at or below which the recruits are required to retest?

   (1) The range between the 3rd standard deviation above the mean and the 3rd standard deviation below the mean is 30.
   (2) The 3rd standard deviation above the mean is 87.

   (A) Statement (1) ALONE is sufficient, but statement (2) alone is not sufficient.
   (B) Statement (2) ALONE is sufficient, but statement (1) alone is not sufficient.
   (C) BOTH statements TOGETHER are sufficient, but NEITHER statement ALONE is sufficient.
   (D) EACH statement ALONE is sufficient.
   (E) Statements (1) and (2) TOGETHER are not sufficient.

APPLIED ARITHMETIC

GMAT is likely to test arithmetic concepts based on scenarios that track to real-world scenarios. In addition, Applied Arithmetic also considers specific strategies for working through some thorny questions.

Many times, these questions come in the form of word problems. This question format is easy to misread and misunderstand, so make sure you're working through those problems carefully and meticulously to prevent any avoidable errors.

RATE PROBLEMS

Any problem that mentions planes, trains, cars, bicycles, distance, miles per hour, or any other travel-related terminology is asking you to solve a rate problem. You may remember that you can use the formula *distance = rate × time* to solve these types of problems.

We're going to use a **Rate Pie** to keep track of the information in a rate problem. Here's what it looks like:

<table>
<tr><td>

Two Out of Three Ain't Bad

For Data Sufficiency problems, as soon as you have two of the pieces of the Rate Pie, you have sufficient information to find the other piece.

</td></tr>
</table>

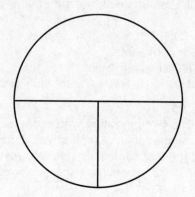

If a problem gives you the rate and time, the pieces on the bottom, you multiply to get the distance. If you have the distance, the piece on the top, and one of the pieces on the bottom, you divide to get the other bottom piece. As soon as you know that you are dealing with a rate problem, draw a Rate Pie and start filling in what you know.

The Rate Pie is really just a different way of writing the *distance = rate × time* formula. It works well for GMAT problems, however, because GMAT problems often involve multiple steps. So, the pie helps you to see what information you have and what you need to find.

Let's try a problem:

Pam and Sue drove in the same car to a business meeting that was 120 miles away. Pam drove to the meeting at 60 miles per hour and Sue drove back, along the same route, at 50 miles per hour. How many more minutes did it take Sue to drive the distance than it took Pam?

(A)   4
(B)   10
(C)   20
(D)   24
(E)   30

Here's How to Crack It

Since the problem deals with rates, you need a Rate Pie. In fact, since there is rate information for both Pam and Sue, you need two Rate Pies—one for Pam and one for Sue.

Pam   Sue

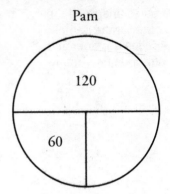   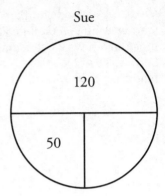

Once you draw the pies, you can transfer the information that you know to each pie. Since Pam and Sue drove along the same route, the distance is 120 miles for each pie. Pam's rate is 60 miles per hour, and Sue's rate is 50 miles per hour. Transfer that information to the pies, too.

To use the pie, remember that if you have the piece at the top and one of the pieces on the bottom, you divide to find the other piece. So, Pam's time is $120 \div 60 = 2$ and Sue's time is $120 \div 50 = 2\frac{2}{5}$. The pies made it easy to see how to find the time for each driver.

Pam   Sue

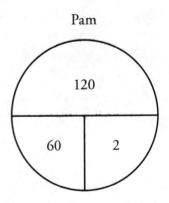   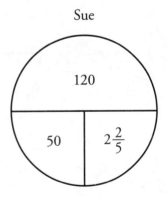

The problem asks how many more minutes it took Sue to drive the distance than it took Pam. Start by subtracting $2\frac{2}{5} - 2 = \frac{2}{5}$ to find that it took Sue $\frac{2}{5}$ of an hour longer. Now, just convert to minutes: $60 \times \frac{2}{5} = 24$. The answer is (D).

Now, let's look at a slightly harder problem:

Easy Eliminations
Choices (A) and (E) are unlikely because they are numbers in the problem. Choice (B) is just 45 ÷ 5, which is Fred's time to walk the whole distance.

Fred and Sam are standing 45 miles apart and they start walking in a straight line toward each other at the same time. If Fred walks at a constant speed of 4 miles per hour and Sam walks at a constant speed of 5 miles per hour, how many miles has Sam walked when they meet?

(A) 5
(B) 9
(C) 25
(D) 30
(E) 45

Here's How to Crack It

Since the problem is about rates, draw a Rate Pie. In this case, you may be wondering if you need one pie or two. You actually need one. Here's why: when dealing with rates, it is often helpful to think about what happens in a certain amount of time, such as an hour. In one hour, Fred walks 4 miles and Sam walks 5 miles. Since they are walking toward each other in a straight line, they have covered 9 miles of the distance between them at the end of an hour. Wait! Nine miles in an hour? That means that their combined rate is 9 miles per hour. That's what goes on the pie for the rate.

Here's A Tip!
When two items travel in a straight line toward each other, you can add their rates.

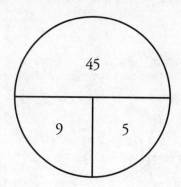

The other piece that you could fill in on the pie from the problem was the distance, 45 miles. Then, use the pie to find that Fred and Sam walk for 5 hours before they meet. (Remember that you divide the top piece of the pie by one of the pieces on the bottom to find the other bottom piece.)

The problem wants to know how many miles Sam had walked when he met Fred. So, set up one more pie. This time you know Sam's rate, 5 miles per hour, and you know that he walked for 5 hours.

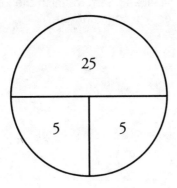

So, Sam walks 25 miles when he meets Fred. The answer is (C).

WORK PROBLEMS

Work problems are a type of rate problem. Rather than asking about a distance, these problems ask about a job or a part of a job. You can use a variation of the Rate Pie to solve these problems. Here's what it looks like:

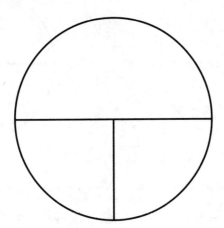

All that changes is that *work* replaces *distance* at the top of the pie. You use the **Work Pie** in the same way as the Rate Pie.

Working at a constant rate, Sam can finish a job in 3 hours. Mark, also working at a constant rate, can finish the same job in 12 hours. How many hours does it take Mark and Sam to finish the job if they work together each at his respective, constant rate?

(A)   1

(B) $2\frac{2}{5}$

(C) $2\frac{5}{8}$

(D) $3\frac{1}{4}$

(E)   4

Here's How to Crack It

Since the problem mentions a job being completed, you can use a Work Pie. You'll actually need two pies for the first step of the problem since you must find each worker's individual rate. Once you draw your pies, you can put each worker's time on the pie. You can also put 1 for the work since they each complete 1 job.

Sam   Mark

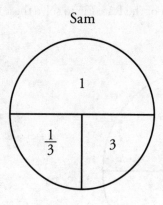   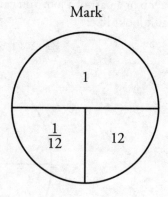

So, Sam's rate is $\frac{1}{3}$ and Mark's rate is $\frac{1}{12}$. What does that mean? Well, it means that Sam completes $\frac{1}{3}$ of the job every hour, while Mark completes $\frac{1}{12}$ of the job every hour.

To finish the problem, note that Mark and Sam work together. Since they are working together, you can combine their rates to find that they complete $\frac{1}{3} + \frac{1}{12} = \frac{5}{12}$ of the job every hour.

When people work together, you can combine their rates. Now, set up one more Work Pie. Use 1 for the amount of work and $\frac{5}{12}$ for the rate.

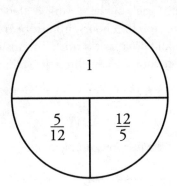

Divide the amount of work by the combined rate to find that the time to complete the job is $1 \div \frac{5}{12} = \frac{12}{5} = 2\frac{2}{5}$ hours. The correct answer is (B).

Same Problem, Different Approach

Another way to look at this problem is to realize that the actual job is never specified. But, wouldn't the problem be much easier to solve if you knew how many of something Sam and Mark needed to make? In other words, this problem can be approached as a Plug In.

Suppose that Sam and Mark were making widgets. Let's say that the complete job is to make 24 widgets. If Sam finishes the job in 3 hours, then he makes 8 widgets per hour. If Mark finishes the job in 12 hours, he makes 2 widgets per hour. Working together, they make $8 + 2 = 10$ widgets per hour.

Now, let's set the last step up using a Work Pie.

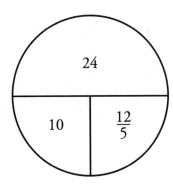

Again, it takes them $\frac{12}{5} = 2\frac{2}{5}$ hours to complete the job. The answer is (B).

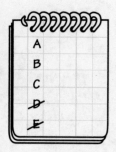

Easy Eliminations

It stands to reason that two men working together would take less time to finish a job than they would if each of them worked alone. Because Sam, working alone, could finish the job in 3 hours, it must be true that the two of them, working together, could do it in less time. The answer to this question has to be less than 3. Therefore, we can eliminate (D) and (E).

Here's a slightly harder version of the previous problem:

Working at a constant rate, Sam can finish a job in 3 hours. Mark, also working at a constant rate, can finish the same job in 12 hours. If they work together for 2 hours, how many minutes will it take Sam to finish the job, working alone at his constant rate?

(A)   5
(B)   20
(C)   30
(D)   60
(E)   120

Here's How to Crack It

This problem starts in the same way, so you can use the same Work Pies to find each worker's rate.

Sam

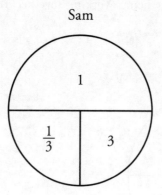

Mark

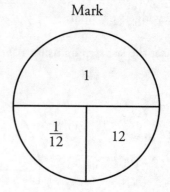

Now you need a new pie. For this pie, you know the combined rate, $\frac{1}{3} + \frac{1}{12} = \frac{5}{12}$, and that they work together for two hours.

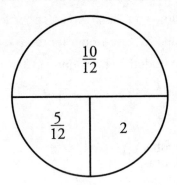

So, you now know that $\frac{5}{12} \times 2 = \frac{10}{12} = \frac{5}{6}$ of the job has been completed when Mark goes home. Sam must finish $\frac{1}{6}$ of the job on his own. Of course, you know Sam's rate, so just set up one last Work Pie.

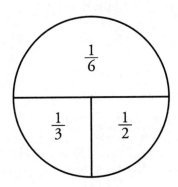

To find the time for Sam to finish the job, use the pie to find that $\frac{1}{6} \div \frac{1}{3} = \frac{1}{2}$, or 30 minutes. The correct answer is (C).

Challenge Question #5

Find the answers to all Challenge Questions in Part V!

James can complete a job in 6 hours and Sarah can complete the same job in $4\frac{1}{2}$ hours. If James works on the job alone for a certain amount of time and Sarah works on the job alone for half as long as James, and it takes 1 hour for them to complete the remainder of the job together, how long did James work on the job alone?

(A) 1 hour, 6 minutes
(B) 1 hour, 10 minutes
(C) 2 hours, 12 minutes
(D) 2 hours, 20 minutes
(E) 3 hours, 18 minutes

DRILL 13

The answers to these questions can be found in Part V.

1. If 2 men and 1 woman drop out of a certain class, the ratio of men to women in the class would be 8 to 7. If the current ratio of men to women in the class is 6 to 5, then how many men are currently in the class?

(A) 14
(B) 16
(C) 18
(D) 20
(E) 22

2. The average (arithmetic mean) of five numbers is 7. If the average of three of the numbers is 5, then what is the average of the other two numbers?

(A)   5
(B) 10
(C) 12
(D) 15
(E) 20

..

3. If $5,000 is invested in an account that earns 8% interest compounded semiannually, then the interest earned after one year would be how much greater than if the $5,000 had been invested at 8% simple yearly interest?

(A) $4
(B) $8
(C) $12
(D) $16
(D) $432

4. If the average of ten numbers is 10, then which of the following could be the standard deviation of the ten numbers?

I   0
II   10
III   20

(A)   I only
(B)   I and II
(C)   I and III
(D)   II and III
(E)   I, II, and III

5. List I: {y, 2, 4, 7, 10, 11}
   List II: {3, 3, 4, 6, 7, 10}

If the median of List I is equal to the sum of the median of List II and the mode of List II, then y equals

(A)   5
(B)   7
(C)   8
(D)   9
(E)   10

6. If Teena is driving at 55 miles per hour and is currently 7.5 miles behind Joe, who is driving at 40 miles per hour in the same direction, then in how many minutes will Teena be 15 miles ahead of Joe ?

(A)   15
(B)   60
(C)   75
(D)   90
(E)   105

7. At a local office, each trainee can stuff $\frac{2}{3}$ as many envelopes per day as a full-time worker. If there are $\frac{2}{5}$ as many trainees as there are full-time workers, then what fraction of all the envelopes stuffed in a day did the trainees stuff?

(A) $\frac{2}{19}$

(B) $\frac{2}{17}$

(C) $\frac{4}{19}$

(D) $\frac{4}{17}$

(E) $\frac{4}{15}$

8. Roger can chop down 4 trees in an hour. How long does it take Vincent to chop down 4 trees?

(1) Vincent spends 6 hours per day chopping down trees.
(2) Vincent takes twice as long as Roger to chop down trees.

(A) Statement (1) ALONE is sufficient, but statement (2) alone is not sufficient.
(B) Statement (2) ALONE is sufficient, but statement (1) alone is not sufficient.
(C) BOTH statements TOGETHER are sufficient, but NEITHER statement ALONE is sufficient.
(D) EACH statement ALONE is sufficient.
(E) Statements (1) and (2) TOGETHER are not sufficient.

9. Automobile A is traveling at two-thirds the speed that Automobile B is traveling. At what speed is Automobile A traveling?

(1) If both automobiles increased their speed by 10 miles per hour, Automobile A would be traveling at three-quarters the speed that Automobile B would be traveling.
(2) If both automobiles decreased their speed by 10 miles per hour, Automobile A would be traveling at half the speed that Automobile B would be traveling.

(A) Statement (1) ALONE is sufficient, but statement (2) alone is not sufficient.
(B) Statement (2) ALONE is sufficient, but statement (1) alone is not sufficient.
(C) BOTH statements TOGETHER are sufficient, but NEITHER statement ALONE is sufficient.
(D) EACH statement ALONE is sufficient.
(E) Statements (1) and (2) TOGETHER are not sufficient.

10. Renee rides her bicycle 20 miles in m minutes. If she rides x miles in 10 minutes at the same rate, which of the following is an expression for x, in terms of m ?

    (A) $\dfrac{m}{200}$

    (B) $\dfrac{m}{20}$

    (C) $\dfrac{m}{2}$

    (D) $2m$

    (E) $\dfrac{200}{m}$

11. Paul jogs along the same route every day at a constant rate for 80 minutes. What distance does he jog?

    (1) Yesterday, Paul began jogging at 5:00 P.M.
    (2) Yesterday, Paul had jogged 5 miles by 5:40 P.M. and 8 miles by 6:04 P.M.

    (A) Statement (1) ALONE is sufficient, but statement (2) alone is not sufficient.
    (B) Statement (2) ALONE is sufficient, but statement (1) alone is not sufficient.
    (C) BOTH statements TOGETHER are sufficient, but NEITHER statement ALONE is sufficient.
    (D) EACH statement ALONE is sufficient.
    (E) Statements (1) and (2) TOGETHER are not sufficient.

12. What is the value of integer x ?

    (1) $\sqrt[x]{64} = 4$
    (2) $x^2 = x + 6$

    (A) Statement (1) ALONE is sufficient, but statement (2) alone is not sufficient.
    (B) Statement (2) ALONE is sufficient, but statement (1) alone is not sufficient.
    (C) BOTH statements TOGETHER are sufficient, but NEITHER statement ALONE is sufficient.
    (D) EACH statement ALONE is sufficient.
    (E) Statements (1) and (2) TOGETHER are not sufficient.

13. If a, b, c, d, and x are all nonzero integers, is the product $ax \cdot (bx)^2 \cdot (cx)^3 \cdot (dx)^4$ negative?

(1) $a < c < x < 0$
(2) $b < d < x < 0$

(A) Statement (1) ALONE is sufficient, but statement (2) alone is not sufficient.
(B) Statement (2) ALONE is sufficient, but statement (1) alone is not sufficient.
(C) BOTH statements TOGETHER are sufficient, but NEITHER statement ALONE is sufficient.
(D) EACH statement ALONE is sufficient.
(E) Statements (1) and (2) TOGETHER are not sufficient.

Challenge Question #6

Find the answers to all Challenge Questions in Part V!

A bar over a digit in a decimal indicates an infinitely repeating decimal.

$333{,}333.\overline{3} \times (10^{-3} - 10^{-5}) =$

(A) $3{,}333.\overline{3}$
(B) $3{,}330$
(C) $333.\overline{3}$
(D) 330
(E) 0

Summary

o   The six arithmetic operations are addition, subtraction, multiplication, division, raising to a power, and finding a square root.

o   These operations must be performed in the proper order (**P**lease **E**xcuse **M**y **D**ear **A**unt **S**ally).

o   If you are adding or multiplying a group of numbers, you can regroup them in any order. This is called the **Associative Law**.

o   If you are adding or subtracting numbers with common factors, you can regroup them in the following way:

$$ab + ac = a(b + c)$$
$$ab - ac = a(b - c)$$

This is called the **Distributive Law**.

o   A fraction can be thought of in two ways:
   *   another way of expressing division
   *   as a $\dfrac{\text{part}}{\text{whole}}$

o   You must know how to add, subtract, multiply, and divide fractions. You must also know how to raise them to a power and find their roots.

o   Always reduce fractions (when you can) before doing a complicated operation. This will reduce your chances of making a careless error.

o   In tough fraction problems, always think $\dfrac{\text{part}}{\text{whole}}$ and *the rest*.

o   A decimal is just another way of expressing a fraction.

o   You must know how to add, subtract, multiply, and divide decimals.

o   In general, it is easier to work with fractions than with decimals, so convert decimals to fractions.

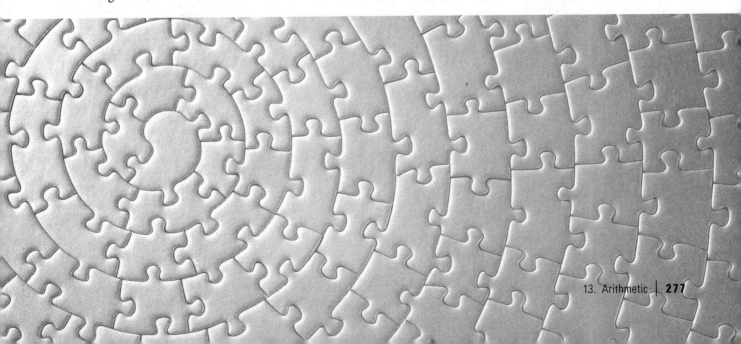

- A ratio is a fraction in all ways but one:

    - A fraction is a $\frac{\text{part}}{\text{whole}}$.

    - A ratio is a $\frac{\text{part}}{\text{part}}$.

    - In a ratio, the whole is the sum of all its parts.

- A percentage is just a fraction whose denominator is always 100.

- You must know the percentage shortcuts outlined in this chapter.

- In tough percent problems, like tough fraction problems, think $\frac{\text{part}}{\text{whole}}$ and *the rest*.

- In a percentage increase or decrease problem, you must put the amount of the increase or decrease over the *original* amount.

- In compound interest problems, the answer will always be *a little bit more* than it would be in a similar simple interest problem.

- To find the average of several values, add the values and divide the total by the number of values.

- Always set up average problems in the same way:

$$\frac{\text{total sum of the items}}{\text{total number of the items}} = \text{average}$$

- To find the median of a list of n numbers, reorder the numbers from least to greatest, and pick the middle number if n is odd. Take the average of the two middle numbers if n is even.

- To find the mode of a list of n numbers, pick the number that occurs most frequently.

- To find the range of a list of n numbers, subtract the smallest number from the greatest number.

- Rate problems and work problems can be solved using your handy Rate or Work Pies.

- The key to work problems is to think about how much of the job can be done in one hour. But remember, it is often easier to simply Plug In.

Chapter 14
Number Theory

Number Theory topics are general principles about numbers and how they interact that can prove useful for solving a variety of math problems. These principles are the Fundamental Theorem of Arithmetic, Least Common Multiples, Greatest Common Factors, Tests for Multiples and Factors, and the Role of Shared Prime Factors.

WHAT IS NUMBER THEORY?

For the purpose of the GMAT, number theory is information about various types of numbers and the interactions between those numbers. An understanding of number theory allows you to work through various problems on the GMAT that may otherwise be inaccessible.

As you work through this chapter, if you come across a concept that is unfamiliar, reference back to the Basic Principles of GMAT Math chapter for a refresher.

PRIMES

Fundamental Theorem of Arithmetic

The Fundamental Theorem of Arithmetic (also known as the Unique Prime Factorization Theorem) is the cornerstone of factorization. It states that every integer greater than 1 is either prime or can be written as the unique product of primes. A prime number has only itself and 1 as factors. Because of this, the number 1 is not prime, and the number 2 is the only even prime number. The list of prime numbers is a familiar cast of characters: 2, 3, 5, 7, 11, ..., 73, 79, 83, 89, 97, ...

Numbers that are not prime are called composite numbers. Each composite number can be factored into a unique set of prime factors that, when multiplied together, equal the number. For example, the prime factors of 42 are 2, 3, and 7. Note that order does not matter. $3 \times 7 \times 2 = 7 \times 3 \times 2 = 42$. The prime factors of 144 are 2, 2, 2, 2, 3, and 3. That is, $2 \times 2 \times 2 \times 2 \times 3 \times 3 = 144$. Every factorization of a composite number is unique to that number, that is, no two distinct composite numbers have the same prime factors. Many times, you'll see the use of exponents as shorthand for representing the prime factorization of a number. For example, the prime factorization of 144 shown above could be written as $2^4 \times 3^2$.

In order to factor an integer, start with the least prime number and continue until all factors are prime. For example, to factor 308, first divide by 2 to get 154, then divide by 2 again to get 77, then divide by 7 to get 11, which means that the prime factors of 308 are 2, 2, 7, and 11, or $2^2 \times 7 \times 11$.

How to Determine If an Integer Is Prime

In order to determine if an integer is prime, start with the least prime number, 2, and test whether the number is divisible by 2. Continue testing prime numbers up to the square root of the number. If none of the prime numbers less than or equal to the square root divide into the number, the number is prime.

Let's try 383. Start with the least prime number, 2. The number 383 is not divisible by 2. The square root of 383 is less than 20, which means that it is not necessary to test any prime greater than 20. Try 3, 5, 7, 11, 13, 17, and 19. None of the primes from 2 to 19 are factors of 383, which means that 383 is prime.

Suppose we want to determine if 3,119 is prime. The square root of 3,119 is less than 56. This means that if we test the prime numbers from 2 to 56 and find that none of those are factors of 3,119, then 3,119 is prime. As it turns out, 3,119 is prime.

How about 3,127? The square root of 3,127 is less than 56. Test to determine if any of the prime numbers from 2 to 56 is a factor of 3,127. When we test 53, we find out that 3,127 divided by 53 equals 59, which means that 3,127 is not prime.

At this point, you may be wondering how you are going to test all the prime factors between 2 and 53 in a reasonable time frame on test day. The good news is the GMAT rarely tests prime factors on numbers greater than 400. So, you'll likely only have to work with the prime numbers up to 20. In addition, knowing a few simple rules about how to determine if certain numbers are factors of another number is useful. These rules are covered in the section on Test for Multiples and Factors in this chapter.

Factorization

The factors of an integer x are comprised of all integers less than x that divide evenly into x. This includes the integer itself and 1. For example, the factors of 12 are 1, 2, 3, 4, 6, and 12. The prime factors of 12 are 2, 2, and 3. The GMAT may ask about distinct prime factors. The distinct prime factors of 12 are 2 and 3.

Every factor pairs with another factor. In the above example, 1 pairs with 12 ($1 \times 12 = 12$), 2 pairs with 6, and 3 pairs with 4.

Let's try another example. What are all the factors of 72? Start with 1 and 72, then 2 and 36, 3 and 24, 4 and 18, 6 and 12, and finally, 8 and 9. The factors of 72 are 1, 2, 3, 4, 6, 8, 9, 12, 18, 24, 36, and 72. The prime factors are 2, 2, 2, 3, and 3. The distinct prime factors are 2 and 3.

Least Common Multiple (LCM)

The least common multiple (LCM), also known as the lowest common multiple, or smallest common multiple of two or more integers, is the least positive integer that is divisible by a set of integers. For example, the LCM of 4 and 6 is 12, because 12 is the least number that is divisible by both 4 and 6.

In order to find the LCM of two numbers, determine the prime factorization of each number. The LCM is the product of each prime factor in either number raised to the higher power in either number. For example, what is the LCM of 36 and 45? The prime factors of 36 are 2, 2, 3, and 3, or $2^2 \times 3^2$. The prime factors of 45 are 3, 3, and 5, or $3^2 \times 5$. This means that the LCM has the factors of 2^2, 3^2, and 5. The LCM of 36 and 45 is $2^2 \times 3^2 \times 5 = 180$.

In order to find the LCM of three or more numbers, follow the same method as above. For example, what is the LCM of 12, 15, and 20? The prime factors of 12 are 2, 2, and 3, or $2^2 \times 3$. The prime factors of 15 are 3×5. The prime factors of 20 are 2, 2, and 5, or $2^2 \times 5$. This means that the LCM of 12, 15, and 20 has the factors 2^2, 3, and 5. So the LCM of 12, 15, and 20 is $2^2 \times 3 \times 5 = 60$.

Here's an example of a GMAT question that requires use of LCM:

A certain light has three bulbs that light up at different intervals. The first lights up every 6 minutes, the second lights up every 8 minutes, and the third lights up every 14 minutes. If all three bulbs lit up simultaneously at 11:04 A.M., at what time will all three bulbs light up simultaneously next?

(A) 12:48 P.M.
(B) 1:48 P.M.
(C) 1:52 P.M.
(D) 2:48 P.M.
(E) 2:52 P.M.

Here's How to Crack It

In order to answer this question, determine the LCM of 6, 8, and 14. The prime factors of 6 are 2 and 3; the prime factors of 8 are 2, 2, and 2, or 2^3; the prime factors of 14 are 2 and 7. The LCM of 6, 8, and 14 is $2^3 \times 3 \times 7 = 168$, which means the three bulbs light up together every 168 minutes, or every 2 hours and 48 minutes. They all lit up together at 11:04 A.M. Adding 2 hours and 48 minutes means that they will light up together again at 1:52 P.M. The correct answer is (C).

Here's another one:

Boris has the same number of orange, purple, and green marbles that he wants to arrange in groups. He wants to arrange the orange marbles in groups of 15, the purple marbles in groups of 13, and the green marbles in groups of 14. What is the least number of marbles of each color Boris must have in order to make these groups and have no marbles left over?

(A)   546
(B)   910
(C) 1,365
(D) 2,730
(E) 5,460

Here's How to Crack It

Begin by determining the LCM of 13, 14, and 15. The only prime factor of 13 is 13. The prime factors of 14 are 2 and 7, and the prime factors of 15 are 3 and 5. All three numbers have no prime factors in common. The LCM of 13, 14, 15 equals $2 \times 3 \times 5 \times 7 \times 13 = 13 \times 14 \times 15 = 2,730$. The correct answer is (D).

Greatest Common Factor (GCF)

The greatest common factor (also known as highest common factor and greatest common divisor) of two or more positive integers is the greatest positive factor they have in common. One way to determine the GCF is to find the product of all the prime numbers that appear in the prime factorization of all members of a set of numbers. For example, to find the GCF of 78 and 130, first determine the prime factors of each number. The prime factors of 78 are 2, 3, and 13, and the prime factors of 130 are 2, 5, and 13. Both numbers have the prime factors 2 and 13 in common, which means the GCF of 78 and 130 is $2 \times 13 = 26$.

Here's an example question that requires use of GCF:

The greatest common factor of 8 and positive integer k is 2, and the greatest common factor of k and 105 is 7. Which of the following could be the greatest common factor of k and 120 ?

(A) 2
(B) 3
(C) 4
(D) 5
(E) 6

Here's How to Crack It

The prime factors of 8 are 2, 2, and 2, or 2^3. The GCF of 8 and k is 2. Because the GCF of 8 and k is 2, k has only one factor of 2. If k had more than one factor of 2, then the GCF of 8 and k would be a multiple of 2. The prime factors of 105 are 3, 5, and 7. The GCF of 105 and k is 7. Because the GCF of 105 and k is 7, k does not have factors of 3 and 5. If k had factors of 3 or 5, then the GCF of 105 and k would be a multiple of 7. The prime factors of 120 are 2, 2, 2, 3, and 5. The question asks which of the following could be the GCF of k and 120. Now look at the answer choices. We know that 2 is a factor of k, so keep (A). Because the GCF of 105 and k is 7, it has already been established that 3 is not a factor of k. Therefore, it is not possible for the GCF of k and 120 to be 3. Eliminate (B). Similarly, because the GCF of k and 8 is 2, 4 is not a factor of k. Eliminate (C). Eliminate (D) because 5 is not a factor of k. Finally, eliminate (E) because 6 is a multiple of 3 and 3 is not a factor of k. The correct answer is (A).

Relation Between LCM and GCF

One interesting property of the LCM and GCF of any two positive integers is that the product of the LCM and GCF of positive integers x and y is equal to the product of x and y. For example, the LCM of 21 and 35 is $3 \times 5 \times 7 = 105$. The GCF of 21 and 35 is 7. The product of 7 and 105 is equal to 735, which is equal to the product of 21 and 35. This property does not hold true for more than two integers.

In other words, for any two positive integers m and n, $mn = \text{LCM}(m, n) \times \text{GCF}(m, n)$. This means that if you know either the LCM or the GCF of any two positive integers, you can determine the other by dividing it into the product of the integers. For example, the GCF of 72 and 48 is 24. What is the LCM? The product of 72 and 48 is 3,456. Divide 3,456 by 24 to get 144, which is the LCM of 72 and 48.

Prime and Coprime Numbers

A number is prime if its factors are only 1 and itself. Two integers are coprime (also known as relatively prime or mutually prime) if the only positive integer that is a factor of both numbers is 1. In other words, two integers are coprime if the GCF of both numbers is 1. For example, 51 and 286 are coprime because they have no common factors other than 1. The numbers 51 and 374 are not coprime, because they both have a factor of 17.

Patterns and Cycles

The GMAT frequently asks questions that require you to recognize various patterns and cycles. For example, consider powers of 7. $7^0 = 1$; $7^1 = 7$; $7^2 = 49$; $7^3 = 343$; $7^4 = 2,401$; $7^5 = 16,807$, etc. Notice the pattern of the units digit of each power of 7: 1, 7, 9, 3, and then the same cycle repeats. Here are some of the frequent examples of patterns that may appear on the GMAT.

Remainder Cycles When Dividing by Integers

When dividing by an integer s, there are s possible remainders, 0 through $s - 1$. These remainders cycle in an infinite loop. For example, 17 divided by 5 has a remainder 2, 18 divided by 5 has a remainder 3, 19 divided by 5 has a remainder 4, 20 divided by 5 has a remainder 0, 21 divided by 5 has a remainder 1, and then the cycle repeats.

Units Digit Cycles

The GMAT sometimes asks questions that require you to determine the units digit of a number raised to a very high power. For example, if integer $g > 0$, what is the remainder when 49^{16g+3} is divided by 5? In order to answer the question, we need to know the units digit of 49^{16g+3}. Plug in $g = 1$. $16 \times 1 + 3 = 19$, which means that we need to know the units digit of 49^{19}. Consider the patterns of the units digit of powers of 9. They are as follows: $9^1 = 9$; $9^2 = 81$; $9^3 = 729$, and so on. The pattern is 9, 1, 9, 1, etc. When 9 is raised to any even power, the units digit is 1, and when 9 is raised to any odd power, the units digit is 9. 19 is odd, so the units digit of 49^{19} is 9. The remainder when 5 is divided into any integer ending in 9 is 4. Plug In $g = 2$. $16 \times 2 + 3 = 35$, which is odd. This means that the units digit of 49^{19} is 9, and the remainder when 49^{19} is divided by 5 is 4.

Tests for Multiples and Factors

The GMAT frequently asks questions that require knowing whether a number is divisible by commonly used integers. The chart below shows divisibility shortcuts for the integers 2 through 13.

Number	Test for divisibility	Examples
2	All even numbers (numbers ending in 0, 2, 4, 6, and 8) are divisible by 2.	4,832 (even) is divisible by 2. 4,831 (odd) is not divisible by 2.
3	If the sum of the digits of a number is divisible by 3, then the number is divisible by 3.	The sum of the digits of 6,711 is 15, which is divisible by 3. So 6,711 is divisible by 3.
4	If the last two digits of a number are divisible by 4, then the number is divisible by 4.	The last two digits of 4,776 are 76, which is divisible by 4. So 4,776 is divisible by 4.
5	Any number ending in 0 or 5 is divisible by 5.	3,745 and 2,670 are divisible by 5.
6	Any even number divisible by 3 is divisible by 6.	The sum of the digits of 2,778 is 24, which is divisible by 3. So 2,778 is an even number divisible by 3, which means it is divisible by 6.
7	Remove the last digit, double it, and then subtract it from the truncated original number. Repeat until what remains is either divisible by 7 or not.	Consider 3,248. $324 - 16 = 308$; $30 - 16 = 14$, which is divisible by 7. So 3,248 is divisible by 7.
8	If the last three digits of a number are divisible by 8, then the number is divisible by 8.	The last three digits of 103,488 are 488, which is divisible by 8. So 103,488 is divisible by 8.
9	If the sum of the digits of a number is divisible by 9, then the number is divisible by 9.	The sum of the digits of 8,343 is 18, which is divisible by 9. So 8,343 is divisible by 9.
10	Any number ending in 0 is divisible by 10.	450, 9,230, and 107,770 are divisible by 10.
11	Remove the last digit and subtract it from the remaining truncated number. Repeat until what remains is either divisible by 11 or not.	Consider 8,173. $817 - 3 = 814$; $81 - 4 = 77$, which is divisible by 11. So 8,173 is divisible by 11.
12	Any number divisible by 3 and 4 is also divisible by 12.	Consider 38,424. The sum of the digits is 21, which is divisible by 3. The last two digits are 24, which is divisible by 4. So 38,424 is divisible by 3 and 4, which means it is divisible by 12.
13	Remove the last number, multiply it by 4, and then add it to the remaining truncated number. Repeat until what remains is divisible by 13 or not.	Consider 18,902. $1,890 + 8 = 1,898$; $189 + 32 = 221$; $22 + 4 = 26$, which is divisible by 13. So 18,902 is divisible by 13.

Here's an example for which divisibility tests may prove useful:

---

b is a multiple of 7. Is *ab* a multiple of 1,638 ?

(1)   *a* is divisible by 39
(2)   Every factor of 42 is a factor of *a*

Here's How to Crack It

This is a Yes/No Data Sufficiency question, so be prepared to Plug In more than once. Begin by working with the question. In order to solve this problem, we need to find the prime factors of 1,638. It is even, so it is divisible by 2. Divide 1,638 by 2 to get 819. The sum of the digits of 819 is 18, which means that 819 is divisible by 9. Divide 819 by 9 to get 91, which is equal to 7×13. The prime factors of 1,638 are 2, 3, 3, 7, and 13. In order for *ab* to be a multiple of 1,638, which is another way of asking if 1,638 is a factor of *ab*, *ab* must share factors with 1,638. In other words, *ab* must have factors of 2, 3, 3, 7, and 13. We know that *b* is a multiple of 7, which means that 7 is a factor of *ab*. If *a* or *b* has the factors 2, 3, 3, and 13, then *ab* has all the factors of 1,638. Evaluate each statement individually.

Statement (1) states that *a* is divisible by 39, which is equal to 3×13. This means that *ab* is a multiple of 3, 7, and 13. However, this provides no information about if *ab* is a multiple of 2 or the second factor of 3. If *ab* is a multiple of 2 and the second factor of 3, then the answer to the question is "Yes." If *ab* is not a multiple of 2 or the second factor of 3, then the answer to the question is "No." Because this statement produces two different answers to the question, the statement is insufficient. Write down BCE.

Statement (2) states that every factor of 42 is a factor of *a*, which is another way of stating that *a* is divisible by 42. The prime factors of 42 are 2, 3, and 7. This statement does not provide any information about whether *ab* is a multiple of 13 or the second factor of 3. If *a* is a multiple of 13 and the second factor of 3, then the answer to the question is "Yes." If *a* is not a multiple of 13 or the second factor of 3, then the answer to the question is "No." Because the statement produces two different answers to the question, the statement is insufficient. Eliminate (B).

Now evaluate the statements together. From Statement (1), we know that 3, 7, and 13 are factors of *ab*, and from Statement (2), we know that 2, 3, and 7 are factors of *ab*. Taken together, 2, 3, 7, and 13 are factors of *ab*. However, this does not provide any information about if *ab* is a multiple of the second factor of 3. This means that statements (1) and (2) together are insufficient. Eliminate (C).

The correct answer is (E).

DRILL 14

The answers to these questions can be found in Part V.

1. What is the remainder when integer n is divided by 13 ?

   (1) When n is divided by 91 the remainder is 83.
   (2) When n is divided by 52 the remainder is 18.

2. If x is an integer, is n prime?

   (1) $x! = n$
   (2) $0 \leq x \leq 2$

3. If $\dfrac{17!}{7^m}$ is an integer, what is the greatest possible value of m ?

   (A) 2
   (B) 3
   (C) 4
   (D) 5
   (E) 6

4. If a is a multiple of 7, is ab a multiple of 21?

   (1) Every factor of 65 is also a factor of b.
   (2) b is divisible by 51.

5. Is m divisible by 14 ?

   (1) The greatest common factor of m and 42 is 6.
   (2) The greatest common factor of m and 72 is 24.

Summary

- Number theory is information about various types of numbers and the interactions between those numbers.

- The Fundamental Theorem of Arithmetic states that every integer greater than 1 is either prime or can be written as the unique product of primes.

- The Least Common Multiple is the least positive integer that is divisible by at least two integers.

- The Greatest Common Factor of two or more positive integers is the greatest positive factor they have in common.

- Prime numbers only have factors of 1 and itself. Coprime numbers are two integers for which 1 is the only positive, common factor.

- Be on the lookout for remainder patterns, units digit patterns, and opportunities to apply divisibility rules to make challenging questions a little less challenging.

Chapter 15
Algebra

Algebra is usually all about writing equations. In this chapter, we'll show you a foolproof way to write the equations you *need* to write, give you a review of the quadratic formula, and teach you how to do simultaneous equations.

Roughly half of the questions on the Quantitative Reasoning section of the GMAT involve traditional algebra. This chapter introduces the algebraic concepts that you will need to know in order to answer questions on the GMAT. It also focuses on ways to find algebraic solutions to common problems on the GMAT.

Earlier in this book we discussed Plugging In—a strategy to turn even the most difficult Algebra problems into Arithmetic. While working through this chapter, be on the lookout for opportunities to practice this critical skill.

However, it is also important to have a firm foundation to effectively deploy the Plugging In strategy. Treat this chapter as a way to build that foundation.

Avoiding Common Errors

We'll add a third rule that you won't find written in any math book.

3. Equations cannot become expressions.

If you've ever started working with one side of an equation without writing down both sides of the equation, you've broken this rule. By always writing down both sides of the equation, you can avoid wasting time and making silly mistakes.

While it is easiest to solve this problem by doing the basic algebra and solve for *x*, it is also possible to solve this question with one of the Plugging In methods. What type of Plugging In strategy could be used to solve this problem?

Two Simple Rules

Before we review some very specific types of algebra that GMAC likes to test, let's review the two basic rules that are true for any algebraic situation. These two rules are used pretty much any time that you solve a problem algebraically.

1. Collect like terms. Get all the *x*s on one side of the equals sign and all the numbers on the other.
2. Whatever you do to one side of an equation, you need to do to the other side of the equation. Did you multiply one side by 5? Then you need to multiply the other side of the equation by 5, as well.

Solving Equalities

If there is one variable in an equation, isolate the variable on one side of the equation and solve it. Let's try an example of this type, although a question this easy wouldn't actually be seen on the GMAT. This one is just for practice.

If $x - 5 = 3x + 2$, then $x =$

(A) -8

(B) -7

(C) $-\dfrac{7}{2}$

(D) $\dfrac{7}{5}$

(E) $\dfrac{10}{3}$

Here's How to Crack It

Get all of the xs on one side of the equation. If we subtract x from both sides, we have:

$$
\begin{aligned}
x - 5 &= 3x + 2 \\
\underline{-x} & \underline{-x} \\
-5 &= 2x + 2
\end{aligned}
$$

Now subtract 2 from both sides:

$$
\begin{aligned}
-5 &= 2x + 2 \\
\underline{-2} & \underline{-2} \\
-7 &= 2x
\end{aligned}
$$

Finally, divide both sides by 2:

$$
\frac{-7}{2} = \frac{2x}{2}
$$

$$
x = -\frac{7}{2}
$$

The answer is (C).

───────────────○───────────────

Solving Inequalities

To solve inequalities, you must be able to recognize the following symbols:

$>$	is greater than
$<$	is less than
$\geq$	is greater than or equal to
$\leq$	is less than or equal to

As with an equation, you can add a number to or subtract a number from both sides of an inequality without changing it; you can collect similar terms and simplify them. In fact, an inequality behaves just like a regular equation except in one way:

> If you multiply or divide both sides of an inequality by a negative number, the direction of the inequality symbol changes.

For example,

$$-2x > 5$$

To solve for x, you would divide both sides by -2, just as you would in an equality. But when you do, the sign flips:

$$\frac{-2x}{-2} < \frac{5}{-2}$$

$$x < -\frac{5}{2}$$

Solving Simultaneous Equations

If there are two equations, both of which have the same two variables, then it is possible to solve for both variables. An easy problem might look like this:

If $3x + 2y = 6$ and $5x - 2y = 10$, then $x = ?$

To solve simultaneous equations, add or subtract the equations so that one of the variables disappears.

$$
\begin{array}{r}
3x + 2y =\ \ 6 \\
+\ \ 5x - 2y = 10 \\
\hline
8x\ \ \ \ \ \ = 16 \\
\end{array}
$$

$$x = 2$$

Q: Are the following equations distinct?
(1) $3x + 21y = 12$
(2) $x + 7y = 4$
Go to page 294 for the answer.

In more difficult simultaneous equations, you'll find that neither of the variables will disappear when you try to add or subtract the two equations. In such cases, you must multiply both sides of one of the equations by some number in order to get the coefficient in front of the variable that you want to disappear to be the same in both equations. This sounds more complicated than it is. A difficult problem might look like this:

If $3x + 2y = 6$ and $5x - y = 10$, then $x = ?$

Let's set it up the same way:

$$3x + 2y = 6$$

$$5x - y = 10$$

Unfortunately, in this example, neither adding nor subtracting the two equations gets rid of either variable. But look what happens when we multiply the bottom equation by 2:

$$3x + 2y = 6 \qquad \text{or} \qquad 3x + 2y = 6$$
$$(2)5x - (2)y = (2)10 \qquad\qquad \underline{+\ 10x - 2y = 20}$$
$$13x \qquad = 26 \qquad x = 2$$

> ### Equation Tricks and Traps
> $x + 3y - 7 = x^2(x^{-1}) + y$
>
> This looks like two variables in one equation, which would mean we need at least one more equation to solve, but look again. Because $x^2(x^{-1}) = x^{(2-1)} = x$, each side of the equation has only one x. The xs can be subtracted, leaving you with just one variable, y. The equation can be solved.

Building Algebraic Expressions

Sometimes, the GMAT provides an equation for you that contains all the information you need to solve the problem. In this case, you can go straight to working the equation by simplifying, substituting, factoring, or whatever method is necessary to solve the equation. For instance, the following equations provide everything you need to know in order to solve for x:

$$7 = x - 2$$
$$2x = 8$$
$$\frac{x + 2}{4} = 12$$

When presented with an equation that looks like one of the above, there is no preparation work to be executed in order to solve for x. However, the GMAT does not always provide fully written out equations like those above. Consider the following statements that describe equations:

7 is 2 less than x
Twice the value of x is 8
The sum of 2 and x, divided by 4, is 12

Statements like these do not lend themselves to immediately having mathematical operations done to them. Before completing any algebraic work, the sentences need to be built into algebraic expressions. Similar work needs to be done for problems that give information such as the following:

If y = 2x and 7 = y + 5, then what value is 4 less than x ?

The problem above combines two algebraic equations and a statement that describes an expression. Before working this question or the three prior statements, you need to build algebraic expressions and equations from the information provided.

Translating from English to Math

One of the skills required to build algebraic expressions correctly is to translate phrases or sentences into expressions or equations. This is a skill most commonly used on Quantitative Reasoning questions, but can show up during the Data Insights section. Use the following table to help translate some of the more common words into a familiar math operation.

Word	Equivalent Symbol
percent	$\overline{100}$
is	=
of, times, product	×
what (or any unknown value)	any variable (x, k, b)
sum	+
difference	−
fraction	$\dfrac{x}{y}$

A: No. Look at what equation (2) looks like multiplied by 3: $3(x + 7y) = 3(4)$ or $3x + 21y = 12$. Multiply both sides by 3 and equations (1) and (2) are identical. When one equation can be multiplied to produce the other, the equations are identical, not distinct.

Less Than, Greater Than

Depending on the context, the phrases *less than* and *greater than* yield different math symbols. For example, in the phrase *7 is less than 9*, the phrase *is less than* indicates an inequality. This is translated as $7 < 9$ and the phrase *is less than* is represented by the symbol <. However, in the phrase *7 less than x is 9*, the phrase *less than* indicates subtraction. This phrase can be rewritten as $x - 7 = 9$, and the phrase *less than* is represented by the subtraction symbol −.

The same is true of the phrases *is greater than* and *greater than*. The phrase *is greater than* is represented by the symbol >. However, the phrase *greater than* indicates addition and is translated to the addition symbol, +.

Order of Operations

The order of operations is the standard rule that dictates which operations are performed in what order. Applying the correct order of operations can dramatically impact the outcome of a set of operations in an equation or expression. As explained earlier, the correct order of operations is most commonly remembered by the acronym PEMDAS, which stands for Parentheses, Exponents, Multiplication, Division, Addition, Subtraction. Begin solving all equations with anything in parentheses, then work with any exponents, then multiply and divide together, working from left to right, and finally add and subtract together, also working from left to right.

When providing information that needs to be used to build algebraic expressions, the GMAT is not going to be as explicit as stating what operation goes where. For instance, the GMAT is not going to provide information that says "3 minus the parenthetical value of 2 plus x." Instead, the GMAT is more likely to write "3 minus the sum of 2 and x." The placement of the word *sum* in the expression implies the parentheses to bracket off the 2 and x. Written out, this expression looks like this:

$$3 - (2 + x)$$

Writing an expression such as the previous one incorrectly can have disastrous consequences. For instance, if $x = 1$, then the previous expression evaluates to $3 - (2 + 1) = 3 - 3 = 0$. However, if you had not set off $2 + x$ in parentheses, then the previous expression is $3 - 2 + 1 = 1 + 1 = 2$. The answer changes because the order of operations changes.

Instead of explicitly telling you to set off items in parentheses, the GMAT uses terms of aggregation, such as *sum*, *difference*, and *product*, to indicate that the value of two items should be calculated first. For instance, the expression "2 times the sum of 4 and 5" is written as $2 \times (4 + 5)$ and is calculated as $2 \times (9) = 18$. This is very different than the expression "2 times 4 plus 5," which is written and calculated as $2 \times 4 + 5 = 8 + 5 = 13$.

Putting It All Together

Let's take another look at the question presented earlier:

If $y = 2x$ and $7 = y + 5$, then what value is 4 less than x?

This question wants to know what value is 4 less than x. Writing this phrase as an expression yields $x - 4$. The word *is* indicates an equals sign, so this can be written as $x - 4 = $. The phrase *what value* indicates a variable, which is what you are solving for. You need to solve for the value of x in order to answer the question. There is only one equation that involves the variable x and that requires a value of y. Solve for y using the equation that has one value of y. If $7 = y + 5$, then $y = 2$. If $y = 2$, then the first equation is $2 = 2x$ and $x = 1$. Therefore, the answer to the question *what value* is 4 *less than x* is $1 - 4 = -3$.

Now that you've gotten an introduction to building algebraic expressions, take a look at the following quiz and build the appropriate equations.

Algebraic Expressions Quiz

The answers can be found in Part V.

1. The sum of x and 4 is 3 less than the sum of y and 8.

2. 35 is what percent of z?

3. 8 plus the product of 3 and 4 is what percent of y?

4. 5 less than the difference between x and 8 is 14.

5. What number is x percent of y?

Using Substitution to Solve

As discussed in the section on solving simultaneous equations, it is almost always impossible to solve a single equation that has two variables. For instance, the equation $x + y = 9$ cannot be solved for either x or y because both variables could be any value so long as the sum is 9. In algebra, if a problem asks to solve for the value of either x or y, there are several ways in which to complete the task. The most commonly known, and widely used, path is to identify a value for one of the variables and use that information to solve for the other variable.

Replacing a variable with a known value is the essence of substitution. In the example above, if you were told that $x = 3$, then it is just a matter of substitution to solve for the value of y. Use the known value of x to replace the variable and solve: $3 + y = 9$, so $y = 6$.

It's All About Relationships

Using substitution to solve for a variable when the known value is an integer or other real number is accomplished by replacing the variable with the known value. But what if the known value of a variable is not an integer or a real number? What if, instead, it is a relationship? For instance, in the equation above, would you be able to solve for y if you knew the value of x is one-half the value of y?

You can! The information provided is enough to solve for the value of y. Write out the equation for the value of x: $x = \frac{1}{2}y$. Apply the rules of substitution for the value of x in the equation to find that $\frac{1}{2}y + y = 9$. Multiply both sides by 2 to produce $y + 2y = 18$ and then combine to find that $3y = 18$ and $y = 6$.

Integers Not Required

When using substitution to solve an algebraic equation or manipulate an expression, you replace a variable with a known quantity for that variable. However, as demonstrated above, the known value does not always need to be an integer or any real number. Knowing the relationship of the variables is enough to use substitution to solve. When the known value is a relationship, the process to apply substitution is no different than when the known value is an integer. Simply replace the variable with the known value and solve!

Solving with Algebra

A key difference between when the known value is a relationship and when it is an integer is how the equation is solved once substitution is complete. It is often easier to solve the equation when the known value is an integer than when it is a relationship to the other variable. When the known value is a relationship, solving can require a more adept use of algebra. However, the use of algebra can be mitigated in certain scenarios by applying the principles of Plugging In. If you are unfamiliar with the Plugging In skill set, check out Chapter 14. It takes a deep dive into how to use this powerful technique to make algebra more like arithmetic, thus making the process of finding solutions to the nastiest of algebra problems far more accessible.

Test out your new skills below.

Substitution Quiz

Solve each of the following equations using substitution. The answers can be found in Part V.

1. What is the value of x in the equation $x + 3y = 6$ if y is one-third the value of x ?

2. If $y = 2x$ and $x + y = 24$, then what is the value of $3x$?

3. If $4x - 2y = 16$ and $12x + 6y = 48$, then what is the value of (x, y) ?

4. What is the value of x if $-6x - 2y = 2$ and $10 = 10x + 10y$?

5. If the area of a rectangle is 18 and the length is twice the width, what is the width of the rectangle?

6. The rate of car A is 3 times that of car B and the combined rate is 88 miles per hour. If car A traveled for 2 hours and car B traveled for 1 hour, then what is the total combined distance the cars traveled?

Hey! What's Up with Those Last Two Questions?

The first four questions in the drill above, as well as all the examples before the drill, all presented two obvious equations that are solvable using substitution. The final question of the drill deviated from that pattern. Instead of providing equations, the questions required that you construct common equations and use the information provided to substitute to find the answer.

Presenting a substitution problem in this format is well within the confines of the content that can be tested on the GMAT. Not all substitution problems are going to contain obvious equations. You may be asked to use substitution in all types of questions, such as geometry and rates.

Three's a Crowd

In addition to asking about substitution in different contexts, the GMAT can also ask about more than two equations and variables. Consider how to solve for x given the following information:

$$x + 2z = 24$$
$$y + x = 12$$
$$4z + 2y = 8$$

There are two equations that contain the variable x. One of the equations also contains the variable z and the other also contains the variable y. In order to solve for x, one of these equations must be set equal to x. The second equation is the simplest, so rewrite that equation as $x = 12 - y$. Now you need a value for y that is expressed in terms of x. The only other equation that contains the variable y is the third equation. Setting this equation equal to y yields results in terms of z. Divide both sides of the equation by 2 and isolate the y to rewrite this equation as $y = 4 - 2z$. Use this value of y in the rewritten second equation, so $x = 12 - (4 - 2z) = 12 - 4 + 2z = 8 + 2z$. The first equation contains values of z and of x, so work there next. The rewritten second equation expresses x in terms of $2z$. The first equation contains $2z$, so rewrite the first equation to provide a value of $2z$. This rewritten first equation is $2z = 24 - x$. Use this value for $2z$ in the rewritten second equation. This yields $x = 8 + 24 - x$. Now solve for x: $2x = 8 + 24 = 32$ and $x = 16$.

When working on substituting with more than two equations, work with the equations one at a time. Begin by isolating the information you want to solve for first and then read through each equation systematically, looking for ways to solve for values present in other equations.

DRILL 15

The answers to these questions can be found in Part V.

1. If x is equal to 1 more than the product of 3 and z, and y is equal to 1 less than the product of 2 and z, then $2x$ is how much greater than $3y$ when z is 4 ?

   (A) 1
   (B) 2
   (C) 3
   (D) 5
   (E) 6

2. A certain town's economic development council has 21 members. If the number of women on the council is 3 less than 3 times the number of men on the council, then the town's economic development council has how many male members?

(A) 5
(B) 6
(C) 7
(D) 9
(E) 15

3. What is the value of x ?

(1) $x^2 - 5x + 4 = 0$
(2) x is not prime.

(A) Statement (1) ALONE is sufficient, but statement (2) alone is not sufficient.
(B) Statement (2) ALONE is sufficient, but statement (1) alone is not sufficient.
(C) BOTH statements TOGETHER are sufficient, but NEITHER statement ALONE is sufficient.
(D) EACH statement ALONE is sufficient.
(E) Statements (1) and (2) TOGETHER are not sufficient.

4. What is the sum of x, y, and z ?

(1) $2x + y + 3z = 45$
(2) $x + 2y = 30$

(A) Statement (1) ALONE is sufficient, but statement (2) alone is not sufficient.
(B) Statement (2) ALONE is sufficient, but statement (1) alone is not sufficient.
(C) BOTH statements TOGETHER are sufficient, but NEITHER statement ALONE is sufficient.
(D) EACH statement ALONE is sufficient.
(E) Statements (1) and (2) TOGETHER are not sufficient.

5. David has three credit cards: a Passport card, an EverywhereCard, and an American Local card. He owes balances on all three cards. Does he owe the greatest balance on the EverywhereCard?

   (1) The sum of the balances on his EverywhereCard and American Local card is $1,350, which is three times the balance on his Passport card.

   (2) The balance on his EverywhereCard is $\frac{4}{3}$ of the balance on his Passport card and $\frac{4}{5}$ of the balance on his American Local card.

   (A) Statement (1) ALONE is sufficient, but statement (2) alone is not sufficient.
   (B) Statement (2) ALONE is sufficient, but statement (1) alone is not sufficient.
   (C) BOTH statements TOGETHER are sufficient, but NEITHER statement ALONE is sufficient.
   (D) EACH statement ALONE is sufficient.
   (E) Statements (1) and (2) TOGETHER are not sufficient.

6. If $a - b = c$, what is the value of b ?

   (1) $c + 6 = a$
   (2) $a = 6$

   (A) Statement (1) ALONE is sufficient, but statement (2) alone is not sufficient.
   (B) Statement (2) ALONE is sufficient, but statement (1) alone is not sufficient.
   (C) BOTH statements TOGETHER are sufficient, but NEITHER statement ALONE is sufficient.
   (D) EACH statement ALONE is sufficient.
   (E) Statements (1) and (2) TOGETHER are not sufficient.

7. Together, Andrea and Brian weigh p pounds and Brian weighs 10 pounds more than Andrea. If Andrea's dog, Cubby, weighs $\frac{p}{4}$ pounds more than Andrea, then, in terms of p, what is Cubby's weight in pounds?

   (A) $\frac{p}{2} - 10$

   (B) $\frac{3p}{4} - 5$

   (C) $\frac{3p}{2} - 5$

   (D) $\frac{5p}{4} - 10$

   (E) $5p - 5$

8. A university awarded grants in the amount of either $7,000 or $10,000 to selected incoming first-year students. If the total amount of all such awards is $2,300,000, did the university award more $7,000 grants than $10,000 grants to the selected incoming first-year students?

   (1) A total of 275 first-year students received grants in one of the two amounts.
   (2) The amount of money awarded in $10,000 grants was $200,000 more than the amount of money awarded in $7,000 grants.

   (A) Statement (1) ALONE is sufficient, but statement (2) alone is not sufficient.
   (B) Statement (2) ALONE is sufficient, but statement (1) alone is not sufficient.
   (C) BOTH statements TOGETHER are sufficient, but NEITHER statement ALONE is sufficient.
   (D) EACH statement ALONE is sufficient.
   (E) Statements (1) and (2) TOGETHER are not sufficient.

Solving by Factoring

The building blocks for solving algebraic equations are addition, subtraction, multiplication, and division. These tools work great when solving for the variable in equations such as $x + 10 = 4$ or $3x = 6$. However, there are occasions when an equation is constructed in such a way that these basic operations alone are not enough to solve the problem. For example, how could you solve for x in the following:

$$2x^2 + 3x = 0$$

Simply subtracting and dividing is not enough to find the value of x. Not even more advanced operations, such as taking the square root, produce a way to solve for the value of x. In this case, solving for x requires factoring out an x from the left-hand side of the equation to produce the following:

$$x(2x + 3) = 0$$

Solving for x in the above equation produces two results. One result is $x = 0$. The other result is $2x + 3 = 0$ and $x = -\dfrac{3}{2}$.

In the above equation, there were two solutions for x. When a variable is factored out of an equation, that variable must be considered as equal to the answer independently from the rest of the equation. In the above example, the x was factored out of the left-hand side of the equation, so the x is considered independently.

When factoring out a variable or value, the variable or value must be present in each of the elements of the expression. For example, in the equation $2x^2 + 4x = 0$, a value of $2x$ can be factored out of the left-hand side of the equation to create $2x(x + 2) = 0$. There are now two separate expressions that need to be considered equal to 0: $2x$ and $x + 2$. Two separate values for x can now be calculated with the basic operations.

> The ability to factor out a value is due to the Distributive Law. This law and a different law, the Associative Law, are discussed in the Arithmetic chapter. We are not going to discuss either of these laws in detail here. If you'd like to know more about either law, and test your skills with a drill, check out the Arithmetic Operations section of the Arithmetic chapter.

Consider the following more complicated equation and use factoring to solve for x.

$$x^3 + 6x^2 + 8x = 0$$

The variable x is present in each element of the expression $x^3 + 6x^2 + 8x$, so x can be factored out of the expression on the left-hand side of the equation above to produce $x(x^2 + 6x + 8) = 0$. As before, there are now two expressions that need to be considered equal to 0: x and $x^2 + 6x + 8$. Setting x equal to 0 reveals one of the possible solutions for x, which is $x = 0$. The other expression is a quadratic.

In the section on solving quadratics (later in this chapter), we discuss the techniques and methodology for solving quadratics. If you are unfamiliar with those techniques, we recommend checking out that section. The quadratic $x^2 + 6x + 8 = 0$ factors to $(x + 4)(x + 2) = 0$. There are now two more expressions that need to be evaluated as equal to 0 : $x + 4$ and $x + 2$. When $x + 4 = 0$, then $x = -4$. When $x + 2 = 0$, then $x = -2$. Therefore, there are three possible solutions for x in the equation above. Those solutions are 0, -4, and -2. Below are all the steps taken to solve this problem written out in order, so you can better visualize them:

$$x^3 + 6x^2 + 8x = 0$$
$$x(x^2 + 6x + 8) = 0$$
$$x((x + 4)(x + 2)) = 0$$
$$x = 0$$
$$x + 4 = 0; x = -4$$
$$x + 2 = 0; x = -2$$
$$x = \{0, -4, -2\}$$

Factoring Equations Not Equal to 0

Thus far, all the examples have been equal to 0. The following equation is not equal to 0. How would your approach to solving this problem differ from your approach for the problem above?

$$2x^3 + 16x^2 - 3x = 24$$

The first step to take is to set the equation equal to 0 by subtracting 24 from both sides to produce:

$$2x^3 + 16x^2 - 3x - 24 = 0$$

At first glance, there is nothing that can be factored out of this equation. However, you can group items together that do have common factors. Group $2x^3$ and $16x^2$ together and group $3x$ and 24 together. By doing this, you can see that $2x^3 + 16x^2$ has a $2x^2$ in common and $3x + 24$ has a -3 in common. So, this equation can be rewritten as:

$$2x^2(x + 8) - 3(x + 8) = 0$$

Because the two terms contain the same factors, you can then combine the factors together. This produces:

$$(2x^2 - 3)(x + 8) = 0$$

Now solve for each of these individually:

$$2x^2 - 3 = 0$$

$$2x^2 = 3$$

$$x^2 = \frac{3}{2} \quad x = \pm\sqrt{\frac{3}{2}}$$

AND

$$x + 8 = 0$$

$$x = -8$$

The solutions for this equation are $x = \pm\sqrt{\dfrac{3}{2}}$ or -8.

Solving Absolute Value Equations and Inequalities

Knowing how to solve absolute value equations and inequalities is a good skill to have for test day. Before considering how to solve these types of questions, let's revisit absolute values and establish a working definition.

In Chapter 6, GMAT Math: Principles and POE, a number line is used to illustrate positive and negative integers. In that same chapter, absolute value is defined as *the distance between a number and 0 on the number line*. Represented visually by the bolded line below, the absolute value of 3 (|3|) is 3 because that is how far that number is from 0 on the number line:

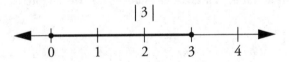

However, the definition of absolute value is not limited to positive numbers only! In fact, the definition states that the absolute value is the distance between *a number and 0*. Therefore, the absolute value of -3 is also 3 because that is how far that number is from 0 on the number line. This is represented again by the bolded bar in the visual below.

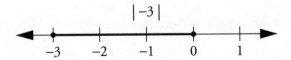

Considering the information above, finding the absolute value of real numbers is an uncomplicated process: simply take the positive value of the number. So, $|6| = 6$, $|-6| = 6$, $\left|-\dfrac{3}{2}\right| = \dfrac{3}{2}$, and so on. It stands to reason, then that the absolute value of a variable follows the same pattern, right?

Let's look at the number line again, but this time map the distance between a positive variable x and 0.

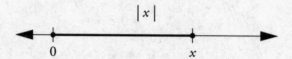

In the example above, the value inside the absolute value brackets is x. The absolute value distance between x and 0 is the positive value of x, so it is true that $|x| = x$. But what happens if the value inside the absolute value brackets is $-x$?

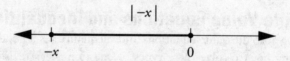

In this case, the absolute distance between $-x$ and 0 is still x. So, it is true that both $|x|$ and $|-x|$ equal x, just like both $|4|$ and $|-4|$ equal 4.

Variable Absolute Values with Real Number Solutions

Now that the basics of absolute values have been covered, let's talk about the first of two specific rules for working with absolute values we'll establish in this chapter. Consider the following question:

What is the value of x in the equation $|x| = 4$?

While the gut reaction to this question is often that $x = 4$, that is not the case. As we established above, there are two values of x that make the equation $|x| = 4$ true. If $x = 4$, then $|4| = 4$ is true. But, if $x = -4$, then $|-4| = 4$ is also true. Therefore, there are two possible values of x: 4 and -4. This is the first specific rule of working with absolute values.

> For the equation $|x| = y$, the value of $x = y$ and $x = -y$

Solving Absolute Value Inequalities

The visual representation of absolute value inequalities is slightly more complicated than the visual representations of absolute values. Consider the inequality $|x| < 4$. The visual representation of all values of x is:

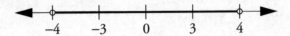

This is true because of the first of the two specific rules stated above. If $|x| < 4$, then $x < 4$, but $x > -4$. When working with absolute value inequalities, the direction of the inequality is always flipped when the value of the number that the variable is being compared to is switched from positive to negative.

The same is true for more complicated absolute value inequalities. What is the range of possible values of x given the following inequality?

$$|x + 4| > 10$$

Because this is an absolute value that involves a variable, there are two solutions for the variable. In this case, both solutions are inequalities. The possible values of x are represented by the inequalities:

$$x + 4 > 10$$
$$x + 4 < -10$$

Solving these inequalities yields both $x > 6$ and $x < -14$. The range of possible values of x is represented by the following number line:

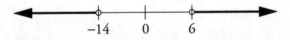

This is the second specific rule for working with absolute values.

> For the equation $|x| > y$, the range of possible values of x is $x > y$ and $x < -y$

The GMAT may ask for values of x in an absolute value inequality multiple-choice question. In this case, if there is only one possible correct answer, look for a value that falls into either range. In this case, the above rule can be read as follows: for the equation $|x| > y$, the possible value of x is $x > y$ OR $x < -y$.

Quadratic Equations

On the GMAT, quadratic equations always come in one of two forms: factored or expanded. Here's an example:

$$\underset{\text{factored}}{(x+2)(x+5)} = \underset{\text{expanded}}{x^2 + 7x + 10}$$

The first thing to do when solving a problem that involves a quadratic equation is to see which form the equation is in. If the quadratic equation is in an unfactored form, factor it immediately. If the quadratic equation is in a factored form, unfactor it. The test-writers like to see whether you know how to do these things.

To unfactor a factored expression, just multiply it using FOIL (First, Outer, Inner, Last):

$$(x+2)(x+5) = (x+2)(x+5)$$

$$= (x \text{ times } x) + (x \text{ times } 5) + (2 \text{ times } x) + (2 \text{ times } 5)$$

$$= x^2 + 5x + 2x + 10$$

$$= x^2 + 7x + 10$$

To factor an unfactored expression, put it into the following format and start by looking for the factors of the first and last terms.

$$x^2 + 2x - 15$$
$$= (\quad)(\quad)$$

For the first term of the unfactored expression to be x^2, the first term of each parentheses of the factored expression has to be x.

$$x^2 + 2x - 15$$
$$= (x \quad)(x \quad)$$

For the last term of the unfactored expression to be 15, the last term in each parentheses of the factored expression must be either 5 and 3 or 15 and 1. Since there is no way to get a middle term for the unfactored expression with a coefficient of 2 if the terms were 15 and 1, we are left with

$$x^2 + 2x - 15$$
$$= (x \quad 5)(x \quad 3)$$

To decide where to put the pluses and minuses in the factored expression, look to see how the inner and outer terms of the factored equation would combine to form the middle term. If we put a minus in front of the 5 and a plus in front of the 3, then the middle term would be $-2x$ (not what we wanted). Therefore, the final factored expression looks like this:

$$x^2 + 2x - 15$$
$$= (x + 5)(x - 3)$$

Quadratic equations are usually set equal to 0. Here's an example:

What are all the values of x that satisfy the equation $x^2 + 4x + 3 = 0$?

(A) −3
(B) −1
(C) −3 and −1
(D) 3 and 4
(E) 4

Here's How to Crack It

This problem contains an unfactored equation, so let's factor it.

$$x^2 + 4x + 3 = 0$$
$$(x \quad)(x \quad) = 0$$
$$(x \quad 3)(x \quad 1) = 0$$
$$(x + 3)(x + 1) = 0$$

In order for this equation to be correct, x must be either −3 or −1. The correct answer is (C).

Note: This problem would also have been easy to solve by Plugging In the Answers (covered in Chapter 7). It asked a specific question, and there were five specific answer choices. One of them was correct. All you had to do was try the choices until you found the right one. Bear in mind, however, that in a quadratic equation there are usually two values that will make the equation work.

> **The Equation Rule**
> For most easy-to-medium level questions, you must have as many equations as you have variables for the data to be sufficient. For example, $x = y + 1$ cannot be solved without another *distinct* equation.

Favorites of GMAT Test-Writers

There are three types of quadratic equations the GMAT test-writers find endlessly fascinating. These equations appear on the GMAT with great regularity in both the Problem Solving format and the Data Sufficiency format:

$$(x + y)^2 = x^2 + 2xy + y^2$$

$$(x + y)(x - y) = x^2 - y^2$$

$$(x - y)^2 = x^2 - 2xy + y^2$$

Memorize all three of these. As with all quadratic equations, if you see the equation in factored form, you should immediately unfactor it; if it's unfactored, factor it immediately.

Here are a couple of examples:

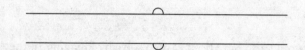

If $\dfrac{x^2 - 4}{x + 2} = 5$, then $x =$

(A) 3
(B) 5
(C) 6
(D) 7
(E) 9

Here's How to Crack It

It's unfactored, so let's factor it:

$$\frac{(x+2)(x-2)}{(x+2)} = 5$$

The $(x + 2)$s cancel out, leaving us with $(x - 2) = 5$. So $x = 7$, and the answer is (D).

$200^2 - 2(200)(199) + 199^2 =$

(A) −79,201
(B)   −200
(C)   1
(D)   200
(E)   79,999

Here's How to Crack It

Although you could solve this problem with lots of tedious multiplication, it's much faster to recognize the common quadratic hidden in the numbers: $x^2 - 2xy + y^2 = (x - y)(x - y)$. That means this calculation can be rewritten as $(200 - 199)(200 - 199)$, or $(1)(1)$. The correct answer is (C).

Since the answer choices vary so widely, you could have applied some POE to the most extreme answer choices, (A) and (E). The product of 200 and 199, which you have to double, is not too different from either 200^2 or 199^2. Thus, the negative value in the equation is roughly equal to the sum of the two positive values in the equation. If you did the math, by the way, and *got* one of those answers, you must have reversed an addition or subtraction sign.

If $x = m - 1$, which of the following is true when $m = \dfrac{1}{2}$?

(A) $x^0 > x^2 > x^3 > x^1$
(B) $x^0 > x^2 > x^1 > x^3$
(C) $x^0 > x^1 > x^2 > x^3$
(D) $x^2 > x^0 > x^3 > x^1$
(E) $x^3 > x^2 > x^1 > x^0$

Here's How to Crack It

Once you've solved for x, which equals $-\dfrac{1}{2}$, this question is just a matter of putting the four values in order. Even better, you already know two of them: $x = -\dfrac{1}{2}$ and $x^0 = 1$. With the other two values, be especially careful about the negative sign: $x^2 = \dfrac{1}{4}$ and $x^3 = -\dfrac{1}{8}$. The correct order is $x^0 > x^2 > x^3 > x^1$, and the answer is (A).

What is the value of $x^2 - y^2$?

(1) $x + y = 0$
(2) $x - y = 2$

(A) Statement (1) ALONE is sufficient, but statement (2) alone is not sufficient.
(B) Statement (2) ALONE is sufficient, but statement (1) alone is not sufficient.
(C) BOTH statements TOGETHER are sufficient, but NEITHER statement ALONE is sufficient.
(D) EACH statement ALONE is sufficient.
(E) Statements (1) and (2) TOGETHER are not sufficient.

Here's How to Crack It

Don't get caught making a careless assumption on this question. You may have immediately recognized that $x^2 - y^2$ factors to $(x + y)(x - y)$. Seeing that Statement (1) provides a value for $(x + y)$ and Statement (2) provides a value for $(x - y)$, you might have automatically assumed that the correct answer to this question is (C). Look more closely, however; Statement (1) tells you that $(x + y) = 0$. Zero times any number equals zero. Therefore, Statement (1) is sufficient to tell you that $(x + y)(x - y) = 0$. Statement (2), however, is not sufficient. Since Statement (2) says that $x - y = 2$, plug this number back into the factored expression from the question stem. Without the value for the other factor (or the values of x and y), Statement (2) cannot be used on its own to answer the question. The correct answer is (A).

Algebraic Functions

The most common notation for function questions on the GMAT is $f(x)$—read as f of x. There are other notations, such as $g(x)$ and $h(x)$, but $f(x)$ is the most common.

Many test-takers are tripped up by function questions because their unfamiliar structure can be intimidating. Before diving into the specifics about solving algebraic functions, let's discuss the components of the function. While knowing the different components of the function is not strictly necessary to solve function questions, knowing this information can be a powerful tool for building familiarity with the topic.

Functions on the GMAT are comprised of two components: domain and range. In the function $f(x) = x + 4$, the domain of the function is all the allowable values of x. The range of the function is all the corresponding values of $x + 4$. The true definitions of domain and range are more complicated than the above information suggests. However, for the purposes of the GMAT, these definitions are sufficient.

A GMAT problem that provides the function $f(x) = x + 4$ and asks to solve for the value of x when $f(x) = 6$ is really asking to solve for the domain in the function $f(x)$ when the range of the function is equal to 6. The range of the function is $x + 4$, so this can be set equal to 6 to yield $x + 4 = 6$. This means that $x = 2$ and the domain of the function $f(x) = 6$ is 2.

The implications of the relationship between the domain and range mean that if a function is defined and then a value for the domain or range is given, the missing piece of information can be solved for. For instance, if a function is defined as $f\left(x\right) = \dfrac{x}{2}$ and you are asked to solve the function for $f(2)$, it could be stated that the domain is 2 and the range is $f\left(2\right) = \dfrac{2}{2} = 1$.

Functions? No Problem

If you can follow a recipe, you can do a GMAT function problem. Many students are uncomfortable with function questions. But, if you can master these questions, you can pick up a couple of points on a question that may trip up some other people.

FUNCTIONS

You know you've hit a function problem by the sensation of panic and fear you get when you see some strange symbol (# or * or Δ) and say, "I studied for two months for this test and somehow managed to miss the part where they told me about # or * or Δ." Relax. Any strange-looking symbol on the GMAT is just a function question. For more information on how to solve function questions, check out that section in the Algebra chapter.

Let's look at an example:

If $\Delta x = x$ for $x \geq 0$ and $2x$ for $x < 0$, $\dfrac{\Delta 30}{\Delta(-5)} =$

(A) −12
(B) −6
(C) −3
(D)   6
(E) 30

Here's How to Crack It

A function is basically a set of directions. In this case, the directions tell you what to do with the number that comes after the symbol Δ. If the number that follows the symbol is greater than or equal to 0, then the output of the function is just the number x. However, if the number that follows the symbol is negative, the output of the Δ function is $2x$. So, we can evaluate the given expression thus:

$$\frac{\Delta 30}{\Delta(-5)} = \frac{30}{2(-5)} = \frac{30}{-10} \text{ or } -3. \text{ The answer is (C).}$$

Mistakes of the Average Test-Taker

The average test-taker has no idea what to do with Δ, so she just ignores it. Because $\dfrac{30}{-5} = -6$, the average test-taker picks (B). On the other hand, the average test-taker might also think she can reduce functions. In other words, she might think she can do this:

$$\frac{\Delta 30}{\Delta(-5)} = \Delta(-6)$$

The function of $-6 = -12$, so she might also select (A).

Find the answers to all Challenge Questions in Part V!

Challenge Question #7

For positive integers x, y, and z, the function $x * y * z$ means that $\frac{z}{x^y}$ is an integer, but $\frac{z}{x^{y+1}}$ is not. If $x * 2 * 144$, then which of the following is NOT a possible value of x?

(A)   2
(B)   3
(C)   4
(D)   6
(E)   12

How to Solve Functions

Solving GMAT function questions is rarely more complicated than following directions. If a function is defined, and the domain or range of that function is provided, then solve for whatever piece of information is missing. If the question contains only variables in the definition of the function, then Plug In.

If you're not already familiar with Plugging In and Plugging In the Answers (PITA), check out the Plugging In chapter to learn more!

The information given is...	So, solve by...
the domain	Plugging In the value of the variable in the function (the domain) for all instances of that variable in the range (what the function is equal to)
the range	Setting the known value of the range equal to the range defined in the function and solving for the variables (the domain)
only variables	Plugging In

Let's try a couple of examples:

For which of the following functions does $f(x) = f(-x)$ for all values of x?

(A) $f(x) = x^3 + 3$
(B) $f(x) = -x$
(C) $f(x) = 2x + 3$
(D) $f(x) = (-x)^2 + 2$
(E) $f(x) = 5x - 4$

Here's How to Crack It

This question only provides variables in the definition of the function, so solve by Plugging In for the variables. Begin with (A). If $x = 2$, then $f(2) = 2^3 + 3 = 11$ and $f(-2) = -2^3 + 3 = 5$. In this case, $f(2) \neq f(-2)$. Eliminate (A). For (B), if $x = 2$, then $f(2) = -2$ and $f(-2) = -(-2) = 2$. The functions are not equal, so eliminate (B). For (C), $f(2) = 2(2) + 3 = 7$ and $f(-2) = 2(-2) + 3 = -1$. Eliminate (C). For (D), $f(2) = (-2)^2 + 2 = 4 + 2 = 6$ and $f(-2) = (-(-2))^2 + 2 = 2^2 + 2 = 4 + 2 = 6$. The functions are equal, so keep (D). For (E), $f(2) = 5(2) - 4 = 10 - 4 = 6$ and $f(-2) = 5(-2) - 4 = -10 - 4 = -14$. The functions are not equal, so eliminate (E). The correct answer is (D).

Let's try another.

If the function $h(x)$ is defined as $h(x) = 3 - \dfrac{1}{x}$, then what is the value of $g(h(x))$?

(1) $x = 1$
(2) $g(2) = 2$

Here's How to Crack It

This is a data sufficiency question, so begin by determining what is known and what is needed to solve the problem. Start by determining what is known. The problem defines $h(x)$ as $h(x) = 3 - \dfrac{1}{x}$ but does not provide any further information. Now consider what is needed from the statements to solve the problem. The problem asks for the value of $g(h(x))$, so the problem needs to define a value for the function g and a way to solve for the value of $h(x)$. Now consider each statement independently.

Statement (1) provides a value of x. This value can be used to Plug In to the function $h(x)$ to solve for $h(x)$ such that $h(1) = 3 - \dfrac{1}{1} = 3 - 1 = 2$, so $h(1) = 2$. Now the function $g(h(x))$ can be rewritten as $g(2)$. However, this statement does not provide any further information about the definition of the function g. Because there is no way to determine the value of the function, this statement is insufficient. Eliminate (A) and (D), and write down BCE.

Now consider Statement (2). This statement states that $g(2) = 2$. While this may seem sufficient to solve the problem, there is no way to verify that $h(x) = 2$ using the information in Statement (2). Because there is no way to determine a value for $h(x)$, there is no way to solve for the value of $g(h(x))$. Eliminate (B).

Now consider both statements together. Statement (1) establishes that $x = 1$. The equation in the question stem can be rewritten as $g(h(1))$. Because $x = 1$, it is true that $h(1) = 2$. The equation in the question stem can be rewritten again as $g(2)$. Statement (2) establishes that $g(2) = 2$. While neither statement provides a definition for the function g, the statements combined are enough to determine that $g(h(x)) = g(2) = 2$. The two statements combined are sufficient. The correct answer is (C).

Sequences

A sequence question on the GMAT is just a special kind of function question. These questions typically present an equation that satisfies a particular element in a sequence often denoted by notation such as A_1 or S_1. Based on the information in the question, you'll likely be asked to find a specific value in the sequence, such as the fourth term.

This style of question is used by GMAC to increase the difficulty of questions, as most test-takers are unfamiliar with that style of notation and that topic. But not you! You know that this is just a special kind of function question, and to solve function questions all you have to do is follow the directions.

Check out the following example:

A sequence of number satisfies the equation $S_n = \dfrac{S_{n+1}}{2} + 4$. If $S_1 = 2$, then what is the value of S_4 ?

(A) −40
(B) −16
(C) −8
(D) 36
(E) 72

Means, Medians, and Modes, Oh My!
Q: For the list of numbers {3, 2, 5, 8, 2, 16}, find the mean, the mode, the median, and the range.
Turn to page 315 for the answer.

Here's How to Crack It

In order to solve this problem, just follow the directions. The problem states that $S_1 = 2$, so use 2 as the value of S_n and solve for the value of S_{n+1}. The equation is now $2 = \dfrac{S_{n+1}}{2} + 4$. In this equation, the value S_{n+1} is the same as the value of S_2 because you started the problem with a value of S_1. Solve for the value of S_{n+1}, or S_2. Subtract 4 from both sides and multiply by 2 to find that $S_2 = -4$.

Now that you have a value of S_2, you can use that value to solve for S_3. Set the original equation equal to 4 and it now reads $-4 = \dfrac{S_3}{2} + 4$. Again, subtract 4 from both sides and multiply by 2. The result is $S_3 = -16$.

Use the value of S_3 to solve for S_4. The equation is now $-16 = \dfrac{S_4}{2} + 4$ and $S_4 = -40$.

The correct answer is (A).

Notice how all that was needed to solve the problem above was just to follow the rules? Just like a function problem!

EXPONENTS

An **exponent** is a short way of writing the value of a number multiplied several times by itself. $4 \times 4 \times 4 \times 4 \times 4$ can also be written as 4^5. This is expressed as "four to the fifth power." The large number (4) is called the base, and the little number (5) is called the exponent.

There are several rules to remember about exponents:

- **Multiplying numbers with the same base:** When you multiply numbers that have the same base, simply add their exponents.

$$6^2 \times 6^3 = 6^{(2+3)} = 6^5 \qquad (y^4)(y^6) = y^{(4+6)} = y^{10}$$

- **Dividing numbers with the same base:** When you divide numbers that have the same base, simply subtract the bottom exponents from the top exponents.

$$\frac{3^6}{3^2} = 3^{(6-2)} = 3^4 \qquad \frac{x^7}{x^4} = x^{(7-4)} = x^3$$

- **Raising a power to a power:** When you raise a number with an exponent to another power, simply multiply the exponents.

$$(4^3)^2 = 4^{(3 \times 2)} = 4^6 \qquad (z^2)^4 = z^{(2 \times 4)} = z^8$$

There are several operations that *seem* like they ought to work with exponents, but don't.

- Does $x^2 + x^3 = x^5$?   NO!
- Does $x^6 - x^2 = x^4$?   NO!

- Does $\dfrac{\left(x^2 + y^2 + z^2\right)}{\left(x^2 + y^2\right)} = z^2$?   NO!

But note that in the first example, $x^2 + x^3$ can be written in another form, using the distributive property: $x^2 + x^3 = x^2(1 + x)$.

> **Means, Medians, and Modes, Oh My!**
> A: Always remember to reorder the numbers.
> In the list of numbers
> {2, 2, 3, 5, 8, 16}:
> The mean is 6.
> The mode is 2.
> The median is 4.
> The range is 14.

The Strange Powers of Powers

If you raise a positive integer to a power, the result is *greater* than the original integer. For example, $6^2 = 36$. However, raising a number to a power can sometimes have unexpected results:

- If you raise a positive fraction that is less than 1 to a power, the result is *less* than the original fraction.

$$\left(\frac{1}{3}\right)^2 = \frac{1}{3} \times \frac{1}{3} = \frac{1}{9}$$

- If you raise a negative number to an odd power, the result is *less* than the original number.

$$(-3)^3 = (-3)(-3)(-3) = -27$$

(Remember, -27 is smaller than -3.)

- If you raise a negative number to an even power, the result is positive.

$$(-3)^2 = (-3)(-3) = 9$$

(Remember, negative times negative = positive.)

- Any number to the first power = itself.

- Any nonzero number raised to the 0 power = 1.

Strange Powers Revealed!

Why is any number to the 0 power equal to 1 when any other time we multiply by 0 the result is 0? The answer is that we aren't multiplying by 0 at all. Watch closely now: 3^0 should equal $3^{-1} \times 3^1$, because when you add the exponents you get 3^0. Now, $3^{-1} \times 3^1$ can be rewritten $\frac{1}{3} \times 3 = \frac{3}{3} = 1$.

RADICALS

The **square root** of a positive number x is the number that, when squared, equals x. By definition, you can take the square root of only a nonnegative number, and the square root function returns only nonnegative values. The symbol for a square root is $\sqrt{\ }$. A number inside the $\sqrt{\ }$ is called a **radical**. Thus, in $\sqrt{4} = 2$, 4 is the radical and 2 is its square root.

The **cube root** of a positive number x is the number that, when cubed, equals x. For example, the cube root of 8 is 2, because $2 \times 2 \times 2 = 8$. The symbol for a cube root is $\sqrt[3]{\ }$. Thus, the cube root of 27 would be represented as $\sqrt[3]{27} = 3$, because $3 \times 3 \times 3 = 27$. The cube root of -27 would be represented as $\sqrt[3]{-27} = -3$ because $-3 \times -3 \times -3 = -27$.

Even More Strange Powers

A radical can be rewritten as a fractional exponent, and vice versa. That is: $\sqrt[3]{5} = 5^{\frac{1}{3}}$.

There are several rules to remember about radicals:

1. $\sqrt{x}\sqrt{y} = \sqrt{xy}$. For example, $\sqrt{12}\sqrt{3} = \sqrt{36} = 6$.

2. $\sqrt{\frac{x}{y}} = \frac{\sqrt{x}}{\sqrt{y}}$. For example, $\sqrt{\frac{3}{16}} = \frac{\sqrt{3}}{\sqrt{16}} = \frac{\sqrt{3}}{4}$.

3. To simplify a radical, try factoring. For example, $\sqrt{32} = \sqrt{16}\sqrt{2} = 4\sqrt{2}$.

4. The square root of a positive fraction less than 1 is actually larger than the original fraction. For example, $\sqrt{\dfrac{1}{4}} = \dfrac{1}{2}$.

DRILL 16 (Algebra)

The answers to these questions can be found in Part V.

1. $\dfrac{\left(\dfrac{1}{3}\right)^6 - \left(\dfrac{1}{3}\right)^4}{\left(\dfrac{1}{3}\right)^5} =$

   (A) $\left(\dfrac{1}{3}\right)^{-3}$

   (B) $-\dfrac{8}{27}$

   (C) $-\dfrac{8}{9}$

   (D) $-\dfrac{8}{3}$

   (E) $-\left(\dfrac{1}{3}\right)^{-3}$

2. The ratio $\dfrac{\sqrt{147} + \sqrt{75}}{14}$ to $\dfrac{28}{7\sqrt{3}}$ is equal to

   (A) $\sqrt{74}$ to 2
   (B) 24 to 7
   (C) 14 to 9
   (D) 9 to 14
   (E) 7 to 24

3. If the operation Δ is defined by $a \, \Delta \, b = \dfrac{(b-a)^2}{a^2}$ for all numbers a and b, and $a \neq 0$, then $-1 \, \Delta \, (1 \, \Delta \, -1) =$

   (A) -1
   (B) 0
   (C) 1
   (D) 9
   (E) 25

4. 5 years ago, Joe was twice as old as Jessica. If in 4 years Joe will be one and a half times as old as Jessica, then how old is Joe now?

   (A)   23
   (B)   25
   (C)   27
   (D)   29
   (E)   31

5. If $\dfrac{x^2 + 2x - 9}{3} \leq x + 1$, then x could be represented by which of the following?

   (A) $-4 \leq x \leq -3$
   (B) $-4 \leq x \leq 3$
   (C) $-3 \leq x \leq 3$
   (D) $-3 \leq x \leq 4$
   (E) $3 \leq x \leq 4$

6. If $x > 0$ and x percent of a is b, then, in terms of x, a is how many times b ?

   (A) $100x$

   (B) $10x$

   (C) x

   (D) $\dfrac{10}{x}$

   (E) $\dfrac{100}{x}$

7. John has s pairs of shoes, which is $\dfrac{1}{3}$ as many as Sheila and twice as many as James. In terms of s, how many pairs of shoes do the three of them have combined?

   (A) $\dfrac{7}{3}s$

   (B) $\dfrac{10}{3}s$

   (C) $\dfrac{7}{2}s$

   (D) $4s$

   (E) $\dfrac{9}{2}s$

8. $\sqrt{\sqrt{\left(1 + \dfrac{17}{64}\right)}} =$

 (A) $\dfrac{\sqrt{34}}{8}$

 (B) $\dfrac{3\sqrt{2}}{4}$

 (C) $\dfrac{9}{8}$

 (D) $\dfrac{\sqrt{68}}{4}$

 (E) $\dfrac{3\sqrt{2}}{2}$

9. An operation $\sim$ is defined by $a \sim b = \dfrac{a+b}{(ab)^2}$ for all numbers a and b such that $ab \neq 0$. If $c \neq 0$ and $a \sim c = 0$, then $c =$

 (A) $-a$
 (B) 0
 (C) $\sqrt{a}$
 (D) a
 (E) a^2

10. A group of 20 friends formed an investment club, with each member contributing an equal amount to the general fund. The club then invested the entire fund, which amounted to d dollars, in Stock X. The value of the stock subsequently increased 40 percent, at which point the stock was sold and the proceeds divided evenly among the members. In terms of d, how much money did each member of the club receive from the sale? (Assume that transaction fees and other associated costs were negligible.)

 (A) $800d$

 (B) $\dfrac{7d}{5}$

 (C) $\dfrac{d}{20} + 40$

 (D) $\dfrac{d}{2}$

 (E) $\dfrac{7d}{100}$

11. The formula $M = \sqrt{l^2 + w^2 + d^2}$ describes the relationship between the length of M, which is the longest line that can be drawn in a rectangular solid, and the length, l, width, w, and depth, d, of that rectangular solid. The longest line that can be drawn in a rectangular solid with a length of 12, a width of 4, and a depth of 3 is how much longer than the longest line that can be drawn in a rectangular solid with a length of 6, a width of 3, and a depth of 2 ?

    (A)   5
    (B)   6
    (C)   7
    (D)   9
    (E)   13

Challenge Question #8

A dealer once sold identical cars at a price of x dollars each (including sales tax). However, the pretax price was recently increased by $2,500 such that 18 cars purchased at the old price would cost the same as purchasing three fewer cars at the new price. If the sales tax rate is 8%, what is the new price of the dealer's cars, including sales tax, in dollars?

    (A) $10,800
    (B) $12,500
    (C) $13,500
    (D) $16,200
    (E) $16,750

Find the answers to all Challenge Questions in Part V!

Summary

o The difficulty of many GMAT questions is reliant on some of the basics of algebra, such as like terms, ensuring you perform operations on both sides of an equation, building algebraic equations, order of operations, and substitution.

o If you see a problem with a quadratic equation in factored form, the easiest way to get the answer is to expand the equation immediately. If the equation is expanded, factor it immediately.

o Memorize the factored and expanded forms of the three most common quadratics on the GMAT:

$$(x + y)^2 = x^2 + 2xy + y^2$$
$$(x + y)(x - y) = x^2 - y^2$$
$$(x - y)^2 = x^2 - 2xy + y^2$$

o On problems containing inequalities, remember that when you multiply or divide both sides of an inequality by a negative number, the sign flips.

o In solving simultaneous equations, add or subtract one equation to or from another so that one of the two variables disappears.

o Problems that involve functions such as $f(x)$ typically require you to follow the directions in the problem or Plug In values for the variable in the function.

o A function problem may have strange symbols like Δ or *, but it is really just a set of directions.

o Sequence questions are just like function questions. Anytime you see a sequence, just follow the instructions in the problem!

Chapter 16
Miscellaneous Math

There are concepts that you can expect to show up on the GMAT that don't fit neatly into any other category. These types of questions typically involve some sort of strange notation or quirk that requires a specialized piece of knowledge to solve. We'll cover those concepts and how to approach solving questions that test them in this chapter.

GROUPS

If we told you that of 900 students who take the GMAT, 700 of them bought this book, how would you calculate the number of students who took the GMAT who did not buy this book?

This is pretty simple! 900 *total students* – 700 *students who bought this book* = 200 *students who did not buy this book*.

Now, if we told you that of those same 900 students, 450 of them bought a different book and no student did not buy any book, how would you calculate the number of students who bought both? How about the number of students who only bought this book or the number of students who only bought a different book?

It's not so simple anymore, is it?

This is a group problem on the GMAT. A characteristic of group problems is that they ask about two or more groups of people engaged in an action. Luckily, there is an equation for working with group problems:

Group Formula
Total = Group 1 + Group 2 – Both + Neither

In our example above, the Total is 900. Group 1 is the number of students who bought this book, or 700. Group 2 is the number of students who bought a different book, or 450. Neither is the number of students who did not buy any book, or 0. Use these numbers as the values of the group formula and solve for the value of Both: 900 = 700 + 450 – *Both* + 0. Subtract 1,150 from both sides to yield –250 = –*Both*. Divide both sides by –1 to get *Both* = 250. The number of students who only bought this book is 700 – 250 = 450. The number of students who only bought a different book is 450 – 250 = 200.

Try this problem that tests the use of the group formula.

In a certain state, 70 percent of the counties received some rain on Monday, and 65 percent of the counties received some rain on Tuesday. No rain fell either day in 25 percent of the counties in the state. What percent of the counties received some rain on Monday and Tuesday?

(A) 12.5%
(B) 40%
(C) 50%
(D) 60%
(E) 67.5%

Here's How to Crack It

This problem introduces groups in the form of counties that either did or did not get rain on Monday and/or Tuesday and asks for the percent of counties that received rain on Monday and Tuesday. Before setting up the equation, realize that this problem would be much easier to solve if you knew an actual value for the total number of counties, so this is a Hidden Plug In problem. Plug In a number for the total number of counties. Because the problem asks about percentages, a good number to Plug In is 100.

Now work with the information in the problem. If there are 100 total counties, then 70 counties received some rain on Monday, 65 counties received some rain on Tuesday, and 25 counties received no rain on either day. Use these values in the group formula to find that $100 = 70 + 65 - Both + 25$. *Both* is the number of counties that received rain on both Monday and Tuesday. Solve to find that *Both* = 60. Therefore, 60 of 100 counties received rain on Monday and Tuesday. Since 60 of 100 counties equals 60%, the correct answer is (D).

Many group problems on the GMAT can be solved by using the group formula, as outlined above. These questions can ask you to solve for any one of the variables in the formula. Regardless, the approach is the same—find the values for the variables and use them as values in the equation.

However, there are group problems on the GMAT that require a different approach. This approach is called the group grid. These problems differ from other group problems in that they present two groups set up in an either/or situation. In order to solve these problems, set up a grid with the two different groups and the total number as columns, and the situation and total as the rows.

Consider the following problem:

Two different buses filled with tourists are going shopping at the local outlet mall. Only 25% of all the tourists plan to pay for their purchases with paper money. If 40% of the tourists arrived on the first bus and 20% of the tourists who arrived on the first bus are going to pay with paper money, what percentage of the tourists arrived on the second bus and do not plan to pay with paper money?

(A) 23%
(B) 35%
(C) 43%
(D) 55%
(E) 63%

Here's How to Crack It

In order to solve this problem, you need to set up a group grid. There are three columns in the grid that can be labeled First Bus, Second Bus, and Total. There are three rows in the grid that can be labeled Paper Money, No Paper Money, and Total. The grid should look like this:

Pay With	First Bus	Second Bus	Total
Paper Money			
No Paper Money			
Total			

Begin filling in the grid with information from the problem. However, notice that this problem would be much easier to solve if you knew the total number of tourists. This is a Hidden Plug In problem. Because the problem is dealing with percents, Plug In 100 for the number of tourists.

The problem starts by stating that 25% of the tourists, or 25 tourists, plan to pay for their purchases with paper money. Therefore, write 25 in the Total column for Paper Money.

Next, the question states that 40% of the tourists, or 40 tourists, arrived on the first bus. Mark 40 in the First Bus column for Total.

Finally, the question states that 20% of the tourists who arrived on the First Bus plan to pay with Paper Money. There are 40 tourists who arrived on the First Bus and 20% of 40 is 8. Write 8 for the First Bus column for Paper Money.

At this point, your grid should look like this:

	First Bus	Second Bus	Total
Paper Money	8		25
No Paper Money			
Total	40		100

Now solve for the missing information by finding the differences that equal the total. For instance, to find the number of tourists that arrived on the First Bus for No Paper Money, subtract 8 from 40 to get 32.

The final grid should look like this:

	First Bus	Second Bus	Total
Paper Money	8	17	25
No Paper Money	32	43	75
Total	40	60	100

The question asks the percentage of the tourists who arrived on the second bus and do not plan to pay with paper money. The answer is 43%. The correct answer is (C).

MEASUREMENT

Measurement problems on the GMAT test your ability to convert between different units. For some measures, GMAT will provide the conversion rates right in the question. For more common conversions, however, GMAT will expect you to know those conversion rates.

Here are some common conversions that may show up on test day for which GMAT is unlikely to provide the information.

1 foot	12 inches
1 hour	60 minutes
1 minute	60 second
1 mile	5,280 feet
1 gram	1,000 milligrams
1 kilogram	100 grams
1 kilometer	1,000 meters

Knowing those conversions is valuable for test day. What also may come in handy is a good familiarity with common units associated with prefixes, such as:

Prefix	Meaning
Kilo	10^3
Deci	10^{-1}
Centi	10^{-2}
Milli	10^{-3}

Pay close attention to the wording of these types of questions—measurement problems will often very subtlety change the units of the problem. For instance, a question might describe a scenario in miles per hour but then ask how many minutes it took to travel a certain distance.

Check out some example measurement problems below.

Honey Brand	Unit Price	Unit Size
Bee's Knees	$3.33	12 oz
Sweet Bear	$2.50	8 oz
Morning Comb	$3.85	16 oz
Buzz Worthy	$5.30	24 oz
Sticky Fingers	$3.70	20 oz

The table above lists the 5 different brands of honey, the price per bottle, and the size of the bottle available for purchase at a local grocery store. Which of the following represents the correct order of the price per pound of different honey brands from least to greatest (1 pound = 16 oz)?

(A) Buzz Worthy, Sticky Fingers, Morning Comb, Bee's Knees, Sweet Bear
(B) Sweet Bear, Bee's Knees, Morning Comb, Sticky Fingers, Buzz Worthy
(C) Sweet Bear, Sticky Fingers, Buzz Worthy, Bee's Knees, Morning Comb
(D) Buzz Worthy, Morning Comb, Sticky Fingers, Sweet Bear, Bee's Knees
(E) Buzz Worth, Sticky Fingers, Morning Comb, Sweet Bear, Bee's Knees

Here's How to Crack It

The question provides a list of honey brands, the price per bottle, and the size of the bottle in ounces for 5 different brands of honey. However, the question asks for the price per pound of the different honey brands. In order to correctly list the brands of honey from least to greatest in price per pound, you'll need to convert the units from ounces to pounds and multiply the unit price by the same number. In order to convert each size to a pound, assign a multiplier to each brand that would make the unit size equal to 16. For instance, to increase 12 ounces to 16 ounces, you need to add 4 ounces, which is one-third of 12. Therefore, the multiplier is 1.33 because 12(1.33) = 16. Below is the table with all the different unit multipliers.

Honey Brand	Unit Price	Unit Size	Multiplier
Bee's Knees	$3.33	12 oz	1.33
Sweet Bear	$2.50	8 oz	2
Morning Comb	$3.85	16 oz	1
Buzz Worthy	$5.30	24 oz	0.66
Sticky Fingers	$4.70	20 oz	0.75

Now apply that multiplier to each of the unit prices in order to get the price per pound. The table below shows the price per pound for each honey brand.

Honey Brand	Unit Price	Unit Size	Multiplier	Price per Pound
Bee's Knees	$3.33	12 oz	1.33	$4.43
Sweet Bear	$2.50	8 oz	2	$5.00
Morning Comb	$3.85	16 oz	1	$3.85
Buzz Worthy	$5.30	24 oz	0.66	$3.50
Sticky Fingers	$4.70	20 oz	0.75	$3.53

Order these values from least to greatest. The correct answer is (A).

Last year, a certain runner was able to run a 10-kilometer race at an average pace of 12 kilometers per hour. If the runner increased their pace by 25%, how many minutes faster did they run the same race?

(A)   5
(B)   10
(C)   25
(D)   30
(E)   40

Here's How to Crack It

Work this problem one piece at a time. The problem begins by stating that last year the runner was able to run a 10-kilometer race at an average pace of 12 kilometers per hour. This means the runner was able to the race in $\frac{10}{12} = \frac{5}{6}$ of an hour, or 50 minutes. The problem then states the runner increased their pace by 25%, so the new pace is 1.25(12) = 15 kilometers per hour. At 15 kilometers per hour, the runner will be able to run 10 kilometers in $\frac{10}{15} = \frac{2}{3}$ of an hour, or $\frac{2}{3}(60) = 40$ minutes. The question asks how many minutes faster the runner was able to run the same race, which is 50 – 40 = 10 minutes. The correct answer is (B).

SCIENTIFIC NOTATION

Scientific notation is a shorthand way of writing either very large or very small numbers that aren't easily written out in their full value or as a decimal. Scientific notation is a means of representing numbers as a number between 1 and 10 multiplied by a power of 10. For instance, the number 10 can be represented in scientific notation as 1×10^1, the number 300 can be written as 3×10^2, and the number 2500 can be written as 2.5×10^3. Similarly, the number 0.1 can be written as 1×10^{-1}, 0.03 can be written as 3×10^{-2}, and 0.0025 can be written as 2.5×10^{-3}.

In order to write a number in scientific notation, consider what it would take to "move" the decimal point of any given number to leave only one non-zero integer to the left of the decimal point. The number of places the decimal point has to "move" represents the number of powers of 10 to multiply by. When the decimal point moves to the left, the number is written to a positive power of 10. When the decimal point moves to the right, the number is written to a negative power of 10.

Consider the number 465. The decimal point in the number 465 is after the units digit, which in this case is the number 5. In order to make a number between 1 and 10 and guarantee that there is only one number to the left of the decimal point, the decimal point needs to "move" 2 spots to the left. Moving the decimal point creates the number 4.65. This can then be multiplied by 10^2 to create the scientific notation 4.65×10^2.

Similar logic could be used on the number 0.00465. In order to create a number between 1 and 10 and guarantee that there is only one number to the left of the decimal point, the decimal point needs to "move" 3 places to the right. Moving the decimal point that many places to the right creates the number 4.65. This can then be multiplied by 10^{-3} to create the scientific notation 4.65×10^{-3}.

The numbers we've used as examples thus far are not numbers typically represented in scientific notation. Generally, scientific notation is used to write very large or very small numbers. For instance, the distance between the Earth and the Sun is 150,000,000,000 meters. This would be represented in scientific notation as 1.5×10^{11}. Similarly, a hydrogen atom is about 0.000000000106 meters in diameter, or 1.06×10^{-10} in scientific notation.

Operations with Scientific Notation

The rules for operations such as addition, subtraction, multiplication, and division depend on the operation.

For addition and subtraction, first make the powers of 10 equal by rewriting the number with the smaller exponents so that it equals that of the larger. Then, apply the operations to the decimal numbers.

For multiplication and division, apply the operation to the decimal number. Then, for multiplication, add the exponents together. For division, subtract the exponents.

According to certain projections, in recent years the total world economy was 1.1×10^{12} dollars. If the average economy of a country included in the projections in the world was approximately $5,500,000,000, then which of the following is closest to the number of countries in the projections?

(A) 20
(B) 40
(C) 120
(D) 200
(E) 400

Here's How to Crack It

The question asks about the number of countries in the projections and provides the total economy size of all the countries and the average economy size of the countries. This is an average problem, so make an average pie. The total is 1.1×10^{12} dollars and the average size is \$5,500,000,000. In order to find the number of countries, divide the total by the average. However, begin by rewriting the average size in scientific notation as 5.5×10^9 dollars. Now divide 1.1 by 5.5 to get 0.2. Subtract the exponents to get 10^3. The total number of countries is $0.2 \times 10^3 = 200$. The correct answer is (D).

Try another one:

If 1 foot is approximately 1.9×10^{-4} miles, then approximately how many miles are in 2.64×10^5 feet?

(A) 5
(B) 15
(C) 25
(D) 40
(E) 50

Here's How to Crack It

In order to solve this problem, set up the ratio. The question provides the distance, in miles, of 1 foot and then asks for the number of miles in a different number of feet, so the equation can be written as $\dfrac{1\ foot}{1.9 \times 10^{-4}\ miles} = \dfrac{2.64 \times 10^5\ feet}{x\ miles}$. Cross multiply to solve for x. The value of x is $x = (2.64 \times 10^5)(1.9 \times 10^{-4}) = 5.016 \times 10 = 50.16$ miles. The correct answer is (E).

MIXTURES

Imagine you have 10ml of salt water that you know has exactly 2 ml of salt. In this scenario, you could say that your solution is a 20% salt solution. If you added another 10ml of water to the solution, what percent salt solution do you have now? The amount of salt hasn't changed at all, so there is now 20 ml of the solution and 2 ml of it is salt, so this is a 10% salt solution.

Now let's say somebody hands you 40 ml of a 15% oil solution, and you combine it with your salt solution. What percent oil is the resulting solution? The amount of oil in the oil solution is 15% of 40 ml, or 6 ml. This solution is added to 20 ml of the salt solution, so there is now 40 ml + 20 ml = 60 ml total of the combined solution. The amount of oil hasn't changed, so there is still 6 ml of oil, which is 10% of the total solution.

Combining substances that have varying portions of different elements is the foundation of mixture problems on the GMAT. These problems can be treated like you are calculating a weighted average. A weighted average has different elements that all contribute to the total, like a normal average. Unlike a normal average, a weighted average will assign different percents, or weights, to the different elements.

For instance, consider a drink that is 1 cup coffee, $\frac{1}{5}$ cup creamer, and $\frac{1}{10}$ cup sweetener. It is technically true to say that this drink is made up of coffee, creamer, and sweetener. However, it is more accurate to say that the drink is approximately 78% coffee, 15% creamer, and 7% sweetener.

In the drink example above, we arrived at those percentages by considering how much each element contributed to the overall total. The total can be calculated arithmetically by converting each of the amounts of the different elements to a fraction and adding. The total is the numerator of the resulting fraction. In this case, this is $\frac{10}{10} + \frac{2}{10} + \frac{1}{10} = \frac{13}{10}$, or 1.3 cups of the drink. To calculate the percentage contributions of each element to the total, simply divide the total by the different amounts and multiply by 100. For instance, there is $\frac{10}{13} \times 100 \approx 78\%$ of the drink that is coffee.

Difficult mixture questions on the GMAT will take this concept of a weighted average and turn it on its head by providing you percentages of different solutions, but then asking you how much of a new solution, with a new percentage, needs to be added to the original solution to result in something entirely different.

Let's return to our coffee example to illustrate this. In order to make our drink even better, we need to make sure it contains 10% chocolate. We have a hot chocolate solution that is 50% chocolate, 50% milk. How much of the hot chocolate solution do we need to add to our coffee drink in order to make sure the drink is 10% chocolate?

Try out some numbers. If you add 1.2 cups of the hot chocolate solution to the 1.3 cups of the drink, you now have a drink that is 2.5 cups. Of this additional 1.2 cups of hot chocolate solution that was added to the drink, 0.6 cups of it are chocolate. This means that 0.6 cups of the 2.5 cups of the drink are chocolate, which is more than 10%. Therefore, you added too much chocolate, and your drink is now ruined!

You can see how these calculations can get complicated quickly. And while there is certainly a mathematical approach to solving problems like this, remember you have tools at your disposal to help! Specifically, Plugging In the Answers! This is a common strategy that you should be on the lookout for opportunities to use for mixture questions.

Take a look at the following example mixture problems for some practice!

A chemist has 600 units of a 10% nitric acid solution and they combined the entire solution with 800 units of a second nitric acid solution to create a 6% nitric acid solution. What percent nitric acid was the second solution?

(A)   1%
(B)   2%
(C)   2.5%
(D)   3%
(E)   4%

Here's How to Crack It

The first solution has $600 \times 0.10 = 60$ units of nitric acid. The final solution is $600 + 800 = 1{,}400$ units of 6% nitric acid, so there is 84 units of nitric acid in the final solution. The problem states that the second nitric acid solution is 800 units. The number of units of nitric acid the second nitric acid solution had to contribute to create the 6% nitric acid solution is $84 - 60 = 24$ units. If the second solution is 800 units and the solution had 24 units of nitric acid, then the second solution was $\dfrac{24}{800} = 0.03 = 3\%$. The correct answer is (D).

Try another!

A baker mixes x grams of a 30% sugar solution with a y grams of a 10% sugar solution to create z grams of a 15% sugar solution. What is the value of z ?

Statement 1
$y = 40$

Statement 2
$x = 16\dfrac{2}{3}$

Here's How to Crack It

The information in the question provides enough details to create two distinct equations. The first is the total volume of the solution. The total is z and z can be defined as the sum of x and y, so the first equation is $x + y = z$.

The second equation is the concentration of sugar in the final solution. This can be defined by the equation $0.3x + 0.1y = 0.15z$.

Therefore, the question provides you two distinct equations but three variables, which means it is impossible to solve without more information. In order to answer the question, the statements need to provide information that reduces the number of variables to one or two.

Statement (1) provides information for the value of y. The two statements are now $x + 40 = z$ and $0.3z + 0.1(40) = z$. There are now two equations and two variables, which means this can be solved. Statement (1) provides a way to answer the question, so it is sufficient. Eliminate (B), (C), and (E). The remaining choices are (A) and (D).

Statement (2) provides information for the value of x. Much like Statement (1), this information means there are now two equations and two variables, which can be solved. Statement (2) provides sufficient information to answer the question. The correct answer is (D).

FACTORIALS

Factorials are denoted by the notation $n!$, *where n is a non-negative integer. A factorial is the product of all positive integers less than or equal to n. For instance, 4! and 10! can be written as:*

$$4! = 4 \times 3 \times 2 \times 1$$

$$10! = 10 \times 9 \times 8 \times 7 \times 6 \times 5 \times 4 \times 3 \times 2 \times 1$$

Common Manipulations of Factorials

There are two common manipulations of factorials you should be aware of on test day.

The first is the prime factorization of factorials. Consider the factorization of 4! discussed earlier. This could be further written as:

$$4! = 4 \times 3 \times 2 \times 1 = (2 \times 2) \times 3 \times 2 \times 1 = 3 \times 2^3$$

When you see factorials of large numbers or factorials as part of fractions, one way to think about reducing or simplifying is by considering the prime factors of the factorials.

The second common manipulation of factorials that may appear on test day is that the factorial of n can also be written as the product of n and the factorial of $n - 1$. For instance:

$$4! = 4 \times (3)!$$

Let's take a look at an example problem to see how factorials may be tested on the GMAT.

$$p = \frac{99!}{50!}$$

$$q = \frac{99!}{75!}$$

What is the value of $\frac{p}{q}$?

(A) 50!

(B) 75!

(C) $\frac{75!}{50!}$

(D) 99! − 75!

(E) 99! − 50!

Here's How to Crack It

There are several ways to solve this problem. The simplest path forward is by substitution. The

value of p and q are provided in the question stem, so substitute them in the fraction. This

results in the expression $\dfrac{\frac{99!}{50!}}{\frac{99!}{75!}}$. Multiply the numerator by the reciprocal of the fraction in the

denominator to simplify the fraction to find that $\frac{99!}{50!} \times \frac{75!}{99!} = \frac{75!}{50!}$. This is the value in (C),

which is the correct answer.

However, let's say that you didn't notice the opportunity to substitute. What does solving this

problem look like by manipulating the factorials? Start with p. The value of p could be written

as $\frac{99 \times 98 \times 97 \times \ldots \times 3 \times 2 \times 1}{50 \times 49 \times 48 \times \ldots \times 3 \times 2 \times 1}$. The value of 50! in the denominator cancels out those same values

in the numerator, which means that p is the value of $99 \times 98 \times 97 \times \ldots 53 \times 52 \times 51$.

The same logic can be used to find the value of q, which is $99 \times 98 \times 97 \times \ldots \times 78 \times 77 \times 76$.

Combing these two values in the fraction $\frac{p}{q} = \frac{99 \times 98 \times 97 \times \ldots \times 53 \times 52 \times 51}{99 \times 98 \times 97 \times \ldots \times 78 \times 77 \times 76}$. Canceling the

values in the fraction leaves you with the value of $75 \times 74 \times 73 \times \ldots 53 \times 52 \times 51$.

Now look at the answer choices. Eliminate (A) and (B) as they do not represent this value. Choice (C) can be expanded to be written as $\dfrac{75\times74\times73\times\ldots\times3\times2\times1}{50\times49\times48\times\ldots\times3\times2\times1}$. This leaves the value of $75\times74\times73\times\ldots53\times52\times51$. This matches the value you solved for earlier. Neither (D) nor (E) match this value either. Eliminate them. The correct answer is (C).

Try another one.

11! is what percent greater than 9! ?

(A)   109%
(B)   110%
(C)   1,100%
(D)   10,900%
(E)   11,000%

Here's How to Crack It
Begin this question by setting up the percent change formula which is $\dfrac{\text{difference}}{\text{original}}\times100$. In this case, the difference is 11! − 9! and the original is 9!. The question can be written as $\dfrac{11!-9!}{9!}\times100$. In order to solve this problem, we need to think about factoring. The largest value that can be factored out between the numerator and the denominator is 9!. Remember that a factorial of n can be written as $n\times(n-1)!$. Use this strategy to factor our 9! From the numerator and denominator. This results in $\dfrac{9!\big((11\times10)-1\big)}{9!}\times100$. Cancel the 9!, which leaves $\dfrac{(11\times10)-1}{1}\times100=(110-1)\times100=10{,}900\%$. The correct answer is (D).

Summary

o   Group problems can be solved with the equation *Total = Group 1 + Group 2 − Both + Neither* or the Group Grid.

o   Measurement problems test your ability to convert from one unit to another.

o   The GMAT may not provide you translation tables between common units, so it's good to have a handful of common measurement conversions and prefixes memorized.

o   Scientific notation is a way of writing either very small or very large numbers as a factor of 10.

o   Mixture questions can be treated like weighted averages and typically ask about the makeup of different substances.

o   Factorials, usually represented by the notation $n!$, are the product of all positive integers less than or equal to n.

o   There are two common methods to working with factorials: prime factorization and that $n! = n \times (n-1)!$.

Chapter 17
Data Methods

On many question types, especially Integrated Reasoning and Data Sufficiency style questions, fluency with how data can be used and manipulated is a key to success. In this chapter, we will cover different methods of deriving information from or manipulating data, including Arrangements and Combinations, Probability, Standard Deviation, Correlation, and advice for Interpreting Charts and Graphs.

WHAT IS DATA METHODS?

Data methods represent the different ways data can be manipulated to derive information on the GRE. Some of the topics in this chapter may not necessarily show up in your graduate class in analytics. Likewise, some of the content covered in other chapters, such as averages, medians, modes, and ranges, are commonly considered part of data analytics.

Nonetheless, the content in this chapter is a combination of technical information about mathematical operations and theoretical content about individual data points or how different data points interact with one another.

Let's dive in!

PERMUTATIONS AND COMBINATIONS

In general, permutation and combination problems tend to show up as medium-hard to hard problems on the GMAT.

Here's a very simple example of a combination problem:

At a certain restaurant, a meal consists of one appetizer, one main course, and one dessert. If the restaurant has 2 appetizers, 3 main courses, and 5 desserts, then how many different meals could the restaurant serve?

(A) 60
(B) 30
(C) 10
(D)   6
(E)   3

Here's How to Crack It
You could just carefully write down all the different combinations:

Shrimp cocktail with meatloaf with cherry pie
Shrimp cocktail with meatloaf with ice cream
Shrimp cocktail with meatloaf with...

You get the idea. But first of all, this is too time consuming, and second of all, there's a much easier way.

For a problem that asks you to choose a number of items to fill specific spots, when each spot is filled from a different source, all you have to do is multiply the number of choices for each of the spots.

So, because there were 2 appetizers, 3 main courses, and 5 possible desserts, the total number of combinations of a full meal at this restaurant would be $2 \times 3 \times 5$, or 30. The answer is (B).

Permutations: Single Source, Order Matters

The same principle applies when you're choosing from a group of similar items—with one slight wrinkle. Take a look at this easy permutation problem:

> Three basketball teams play in a league against each other. At the end of the season, how many different ways could the 3 teams end up ranked against each other?
>
> (A) 1
> (B) 3
> (C) 6
> (D) 36
> (E) 72

Here's How to Crack It

You could just carefully write down all the different combinations. If we call the three teams A, B, and C, then here are the different ways they could end up in the standings:

ABC   ACB   BAC   BCA   CAB   CBA

But again, this approach is time-consuming (even more so for more difficult problems). As you probably suspected, there's a simpler and faster way to solve this problem.

> For a problem that asks you to choose from the same source to fill specific spots, all you have to do is multiply the number of choices for each of the spots—but the number of choices keeps getting smaller.

Let's think for a moment about how many teams could possibly end up in first place. If you said 3, you're doing just fine.

Now, let's think about how many teams could finish second. Are there still 3 possibilities? Not really, because one team has already finished first. There are, in fact, only 2 possible teams that could finish second.

And finally, let's think about how many teams could finish third. In fact, there is only 1 team that could finish third.

To find the number of different ways these teams could end up in the rankings, just multiply the number of choices for first place (in this case, 3) by the number of choices for second place (in this case, 2) by the number of choices for third place (in this case, 1).

$$3 \times 2 \times 1 = 6$$

The correct answer is (C).

In general, no matter how many items there are to arrange, you can figure out the number of permutations of a group of n similar objects with the formula:

$$n(n-1)(n-2)\ldots \times 3 \times 2 \times 1, \text{ or } n!$$

So, if there were 9 baseball teams, the total number of permutations of their standings would be $9 \times 8 \times 7 \times 6 \times 5 \times 4 \times 3 \times 2 \times 1$, also sometimes written as 9!. If 4 sailboats sailed a race, the total number of permutations of the orders in which they could cross the finish line would be $4 \times 3 \times 2 \times 1$, also sometimes written as 4!.

Single Source, Order Matters but Only for a Selection

The problems we've shown you so far were necessary to show you the concepts behind permutation problems—but were much too easy to be on the GMAT. Here's a problem that would be more likely to appear on the test:

---○---

Seven basketball teams play in a league against each other. At the end of the season, how many different arrangements are there for the top 3 teams in the rankings?

(A)   6
(B)   42
(C)   210
(D) 5,040
(E) 50,450

Easy Eliminations

If you were to see this problem on the computer-adaptive section of the actual GMAT, you should first stop and give yourself a pat on the back, because it means you're doing pretty well—permutation and combination problems usually show up only among the more difficult problems. But after you've congratulated yourself, stop and think for a moment. Could the answer to this difficult problem simply be a matter of finding $7 \times 6 \times 5 \times 4 \times 3 \times 2 \times 1$, (D)? Too easy. Because the question is asking for the permutations for only 3 of the 7 slots, the number must be less than that. So get rid of (D) and (E).

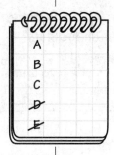

Here's How to Crack It

To find all the possible permutations of the top 3 out of 7 baseball teams, simply multiply the number of combinations for each spot in the standings. How many teams are possibilities for the first place slot? If you said 7, you're right. How about for the second slot? Well, one team is already occupying the first place slot, so there are only 6 contenders left. And for the third place slot? That's right: 5.

So, the correct answer is $7 \times 6 \times 5 = 210$, or (C).

---○---

In general, no matter how many items there are to arrange, you can figure out the number of permutations of r objects chosen from a set of n objects with the formula:

$$n(n-1)(n-2) \ldots \times (n-r+1)$$

So if there were 9 baseball teams (*n*), the total number of permutations of the top 4 teams (*r*) would be $9 \times 8 \times 7 \times 6$. If 4 sailboats sailed a race (*n*), the total number of permutations of the first 3 boats to cross the finish line (*r*) would be $4 \times 3 \times 2$. Here is another way to write this same formula:

$$\frac{n!}{(n-r)!}$$

(where *n* = total items and *r* = the number selected)

Because $9 \times 8 \times 7 \times 6$ is the same as $\dfrac{9 \times 8 \times 7 \times 6 \times \cancel{5}!}{\cancel{5}!}$

Combinations: Single Source, Order Doesn't Matter

In the previous problems, the order in which the items are arranged actually matters to the problem. For example, if the order in which the three teams finish a season is Yankees, Red Sox, Orioles—that's entirely different than if the order were Red Sox, Yankees, Orioles, especially if you're from Boston.

However, combination problems don't care about the order of the items.

> **Not Sure If It's a Permutation or a Combination Problem?**
> Here's a good clue:
> Permutation problems usually ask for "arrangements."
> Combination problems usually ask for "groups."

Six horses are running in a race. How many different groups of horses could make up the first 3 finishers?

(A)   6
(B)   18
(C)   20
(D) 120
(E) 720

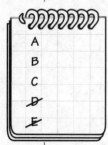

> **Easy Eliminations**
> If we cared about the order in which the top 3 horses finished the race, then the answer would be the number of permutations: $6 \times 5 \times 4$, or 120. But in this case, we care only about the number of *unique* permutations, and that means the number will be smaller because we don't have to count the set of, for example, (Secretariat, Seattle Slew, and Affirmed) and the set of (Seattle Slew, Secretariat, and Affirmed) as two different permutations. If the correct answer must be smaller than 120, then we can eliminate (D) and (E)—they're too big.

Here's How to Crack It

To find the number of combinations, first find the number of permutations. If 6 horses run in the race, and we are interested in the top 3 finishers, then the number of permutations would be $6 \times 5 \times 4$, or 120. But if we don't care about the order in which they finished, then a bunch of these 120 permutations turn out to be duplicates.

How many? Let's think of one of those permutations. Let's say the first 3 finishers were Secretariat, Seattle Slew, and Affirmed. How many different ways could we arrange these 3 horses? If you said 6, you're thinking like a permutation expert. There are 3!, or $3 \times 2 \times 1$ permutations of any 3 objects. So, of those 120 permutations of the top 3 horses, each combination is being counted 3!, or 6 times. To find the number of combinations, we need to divide 120 by 6. The correct answer is (C).

In general, no matter how many items there are to arrange, you can figure out the number of combinations of r objects chosen from a set of n objects with the formula:

$$\frac{n(n-1)(n-2)...\times(n-r+1)}{r!}$$

So if there were 9 baseball teams, the total number of combinations of the top 4 teams would be:

$$\frac{9 \times 8 \times 7 \times 6}{4 \times 3 \times 2 \times 1}$$

Another way to write this same formula is:

$$\frac{n!}{r!(n-r)!}$$

because $\dfrac{9 \times 8 \times 7 \times 6}{4 \times 3 \times 2 \times 1}$ is the same as $\dfrac{9 \times 8 \times 7 \times 6 \times \cancel{5}!}{(4 \times 3 \times 2 \times 1) \times \cancel{5}!}$

PROBABILITY

Probability, Part 1

Just the word is enough to cause math-phobes to run for the exits—but, at least as it appears on the GMAT, probability really isn't all that bad. Check out the easy example below:

> A fair, six-sided die with faces numbered one through six is rolled once. What is the probability that this roll results in a 2 ?

Well, of course, there's only one possibility of this happening, and there are six possible outcomes, so there's a one-in-six chance. In essence, this is all that probability is about. On the GMAT, probability is usually expressed as a fraction: the total number of possibilities is always the denominator. The number of possibilities that match what you want is the numerator. In the example above, that translates to $\frac{1}{6}$.

$$\text{Basic probability formula} = \frac{\text{number of outcomes you want}}{\text{total number of possible outcomes}}$$

Let's make this example a little harder:

> A fair, six-sided die with faces numbered one through six is rolled once. What is the probability that this roll results in either a 2 or a 3 ?

The total number of possible outcomes (the denominator) is still the same: 6. But the numerator is different now. There are two possibilities that would match what we want, so the numerator becomes 2. The probability is $\frac{2}{6}$, or $\frac{1}{3}$.

Let's make the example a little harder still.

> A fair, six-sided die with faces numbered one through six is rolled twice. What is the probability that both rolls result in a 2 ?

Obviously, the odds of this happening are much smaller. How do you figure out the probability of something happening over a series of events? To find the probability of a series of events, you multiply the probabilities of each of the individual events. Let's start with the first roll of the die. We already figured out that the probability of the die landing with its "2" side facing up on a single toss is $\frac{1}{6}$. Now, let's think about the second toss. Well, actually, the probability of this happening on the second toss is exactly the same: $\frac{1}{6}$.

However, to figure out the probability of the "2" side facing upward on *both* tosses, you multiply the first probability by the second probability: $\frac{1}{6} \times \frac{1}{6} = \frac{1}{36}$.

The probability that A **and** B will both happen:
p(A and B) = p(A) × p(B)

Here's an example of a moderately difficult GMAT problem.

There are 8 job applicants sitting in a waiting room—4 women and 4 men. If 2 of the applicants are selected at random, what is the probability that both will be women?

(A) $\frac{1}{2}$

(B) $\frac{3}{7}$

(C) $\frac{1}{4}$

(D) $\frac{3}{14}$

(E) $\frac{1}{10}$

Admissions Insight No. 2: Letters of Recommendation, Part 2

Most MBA programs require two to three letters of recommendation. The best recommendations are from people who know you well in a professional capacity and can discuss the same points you have already made in your essays.

Unlike admissions committees for other graduate programs, MBA admissions committees generally prefer professional recommendations to academic ones.

Here's How to Crack It

Let's take the first event in the series. The total number of possibilities for the first selection is 8, because there are 8 applicants in the room. Of those 8 people, 4 are women, so the probability that the first person chosen will be a woman is $\frac{4}{8}$, or $\frac{1}{2}$. You might think that the probability would be exactly the same for the second choice (in which case you would multiply $\frac{1}{2} \times \frac{1}{2}$ and choose (C)), but in fact, that's not true. Let's consider: the first woman has just left the room, and they are about to choose another applicant at random. How many total people are now in the room? Aha! Only 7. And how many of those 7 are women? Only 3. So the probability that the second choice will be a woman is actually only $\frac{3}{7}$, which is (B). But we aren't done yet. We have to figure out the probability that BOTH choices in this series of two choices will be women. The probability that the first will be a woman is $\frac{1}{2}$. The probability that the second will be a woman is $\frac{3}{7}$. The probability that they both will be women is $\frac{1}{2} \times \frac{3}{7}$, or $\frac{3}{14}$. The answer is (D).

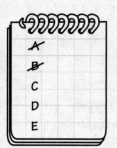

Easy Eliminations

The GMAT test-writers like to see if they can trick you into picking partial answers—i.e., numbers that you get in the course of solving a problem that are not quite the final answer. The probability that the first choice will be a woman is $\frac{1}{2}$, (A)—but does it feel like you've done enough work to "deserve" to get this problem right yet? Nope—this is only an intermediate step. The probability that the second choice will be a woman is $\frac{3}{7}$, (B). But again, this is just another intermediate step. Don't fall for these trick choices—cross off (A) and (B).

Probability, Part 2: One Thing or Another

So far, we've been dealing with the probability of one event happening and then another event happening (for example, in that last problem, the first event was choosing a female job applicant; the second event was choosing ANOTHER female job applicant). But what if you are asked to find the probability of either one thing OR another thing happening? To solve this type of problem, you simply add the probabilities. Note that pure versions of these "or" problems are incredibly rare on the GMAT. Understanding the idea can be helpful on other problems, however.

The probability that A or B will happen: p(A or B) = p(A) + p(B).

This is the formula used if the probabilities are mutually exclusive, that is, if they cannot happen together. Use this formula because **on the GMAT, probabilities are almost always mutually exclusive**. In case you're curious, the formula used to show the probability that A or B will happen, if the events are NOT mutually exclusive, is

p(A or B) = p(A) + p(B) − p(A and B).

Here's an example:

Sally and Sam are watching a magician perform with 16 of their friends. If the magician chooses one audience member at random to assist with a trick, what is the probability that either Sally or Sam is chosen?

Here's How to Crack It

By this point, you should have no problem figuring out that the probability of Sally being chosen is $\frac{1}{18}$. And the probability of Sam being chosen? That's right: $\frac{1}{18}$. So what is the probability of Sally or Sam being chosen?

$$\frac{1}{18} + \frac{1}{18} = \frac{2}{18} \ or \ \frac{1}{9}$$

Probability, Part 3:
The Odds That Something Doesn't Happen

But what if you are asked to find the probability that something will NOT happen? Well, think of it this way: if the probability of snow is 70%, or $\frac{7}{10}$, what's the probability that it won't snow? That's right: 30%, or $\frac{3}{10}$. To figure out the probability that something won't happen, simply figure out the probability that it WILL happen and then subtract that fraction from 1.

---

p(event happens) + p(event does NOT happen) = 1

Here's an example:

Sally and Sam are watching a magician perform with 16 of their friends. If one audience member is chosen at random to assist with a trick, what is the probability that neither Sally nor Sam is chosen?

Here's How to Crack It

As we already know, the probability that Sally will be chosen is $\frac{1}{18}$. The probability that Sam will be chosen is also $\frac{1}{18}$. So what is the probability that neither Sally nor Sam will be chosen?

$$1 - \frac{2}{18} = \frac{16}{18} = \frac{8}{9}$$

Probability, Part 4:
The Odds That at Least One Thing Will Happen

What if the problem asks the probability of something happening at least once? To calculate the probability of at least one thing happening, just use this equation: the probability of what you WANT to happen plus the probability of what you DON'T want to happen equals one. Or, to put it another way:

$$p(\text{event happens}) = 1 - p(\text{event does NOT happen})$$

Here's an example:

Nine boys and nine girls are watching a magician perform. Four times during the performance a child is chosen at random to assist with a trick. If any of the children can be chosen to assist with each of the four tricks, what is the probability that at least one girl is chosen?

Here's How to Crack It

To find the odds of at least one girl being chosen, let's begin by figuring out the odds that a girl isn't chosen. The magician will make a total of four choices. What are the odds that the magician will not pick a girl in the first round? If you said $\frac{9}{18}$ or $\frac{1}{2}$, you are doing just fine. And what are the odds that the magician will not pick a girl the second, third, and fourth round? Each time, the odds of not picking a girl stay the same, because the children are returned to the pool of possible candidates, so each time the odds will be $\frac{9}{18}$ or $\frac{1}{2}$. The probability of not picking a girl all four times is:

$$\frac{1}{2} \times \frac{1}{2} \times \frac{1}{2} \times \frac{1}{2} = \frac{1}{16}$$

But we aren't done. The probability of a girl being picked at least once is 1 minus the probability that she will not be picked. So the correct answer is:

$$1 - \frac{1}{16} = \frac{15}{16}$$

STANDARD DEVIATION

Standard deviation is another way that the dispersion of a group of numbers is calculated.

A Question of Spread

The first thing to know is what is meant by standard deviation on the GMAT. Standard deviation is a measure of the amount of spread, or variation, of a set of data values. A low standard deviation indicates that the data values tend to be close to the mean (thus, to have little spread), while a high standard deviation indicates that the values are spread out over a wider range. So, the further the distance between the members of a set and the set's average, the greater the standard deviation of the set.

Consider two sets of numbers, {4,4,4} and {3,4,5}. The first set, {4,4,4}, has a mean value of 4, as $\left(\dfrac{4+4+4}{3}\right)$ is equal to 4. However, since each member of the set is equal to the mean (and thus to each other member of the set), there is no distance between the members of the set and the mean of the set, so there is no spread among the numbers. Now look at the second set, {3,4,5}. This set also has a mean of 4, as $\left(\dfrac{3+4+5}{3}\right)$ is equal to 4. However, in this group, instead of all numbers being equal to the mean, two members of the set have some distance from the mean (3 and 5 are not equal to the mean of 4). Therefore, since the second set has more spread (the members of the set have more distance from the mean), the second set has a greater standard deviation.

Here's an example of how GMAC might test standard deviation:

What is the standard deviation of set R ?

(1)   The value of all elements of set R is between 5 and 20.
(2)   The mean of set R is 12.

Here's How to Crack It

This is a Value Data Sufficiency question, so begin by determining what is known from the question stem and what is needed from the statements in order to answer the question. Begin by determining what is known. The question stem only provides that there is a set R. Next, determine what is needed. In order to be sufficient, the statements need to provide information necessary to determine the standard deviation. In order to determine the standard deviation, the statements need to provide a way to determine the values in set R. Evaluate the statements individually.

Statement (1) provides a range of the value of all elements of set R, but does not state how many elements there are, or what the average is, so there is no way to determine the standard deviation of set R from this information. Write down BCE.

Statement (2) provides the mean of set R. However, this does not provide information that indicates the actual values of R or how many elements are in set R, so eliminate (B).

The statements combined provide a range of values and a mean for set R. However, this information is still not sufficient. For example, the values of set R could be 11 and 13, which are between 5 and 20 and have an average of 12. Alternatively, set R could contain 6 instances of the number 12. Both options satisfy the statements, but there is not a consistent answer for the question. Therefore, the statements combined are not sufficient. Eliminate (C).

The correct answer is (E).

———————————○———————————

Now, let's try a question that deals with standard deviation differently.

———————————○———————————

For a certain distribution, the value 12.0 is one standard deviation above the mean and the value 15.0 is three standard deviations above the mean. What is the mean of the data set?

(A) 9.0
(B) 9.5
(C) 10.0
(D) 10.5
(E) 11.0

Here's How to Crack It

This one's a little tougher than the previous question. The question provides neither the individual data points nor the mean, and GMAC is hoping that this will throw you off. But remember that standard deviation deals with the distance from the mean. Start by determining the size of one standard deviation. Since 12.0 is one standard deviation above the mean and 15.0 is three standard deviations above the mean, then the difference between the data values represents the difference in the number of standard deviations. Therefore:

$$15.0 - 12.0 = 3.0 \text{ st dev} - 1.0 \text{ st dev, so } 3.0 = 2.0 \text{ st dev}$$

Now set up a proportion to find the size of one standard deviation:

$$\frac{3.0}{2.0 \text{ st dev}} = \frac{x}{1 \text{ st dev}}$$

Solve to find that $x = 1.5$, which means that one standard deviation for this data set is equal to 1.5. Since 12.0 is one standard deviation above the mean, the mean of the data set is $12.0 - 1.5 = 10.5$, so the answer is (D).

CORRELATION

Questions that involve charts or tables may ask about the correlation between two variables. Correlation refers to the way in which variables are related to one another. In statistics, there are a number of techniques and methods for measuring the correlation between two variables. And while most of these are beyond the scope of the GMAT, it's useful to introduce a couple of concepts to prepare you for any correlation questions on the GMAT.

Two variables can show negative correlation, positive correlation, or no correlation at all. The strength of the correlation can range from perfectly correlated to no correlation. We can use correlation to begin to determine what impact a change in one variable would have on another variable.

A perfectly positive correlation tells us that for every increase in one variable, we get a consistent and expected increase in the other variable. If you were to plot two variables with a perfectly positive correlation on a scatter plot, the line connecting all the data points would look like this:

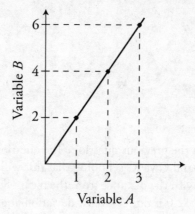

For every 1 unit of Variable A, Variable B increases 2 units. This happens with every increase of Variable A with no deviation, so this is a perfectly positively correlated relationship between two variables.

A perfectly negatively correlated relationship between two variables looks like this:

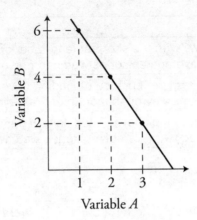

For every 1 unit of Variable A, Variable B decreases by 2 units. Similar to the perfectly positively correlated relationship, there is no deviation in this relationship.

It's important to remember that a correlation does not have to be perfectly positive or perfectly negative in order to be simply positive or negative. There can be fluctuations in the data points. So long as the general trend of the data points follows the pattern, there can be negative or positive correlation.

The GMAT will test vocabulary such as positive and negative correlation, but will also ask questions about relationships between the data points in the chart or table without describing the correlation.

Consider the following questions that test correlation.

The table displays viewership statistics for six different reality television shows on a streaming service.

Show	Viewers per Episode (000s)	Length per Episodes (minutes)	Average Episodes Watched per Login	Viewer Abandonment Rate
People Living Under a Ship	369	60	1.2	26%
Finding Love	365	45	1	27%
Finding Love: Island	374	48	1.5	29%
Cast Away	373	55	1.2	25%
By Yourself	382	75	2	25%
Lifestyle Advice	396	65	1.8	26%

For each of the following statements, select Yes if the statement is true based on the information in the table. Otherwise, select No.

Yes	No	
		The show with the shortest length per episode also has the fewest average episodes watched per login.
		If the length per episode of Finding Love: Island were increased, its viewer abandonment rate would decrease.
		For each of the shows listed, length per episode is negatively correlated with average episodes watched per login.

Sort by: Viewers per Episode

Show	Viewers per Episode (000s)	Length per Episodes (minutes)	Average Episodes Watched per Login	Viewer Abandonment Rate
Finding Love	365	45	1	27%
People Living Under a Ship	369	60	1.2	26%
Cast Away	373	55	1.2	25%
Finding Love: Island	374	48	1.5	29%
By Yourself	382	75	2	25%
Lifestyle Advice	396	65	1.8	26%

Sort by: Length per Episode

Show	Viewers per Episode (000s)	Length per Episodes (minutes)	Average Episodes Watched per Login	Viewer Abandonment Rate
Finding Love	365	45	1	27%
Finding Love: Island	374	48	1.5	29%
Cast Away	373	55	1.2	25%
People Living Under a Ship	369	60	1.2	26%
Lifestyle Advice	396	65	1.8	26%
By Yourself	382	75	2	25%

Sort by: Average Episodes Watched per Login

Show	Viewers per Episode (000s)	Length per Episodes (minutes)	Average Episodes Watched per Login	Viewer Abandonment Rate
Finding Love	365	45	1	27%
People Living Under a Ship	369	60	1.2	26%
Cast Away	373	55	1.2	25%
Finding Love: Island	374	48	1.5	29%
Lifestyle Advice	396	65	1.8	26%
By Yourself	382	75	2	25%

Sort by: Viewer Abandonment Rate

Show	Viewers per Episode (000s)	Length per Episodes (minutes)	Average Episodes Watched per Login	Viewer Abandonment Rate
Cast Away	373	55	1.2	25%
By Yourself	382	75	2	25%
People Living Under a Ship	369	60	1.2	26%
Lifestyle Advice	396	65	1.8	26%
Finding Love	365	45	1	27%
Finding Love: Island	374	48	1.5	29%

Here's How to Crack It

This is a Table Analysis question, so begin by reading the headers and row labels to understand the information in the table. This table shows statistics about six different television shows. The questions are in *Yes/No* format, so your task is to evaluate each question and determine if the answer is Yes or No based on the information in the table.

Look at the first statement, which is that the show with the shortest length per episode also has the fewest average episodes watched per login. Determine if you need to sort the table to answer this question. Because there are only six shows, it's not necessary to sort the table here. Find the show with the shortest length per episode, which is Finding Love. Now determine if it has the fewest average episodes watched per login. Its average episodes watched per login is 1, which is the least of all 6 shows. Therefore, the answer to this question is *Yes*.

Now look at the second statement, which is that if the length per episode of Finding Love: Island were increased, its viewer abandonment rate would decrease. Determine if you need to sort the table to answer this question. Because this statement asks about the relationship between two of the variables and it wants you to consider the full dataset, it might be easiest to sort by length per episode. When sorted by length per episode, it becomes clear that as the length per episode increases, the viewer abandonment rate decreases. Therefore, the answer to this question is *Yes*.

Lastly, look at the third statement, which is that for each of the shows listed, length per episode is negatively correlated with average episodes watched per login. Keep the table sorted by length per episode and evaluate the relationship between length per episode and average episodes watched per login. The statement is that these two items are negatively correlated, which would suggest that as length per episode increases, average episodes watched per login decreases. This is not true based on the information in the data. Therefore, the answer to this question is *No*.

INTERPRETING CHARTS AND GRAPHS

As businesses have evolved to rely more and more on data and analytics, MBA programs have followed suit, launching data analytics courses in droves. The GMAT has followed this trend and tests general ability to understand and interpret charts and graphs now more heavily than ever before.

Charts and graphs on the GMAT can come in all shapes and sizes. It would be impossible to write a section of this book that covers all possible iterations of the types of charts you might encounter on test day. In lieu of that, we've developed some advice on the best way to think about the information on a chart or graph to make sure you've interpreted it quickly and accurately.

Advice: Always understand the topic

Charts and graphs are meant to tell a story or the details of a specific piece of data. In order to know the details of the story, you first need to understand what the story is about! Many charts on the GMAT will contain text that explains the information in the chart. While you can read this information, it can also be an unnecessary expenditure of time.

Instead, start by reading the title, *x*- and *y*-axis titles, and any column or row names associated with the chart. Oftentimes, it's possible to get an understanding of the content in the chart or graph just by looking at these items.

If you look at those details and are still a bit unsure about the details of the chart, then it is probably worth the time to read the associated text.

Either way, attempting to answer questions about a chart that you don't understand the details of is a lost cause. Always make sure you orient yourself to the details before rushing to answer the questions.

Advice: Observe the x- and y-axis

Not all charts have an *x*- and a *y*-axis. But, for those that do, it's important to observe two distinct elements of each of the axes: the title and the tick marks.

The title of the axes will typically tell you the measure represented by the axis and any necessary units that might be important to understanding the measure.

The tick marks tell you the scale of the measure, which is important to gauging the impact of any given point in the chart.

Advice: How are any special markings or colors being used?

One of the most eye-catching parts of a chart or graph is any colors, symbols, or special markings associated with the image. Sometimes, these markings can be used to highlight important pieces of information. Other times, they can be used to delineate between different measurements or dimensions in the data.

Regardless of how they are being used, knowing what colors, symbols, or special markings represent in a chart goes a long way to being able to interpret and mine information from the graph.

Typically, the fastest way to find out what each of the different markings or colors represent is by looking for the legend. However, in some question types such as Multi-Source Reasoning, the details of the legend may be tucked into the text or even on a different tab of the question!

Advice: Be able to state, in your own words, what a single point in the graph represents

A single point on a graph can be a dot on a scatter plot, a bar in a bar chart, a section of a pie chart, a line in a line chart, the colored area of an area chart, etc. It's important to be able to articulate what a single point on the graph represents.

For instance, a point on a scatter plot represents the interaction of two measures in the dataset—the measure on the *x*-axis and the measure on the *y*-axis. A bar on a bar chart typically will represent the amount of a certain measure by the length of the bar and the subsections of a particular dimension by the presence of different bars. A section of a pie chart will represent a portion of a total measure by a specific subsection of a dimension.

But, it's not enough to know what these different points are in theory. You need to be able to state clearly and accurately the details of the measures. For instance, say you have a scatterplot of different heights and weights from a doctor's office colored by gender. It's not enough to say that a single point is the interaction of two measures—you need to be able to articulate that a single point is the height and weight of a person of a certain gender.

DRILL 17

The answers to these questions can be found in Part V.

1. On a certain two-part test, a student must choose one of 4 short essays and one of 2 long essays in Part One, and then choose one of x short essays and one of y long essays in Part Two. If there is a total of 144 different lineups of essays that the student could choose, and the ratio of available long essays to short essays remains constant in both parts of the test, then what is the value of x ?

    (A)   3
    (B)   6
    (C)   8
    (D)   9
    (E)   12

2. A focus group is currently made up of x men and y women. If 2 men and 4 women are added to the group, and if one person is selected at random from the larger focus group, then what is the probability that a man is selected?

    (A) $\dfrac{x}{x+2}$

    (B) $\dfrac{x}{x+y}$

    (C) $\dfrac{x+2}{x+y+2}$

    (D) $\dfrac{y+4}{x+y+6}$

    (E) $\dfrac{x+2}{x+y+6}$

3. If there are g girls and b boys on a team, and two members of the team are randomly selected, then what is the probability, in terms of g and b, that at least one selected player is a girl?

    (A) $\dfrac{g(g-1)}{(b+g)(b+g-1)}$

    (B) $\dfrac{b(b-1)}{(b+g)(b+g-1)}$

    (C) $\dfrac{2bg}{(b+g)(b+g-1)}$

    (D) $\dfrac{g(2b+g-1)}{(b+g)(b+g-1)}$

    (E) $\dfrac{b(2g+b-1)}{(b+g)(b+g-1)}$

4. The new recruits of a military organization who score more than 2 standard deviations below the mean of their physical conditioning test are required to retest. If the test scores are normally distributed and have an arithmetic mean of 72, what is the score at or below which the recruits are required to retest?

   (1) The range between the 3rd standard deviation above the mean and the 3rd standard deviation below the mean is 30.
   (2) The 3rd standard deviation above the mean is 87.

   (A) Statement (1) ALONE is sufficient, but statement (2) alone is not sufficient.
   (B) Statement (2) ALONE is sufficient, but statement (1) alone is not sufficient.
   (C) BOTH statements TOGETHER are sufficient, but NEITHER statement ALONE is sufficient.
   (D) EACH statement ALONE is sufficient.
   (E) Statements (1) and (2) TOGETHER are not sufficient.

5. Which of the following contains the interval two standard deviations from the mean of a set of data with an arithmetic mean of 46 and a standard deviation of 4 ?

   (A) 38 to 46
   (B) 38 to 54
   (C) 42 to 50
   (D) 44 to 48
   (E) 46 to 50

6. For the set of measurements 3, x_2, x_3, what is the value of x_3 ?

   (1) The range of the set of measurements is 0.
   (2) The standard deviation of the set of measurements is 0.

   (A) Statement (1) ALONE is sufficient, but statement (2) alone is not sufficient.
   (B) Statement (2) ALONE is sufficient, but statement (1) alone is not sufficient.
   (C) BOTH statements TOGETHER are sufficient, but NEITHER statement ALONE is sufficient.
   (D) EACH statement ALONE is sufficient.
   (E) Statements (1) and (2) TOGETHER are not sufficient.

$$X = \{9, 10, 11, 12\}$$

$$Y = \{2, 3, 4, 5\}$$

7. If one number is chosen at random from each of the sets above and the number from Set X is divided by the number from Set Y, what is the probability that the result is an integer?

    (A) $\dfrac{1}{16}$

    (B) $\dfrac{3}{8}$

    (C) $\dfrac{1}{2}$

    (D) $\dfrac{3}{4}$

    (E) $\dfrac{15}{16}$

8. Sam and Jessica are invited to a dance. If there are 7 men and 7 women in total at the dance, and one woman and one man are chosen to lead the dance, what is the probability that Sam and Jessica will NOT be the pair chosen to lead the dance?

    (A) $\dfrac{1}{49}$

    (B) $\dfrac{1}{7}$

    (C) $\dfrac{6}{7}$

    (D) $\dfrac{47}{49}$

    (E) $\dfrac{48}{49}$

9. A six-sided die with faces numbered one through six is rolled three times. What is the probability that the face with the number 6 on it will NOT be facing upward on all three rolls?

    (A) $\dfrac{1}{216}$

    (B) $\dfrac{1}{6}$

    (C) $\dfrac{2}{3}$

    (D) $\dfrac{17}{18}$

    (E) $\dfrac{215}{216}$

10. For a certain foot race, how many different arrangements of medal winners are possible?

    (1)   Medals will be given for 1st, 2nd, and 3rd place.
    (2)   There are 10 runners in the race.

    (A)   Statement (1) ALONE is sufficient, but statement (2) alone is not sufficient.
    (B)   Statement (2) ALONE is sufficient, but statement (1) alone is not sufficient.
    (C)   BOTH statements TOGETHER are sufficient, but NEITHER statement ALONE is sufficient.
    (D)   EACH statement ALONE is sufficient.
    (E)   Statements (1) and (2) TOGETHER are not sufficient.

11. An employer has 6 applicants for a programming position and 4 applicants for a manager position. If the employer must hire 3 programmers and 2 managers, what is the total number of ways the employer can make the selection?

    (A)   1,490
    (B)   132
    (C)   120
    (D)   60
    (E)   23

12. If a fair two-sided coin is flipped 6 times, what is the probability that tails is the result at least twice but at most 5 times?

    (A) $\dfrac{5}{8}$

    (B) $\dfrac{3}{4}$

    (C) $\dfrac{7}{8}$

    (D) $\dfrac{57}{64}$

    (E) $\dfrac{15}{16}$

13. Each of the integers from 1 to 20 is written on a separate index card and placed in a box. If the cards are drawn from the box at random without replacement, how many cards must be drawn to ensure that the product of all the integers drawn is even?

    (A)   19
    (B)   12
    (C)   11
    (D)   10
    (E)   3

14. A four-character password consists of one letter from the English alphabet and three different digits from 0 to 9. If the letter is the second or third character of the password, how many different passwords are possible?

   (A)   5,040
   (B)   18,720
   (C)   26,000
   (D)   37,440
   (E)   52,000

15. A first-grade teacher uses ten flash cards, numbered 1 through 10, to teach her students to order numbers correctly. She has students choose four flash cards at random and arrange the cards in ascending order. If she removes the cards numbered 2 and 4, how many different correctly ordered arrangements of the four selected cards are possible?

   (A)   70
   (B)   210
   (C)   336
   (D)   840
   (E)   1,680

Summary

- o Permutation and combination problems ask you to choose or arrange a group of objects.
  - To choose a number of items to fill specific spots, when each spot is filled from a different source, multiply the number of choices for each of the spots.
  - To choose from a set of n objects from the same source to fill specific spots, when order matters, multiply the number of choices for each of the spots—but the number of choices keeps getting smaller, according to the formula:

    $n(n-1)(n-2) \ldots \times 3 \times 2 \times 1$, or $n!$

  - To find the number of permutations of r objects chosen from a set of n objects, when order matters, use the formula $n(n-1)(n-2) \ldots \times (n-r+1)$, also expressed as $\dfrac{n!}{(n-r)!}$.

  - To find the number of combinations of r objects chosen from a set of n objects, use the formula $\dfrac{n(n-1)(n-2)\ldots\times(n-r+1)}{r!}$

- o Probability problems can be solved by putting the total number of possibilities in the denominator and the number of possibilities that match what you are looking for in the numerator.

- o Standard deviation is a measure of spread of a set of numbers.

- o Correlation refers to the way in which data points are related to one another and is an expression of the general trend of the dataset.

- o Quickly and accurately interpreting the information in charts and graphs is an important step to successfully analyzing data for information that may help you answer questions.

Part IV
How to
Crack the
Verbal GMAT

Chapter 18
Reading
Comprehension

Reading Comprehension questions make up about half of the questions in the Verbal section. Reading passages occur at any point in the Verbal section, but all questions related to a passage will be presented together.

READING COMPREHENSION OVERVIEW

In most cases, you'll see three or four reading passages on the test. There are usually two short passages, which average around 250 words and are typically followed by three questions, and one or two long passages, which average around 350 words and are typically followed by four questions.

Reading Comprehension passages can be intimidating to test-takers, as there is a sudden rush of information on the screen and the test-taker prepares for the task of reading and answering questions on a passage that is often dense, wordy, and boring. During Reading Comprehension passages, it is common for test-takers to feel rushed, which makes it hard to pay attention to a passage that covers a topic area that most find dry. However, contrary to popular belief, everything you need to know to crack Reading Comprehension questions can be found in the text. This chapter is going to teach you how to crack the passages and questions, leading you to the correct answers.

MORE INFORMATION ON READING COMPREHENSION PASSAGES

GMAT passages cover a variety of topics but typically come from four primary areas.

- *Social Science*: social or historical issues, such as the civil rights movement or World War I
- *Physical Sciences*: natural science topics, such as photosynthesis or black holes
- *Biological Sciences:* topics related to living organisms and how they interact with their environment
- *Business*: business-related topics, such as management strategies or the loosening of international trade restrictions

The passage appears on the left side of the screen. The passage may be too long to fit in the window, so you may have to use the scroll bar to read it completely. The questions appear on the right side of the screen, one at a time. After you answer the first question, another appears in its place. The passage remains unchanged and in place so you can always refer to it. As with any other type of question on the GMAT, you must answer Reading Comprehension questions in the order that they appear on your screen. So if a question that asks for the main idea appears first, that's the question you must answer first.

THE BASIC APPROACH TO CRACKING GMAT READING COMPREHENSION

Before we begin to crack the Reading Comprehension passages and questions, it is important to establish The Basic Approach, which allows you to:

- actively read the passages and seek out the most important information
- understand the different types of questions and what they require you to do
- quickly find the credited response by eliminating incorrect answers

Don't Be Predictable

The typical test-taker is predictable and approaches questions on the test in a certain way. The people who write the GMAT create questions and passages that are designed with those people in mind. They will make questions that trick and confuse test-takers who follow the typical approach. However, if you approach the test in a better way, you improve your chance of getting a better score. One hard-and-fast rule of test taking is that whenever you do what the test-writers expect, you don't get the best score that you could. When you do things in a different way, you increase your chances of getting a better score. So, our approach to reading needs to be that "different way." The different ways you are going to learn are The Basics of Cracking the Passage, The Basics of Cracking the Questions, and The Basics of Cracking the Answer Choices. These combine to form the foundation that is used for the Basic Approach to Cracking Reading Comprehension.

The Basics of Cracking the Passage

Let's start with the approach to cracking the passage. The typical test-taker reads the passage without a plan. So to crack the passage, you need to have a plan for reading the passage. The typical test-taker concentrates on the facts in the passage rather than why those facts are there. So to crack the passage, you also need to read for the main idea of the passage.

The Basics of Cracking the Questions

The typical test-taker reads the question but doesn't identify the question task. To crack the questions, you must learn to locate both the subject and the task of the question. The **subject** of the question is what you need to find in the passage. The **question task** tells you what type of information you need to find about the subject of the question. For example, do you need to locate what the author said about the subject, or do you need to find out why the author mentioned the subject?

The Basics of Cracking the Answer Choices

The typical test-taker is focused on simply finding the correct answer. While that may seem a reasonable goal, it's actually a more effective strategy to utilize Process of Elimination (POE) and eliminate wrong answers. Cracking the answer choices is all about understanding how the

GMAC constructs incorrect answer choices. If you can learn to identify common trap answer choices, you can often eliminate them with confidence.

Additionally, the typical test-taker relies a lot on memory and reads only parts of sentences that are referenced by the question or answer choices. Reading only parts of sentences makes it easy to misconstrue the context of the sentence. Flipping this behavior around by not only reading full sentences but also reading sentences before and after it is crucial to cracking both the question and the answer choices. Remember, the correct answer is always found in the text. Always refer back to the passage and always read full sentences when you do so.

THE STEPS OF THE BASIC APPROACH TO CRACKING GMAT READING COMPREHENSION

Here are the steps of the Basic Approach:

1. **Work the Passage**

   In this step, apply The Basics of Cracking the Passage. You must have a plan for reading the passage, and you must learn to read actively. As you read, always be on the lookout for the main idea of the passage. To find the main idea, ask yourself questions such as what does the author want me to remember or believe about the topic under discussion? What's the author's conclusion? How is that conclusion supported?

2. **Understand the Question Task**

   Apply The Basics of Cracking the Questions. Try to break the question down. First, look for the subject of the question. Then, find the words that indicate the task.

3. **Find the Information in the Passage That Addresses the Task of the Question**

   Refer back to the passage. GMAC needs to be able to justify its credited responses by referring to specific information mentioned in the passage. When you understand the task of the question, it becomes easier to find this information. Once you locate the information in the passage that addresses the question task, you're ready to look at the answer choices.

4. **Use POE to Find the Answer**

   Use The Basics of Cracking the Answer Choices. Approach each answer choice with a healthy level of suspicion. Since there are four incorrect answers for every question, you are more likely to be reading a wrong answer than a right answer. Look for signs that are more likely to make an answer wrong, such as the answer sounding too much like the passage. Don't be afraid to just pick the answer that remains if you can find good reasons to eliminate the other four answer choices. An overview of common trap answer choices can be found later in this section.

STEP 1: WORK THE PASSAGE

Overview

Working the passage is the first step of The Basic Approach to Cracking GMAT Reading Comprehension Passages. By following the recommendations here on how to Work The Passage, you will be able to follow a strategic plan for reading the passage, avoid wasting time by actively reading the passage, learn a little about common passage structures, and map the passage to glean all the relevant information from the passage, which enables you to answer the questions later on. All in all, you will know what it takes to Crack the Passage. From there on, it's time to practice!

How Do You Plan to Read?

Before we talk about how to Crack the Passage, let's quickly explore how you can plan to read. You saw the idea of planning to read a handful of times in the previous section, but what does it mean? Let's first explore how the typical test-taker handles the passage. Typical test-takers approach the Reading Comprehension passage in the same way they would approach any reading assignment. They read as quickly as possible, only barely scratching the surface of the major points of the passage that the author was trying to express. Often about halfway through the passage, they realize they have not retained a single major point of the passage. The test-taker is now either forced to reread the entire passage, or move on to the answer choices without a full comprehension of the material. This strategy is ineffective and wastes a lot of time!

A better way to approach the passage is to plan to read! Central to the plan is the test-taker's ability to comprehend the passage by Active Reading. Active Reading keeps you engaged with the passage, fights off the tendency to let your mind wander away from the task at hand, and leaves you with a better understanding of the author's main point once you are finished. But what is Active Reading, and how do you do it?

The Basics of Cracking the Passage

Active Reading

The easiest way to define "Active Reading" is to define the opposite, or "Passive Reading." During passive reading, you look at the words but the content just isn't registering. You may remember some of the details from the passage, but you probably missed why the author told you about those details. This is common on GMAT passages, as the content can often be dense.

Active reading, on the other hand, means that you follow the author's argument. Put another way, you try to separate the author's claims from the facts and other evidence used to back up those claims. This is an essential ingredient for Cracking the Passage.

Effective active reading involves:

- *Asking questions as you read:* Asking questions helps to engage your mind. For example, ask yourself key questions about the passage and its author. What is the author's purpose for writing the passage? What are the big ideas? Where in the passage are the big ideas located? What kind of tone is the author adopting (scholarly, friendly, critical, objective, biased)? At the end of a paragraph, try to predict where the author takes the argument next. These practices help to create a full understanding of the passage.

- *Identifying the Structure of the Passage*: The structure of a passage is an undervalued hint to deciphering the intentions of the author and the main point of the passage. Passages written in a conventional manner usually proceed from the general to the specific and then return to the general. Individual paragraphs are also usually written that way. Authors may open with a topic sentence, elaborate on the topic with explanations and examples, and then conclude the paragraph with a general statement that transitions to the next paragraph. Be on the lookout for trigger words or phrases in the middle of a paragraph (*however, on the contrary, on the other hand*). These words are indicators of the author's perspective on the topic of the passage. Often the author follows up one of these trigger words with the perspective they are trying to convince you to adopt.

- *Look for Topic Sentences*: Topic sentences usually can be found at the start of each paragraph and are not only a great tool to keep you engaged in the passage but also a way to easily find your way back to the appropriate point in the passage when you need to consult the passage to answer a question. A bit further in the paragraph you usually find explanations and examples of that topic. Like before, be on watch for trigger words mid-paragraph. Note how each new paragraph follows the one that precedes it, and look to the end of a paragraph for clues about the next idea. Use the noteboard to record the flow of ideas from one paragraph to the next. Sometimes two or more paragraphs may act as a "chunk" of the passage. Ideas can flow between these chunks in the same way they flow from paragraph to paragraph.

The Main Idea

One of the central goals of Active Reading is to find the main idea and try to follow it. The main idea of the passage is what the author wants you to believe about the issue being presented in the passage.

Note here that this does not mean that the topic of the passage is the main idea. The topic of the passage—which is usually on one of the four primary areas of GMAT passages outlined in the previous section as social science, physical science, biological science, or business—is the overarching theme of the entire passage. The main idea is what the author wants you to believe about the topic. So, if you find yourself agreeing or disagreeing with the author, or noticing the author pushing an opinion or arguing a point, chances are that is the main idea of the passage.

By identifying the main idea of the passage, you can quickly and easily determine the purpose of the passage, which is one of the key components of successfully Cracking the Passage.

The Purpose of the Passage

The purpose of the passage is what the author wants you to believe after reading the passage. The purpose of most passages is to persuade the reader to accept the author's main point. However, there are other reasons an author may write a passage. Broadly, the purpose behind a passage falls into one of three categories.

- *To Persuade*: The most common purpose for a GMAT passage is to persuade. As stated earlier, the author typically tries to convince you that their viewpoint (the main idea) is correct. In that sense, the main idea and the purpose are intimately connected.

- *To Criticize or Evaluate*: The second most common passage purpose is criticism or evaluation. The author may favor a new view over an existing one, or may criticize someone else's ideas. But criticism need not be negative; authors may play up the merits of a particular theory, book, technique, or other idea.

  When the author's purpose is to criticize or evaluate an idea, the passage almost always starts with a review of that idea. The author generally gives a quick over-view in a neutral tone. The author's tone changes from neutral to critical (or perhaps complimentary) shortly after the main conclusions of the theory or idea are presented.

- *To Explain or Analyze*: While most passages involve some explanations and some analysis, passages that only explain or analyze are infrequent on the GMAT. Most authors have a point of view about the topic under discussion. However, a passage that deals with some sort of problem or puzzle may be purely explanatory in nature.

Mapping the Passage

Mapping the Passage is the final tool in learning how to Crack the Passage. By Mapping the Passage you can easily identify the main idea and purpose of the passage, and doing so will keep you engaged and save you time as you move on to the questions. But, to successfully map the passage, you must do something that a typical test-taker never does. You must write things down. Just because you reach a reading comprehension passage does not give you an excuse to stop writing things down. In fact, as a time-saving tactic alone, writing things down while working on a reading comprehension passage is worth the effort. Writing things down also helps you get a better understanding of the topic being presented, which yields a more complete appreciation for the passage and makes answering the questions a lot more manageable!

The best strategy for Mapping the Passage is called Key Sentences. In this approach, read the passage one paragraph at a time. At the end of each paragraph, stop and try to identify the one sentence that seems the most like an opinion, recommendation, conclusion, or reason. Write a short summary of that sentence down on the noteboard. You don't need to write the entire sentence, but you do want to write more than one or two words. It's also a good idea to label the sentence as either a claim (a primary or secondary conclusion of the passage) or a reason that supports a previous claim. The idea of mapping the passage in this fashion is to uncover the author's original outline for the passage. When you are finished mapping the passage, you should be able to string together your key sentences to produce the main idea of the passage.

STEP 2: UNDERSTAND THE QUESTION TASK

Overview

Understanding the question task is important to Cracking GMAT Reading Comprehension, and it is largely overlooked by the average test-taker. The Basics of Cracking the Questions can be broken down into two parts: identifying the subject and understanding the task.

The Basics of Cracking the Questions

Part 1: Identifying the Subject

When cracking GMAT Reading Comprehension questions, you must identify the subject of the question. For example, in the question "The author mentions land management policy in order to," the subject is *land management policy*. The subject helps you locate what you need to read *about* to answer the question.

By identifying the subject, you'll know what the question writer is testing you on. This is important for two reasons. First, by knowing the content that the question writer is testing you on, you are able to locate that information in the passage more easily. This is outlined in Step 3 of the Basic Approach. Secondly, without identifying the subject, you may struggle to eventually answer the question and are susceptible to some of the common trap answer choices. Identifying the subject is critical to Cracking the Questions, but equally important is understanding the task of the question.

Part 2: Understanding the Task

If you have been actively reading, you may have been able to predict that the second part of Cracking the Questions is understanding the task of the question. The task of the question is what you need to find out about the subject. For example, is the question asking for a detail from the passage, or is it asking why that detail is in the passage? Are you required merely to describe something, or does the question expect you to analyze it? Meanwhile, you should also be on the lookout for words such as EXCEPT, LEAST, and NOT.

In the example question given earlier, "The author mentions land management policy in order to," the task words are *in order to*. The tasks that questions can ask about are diverse and can be categorized as *general*, *specific*, or *complex* tasks.

Specific: Specific tasks reference a small part of the passage. There are four different ways specific questions can be asked. They are retrieval, inference, purpose, and vocab-in-context.

- **Retrieval** questions ask you to find information in the passage and may make reference to a detail or fact (a person's name, a theory, a time period). The answer is typically just a paraphrase of this information in the passage. These questions are highlighted by phrases such as *According to the passage,* and any reference to things that are mentioned by the author.

- **Inference** questions make test-takers nervous because they appear to suggest that the answer has to be figured out using knowledge about the author. Remember that all answers are found directly in the passage. In fact, inference tasks are a lot like retrieval tasks, particularly since a good portion of inference questions ask about a small detail that is easily overlooked. Keywords that identify a question as an inference include *infer, suggest, conclude,* or *imply,* among others. Because of the nature of these questions, it's easy to go wrong by drawing on outside information or making assumptions. Many wrong answers are based on the ways that people read into or interpret the information in the passage.

- **Purpose** questions ask *why* the author included the subject or some particular piece of information. Typically, the answers to these questions are closely related to the main point of the subject of the question. These questions can be identified by phrases such as *in order to* and *serves which of the following functions.* To answer these questions, identify what the author said about the subject of the question and find an answer choice that reflects that idea.

- **Vocabulary-in-Context** questions ask you to state what the author means by a certain word or phrase. These questions are very similar to inference questions, because they usually ask what the author is suggesting or implying by the use of a particular term. The correct answer must fit the context of its sentence and the paragraph containing that sentence and match the main point of the passage.

General: General tasks ask about the passage as a whole. General questions can be asked in four different ways as well: primary purpose, main idea, tone, and structure.

- **Primary Purpose** questions may seem similar to Main Idea questions, but they differ in one critical way. Primary Purpose questions ask *why* the author wrote the passage. Therefore, the answers are typically more general than those for Main Idea questions. The subject of Primary Purpose questions is usually the whole passage. These questions can be identified by the phrase *primary purpose* and *chiefly concerned.* Not to be confused with Purpose questions, Primary Purpose questions test very broad ideas. This is an instance in which, if you have carefully Cracked the Passage, you should be able to answer these questions easily.

- The task of **Main Idea** questions is to figure out what the author wants you to believe. The main idea is the overall claim, supported by the evidence contained in the rest of the text—in other words, what does the author want you to accept as true? Main Idea questions differ from Primary Purpose questions in that the former deal with *what* the passage is about rather than *why* the author wrote it. These questions can be identified by any phrase that indicates a need for a general understanding of the passage, such as *overall claims* and *main point*. However, much like Primary Purpose questions, these questions are easily answerable if you have successfully Cracked the Passage.

- **Tone** questions ask you to evaluate how strongly or negatively the author feels about the subject of the question. Find the subject in the passage and look for words that reveal the author's feelings. Examples of such words and phrases include *misrepresenting*, *unlikely*, *considerable importance*, *unfortunately*, and *a poor grasp*, among others. Questions that ask about the author's tone generally use the words *tone* or *attitude*.

- Some **Structure** questions ask about the overall sequence of the passage, while others ask about a smaller piece of it, such as a single paragraph. Either way, these questions test the general flow of the passage. If you can describe the flow of ideas—a task made easier by Mapping the Passage on the noteboard—you'll be able to narrow down the answer choices, crossing off answers that describe things that didn't happen in the passage.

Complex: Complex tasks require a good understanding of the main idea, so Cracking the Passage is essential. Complex questions also can be asked in four different ways. Those ways are evaluation, weaken/strengthen, analogy, and application.

- **Evaluation** questions on the GMAT are pretty rare, but they do exist. These questions test your ability to compare or analyze information from the passage. For example, you may be asked to assess the relationship between two pieces of information from the passage. There aren't many common forms of questions like this, so an example of this type of question would be *Which of the following most accurately summarizes the relationship between nineteenth-century American women and eighteenth-century American women in the highlighted text?*

- Slightly more common than evaluation questions, **Weaken/Strengthen** questions ask the test-taker to weaken or strengthen an assertion made in the passage. These questions can be identified by the presence of the word *weaken* or *strengthen* in the question.

- **Analogy** questions typically use the answer choices to draw comparisons to information discussed in the passage. The correct answer is the one that completes a reasonable analogy. Mostly, these questions can be identified by the key phrase *most similar*.

- Sometimes questions ask you to apply information from the passage to a new scenario. These are **Application** questions and can be easily spotted when the question stem refers to the answer choices as either "scenarios," "situations," or "assertions."

STEP 3: FIND INFORMATION IN THE PASSAGE THAT ADDRESSES THE TASK

Overview

Step 3 of the Basic Approach to Cracking the GMAT Reading Comprehension is finding the information in the passage that addresses the question task. After you have Cracked the Question by identifying the subject and the task, look for the subject in the passage. Once you locate the subject, find the information about the subject that addresses the task of the question.

This is when Cracking the Passage from Step 1 of The Basic Approach is invaluable. Use your notes to find the appropriate place in the passage that addresses the subject and start reading. Try to read 8 to 10 lines. Then make sure you understand what you have read. It is important for you to not attempt to answer the question in your own words. Attempting to do so may cause you to interpret the passage, which is not your goal. Your goal is to find the information from the passage that addresses the task of the question. And, as always, the answers to the questions can be found in the passage.

It is important for this step to use the **Active Reading** strategies from Step 1 again. After you have found the appropriate place to begin reading, keep the task of the question in the back of your mind and be on constant lookout for any information that addresses the task of the question. After you have found this information, and have taken measures to ensure you truly understand the information, you are ready to move on to Step 4 of The Basic Approach to Cracking GMAT Reading Comprehension—examining and eliminating the answer choices.

STEP 4: USE POE TO FIND THE ANSWER

Overview

The final step of The Basic Approach to Cracking GMAT Reading Comprehension is using POE to find the answer. If you have followed all of the steps up to this point, then you have worked the passage and have a thorough understanding of it through Active Reading, analyzed and achieved understanding of the question subject and task, and located and read the information about the question subject and task in the passage. Now it's time to look at the answer choices and find the correct answer by using POE (Process of Elimination).

As discussed throughout this entire book thus far, POE is one of the most powerful tools at your disposal on test day. Reading Comprehension is no different as POE is the best tool to help you find the correct answer by eliminating the incorrect ones. Once you understand the task of the question and have been able to locate its information in the passage, eliminating wrong answer choices is the most effective way to answer the question correctly.

Many test-takers do exactly what the writers of the test want them to do—they answer questions based on memory or what sounds correct. However, if you learn how test-writers create incorrect answer choices, you can eliminate answers quickly and stand your best chance at achieving the highest score possible for you.

In light of that, the final step in learning how to crack GMAT Reading Comprehension is learning about the different ways that the test-writers create wrong answer choices. Once you know their methodology, you can learn how to spot wrong answers and then confidently eliminate the offending answer choices.

The Basics of Cracking the Answer Choices

Knowing the types of answer choices that test-writers use to create wrong answers is the key to being prepared to use POE on test day. Test-writers use certain kinds of answer choices to make an answer choice look attractive. The problem is, even if you have read the passage and followed the steps, a lot of times the incorrect answer choices still look correct! The test-writers have to write hard answer choices like this, or else the questions are too easy. Your job is to become familiar with the ways by which they create these wrong answers so that when you read an answer choice constructed in a certain way, it raises suspicion. The more skeptical you are of the answer choices, the more likely you are to be able to eliminate them.

The following are the ways in which test-writers create wrong answers:

Watch out for these
tricks and traps!

- Recycled Language and Memory Traps
- Extreme Language
- No Such Comparison
- Reversals
- Emotional Appeals
- Outside Knowledge

Become familiar with these, and you will be one step closer to cracking GMAT Reading Comprehension.

Recycled Language and Memory Traps

One of the easiest and most common ways that test-writers create wrong answer choices is by repeating memorable words or phrases from the passage. The correct answers for GMAT Reading Comprehension questions are generally paraphrases of the passage. So the presence of words or phrases that are very reminiscent of the passage is a reason to be skeptical of the answer choice.

Recycled language is one of the most common forms of memory traps. Recycled language in an answer choice is easily identified because recycled language includes words or phrases that are direct quotes from the text. If you see words or phrases that fit the description of recycled language, you should be very skeptical of the answer choice. Did the passage say exactly what the answer choice says regarding the recycled language? If it doesn't, the answer choice is incorrect.

More commonly, memory traps are words or phrases that evoke a strong memory from the passage. These answer choices are designed to make the average test-taker think, "Oh, I remember reading that in the passage" and, because of that, they make for very appealing answer choices. Memory traps evoke a stronger memory than actual correct answers do, so if you find yourself attracted to an answer choice because of the mention of something you remember, be wary! Make sure that the answer choice hasn't taken that piece of information out of context or confused it with another part of the passage.

Extreme Language

Another common way to create wrong answer choices is by using language that is too "powerful" or overt. Common ways to do that are by using words such as *must, always, never, only, best,* and other very strong words, or with answers that include strong verbs, such as *prove* or *fail.*

For instance, a primary purpose question may have answer choices that use a powerful verb such as *defend* or *criticize.* If the passage does not explicitly defend or criticize the main idea, this answer choice is incorrect because it contains the extreme language. Below is a chart of common words that should cause skepticism for extreme language.

Common Extreme Words			
Never	Not	Defend	Contradict
Always	No	Attack	Failure
Only	Must	Denounce	
None	Prove	Counter	

No Such Comparison

Comparison words such as *better, more, reconcile, less, decide,* or *more than* are used by test-writers to make answer choices more appealing by drawing a comparison between two items referenced in the passage. If you see them, you should be skeptical. As with every answer choice, make sure to reference them against the information in the passage. Often the ideas being compared in the answer choices were discussed in the passage but not explicitly compared.

Reversals

Reversal answer choices seek to confuse the test-taker by saying the opposite of the main idea or a detail from the passage. These answer choices are more difficult to spot because there isn't a list of common words. However, if you have successfully Cracked the Passage and found the information in the passage that references the task of the question, then identifying reversals of the answer choices becomes a lot more manageable.

Emotional Appeals

This answer choice type is fairly rare on the GMAT. However, it is still worth mentioning. Some answer choices may try to appeal to the beliefs of the test-taker. For instance, a political passage may contain an answer choice that values one political stance over another, even if the passage made no such claim. If you have successfully followed the steps to Crack the Passage and identified the main idea and the task of the question, these answer choices are easily eliminated.

Outside Knowledge

Much like emotional appeal answer choices, outside knowledge answer choices are also fairly rare on the GMAT. Correct answer choices on the GMAT contain information that is found only in the passage. However, these answer choices can be very tempting to you because you may know a piece of information that is not mentioned in the passage but is reflected in an answer choice. Remember, you should rely on the information in the passage only to answer questions on the GMAT.

DRILL 18 (Reading Comprehension)

The answers to the questions in this drill can be found in Part V.

Questions 1–4 are based on the following passage.

The practice of mindfulness meditation originated as an ancient Buddhist meditation technique in which the meditator focuses on being aware of the present moment and acknowledging feelings and thoughts as they come and go. In recent years, brain
Line imaging techniques have shed light on the effects on the brain and body of those
(5) who participate in a couple of hours of mindfulness meditation each week.

MRI scans conducted on the brains of people who engaged in an eight-week meditation practice showed an apparent reduction in the size of the amygdala. Commonly thought of as the primal "fight or flight" center of the brain, the amygdala dictates the response to stress. While the amygdala appears to shrink because of
(10) meditation, the prefrontal cortex, the area of the brain associated with concentration and awareness, thickens, and the relationship between the amygdala and the rest of the brain appears to weaken. These findings prompted researchers to hypothesize that increased meditation may be capable of replacing our fearful responses to stress with more rational ones.

(15) While researchers have called for more studies to be done on the mental and physical ramifications of mindfulness meditation, a new debate has emerged over whether meditation itself is a science. Proponents of meditation-as-science argue that science is the study of the natural world through observation and experiment to produce a unified body of knowledge on a given subject. Meditation, says the
(20) argument, is the observation of one's own mind, and a body of knowledge has been built over thousands of years as the result of consistent experimentation of techniques to observe and better understand the consciousness of the mind.

1. According to the passage, which of the following is true about
   the amygdala?

   (A) Extended meditation causes long-term damage to the amygdala.
   (B) The response to stress produced by the amygdala is less valuable than the
       response produced by the prefrontal cortex.
   (C) There is a direct correlation between the size of the amygdala and the
       thickness of the prefrontal cortex.
   (D) The size difference of the amygdala between those who practice meditation
       and those who do not may impact their responses to stress.
   (E) The relationship between the amygdala and the rest of the brain is weakened
       as a result of the thickening of the prefrontal cortex.

2. The passage is primarily concerned with

   (A) convincing the reader of the benefits of meditation
   (B) outlining the science of the response the brain has to meditation and the
       debates the practice inspires
   (C) arguing that meditation is the most effective way to depress the "fight or
       flight" response
   (D) validating the stance of those who believe meditation is a science
   (E) teaching people how to better handle stress

3. Based on the information in the passage, which of the following can
   be inferred about fearful responses to stress?

   (A) Fearful responses to stress can be replaced with more rational responses if
       the person engages in a couple of hours of meditation per week.
   (B) Fearful responses to stress occur more regularly in people with a thin
       prefrontal cortex.
   (C) There is some debate over whether the research behind reducing fearful
       responses to stress should be considered science.
   (D) Researchers believe that further study regarding fearful responses to stress
       and the relationship those responses have to mindfulness meditation
       is warranted.
   (E) Fearful responses to stress can be seen on an MRI scan.

4. Which of the following scenarios would a proponent of meditation-as-
   science be most likely to argue is not a science?

   (A) A worldwide effort to uncover the secrets of a little-known video game
   (B) A thorough review of popular literature with the goal of analyzing sentence
       structure and word choice for similarities
   (C) The study of stars and planet movement to notice patterns that correlate to
       terrestrial events
   (D) The observation of fashion trends over the course of hundreds of years to
       predict fashion in the future
   (E) Collecting samples of wood used in the construction of log cabins to
       determine which wood produces the most stable product

Questions 5–7 are based on the following passage.

Artificial neural networks, named so as to distinguish them from real neural networks found inside a brain, are designed to simulate the activity of real neural networks by packing interconnected "brain cells," or units, so a computer can learn
Line and recognize patterns on its own. Artificial neural networks typically consist of three
(5) types of units: input units which receive information to learn about, output units which signal how the network has responded to the items it learned about, and hidden units which sit in layers between the input and output units. The connections made between the units are given weight, which dictates the influence of a given connection.
(10) By constructing artificial neural networks in this way, the networks can learn through information flow in a manner similar to how a real brain learns. Information is passed to the input units, which trigger the hidden units. The hidden units are activated and the sum of the inputs it receives triggers the next unit to fire if the sum exceeds a certain threshold. By giving the output units a model to compare the result of the learning
(15) process to, the artificial neural network can learn where to place more weight in order to make the result of the output unit more closely resemble that of the model.

5. The primary purpose of the passage is to

   (A) describe artificial neural networks
   (B) contrast artificial neural networks with neural networks found in brains
   (C) illustrate how to build an artificial neural network
   (D) argue for the wider adoption of artificial neural networks
   (E) outline the different units of an artificial neural network and their roles in producing intelligence

6. It can be inferred from the passage that real neural networks

   (A) are to be considered superior to artificial neural networks
   (B) consist of input, hidden, and output units
   (C) inspired the development of artificial neural networks
   (D) are more capable of recognizing patterns than artificial neural networks
   (E) will someday become obsolete

7. According to the passage, which of the following best represents the optimal flow of information through an artificial neural network?

   (A) A model is shown to the input units which pass information to the output units which describe the model.
   (B) Information is fed to the input units which activate the hidden units which then change the input units to more closely resemble the model.
   (C) The input units receive information to give to the hidden units which then forward information to the output units to compare against a model.
   (D) A model is shown to the input units which then attempt to recreate the model using different information.
   (E) The input units are activated by information fed to them via the output units which analyze a model and improve the information before handing it to the input units.

Questions 8–11 are based on the following passage:

As a business model, the world of publishing has always been a somewhat sleepy enclave, but now all that seems poised to change. Several companies have moved aggressively into a new business endeavor whose genesis comes from the question:
Line Who owns the great works of literature?
(5)   Text-on-demand is not a completely new idea, of course. In the 1990s, the Gutenberg project sought volunteers to type literary classics that had expired copyrights into word processing files so that scholars would have searchable databases for their research. Most of the works of Shakespeare, Cervantes, Proust, and Molière were to be found free online by as early as 1995.
(10)   However, now large-scale companies have moved into the market, with scanners and business plans, and are looking for bargain basement content. These companies are striking deals with libraries, and some publishers, to be able to provide their content, for a price, to individual buyers over the Internet.
        At stake are the rights to an estimated store of 30 million books, most of which
(15) are now out of print. Many of these books are now also in the public domain, giving any company the right to sell them online. Still, a good portion of the books a general audience might actually want to buy is still under copyright. The urgent question: Who owns those copyrights? In the case of all too many books put out more than 20 years ago by now-defunct publishing companies, the answer is unclear—a situation
(20) the new text-on-demand companies are eager to exploit. An association of publishers has sued, claiming massive copyright infringement. The case is several years away from trial.

8. The primary purpose of the passage is to

    (A) present the results of a statistical analysis and propose further study
    (B) explain a recent development and explore its consequences
    (C) identify the reasons for a trend and recommend measures to address it
    (D) outline several theories about a phenomenon and advocate one of them
    (E) describe the potential consequences of implementing a new policy and argue in favor of that policy

9. It can be inferred from the passage that the works of Shakespeare, Cervantes, and Molière

    (A) are some of the most popular works of literature
    (B) are no longer copyrighted
    (C) are among the works for which the association of publishers is suing text-on-demand companies
    (D) do not currently exist as searchable databases
    (E) were owned by now-defunct publishing companies

10. Which of the following is an example of a book that a text-on-demand company would not have to acquire the rights to?

    (A) A book still under copyright
    (B) A book more than 20 years old
    (C) A book in the public domain
    (D) A book a general audience might want to buy
    (E) A book not already owned by publishers the company has a deal with

11. It can be inferred from the passage that a common practice of text-on-demand companies is to

    (A)   use scanners to find books they want to acquire
    (B)   create business plans well before they have any actual business
    (C)   buy content at premium prices
    (D)   acquire the rights to books for as little as possible
    (E)   attempt to supplant the role of traditional publishers

Questions 12–15 are based on the following passage:

Founded at the dawn of the modern industrial era, the nearly forgotten Women's Trade Union League (WTUL) played an instrumental role in advancing the cause of working women throughout the early part of the twentieth century. In the face of
Line considerable adversity, the WTUL made a contribution far greater than did most
(5) historical footnotes.

The organization's successes did not come easily; conflict beset the WTUL in many forms. During those early days of American unions, organized labor was aggressively opposed by both industry and government. The WTUL, which represented a largely unskilled labor force, had little leverage against these powerful opponents. Also,
(10) because of the skill level of its workers as well as inherent societal gender bias, the WTUL had great difficulty finding allies among other unions. Even the large and powerful American Federation of Labor (AFL), which nominally took the WTUL under its wing, kept it at a distance. Because the AFL's power stemmed from its highly skilled labor force, the organization saw little economic benefit in working with the WTUL. The
(15) affiliation provided the AFL with political cover, allowing it to claim support for women workers; in return, the WTUL gained a potent but largely absent ally.

The WTUL also had to overcome internal discord. While the majority of the group's members were working women, a sizeable and powerful minority consisted of middle- and upper-class social reformers whose goals extended beyond labor reform.
(20) While workers argued that the WTUL should focus its efforts on collective bargaining and working conditions, the reformers looked beyond the workplace, seeking state and national legislation aimed at education reform and urban poverty relief as well as workplace issues.

Despite these obstacles, the WTUL accomplished a great deal. The organization
(25) was instrumental in the passage of state laws mandating an eight-hour workday, a minimum wage for women, and a ban on child labor. It provided seed money to women who organized workers in specific plants and industries, and it also established strike funds and soup kitchens to support striking unionists. After the tragic Triangle Shirtwaist Company fire of 1911, the WTUL launched a four-year
(30) investigation whose conclusions formed the basis of much subsequent workplace safety legislation. The organization also offered a political base for all reform-minded women, and thus helped develop the next generation of American leaders. Eleanor Roosevelt was one of many prominent figures to emerge from the WTUL.

The organization began a slow death in the late 1920s, when the Great Depression
(35) choked off its funding. The organization limped through the 1940s; the death knell eventually rang in 1950, at the onset of the McCarthy era. A turn-of-the-century labor organization dedicated to social reform, one that during its heyday was regarded by many as "radical," stood little chance of weathering that storm. This humble ending, however, does nothing to diminish the accomplishments of an organization that is yet
(40) to receive its historical due.

12. The primary purpose of this passage is to

   (A) describe the barriers confronting women in the contemporary workplace
   (B) compare and contrast the methods of two labor unions of the early industrial era
   (C) critique the methods employed by an important labor union
   (D) rebuke historians for failing to cover the women's labor movement adequately
   (E) call readers' attention to an overlooked contributor to American history

13. Which of the following best characterizes the American Federation of Labor's view of the Women's Trade Union League, as it is presented in the passage?

   (A) The WTUL was an important component of the AFL's multifront assault on industry and its treatment of workers.
   (B) Because of Eleanor Roosevelt's affiliation with the organization, the WTUL was a vehicle through which the AFL could gain access to the White House.
   (C) The WTUL was to be avoided because the radical element within it attracted unwanted government scrutiny.
   (D) The WTUL offered the AFL some political capital but little that would assist it in labor negotiations.
   (E) The WTUL was weakened by its hesitance in pursuing widespread social reform beyond the workplace.

14. Each of the following is cited in the passage as an accomplishment of the Women's Trade Union League EXCEPT

   (A) It organized a highly skilled workforce to increase its bargaining power.
   (B) It contributed to the development of a group of leaders in America.
   (C) It provided essential support to striking women.
   (D) It helped fund start-up unions for women.
   (E) It contributed to the passage of important social and labor reform legislation.

15. The passage suggests which of the following about the "middle- and upper-class social reformers" mentioned in lines 32–33 ?

   (A) They did not understand, nor were they sympathetic to, the plight of poor women workers.
   (B) Their naive interest in Communism was ultimately detrimental to the Women's Trade Union League.
   (C) It was because of their social and political power that the Women's Trade Union League was able to form an alliance with the American Federation of Labor.
   (D) They represented only an insignificant fraction of the leadership of the Women's Trade Union League.
   (E) They sought to advance a broad political agenda of societal improvement.

<u>Questions 16–19</u> are based on the following passage:

It has long been a tenet of business theory that the best decisions are made after careful review and consideration. Only after weighing all the options and studying projections, say most professors of business, can a practical decision be made.

Line
(5) Now, that model is being questioned by some business thinkers in the light of the theories of Malcolm Gladwell, who states that human beings often make better decisions in the blink of an eye.

It is, at first glance, a theory so counter-intuitive as to seem almost ludicrous. Behind any decision, Gladwell posits, there is a behind-the-scenes subconscious process in which the brain analyzes; ranks in order of importance; compares and
(10) contrasts vast amounts of information; and dismisses extraneous factors, seemingly almost instantaneously, often arriving at a conclusion in less than two seconds. Citing a multitude of studies and examples from life, Gladwell shows how that split-second decision is often better informed than a drawn-out examination.

Evanston and Cramer were the first to apply this theory to the business world.
(15) Evanston videotaped the job interviews of 400 applicants at different firms. He then played only 10 seconds of each videotape to independent human resources specialists. The specialists were able to pick out the applicants who were hired with an accuracy of over 90%.

Cramer took the experiment even further, using only five seconds of videotape,
(20) without sound. To his astonishment, the rate of accuracy with which the HR specialists were able to predict the successful applicants fell only to 82%.

Critics argue that these results illustrate a problem with stereotyping that impedes human resources specialists from hiring the best candidates even when they have the time to get below the surface: going for the candidate who "looks the part."
(25) Gladwell argues that, on the contrary, the human mind is able to make complicated decisions quickly and that intuition often trumps an extended decision-making process.

16. The primary purpose of the passage is to

   (A)   discuss reasons an accepted business theory is being reexamined
   (B)   present evidence that resolves a contradiction in business theory
   (C)   describe a tenet of business practices and how that tenet can be tested in today's economic environment
   (D)   argue that a counter-intuitive new business idea is, in the final analysis, incorrect
   (E)   present evidence that invalidates a new business model

17. According to the passage, all of the following are examples of the subconscious processes by which the brain makes a decision EXCEPT

   (A)   analysis of information
   (B)   ranking of information
   (C)   comparison and contrast of information
   (D)   rejecting information that is not pertinent
   (E)   consulting a multitude of studies and examples

18. The author most likely `mentions the results of Cramer's extension of Evanston's experiment in order to

    (A) show that Cramer's hypothesis was correct, while Evanston's hypothesis turned out to be incorrect
    (B) show that Evanston's hypothesis was correct, while Cramer's hypothesis turned out to be incorrect
    (C) demonstrate that while both experiments were scientifically rigorous, neither ended up being scientifically valid
    (D) illustrate that the principle of subconscious decisions continues to work even when less information is available
    (E) demonstrate that Cramer's experiment was 8% more accurate than Evanston's, even though his subjects had less information to work with

19. It can be inferred that the critics referred to in line 36 believed the results of the two experiments had less to do with the innate decision-making of the subjects than with

    (A) the excellent decision-making of Evanston and Cramer
    (B) the expertise of Malcolm Gladwell, who originated the theory
    (C) not choosing candidates who "looked the part"
    (D) the use of videotape as a method of choosing candidates
    (E) their unconscious use of visual stereotypes in making their selections

Summary

○ Most likely you will see four Reading Comprehension passages. There are usually three short passages, followed by three questions each, and one long passage, followed by four questions.

○ GMAT Reading Comprehension passage topics are usually from four areas: social sciences, biological science, physical science, and business.

○ GMAT test-writers create questions in a certain way. For you to be successful, follow the steps of The Basic Approach to Cracking GMAT Reading Comprehension:
- Step 1: Work the Passage
- Step 2: Understand the Question Task
- Step 3: Find Information in the Passage That Addresses the Task
- Step 4: Use POE to Find the Answer

○ The Basics of cracking the passage start with Active Reading. Active Reading enables you to gain a greater understanding of the passage by asking questions, identifying the structure of the passage, and looking for topic sentences.

○ Crack the passage by identifying the main point and the purpose of the passage. The main point is what the author wants you to believe about something, and the purpose is why the author wrote the passage (to persuade, to criticize or evaluate, or to explain or analyze).

○ Mapping the passage is an effective tool for keeping yourself organized in order to work efficiently while cracking the passage.

○ Test-writers deliberately create wrong answers using recycled language and memory traps, extreme language, no such comparison, reversals, emotional appeals, and outside knowledge.

Chapter 19
Critical Reasoning

To perform well on Critical Reasoning questions, you need to know how GMAT arguments are constructed and how they are commonly reasoned. It is also helpful to know how incorrect answer choices are typically created so you can recognize them on test day. In this chapter, we will show you how to recognize and master the eight types of argument questions that appear on the GMAT.

CRITICAL REASONING OVERVIEW

Critical Reasoning questions comprise about half of the questions in the Verbal Reasoning section of the GMAT. Each question consists of a short reading passage, followed by a single question and 5 multiple choice answers. Critical Reasoning passages are based on a short argument, a set of statements, or a plan of action. For each question, select the best answer from among the choices provided.

The Passage

Critical Reasoning passages tend to be short (usually 20–100 words) and oftentimes take the form of an argument. The subjects they consider don't often fall into neat categories, and the scenarios they present are commonly hypothetical. Read the passages carefully, pay attention to the language employed, and interpret that language literally. It is important to be precise when reading the passage for Critical Reasoning questions. As you'll see in the pages to come, the difference between getting a Critical Reasoning question correct and falling for a trap answer often lies in the particulars of the passage's wording.

The Question

There are eight types of Critical Reasoning questions, each of which involves a different task with respect to the passage. Most questions test your ability to evaluate the reasoning employed in an argument, but some test your ability to reason on the basis of information. This chapter will outline the different types of questions you will see, how to identify them, and what to look for in the passage based on the type of question. So much of your evaluation of the passage depends on what the question is asking you to identify in the passage. Because of this, you should read the question first, and then read the passage.

The Answer Choices

All things verbal come down to Process of Elimination, and Critical Reasoning is no exception. Each question type for Critical Reasoning questions has its own set of POE tools. These tools are based on the common trap answers constructed by the test-writers. Because the question types all vary, the common trap answers and POE tools to employ also vary based on question type. After mastering the different types of questions, you'll learn how answer choices for those question types are constructed and, with enough practice, you'll be able to spot a bad answer choice with confidence.

HOW GMAT ARGUMENTS ARE CONSTRUCTED

Most Critical Reasoning passages take the form of *arguments* in which the writer tries to convince the reader of something. Here's an example:

> During the past 10 years, advertising revenues for the magazine *True Investor* have fallen by 30 percent. The magazine has failed to attract new subscribers, and publication sales are at an all-time low. Thus, sweeping changes to the editorial board will be necessary for the magazine to survive.

GMAT arguments consist of three connected parts:

- Conclusion—what the author tries to persuade the reader to accept
- Premise—evidence provided in support of a conclusion
- Assumption—unstated ideas upon which an argument's validity rests

Conclusions

A conclusion is the primary claim made in an argument. The easiest way to identify the conclusion is to ask yourself what its author wants you to believe. In the argument above, the conclusion is found in the last sentence, where the author attempts to persuade the reader that *sweeping changes to the editorial board will be necessary for the magazine to survive.*

In some cases, indicator words can help you to find the conclusion. These include:

Therefore	Hence
Clearly	Consequently
Thus	So

Indicator words can help you to identify the parts of an argument, but not every argument uses them. However, almost every argument will have a conclusion of some kind. A conclusion can be a plan or course of action, an argument, a statement of supposed truth, or any number of resolutions to the contents of the passage.

Learning to identify the conclusion is the first important step in evaluating the passage. Once you've identified the conclusion, the remaining information in the passage should reveal evidence that is used in support of the conclusion.

Premises

The premise of an argument includes any reasons, statistics, or other evidence provided in support of the conclusion. In the case of GMAT arguments, you must accept the truth of the premise, whether you agree with it or not. The easiest way to identify the premise is to ask what information the author has provided to justify the truth of the conclusion.

In the argument above, the premise can be found in the first two sentences, where the author provides three pieces of evidence in support of the conclusion: *advertising revenues have fallen by 30 percent*, *the magazine has failed to attract new subscribers*, and *sales are at an all-time low*.

Sometimes you'll see indicator words that can help you to find the premise. These include:

Because	In view of
Given that	Since
As a result of	Supposing that

Assumptions

Assumptions are unstated premises on which the author relies to prove their conclusion. Even well-reasoned arguments rest on assumptions; because it's impossible to say everything, some things must go unsaid. Therefore, assumptions play a crucial role in the structure of an argument, bridging gaps in reasoning from the premise to the conclusion.

The argument above assumes that the editorial board *caused* the problems now attributed to the magazine. If something other than the editorial board were responsible, then sweeping changes to the board might do little to improve the magazine's financial situation. In this case, the connection between the premise (the magazine's problems) and the conclusion (changes to the editorial board) falls apart. The reader is no longer persuaded that *changes to the editorial board will be necessary for the magazine to survive*. The argument collapses.

The easiest way to identify an assumption is to distinguish an argument's conclusion from its premise. Then, ask what additional information is required to link the conclusion to the premise.

Gaps

In many cases, gaps in reasoning are indicated by gaps in language. Look for words or phrases in the conclusion that do not come from the premise. Identify an assumption in the following example:

> Cream cheese contains half as many calories per tablespoon as does butter or margarine. Therefore, a bagel with cream cheese is more healthful than is a bagel with butter.

First, find the conclusion. The word *therefore* gives the conclusion away: *a bagel with cream cheese is more healthful than is a bagel with butter*.

Second, find the premise. What information does the author provide to support the conclusion? The premise states that *cream cheese contains half as many calories per tablespoon*.

Third, look for shifts in language between the premise and conclusion. The premise compares the calorie content of a tablespoon of cream cheese to that of a tablespoon of butter or margarine. The conclusion introduces the word *healthful*, which does not appear in the premise. This shift in the argument's language is indicative of a gap in reasoning—the argument leaps from a thing that *has fewer calories per tablespoon* to a thing that *is more healthful*. Therefore, this argument rests on the assumption that a food with *fewer calories* is a food that is *more healthful*.

Although most Critical Reasoning passages consist of three basic parts—conclusions, premises, and assumptions—some passages also include extraneous ideas, background information, or opposing points of view. The efficiency with which you identify assumptions depends in large part on the accuracy with which you identify conclusions and premises, so don't be distracted by nonessential information.

COMMON REASONING PATTERNS

Like the other question formats on the GMAT, Critical Reasoning questions tend to be predictable. While you'll never see the same question twice, many Critical Reasoning passages employ similar patterns of reasoning. Learning to recognize these patterns provides you with another means of identifying assumptions.

Not every GMAT argument models one of the common reasoning patterns, so you'll sometimes still need to look for shifts in language. However, when one of the common reasoning patterns is present, it can help you to locate information needed to strengthen or weaken an argument. Each of the five common patterns involves its own standard assumption or assumptions. Learning to recognize these patterns, and the assumptions they incorporate, will help you to identify unstated presuppositions and pinpoint an argument's flaws.

Causal Patterns

In a causal argument, the premise usually states that two things happened, from which the author concludes that one thing caused the other. Consider the following simple example:

> A study indicated that adults who listen to classical music regularly
> are less likely to have anxiety disorders. Clearly, classical music calms
> the nerves and reduces anxiety.

The author of this argument concludes that *classical music calms the nerves and reduces anxiety*. This conclusion is based on a study indicating that *adults who listen to classical music regularly are less likely to have anxiety disorders*. Thus, the premise posits a correlation between two things—exposure to classical music and reduced likelihood of anxiety disorders—and the conclusion makes a leap from correlation to causation.

Every causal argument involves two standard assumptions:

- There's no other cause.
- It's not a coincidence.

Our argument assumes that it's not a coincidence that adults who listened to classical music were less likely to have anxiety disorders, and that makes sense because it also assumes that nothing other than classical music caused study participants to experience fewer anxiety disorders.

The first standard assumption suggests that classical music, and only classical music, caused participants in the study to experience fewer anxiety disorders. But what if something else was responsible? The passage doesn't rule out the possibility that study participants used anxiety-reducing medication, or that they simply happened to be calm people to begin with. In neither of these cases would it follow that *classical music calms the nerves and reduces anxiety*. Thus, the argument must assume that a causal relationship exists.

The second standard assumption denies that the correlation between classical music and anxiety is a coincidence. But what if a different study indicated that adults who listen to classical music regularly were more likely to have anxiety disorders? In that case, it no longer follows that classical music calms the nerves and reduces anxiety—on the contrary, the counterexample suggests that the first study's results were coincidental. Thus, the argument must assume that the correlation between classical music and lower anxiety is not a coincidence.

When you spot an argument that employs a causal reasoning pattern, remember that the argument relies on two assumptions: first, there's no other cause; and second, it's not a coincidence.

Planning Patterns

Many GMAT arguments introduce plans that are designed to solve problems: a municipal government's plan to improve water quality, a transit authority's plan to reduce traffic congestion, or a town board's plan to increase voter turnout. The premise of planning arguments describes what the plan is supposed to accomplish and how it is supposed to work. For example:

> During the past 5 years, Meridian Township has seen a dramatic rise in crime. As a result, Meridian's police force plans to install video surveillance cameras at major intersections in neighborhoods that suffer the worst crime rates. Clearly, the crime rate in Meridian Township will drop.

Consider this argument in terms of its parts. Meridian Township has a problem: *a dramatic rise in crime*. To address this problem, the police force plans to *install video surveillance cameras*. This is the premise of the argument because it outlines the plan for addressing the problem. The argument concludes that, as a result of instituting the plan, the crime rate will drop. In general, the conclusion of an argument that employs the planning pattern can simply be expressed: *do the plan*.

Every planning argument involves one standard assumption:

- There's no problem with the plan.

Evaluating an argument with a planning reasoning pattern will revolve around the plan itself. For instance, what if there *is* a problem with the plan to reduce crime by installing video cameras at major intersections? After all, crime is not limited to major intersections. Perhaps the cameras will malfunction or produce poor quality images. Perhaps criminals will simply relocate to neighborhoods without cameras. In these cases, our confidence in the conclusion is shaken. On the basis of the premise alone, it no longer seems to follow that *the crime rate will drop*. Thus, in order for the argument to "work," its author must assume that installing the cameras really will reduce crime, or that there's no problem with the plan. A question could ask to identify a potential problem with the plan, or to strengthen the plan with the addition of some other fact.

No matter what the question asks, when you encounter an argument that employs a planning pattern, remember the standard assumption at play: there's no problem with the plan.

Sampling Patterns

Arguments that exhibit a sampling pattern are less common than causal or planning arguments. In a sampling argument, the author reaches a general conclusion about a population based on evidence about some members of the population. Sampling arguments assume that a smaller group is typical of a larger group and accurately reflects the relevant characteristics or feelings of the larger group. Here is an example:

> Contrary to popular belief, football fans overwhelmingly approve of the decisions made by the administrative staffs of their local teams. We know this to be true because a large group of fans leaving a stadium expressed admiration for their teams' coaches and coordinators in an interview last week.

The author of this argument concludes that *football fans overwhelmingly approve of the decisions made by the administrative staffs of their local teams*. This conclusion is based on the premise that *a large group of fans leaving a stadium expressed admiration for their teams' coaches and coordinators in an interview last week*. Thus, the conclusion makes a leap from the opinion of one group of fans at a particular moment to the opinion of football fans in general.

Every sampling argument involves one standard assumption:

*   The sample is representative.

When you encounter a sampling reasoning pattern, look for reasons why the sample itself is either representative or not. What if the opinion of the interviewed group of football fans isn't representative of the opinions of football fans in general? Perhaps the interviewed fans attended a game their team won, and perhaps their local team has long enjoyed a winning record. It does not follow from this that fans of every team approve of the decisions made by their team's administrative staff. To properly link the argument's conclusion to its premise, the author must assume that the opinions of interviewed fans accurately reflect those of football fans in general.

When you run into an argument that employs a sampling pattern, remember that the argument relies on the assumption that a sample is representative of a larger population.

Interpretation of Evidence Patterns

In some GMAT arguments, the author understands the conclusion to be synonymous with one or more of the premises. In other words, information in the premise is interpreted to mean information in the conclusion. These arguments exhibit the interpretation of evidence pattern.

One particularly common instance of this pattern involves the misinterpretation of statistical data. Not every argument that incorporates statistics is an interpretation of evidence argument, but arguments that exhibit this pattern frequently involve statistics. Most often, the argument confuses percentages with actual values. Consider the following example:

> Local grocer: Ninety percent of customers bought store brand soup last winter, but only eighty percent bought store brand soup this winter. Obviously, more customers bought store brand soup last winter.

The author concludes that *more customers bought store brand soup last winter*. This conclusion is based on the premise that *ninety percent of customers bought soup last winter, but only eighty percent bought soup this winter*. The premise describes a change in the percentage of customers who bought store brand soup, and the conclusion leaps from percentages to actual numbers.

Every interpretation of evidence argument involves one standard assumption:

• There's no other way to interpret the evidence.

What if there's another way to interpret the data? If 100 customers visited the grocer last winter, and ninety percent bought store brand soup, then 90 people bought store brand soup last winter. But if 200 customers visited the grocer this winter, and eighty percent bought store brand soup, then 160 people bought store brand soup this winter. In this case, it no longer follows that more people bought store brand soup last winter—the author misinterprets the statistical data.

When you come across an interpretation of evidence pattern, the argument most likely relies on the standard assumption that there's no other way to interpret the evidence.

Analogy Patterns

Reasoning by analogy is relatively rare on the GMAT, but that doesn't mean you won't see arguments by analogy. These arguments characteristically assume that what is appropriate in one case is also appropriate in another. They typically rely on the assumption that two things are similar enough to sustain a comparison. Here is a simple example:

> Using this line of products has been shown to cause cancer in laboratory animals. Therefore, you should stop using this line of products.

The author concludes that *you should stop using this line of products.* This conclusion is based on the premise that *this line of products has been shown to cause cancer in laboratory animals.* The premise concerns lab animals, and the conclusion leaps to humans. Thus, the argument relies on the assumption that humans and lab animals are similar: what causes cancer in laboratory animals also causes cancer in humans.

Arguments by analogy involve one standard assumption:

- One thing is similar to another.

What if humans are significantly different from laboratory animals? For example, if a feature of human physiology not shared by lab animals prevented the growth of cancers in humans who used the products, it would no longer follow that you should stop using the products.

When you encounter an argument that employs an analogy pattern, it probably relies on the assumption that one thing is similar to another in some relevant way.

THE BASIC APPROACH TO CRITICAL REASONING QUESTIONS

Critical Reasoning questions come in eight flavors. The majority of the questions are either *assumption*, *weaken*, or *strengthen* questions. However, there are some minor question types, such as *inference*, *resolve/explain*, *evaluate*, *identify the reasoning*, and *flaw* questions, of which you should be aware. Each of these question types has its own unique task and common trap answers.

Most Critical Reasoning questions will present you with an argument, but not all questions involve arguments. In fact, some Critical Reasoning passages don't look like arguments at all. In order to master the Critical Reasoning format, you need a basic approach that can be applied to any Critical Reasoning question you encounter, no matter what kind of question it is.

Here are the steps of the Basic Approach:

1. **Identify the Question**

   Look for words or phrases in the question stem that can be used to identify the question type. Your knowledge of the question type informs your approach to the passage, so always read the question stem before you read the passage.

2. **Work the Passage**

   For most question types, begin working an argument by distinguishing its conclusion from its premise. Then, look for shifts in language or reasoning patterns that can help you to identify the argument's assumption.

3. **Predict What the Answer Should Do**

   While it's often difficult to predict the answer, it's usually easier to predict what the answer should do. Before turning to the answer choices, use your knowledge of the question and the information in the passage to determine what the correct answer needs to accomplish.

4. **Use POE to Find the Answer**

   It's often easier to identify incorrect answers than it is to identify correct answers, so use POE aggressively. The POE tools change based on the question type, which is why it is critically important for you to become familiar with the different types of questions and how answer choices are constructed for them.

Step 1: Identify the Question

The surest way to improve performance and boost confidence in your Critical Reasoning ability is to take control of your approach to Critical Reasoning questions. Every question includes a word or phrase that can help you to identify what kind of question it is, and each question type involves a unique task with respect to the passage. Not all tasks are created equally, so it's important to know what's required of you.

Your knowledge of the question type should inform your approach, suggesting what kind of information to look for in the passage and what kind of answers to avoid. For now, we'll introduce the different question types, saving a more detailed discussion for later in the chapter.

Assumption Questions

Assumptions are necessary but invisible parts of an argument that bridge gaps in reasoning between its premise and conclusion. Here's where all that practice identifying the parts of an argument really begins to pay off. Simply put, assumption questions ask you to identify an unstated premise on which an argument depends.

Assumption questions typically ask:

- The argument above assumes which of the following?
- The author of the argument above presupposes which of the following to be true?
- Which of the following is an assumption on which the truth of the author's conclusion depends?

Different forms of the words *presupposition*, *expectation*, and *assumption* can alert you to the fact that you've encountered an assumption question.

Weaken Questions

Weaken questions ask to find a reason why the information in the passage could be wrong, or is incomplete. The vast majority of weaken questions require you to undermine the conclusion by attacking one of the argument's assumptions. Most commonly, the real job when answering weaken questions is not to attack the conclusion, but to attack *the way the conclusion follows from the premise.*

Weaken questions typically ask:

- Which of the following, if true, most seriously weakens the argument above?
- Which of the following casts the most doubt on the author's conclusion?
- Which of the following calls into question the reasoning above?

Indicator words such as *weaken*, *undermine*, and *cast doubt* can help you to spot a weaken question.

Strengthen Questions

Strengthen questions require you to reinforce an argument's conclusion. This is usually accomplished by strengthening one of the argument's assumptions. In order to answer a strengthen question with confidence, therefore, you must first identify an assumption. Once the pivotal assumption has been found, your job is to strengthen it—support the conclusion by strengthening the assumption.

Strengthen questions typically ask:

- Which of the following provides the best support for the claims made above?
- Which of the following statements, if true, most strengthens the argument's conclusion?
- Which of the following, if true, increases the likelihood that the author's claim is also true?

Words such as *strengthen*, *support*, and *justify* can help you to recognize a strengthen question.

Inference Questions

In one sense, an inference question is like a strengthen question in reverse. In a strengthen question, the correct answer strengthens the passage, but in an inference question, the passage strengthens the correct answer. As a result, many indicator words associated with strengthen questions—words such as *strengthen*, *support*, and *bolster*—are also associated with inference questions. Distinguish an inference question from a strengthen question by determining the direction of support.

In another sense, inference questions are unlike any of the question types we've discussed so far, because they don't require you to break an argument into its parts. In fact, inference passages tend not to resemble arguments at all. Instead, they merely present you with information—usually a collection of facts or opinions that lead to a particular conclusion. Once you're clear on the facts, your job is to select the answer that necessarily follows from them.

Inference questions typically ask:

- Which of the following can be inferred from the information above?
- On the basis of the statements above, which of the following must be true?
- With which of the following statements would the author of the passage most agree?

Words such as *inference*, *support*, and *strengthen* can help you spot an inference question.

Resolve/Explain Questions

Some Critical Reasoning questions ask you to resolve an apparent discrepancy or explain a paradoxical situation. The passages that accompany these questions almost never resemble arguments. Like inference passages, they merely present you with information. Resolve/Explain questions ask how two seemingly incongruous statements can be true at the same time. Clearly state the two ideas that seem to be opposed, and then select the answer that allows both ideas to be true.

Resolve/Explain questions typically ask:

- Which of the following, if true, resolves the paradox outlined above?
- Which of the following best explains the apparent contradiction?
- Which of the following statements goes farthest in explaining the situation above?

Resolve/Explain questions are easy to recognize because they include the word *resolve* or *explain*. Words such as *paradox* and *discrepancy* can also help you identify resolve/explain questions.

Evaluate Questions

Evaluate questions target your ability to spot a question (or test) that could be answered (or performed) to *evaluate* or *assess* an argument. Your job is to identify the question that, if answered, would allow you to test the argument's key assumption. Thus, evaluate questions are similar to strengthen and weaken questions in that they first require you to identify an unstated premise.

However, once the key assumption has been found, your task is not to weaken or strengthen it, but to identify the test that could help determine whether the argument is weak or strong.

Evaluate questions typically ask:

- The answer to which of the following questions would most likely yield information that could be used to assess the author's claim?
- Which of the following experiments would be most useful in evaluating the argument above?
- Which of the following tests could be performed to determine the truth of the argument's conclusion?

Indicator words such as *evaluate* and *assess* can help you to recognize an evaluate question.

Identify the Reasoning Questions

Occasionally, a Critical Reasoning question will ask you to identify the method, technique, or strategy used by the author of an argument, or to describe the roles played by bolded phrases in an argument. Identify the reasoning questions concern the relationships that exist between an argument's parts. Before you can answer a question about that relationship, you must first identify those parts. Distinguish the argument's conclusion from its premise, and then select the answer that accurately describes the structure of the argument.

Identify the reasoning questions typically ask:

- The author provides support for the argument above by…
- Which of the following methods of reasoning does the argument above exhibit?
- The bolded phrases play which of the following roles in the argument above?

Words such as *technique, strategy, method*, and *by* can help you to spot an identify the reasoning question.

Flaw Questions

Flaw questions ask you to describe what went wrong in an argument. The question stem already acknowledges that you're dealing with a bad argument. Your job is to identify its vulnerability. Flaw questions tend to resemble a blend of the identify the reasoning and weaken question types. Select the answer that accurately describes a vulnerability in the argument's reasoning.

Flaw questions typically ask:

- Which of the following statements describes a flaw in the argument above?
- The argument above is vulnerable to criticism for which of the following reasons?

To identify a flaw question, look for the words *vulnerable, criticism*, and *flaw*.

Step 2: Work the Argument

After you've read a Critical Reasoning question, read the accompanying passage. Allow your knowledge of the question type to guide you to relevant information.

Most Critical Reasoning questions—assumption, weaken, strengthen, evaluate, flaw, and identify the reasoning questions—provide you with an argument, and then ask you to perform a task related to the reasoning that argument employs.

- **Assumption questions** ask for an assumption required to make the argument valid. The correct answer will bridge a gap in an argument's reasoning from premise to conclusion, so begin by distinguishing the conclusion from the premise that supports it. Then, identify the assumption that links the conclusion to the premise, choosing the answer that bridges the gap. Shifts in language and reasoning patterns can help you to spot assumptions.

- **Weaken questions**: Weakening a GMAT argument is almost always accomplished by attacking one of the argument's key assumptions. Therefore, begin a weaken question the same way you begin an assumption question, by using the argument's premise and conclusion to identify unstated information on which the argument depends. Once you've spotted the pivotal assumption, choose the answer that offers good reason to believe it isn't true.

- **Strengthen questions**: Strengthening a GMAT argument is almost always accomplished by reinforcing one of the argument's key assumptions. Begin a strengthen question by identifying the argument's premise and conclusion, as well as any gaps in reasoning between them. Once you've found the pivotal assumption, choose the answer that suggests it's true.

- **Evaluate questions** are similar to weaken and strengthen questions in that they ask you to consider the unstated piece of information that, if you knew it, would tell you whether you're looking at a weak argument or a strong argument. Evaluating a GMAT argument is almost always accomplished by identifying a test you could perform or a question you could answer to determine the truth or falsity of an assumption.

- **Identify the Reasoning questions** ask you to describe the structure of an argument or how it works. Some identify the reasoning questions concern the logical function of bolded phrases in the passage. For any identify the reasoning question, determine which part of the argument functions as its claim and which parts function as evidence. Choose the answer that accurately describes the structure of the argument. There's no need to worry about assumptions.

- **Flaw questions** combine the tasks involved in identify the reasoning and weaken questions. You're looking for the answer that accurately describes the structure of the argument (identify the reasoning), usually by exposing the weakness of an assumption made by the author (weaken). Begin by distinguishing the argument's conclusion from its premise. Use shifts in language or reasoning patterns to identify the faulty assumption.

- **Inference questions**: Passages that accompany inference questions tend to look like collections of facts without any logical progression from premise to conclusion. There's usually no way to differentiate claims from evidence, so don't bother. In fact, you may feel as though the question gives you the evidence and asks you to provide the conclusion. Begin an inference question by familiarizing yourself with the information provided; if it helps, use your noteboard to create a list of facts. Then, choose the answer that must be true on the basis of the facts.

- **Resolve/Explain questions**: Like inference passages, the passages that accompany resolve/explain questions tend not to exhibit the structural elements of an argument. Instead, they present two ideas that seem to be opposed. Rather than looking for the premise and conclusion, begin by using your noteboard to clarify the apparent conflict: "On the one hand, *X*, but on the other, *Y*." Indicator words such as *but*, *yet*, and *however* can draw your attention to opposing ideas and help you to articulate the apparent conflict. Choose the answer that explains how *X* and *Y* might both be true at the same time.

Step 3: Predict What the Answer Should Do

Just as your knowledge of the question type can help you to identify relevant information in a Critical Reasoning passage, your knowledge of the question type can help you to recognize the characteristics of the answer you're looking for.

Predicting the answer to a Critical Reasoning question is often quite difficult. Predicting what the answer should do is usually easier. Before turning to the answers, think about what the correct answer needs to accomplish based on the question type and information in the argument. In this way, you continue to exercise control over a question as you move from information gathering to answer selection.

- **Assumption questions:** Good answers to assumption questions bridge a gap in reasoning between the premise of an argument and its conclusion. For this reason, they often employ words or phrases that appear in the premise, as well as language from the conclusion. A good answer links the author's claim to evidence that supports it, or rules out obstacles to that link.

- **Weaken questions:** Good answers to weaken questions widen a gap in reasoning between the premise of an argument and its conclusion. In order to do so, they often introduce new information that attacks one of the argument's assumptions. A good answer makes the truth of an author's claim seem less likely by disrupting the link between that claim and the evidence that supports it.

- **Strengthen questions:** Good answers to strengthen questions are very similar to those for assumption questions. That's because both question types require you to find an assumption that supports the argument's conclusion. A good answer will confirm the pivotal assumption or introduce new information that rules out obstacles to it.

- **Inference questions:** Like inference questions in the Reading Comprehension format, inference questions in the Critical Reasoning format don't really ask you to make an inference beyond the scope of the information provided. It can be difficult to come up with your own answer to an inference question, so let the test-writers worry about the phrasing. Simply keep in mind that you want the answer best supported by the facts. An answer that paraphrases a fact from the passage is often the credited response.

- **Resolve/Explain questions:** Passages that accompany resolve/explain questions introduce a pair of facts or ideas that seem to oppose one another. Once you've clarified the apparent conflict, look for answer choices that allow both facts to be true simultaneously. Good answers address both sides of the issue, rather than ignoring one side or the other.

- **Evaluate questions:** Evaluate questions require you to select a test you could perform, or a question you could ask, to assess the validity of an argument. If the answer choices are phrased as questions, try answering each question "Yes" and "No" to see whether different answers change your belief in the argument's conclusion. If so, you're probably dealing with the credited response. Good answers make it possible to determine the truth or falsity of an assumption made in the argument.

- **Identify the Reasoning questions:** Once you've identified the premise and conclusion of an identify the reasoning passage, look for answer choices that accurately describe the relationships between an argument's parts. There's no reason to look for gaps or assumptions; the task is purely descriptive. Keep an eye out for answers that focus on the structure of the argument rather than its content. Good answer choices accurately mirror the argument's structure.

- **Flaw questions:** Good answers to flaw questions accurately reflect the structure of the argument. They differ from good answers to identify the reasoning questions only because they invariably describe flaws in reasoning. The correct answer most often articulates a faulty assumption.

Step 4: Use POE to Find the Answer

This is the last step in the basic approach to Critical Reasoning questions. You've done most of the work required to answer the question. All that remains is to select and confirm your answer. You're already armed with a sense of what the correct answer needs to accomplish. Now supplement that understanding with an efficient, effective process for weeding out bad answers and avoiding traps—tempting answers that are nevertheless incorrect.

Just as your knowledge of question types can help you find relevant information in a passage and predict what the correct answer should do, it can help you to narrow your search for the correct answer by enabling you to quickly eliminate answers that are flawed. You've read about the characteristics of good answers. It's time to consider the characteristics of poor answers. Each Critical Reasoning question type has its own set of attractor answers that you will learn to anticipate. GMAT arguments are often quite specific, so read them carefully and interpret them literally. Pay close attention to the language used in arguments and answer choices.

Assumption questions ask you for the unstated premise in the argument. Correct answers link conclusions to the premises that support them, so ask how each answer affects the author's claim. When you think you've found the correct answer, apply the **Negation Test**. Negate your preferred answer, and if your belief in the argument's conclusion isn't affected, the answer is incorrect. Avoid answers that:

- are out of scope
- use extreme language

Weaken questions ask you to select the answer that disrupts the link between the premise and the conclusion. Ask yourself how each choice affects the author's claim. Eliminate answers that:

- are out of scope
- use extreme language
- strengthen the argument

Strengthen questions ask you to select the answer that reinforces the link between the premise and the conclusion. Ask yourself how each choice affects the author's claim. Eliminate answers that:

- are out of scope
- use extreme language
- weaken the argument

Inference questions ask for the answer choice that follows necessarily from the facts in the passage. The answers to inference questions generally don't stray far from the information provided, so look to eliminate answers that require additional assumptions. Avoid answers that:

- are out of scope
- use extreme language

Resolve/Explain questions ask for the answer that resolves an apparent conflict between two ideas, or that explains the conflict away. When you consider the answer choices, adhere closely to the opposing ideas. Avoid answers that:

- are out of scope
- make the conflict worse
- address only one side of the conflict

Evaluate questions ask you to select the answer that allows the strength or weakness of an argument to be determined. Incorrect answers offer new information that does not connect the argument's conclusion to its premise in a meaningful way. Eliminate answers that:

- are out of scope

Identify the Reasoning questions ask you to find the answer that accurately describes the structure of an argument. Avoid answers that:

- do not match the structure of the argument
- only partially match the structure

Flaw questions ask you to choose the answer that accurately describes a flaw in the structure of an argument. Watch out for answers that describe the argument faithfully, but neglect to mention a flaw. Eliminate answers that:

- are out of scope
- cannot be matched to the argument or are only partial matches

PRACTICE QUESTIONS

Now that you've been introduced to the parts of a GMAT argument, the reasoning patterns typical of GMAT arguments, and the basic approach to Critical Reasoning questions, work through some example questions to bolster your understanding of the Critical Reasoning question format.

Here is an example of an **Assumption question.**

Most people believe that gold and platinum are the most valuable commodities. To the true entrepreneur, however, gold and platinum are less valuable than the knowledge of opportunities is. Thus, in the world of high finance, information is the most valuable commodity.

The author of the passage above makes which of the following assumptions?

(A) Gold and platinum are not the most valuable commodities.
(B) Entrepreneurs are not like most people.
(C) The value of information is incalculably high.
(D) Information about business opportunities is accurate and leads to increased wealth.
(E) Only entrepreneurs feel that information is the most valuable commodity.

Here's How to Crack It

The question asks for the *assumption* made by the author, so this is an assumption question.

An assumption supports the conclusion of an argument, so when you read the passage, look for the conclusion. The word *thus* in the passage's final sentence gives it away: *in the world of high finance, information is the most valuable commodity.*

Now determine what information in the passage is in support of the conclusion. Two pieces of information are provided in support of the conclusion. One group of people—*most people*—believe that *gold and platinum are the most valuable commodities*. Another group—*true entrepreneurs*—believe that *gold and platinum are less valuable than is the knowledge of opportunities*.

From the opinions of two groups of people, the author concludes that the opinion of one group is to be preferred, but the passage doesn't say why. Therefore, it's likely that the correct answer will explain why the opinion of *the true entrepreneur* is to be preferred. With that in mind, you're ready to attack the answer choices:

(A)   Gold and platinum are not the most valuable commodities.

This answer appears to support the conclusion. If *gold and platinum are not the most valuable commodities*, there's a chance that *information is*. By itself, however, the idea that gold and platinum *are not* the most valuable commodities doesn't mean information *is* the most valuable commodity. This assumption provides no reason why the author should agree with *the true entrepreneur*; it doesn't link the argument's premise to its conclusion. Eliminate (A).

(B)   Entrepreneurs are not like most people.

This answer choice doesn't tell you anything you don't already know: if the true entrepreneur doesn't share the opinion of most people, then entrepreneurs aren't like most people (at least not in the way they value commodities). In any case, this answer doesn't provide a reason to favor the opinion of the true entrepreneur. Eliminate (B).

(C)   The value of information is incalculably high.

Be wary of the extreme language in this answer choice. The author needn't assume the value of information is incalculable in order to believe that it's the most valuable commodity. On the other hand, the value of many commodities might be incalculable; it doesn't follow from this that information is most valuable. Eliminate (C).

(D)   Information about business opportunities is accurate and leads to increased wealth.

This answer links the argument's conclusion to its premise by providing a reason to side with the true entrepreneur. To check whether this assumption is required by the argument, apply the Negation Test. If information *isn't* accurate and *doesn't* lead to increased wealth, it's unclear why the author believes it to be most valuable. Negating this answer disrupts the argument, so keep (D).

(E)   Only entrepreneurs feel that information is the most valuable commodity.

This answer is out of scope. It doesn't matter *who* believes information to be most valuable. What matters is *why* the author believes it to be most valuable. Eliminate (E).

The correct answer is (D).

Here is an example of a **Weaken question.**

An artist who sells her paintings for a fixed price decides that she must increase her income. Because she does not believe that customers will pay more for her paintings, she decides to cut costs by using cheaper paints and canvases. She expects that, by cutting costs, she will increase her profit margin per painting and thus increase her annual net income.

Which of the following, if true, most weakens the argument above?

(A)   Other area artists charge more for their paintings than the artist charges for hers.
(B)   The artist has failed to consider other options, such as renting cheaper studio space.
(C)   The artist's plan will result in the production of inferior paintings which, in turn, will cause a reduction in sales.
(D)   If the economy were to enter a period of inflation, the artist's projected increase in income could be wiped out by increases in the price of art supplies.
(E)   The artist considered trying to complete paintings more quickly and thus increase production, but concluded that it would be impossible.

Here's How to Crack It

The question asks which of the answer choices *weakens* the argument, so this is a weaken question.

Begin by breaking this question down into its component parts. The argument contains a planning pattern. The conclusion of the argument is that *by cutting costs, she* [the artist] *will increase her profit margin per painting and thus increase her annual net income.* The premise of the argument is that the artist *decides she must increase her income* and that she *does not believe that customers will pay more for her paintings.* The plan is that *she decides to cut costs by using cheaper paints and canvases.*

The standard assumption of a planning argument is that there is no problem with the plan. In order to weaken the argument, the correct answer choice will highlight a potential problem with the plan. Evaluate the answer choices one at a time.

(A)   Other area artists charge more for their paintings than the artist charges for hers.

This answer choice introduces the idea of *other area artists*, which is beyond the scope of the argument. Additionally, this answer choice does not address a potential problem with the plan. If anything, it strengthens the plan because it suggests people are willing to pay more for paintings than what the artist is charging. Eliminate (A).

(B)　The artist has failed to consider other options, such as renting cheaper studio space.

This answer choice introduces the idea of *renting cheaper studio space*, which is out of scope. This does not address a problem with the plan to *cut costs by using cheaper paints and canvases*. Eliminate (B).

(C)　The artist's plan will result in the production of inferior paintings which, in turn, will cause a reduction in sales.

This answer choice mentions a potential problem with the plan. If the artist's plan will result in *inferior paintings* that *will cause a reduction in sales*, then the plan to *cut costs by using cheaper paints and canvases* in order to *increase her profit margin per painting and thus increase her annual net income* is called into question. If the artist sells fewer paintings, then the increase in her profit margin from using cheaper materials may not result in an increase in her annual net income. Keep (C).

(D)　If the economy were to enter a period of inflation, the artist's projected increase in income could be wiped out by increases in the price of art supplies.

This answer choice introduces the idea of *a period of inflation*, which is both out of scope and does not address the plan in the argument. Eliminate (D).

(E)　The artist considered trying to complete paintings more quickly and thus increase production, but concluded that would be impossible.

If the artist has eliminated another possible plan in order to increase annual income, then it de facto strengthens the argument to increase net revenue by using cheaper materials because it eliminates another possible plan. Eliminate (E).

The correct answer is (C).

Challenge Question #9

In an effort to stimulate economic growth, the parliament of Sapland is promoting new legislation which halves the corporate tax rate. Members of parliament claim the move will lead to job creation and investment by the impacted corporations. Critics disagree vocally, pointing to a plethora of studies indicating that such tax savings tend to be kept as profit rather than reinvested, and therefore are unlikely to spur job creation or corporate investment.

Which of the following, if true, most undermines the critics' objection to the tax plan promoted by parliament to spur job creation and corporate investment by halving the corporate tax rate?

(A) The legislation halving the corporate tax rate includes a stipulation that funds equal to those owed in the form of taxes must be used by the impacted corporation to promote its primary business purpose.

(B) The tax savings will induce the shareholders of many impacted corporations to increase their personal investment portfolios significantly.

(C) Many corporate shareholders consider their respective corporations' performance to be more than sufficient, and see no reason to expand either their workforces or capital investments.

(D) The majority of the tax revenue lost due to the corporate tax rate reduction can be reclaimed by raising property taxes on large estates.

(E) Sapland currently suffers from high unemployment, brought on by years of government-mandated anti-discrimination policies and environmental regulations.

Find the answers to all Challenge Questions in Part V!

Here is an example of a **Strengthen question**.

It has recently been proposed that Country X adopt an all-volunteer army. This policy was tried on a limited basis several years ago and was a miserable failure. The level of education of the volunteers was unacceptably low, while levels of drug use and crime soared among army personnel. Can Country X trust its national defense to a volunteer army? The answer is clearly "No."

Which of the following statements, if true, provides the most support for the claim that an all-volunteer army should not be implemented?

(A)   The population's level of education has risen since the first time an all-volunteer army was tried.

(B)   The proposal was made by an organization called Citizens for Peace.

(C)   The first attempt to create a volunteer army was carried out according to the same plan now under proposal and under the same conditions as those that exist today.

(D)   A volunteer army would be less expensive than an army that relies on the draft.

(E)   Armies are smaller today than they were when a volunteer army was last proposed.

Here's How to Crack It

The question asks for the statement that *provides the most support for the claim*, so this is a strengthen question. Begin by distinguishing the argument's conclusion from its premise, and then find the assumption.

The conclusion of the argument is easy to identify because it's stated in the question stem: *an all-volunteer army should not be implemented*. As you read the passage, be on the lookout for a premise that supports the author's claim.

The author provides only one piece of evidence to suggest that an all-volunteer army shouldn't be implemented: it was *tried on a limited basis several years ago and was a miserable failure*. According to the argument, Country X shouldn't implement an all-volunteer army now because it didn't work out then. This argument exhibits the analogy pattern; it assumes that the current attempt to institute an all-volunteer army will be like the previous attempt.

Because this is a strengthen question, look for answer choices that suggest the two attempts are similar. The more similar they are, the more likely the current attempt will end in failure, and the easier it is to conclude that Country X shouldn't implement an all-volunteer army.

(A)   The population's level of education has risen since the first time
        an all-volunteer army was tried.

This answer choice introduces a difference between the current attempt to implement an all-volunteer army and the past attempt. If the education level of the population increased, there's reason to expect a different result this time around. Rather than strengthen the argument against an all-volunteer army, this answer weakens it. Eliminate (A).

(B)   The proposal was made by an organization called Citizens for Peace.

The identity of the group that made the proposal is out of scope. The relevant question asks whether there's good reason to believe that acting on the proposal will end in failure. Eliminate (B).

(C)   The first attempt to create a volunteer army was carried out
        according to the same plan now under proposal and under the
        same conditions as those that exist today.

Eureka! This answer introduces a relevant similarity between the two attempts to institute an all-volunteer army. If the last attempt ended in disaster, and the current attempt follows the same plan under the same conditions, there's reason to believe the outcome will be similar. Choice (C) strengthens the argument against an all-volunteer army, so keep it.

(D)   A volunteer army would be less expensive than an army that
        relies on the draft.

The cost of a volunteer army is out of scope. The argument concerns the trustworthiness of such an army, not its cost. Eliminate (D).

(E)   Armies are smaller today than they were when a volunteer army
        was last proposed.

Like (A), (E) introduces a dissimilarity between the two attempts to institute a volunteer army. For that reason, it's unlikely to be the correct answer. More importantly, like (B) and (D), it's out of scope. It doesn't matter how big the army is or was, but whether it's staffed by trustworthy people or fools and criminals. Eliminate (E).

The correct answer is (C).

Here is an example of an **Inference question.**

In film and television, it's possible to induce viewers to project their feelings onto characters on the screen. In one study, a camera shot of a woman's face was preceded by images of a baby. The audience thought the woman's face registered contentment. When the same woman's face was preceded by images of a shark attack, the audience thought the woman's face registered fear. Television news teams must be careful to avoid such manipulation of their viewers.

Which of the following is best supported by the information in the passage?

(A) Television news teams have abused their position of trust in the past.
(B) The expression on the woman's face was, in actuality, blank.
(C) Images of a baby engendered feelings of happiness in the audience.
(D) Audiences should strive to be less gullible.
(E) The technique for manipulating audiences described in the passage would also work in a radio program that played dramatic music.

Here's How to Crack It

The question asks for the answer *best supported by the information in the passage.* The direction of support is from the passage to the answer choices, so this is an inference question. Begin by getting clear on the facts.

> Fact 1: *In film and television, it's possible to induce viewers to project their feelings onto characters on the screen, making it possible for news teams to manipulate viewers.*

> Fact 2: *When a camera shot of a woman's face was preceded by images of a baby, the audience thought the woman's face registered contentment.*

> Fact 3: *When the same woman's face was preceded by images of a shark attack, the audience thought the woman's face registered fear.*

Once you're clear on the facts, look for the answer that must be true on their basis. Be wary of extreme language and eliminate answers that are beyond the scope of the information provided. The correct answer is likely to paraphrase information in the passage.

(A) Television news teams have abused their position of trust in the past.

This answer goes well beyond the scope of the passage. We have no idea what news teams did in the past based on the information provided. Eliminate (A).

(B)   The expression on the woman's face was, in actuality, blank.

Like the previous choice, this answer is out of scope. Based on the information provided, we simply don't know whether the woman's face was expressionless. Eliminate (B).

(C)   Images of a baby engendered feelings of happiness in the audience.

Images of a baby led the audience to believe the woman's face registered contentment. If audience members projected their feelings onto the woman, then audience members must have experienced contentment, and it's likely the images of a baby were responsible. Keep (C).

(D)   Audiences should strive to be less gullible.

Of course, we should all strive to be less gullible, but we know that simply because we know what "gullible" means, not because of the information provided. Nothing in the passage suggests that audience members were gullible. Eliminate (D).

(E)   The technique for manipulating audiences described in the passage would also work in a radio program that played dramatic music.

It's possible that the information in this answer choice is true, but possible isn't good enough. We need an answer that *must be* true, and the passage provides no information about the projection of emotion in the medium of sound. Eliminate (E).

The correct answer is (C).

Find the answers to all Challenge Questions in Part V!

Challenge Question #10

Glacial ablation is the term for a loss of glacial mass in terms of ice. Ablation rates vary based on a wide number of factors, one of which is submarine melt: ice loss due to contact between the glacier and seawater. While factors such as air temperature, precipitation, and snow accumulation play significant roles, glacial ablation along coastlines tends to proceed at its greatest rate when warm ocean currents come into contact with the base of the glacier and produce a high degree of submarine melt. Warm ocean currents along glacial coastline areas increase in frequency as overall ocean temperatures rise.

Which of the following can be most readily inferred from the information in the passage?

(A)   Regions with the greatest rate of glacial ablation have the greatest proximity to the strongest warm ocean currents.
(B)   Very few glaciers in regions without warm ocean currents suffer from high rates of glacial ablation.
(C)   Glacial ablation due to submarine melt rates was lower on average during periods of lower overall ocean temperatures.
(D)   Submarine melt rates have become an important factor to glacial ablation only with the onset of global climatic shifts.
(E)   The lower the overall ocean temperature, the more likely that factors such as snow accumulation are to play a significant role in glacial ablation.

Here is an example of a **Resolve/Explain question.**

In recent years, the world's airlines reported an increase in the total number of passengers carried, but a decrease in total revenues, even though prices for airline tickets on all routes remained unchanged from the year before.

Which of the following resolves the paradox described above?

(A)   The airline industry was a victim of a recent recession.
(B)   Total passenger miles were up in recent years.
(C)   Fuel costs remained constant over recent years.
(D)   Passengers traveled shorter distances on less expensive flights in recent years.
(E)   No new aircraft were purchased by any carrier in recent years.

Here's How to Crack It

The question asks for the answer that *resolves the paradox*, so this is a resolve/explain question. Your knowledge of question types suggests that the accompanying passage will present two pieces of information which seem to be in conflict. State that opposition as clearly as possible.

On the one hand, more passengers traveled by air.

On the other, airline revenues decreased, even though ticket prices remained unchanged.

The correct answer to a resolve/explain question will allow both pieces of information to be true simultaneously. Eliminate answers that are out of scope, address only one side of the conflict, or make the conflict worse.

(A)   The airline industry was a victim of a recent recession.

A recession might account for the decrease in revenue, but if ticket prices remained the same, it's unclear how the number of passengers could have increased. Choice (A) addresses only one side of the conflict, so eliminate it.

(B)   Total passenger miles were up in recent years.

If passengers flew farther and ticket prices remained the same, it's unclear how revenues could have decreased. Like (A), this answer addresses only one side of the conflict. Eliminate (B).

(C)   Fuel costs remained constant over recent years.

Fuel costs are out of scope. An increase in fuel costs might have affected airline profits, but profits are not revenues. This answer has no bearing on either side of the conflict. Eliminate (C).

(D)   Passengers traveled shorter distances on less expensive flights in recent years.

This answer looks promising. If the increase in passengers was offset by passengers taking cheaper flights, then revenues could have decreased even as the number of passengers increased. Keep (D).

(E)   No new aircraft were purchased by any carrier in recent years.

New aircraft are out of scope. The purchase of new aircraft might have affected airline profits, but if no new aircraft were purchased, then new aircraft affected neither profits nor revenues, and this answer has no relevance at all. Eliminate (E).

The correct answer is (D).

Here is an example of an **Evaluate question.**

During a period of low growth after a recent and remarkable boom in the solar energy sector, Company X, a major manufacturer of solar-powered generators, attributed its success during the boom to the sale of excess inventory it had discovered in one of its warehouses.

Which of the following tests would most help to evaluate the company's hypothesis as to the cause of its success?

(A)   Comparing the length of the low-growth period to the length of the preceding boom
(B)   Comparing the boom experienced by Company X to those experienced by similarly-sized manufacturers of solar-powered generators that did not have inventory on hand
(C)   Calculating average sales increases within the individual divisions of Company X
(D)   Comparing the total number of generators sold by Company X during the boom to the total number sold by Company X during the period of low growth
(E)   Using economic theory to predict the next economic boom for Company X

Here's How to Crack It

The question asks for the test that would most help to *evaluate* the company's hypothesis, so this is an evaluate question. According to the question stem, the hypothesis concerns the cause of Company X's success. As you begin to work the argument, look for claims that provide a reason company X succeeded.

The passage's final sentence states that Company X *attributed its success during the boom to the sale of excess inventory*, but how does Company X come to believe that? The only other piece of information we get from the passage is that there was a *boom in the solar energy sector*, followed by a *period of low growth.*

Without additional information, it's unclear how changes in the solar energy sector relate to the company's claim about its own success. However, if you noticed the word *cause* in the question stem, then you probably recognized that Company X makes a causal argument.

Take advantage of the causal reasoning pattern by recalling its standard assumptions: there's no other cause, and it's not a coincidence. The former assumption seems more relevant here, because Company X assumes the sale of excess inventory alone was responsible for its success.

Evaluate the answer choices one at a time, looking for the test that would allow you to determine whether there isn't another reason for Company X's success.

(A) Comparing the length of the low-growth period to the length of the preceding boom

Executing this comparison would tell us how long each of the periods lasted, but connecting that information to the sale of excess inventory would require inferences beyond the scope of the information provided. Eliminate (A).

(B) Comparing the boom experienced by Company X to those experienced by similarly-sized manufacturers of solar-powered generators that did not have inventory on hand

This answer choice is tempting. We're looking for a way to determine whether something other than the sale of excess inventory might have caused Company X's success. If competitors without excess inventory to sell experienced booms comparable to that of Company X, then the company's claim might be incorrect. On the other hand, if competitors didn't experience as big a boom, it appears more likely that the sale of excess inventory was responsible for Company X's success. Keep (B).

(C) Calculating average sales increases within the individual divisions of Company X

Individual divisions of Company X are out of scope. We already know that the company sold excess inventory; which divisions saw sales increases is irrelevant. Eliminate (C).

(D) Comparing the total number of generators sold by Company X during the boom to the total number sold by Company X during the period of low growth

At first glance, this answer choice looks appealing. The comparison described here would allow us to determine how many generators were sold during each period. If more generators were sold during the boom than during the low-growth period, it might seem as though Company X's success during the boom resulted from the sale of excess inventory. However, the passage states that the period of low growth *followed* the boom. If more generators were sold during the boom, then at best, we could infer that a *decline* in sales led to *decreased* success. To determine whether the sale of excess inventory *caused* Company X's success during the boom, we'd need sales numbers from the period *before* the boom, not the period *after* it. Eliminate (D).

(E)   Using economic theory to predict when the next economic boom
       for Company X will occur

Of the five answer choices, this one is most obviously out of scope. An estimate of the time that will elapse before the next boom needn't have any relevance to the cause of the last boom. Eliminate (E).

The correct answer is (B).

Here is an example of an **Identify the Reasoning question.**

Although measuring the productivity of outside consultants is a complex endeavor, **Company K, which relies heavily on consultants, must find ways to assess the performance of these workers.** The risks to a company that does not review the productivity of its human resources are simply too great. **Last year, Company L was forced into receivership after its productivity declined for three consecutive quarters.**

The bolded clauses play which of the following roles in the argument above?

(A)   The first bolded clause states the author's conclusion, and the second introduces unrelated information.
(B)   The first bolded clause provides background information, and the second offers evidence to contradict that information.
(C)   The first bolded clause states one of the author's premises, while the second states the author's conclusion.
(D)   The first bolded clause expresses a position, and the second warns against the adoption of that position.
(E)   The first bolded clause represents the author's conclusion, and the second supports the conclusion with an analogy.

Here's How to Crack It

The bolded clauses in the passage immediately indicate that this is an identify the reasoning question, so begin by distinguishing the argument's conclusion from the premise that supports it. Don't worry about finding assumptions.

The phrase *must find ways to assess* is strong language, making the first bolded phrase a good candidate for the argument's conclusion. Why must Company K find ways to assess the performance of its outside consultants? Because companies that don't review the productivity of human resources face risks—just look at Company L! Both of the passage's remaining sentences operate in support of the first bolded phrase. The second bolded clause supports the conclusion by offering the example of a company that was *forced into receivership after its productivity declined*.

Now that you've got a good sense of the argument's structure, look for the answer that correctly mirrors it.

(A)   The first bolded clause states the author's conclusion, and the
      second introduces unrelated information.

The first part of this answer looks good, because the first bolded clause *does* state the author's conclusion. However, the second bolded clause supports the conclusion; it does not introduce unrelated information. Choice (A) only partially matches the argument's structure, so eliminate it.

(B)   The first bolded clause provides background information, and the
      second offers evidence to contradict that information.

Part of the first bolded clause states that Company K *relies heavily on consultants*, which does resemble background information. However, nothing in the second bolded clause contradicts that information. Choice (B) is a partial match. Eliminate it.

(C)   The first bolded clause states one of the author's premises, while
      the second states the author's conclusion.

This answer choice reverses the roles played by the bolded clauses. Since it doesn't match the structure of the argument, eliminate (C).

(D)   The first bolded clause expresses a position, and the second
      warns against the adoption of that position.

Like (A) and (B), (D) is a partial match. The first bolded clause expresses a position, but the second doesn't warn against the adoption of that position. Eliminate (D).

(E)   The first bolded clause represents the author's conclusion, and
      the second supports the conclusion with an analogy.

This answer accurately reflects the relationship between the bolded clauses: the first is the author's conclusion, and the second supports the conclusion by offering the example of analogous Company L. Keep (E).

The correct answer is (E).

Here is an example of a **Flaw question**.

A telephone poll conducted in two states asked respondents whether their homes were cold during the winter months. Ninety-nine percent of respondents said their houses were always warm during the winter. The pollsters published their findings, concluding that ninety-nine percent of all homes in the United States have adequate heating.

Which of the following most accurately describes a questionable technique employed by the pollsters in drawing their conclusion?

(A) The poll wrongly ascribes the underlying causes of the problem.
(B) The poll assumes conditions in the two states are representative of the entire country.
(C) The pollsters conducted the poll by telephone, thereby relying on the veracity of respondents.
(D) The pollsters didn't visit respondents' houses in person, so no measure of the temperature in a subject's home was actually made.
(E) The pollsters never defined the term "cold" in terms of a specific temperature.

Here's How to Crack It

The question asks for a *questionable technique* used by the pollsters, so this is a flaw question.

You already know from the question stem that the argument has a serious problem. Your job is to figure out what that problem is. Begin by identifying the argument's premise and conclusion. Then, use a gap in the reasoning to focus on the assumption. Because this is a flaw question, be on the lookout for common reasoning patterns.

The word *concluding* in the last sentence of the passage gives away the conclusion: *ninety-nine percent of all homes in the United States have adequate heating*. Why did the pollsters conclude this? Their findings were based on the results of *a telephone poll conducted in two states*, in which *ninety-nine percent of respondents said their houses were always warm during the winter*.

Did you recognize the pattern of reasoning in this argument? Information about one group of people (the poll was conducted in two states) is used to make a claim about a much larger group (all households in the United States). This argument employs the sampling pattern. The standard assumption involved in the sampling pattern is that the sample is representative of the larger population. Look for answers that call attention to this assumption.

    (A)   The poll wrongly ascribes the underlying causes of a problem.

Underlying causes are out of scope. The pollsters ask whether people's homes are cold. The reason they might be cold is irrelevant. Eliminate (A).

    (B)   The poll assumes conditions in the two states are representative of the entire country.

This answer expresses the standard assumption involved in the sampling pattern. Nothing in the passage suggests that the households surveyed are representative of U.S. householders in general. Keep (B).

    (C)   The pollsters conducted the poll by telephone, thereby relying on the veracity of respondents.

The information in this answer might betray a weakness in the pollsters' methodology, but it isn't a weakness in the pollsters' reasoning. Eliminate (C).

    (D)   The pollsters didn't visit respondents' houses in person, so no measurement of the temperature in a subject's home was actually made.

Like (C), this answer describes a problem with the poll, not with the argument. Eliminate (D).

    (E)   The pollsters never defined the term "cold" in terms of a specific temperature.

It's true that the pollsters never defined the term "cold," but does that represent a flaw in the pollsters' reasoning? The flaw identified here concerns the poll itself, not the argument. Eliminate (E).

The correct answer is (B).

Now that you know how to identify and approach each of the eight Critical Reasoning question types, the best way to proceed is to practice. The more you experience through preparation, the less likely you are to be surprised on test day.

As you complete Critical Reasoning drills and exercises, force yourself to follow the basic approach. Your knowledge of the question type informs every step of the basic approach to Critical Reasoning questions, from reading the passage to eliminating incorrect answers, so always read the question first. Memorize the common reasoning patterns and the assumptions that go with them, develop a familiarity with the characteristics of good and bad answers, and you'll be well on your way to mastering the Critical Reasoning format.

DRILL 19 (Spotting Critical Reasoning Question Types)

The answers to questions in this drill can be found in Part V.

For each of the questions below, decide which question type it belongs to. For extra credit, list what you should look for in the passage that would normally precede the question.

1. Which of the following, if true, gives the most support to the recommendations above?
2. Which of the following statements can properly be inferred on the basis of the statements above?
3. The answer to which of the following questions would most help the CEO to evaluate the manager's claim?
4. The argument in the passage depends on which of the following assumptions?
5. The argument above is vulnerable to criticism for which of the following reasons?
6. The author's argument would be most seriously weakened if it were true that…
7. The senator responds to the constituent's assertion by…
8. Which of the following statements best explains the apparent discrepancy described above?

DRILL 20

The answers to questions in this drill can be found in Part V.

1. A fashion designer's fall line for women utilizing new soft fabrics broke all sales records last year. To capitalize on her success, the designer plans to launch a line of clothing for men this year that makes use of the same new soft fabrics.

   The designer's plan assumes that

   (A) other designers are not planning to introduce new lines for men utilizing the same soft fabrics
   (B) men will be as interested in the new soft fabrics as women were the year before
   (C) the designer will have time to develop new lines for both men and women
   (D) the line for men will be considered innovative and daring because of its use of fabrics
   (E) women who bought the new line last year will continue to buy it this year

2. According to a recent report, the original tires supplied with the Impressivo, a new sedan-class automobile, wore much more quickly than tires conventionally wear. The report suggested two possible causes: (1) defects in the tires and (2) improper wheel alignment of the automobile.

    Which of the following would best help the authors of the report determine which of the two causes identified was responsible for the extra wear?

    (A) A study in which the rate of tire wear in the Impressivo is compared to the rate of tire wear in all automobiles in the same class
    (B) A study in which a second set of tires, manufactured by a different company from the one that made the first set, is installed on all Impressivos and the rate of wear is measured
    (C) A study in which the level of satisfaction of workers in the Impressivo manufacturing plant is measured and compared to that of workers at other automobile manufacturing plants
    (D) A study that determines how often improper wheel alignment results in major problems for manufacturers of other automobiles in the Impressivo's class
    (E) A study that determines the degree to which faulty driving techniques employed by Impressivo drivers contributed to tire wear

3. Scientists wishing to understand the kinetic movements of ancient dinosaurs are today studying the movements of modern-day birds, which many scientists believe are descended from dinosaurs. A flaw in this strategy is that birds, although once genetically linked to dinosaurs, have evolved so far that any comparison is effectively meaningless.

    Which of the following, if true, would most weaken the criticism made above of the scientists' strategy?

    (A) Birds and dinosaurs have a number of important features in common that exist in no other living species.
    (B) Birds are separated from dinosaurs by 65 million years of evolution.
    (C) Our theories of dinosaur movements have recently undergone a radical reappraisal.
    (D) The study of kinetic movement is a relatively new discipline.
    (E) Many bird experts do not study dinosaurs to draw inferences about birds.

4. A proposal for a new building fire safety code requires that fire-retardant insulation no longer be sprayed on steel girders in the factory, but be sprayed on once the girders have arrived at the building site. This will eliminate the dislodging of the insulation in transit and reduce fatalities in catastrophic fires by an estimated 20%.

   Which of the following, if true, represents the strongest challenge to the new proposal?

   (A) The fire-retardant insulation will also be required to be one inch thicker than in the past.
   (B) Studies have shown that most dislodgement of insulation occurs after the girders arrive on site.
   (C) Catastrophic fires represent only 4% of the fires reported nationally.
   (D) The proposed safety code will add considerably to the cost of new construction.
   (E) In most of Europe, spraying fire-retardant insulation onto steel girders at the building site has been required for the past ten years.

5. Because of a quality control problem, a supplier of flu vaccines will not be able to ship any supplies of the vaccine for the upcoming flu season. This will create a shortage of flu vaccines and result in a loss of productivity as workers call in sick.

   Which of the following, if true, most seriously weakens the argument above?

   (A) The quality control problem of the supplier is not as severe as some experts had initially predicted.
   (B) Other suppliers of flu vaccine have not been affected by the quality control problem.
   (C) Last year there was also a shortage of flu vaccine available.
   (D) The price of flu vaccines is expected to fall in the next ten years.
   (E) The flu season is expected to last longer than usual this year.

6. The women's volleyball team at a local college finished fifth in its division, prompting the college to fire the team's general manager. The manager responded by suing the college, saying that the team's performance put it among the top teams in the country.

   Which of the following statements, if true, would support the claim of the team's manager, and resolve the apparent contradiction?

   (A) The team won all of its "away" games during the season in question.
   (B) Attendance at the volleyball team's games was up 35% from the year before.
   (C) Of the starting team, three team members were unable to play for at least half the season because of injuries.
   (D) There are 80 teams in this particular volleyball team's division.
   (E) The team lost more games this year than it did the year before.

7. Experts studying patterns of shark attacks on humans have noted that attacks tend to diminish when the water temperature drops below 65 degrees Fahrenheit. Until recently, researchers believed this was because sharks prefer warmer water, and thus are present in fewer numbers in colder water. However, new research shows that sharks are present in equal numbers in cold and warm water.

Which of the following, if true, best explains the apparent paradox?

(A) In general, humans prefer warm water.
(B) Sharks' keen sense of smell is enhanced in cold water.
(C) In the Pacific, shark attacks tend to occur more frequently in the daytime.
(D) Of the more than 200 types of sharks present in the ocean, only three attack humans.
(E) The average temperature of the Earth's oceans is 55 degrees.

8. MoviesNow! streaming service is projected to buy more licenses to stream more movies in the next 5 years than in any previous 5-year window. This is because MoviesNow!'s board of directors has encouraged the pursuit of subscribers who are parents of children under the age of 12 and the current selection of movies to stream in the MoviesNow! database is targeted at subscribers ages 18–35.

Which of the following, if true, would most strengthen the argument from MoviesNow!'s board of directors that they should pursue subscribers who are parents of children under the age of 12?

(A) The board monitors the demographic targets of large advertising companies and chooses target audiences for their streaming service based on those trends.
(B) A population study conducted by an independent research group has uncovered a large uptick in the number of parents who are raising children under the age of 12.
(C) People aged 18–35 generally have less disposable income than other age demographics.
(D) The licensing agreement MoviesNow! has with the largest movie production company is set to expire within the next 5 years.
(E) The board of MoviesNow! is comprised of parents of children under the age of 12.

9. In order to understand the dangers of the current real-estate bubble in Country Y, one has only to look to the real-estate bubble of the last decade in Country Z. In that country, incautious investors used the inflated value of their real estate as collateral in risky margin loans. When the real-estate market collapsed, many investors went bankrupt, creating a major recession. Country Y is in real danger of a similar recession if more-stringent laws restricting margin loans are not enacted promptly.

    The answer to which of the following questions would be most useful in evaluating the significance of the author's claims?

    (A) Was the real estate in Country Z located principally in rural areas or was it located in more urban communities?
    (B) Could the bankruptcies in Country Z have been prevented by a private bailout plan by the nation's banks?
    (C) Does Country Y currently have any laws on its books regarding margin loans?
    (D) Are there business ties and connections between Country Y and Country Z?
    (E) Were there other factors in the case of Country Y that would make the comparison with Country Z less meaningful?

10. A prolonged period of low mortgage rates resulted in a period of the most robust home sales ever. At the same time, the average sale price of resale homes actually dropped, when adjusted for inflation.

    Which of the following, if true, would explain the apparent contradiction between the robust home sales and the drop in the average sale price of resale homes?

    (A) The inflation rate during this period exceeded the increase in the average salary, thus preventing many buyers from securing mortgages.
    (B) Resale homes represent the best value on the real estate market.
    (C) Without the adjustment for inflation, the price of resale homes actually increased by a very slight amount.
    (D) The decrease in mortgage rates was accompanied by a widening of the types of mortgages from which borrowers could choose.
    (E) The increase in home sales was due entirely to an increase in the sale of new homes.

11. A study showed that only ten percent of American dog owners enroll their dogs in formal obedience training classes. More than twenty percent of these dog owners, the study also showed, participate in dog shows. Thus, it is obvious that people who train their dogs are more likely to participate in dog shows than are people who do not train their dogs.

The conclusion above is correct provided which of the following statements is also true?

(A) It is impossible for a dog to compete in a dog show if the dog has not completed at least one formal obedience training class.

(B) The proportion of dog owners who enroll their dogs in formal obedience training classes is representative of the proportion who train their dogs outside such classes.

(C) Dog owners who participate in dog shows only train their dogs by enrolling them in formal obedience training lessons.

(D) Participation in dog shows is a reliable indicator of how much attention a dog owner pays to his dog.

(E) Only purebred dogs can participate in dog shows, so many owners who enroll their dogs in formal obedience training classes are excluded from this activity.

12. A bullet train travels in excess of 150 miles per hour. Therefore, if a train travels slower than 150 miles per hour, it is not a bullet train.

Which of the following most closely parallels the reasoning used in the argument above?

(A) An orange ripens only on the vine. If it ripens on the vine, then it is not an orange.

(B) Newspapers are often read by more than one person. Therefore, magazines are also likely to be read by more than one person.

(C) An earthquake of 5.0 or above on the Richter scale causes massive damage. If there is not massive damage, then the earthquake did not attain a 5.0 or above.

(D) A supersonic plane travels at speeds in excess of Mach 1. If it is not supersonic, then it will travel at speeds below Mach 1.

(E) Fluoride generally prevents cavities. If there are no cavities, then there was no fluoride used.

Challenge Question #11

It is widely believed that dogs need to engage in play with other dogs in order to maintain proper socialization as they grow older. In truth, however, merely sharing the same physical space with another dog is sufficient to maintain proper socialization. Supporting evidence to this effect comes from a study demonstrating that the more often a dog shares a physical space with another dog, the better its socialization.

Which of the following, if true, most seriously weakens the influence of the evidence cited?

(A) As dogs age, it is necessary to challenge their physical and mental capacities in order to avoid the deterioration of these capacities.

(B) Many behavioral reasons that negatively impact a dog's proper socialization also increase the likelihood that a dog is not sharing physical space with another dog.

(C) Many dogs are capable of both play and simply sharing space with other dogs.

(D) The study itself did not observe dog socialization, but analyzed observations on the issue from other studies.

(E) The metrics for evaluating socialization that the study measured more resembled play than simply sharing physical space.

Find the answers to all Challenge Questions in Part V!

Summary

o Critical Reasoning is made up of short passages. Each of these passages is followed by one question, for a total of roughly 11 questions.

o There are three parts to an argument:
   - Conclusion
   - Premise
   - Assumptions

o Critical Reasoning is **not** like Reading Comprehension.
   - You should never skim: each word is important.
   - Most of the Reading Comprehension techniques we have shown you are inappropriate for Critical Reasoning.

o Follow the basic approach and make sure to read the question first.

o Learn to identify the common reasoning patterns in argument passages:
   - Causal patterns
   - Planning patterns
   - Sampling patterns
   - Interpretation of Evidence patterns
   - Analogy patterns

o There are eight question types. Each type has its own strategy.
   - **Assumption questions**
     Assumptions are unstated premises that support the conclusion.

   - **Strengthen questions**
     Look for an answer choice with information that supports the conclusion.

   - **Weaken questions**
     These questions ask you to find the answer choice that provides information that weakens the conclusion.

- **Inference questions**

  Like Reading Comprehension inference questions, these questions do not actually want you to infer. Unlike most Critical Reasoning questions, these questions typically concern the *premise,* not the conclusion.

- **Resolve/Explain questions**

  This type of question asks you to pick an answer choice that explains an apparent contradiction between two incompatible facts.

- **Evaluate questions**

  This type of question asks you to pick an answer choice that would help to evaluate an unspoken assumption about the argument.

- **Identify the Reasoning questions**

  This type of question asks you to pick an answer choice that identifies the purpose of a word or phrase, or the type of reasoning used in an argument.

- **Flaw questions**

  Flaw questions ask you to choose the answer that accurately describes a flaw in the structure of an argument.

Part V
Answer Key to Drills

Which Plugging In Method Should I Use? Quiz (page 99)

Question	Should You Plug In?	Plugging In Method
1. If Mark's current age is three times greater than Jenny's age was 5 years ago, then, in terms of Jenny's current age, what is Mark's current age?	Yes	Hidden Plug In. Plug In a value for Jenny's current age.
2. What number is 625% of 3,420?	No	None
3. If $x^2 > 17$ and $x^3 > -512$, then which of the following must be true of x?	Yes	Plug In more than once. Plug In values of x and use POE.
4. The original price of a shirt was increased by 25% and then decreased by 15% to a final price of $105. What was the original price of the shirt?	Yes	Plug In the Answers. Beginning with (C), Plug in the answer choices for the value of the original price of the shirt.
5. A certain square has an area of 24 and a height that is 1.5 times its width. What is the perimeter of the square?	No	None

DRILL 1 (Plugging In) (Page 100)

1. **D** The problem contains a variable, and the answer choices provide a specific value for that variable, so Plug In the Answers. Begin with (C). If $x = 2$, then list L is 1, $\sqrt{2}$, 2, 4. This does not meet the requirement that the range of numbers is 4, so eliminate (C). The range needs to be greater, so choose a greater number such as (B), 4. If $x = 4$, then list L is 1, $\sqrt{2}$, 4, 16. This is incorrect as the range is too great, so eliminate (B). Try (D). If $x = \sqrt{5}$, then list L is 1, $\sqrt{2}$, $\sqrt{5}$, 5. The range of this list is 4. The correct answer is (D).

2. **B** There are variables in the question stem and answer choices, so Plug In. This is a "must be" question, so be prepared to Plug In more than once. Begin with easy values for r, s, and t that abide by the parameters of the problem such as $r = 2$, $s = 3$, and $t = 4$. Plug In these values for the variables into each of the answer choices and eliminate any that are not true. In this case, (A) is not true because it evaluates to $-4 > 0$, so eliminate (A). Choice (B) is true, as well as (C) and (D). Choice (E) evaluates to $-4 > -\dfrac{1}{4}$, which is not true, so eliminate (E). Now Plug In again. If $r = -2$, $s = 3$, and $t = 4$, then (B)

is still true. Keep (B). Choice (C) is $-8 + 12 > 0$, which is true, so keep (C). Choice (D) is $(4 - 9) \times 4 = -20$, which is less than 0 so eliminate (D). Try Extreme numbers. If $r = -100$, $s = 3$, and $t = 4$, then (B) is still true but (C) is now $-388 > 0$. This is not true, so eliminate (C). The correct answer is (B).

3. **D** This is a Yes/No Data Sufficiency problem, so be prepared to Plug In more than once. The question asks if $xy > 0$, so be prepared to Plug In for x or y values. Evaluate each statement individually. Statement (1) provides that $|x| + 8|y| = 0$, so Plug In values for x and y that make this statement true. Plugging In various values for x and y reveals that the only way the statement is true is if both x and y are equal to 0. Therefore, the answer to the question is "No" because xy is not greater than 0. Because this statement produces only one correct answer to the question, the statement is sufficient. Write down AD. Now work with Statement (2). Statement (2) states that $8|x| + |y| = 0$. Plug In for values of x and y. Plugging In various values for x and y also reveals that the only way the statement is true is if both x and y equal 0. Therefore, the answer to the question is "No" because xy is not greater than 0. Because this statement produces only one correct answer to the question, the statement is sufficient. The correct answer is (D).

4. **B** This is a Hidden Plug In question. Plug In a number for the total number of majors in 2015, such as 100. If there were 100 total majors in 2015 and 18% of them were math majors, then there were 18 math majors in 2015. The problem states that $\frac{2}{6}$ of the math majors focused on statistics, so there are $\frac{2}{6} \times 18 = 6$ majors focused on statistics. Therefore, the correct answer is (B), 6%.

5. **E** This question contains variables in the question stem and answer choices, so Plug In. Begin by establishing what information is provided by the question stem. The stem provides that x and y are integers, $x^2 + y^2 < 46$, and $0 < x \le 5$. So, x is either 1, 2, 3, 4, or 5. Plug In values of x and solve for the possible values of y. If $x = 1$, then y can be any of the integers between -6 and 6, inclusive, because $1^2 + \pm6^2 < 46$. So, $-6 \le y \le 6$ is the value of y when $x = 1$. If $x = 2$, then y can be any integer between -6 and 6, inclusive, so this is the same information as when $x = 1$. If $x = 3$, then y can be any of the integers between -6 and 6, inclusive, which is the same information as when $x = 1$ or 2. However, when $x = 4$, y can only be values between -5 and 5, inclusive because $4^2 + \pm5^2 < 46$, but $4^2 + \pm6^2 > 46$. So, the possible values of y are represented by $-5 \le y \le 5$. Eliminate (A) and (B). When $x = 5$, y is between the values of -4 and 4 because $5^2 + \pm4^2 < 46$, but $5^2 + \pm5^2 > 46$. So, the values of y are now restricted to $-4 \le y \le 4$. There are no further values of x possible, so the correct answer is (E).

6. **E** This is a Yes/No Data Sufficiency problem, so be prepared to Plug In more than once. The question asks if the integers x, y, and z are consecutive. Plug In values for the variables that satisfy the conditions of the statements. Begin with Statement (1), which states that the average (arithmetic mean) of x, y, and z is y. Plug In values that make this statement true. If $x = 2$, $y = 3$, and $z = 4$, then the average is $\frac{2 + 3 + 4}{3} = 3$. This satisfies that statement, and the answer to the question

is "Yes" because the integers are consecutive. Now Plug In again and attempt to produce a "No" answer to the question. If $x = 2$, $y = 4$, and $z = 6$, then the average is $\frac{2+4+6}{3} = 4$. This satisfies the statements. However, the answer to the question is now "No" because x, y, and z are not consecutive. When the statement produces two different answers to the question, the statement is insufficient. Write down BCE. Now evaluate Statement (2). Statement (2) is that $y - x = z - y$. Plug In. If $x = 2$, $y = 3$, and $z = 4$, then the statement is satisfied because $3 - 2 = 4 - 3$. The answer to the question is "Yes" because the integers are consecutive. Plug In again in an attempt to produce a "No" answer. If $x = 2$, $y = 4$, and $z = 6$, then the statement is satisfied because $4 - 2 = 6 - 4$. The answer to the question is now "No" because the integers are not consecutive. Eliminate (B). Now consider the two statements together. The numbers that were Plugged In for both statements individually are the same numbers that can be Plugged In for both statements combined. Therefore, it is possible to produce both a "Yes" and a "No" answer to the question. Eliminate (C). The correct answer is (E).

7. **B** The problem contains a variable, and the answer choices provide a specific value for that variable, so Plug In the Answers. Begin with (C). If the total number of marbles in the bag is 55, then the probability of pulling 2 red marbles is $\left(\frac{3}{55}\right)\left(\frac{2}{54}\right)$, which does not equal $\frac{3}{55}$. The denominator is too great. Eliminate (C) as well as (D) and (E), as they will make the denominator even greater. Try (B). If the total number of marbles in the bag is 11, then the probability is $\left(\frac{3}{11}\right)\left(\frac{2}{10}\right) = \frac{6}{110} = \frac{3}{55}$. The correct answer is (B).

8. **C** This is a Yes/No Data Sufficiency problem, so be prepared to Plug In more than once. The question states that y is an integer, so Plug In a value for y where possible. Evaluate the statements individually. Statement (1) is that $y > 5$. Plug In for y. If $y = 6$, then the answer to the question is "No" because the remainder of $\frac{6}{2}$ is not 1. However, if $y = 7$, then the answer to the question is "Yes" because the remainder of $\frac{7}{2}$ is 1. This statement produces two different answers to the question, so it is insufficient. Write down BCE. Now work with the second statement. Statement (2) is that y is prime. All prime numbers are odd numbers except for the number 2. Plug In. If $y = 2$, then the answer to the question is "No." However, if y is any prime value other than 2, the answer is "Yes." This statement provides two different answers to the question, so it is not sufficient. Eliminate (B). Now combine the statements. All prime numbers greater than 5 are odd numbers, so any value of y that can be Plugged In is going to have a remainder of 1 when divided by 2. The two statements combined are sufficient to answer the question. The correct answer is (C).

9. **A** There are fractions in the answer choices and the question has a missing piece of information (the total number of cars), so this is a Hidden Plug In question. Plug In for the total number of cars that the automobile manufacturer produces. When working with fractions, the best number to Plug In is the product of the denominators of all the fractions in the question stem. The fractions in the question stem are $\frac{1}{4}$, $\frac{1}{5}$, and $\frac{1}{3}$. So, Plug In $4 \times 5 \times 3 = 60$. If the manufacturer produces 60 cars, then $60 \times \frac{1}{4} = 15$ of them are sports cars, which means that $60 - 15 = 45$ are sedans. The problem then states that $60 \times \frac{1}{5} = 12$ of the cars manufactured are red and that $15 \times \frac{1}{3} = 5$ of the sports cars are red. Therefore, $12 - 5 = 7$ of the 45 sedans are red. The fraction of sedans that are red is $\frac{7}{45}$. The correct answer is (A).

10. **A** This is a Yes/No Data Sufficiency question, so be ready to Plug In more than once. The question asks if Amy's average speed was greater than 60 miles per hour. The question states that she drove the distance in less than 2 hours. In order for the statements to be sufficient, they need to provide information that produces a consistent Yes or No answer to the question.

    Evaluate Statement (1). The statement provides information that the distance Amy drove is less than 125 miles. Plug In a distance that meets these parameters. If The distance was 124 miles and Amy drove that distance in less than 2 hours, then her average speed is greater than 60 miles per hour and the answer to the question is Yes. However, if the distance was 20 miles and Amy drove that distance in 2 hours, then her average speed is less than 60 miles per hour and the answer to the question is No. This statement does not provide a consistent answer to the question, so it is not sufficient. Eliminate (A) and (D). The only remaining possible answers are (B), (C), and (E).

    Next, evaluate Statement (2). The statement provides information that the distance Amy drove is greater than 122 miles. Plug In a distance that meets these parameters. If Amy drove 122 miles exactly and she did it in less than 2 hours, then her average speed has to be greater than 61 miles per hour. The answer to the question is Yes. Because the least distance Amy could have driven is greater than 122 miles, her average miles per hour is always greater than 60. Statement (2) provides information that always produces a consistent Yes answer to the question, so it is sufficient. The correct answer is (B).

DRILL 2 (AD/BCE) (Page 159)

1. **BCE**   Statement (1) gives a value for y but no information on the value of x. Since the problem asks for a value of x, Statement (1) is insufficient.

2. **BCE**   Statement (1) states that $2y$ is an integer. Consider what values of y are possible. The value of y could be an integer, such as 2, but it could also be a fraction, such as $\frac{1}{2}$. Statement (1) is insufficient.

3. **AD**   The question states that there are 12 boys and girls in the room. Statement (1) provides the number of girls, so both the number of boys and the difference between the number of boys and the number of girls can be determined. Since the difference can be determined, Statement (1) is sufficient.

4. **AD**   Statement (1) can be rewritten as the equation $\left(\frac{10}{100}\right)x = 5$, which can be used to solve for x. If the value of x is known, then the question can be answered. Statement (1) is sufficient.

DRILL 3 (Data Sufficiency Parts and Wholes) (Page 166)

1. **C**   Statement (1) provides the number of people who *paid deposits*, which may seem sufficient, but the question allows for the possibility that a person may pay a deposit and yet not attend, so Statement (1) is insufficient. Write down BCE. Statement (2) provides the percent of people who attended after paying a deposit, but it does not indicate the number of people who paid a deposit, so Statement (2) is insufficient. Eliminate (B). The statements together indicate that 60% of the 70 people who paid deposits attend, which allows the question to be answered. The correct answer is (C).

2. **D**   Statement (1) provides an amount of pigment and a total volume, which allows solving for the amount of alcohol and subsequently the ratio of alcohol to pigment, as there are only two ingredients in the paint. Statement (1) is sufficient. Write down AD. Similarly, Statement (2) provides an amount of alcohol and a total volume, which also allows solving for the ratio of alcohol to pigment. Statement (2) is sufficient. The correct answer is (D).

3. **C**   Statement (1) provides the proportional distances between the three towns, but no specific values, so Statement (1) is insufficient. Write down BCE. Statement (2) provides the distance from Ferristown to Laredo, but it provides no information about the distance from Smithville to Ferristown, so Statement (2) is insufficient. Eliminate (B). Together, the statements provide that Ferristown to Laredo is 12 miles, which is $\frac{2}{5}$ of the distance from Smithville to Laredo, and allows the question to be answered. The correct answer is (C).

4. **D**   This is a Value Data Sufficiency question, so begin by determining what is known and what is needed in order to answer the question. The question states that a store sold 30 more televisions in this month than it did last month. The question asks about the percent increase of televisions

sold from last month to this month. This suggests the need for the percent change formula, which is $\% \text{ change} = \dfrac{\text{difference}}{\text{original}} \times 100$. The question as already provided the value for "difference", so the equation can be rewritten as $\% \text{ change} = \dfrac{30}{\text{original}} \times 100$. In order to answer this question, the statements need to provide a way to determine the number of televisions sold either this month or last month. Evaluate the statements individually.

Statement 1 provides the number of televisions sold this month. If the store sold 15 televisions this month and that is an increase of 30 televisions, then the original value is 120 televisions. This statement provides enough information to answer the question, so it is sufficient. Eliminate (B), (C), and (E). The possible answer is (A) or (D).

Now work with the second statement. Statement 2 provides the percent of televisions sold last month that were sold this month. If last month's sales were 80% of this month's sales and there were an additional 30 televisions sold, that means that 30 televisions is 20% of the total. This means there were 150 televisions sold this month and 150 − 30 = 120 televisions sold last month. Statement 2 also provides enough information to answer the question, so it is sufficient. Eliminate (A). The correct answer is (D).

5. **B**   This is a Value Data Sufficiency question, so determine what is known and what is needed in order to solve the problem. The question asks about an average. Averages can be calculated based on the sum of the items being averaged and the number of those items. In this case, the question states there are 6 consecutive integers from 10-99, inclusive. In order to answer the question, the statements could provide the sum of the six numbers, one of the integers and its position on the list, or any other type of information that might help determine the 6 consecutive integers. Evaluate the statements individually.

Statement 1 provides information about the remainder when the fourth integer is divided by 5. Plug In some possible numbers that satisfy this statement. If the fourth integer is 18, then the first integer is 15 and the complete list is 15, 16, 17, 18, 19, 20, which has an average of 17.5. However, the fourth integer could also be 33, which would make the average of the six integers 32.5. Statement 1 does not provide enough information to determine a consistent answer to the question, so it is not sufficient. Eliminate (A) and (D). The remaining possible answers are (B), (C), and (E).

Now evaluate Statement 2. The only integers that satisfy this statement are 20 and 25 because there needs to be 6 integers in the list. Therefore, this statement provides a consistent answer to the question and is sufficient. Eliminate (C) and (E). The correct answer is (B).

DRILL 4 (Yes or No) (Page 171)

1. **A**   Statement (1) states that $2x < 1$. Divide by 2 to yield that $x < \frac{1}{2}$. The answer to the question is "Yes." Statement (1) is sufficient. Write down AD. Statement (2) states that $2x \leq 2$. Divide by 2 to yield that $x \leq 1$. x can equal 1, and the answer to the question is "No." x can also equal $\frac{1}{2}$, and the answer to the question is "Yes." When two values that satisfy a statement yield different answers to the question, the statement is insufficient. The correct answer is (A).

2. **B**   Statement (1) states that $xy = 6$. Let $x = 2$ and $y = 3$. These values satisfy the statement and the answer to the question is "Yes." Try to arrive at an answer of "No." Let $x = -2$ and $y = -3$. These values satisfy the statement and the answer to the question is "No." When two values that satisfy a statement yield different answers to the question, the statement is insufficient. Write down BCE. Statement (2) states that $xy^2 = 12$. Let $x = 3$ and $y = 2$. These values satisfy the statement and the answer to the question is "Yes." Try to arrive at an answer of "No." Because the product is not equal to 0, y^2 must be positive. Thus, x must also be positive in order to yield a product of positive 12. Statement (2) is sufficient. The correct answer is (B).

3. **E**   Statement (1) states that xy is an integer. Let $x = 2$ and $y = 3$. These values satisfy the statement and the answer to the question is "Yes." Try to arrive at an answer of "No." Let $x = \frac{1}{2}$ and $y = 2$. These values satisfy the statement and the answer to the question is "No." When two values that satisfy a statement yield different answers to the question, the statement is insufficient. Write down BCE. Statement (2) states that $x + y$ is an integer. Let $x = 2$ and $y = 3$. These values satisfy the statement and the answer to the question is "Yes." Try to arrive at an answer of "No." Let $x = \frac{1}{2}$ and $y = \frac{1}{2}$. These values satisfy the statement, and the answer to the question is "No." Statement (2) is insufficient. Eliminate (B). Now consider both statements combined. The only values that satisfy the requirements of both statements (1) and (2) are when x and y are both integers. The correct answer is (E).

4. **E**   This is a Yes/No Data Sufficiency question, so be prepared to Plug In more than once. Start by evaluating Statement (1) alone. Pick an easy number for n. If $n = 2$, then $k = 3$. The numbers satisfy the statement, so it's time to use them to answer the question. Is $3^2 > 2^3$? Yes. Remember, however, that you can't properly evaluate the statement based on the results from only one set of numbers. Suppose we tried something a little weirder for n? If $n - -1$, then $k = 0$. Is $3 - 1 > 2^0$? No. (Remember that negative exponents are just another way of writing a reciprocal and that any nonzero number raised to 0 is 1.) So, we don't actually know what the answer to the question is based only on Statement (1). It looks as though the answer depends on the numbers we choose. Write down BCE.

    For Statement (2), we can also Plug In. Notice that the statement doesn't tell us anything about k, however. So we could say that $n = 2$ and $k = 1$ to get an answer of yes to the question. But we could also say that $n = 2$ and $k = 4$ to get an answer of no. Cross off (B).

    When we combine the statements, we can still use $n = 2$ and $k = 3$, which, as we saw when we looked at Statement (1), gives us an answer of yes to the question. However, we could also use $n = 1$ and $k = 2$ to satisfy the combined statements. Is $3^1 > 2^2$? No. So, the answer to this problem is (E).

DRILL 5 (Page 196)

1. **E** This is a Yes/No Data Sufficiency question, so be prepared to Plug In more than once. The question stipulates that x is a positive integer and asks if x is divisible by 48. In order for a number to be divisible by 48, it needs to be divisible by all the prime factors of 48. So, begin this question by writing out the prime factors of 48, which results in $2^4 \times 3$. Any number that is divisible by 48 must contain four 2s and one 3 as part of its prime factorization.

   Evaluate Statement (1), which provides that x is divisible by 8. The prime factorization of 8 is 2^3. Therefore, a number divisible by 8 does not have to be divisible by 48 because the prime factors of 8 do not encompass all the prime factors of 48. For instance, if $x = 16$, the answer to the question is No. But, if $x = 48$, which is divisible by 8, then the answer is Yes. This statement does not provide a consistent answer to the question, so it is not sufficient. Eliminate (A) and (D). The remaining possible answers are (B), (C), and (E).

   Now look at Statement (2). Similar to Statement (1), the prime factorization of 6, which is 2×3, does not encompass all the prime factors of 48. Plug In some examples. If $x = 12$, the answer to the question is No. If $x = 48$, the answer to the question is Yes. The statement is not sufficient, so eliminate (B).

   Now evaluate both statements together. Plug In values that are divisible by both 8 and 6. If $x = 48$, then the answer to the question is Yes. However, x could also equal 24, which is not divisible by 48. Because the statements combined do not produce a consistent answer to the question, they are not sufficient. Eliminate (C). The correct answer is (E).

2. **C** This is a Yes/No Plug In question, so be prepared to Plug In more than once. The question states that x is a positive integer and asks if the greatest common factor of x and 150 is a prime number. The factors of 150 are 1 and 150, 2 and 75, 3 and 50, 5 and 30, 6 and 25, and 10 and 15. Evaluate the statements individually, looking to evaluate if the greatest common factor of x and 150 is one of the prime factors of 150 (2, 3, or 5).

   Evaluate Statement (1). Based on this information, there is not enough to determine a specific, consistent value of x, as x could be any prime number. Statement (1) is not sufficient. Eliminate (A) and (D). The remaining answers are (B), (C), and (E).

   Next evaluate Statement (2), which states that $x < 4$. If $x = 3$ or $x = 2$, then the answer to the question is Yes because both 3 and 2 are prime numbers. However, if $x = 1$, then the answer to the question is No because 1 is not prime. This statement provides two different answers to the question, so it is not sufficient. Eliminate (B).

   Now evaluate both statements together. When combined, the only possible values of x are 2 or 3. Regardless of whether x is equal to 2 or 3, the answer to the question is Yes. The statements combined contain enough information to provide a consistent answer to the question. The correct answer is (C).

3. **E** This is a Yes/No data sufficiency question, so be prepared to Plug In more than once. The question asks if x is a prime number and states that both x and y are integers greater than 1. Evaluate the statements individually. Statement (1) provides information about the factors of y, but does not give any information about x. Without the information about x, there is no way to determine if x is prime. Statement (1) is insufficient. Write down BCE. Consider Statement (2). Plug In values of x and y. If $x = 5$ and $y = 7$, then Statement (2) is satisfied because 35 is the least common multiple of 5 and 7. In this case, the answer to the question is Yes. Plug In again in an attempt to get an answer of No to the question. If $x = 4$ and $y = 7$, then the statement is satisfied because 28 is the least common multiple of 4 and 7. In this case, the answer to the question is No. The statement produces both a Yes and a No answer to the question, so Statement (2) is insufficient. Eliminate (B). Consider Statements (1) and (2). All of the values used in Statement (2) satisfy the requirements of Statement (1), which means that Statements (1) and (2) together are insufficient. Eliminate (C). The correct answer is (E).

4. **D** Plug In values for x and y according to the information in the answer choices, looking for ways to eliminate each. For (A), if $x = 2$ and $y = 4$, then the result of the expression in the question stem is 9, which makes (A) true. However, if $x = 3$ and $y = 6$, then the result of the expression in the question stem is 16. Now (A) is false. Eliminate it. For (B), if $x = 3$ and $y = 5$, then the result is 15. Choice (B) is false, so eliminate it. For (C), if $y = 3$ and $x = 6$, then the result is 40. Choice (C) is false, so eliminate it. For (D), if $x = 2$ and $y = 3$, then the result is 8. No matter what values for x and y are used, (D) is true. Keep it. Choice (E) is false when $x = 3$ and $y = 2$, so eliminate (E). The correct answer is (D).

5. **E** This is a Yes/No data sufficiency question, so be prepared to Plug In more than once. The question asks if P is divisible by 15. The prime factorization of 15 is 3×5, so for P to be divisible by 15, P must have at least one 3 and one 5 as part of its prime factorization. Consider Statement (1). The prime factorization of 65 is 5×13. Plug In numbers for P that satisfy the statement. If $P = 39$, then the greatest common prime factor of P and 65 is 13. The statement is satisfied. The prime factorization of 39 is 3×13. In this case, the answer to the question is No because P does not have a prime factor of 5. Plug In again in an attempt to get a Yes answer to the question. If $P = 195$, then the prime factorization of P is $3 \times 5 \times 13$. In this case, the answer to the question is Yes because P has both 3 and 5 as prime factors. This statement provides two different answers to the question, so it is not sufficient. Write down BCE. Consider Statement (2). The prime factorization of 95 is 5×19. Plug In numbers for P that satisfy the statement. If $P = 57$, then the greatest common prime factor of P and 95 is 19. The statement is satisfied. The prime factorization of 57 is 3×19. In this case, the answer to the question is No because P does not have a prime factor of 5. Plug In again in an attempt to get a Yes answer to the question. If $P = 285$, then the prime factorization of P is $3 \times 5 \times 19$. In this case, the answer to the question is Yes because P has both 3 and 5 as prime factors. This statement provides two different answers to the question, so it is not sufficient. Eliminate (B). Consider the two statements combined. If $P = 3 \times 5 \times 13 \times 19 = 3,705$, then both statements are satisfied and the answer to the question is Yes because P has both 3 and 5 as prime factors. However,

if $P = 3 \times 13 \times 19 = 741$, then both statements are satisfied but the answer to the question is No because P does not have 5 as a prime factor. The two statements combined do not produce a consistent Yes or No answer to the question, so the statements combined are insufficient. The correct answer is (E).

6. **C** This is a value data sufficiency question, so determine what is known and what is needed to answer the question. The question asks about the value of w. The statements need to provide a way to solve for a single value of w. Evaluate each statement individually. Statement (1) is that w is a factor of 51. The factors of 51 are 1, 3, 17, and 51. There are no further restrictions on this, so w can be equal to 1, 3, 17, or 51. Statement (1) is insufficient. Write down BCE. Statement (2) provides that w is greater than 17. This can be any value, which means that Statement (2) is insufficient. Eliminate (B). Consider Statements (1) and (2) together. From Statement (1), w is 1, 3, 17, or 51, and from Statement (2), w is greater than 17. When combined, these statements provide enough information to determine that $w = 51$. Statements (1) and (2) together are sufficient. The correct answer is (C).

DRILL 6 (Page 229)

1. **77** $74 + (27 - 24) = 74 + 3 = 77$

2. **79** $(8 \times 9) + 7 = 72 + 7 = 79$

3. **10** $2(9 - (8 \div 2)) = 2(9 - 4)$, which simplifies to $2(5) = 10$.

4. **16** $2(7 - 3) + (-4)(5 - 7) = 2(4) + (-4)(-2)$, which simplifies to $8 + 8 = 16$.

5. **B** $4(-3(3 - 5) + 10 - 17) = 4(-3(-2) + 10 - 17)$, which simplifies to $4(6 + 10 - 17) = 4(-1)$, or -4. The correct answer is (B).

6. **A** Statement (1) states that $x^3 = 8$. If $x^3 = 8$, then x equals 2. Since there is only one possible value of x that satisfies the equation, Statement (1) is sufficient. Write down AD. Statement (2) states that $x^2 = 4$. In this case, x could be 2 or -2. Statement (2) is therefore insufficient. The correct answer is (A).

DRILL 7 (Page 230)

1. $x^2 + x = x(x + 1)$

2. $(55 \times 12) + (55 \times 88) = 55(12 + 88)$, which simplifies to $55(100) = 5,500$.

3. $a(b + c - d) = ab + ac - ad$

4. $abc + xyc = c(ab + xy)$

5. **B** If $x = 6$, then $\dfrac{2xy - xy}{y} = \dfrac{2(6)y - (6)y}{y}$, which simplifies to $\dfrac{12y - 6y}{y} = \dfrac{6y}{y}$, and reduces to 6. The correct answer is (B).

6. **B** Statement (1) provides a value for x, but provides no information about y and z, so Statement (1) is insufficient. Write down BCE. Statement (2) provides a value for a. Factor the equation given to yield $a(x + y + z) = 15$. If $a = 5$, then $x + y + z = 3$, and Statement (2) is sufficient. The correct answer is (B).

DRILL 8 (Page 238)

1. $\dfrac{49}{8}$ or $6\dfrac{1}{8}$

   $5\dfrac{3}{4} + \dfrac{3}{8} = \dfrac{23}{4} + \dfrac{3}{8}$, which may be rewritten as $\dfrac{46}{8} + \dfrac{3}{8} = \dfrac{49}{8}$.

2. $\dfrac{1}{5}$ $\dfrac{12}{60} = \dfrac{12 \times 1}{12 \times 5}$, which reduces to $\dfrac{1}{5}$.

3. $\dfrac{29}{3}$ $9\dfrac{2}{3} = \dfrac{9 \times 3}{3} + \dfrac{2}{3}$, which yields $\dfrac{27}{3} + \dfrac{2}{3} = \dfrac{29}{3}$

4. **18**   Cross-multiply to get $2x = 36$. Divide both sides of the equation by 2 to get $x = 18$.

5. **C** $\dfrac{\left(\dfrac{\frac{4}{5}}{\frac{3}{5}}\right)\left(\dfrac{\frac{1}{8}}{\frac{2}{3}}\right)}{\dfrac{3}{4}} = \dfrac{\left(\dfrac{4}{5} \times \dfrac{5}{3}\right)\left(\dfrac{1}{8} \times \dfrac{3}{2}\right)}{\dfrac{3}{4}}$, which yields $\dfrac{\dfrac{4}{3} \times \dfrac{3}{16}}{\dfrac{3}{4}} = \dfrac{\dfrac{4}{16}}{\dfrac{3}{4}}$, which further yields $\dfrac{1}{4} \times \dfrac{4}{3} = \dfrac{4}{12}$,

   or $\dfrac{1}{3}$. The correct answer is (C).

6. **C** You could start by converting all the fractions to their least common denominator of 81—an understandable temptation. However, in this case, it's quicker and simpler to reduce the fractions instead. They all reduce to $\dfrac{5}{9}$, so $x = \dfrac{\dfrac{5}{9} + \dfrac{5}{9} + \dfrac{5}{9}}{3}$, or $\dfrac{3\left(\dfrac{5}{9}\right)}{3}$... or $\dfrac{5}{9}$. Now that you know the value of x, you can solve for $\sqrt{(1-x)}$: $\sqrt{\left(1 - \dfrac{5}{9}\right)} = \sqrt{\dfrac{4}{9}} = \dfrac{\sqrt{4}}{\sqrt{9}} = \dfrac{2}{3}$. The correct answer is (C). Choice (B), of course, is x itself, and (D) is $\sqrt{x}$.

7. **C**   First, solve for y. Since $2\frac{2}{3}=\frac{8}{3}$, $\frac{1}{y}=\frac{8}{3}$ and thus $y=\frac{3}{8}$. Now plug the value for y into the expression:

$$\left(\dfrac{1}{\dfrac{3}{8}+1}\right)^2 \quad \left(\dfrac{1}{\left(\dfrac{11}{8}\right)}\right)^2 \quad \dfrac{1^2}{\left(\dfrac{11}{8}\right)^2} \quad \dfrac{\dfrac{1}{121}}{\dfrac{1}{64}}=\dfrac{64}{121}.$$

The correct answer is (C).

Choice (B), of course, is the value of y. Choice (D) is the reciprocal of the correct answer, which could indicate that you didn't do the last step of the calculation. If you chose (A), you forgot to add 1 when you put the value for y into the expression. And if you chose (E), you did both.

DRILL 9 (Page 246)

1. **33.30**   Since the numbers are lined up, just subtract down, remembering to borrow when dealing with the tenths digit.

2. **266.175**   Multiply 273 by 975 as normal and then move the decimal point over 3 spots.

3. **6.125**   Set up to do long division: $3.2\overline{)19.6}$. Move the decimal point over one to the right to get $32\overline{)196}$. Since 32 goes into 196 a total of 6 times, $32\overset{6}{\overline{)196}}$. Next, multiply 6 by 32 to get 192 and subtract 192 from 196 to get 4. Then add a decimal point and a 0, bring that 0 down, and see that 32 goes into 40 one time, so multiply 1 by 32 and then subtract 32 from 40 to get 8. Add another 0, bring it down, and see that 32 goes into 80 two times, so multiply 32 by 2 to get 64 and then subtract that from 80. Finally, add one more 0 and see that 32 goes into 160 exactly 5 times:

$$
\begin{array}{r}
6.125 \\
32\overline{)196.000} \\
192\\
\hline
40\\
32\\
\hline
80\\
64\\
\hline
160\\
160\\
\hline
0
\end{array}
$$

The correct answer is 6.125.

4. **800** $\dfrac{\frac{4}{0.25}}{\frac{1}{50}} = \dfrac{\frac{4}{1}}{\frac{1}{50}}$, which may be rewritten as $\dfrac{4 \times \frac{4}{1}}{\frac{1}{50}} = \dfrac{16}{\frac{1}{50}}$, and yields $16 \times \dfrac{50}{1} = 800$.

5. **C** $\dfrac{\frac{3}{10} \times 4 \times 0.8}{0.32} = \dfrac{\frac{3}{10} \times \frac{4}{1} \times \frac{8}{10}}{\frac{32}{100}}$, which yields $\dfrac{\frac{96}{100}}{\frac{32}{100}} = \dfrac{96}{100} \times \dfrac{100}{32}$, which reduces to $\dfrac{96}{32} = 3$.

The correct answer is (C).

6. **D** The question states that x and y are reciprocals, which means that determining the value of either variable provides the value of the other. Therefore, Statement (1) provides the values of both x and y, which allows the question to be answered. Write down AD. Statement (2) also provides the values of both y and x, so the correct answer is (D).

DRILL 10 (Page 250)

1. **C** If 30% of the players on the soccer team scored goals during the season, then 70% did not score goals. The ratio of those who scored to those who did not is 30 to 70, which reduces to 3 to 7.

   Some will find that Plugging In is the easiest way to solve this problem. Plug in 10 for the number of players on the team (choose this number because it is easy to work with in a percentage problem). 30% of the 10 players—that is to say, 3 players—scored goals. The other 7, it then follows, did not score goals. The ratio of those who scored to those who did not is 3 to 7. The correct answer is (C).

2. **A** Plug In the Answers! Start with (C). If this is the correct answer, then the Binary Ice Cream Shoppe sold 42 vanilla cones on Friday. Because vanilla cones sold at a 2-to-3 ratio to chocolate cones, this means that the shop sold 63 chocolate cones $\left(\dfrac{2}{3} = \dfrac{42}{63} \right)$. If this is the correct answer, then the ratio of 46, the result of adding 4 to the number of vanilla cones sold, to 63 is 3 to 4. It is not, so this answer is incorrect.

   You must decide next whether the correct answer is more or less than 42. Since the situation is complicated, you may not be sure in which direction to go so just pick a direction; you'll find the correct answer soon enough. Note that the answer cannot be (B) because 35 is not divisible by 2;

thus it cannot be the number of vanilla cones sold. Choice (A) is the correct answer. 32 to 48 is a 2-to-3 ratio; add 4 more vanilla cones to get a ratio of 36 to 48, which reduces to 3 to 4.

3. **C** Create a table to solve this proportions question. It should look something like this:

	Red	Blue	TOTAL
Coupes			
Sedans			
TOTAL	4,500	4,500	9,000

The question stem says how many cars were sold last year. Because it says that half the cars sold were red, it also says the number of blue cars sold last year.

Statement (1) says, "The dealership sold three times as many blue coupes as red sedans last year." Enter this information into the table in algebraic terms:

	Red	Blue	TOTAL
Coupes		$3x$	
Sedans	x		
TOTAL	4,500	4,500	9,000

Because two unknowns—red coupes and blue sedans—remain, Statement (1) does not provide enough information to solve the problem. Write down BCE.

Use the same procedure to test Statement (2): "The dealership sold half as many blue sedans as blue coupes last year":

	Red	Blue	TOTAL
Coupes		$2x$	
Sedans		x	
TOTAL	4,500	4,500	9,000

Again, two unknowns remain. *This* time, though, you have all the information you need to write a solvable equation. You know that $2x + x = 4,500$. Therefore, x equals 1,500. You now know the following:

	Red	Blue	TOTAL
Coupes		3,000	
Sedans		1,500	
TOTAL	4,500	4,500	9,500

Unfortunately, this still isn't enough information to answer the question. The answer is (C) or (E). Combine the information from the two statements. Statement (2) says that the dealership sold 3,000 blue coupes; combined with Statement (1), this says that the dealership sold 1,000 red sedans. Now subtract 1,000 from 4,500 to determine that the dealership sold 3,500 red coupes. Therefore, it sold 6,500 coupes last year. The correct answer is (C).

DRILL 11 (Page 256)

1. **D**   Before you worry about the division, solve for the two values. The second one is easier, so start there: "of" means multiply, so 0.25 × 600 = 150. With the first value, you have to be sure to take into account both the decimal *and* the percent sign: 0.25% can be represented as $\frac{0.25}{100}$, or 0.0025. Either way, when you multiply by 600, the result is 1.5. The quotient is thus 1.5 divided by 150, or 0.01. The answer is (D).

2. **D**   To answer this question, break the problem down into small, manageable steps. The first job at hand is to determine the selling price of the shirt, both during the first month they were on sale and then during subsequent months. Because the store bought 1,000 shirts for $9,000, the cost of each shirt was $9.00. The store sold the shirts at an 80% markup during the first month. 1.8 × $9.00 = $16.20, so during the first month, the shirts sold for $16.20 each. After the first month, the selling price was 20% above cost. 1.20 × $9.00 = $10.80, so that was the selling price after the first month.

    The store sold 75% of the shirts during the first month. 75% of 1,000 is 750; the store sold 750 shirts at $16.20 each. 750 × $16.20 = $12,150. Note that this partial answer is (C). Test-takers who only half-finish their work will choose this incorrect answer. The store then sold 50% of its remaining stock at $10.80 per shirt. The remaining stock is 250 shirts (1,000 − 750), half of which is 125. The store, then, sold 125 shirts at $10.80 each. 125 × $10.80 = $1,350. The store's gross income from the sale of these shirts, then, is $12,150 + $1,350 = $13,500. The correct answer is (D).

3. **D**   This problem never specifies the cost of a gallon of gas, so plug in $1. If the price per gallon is $1 for the first 10 gallons, then the price for every subsequent gallon is $0.90. Now calculate the per gallon discount for 20 gallons. First, calculate the total cost for 20 gallons. The cost is $10 for the first 10 gallons and 10 × $0.90 = $9 for the next 10 gallons, for a total of $19 and an average price per gallon of $0.95. So the per gallon discount is 5 cents. Repeat this process to calculate the per gallon discount for 25 gallons. The total price for 25 gallons is $23.50, for an average per gallon price of $0.94 and a discount of 6 cents. The question asks you to relate the per gallon discounts as a percentage, so 6 is 120% of 5 and the correct answer is (D).

4. **C**   This is a question about an unspecified amount, so it is a great opportunity to Plug In! Since the answers are percentages, let's plug in 100 for the total number of seniors. That means there are 60 females, of whom 70%, or 42, are going on the senior trip; they'll be joined by 90% of the 40 males, which gives 36 males on the trip. That's a total of 42 + 36 = 78 students who are going on the trip. Seventy-eight out of our senior class of 100 is, of course, 78%, so the correct answer is (C).

5. **E**   This is a group formula problem. The group formula is *Total = Group 1 + Group 2 − Both + Neither*. Assume the total is 100. If there are 100 total Americans, then 75 own an automobile (which is Group 1), 15 own a bicycle (Group 2), and 20 own neither. So the equation now reads 100 = 75 + 15 − Both + 20. Solve for Both and discover that it equals 10. Since 10 is 10% of 100, the correct answer is (E).

DRILL 12 (Page 261)

1. **A** The average of all four numbers is 6, so the numbers must add up to 6 times 4, or 24. That means y must equal 13. And if y equals 13, the median must be 5—that is, the average of the two middle numbers in the set. Even if y is very large, the middle numbers will still be 4 and 6, so (D) and (E) are much too large. The correct answer is (A).

2. **B** This is a multistep average problem involving an unknown quantity—in short, a perfect place to Plug In the Answers! Start with (C). If Steven has already run 6 laps, then he has run for a total of 6×51, or 306, seconds. One more lap in 39 seconds gives him a total of 7 laps in 345 seconds, and the average works out to be a little greater than 49 seconds ($49\frac{2}{7}$, to be exact). Close, but not quite. Fewer laps will reduce Steven's average speed, so (B) is the next logical choice to try. Five laps in 51 seconds means Steven has run 5×51, or 255, seconds so far, and the additional 39-second lap gives a total of 6 laps run in 294 seconds. The average is now $\frac{294}{6} = 49$ seconds, and (B) is the correct answer.

3. **D** Since the answer choices contain variables, this is a good place to Plug In. Make $d = 10$, $c = 200$ (a particularly helpful number, because it allows you to work the problem in whole dollar amounts), and $x = 5$. If the restaurant has an average of 5 items per day delivered, then it had a total of 35 items delivered for the week. Multiplied by the 200 cents (or $2) charge per item, that's a total of $70 in per-item charges. When you add that amount to the $70 total for the per-delivery charges—7 deliveries at $10 per delivery—you get a total of $140 for the week. The target answer, then, is 140; only (D) gives 140 when you plug the values into the answer choices, and, therefore, (D) is the correct answer.

    If you got (C), by the way, check your calculations for your target answer. You likely calculated the per-item charges as though x were the total, rather than the daily average, of the items delivered.

4. **A** You *could* solve this problem algebraically, although it's a bit of a chore. If you assign x to represent the smallest integer in the set, then $x + (x + 1) + (x + 2) + (x + 3) + (x + 4) = 265$, so $5x + 10 = 265$, $5x = 255$, and $x = 51$. The five least consecutive integers are thus 51 through 55; you can now add the five greatest consecutive integers, which are 56 through 60. The total is 290, and the correct answer is (A).

    A much simpler way to solve the problem, though, is to recognize that the difference between the sums of *any* two adjacent sets of five consecutive integers is the same; you can, therefore, find this difference using much smaller, easier-to-work-with numbers, and then add this difference to the total given in the problem. The sum of the integers from 1 to 5 is 15, and the sum of the integers from 6 to 10 is 40; our difference, thus, is 25, and $265 + 25 = 290$.

5. **D** This problem is a great opportunity to Plug In the Answers. Start with (C) and substitute 10 for y in the problem. The average of the numbers {3, 5, 9, 13, 10} is 8, but the median of those numbers is 9. Eliminate (C). The value of y needs to be greater, so try (D), 15. The average of the numbers {3, 5, 9, 13, 15} is 9, and the median of those numbers is also 9. You're done. The correct answer is (D).

6. **D** The question stem states that the average high temperature for the five-day period was 86°; therefore, the sum of the high temperatures for those days was $5 \times 86 = 430°$. Statement (1) says that the average high temperature for the first four days was 87°; therefore, the sum of the high temperatures for those days was $4 \times 87 = 348°$. $430 - 348 = 82°$, the high temperature on Friday. Statement (1) is sufficient; write down AD.

Statement (2) says that Friday's temperature reduced the average high for the five-day period by 1 degree. This means that the average high for the first four days was 87°; thus, Statement (2) is sufficient for the same reason that Statement (1) is sufficient. The correct answer is (D).

7. **E** This is a yes-or-no question. Statement (1) says that three of the five integers are less than 50. This information by itself does not ensure that the other two integers *are* greater than 100. Both remaining values *could* be greater than 100; the solution set {10, 20, 30, 140, 300}, for example, satisfies this condition. However, the set {1, 2, 3, 4, 490} *also* satisfies the conditions of the problem, and it contains only one value greater than 100. Statement (1) is insufficient on its own; the correct answer must be BCE. Statement (2) says only that none of the integers is equal to 100. By itself, this is clearly not sufficient to tell you that exactly two of the integers are greater than 100; eliminate (B). In fact, the statement provides no more useful information than that provided in Statement (1); both of the solutions provided above satisfy this statement as well. The correct answer is (E).

8. **B** Statement (1) provides no information about the non-executive employees at Company *R*. It is not sufficient by itself, so you're down to BCE. Statement (2) provides a ratio of executive employees to non-executive employees at Company *R*. This information is sufficient on its own to determine the average age of all employees at Company *R*. Regardless of whether Company *R* has 2 executives and 8 non-executives or 200 executives and 800 non-executives, the resulting average for all employees is the same, because the proportional contribution of each group to the average remains fixed. The best way to prove this is simply to plug in some numbers and see for yourself. The average age of 1 executive and 4 non-executives is $\dfrac{54 + 4(34)}{5} = 38$. The average age of 30 executives and 120 non-executives is $\dfrac{30(54) + 120(34)}{150} = 38$. Thus, the correct answer is (B).

9. **D** This is a Value Data Sufficiency question, so begin by determining what is known from the information in the question stem. The question stem provides that the mean of the scores for the physical conditioning test is 72 and that the test scores are normally distributed. The test scores being normally distributed indicates that the distance between each of the standard deviations is going to be equal. Next, determine what is needed in order to answer the question. The question asks for the score at or below which the recruits are required to retest and the question states that recruits must retest if they are more than 2 standard deviations below the mean. In order to be sufficient, the statements must provide a way to determine the value that is 2 standard deviations below the mean. Evaluate the statements one at a time.

Statement (1) provides that the range between the 3rd standard deviations above and below the mean is 30. Because the scores are normally distributed, it is possible to calculate the distance of each standard deviation. The distance between the 3rd standard deviations is 30 and there are 6 standard deviations in total, which means each standard deviation is worth 5 points. Therefore, the score that is 2 standard deviations below the mean is 62. This statement provides a consistent answer to the question, so it is sufficient to answer the question. Eliminate (B), (C), and (E). The remaining choices are (A) and (D).

Evaluate Statement (2). This statement provides that the 3rd standard deviation above the mean is 87. If 3 standard deviations above the mean is 87 − 72 = 15 points above the mean, then each standard deviation is worth 5 points. Therefore, the second standard deviation below the mean is 10 points below 72, or 72 − 10 = 62. This statement provides a consistent answer to the question, so it is sufficient to answer the question. Eliminate (A). The correct answer is (D).

DRILL 13 (Page 272)

1. **C** The question involves ratios, so set up a Ratio Box. Since there are 2 ratios given, set up 2 Ratio Boxes—the current situation and the hypothetical if the students drop out.

Current:

	Men	Women	Total
Ratio	6	5	11
Multiplier			
Actual			

After drop outs:

	Men	Women	Total
Ratio	8	7	15
Multiplier			
Actual			

Since the algebra seems somewhat complicated, Plug In the Answers. Start with (C). The answers represent the number of men currently in the class. Plugging 18 in gives

Current

	Men	Women	Total
Ratio	6	5	11
Multiplier	3	3	3
Actual	18	15	33

The problem then states that 2 men and 1 woman drop out, so subtract 2 from the total men and 1 from the total women and check if that fits an 8 to 7 ratio in the After drop outs box:

After drop outs:

	Men	Women	Total
Ratio	8	7	15
Multiplier			
Actual	16	14	

16 to 14 is an 8 to 7 ratio. Since the condition is met, the correct answer is (C).

2. **B** If the average of 5 numbers is 7, then the numbers must add up to 35. If three of those numbers average 5, then those 3 numbers must add up to 15. The sum of the two numbers left is therefore $35 - 15 = 20$. If the sum of the two numbers is 20, then the average of those two numbers is 10. The correct answer is (B).

3. **B** Determine the two amounts of interest. $5,000 earning 8% interest, compounded semiannually, earns 4% interest compounded every 6 months. 4% of 5,000 is $5,000 \times \dfrac{4}{100} = 200$. Then, 4% of the new $5,200 balance is $5,200 \times \dfrac{4}{100} = 208$, and the account contains $5,408 at the end of one year. For the other account, 8% of 5,000 is $5,000 \times \dfrac{8}{100} = 400$, so the account contains $5,400 at the end of one year. The difference is $\$5,408 - \$5,400 = \$8$. The correct answer is (B).

4. **E** If the average of ten numbers is 10, then the numbers have to add up to 100. However, the numbers could be anything. For example, if all ten numbers are 10, then the standard deviation is 0. However, since standard deviation is defined as the spread of numbers away from the average, the standard deviation could be anything—as the numbers could be negative numbers, really big numbers, and so on—as long as the sum is 100. So, 0, 10, and 20 could all be standard deviations. The correct answer is (E).

5. **D** Start by figuring out the median and mode of List II. The mode is 3 and the median is 5. Their sum is 8. So, the median of List I must also be 8. Since there are 6 elements in List I, the median will be the average of the third and fourth numbers. Therefore, those two numbers must add up to 16. Since 7 is already listed, the only possible way to get a median of 8 is if y is 9. The correct answer is (D).

6. **D** When objects move in the same direction, the difference in their rates may be calculated by subtraction. Teena's rate of 55 miles per hour minus Joe's rate of 40 miles per hour yields $55 - 40 = 15$ miles per hour. Thus, Teena travels 15 miles further than Joe every hour. Because Teena is currently 7.5 miles behind Joe, and the question asks in how many minutes she will be 15 miles ahead of Joe, Teena needs to cover a relative distance of $15 + 7.5 = 22.5$ miles. Use $D = RT$, and solve for T. Therefore, $22.5 = 15 \times T$, which yields that $T = \dfrac{22.5}{15}$, or $T = 1.5$ hours. Because there are 60 minutes in each hour, multiply 1.5 by 60 to determine the number of minutes. $1.5 \times 60 = 90$ minutes. The correct answer is (D).

7. **C** The problem does not specify the number of workers or envelopes each worker can stuff, so Plug In. Let the number of full-time workers be 5. There are $\dfrac{2}{5}$ as many trainees as there are full-time workers, so there are $\dfrac{2}{5} \times 5 = 2$ trainees. Let the number of envelopes each full-time worker can stuff per day be 3. Each trainee can stuff $\dfrac{2}{3}$ as many envelopes as can a full-time worker, so each trainee can stuff $\dfrac{2}{3} \times 3 = 2$ envelopes per day. Thus, each day the full-time workers stuff $5 \times 3 = 15$ envelopes, the trainees stuff $2 \times 2 = 4$ envelopes, and together the two groups stuff $15 + 4 = 19$ envelopes. The trainees stuff 4 envelopes, so they stuffed $\dfrac{4}{19}$ of the envelopes. The correct answer is (C).

8. **B** Statement (1) tells you how many hours Vincent spends chopping down trees in a day, but it provides no data to help you determine how long it takes him to chop down 4 trees. This statement is clearly insufficient to answer the question. The answer must be (B), (C), or (E).

   Statement (2) tells you that Vincent takes twice as long as Roger to chop down trees. Because the question stem tells you that Roger chops down 4 trees per hour, you can deduce that Vincent chops down 4 trees every 2 hours. Thus, Statement (2) is sufficient to answer the question. The correct answer is (B).

9. **D** To solve this problem, you need to write some equations. Let's call Automobile A's current speed A and Automobile B's current speed B. The question stem tells you that $A = \dfrac{2}{3}B$. Statement (1) tells you that $A + 10 = \dfrac{3}{4}(B + 10)$. Thus, between the question stem and Statement (1), you have two distinct equations, which means you can solve for the two variables. The possible answers are (A) or (D).

   Statement (2) tells you that $A - 10 = \dfrac{1}{2}(B - 10)$. Once again, you have two distinct equations and two variables. Statement (2) is sufficient, and the correct answer is (D).

10. **E** Solve this problem by Plugging In. Set m equal to a value that turns the question into an easy arithmetic problem. For example, $m = 40$ is a good, easy value. It tells you that Renee can ride 1 mile every 2 minutes. How many miles, then, can she ride in 10 minutes? She can ride 5 miles in 10 minutes.

    Now, plug in 40 for m in each of the answer choices. The correct answer will calculate to 5, the value of x when $m = 40$. Because (E) is the only answer that equals 5, (E) is the correct answer.

11. **B** Statement (1) clearly is not sufficient to answer the question because the only information it provides is Paul's starting time. The correct answer to this question must be BCE. Statement (2) says that Paul had jogged 5 miles by 5:40 P.M. and 8 miles by 6:04 P.M. You might be tempted to choose (C) at this point; after all, you now know when Paul began jogging and how far he had jogged at various intervals, so you could easily figure out how far he had run by 6:20 P.M., the end of the 80-minute period beginning at 5:00 P.M. Resist the temptation! Look more closely at Statement (2). It says that Paul covered 3 miles between 5:40 P.M. and 6:04 P.M. Thus, you know that Paul ran eight-minute

miles during that 24-minute period. The question stem says that Paul jogs at a constant rate, and that he jogs for 80 minutes. Therefore, Statement (2), in combination with the question stem, provides all the information you need; Paul jogs eight-minute miles for 80 minutes, so the route along which he jogs is 10 miles long. The correct answer is (B).

12. **A** The only solution to the equation in Statement (1) is $x = 3$. That narrows it down to AD.

To determine whether Statement (2) is sufficient, subtract $x + 6$ from both sides of the equation to get

$$x^2 - x - 6 = 0$$

This equation can be factored to

$$(x - 3)(x + 2) = 0$$

Thus, the equation has two solutions: x can equal 3 or -2. Statement (2) is not sufficient. The correct answer is (A).

13. **A** Statement (1) says that a, c, and x are negative. Instinctively, you might conclude that this isn't enough information, because it says nothing about b or d. Look at the expression in the question stem again, though; b and d appear only in the expressions $(bx)^2$ and $(dx)^4$. Both of these expressions contain even exponents; you know, therefore, that these expressions are positive regardless of the values b and d represent, because nonzero integers raised to an even power are always positive. From Statement (1), you know that ax is positive (a negative times a negative equals a positive) and, similarly, that $(cx)^3$ is positive. Statement (1) is sufficient even though the answer to the question is "No." The possible answers are AD. Statement (2) provides no valuable information. The values of b and d do not matter, as they are used only in expressions that result in positive numbers. The values of a and c, however, do matter because they are raised to an odd exponent. Any number raised to an odd exponent retains the positive or negative nature of the original number. There is no way to ensure, then, that ax or cx, when raised to an odd exponent, is positive or negative. The correct answer is (A).

DRILL 14 (Page 287)

1. **D** This is a Value Data Sufficiency question, so begin by determining what is known and what is needed to answer the question. The question asks for the remainder when integer n is divided by 13. So, determining possible values of n is necessary to solve the question. Evaluate the statements individually.

Statement (1) states that when n is divided by 91, the remainder is 83, which means that $\frac{n}{91} = k + \frac{83}{91}$, and that $n = 91k + 83$ for some integer k. Plug In. If $k = 1$, then $n = 91(1) + 83 = 174$. When 174 is divided by 13, the remainder is 5 because $13 \times 13 = 169$ and $174 - 169 = 5$. Plug In again. If $k = 0$, then $n = 83$. The remainder when 83 is divided by 13 is 5 because $13 \times 6 = 78$ and $83 - 78 = 5$. In fact, no matter what number is used for k, the remainder when n is divided by 13 is always 5.

This statement produces the same result no matter what the numbers are, so the statement is sufficient. Write down AD.

Statement (2) states that when n is divided by 52 the remainder is 18, which means that $\frac{n}{52} = j + \frac{18}{52}$, and that $n = 52j + 18$ for some integer j. Plug In. If $j = 1$, then $n = 52(1) + 18 = 70$. When 70 is divided by 13, the remainder is 5 because $13 \times 5 = 65$ and $70 - 65 = 5$. Plug In again. If $k = 0$, then $n = 18$. The remainder when 18 is divided by 13 is 5 because $13 \times 1 = 13$ and $18 - 13 = 5$. Plug In one more time. If $j = 2$, then $n = 122$. The remainder when 122 is divided by 13 is 5 because $13 \times 9 = 117$ and $122 - 117 = 5$. No matter what number is used for the value of j, this statement produces the same answer to the question. When a statement produces the same answer to the question, that statement is sufficient. Eliminate (A). The correct answer is (D).

2. **E** This is a Yes/No Data Sufficiency question, so be prepared to Plug In more than once. The question asks if n is prime and provides that x is an integer. Evaluate the statements individually.

Consider Statement (1), which states that $x! = n$. This means that x could be equal to 2 or any other number. Statement (1) is not sufficient. Write down BCE.

Statement (2) states that $0 \le x \le 2$, which means that x could be equal to 2, 1, or 0. This does not provide any information about n, so eliminate (B).

Now consider both statements together. According to Statement (2), x could be equal to 0, 1, or 2. Any of these values for x satisfies Statement (1). Plug In. If $x = 1$, the answer to the question is "No." If $x = 2$, the answer to the question is "Yes." The statements combined result in two different answers to the question, so the statements combined are insufficient. Eliminate (C). The correct answer is (E).

3. **A** The question states that $\frac{17!}{7^m}$ is an integer, so expand this factorial to find that $\frac{17!}{7^m} = \frac{17 \times 16 \times 15 \times 14 \times 13 \times 12 \times 11 \times 10 \times 9 \times 8 \times 7 \times 6 \times 5 \times 4 \times 3 \times 2 \times 1}{7^m}$. In order for $\frac{17!}{7^m}$ to be an integer, 17! must be divisible by 7^m. Because 7 is prime, there must be at least as many factors of 7 in the numerator as in the denominator. The numerator has two factors of 7, one at 7 and one at 14. For $\frac{17!}{7^m}$ to be an integer, the denominator can have at most two factors of 7. The correct answer is (A).

4. **B** This is a Yes/No Data Sufficiency question, so be prepared to Plug In more than once. The prime factors of 21 are 3 and 7, which means that for ab to be a multiple of 21, it must have factors of 3 and 7. The question states that a is a multiple of 7, which means that ab has at least one factor of 7. So, it is necessary to find out if either a or b has a factor of 3.

Statement (1) states that every factor of 65 is also a factor of b. The prime factors of 65 are 5 and 13. If these are the only factors of b, then the answer to the question is "No." However, if b has a factor of 3 as well, the answer to the question is "Yes." The statement produces two different answers to the question, so it is insufficient. Write down BCE.

Statement (2) states that b is divisible by 51. The prime factors of 51 are 3 and 17, which means that b has at least one factor of 3. Statement (2) is sufficient. Eliminate (C) and (E). The correct answer is (B).

5. **A**   This is a Yes/No Data Sufficiency question, so be prepared to Plug In more than once. The question asks if the variable m is divisible by 14. Begin by finding the prime factors of 14, which are 2 and 7. For m to be divisible by 14, both 2 and 7 must be factors of m.

Statement (1) states that the GCF of m and 42 is 6. The prime factors of 42 are 2, 3, and 7. Because the GCF of m and 42 is 6 and $2 \times 3 = 6$, two of the factors of m are 2 and 3. Alternatively, m does not have 7 as a factor. Because 7 is not a factor of m, it is impossible for m to be divisible by 14. Therefore, the answer to the question is "No." There is no way to produce an answer of "Yes" to the question. When a statement consistently produces the same answer to a question, that statement is sufficient. Write down AD.

Statement (2) states that the GCF of m and 72 is 24. The prime factors of 72 are 2, 2, 2, 3, and 3, or $2^3 \times 3^2$, and the prime factors of 24 are 2, 2, 2, and 3, or $2^3 \times 3$, which means that the prime factors of m include 2^3 and one factor of 3. This information does not provide enough data to determine if m is divisible by 14 because it does not give any indication if 7 is a factor of m. If m has a factor of 7, then the answer to the question is "Yes." However, if m does not have a factor of 7, then the answer to the question is "No." The statement produces two different answers to the question, so the statement is insufficient. Eliminate (D). The correct answer is (A).

Algebraic Expressions Quiz (Page 296)

1. $x + 4 = y + 8 - 3$

2. $35 = \left(\dfrac{x}{100} \right) z$

3. $8 + 3 \times 4 = \left(\dfrac{x}{100} \right) y$

4. $(x - 8) - 5 = 14$

5. $z = \left(\dfrac{x}{100} \right) y$

Substitution Quiz (Page 297)

1. This problem states that $x + 3y = 6$ and $y = \frac{1}{3}x$. Use substitution to solve for x: $x + 3\left(\frac{1}{3}x\right) = 6$. This results in $x + x = 6$, so $2x = 6$ and $x = 3$.

2. This problem states that $y = 2x$ and $x + y = 24$ and asks for the value of $3x$. Use substitution to solve: $x + 2x = 24$, so $3x = 24$.

3. This problem states that $4x - 2y = 16$ and $12x + 6y = 48$ and asks for the value of (x, y). Solve for one of the variables first. The first equation can be rewritten as $x = 4 + \frac{1}{2}y$. Solve the second equation for y to produce $y = 8 - 2x$. Use substitution to solve for x in the first equation: $x = 4 + \frac{1}{2}(8 - 2x) = 4 + 4 - x$. Combine like terms to find that $2x = 8$ and $x = 4$. Use this value of x to solve for y. In the first equation, $4(4) + 2y = 16$, so $2y = 0$ and $y = 0$. The answer is $(4, 0)$.

4. This problem states that $-6x - 2y = 2$ and $10 = 10x + 10y$ and asks to solve for the value of x. Use the second equation and solve for y. Isolate $10y$ on one side, which produces $10y = 10 - 10x$. Divide both sides by 10 to produce $y = 1 - x$. Use substitution in the first equation to produce $-6x - 2(1 - x) = 2$. Solve for x by distributing the 2, combining similar terms, and isolating the x: $-6x - 2 + 2x = 2$ yields $-4x = 4$ and $x = -1$.

5. The problem states that the area of a rectangle is 18. The area of a rectangle is found by the expression *length* $\times$ *width*. The problem also states that the length is twice the width, which can be written as $l = 2w$. The question asks for the width, so use substitution to solve: $2w \times w = 18$ produces $2w^2 = 18$ and $w^2 = 9$. Therefore, $w = 3$.

6. The problem states that the rate of car A is 3 times that of car B, which can be written as $A = 3B$. The problem then states that the combined rate is 88 miles per hour, which can be written as $A + B = 88$. The problem then states that car A travels for 2 hours and car B travels for 1 hour and asks for the combined distance they each covered. This is a distance problem, so use the distance formula, which is *Distance* = *Rate* $\times$ *Time*. The problem provides the time each car traveled and provides formulas that concern the rate. Use substitution to solve for the rate of each car. The first equation defines A, so use that information and substitute into the second equation to solve for B. This yields $3B + B = 88$ and $4B = 88$, so $B = 22$. Use this information to solve for A: $A + 22 = 88$ and $A = 66$. Now use the rate formula to determine the total distance traveled by each car. Car A traveled at a rate of 66 miles per hour for 2 hours, so car A traveled $66 \times 2 = 132$ miles. Car B traveled 22 miles per hour for 1 hour, so car B traveled $22 \times 1 = 22$ miles. The combined distance is $132 + 22 = 154$.

DRILL 15 (Page 298)

1. **D** Start by translating the two original equations: $x = 3z + 1$ and $y = 2z - 1$. If z is 4, then $x = 13$ and $y = 7$. Thus, $2x$ is 26 and $3y$ is 21. The difference between the two values is 5, so the correct answer is (D).

   If you chose (A), you may have mistakenly added when the problem asked for a product. If you got (E), you may have solved for $x - y$ when the problem asked for $2x - 3y$. And if you got (C), you may have done both.

2. **B** Although you could solve this by writing a pair of algebraic equations ($f + m = 21$ and $f = m - 3$), it's simpler to Plug In the Answers. Start with (C), 7 men. The number of women would be 3 less than 3 times that number, or $21 - 3 = 18$ women. That's a total of 25 council members altogether, and you're looking for 21. Now that you know that (C) is too big, eliminate (C), (D), and (E).

   If you try (B), 6 men, then you have $18 - 3 = 15$ women. This gives the desired total of 21 council members, so the correct answer is (B). If you got (E), by the way, you solved for the number of women on the board.

3. **E** Statement (1) is a quadratic equation, so factor it and see what the options are for x: $x^2 - 5x + 4 = 0$ factors into $(x - 4)(x - 1) = 0$, so x could be 4 or 1. Since there's more than one value for x, Statement (1) alone is insufficient, and you're down to BCE.

   Statement (2) alone leaves you with the vast majority of all numbers—this statement is *definitely* not sufficient, so you're down to (C) or (E).

   When you combine the statements, they're still not sufficient. Be careful not to fall for one of the classic GMAT traps: 1 is *not* prime. Because 4 is also not prime, you're left with both values, and the correct answer is (E).

4. **C** Gut instinct may lead to you select (E) on this one; after all, Statement (1) provides a three-variable equation, which does not have a unique solution. Statement (2) refers to only two of the three variables mentioned in the question stem, so clearly it cannot be sufficient. At first glance, it may be hard to imagine how the two statements together could be any more helpful than each is on its own.

   Statement (1) is, in fact, insufficient on its own, for the reason stated above. The possible answers are BCE. Statement (2) is also insufficient, again for the reason stated above. Eliminate (B). The answer is (C) or (E).

   Now, add the two equations provided by Statements (1) and (2) to get $3x + 3y + 3z = 75$. Factor a 3 out of both sides of the equation, and you end up with $x + y + z = 25$. Thus, the two statements together *are* sufficient to answer the question. The correct answer is (C).

5. **B** Statement (1) provides information only about the sum of the balances on David's EverywhereCard and his American Local card. Therefore, the statement is insufficient to determine whether the balance on David's EverywhereCard is his highest balance, because it does not provide any information that allows you to compare the balance on the EverywhereCard to the balances on the other two cards. The possible answers are BCE.

Statement (2) tells you that the balance on David's EverywhereCard is greater than the balance on his Passport card and less than the balance on his American Local card. Thus, it provides enough information to answer the question. The correct answer is (B).

There are a couple of places where you can go wrong on this question. The first involves the fact that Statement (2) answers the question this way: "No, he does not owe the greatest balance on the EverywhereCard." Some test-takers get confused and use a "no" answer to decide that a statement is insufficient. Remember, it doesn't matter how you answer a yes-or-no question, just so long as you can answer it conclusively.

Some test-takers might realize that Statements (1) and (2) together provide enough information to calculate the exact balance on each credit card, and thus may choose (C). But because Statement (2) is sufficient on its own, (C) cannot be the correct answer to this question.

6. **A**   It can be a good idea to simplify before heading into the statements. If you have the equation $a - b = c$ and want b, then you could simply write it as $b = a - c$. Now, consider Statement (1) on its own. Statement (1) can be rewritten as $a - c = 6$. Since $a - c = b$ from the question stem, you know that $b = 6$. Statement (1) is sufficient, and you're down to AD. Statement (2) provides information about only one of the three variables in the original equation, so it cannot be sufficient on its own. The correct answer is (A).

7. **B**   Variables in the answer choices mean it's time to Plug In. For the purposes of this problem, it's probably easiest to plug in weights for Andrea and Brian, add them, and use the sum for the value of p. Remember to plug in values that conform to the rules of the problem; Brian must weigh exactly 10 pounds more than Andrea. Try to make p a value that is divisible by 4; that will make it easier to calculate Cubby's weight. Let's say Andrea weighs 45 pounds and Brian weighs 55 pounds. That makes p equal to 100, a nice, round number that is easily divisible by 4. Cubby weighs $\frac{p}{4}$ pounds more than Andrea, so he weighs 25 pounds more than Andrea, or 70 pounds. Plug 100 in for p in each of the answer choices and eliminate those that do not yield an answer of 70. The correct answer is (B).

8. **D**   This is a simultaneous equation problem dressed up as a word problem. The question stem says that two types of grants were awarded; it also provides the sum of the grants. Let's call the group of first-years who received \$7,000 grants x and the group of first-years who received \$10,000 grants y. The question stem says that $7,000x + 10,000y = 2,300,000$. That's one equation; to solve simultaneous equations, you need two equations. Statement (1) provides a second equation. That equation is $x + y = 275$. You can solve simultaneously—although, of course, you don't have to because this is Data Sufficiency, not Problem Solving—to determine that $x = 150$ and $y = 125$. Statement (1) is sufficient; the answer is (A) or (D). Statement (2) also provides a second equation. That equation is $10,000y = 7,000x + 200,000$. Again, you can solve to determine that $x = 150$ and $y = 125$. Choice (D) is the correct answer.

DRILL 16 (Algebra) (Page 317)

1. **D** $\dfrac{\dfrac{1^6}{3}-\dfrac{1^4}{3}}{\dfrac{1^5}{3}}$ may be factored to yield $\dfrac{\left(\dfrac{1}{3}\right)^4\left(\left(\dfrac{1}{3}\right)^2-1\right)}{\dfrac{1^5}{3}}=\dfrac{\left(\dfrac{1}{3}\right)^4\left(\left(\dfrac{1}{3}\right)^2-1\right)}{\left(\dfrac{1}{3}\right)^4\left(\dfrac{1}{3}\right)}$, which reduces to

   $\dfrac{\left(\dfrac{1}{3}\right)^2-1}{\dfrac{1}{3}}=\dfrac{\dfrac{1}{9}-1}{\dfrac{1}{3}}$, which yields $\dfrac{-\dfrac{8}{9}}{\dfrac{1}{3}}=-\dfrac{8}{9}\times\dfrac{3}{1}$, which results in $-\dfrac{8\times 3}{3\times 3}=-\dfrac{8}{3}$. The correct answer

   is (D).

2. **D** Factor $\dfrac{\sqrt{147}+\sqrt{75}}{14}$ as $\dfrac{\sqrt{7\times 7\times 3}+\sqrt{5\times 5\times 3}}{14}=\dfrac{7\sqrt{3}+5\sqrt{3}}{14}$, which simplifies to

   $\dfrac{12\sqrt{3}}{14}=\dfrac{6\sqrt{3}}{7}$. The second expression simplifies to $\dfrac{28}{7\sqrt{3}}=\dfrac{4}{\sqrt{3}}$. In order to evaluate the

   ratio between the expressions, express them as the fraction $\dfrac{\dfrac{6\sqrt{3}}{7}}{\dfrac{4}{\sqrt{3}}}=\dfrac{6\sqrt{3}}{7}\times\dfrac{\sqrt{3}}{4}$, which yields

   $\dfrac{6\sqrt{3\times 3}}{28}=\dfrac{6\times 3}{28}$, and reduces to $\dfrac{9}{14}$, or a 9 to 14 ratio. The correct answer is (D).

3. **E** The problem provides the definition of the function $a\Delta b$ and asks for the value of $-1\Delta(1\Delta-1)$,

   so evaluate the expression in the parenthesis first. $(1\Delta-1)=\dfrac{(-1-1)^2}{1^2}$, which simplifies to

   $\dfrac{(-2)^2}{1}=4$. Now, evaluate $-1\Delta 4$. $-1\Delta 4=\dfrac{(4-(-1))^2}{(-1)^2}$, which simplifies to $\dfrac{(5)^2}{1}=25$. The correct

   answer is (E).

4. **A** There are numbers in the answer choices, so Plug In the Answers. Start with (C) and label the columns as Joe's current age. Draw a new column for Joe's age 5 years ago, which is $27-5=22$. Draw a new column for Jessica's age 5 years ago, which is $22\div 2=11$. Draw a new column for Jessica's current age, which is $11+5=16$. Draw a new column for Jessica's age in 4 years, which is $16+4=20$. Draw a new column for Joe's age in 4 years, which is $27+4=31$. Finally, evaluate the condition that Joe's age in 4 years *will be one and half times as old* as Jessica's age in 4 years, which is incorrect for (C). Eliminate (C). Because Joe's age in 4 years is greater than *one and a half times* that of Jessica, try (B), which is a smaller number. If Joe's current age is 25, then Joe's age 5 years ago is $25-5=20$, Jessica's age 5 years ago is $20\div 2=10$, Jessica's current age is $10+5=15$, Jessica's age in 4 years is $15+4=19$, and Joe's age in 4 years is $25+4=29$. Joe's age in 4 years is still greater

than *one and half times* that of Jessica, so eliminate (B) and check (A) to confirm that it is the correct answer. If Joe's current age is 23, then Joe's age 5 years ago is $23 - 5 = 18$, Jessica's age 5 years ago is $18 \div 2 = 9$, Jessica's current age is $9 + 5 = 14$, Jessica's age in 4 years is $14 + 4 = 18$, and Joe's age in 4 years is 27. Since 27 is *one and a half times* 18, (A) meets the condition. The correct answer is (A).

5. **D** $\dfrac{x^2 + 2x - 9}{3} \le x + 1$ can be rewritten as $x^2 + 2x - 9 \le 3(x + 1)$ or $x^2 + 2x - 9 \le 3x + 3$. Subtract $3x$ and 3 from both sides to yield $x^2 + 2x - 3x - 9 - 3 \le 0$, or $x^2 - x - 12 \le 0$. Factor the quadratic expression to yield $(x - 4)(x + 3) \le 0$. Thus, the parabola defined by the quadratic expression has x-intercepts of $(4, 0)$ and $(-3, 0)$. Because the term x^2 is positive, the y-value of the parabola is negative between its x-intercepts, and the values of x that satisfy the inequality are those values from -3 to 4, inclusive, which may be represented as $-3 \le x \le 4$. The correct answer is (D).

6. **E** There are variables in the answer choices, so Plug In. Let $x = 20$ and $a = 100$. Since 20% of 100 is 20, then $b = 20$. Since 100 is 5 times 20, the target is 5. Now, plug $x = 20$ into the answer choices, looking for the target of 5. Only (E) matches. The correct answer is (E).

7. **E** There are variables in the answer choices, so Plug In. Let $s = 6$. John has 6 pairs of shoes, so Sheila has 18 and James has 3. The *three of them combined* have 27 pairs of shoes, and 27 is the target. Now, plug $s = 6$ into the answer choices, looking for a target of 27. Only (E) matches. The correct answer is (E).

8. **B** Since you should always calculate things inside the parentheses first—don't forget PEMDAS!—start by adding 1 and $\dfrac{17}{64}$ to get $\dfrac{81}{64}$. Those are both perfect squares, so the inner root sign will be easy to handle: $\sqrt{\dfrac{81}{64}} = \dfrac{\sqrt{81}}{\sqrt{64}} = \dfrac{9}{8}$. Don't grab (C), though—you still need to work the outer sign: $\sqrt{\dfrac{9}{8}} = \dfrac{\sqrt{9}}{\sqrt{8}} = \dfrac{3}{2\sqrt{2}}$. Like in high school, you can't leave a radical on the bottom of a fraction, so you'll need to multiply your answer by $\dfrac{\sqrt{2}}{\sqrt{2}}$ to get the final answer of (B), $\dfrac{3\sqrt{2}}{4}$.

If you're comfortable estimating fractions and roots, you can apply POE to this question. $1 + \dfrac{17}{64}$ is a little greater than 1; the square root of something a little greater than 1 is also something a little greater than 1; and the square root of that number is, again, something a little greater than 1. Only (B) and (C) are a little greater than 1.

9. **A** Answering a function problem on the GMAT is simply a matter of following the directions provided by the definition of the function. In this case, the operation signified by two numbers with the ~ between them is defined as the sum of the numbers on either side of the ~ sign divided by the square of the product of the two numbers. If $a \sim c = 0$, then $\dfrac{a+c}{(ac)^2} = 0$; since the numerator must be zero in order for the fraction itself to equal zero, you know that $a + c = 0$. Subtract a from both sides and $c = -a$. The answer is (A).

10. **E** The variables in the answer choices should tell you that this is a great problem for Plugging In. Choose a value easily divisible by 20 (the number of friends in the group) and one for which percentages are easy to calculate (because the value of the stock increases by a percentage). Set d equal to 100. The general fund of $100, then, was invested in Stock X, which subsequently increased in value by 40 percent; thus, its value increased to $140. At this point, the club sold the stock and divvied up the proceeds. Each member received $140 ÷ 20 = $7 in the process. Therefore, when d equals 100, the correct answer choice yields a result of 7. Check each answer choice, plugging in 100 for d. The correct answer is (E).

11. **B** Although the relationship provided in the problem is based on geometry, this isn't really a geometry problem: you can simply plug the given numbers into the formula. Starting with the larger rectangular solid, $\sqrt{12^2 + 4^2 + 3^2} = \sqrt{144 + 16 + 9} = \sqrt{169} = 13$. For the smaller rectangular solid, $\sqrt{6^2 + 3^2 + 2^2} = \sqrt{36 + 9 + 4} = \sqrt{49} = 7$. Both 13 and 7 are, of course, answer choices, but the problem asked you for the *difference* between the two values, so the correct answer is 6, (B).

DRILL 17 (Page 360)

1. **B** The answer choices represent the information directly asked for by the question, so Plug In the Answers. However, there is information in the question that should first be considered. Variables x and y represent the number of short and long essays available in Part Two of the test, respectively. The ratio of available long essays to short essays remains a constant in both parts of the test, and the ratio of short to long essays in Part One is 2:1. Therefore, the ratio of short to long essays in Part Two is 2:1, and the value of x must be twice the value of y. Eliminate (A) and (D), in which x is an odd number, because they entail non-integer values of y. Now, Plug In the Answers, beginning with (C).

If $x = 8$, then there are 8 short essays and 4 long essays available in Part Two, and $8 \times 4 = 32$ ways to select these essays. In this case, because there are $4 \times 2 = 8$ ways to select essays in Part One, there are $8 \times 32 = 256$ different lineups of essays a student can choose. This does not match the criterion in the question stem, which states that there are 144 different lineups. Since the number of essays in Part One is fixed, there must be fewer essays available in Part Two. Try (B).

If $x = 6$, then there are 6 short essays and 3 long essays available in Part Two, and $6 \times 3 = 18$ ways to select these essays. In this case, because there are 8 ways to select essays in Part One, there are $8 \times 18 = 144$ different lineups of essays a student can choose. This matches the criterion in the question stem, so the correct answer is (B).

2. **E** There are variables in the answer choices, so Plug In. Let $x = 3$ and $y = 5$. The larger group consists of $3 + 2 = 5$ men and $5 + 4 = 9$ women, for a total of $5 + 9 = 14$ members. The probability of selecting a man from the larger group is $\dfrac{5}{14}$, and that is the target. Plug $x = 3$ and $y = 5$ into the answer choices, looking for the target of $\dfrac{5}{14}$. The correct answer is (E).

3. **D** There are variables in the answer choices, so plug values in for g and b. Let $g = 2$ and $b = 3$. The question asks for the probability that at least one of two randomly selected players is a girl, which is equivalent to 1 minus the probability that both of the selected players are boys. The probability that the first player selected is a boy is $\dfrac{3}{5}$, and the probability that the second player selected is a boy is $\dfrac{2}{4}$. Therefore, the probability that both selected players are boys is $\dfrac{3}{5} \times \dfrac{2}{4} = \dfrac{6}{20}$, and the probability that at least one of the players is a girl is $1 - \dfrac{6}{20} = \dfrac{14}{20}$. Plug $g = 2$ and $b = 3$ into each of the answer choices, looking for the answer that equals $\dfrac{14}{20}$.

Choice (A) is $\dfrac{2(2-1)}{(3+2)(3+2-1)} = \dfrac{2}{20}$, so eliminate (A). Choice (B) is $\dfrac{3(3-1)}{(3+2)(3+2-1)} = \dfrac{6}{20}$, so eliminate (B). Choice (C) is $\dfrac{2(3)(2)}{(3+2)(3+2-1)} = \dfrac{12}{20}$, so eliminate (C). Choice (D) is $\dfrac{2(2 \times 3 + 2 - 1)}{(3+2)(3+2-1)} = \dfrac{14}{20}$, so keep (D). Choice (E) is $\dfrac{3(2 \times 2 + 3 - 1)}{(3+2)(3+2-1)} = \dfrac{18}{20}$, so eliminate (E). The correct answer is (D).

4, **D** This is a Value Data Sufficiency question, so begin by determining what is known from the information in the question stem. The question stem provides that the mean of the scores for the physical conditioning test is 72 and that the test scores are normally distributed. The test scores being normally distributed indicates that the distance between each of the standard deviations is going to be equal. Next, determine what is needed in order to answer the question. The question asks for the score at or below which the recruits are required to retest, and the question states that recruits must retest if they are more than 2 standard deviations below the mean. In order to be sufficient, the statements must provide a way to determine the value that is 2 standard deviations below the mean. Evaluate the statements one at a time.

Statement (1) provides that the range between the 3rd standard deviations above and below the mean is 30. Because the scores are normally distributed, it is possible to calculate the distance of each standard deviation. The distance between the 3rd standard deviations is 30 and there are 6 standard deviations in total, which means each standard deviation is worth 5 points. Therefore, the score that is 2 standard deviations below the mean is 62. This statement provides a consistent answer to the question, so it is sufficient to answer the question. Eliminate (B), (C), and (E). The remaining choices are (A) and (D).

Evaluate Statement (2). This statement provides that the 3rd standard deviation above the mean is 87. If 3 standard deviations above the mean is $87 - 72 = 15$ points above the mean, then each standard deviation is worth 5 points. Therefore, the second standard deviation below the mean is 10 points below 72, or $72 - 10 = 62$. This statement provides a consistent answer to the question, so it is sufficient to answer the question. Eliminate (A). The correct answer is (D).

5. **B** Standard deviation is the measure of how greatly the individual elements in a data set vary from the arithmetic mean of the set. As a general rule, the more widely dispersed the data in a set, the greater the standard deviation.

For the GMAT, you mostly need to know that standard deviation is measured from the arithmetic mean of a data set. If a data set has an arithmetic mean of 10 and a standard deviation of 2, then 8 and 12 are the values that are exactly one standard deviation from the arithmetic mean of the set.

In this problem, the standard deviation is 4, and the question asks for an interval that covers two standard deviations from the arithmetic mean of 46. It's key here to remember that "two standard deviations" means two *in each direction*—that is, both above *and* below the mean. Thus, you need an interval that covers 2×4, or 8, from the mean in each direction: $46 - 8 = 38$, so the bottom end of the interval is 38, and $46 + 8 = 54$, so the top end of the interval is 54. The correct answer is (B).

If you chose (A), by the way, you accounted for only the two standard deviations below the mean. If you chose (E), you accounted only for the two standard deviations above the mean. And if you chose (C), you forgot to take two standard deviations in each direction.

6. **D** The range of any set of measurements is equal to the greatest item in the set minus the least. Statement (1) gives a value for the range. If that value were anything other than 0, you would not be able to solve the problem based only on this statement. Because Statement (1) says that the range is 0, you actually know more than you might think about these three numbers. Because the problem says that the first measurement is 3, Plug In values for x_2 and x_3, just to see what happens. For example, if x_2 and x_3 both equal 5, the range does not equal 0. When you start plugging in numbers, you realize that the only way for the range of these three numbers to be 0 is if each of the numbers is exactly the same. And because you know the first value is 3, that means both x_2 and x_3 equal 3 as well. The possible answers are AD.

Statement (2) says that all the measurements correspond exactly to the arithmetic mean—which says that all three measurements are equal to 3. Statement (2) is also sufficient, so the correct answer is (D).

7. **B** As with all probability problems, find a fraction that has the total number of possibilities in the denominator and the number of those possibilities that meet a certain requirement in the numerator. The denominator is the easy part: because there are 4 members of each set, there are $4 \times 4 = 16$ total possibilities for the quotient when one member of X is divided by one member of Y. Now just figure out how many of those possibilities meet the requirement.

The requirement, in this case, is that the quotient is an integer—in other words, that the member chosen from X is divisible by the member chosen from Y—and you can count out all of the combinations that meet that requirement quickly and easily. The first member of Set X, 9, is divisible by only one member of Set Y, 3, so that's one. Then, working through Set X: 10 is divisible by both 2 and 5, so there are two other possibilities; 11 is prime, so it's not divisible by any members of Set Y; and 12 gives three other possibilities, because it's divisible by 2, 3, and 4. Thus, 6 of the total of 16 possibilities meet our requirement, and our probability is $\frac{6}{16}$, or $\frac{3}{8}$. The answer is (B).

8. **E** The probability that John will be chosen is $\frac{1}{7}$. The probability that Jessica will be chosen is also $\frac{1}{7}$. The probability that they will both be chosen is $\frac{1}{7} \times \frac{1}{7} = \frac{1}{49}$ This is (A), but you aren't done yet. The question asks for the probability that they will NOT both be chosen. The probability that an event does NOT happen can be expressed as 1 minus the probability that the event DOES happen. So $1 - \frac{1}{49} = \frac{48}{49}$, or (E).

9. **E** Before you start calculating, it is always helpful to think about what is reasonable. The probability that the number 6 is going to come up three times in a row is pretty low, which is another way of saying that the probability that 6 is NOT going to come up three times in a row is pretty high. So eliminate (A), (B), and (C). Now, figure out the problem. The probability that the first roll yields the number 6 is $\frac{1}{6}$. The probability that the second roll yields the number 6 is also $\frac{1}{6}$. The probability that the third roll yields the number 6? You guessed it: $\frac{1}{6}$. To find the probability of the series of these three events happening, you multiply the probabilities of each of the individual events: $\frac{1}{6} \times \frac{1}{6} \times \frac{1}{6} = \frac{1}{216}$. That's (A), but you aren't done yet. $\frac{1}{216}$ is the probability that the number 6 WILL land face up on all three rolls. The probability that an event does NOT happen can be expressed as 1 minus the probability that the event DOES happen: $1 - \frac{1}{216} = \frac{215}{216}$. The correct answer is (E).

10. **C** This is a permutation problem. Looking at Statement (1), it might seem enough to know that medals will be awarded for 1st, 2nd, and 3rd place. While some test-takers might be quick to assume that there are $3 \times 2 \times 1$ possible arrangements of medal winners, until you know the number of runners, you don't know enough. Statement (1) is not sufficient, so the possible answers are BCE.

Statement (2) gives the number of runners. Since you cannot use the information from Statement (1) while evaluating Statement (2), you now do not know how many medals are to be given. Statement (2) is also insufficient, so you're down to (C) or (E).

Putting the two statements together, you can now find out how many different arrangements of medal winners there are: $10 \times 9 \times 8 = 720$. The correct answer is (C).

11.   **C**   In this combination problem, the employer's choice of a programmer can be written as

$$\frac{6 \times 5 \times 4}{3 \times 2 \times 1} \text{ or } 20$$

The employer's choice of a manager can be written as

$$\frac{4 \times 3}{2 \times 1} \text{ or } 6$$

To find the total number of ways she could make her selection, multiply the respective number of possibilities: $6 \times 20 = 120$. The correct answer is (C).

12.   **C**   As is often the case with difficult probability questions, the bottom part of the fraction—the total number of possibilities—is a permutation problem in itself. In this case, you need to figure out how many different outcomes you can get if you flip a coin 6 times. Since you have 6 events with 2 possible outcomes each, the total number of different outcomes is $2 \times 2 \times 2 \times 2 \times 2 \times 2$, or 2^6, or 64. Now you just need to figure out how many of those possibilities meet the requirement.

For this problem, however, since there are so many different ways to meet the requirement, you'll

be better off figuring out how many outcomes *don't* meet the requirement; you can then subtract

this number from the total of 64. There are only three ways to *not* meet the requirement of 2 to 5

tails on 6 flips—you could get 0, 1, or 6 tails—and these can be quickly and easily counted out.

There is only one way to get 6 tails, and, likewise, there is only one way to get 0 tails, which is

another way of saying 6 heads. That's two possibilities. And there are only six different ways to get

tails once: the single tails can come up in the first spot, the second spot, and so on. That's 8 out of

the total of 64 possible outcomes that don't meet our requirement, so 56 do. The probability, there-

fore, is $\frac{56}{64}$, which reduces to $\frac{7}{8}$. The correct answer is (C).

13.   **C**   To determine how many cards must be drawn to ensure that the product is even, determine the worst-case scenario. Start by figuring out the maximum number of cards that can be drawn so that the product of the numbers on the cards is odd. The first card, obviously, is an odd-numbered card. If the second card is an odd-numbered card, then the product of the numbers on the cards is odd. If the third card is odd, then the product remains odd. As long as the numbers on the cards drawn are odd, the product of those numbers is odd. Thus, in the worst-case scenario, all ten odd numbered cards are drawn in succession. At this point, the eleventh card must be even, which would make the product of the 11 cards even. Therefore, 11 cards must be drawn to ensure an even product. The correct answer is (C).

14.   **D**   According to the problem, an acceptable password consists of either *DLDD* or *DDLD*, where *D* represents a digit and *L* represents a letter of the alphabet. Remember also that the digits must be different. First, consider *DLDD*. The first character can be any of the ten digits, 0 through 9. The

second character can be any of the 26 letters of the English alphabet. There are only 9 possible digits for the third character, because the third character cannot repeat the digit used for the first character. By the same reasoning, there are only 8 possible digits for the fourth character.

Thus, there are $10 \times 26 \times 9 \times 8 = 18{,}720$ possible passwords that follow the *DLDD* pattern. Now consider *DDLD*. There are an equal number of possible passwords that follow this pattern. The first character can be any of 10 digits; the second character can be any of the 9 remaining digits; the third character can be any of the 26 letters of the alphabet; and the fourth character can be any of the remaining 8 digits: $10 \times 9 \times 26 \times 8 = 18{,}720$. There are $18{,}720 + 18{,}720 = 37{,}440$ different passwords possible, and the correct answer is (D).

15. **A** This question is easier than it first appears. At first glance, the restrictive rules—the cards must be arranged in order, some cards have been removed from the deck—seem to complicate the problem. In fact, they do not; because there is only one correct solution for each set of cards chosen, you must determine only the number of possible combinations of the cards in order to determine the number of possible correct arrangements. The one-to-one correlation between combinations and correct solutions actually simplifies the problem. Because the teacher has removed two cards from the deck, only 8 cards remain. The values on the selected cards are immaterial and are presented merely as a distractor; the answer to this question is the same regardless of the values written on the two cards she removes. Make four spots for the cards chosen; then fill in the number of options for each spot: $8 \times 7 \times 6 \times 5$. Then, divide by the number of ways to arrange these four cards: $4 \times 3 \times 2 \times 1$. Reduce and solve to find 70. The correct answer is (A).

DRILL 18 (Reading Comprehension) (Page 382)

1. **D** The subject of the question is the *amygdala* and the task of the question is revealed by the statement *is true*, which indicates this is a purpose question. The question asks which of the answer choices is true. Begin by determining what the passage says about the amygdala. The amygdala is discussed in the second paragraph, which states that *MRI scans* showed a *reduction in the size of the amygdala* for people who engaged in an *eight-week meditation practice*. The passage then goes on to state the purpose of the amygdala as the *"fight or flight" part of the brain* that dictates the *response to stress*. Next, the passage relates the amygdala's response to mindfulness meditation to the prefrontal cortex's response. Evaluate the answer choices one at a time, looking for one that is supported by the information in the passage.

Choice (A) uses the extreme language *long-term damage*, which is cause for suspicion. The passage mentions that meditation reduces the size of the amygdala but does not state anything about the long-term implications of the reductions in size, nor does the passage suggest any *damage* to the amygdala is caused by meditation. Eliminate (A). Choice (B) uses the extreme language *less valuable*, so be suspicious of this answer choice as well. While the passage discusses the differences in the responses of the amygdala and the prefrontal cortex, the passage does not make any indication about the value of one over the other. Eliminate (B). Choice (C) also utilizes extreme language with the phrase *direct correlation.* The passage does not state that there is a correlation between the size of the amygdala and the thickness of the prefrontal cortex. The passage mentions both the size of the amygdala and the thickness of the prefrontal cortex but does not state they are correlated, simply that they both occur. Eliminate (C). Choice (D) is supported by the passage, which discusses the size of the amygdala based on a response to meditation and then states that *increased meditation may be capable of replacing our fearful responses to stress.* In other words, the size of the amygdala has some link to the type of response exhibited under stress. Keep (D). Choice (E) utilizes recycled language as the passage does mention the *relationship between the amygdala and the rest of the brain.* However, the passage does not state that this relationship is impacted by the thickness of the prefrontal cortex. Eliminate (E). The correct answer is (D).

2. **B** The subject of the question is the passage as a whole and the task is identified by the phrase *primarily concerned with,* so this is a primary purpose question. Evaluate the statements individually to determine which best describes the primary purpose of the passage.

Choice (A) is an example of extreme language because the passage does not attempt to *convince* the reader of anything. Eliminate (A). Choice (B) is a good description of the primary purpose of the passage, as the passage is *primarily concerned with* spreading information about the science and the debates regarding the brain's response to meditation. Keep (B). Choice (C) is an example of extreme language, as the passage does not argue that meditation is the *most effective* way to do anything. The passage is not concerned with the level of effectiveness of meditation. Eliminate (C). Choice (D) is a memory trap because the passage does mention those who believe that meditation should be considered a science in the last paragraph. However, this is not the primary purpose of the passage. Eliminate (D). Choice (E) appeals to outside knowledge and is also a memory trap as the passage is not primarily concerned with ways to better handle stress but rather that meditation is commonly thought to be a way to handle stress, and the response to stress is discussed in the passage. Eliminate (E). The correct answer is (B).

3. **D** The subject of the passage is the *fearful response to stress,* and the task of the passage is identified by the word *inferred,* so this is an inference question. The correct answer to inference questions must be true based on the information in the passage, so look for an answer choice that is definitely true given the contents of the passage.

While (A) is tempting, it is actually an example of extreme language. The passage states that responses to stress *may be altered* by practicing meditation, from fearful to rational. The passage does not definitively state if fearful responses *can be replaced.* Eliminate (A). Choice (B) is a memory trap from the passage's statement that meditation may cause the thickness of the prefrontal cortex to increase but does not mention the likelihood of having a fearful response to stress based on the thickness of the prefrontal cortex. Eliminate (B). Choice (C) is a memory trap, as the passage discusses whether meditation should be considered a science but does not have that same debate over the research regarding fearful responses. Eliminate (C). Choice (D) is supported by the last sentence of the second paragraph and the first sentence of the third paragraph, which state *These findings prompted researchers to hypothesize that increased meditation may be capable of replacing our fearful responses to stress with more rational ones. While researchers have called for more studies to be done on the mental and physical ramifications of mindfulness meditation....* Keep (D). Choice (E) is a recycled language trap. The word *MRI* is used in the passage, but the passage states that MRIs show the amygdala. The passage does not state that MRI scans show fearful responses. Eliminate (E). The correct answer is (D).

4. **A** The subject of the question is *proponent of meditation-as-science,* and the task of the question is found in the phrase *most likely to argue is not a science.* This is an application question, so begin by determining what the passage states about proponents of meditation as a science. The passage states that these individuals define science as *the study of the natural world through observation and experiment to produce a unified body of knowledge on a given subject.* The question asks to identify which one of the answer choices is *not* considered a science based on that definition. Evaluate the answer choices individually.

Choice (A) does not meet the requirement that the study be of the *natural world,* nor does it seek to create a *unified body of knowledge* through *observation and experiment.* Keep (A). Choice (B) pertains to the natural world and produces a unified body of knowledge through observation. This fits the definition of science, so eliminate (B). Choice (C) is a study of the natural world that seeks to explain events based on observation, so eliminate (C). Choice (D) deals with observations of the natural world and experiments to predict future events. This matches the definition of science, so eliminate (D). Choice (E) produces a unified body of knowledge pertaining to the natural world through observation and experimentation with samples of wood. Eliminate (E). The correct answer is (A).

5. **A** The subject of the question is the passage as a whole. The task of the question is found in the phrase *primary purpose,* so this is a primary purpose question. Evaluate the answer choices individually to determine which best describes the primary purpose of the passage.

Choice (A) is a good description of the primary purpose of the passage as the passage does seek to *describe* artificial neural networks, so keep (A). Choice (B) is a no such comparison trap answer. While the passage does discuss artificial neural networks and neural networks found in the brain, the passage does not *contrast* these different networks. Eliminate (B). Choice (C) is a memory trap. The passage does discuss the general construction of artificial neural networks but does not *illustrate how to build* them. Eliminate (C). Choice (D) is an example of extreme language as the passage does not *argue* for anything. The passage only provides information about neural networks. Eliminate (D). Choice (E) is a recycled language trap. The passage does mention the different *units* of an artificial neural network and their roles in producing intelligence, but this is not the primary purpose of the passage. The information about the units of the artificial neural network is only half of the information contained in the passage. Eliminate (E). The correct answer is (A).

6. **C** The subject of the question is *real neural networks.* The task of the question is *inferred,* which indicates this is an inference question. The correct answer for inference questions must be true based on the information in the passage, so determine what the passage states about real neural networks. The passage states that real neural networks are *found inside a brain* and that artificial neural networks *are designed to simulate the activity of real neural networks.* Evaluate the answer choices, looking for one that is true based on this information.

Choice (A) is an example of extreme language as the passage does not suggest that real neural networks *are to be considered superior to artificial neural networks*. Eliminate (A). Choice (B) is a recycled language trap. The passage states that artificial neural networks have *input, hidden, and output units* and are designed to simulate real neural networks. However, the passage does not state that real neural networks contain those units. Eliminate (B). Choice (C) is true based on the information in the passage. If artificial neural networks *are designed to simulate the activity of real neural networks*, then it can be said that real neural networks *inspired the development of artificial neural networks*. Keep (C). Choice (D) is a no-such-comparison answer, as the passage does not compare the capability of real and artificial neural networks. Eliminate (D). Choice (E) is an example of extreme language, as the passage does not suggest that real neural networks *will someday become obsolete*. Eliminate (E). The correct answer is (C).

7.　**C**　The subject of the question is *the optimal flow of information through an artificial neural network*. The task of the question is revealed by the phrase *according to the passage,* so this is a retrieval question. Determine which of the answer choices best represents the subject of the question by first determining what the passage says about the flow of information through an artificial neural network. The second paragraph of the passage gives *the flow of information through as Information is passed to the input units, which trigger the hidden units. The hidden units are activated and the sum of the inputs it receives triggers the next unit to fire if the sum exceeds a certain threshold. By giving the output units a model to compare the result of the learning process to, the artificial neural network can learn where to place more weight in order to make the result of the output unit more closely resemble that of the model*. Evaluate the answer choices individually, looking for one that optimizes this path.

Choice (A) is incorrect, as the input units do not directly pass information to the output units. Eliminate (A). Choice (B) is incorrect as the hidden units do not *change the input units to more closely resemble the model*. Eliminate (B). Choice (C) accurately reflects the optimized path for an artificial neural network as stated in the passage, so keep (C). Choice (D) does not mention the hidden units or the output units, so eliminate (D). Choice (E) states that the output units analyze a model and improve it before handing the model to the input units, which does not match the information in the passage. Eliminate (E). The correct answer is (C).

8.　**B**　Process of Elimination is useful here. Does the author present a statistical analysis? No, so eliminate (A). While the author might be said to identify the reasons for a trend, does she recommend measures to address it? No, so eliminate (C). Does the author advocate anything whatsoever? No, so eliminate (D). Does the author argue in favor of any policy? No, so eliminate (E). The correct answer is (B).

9.　**B**　Look for information about the authors mentioned in the question: it's in the end of the second paragraph. Make sure to read the context and not just those lines. Based on the previous sentence, these books are examples of ones with expired copyrights that were typed and put online. This supports (B). Choices (A) and (E) might be true but cannot be inferred. Choice (C) is out of scope, as lawsuits apply to other works than the subject of this question. Choice (D) directly contradicts the passage. The correct answer is (B).

10. **C** The passage states in the last paragraph that these companies want to exploit the unclear situation of who owns the copyrights to certain books. They would want to print something that is not under copyright, so it would be in the public domain, as the passage indicates in lines 24–26. For (B), the passage does not say that all books over 20 years old may be freely printed. The correct answer is (C).

11. **D** Use Process of Elimination. Choices (A) and (B) are recycled language—the passage mentions scanners and business plans but not in the same way as these two choices. Choice (C) is a reversal—the passage states that these companies are *looking for bargain basement content.* Choice (D) fits with this statement. Choice (E) is not supported because the passage doesn't explain what these practices have to do with *the role of traditional publishers.* The correct answer is (D).

12. **E** Use Process of Elimination. Choice (A) is incorrect because the passage is focused on a historical group, not contemporary conditions. Choice (B) is incorrect because the passage is about only one union. Choice (C) is incorrect because the author doesn't critique the union's methods. Choice (D) is close but highlights why (E) is correct. The author notes that the WTUL is *nearly forgotten* but doesn't criticize historians for not drawing attention to it. The passage serves to remind readers of the WTUL. The correct answer is (E).

13. **D** The passage states that the AFL was a *potent but largely absent ally,* and that the AFL *saw little economic benefit in working with the WTUL,* which served as *political cover* for the AFL. This does not support (A), (B), (C), or (E). The correct answer is (D).

14. **A** Search the passage for each answer choice. Choice (B) is in lines 54–55. Choice (C) is in lines 47–48. Choice (D) is in lines 45–46. Choice (E) is in lines 42–44. Choice (A) is not supported by the passage because in line 14 it states that the WTUL *represented a largely unskilled labor force.* The correct answer is (A).

15. **E** The passage states that these women were a *powerful minority* within the WTUL and that they were *looking beyond the workplace* to influence legislation. Choices (A), (B), (C), and (D) are not supported by the text in this part of the passage, whereas (E) matches the meaning of the passage. The correct answer is (E).

16. **A** In this passage, the accepted practice of making thoughtful business decisions based on careful review is being questioned in light of a new theory. Both (D) and (E) imply that the author has rejected this new model. Choice (C) uses a catchy word from the passage (*tenet*) and fails to indicate that there is a new idea that goes against that tenet. Choice (B) implies that the contradiction between the theory of making decisions based on careful review and the theory of making split-second decisions has in fact been resolved. The correct answer is (A).

17. **E** Where do you find the key words *subconscious process*? In the third paragraph. Choices (A), (B), (C), and (D) are all paraphrases of examples of the processes cited in that paragraph. Only (E) is not. In fact, the multitude of studies and examples are cited in support of Gladwell's hypothesis. The correct answer is (E).

18. **D** The information about Cramer's *extension* is in lines 31–35. Choices (A) and (B) are incorrect because the passage doesn't mention what the researchers' hypotheses were. Choice (C) is incorrect because the author doesn't say their work was invalid. Choice (D) is supported by the passage because Cramer found that with even less information, the specialists were still highly successful at predicting. Choice (E) is incorrect; in Cramer's study the participants did somewhat worse with less information, not better. The correct answer is (D).

19. **E** The passage states that the critics believe that human resources specialists prefer someone *who looks the part*, and that is the reason successful candidates can be predicted from brief observations. This supports (E) because [looking] *the part* is the same as *visual stereotypes*. Watch out for trap answer (C), which is a reversal. The correct answer is (E).

DRILL 19 (Spotting Critical Reasoning Question Types) (Page 424)

1. **Strengthen question.**
    Look for the conclusion and premise in the question. The correct answer will strengthen a premise that supports the conclusion.

2. **Inference question.**
    Look for information in the passage that pertains to the subject of the question.

3. **Evaluate question.**
    Look for assumptions in the passage.

4. **Assumption question.**
    To find the correct answer, look for the gap in the argument.

5. **Flaw question.**
    The passage should contain information that can be disputed. Find that information and anything that contradicts it.

6. **Weaken question.**
    Look for the conclusion and premise in the argument. The correct answer will weaken a premise that supports the conclusion.

7. **Identify the reasoning question.**
    The passage will provide a response to an assertion and the correct answer will reveal how the response was made.

8. **Resolve/Explain question.**
    Look for two incongruent facts in the passage and find a way to explain why both facts could be simultaneously true.

DRILL 20 (Page 424)

1. **B** This is an analogy argument. The men's line is being introduced in the hope that men will like the new soft fabrics as much as women did the year before. The key word in the passage that might have alerted you to the analogy was the word *same*. The assumption on which this argument depends is that men and women will like the same new fabric. Choices (A), (C), (D), and (E) are all outside the scope of the argument. The correct answer is (B).

2. **B** Because the report identifies two possible causes of the tire wear, the best answer must identify a study that focuses on one of these possible causes. Studies focusing on car models other than the Impressivo, (A) and (D), worker satisfaction, (C), or driver error, (E), are all irrelevant to this study. The study described in (B) removes one of the two possible causes. If the newly installed tires made by another manufacturer also turn out to wear abnormally, then the authors will have good reason to suspect that faulty alignment caused the initial problem. If the new tires wear normally, then they will know that the original tires were faulty. The correct answer is (B).

3. **A** In this passage, the author is questioning an analogical argument. To understand the kinetic movement of dinosaurs, says the argument, you should study the kinetic movement of birds, which are a lot like dinosaurs. The author is trying to weaken this analogy by saying that dinosaurs and birds are actually not very similar. Your job is to weaken the author's attempt to demonstrate that the argument is flawed. How do you do that? By showing that dinosaurs and birds *are* in fact alike. Choice (B), if anything, actually strengthens the author's criticism of the analogy. Choices (C) and (D) are outside the scope of the argument. Choice (E) seems to strengthen the author's criticism of the analogy. It is also out of scope since the fact that some bird experts don't study dinosaurs doesn't mean that dinosaur experts shouldn't study birds. Choice (A) shows how birds and dinosaurs are alike. The correct answer is (A).

4. **B** The words *strongest challenge* in the question mean that you are trying to weaken the argument. Choice (A), if anything, appears to support the argument rather than weaken it, so you can eliminate it. Choices (C) and (D) do seem negative toward the argument, but both are outside the scope, as is (E). For (B), if the insulation comes loose *after* the girders arrive on site, then making an effort to prevent its dislodgement in transit to the building site will not have any effect and will not necessarily reduce fatalities. The correct answer is (B).

5. **B** You might have been tempted by (A), which seems to weaken the argument by saying the quality control problem of the supplier is not as severe as experts had predicted. However, the initial predictions of experts are outside the scope of the argument, because they don't change the fact that this supplier will not be supplying any vaccines, regardless of how minor the problems might be. Similarly, what happened last year, (C), or what will happen in the next 10 years, (D), is also outside the scope of the argument; you want to know what will happen *this* year. Choice (E) seems to strengthen the argument since a longer flu season will presumably result in more people getting sick. For (B), if other suppliers have not been affected by quality control problems, then the overall shortage may be less severe. The correct answer is (B).

6. **D** The manager was apparently fired because of his team's end-of-season statistics. If this made you wonder if the statistics were actually representative, your thinking was right on the money. To support the manager's claim, you have to show that the team's fifth-place finish was actually better than it looked. Choices (A), (B), and (C), while generally positive about the team (and by extension, perhaps, its manager), are outside the scope of the argument. Choice (E) actually puts the team's performance in a more negative light. On the other hand, (D) puts the team's fifth-place finish in a very positive perspective: if the division was made up of 80 teams, finishing in fifth place is actually extremely good. The correct answer is (D).

7. **A** People tend to try to explain shark attacks by thinking about the *shark's* behavior. But (A) points out that it takes two to tango. A shark attack requires one shark and one human to be attacked. One reason there might be fewer shark attacks on humans in cold water is that there are fewer humans swimming in cold water in the first place. If you were looking at (B) and saying, "Hmm, if a shark's olfactory powers were enhanced by cold water, then presumably he'd be better at attacking," or if you were thinking that if his olfactory powers were enhanced, he would know enough *not* to attack a human, then either way, you were having to think way too hard for this to be inside the scope. Choice (C) is outside the scope, too, since it is dealing with only one ocean and does not address temperature at all. Choice (D) provides extraneous information, and (E) does not help to explain the apparent paradox. The correct answer is (A).

8. **B** This is a strengthen problem, as evidenced by the question asking which answer choice *would most strengthen the argument*. This argument uses a planning pattern, as evidenced by the presence of the plan of *MovieNow!'s board of directors*. The assumption of a planning reasoning pattern is that there are no problems with the plan. In this case, the assumption is that there are no problems with the plan to pursue *subscribers who are parents of children under the age of 12*. Because this is a strengthen question, the correct answer will provide information that makes the plan stronger, or removes a potential objection to the plan. Evaluate the answer choices individually. Choice (A) introduces *large advertising companies* and states that *the board monitors the demographic targets* of those companies to help *choose target audiences for their streaming service*. This choice is out of scope because it is not possible to know that the demographic targets of large advertising companies are the same demographics that the board of MoviesNow! is interested in pursuing. Eliminate (A).

9. **E** To evaluate the significance of the author's claims, you need to recognize what kind of argument it is: an analogy. The author is saying that the situation in Country Y is analogous to that of Country Z. To weaken an analogy, you merely have to question whether the two situations were really analogous. Choices (A) and (B) are outside the scope of the argument. Choice (C) is incorrect because the author's argument stated that more-stringent laws were needed, making it irrelevant whether Country Y had any laws about this in the first place. Choice (D) goes off on an interesting tangent by asking if there were business ties between the two countries, but it does not weaken the argument's analogy. Only (E) questions whether the two situations are in fact analogous. The correct answer is (E).

10. **E** During a period of robust home sales, one would expect the prices of all homes to increase; that would be the natural effect of the law of supply and demand. The question states, however, that the real price of resale homes during this period actually decreased. Thus, it is reasonable to assume that the demand for resale homes decreased. How can you resolve this apparent contradiction? If all the increased demand for homes was in the new home market, then it would be possible that the overall increase in home sales would not result in an increase in resale home prices and may, in fact, even accompany a drop in those prices. The correct answer is (E).

11. **B** The statement draws a conclusion about *people who train their dogs* based on statistics relating only to people who take their dogs to formal obedience training classes. In order for the statement to be correct, then, these statistics must be valid for all people who train their dogs, not only those who train them in formal classes. Choice (B) plugs this hole in the argument, thus making the conclusion necessarily true. The correct answer is (B).

12. **C** To answer this parallel-the-reasoning question, you have to break down the original argument, and then find an answer choice that mimics it exactly. In this case, the argument says a bullet train travels in excess of 150 miles per hour (if A, then B). Therefore, if a train travels less than 150 miles per hour, then it is not a bullet train (if not B, then not A). Now all you have to do is find an answer choice that mimics that reasoning exactly. Choice (A), broken down, reads, "if A, then B...so if B, then not A." This isn't it. Eliminate it. Choice (B) breaks down to "if A, then B...therefore C will also cause B." That's not it either. Choice (C) breaks down to "if A, then B...therefore if not B, then not A." Keep (C).

Choice (D) might seem tempting because it also has to do with a fast means of transportation, but what counts here is the reasoning: "if A, then B...if not A, then not B." This is close, but no cigar. Choice (E) is also appealing; you may even think it mimics the argument exactly. But there's a trick. The first half of the sentence reads, *Fluoride generally prevents cavities* (if A, then B). Note that the B part is about the prevention—not the presence—of cavities. So the second half, *If there are no cavities, there was no fluoride*, actually breaks down to "if B, then not A." The correct answer is (C).

ANSWERS TO CHALLENGE QUESTIONS

Page 168—Challenge Question #1

E   This is a Value Data Sufficiency question, so begin by determining what is known and what is needed to answer the question. What is known is that Angela is twice as old as the sum of Bill's and Charlie's ages. This information can be expressed algebraically: let a be Angela's age, b be Bill's age, and c be Charlie's age. Thus, $a = 2(b + c)$. To solve this equation, what is needed are values for both a and b or two more distinct equations with all three variables.

Evaluate Statement (1). In four years, each of the people will have aged, so make sure to include this information in an algebraic equation: $(a + 4) + (b + 4) + (c + 4) = 108$. This equation simplifies into $a + b + c = 96$. This statement gives another equation with all 3 variables. However, there are still 3 variables and only 2 equations. This statement is therefore insufficient. Write down BCE.

Evaluate Statement (2). Remember that an average is calculated by adding the values and dividing by the number of values. Also, "five years ago" will affect each person's age, so make sure this information is included in the algebraic expression: $\frac{(a - 5) + (b - 5) + (c - 5)}{3} = 27$, which simplifies to $a + b + c - 15 = 81$ or $a + b + c = 96$. This statement gives an equation with all 3 variables. But, there are still 3 variables and only 2 equations. This statement is therefore insufficient. Eliminate (B).

Finally, evaluate the two statements combined. The rules for simultaneous equations require that each of the three equations be distinct. Since the equation for Statement (1) is identical to that of Statement (2), the combination of the two statements still gives only 2 equations and 3 variables. The two statements together are therefore insufficient. The correct answer is (E).

Page 172—Challenge Question #2

A   This is a Yes/No Data Sufficiency question, so be prepared to Plug In more than once. Because both sides of the inequality involve cube roots, take the cube of both sides to remove the cube roots and simplify even further. Therefore, the inequality is $8a < a + b$. Subtract a from both sides to find that $7a < b$. Now that the inequality has been simplified as far as possible, evaluate the statements individually. For Statement (1), if it is true that $7a < b$, then the inequality in the question stem is always true, and the answer to the question is "Yes." Write down AD.

For Statement (2), begin by manipulating the statement to produce $6a < b$. Plug in values for a and b that satisfy that statement. If $a = 1$ and $b = 7$, then the statement is satisfied because $6 < 7$. In this case, the inequality from the question stem, $7a < b$, is not true because $7 = 7$, so the answer is "No." Plug In again to see if there is a way to produce a "Yes" answer to the question. If $a = 1$ and $b = 8$, then the statement is satisfied, and the inequality in the question stem is now true because $7 < 8$. Now the answer to the question is "Yes." Because the statement produces two different answers to the question, the statement is insufficient. Eliminate (D). The correct answer is (A).

Page 197—Challenge Question #3

C   Begin by considering the possible values of x and y. Prime numbers with squares less than 60 are 2, 3, 5, and 7, for squares of 4, 9, 25, and 49, respectively. Therefore, possible sums of distinct pairs of squares are $4 + 9 = 13$, $4 + 25 = 29$, $4 + 49 = 53$, $9 + 25 = 34$, and $9 + 49 = 58$. Thus, x can be 13, 29, 34, 53, or 58. For y, multiples of 17 less than 60 are 17, 34, and 51. Now consider the answer choices. Choice (A) is −19, so look for combinations of answer choices that could result in −19. The only possible values that are close are $13 - 34 = -21$, $29 - 51 = -22$, and $34 - 51 = -17$. None of these values match −19, so eliminate (A). Choice (B) is −7, so consider whether that value might be used. $13 - 17 = -4$ and $29 - 34 = -5$, neither of which matches −7, so eliminate (B). Choice (C) is 0, and $34 - 34 = 0$. The correct answer is (C).

Page 231—Challenge Question #4

D   The question asks for the factor by which the value of a gem with a rating of p would have to be multiplied to equal the value of a gem with a rating of $p - r$. According to the rating system described by the question stem, the value of a gem with a rating of $q - 1$ is 5 times greater, and the value of a gem with a rating of $q - 4$ is 625 times greater, than the value of a gem with a rating of q. The first example provides the information that subtracting 1 from the rating corresponds to a 5-fold increase in value. The second example provides the value increase by a factor of 625, which can be rewritten as 5^4. Therefore, the pattern in the question is that for each value subtracted from a rating of q, the value is 5^x, where x is the value subtracted from the rating of q. Following the pattern suggested by the question stem, the value of a gem with a $q - 2$ rating is greater than the value of a gem with a q rating by a factor of 25, or 5^2. Similarly, the value of a gem with a $q - 3$ rating is greater than the value of a gem with a q rating by a factor of 125, or 5^3. Apply this pattern to gems rated $p - r$ and p. The easiest way to do this is to Plug In values for p and r. Let $p = 5$ and $r = 2$. In this case, the gems to be compared are rated $5 - 2$ and 5. Based on the pattern above, the value of the gem rated $5 - 2$ is greater than the value of the gem rated 5 by a factor of 25. Substitute $p = 5$ and $r = 2$ into the answer choices, looking for the answer that equals 25. Choice (A) is $5^5 - 2^5$, a number much greater than 25. Eliminate (A). Choice (B) is $2^5 = 32$. Eliminate (B). Choice (C) is $(5 - 2)^5 = 243$. Eliminate (C). Choice (D) is 5^2, or 25. Keep (D). Choice (E) is $5(2) = 10$. Eliminate (E). The correct answer is (D).

Page 272—Challenge Question #5

C   If James can complete the job in 6 hours, then James's rate is $\frac{1}{6}$ of a job per hour. If Sarah can complete the job in 4.5 hours, then Sarah's rate is $\frac{1}{4.5}$ or $\frac{2}{9}$ of a job per hour. Together, James and Sarah work at a rate of $\frac{1}{6}+\frac{2}{9}$ or $\frac{3}{18}+\frac{4}{18}=\frac{7}{18}$ of a job per hour.

During the hour that James and Sarah work together, they complete $\frac{7}{18}$ of the job, leaving $\frac{11}{18}$ of the job unfinished. James will complete some of the unfinished work at a rate of $\frac{1}{6}$ per hour, and Sarah will finish the rest at a rate of $\frac{2}{9}$ per hour, such that Sarah works by herself half as long as James does. Translate this information into an algebraic equation. If t represents the number of hours during which James works alone, then $t\times\frac{1}{6}+\frac{t}{2}\times\frac{2}{9}=\frac{11}{18}$. Multiply both sides of the equation by 18 and simplify to find that $3t+2t=11$. Simplify the equation further so that $5t=11$. Divide both sides of the equation by 5, so that $t=2.2$ hours, or 2 hours and 12 minutes. The correct answer is (C).

Page 276—Challenge Question #6

D   The question asks for the value of $333,333.\overline{3}\times\left(10^{-3}-10^{-5}\right)$. Rewrite the expression without the negative exponents, yielding $333,333.\overline{3}\times\left(\frac{1}{10^3}-\frac{1}{10^5}\right)$. Use the distributive property of multiplication to rewrite the expression, $\frac{333,333.\overline{3}}{10^3}-\frac{333,333.\overline{3}}{10^5}$. Eliminate the fractions by shifting the decimal places in the numerators the appropriate number of places to the left, resulting in a subtraction problem, $333.\overline{3}-3.\overline{3}=330$. The correct answer is (D).

Page 312—Challenge Question #7

A   First, plug in the values from the question stem. Plug 2 in for y and 144 in for z to get that $\frac{144}{x^2}$ is

an integer, while $\frac{144}{x^3}$ is not, which means that x^2 divides evenly into 144, but x^3 does not. To easily

determine if a number divides evenly into another, find the prime factors. In this case, the prime fac-

torization of 144 is $144 = 2^4 \times 3^2$. Now Plug In the Answers for the value of x and determine if $\frac{144}{x^2}$

is an integer, while $\frac{144}{x^3}$ is not. Choice (A) is 2 and 2^2 and 2^3 are factors of 144. Because the question

asks which answer choice is NOT a factor of 144, keep (A). Because the answer choices were used

to determine the factors and there can be only one answer choice that works, there is no need to test

other answer choices. In fact, if the remaining answer choices are all taken down to their prime fac-

tors and plugged in for x, they will all abide by the rules in the problem that $\frac{144}{x^2}$ is an integer, while

$\frac{144}{x^3}$ is not. The correct answer is (A).

Page 320—Challenge Question #8

D   The answer choices represent the information directly asked for by the question, so Plug In the An-

swers. Begin with (C). If the new after-tax price of a car is $13,500, then the new pretax price

is $\frac{\$13,500}{1.08} = \$12,500$, the old pretax price is $12,500 − $2,500 = $10,000, and the old after-tax

price is $10,000 × 1.08 = $10,800. In this case, the cost of 18 cars at the old after-tax price is 18 ×

$10,800 = $194,400, and the cost of 15 cars at the new after-tax price is 15 × $13,500 = $202,500.

Since these costs should be equal, eliminate (C).

When the new after-tax price of a car was $13,500, the cost of 15 cars at the new after-tax price was

too great, and the cost of 18 cars at the old after-tax price was less than necessary. Two factors con-

tributed to the unwanted gap between these values. First, fewer cars were purchased at the new price

than at the old price. Nothing can be done about this, since the quantities purchased are built into

the question. Second, the difference between the new pretax price and the old pretax price is $2,500.

This difference was too great relative to a new after-tax price of $13,500. To lessen the impact of the

$2,500 pretax price difference, therefore, increase the new after-tax price of a car. Try (D).

If the new after-tax price of a car is $16,200, then the new pretax price is $\frac{\$16,200}{1.08} = \$15,000$,

the old pretax price is $15,000 − $2,500 = $12,500, and the old after-tax price is $12,500 × 1.08 =

$13,500. In this case, the cost of 18 cars at the old after-tax price is 18 × $13,500 = $243,000, and

the cost of 15 cars at the new after-tax price is 15 × $16,200 = $243,000. Since these costs are equal,

the correct answer is (D).

Page 412—Challenge Question #9

A   The task of the question is to weaken the objection, which means to provide a reason that the proposed tax plan might work despite the objection. The objection is that *such tax savings tend to be kept as profit rather than reinvested.* This objection is significant, because if the savings are not reinvested, there will be no *job creation or corporate investment* as a result of the savings. Thus, the correct answer needs to change something about what happens to the tax savings. Choice (A) indicates that the savings are required to be reinvested, which addresses the objection. Keep (A). Choice (B) is out of scope, as it discusses *personal* investments, so eliminate (B). Choice (C) is reversal—it strengthens the objection, so eliminate (C). Choice (D) is out of scope. It provides a mechanism by which the lower tax rate may not significantly hurt overall government revenue, which is irrelevant to whether the tax plan will produce *job creation or corporate investment,* so eliminate (D). Choice (E) is out of scope, as it discusses reasons for economic issues that cannot be directly tied to a reason that tax savings would be used to create jobs, so eliminate (E). The correct answer is (A).

Page 416—Challenge Question #10

C   Treat the passage as a series of facts and consider whether each answer choice can be proven. Choice (A) is out of scope. Proximity to the strongest warm ocean currents may not mean that any warm ocean currents impact that portion of coastline directly. Eliminate (A). Choice (B) is extreme language, as the other factors of glacial ablation may lead to *high rates* of ablation without warm ocean currents, so eliminate (B). Choice (C) matches the information in the passage. If a rise in ocean temperatures leads to a rise in warm ocean currents along glacial coasts, those currents will cause a rise in submarine melt rates. Thus, submarine melt rates are higher in the presence of warm ocean currents than they are in the absence of warm ocean currents. Keep (C). Choice (D) is extreme. While global climatic shifts may increase the occurrence of submarine melt rates, submarine melt may still have been an important factor in prior periods, so eliminate (D). Choice (E) is extreme language. Lower ocean temperatures may lead to a reduction in submarine melt rates, but that doesn't prove that snow accumulation will be a more significant factor. Eliminate (E). The correct answer is (C).

Page 430—Challenge Question #11

B   This is a weaken question, so find the conclusion, premise, and any assumptions in the argument. The conclusion of the argument is that *merely sharing the same physical space with another dog is sufficient to maintain proper socialization* in dogs as they grow older. The premise for the conclusion comes from the last sentence, which cites evidence *from a study demonstrating that the more often a dog shares a physical space with another dog, the better its socialization*. A study shows that the more often a dog shares a physical space, the better its socialization is, so sharing a physical space is sufficient for maintaining proper socialization. This argument exhibits a causal reasoning pattern, in effect stating that shared physical space causes socialization in dogs. The standard assumption for causality is that there is no other cause, and it is not a coincidence. To weaken an argument based on the causality pattern, the correct answer will usually either provide an alternate cause or present a situation in which the supposed cause (shared physical space) is present, but the supposed effect (socialization) did not occur. It is also possible that the answer may indicate that the supposed cause and effect have been reversed. Here, that would mean that the answer could indicate that shared physical space is a result of socialization rather than socialization being the result of shared physical space. Evaluate the answer choices one at a time.

Choice (A) is out of scope because challenging a dog's *physical and mental capacities* and avoiding *the deterioration of these capacities* is not the focus of the argument. Eliminate (A). Choice (B) indicates that the causality may have been reversed. In effect, well-socialized dogs often share physical space with other dogs, while poorly socialized dogs (for example, dogs that are aggressive toward other dogs) do not. Keep (B). Choice (C) is out of scope because dogs that are capable of both play and sharing space are not the focus of the passage. Eliminate (C). Choice (D) is out of scope. A study that analyzes other studies is just as valid as a study that collects its own data. Eliminate (D). Choice (E) casts doubt on the validity of the metrics used for measuring socialization, but this is out of scope. Eliminate (E). The correct answer is (B).

Part VI
Diagnostic Test 2

Chapter 20
Diagnostic Test 2

TAKING THE SECOND DIAGNOSTIC

The purpose of the second diagnostic is to gauge how far you've come!

To maximize the effectiveness of this second diagnostic, don't rush to take it. If there are a couple of topics you are still uneasy with, take the time to review them, practice them, and turn them into strengths. Make sure you've overturned every stone this book has to offer before taking this test. Why? Because using this test as a measure of progress is effective only once. If your brain is giving you any sense that you may want to work through another section again before starting this section, listen to that instinct.

HOW TO SCORE THE SECOND DIAGNOSTIC

At the end of the diagnostic, we provide both a diagnostic answer key and explanations for each question. Keep track of the number of questions you get correct and the content areas of the questions that you missed. The total number of questions you get correct is considered your "score." While this is not an accurate representation of an actual GMAT score, it is a way for you to monitor progress and compare how you perform on this diagnostic with how well you performed on the first diagnostic.

Once done, compare the content areas that you answer questions incorrectly in the second diagnostic to the content areas of incorrect questions on the first diagnostic. How have you improved? Are there areas you are still struggling with?

WHAT TO DO AFTER THE SECOND DIAGNOSTIC?

What happens if the results of this second diagnostic reveal that you are still struggling in some of the same areas you struggled with on the first? If you've read through every page on this topic and answered every practice question in this book about it, then don't fear. You are not out of options. There are many resources from The Princeton Review available to you to continue pushing your studies forward. You can check out one of our other titles that contain even more practice questions. You can contact your local office and inquire about picking up a few hours of private tutoring. You can email our editorial support team to ask specific questions about what you did wrong on any given question and get another explanation for how to approach a problem.

We are here to help achieve the goal we outlined in the letter at the beginning of this book: to help you achieve the GMAT score of your dreams. Don't be afraid to reach out to us to lament your struggles and celebrate your successes. We will gladly be one of your biggest fans.

Clear your calendar and get ready for the second diagnostic. Best of luck!

Arithmetic

1. If k is a positive, two-digit integer, what is the value of k?

   (1) The remainder when k is divided by 9 is 8
   (2) The remainder when k is divided by 8 is 7

   (A) Statement (1) ALONE is sufficient, but statement (2) alone is not sufficient.
   (B) Statement (2) ALONE is sufficient, but statement (1) alone is not sufficient.
   (C) BOTH statements TOGETHER are sufficient, but NEITHER statement ALONE is sufficient.
   (D) EACH statement ALONE is sufficient.
   (E) Statements (1) and (2) TOGETHER are not sufficient.

2. If the size of a rug is 25,000 square millimeters, what is the size of the rug in square centimeters? (1 millimeter = 0.1 centimeter)

   (A) 0.25
   (B) 2.5
   (C) 25
   (D) 250
   (E) 2,500

3. Set $P = \{1, 3, 4, 7, 9\}$

   If d is a random two-digit integer formed by any two distinct members chosen from set P, what is the probability that d is prime?

   (A) $\dfrac{7}{20}$

   (B) $\dfrac{2}{5}$

   (C) $\dfrac{1}{2}$

   (D) $\dfrac{3}{5}$

   (E) $\dfrac{13}{20}$

4. During a summer Chemistry course, Phyllis earned 1 hour of course credit for every 3 labs she completed and 0.25 hours of course credit for every hour of class she attended. The course lasted 8 weeks, offering 2 three-hour classes per week. If Phyllis went to all classes and completed 9 labs, how much course credit did she earn?

   (A) 3.5
   (B) 5
   (C) 9.5
   (D) 15
   (E) 17

GO ON TO THE NEXT PAGE.

5. If $a + b$ is the average (arithmetic mean) of c and d, what is the average of a, b, c, and d ?

   (1) $a + b = 2$
   (2) $c + d = 4$

   (A) Statement (1) ALONE is sufficient, but statement (2) alone is not sufficient.
   (B) Statement (2) ALONE is sufficient, but statement (1) alone is not sufficient.
   (C) BOTH statements TOGETHER are sufficient, but NEITHER statement ALONE is sufficient.
   (D) EACH statement ALONE is sufficient.
   (E) Statements (1) and (2) TOGETHER are not sufficient.

6. The yield last week from a garden was 15 apples and 20% more pears than apples. How many total pears and apples did the garden yield last week?

   (A) 3
   (B) 6
   (C) 15
   (D) 18
   (E) 33

7. If x is an even integer, then what is the value of x ?

   (1) $x + 5$ is prime
   (2) $x - 16$ is prime

   (A) Statement (1) ALONE is sufficient, but statement (2) alone is not sufficient.
   (B) Statement (2) ALONE is sufficient, but statement (1) alone is not sufficient.
   (C) BOTH statements TOGETHER are sufficient, but NEITHER statement ALONE is sufficient.
   (D) EACH statement ALONE is sufficient.
   (E) Statements (1) and (2) TOGETHER are not sufficient.

8. In a gumball machine, the probability of not getting a red gumball is 60%. The probability of not getting a lettered gumball is 45%. If none of the red gumballs are lettered, what is the probability of getting a red gumball or a lettered gumball?

   (A) 18%
   (B) 33%
   (C) 51%
   (D) 73%
   (E) 95%

GO ON TO THE NEXT PAGE.

9. The combination of a certain lock is comprised of 5 alpha-numeric characters. The alphabetic characters can be any of the letters A through H of the English alphabet and the numeric characters can be any number 0 through 9. The first character of the combination is a letter, the last two characters are numbers, and the letters and numbers can be used more than once. If a computer can code one possible combination per second, how many hours will it take to code every possible combination?

    (A)   72
    (B)   80
    (C)   104
    (D)   4,320
    (E)   259,200

10. $a, b, c,$ and d are numbers on the number line shown. If the distance between each variable is $n,$ then what is the value of $a + d$?

    (1) $a + 2n = 6$
    (2) $b = 2$

    (A)   Statement (1) ALONE is sufficient, but statement (2) alone is not sufficient.
    (B)   Statement (2) ALONE is sufficient, but statement (1) alone is not sufficient.
    (C)   BOTH statements TOGETHER are sufficient, but NEITHER statement ALONE is sufficient.
    (D)   EACH statement ALONE is sufficient.
    (E)   Statements (1) and (2) TOGETHER are not sufficient.

GO ON TO THE NEXT PAGE.

Algebra

1. If x is an integer, is $x^6 = 64$?

   (1) $x^{-5} = \dfrac{1}{32}$

   (2) x is prime

   (A) Statement (1) ALONE is sufficient, but statement (2) alone is not sufficient.
   (B) Statement (2) ALONE is sufficient, but statement (1) alone is not sufficient.
   (C) BOTH statements TOGETHER are sufficient, but NEITHER statement ALONE is sufficient.
   (D) EACH statement ALONE is sufficient.
   (E) Statements (1) and (2) TOGETHER are not sufficient.

2. What is the value of $a + b + c$?

   (1) $4a - 3b + 5c = 65$
   (2) $-2a - 9b - c = 23$

   (A) Statement (1) ALONE is sufficient, but statement (2) alone is not sufficient.
   (B) Statement (2) ALONE is sufficient, but statement (1) alone is not sufficient.
   (C) BOTH statements TOGETHER are sufficient, but NEITHER statement ALONE is sufficient.
   (D) EACH statement ALONE is sufficient.
   (E) Statements (1) and (2) TOGETHER are not sufficient.

3. What is the value of $\dfrac{g-1}{h+1}$?

   (1) $7g - 6h = 0$
   (2) $h = 42$

   (A) Statement (1) ALONE is sufficient, but statement (2) alone is not sufficient.
   (B) Statement (2) ALONE is sufficient, but statement (1) alone is not sufficient.
   (C) BOTH statements TOGETHER are sufficient, but NEITHER statement ALONE is sufficient.
   (D) EACH statement ALONE is sufficient.
   (E) Statements (1) and (2) TOGETHER are not sufficient.

4. In 3 years, Calvin will be 3 times as old as Jill. In 6 years, Jill will be half as old as Tom. If Calvin is currently c years old, then, in terms of c, how old is Tom?

   (A) $\dfrac{2c}{3}$

   (B) $\dfrac{2c}{3} + 2$

   (C) $\dfrac{c+3}{3} + 6$

   (D) $\dfrac{3c+6}{2}$

   (E) $\dfrac{3c}{2} + 2$

GO ON TO THE NEXT PAGE.

5. If $6^{2x+2} = 36^{2x-2}$, then what is the value of x ?

(A) $\dfrac{1}{2}$

(B) 2

(C) $\dfrac{3}{2}$

(D) 3

(E) 4

6. r, s, and t are negative consecutive odd digits, and $r < s < t$. All of the following could be the units digit of s^5 EXCEPT

(A) 1
(B) 3
(C) 5
(D) 7
(E) 9

7. Is m a positive integer?

(1) $-m^3 \leq -1$
(2) $-m^2 \geq -1$

(A) Statement (1) ALONE is sufficient, but statement (2) alone is not sufficient.
(B) Statement (2) ALONE is sufficient, but statement (1) alone is not sufficient.
(C) BOTH statements TOGETHER are sufficient, but NEITHER statement ALONE is sufficient.
(D) EACH statement ALONE is sufficient.
(E) Statements (1) and (2) TOGETHER are not sufficient.

8. If $f(x) = 3x + w$ and $g(x) = 4x - w$, then what is the value of $g(f(5)) - f(g(5))$?

(A) $x + 5w$
(B) $2x - w$
(C) $5w$
(D) $-5w$
(E) $2x + 5w$

GO ON TO THE NEXT PAGE.

Reading Comprehension

Questions 1–3 are based on the following passage:

Creative thinking, adaptability, and collaboration are part of human nature. Unfortunately, however, the hierarchical structures at workplaces
Line unwittingly discourage these traits. Paradoxically,
(5) the preeminent organizational strategy designed to maximize efficient productivity may actually be detrimental. The long-term success of a corporation requires flexibility and new ideas to respond to ever-evolving political, social, and
(10) economic conditions.

Becoming a "flat organization" will best ensure a company's survival. Such enterprises abolish middle management structures and instead assign most workers to the same level, with only
(15) a few superiors. In doing so, corporations must reconsider their view of employees: rather than workers reporting to a manager responsible for making decisions, non-hierarchical committees share in a decentralized decision-making process.
(20) Collaboration is encouraged and innovation is rewarded; new ideas can be implemented more quickly without requiring the traditional levels of ascension through middle management. Limiting specialization in job titles fosters flexibility as
(25) workers can take on a variety of roles depending on individual project needs, which leads to an increase in employee learning. Simply put, leaders in flat organizations have the responsibility to construct organizations in which members
(30) maximize their abilities and directly contribute to the company's success.

1. Which of the following could best serve as an example of how a company might become a flat organization, as such organizations are described in the passage?

   (A) Outsourcing middle management to a separate company
   (B) Abolishing job titles and rotating responsibility for leading meetings
   (C) Denoting specific guidelines for approval of new ideas
   (D) Hiring a specialist for each stage of a project's completion
   (E) Assigning each employee another employee to oversee

2. The primary purpose of the passage is to

   (A) compare various corporate organizational strategies
   (B) explain and endorse an alternative business structure
   (C) propose a traditional corporate approach
   (D) evaluate and then criticize a new method of conducting business
   (E) acknowledge the similarities between two management theories

3. Which of the following can be inferred from the passage about hierarchical workplaces?

   (A) They may result in a delayed approval process for new ideas.
   (B) They often contain more middle managers than upper managers.
   (C) They maximize efficiency by promoting specialization.
   (D) They are more beneficial for larger companies than for smaller companies.
   (E) They do not allow employees to have flexible roles.

GO ON TO THE NEXT PAGE.

Questions 4–6 are based on the following passage:

Eighteenth-century economist Adam Smith
introduced the "invisible hand" as a metaphor for
the societal results of individuals' self-interested
Line actions. Subsequent theorists expanded Smith's
(5) idea to form the "general equilibrium theory,"
in which invisible market forces guided the
interaction of supply and demand toward a natural
balance as individuals act in their own interest and
firms pursue the goal of maximizing profit.

(10)   Despite the ubiquity of this model in both
popular and scholarly thinking, there is no evidence
for its truth. Although academic economists have
demonstrated that an optimal equilibrium of
supply and demand exists, the guiding influence
(15) of Smith's invisible hand in moving markets
toward such a balance has not been shown. The
dubious belief that markets actively move toward
an equilibrium has been used by proponents of
deregulation, who insist that removing government
(20) interventions promotes economic strength, and
the presumption of its accuracy has prevented
some leaders and economists from identifying
critical signs of impending crises. The general
equilibrium theory presents an optimistic view
(25) of self-correction that has not been borne out by
actual economic conditions—a defect that calls
into question Smith's antecedent hypotheses.

4. The author of the passage implies which of the
following regarding the originators of the general
equilibrium theory?

(A) There is ample evidence to support the
basis of the theory.
(B) They developed the theory sometime in the
eighteenth century.
(C) Their theories were immediately popular
among the general public.
(D) They were aware of Smith's beliefs about
the relationship between individual actions
and the economy.
(E) Some of them worked closely with Smith
during the time in which he formulated
his theory.

5. The author of the passage is primarily concerned
with

(A) exploring the argument for
economic regulation
(B) questioning the foundation of the general
equilibrium theory
(C) defending Smith's beliefs with
supporting evidence
(D) asserting that market forces naturally
maintain balance
(E) comparing several economic theories

6. It can be inferred from the passage that
defenders of the general equilibrium theory
would most likely regard economic regulations as

(A) imperative
(B) catastrophic
(C) salutary
(D) insufficient
(E) unnecessary

GO ON TO THE NEXT PAGE.

Reading Comprehension

Questions 7–10 are based on the following passage:

A critical aspect of product advertising is the choice between positive and negative approaches. Positive advertisements tout the benefits of a
(Line)
(5) product to convince consumers that they want or need the item for sale. Negative advertisements, by contrast, involve attacks on competing companies or products to dissuade their audience from considering those options.

An advantage of positive advertising is its
(10) ability to evoke emotions such as happiness, nostalgia, and optimism in its audience, creating a psychological association between the brand and feelings of warmth. Despite this, some consumers may view such campaigns as insincere
(15) or predatory due to their reliance on manipulating emotions rather than presenting factual information. The resulting distrust can then lead to skepticism regarding appeals that are based more on logic, as consumers assume they are
(20) still being manipulated for the goal of producing positive feelings. By contrast, negative advertising can appear more truthful: the company is not painting a rosy sheen over its own products but rather warning consumers of a competitor's flaw.
(25) Consumers may thus more readily believe negative information compared to arguments made in favor of a brand or product, and the former often makes a stronger mental impression.

Psychological research explains why such
(30) advertising can be more memorable: negativity bias. People tend to give more attention to negative, rather than positive, events, and make more decisions based on negative information. Furthermore, negative advertising has other
(35) applications aside from attacking competitors: many firms have found success in advertising by highlighting a problem that the promoted product can solve or by suggesting that it could prevent the consumer from losing something—rather than
(40) positive advertising, which might focus on what the audience has to gain.

In spite of these benefits, negativity in advertising is not always more effective than the alternative. For instance, featuring a competitor
(45) in an advertisement can inadvertently provide a boost to the competing brand, even if the message is ultimately defamatory. Furthermore, negative advertising poses a risk that the audience will be alienated from both the competitor and the
(50) company criticizing it. Consumers who choose a brand simply because the alternative is presented as flawed are not as loyal as those for whom merit guides the decision. A final concern is that consumers may view attacks on competitors as
(55) petty and untoward.

7. The primary purpose of the passage is to

(A) argue the inferiority of one advertising approach to another
(B) explore the advantages of different forms of advertising on different audiences
(C) consider the benefits and risks of two marketing strategies
(D) explain what makes a particular advertising strategy effective
(E) illustrate the need for companies to advertise their products

8. All of the following are mentioned as potential risks in advertising EXCEPT

(A) Consumers may lose interest in petty feuds between rival companies.
(B) Consumers may reject both the advertiser and a named competitor.
(C) Consumers may not believe claims made in advertising.
(D) A company could lose its audience's trust.
(E) A company could give attention to a competitor's products.

GO ON TO THE NEXT PAGE.

9. Which of the following could best serve as an example of negative advertising as it is described in the passage?

   (A) A packaging company uses a bittersweet story about an animal shelter to provoke an emotional response.

   (B) A restaurant advertises that its fruits and vegetables do not contain pesticides.

   (C) A beauty company claims its competitor's product has long-term health implications.

   (D) An environmental group criticizes the airline industry for its lack of sustainability.

   (E) A construction firm provides data and customer reviews to attract new clients.

10. Which of the following best describes the function of the highlighted sentence in the context of the passage as a whole?

    (A) It explains why a particular strategy is demonstrably superior to the approach that was previously discussed.

    (B) It summarizes the main differences between the two strategies described in the passage and introduces a new perspective.

    (C) It refutes the argument made in the first paragraph and provides the foundation for an assertion made in the following paragraph.

    (D) It describes an alternative to a potential problem mentioned earlier in the paragraph and previews the topic of the following paragraph.

    (E) It suggests that a method mentioned earlier in the paragraph is less effective than most experts believe.

GO ON TO THE NEXT PAGE.

Critical Reasoning

1. **Physiotherapist:** Although the patient's health would improve with daily outdoor walks, I have advised against it in the health plan. Since she is overweight, an increase in walking exercise would stress the already overstressed knee joints and would therefore put the patient at increased risk of injury.

   The physiotherapist's argument depends on which of the following?

   (A) The patient would use her knees during daily walks more than she currently does in other activities, such as bicycling.
   (B) The amount of exercise the patient currently undertakes does not put her at risk of joint injury.
   (C) Any patient is apt to be healthier with some exercise than with none at all.
   (D) The patient will not attempt to take daily walks despite the recommendation of the physiotherapist.
   (E) The physiotherapist should have the patient's best well-being as the foremost concern.

2. Cancer is a disease that involves the uncontrolled division of abnormal cells in the body. It stands to reason that the more cells an organism has, the more likely that organism would get cancer. However, the incidence of cancer in mice is many times that of humans, even though humans have over 1,000 times as many cells as mice do. Furthermore, elephants have even more cells than humans do, but the incidence of cancer in elephants is much lower.

   The statements above, if true, provide the most support for which of the following conclusions?

   (A) The incidence of cancer in an organism is due in part to factors other than body size.
   (B) A higher incidence of cancer correlates to an increase in body size.
   (C) The number of cells in any organism's body is not a predictor of likelihood of cancer.
   (D) Within a species, the number of abnormal cells in an organism can contribute to the uncontrolled division of those cells.
   (E) Abnormal cell division is the key to understanding and curing cancer in humans.

GO ON TO THE NEXT PAGE.

3. **Lawyer:** Although there is no eyewitness to the crime, it is evident that it must have been committed by Jones, Alyers, or Singh, all of whom were working in the electronics supply warehouse at the time the theft of the case of new tablets occurred. Electronic timestamps indicate that all three men were checking inventory at the time of the theft. Singh, the more senior employee with the higher pay grade, was supervising Jones and Alyers, who were processing the inventory. Singh has already testified that both Jones and Alyers were out of his sight numerous times throughout the shift. Therefore, Jones or Alyers had the most motive and opportunity to commit the theft.

The lawyer's argument assumes which of the following?

(A) All theft by employees of a company is done during the processing of inventory.
(B) Jones was out of Singh's sight more often than Alyers.
(C) Any testimony in court should be treated skeptically.
(D) The number of trucks with stolen items is growing.
(E) Tenure of employment and salary are directly related to the likelihood of committing theft.

4. **Social Media Officer:** Our biggest competitor allows many more advertisements per page view on its website than we currently allow on ours. Because revenue depends on page views, this means that we are not generating as much revenue for our content as we could. I propose that we increase the rotation of banner ads on the header of our homepage as well as include more thumbnail ads on the left margin of each subpage. Although I think this will generate more profits in the long run, be prepared for an initial loss, since _____.

Which of the following is the most logical completion of the passage?

(A) our biggest competitor has standing relationships with all the advertisers to whom we are likely to sell the new inventory
(B) the percent of ads devoted to our current advertisers will decrease, since the additional ads will be devoted to new advertisers
(C) creating the infrastructure to host more advertisements at different locations on our website requires a large up-front investment
(D) none of our current customers want to engage with more advertisements
(E) the rates we will charge for these new ads will be slightly lower to encourage new advertisers to utilize our site

GO ON TO THE NEXT PAGE.

5. **Store manager:** The majority of the profits in our hardware store during the last quarter depended on the sales of paint and household tools. Regrettably, the reliability of our deliveries has diminished due to nationwide strikes on the part of the truckers' union. Therefore, to keep our store profits at the same level, we will have to raise the prices of products in these categories until the nationwide truckers' strike is over.

Which of the following is an assumption on which the store manager's argument depends?

(A) It is only the actions of the truckers' union that caused the shortages of paint and household tools in the hardware store.

(B) Raising prices of paint and household tools until the end of the truckers' strike would not decrease patronage at the grocery store.

(C) Raising prices of paint and household tools is more important than diversifying the hardware store's inventory and offering a broader selection of products.

(D) Other stores have maintained their profits by raising the prices of their most popular goods to cope with the diminished supply due to the truckers' strike.

(E) If the prices of popular goods increase, there will be increased pressure nationwide to end the truckers' strike.

6. **Gardener:** Under normal weather conditions, any major brand of soil provides nutrients to your plants as well as Q-Earth does. However, when conditions are not ideal, Q-Earth's nutrient generation technology provides better support for your plants when natural nutrient formation is inhibited due to lack of sunlight, rain, or heat. So, if you want your garden to thrive under any condition, use Q-Earth.

Which of the following, if true, most strengthens the gardener's argument?

(A) Q-Earth provides about average support for plants that tend to grow quickly.

(B) Q-Earth is the preferred soil of interior gardeners—those who build gardens inside homes using plants that typically thrive outside.

(C) Q-Earth's share of the soil market has climbed steadily for the past 5 years.

(D) Q-Earth, like all branded soil, is more effective under normal weather conditions than conditions that are not ideal.

(E) Q-Earth is manufactured at only one location and distributed from there to all markets.

GO ON TO THE NEXT PAGE.

7. **Principal:** The average grade of honors students on the last test was 102 points. Most students in the school are honors students. Furthermore, the amount of extra credit per test earned by any student generally does not fluctuate from test to test. It is clear that most students in the school earn at least some extra credit.

The principal's conclusion is most vulnerable to which of the following criticisms?

(A) It takes for granted that classes with honors students are typical of the classes at the whole school with regard to the average amount of extra credit earned per test.

(B) It takes for granted that if a certain average amount of extra credit is earned on a test by each student in the school, then approximately the same amount of extra credit must be earned each test by each honors student.

(C) It confuses a claim from which the argument's conclusion about the test scores would necessarily follow with a claim that would follow from the argument's conclusion only with a high degree of probability.

(D) It overlooks the possibility that even if, on average, a certain amount of extra credit is earned by some types of students, many students may earn no

(E) It overlooks the possibility that even if most students in the class earn some extra credit each test, any one student may, on some tests, earn no extra credit.

8. The troubling discovery of cheating on the most common college entrance examination should not impact the reputation of the College Admissions Board. **The revelation confirms that the system works**, since the students themselves were the ones who reported their peers for unethical behavior.

The bolded phrase plays which of the following roles in the argument?

(A) It is a claim for which the argument gives evidence, and which is used to support the primary claim.

(B) It is the argument's primary position, and another conclusion provides support for it.

(C) It is an assumption that has no stated evidence in the argument.

(D) It is the main conclusion of the argument.

(E) It is a statement that contains both a premise and an assumption that support the conclusion.

GO ON TO THE NEXT PAGE.

9. **Chef:** I have noticed that savory recipes invented by culinary experts with over 20 years of experience in general yield better dishes that enjoy a much broader popularity than savory dishes based on recipes by chefs with less than 20 years of experience. Dishes derived from recipes by less experienced chefs are more prone to error and clashing flavors and, as a result, are not as popular. It seems that more experienced chefs are more precise and careful when designing their savory recipes than their counterparts, who may just be experimenting with trendy cuisines.

Which of the following, if true, most seriously weakens the chef's argument?

(A) The quality of recipes for savory dishes is generally much better than the quality of recipes for sweet dishes, such as cakes and sweetbreads.

(B) Savory recipes created by less experienced chefs are generally easier for the domestic cook to follow than savory recipes created by more experienced chefs.

(C) Chefs of all experience levels use the same range of spices when creating their savory recipes.

(D) The most popular recipes are first discovered by individuals in cooking magazines which often feature recipes by those with industry connections.

(E) In general, a culinary expert with over 20 years of experience is older than one with less than 20 years experience.

END OF DIAGNOSTIC TEST

Chapter 21
Diagnostic Test 2:
Answers and
Explanations

DIAGNOSTIC TEST 2: MULTIPLE CHOICE ANSWER KEY

STEP 1 » Check your answers and mark any correct answers with a ✔ in the appropriate column.

Arithmetic									
Q. #	Ans.	✔	Chap. #	Section	Q. #	Ans.	✔	Chap. #	Section
1	C		17	Patterns and Cycles	6	E		12	Percentages
2	D		12	Ratios	7	B		18	More Ways to Plug In
3	D		9	Remainders	8	E		15	Probability
4	D		13	Building Algebraic Expressions	9	A		15	Permutations and Combinations
5	D		12	Averages	10	C		18	Pieces of the Puzzle

Algebra									
1	A		18	Data Sufficiency and the Strange Power of Powers	5	D		17	Factorization
2	C		13	Using Substitution to Solve	6	A		17	Patterns and Cycles
3	C		13	Using Substitution to Solve	7	E		18	Plugging In on Yes/No Questions
4	B		14	Not Exactly Algebra: Basic Principles	8	C		15	Functions

STEP 2 » Add the total number of correct answers for each test section. Then, divide the number correct by the number of total questions to get your percent correct.

Test Section	# Correct	Total Questions	% Correct
Arithmetic		10	
Algebra		8	

STEP 3 » Compare performance to Diagnostic Test 1.

Test Section	Test 1 Results	Test 2 Results
Arithmetic		
Algebra		

DIAGNOSTIC TEST 2: MULTIPLE CHOICE ANSWER KEY

 **STEP 1 »** Check your answers and mark any correct answers with a ✔ in the appropriate column.

Reading Comprehension							
1	B		21	Retrieval	6	E	21	Inference
2	B		21	Primary Purpose	7	C	21	Primary Purpose
3	A		21	Inference	8	A	21	Retrieval
4	D		21	Inference	9	C	21	Retrieval
5	B		21	Primary Purpose	10	D	21	Specific Purpose

Reading Comprehension							
1	B	21	Retrieval	6	E	21	Inference
2	B	21	Primary Purpose	7	C	21	Primary Purpose
3	A	21	Inference	8	A	21	Retrieval
4	D	21	Inference	9	C	21	Retrieval
5	B	21	Primary Purpose	10	D	21	Specific Purpose

Critical Reasoning							
1	A	22	Assumption Question	6	B	22	Strengthen Questions
2	A	22	Strengthen Questions	7	D	22	Flaw Questions
3	E	22	Assumption Question	8	A	22	Quantify the Reasoning Questions
4	C	22	Inference Questions	9	D	22	Weaken Questions
5	B	22	Assumption Questions				

 **STEP 2 »** Add the total number of correct answers for each test section. Then, divide the number correct by the number of total questions to get your percent correct.

Test Section	# Correct	Total Questions	% Correct
Reading Comprehension		10	
Critical Reasoning		9	

STEP 3 » Compare performance to Diagnostic Test 1.

Test Section	Test 1 Results	Test 2 Results
Reading Comprehension		
Critical Reasoning		

ARITHMETIC

1. **C** This is a value data sufficiency question, so begin by determining what is known and what is need-ed to solve the problem. The problem states that k is a two-digit positive integer and asks for the value of k. In order to be sufficient, the statements need to provide a way to solve for the value of k. Consider Statement (1). For a number to have a remainder of 8 when divided by 9, that number has to be 1 less than a multiple of 9. Therefore, the possible values of k according to this statement are 17, 26, 35, 44, 53, 62, 71, 80, 89, and 98. Because k can be any of those values, the statement is not sufficient. Write down BCE. Consider Statement (2). For a number to have a remainder of 7 when divided by 8, that number has to be 1 less than a multiple of 8. Therefore, the possible values of k according to this statement are 15, 23, 31, 39, 47, 55, 63, 71, 79, 87, and 95. Because k can be any of those values, the statement is not sufficient. Eliminate (B). Consider both statements com-bined. The only number that is part of both lists is 71. Therefore, $k = 71$. The combined statements provide a single answer to the question, so they are sufficient. The correct answer is (C).

2. **D** Because 1 mm = 0.1 cm, it follows that 1 mm² = 0.1² cm² = 0.01 cm². Therefore, 25,000 mm² = 25,000(0.01) cm² = 250 cm². The correct answer is (D).

3. **D** Begin by determining the number of 2-digit integers that can be formed by distinct members of set P. There are 5 options for the first digit and 4 options for the second digit, so there are 5 × 4 = 20 possible 2-digit numbers. Next, determine how many possible 2-digit prime numbers can be made from distinct members of set P. The prime numbers that can be created are 13, 17, 19, 31, 37, 41, 43, 47, 71, 73, 79, and 97. There are 12 prime numbers and 20 possible numbers, so the probability is $\frac{12}{20} = \frac{3}{5}$. The correct answer is (D).

4. **D** The problem states there were 2 three-hour classes per week for 8 weeks, which means there was a total of 48 hours of class. If Phyllis attended all classes, she would have earned 48(0.25) = 12 hours of credit for classes. If Phyllis completed 9 labs and received 1 hour of course credit for every 3 labs, she would have earned 9 ÷ 3 = 3 hours of course credit for labs. In total, Phyllis received 12 + 3 = 15 hours of course credit. The correct answer is (D).

5. **D** This is a value data sufficiency question, so determine what is known and what is needed to answer the question. The question states that $a + b$ is the average of c and d. Therefore, $a + b = \frac{c + d}{2}$. Simplified, this is $2(a + b) = c + d$. The average of a, b, c, and d can be found by obtaining the sum $a + b + c + d$ and dividing by 4. Thus, since $2(a + b) = c + d$, the statements need to provide values for $(a + b)$ or $(c + d)$. Consider Statement (1). If $a + b = 2$, that means that the average of c and d is 2. In that case, $2 = \frac{c + d}{2}$ and so $c + d = 4$. This means that $a + b + c + d = 6$, and the average can be determined, so Statement (1) is sufficient. Write down AD. Consider Statement (2). If $c + d = 4$, that means that the average of c and d is $\frac{4}{2} = 2$. Since $a + b$ is the average of c and d, this means $a + b = 2$, and $a + b + c + d = 6$ and the average can be determined. Statement (2) is sufficient. Eliminate (A). The correct answer is (D).

6. **E**   The problem states that the garden yielded 15 apples and 20% more pears than apples. The number of pears is 20% more than apples. The number of pears can be calculated by taking 120% of the number of apples: pears = 1.2 × 15 = 18. The question asks for the number of pears and apples combined, which is 15 + 18 = 33. The correct answer is (E).

7. **B**   This is a value data sufficiency question, so begin by determining what is known and what is needed to answer the question. The problem states that x is an even integer and asks for a value of x. To answer the question, the statements need to provide a way to determine the value of x. Consider Statement (1). Plug In values that satisfy the statement. If $x = 18$, then the statement is satisfied because 18 + 5 = 23. This satisfies the statement. However, if $x = 24$, then the statement is also satisfied because 24 + 5 = 29. Because the statement produces two different values of x, the statement is insufficient. Write down BCE. Consider Statement (2). Because x is an even integer and the statement subtracts another even number from it, the result is going to be another even integer because *even − even = even*. The only even prime number is 2. Therefore, $x - 16 = 2$ and $x = 18$. The statement produces one value for the question, so it is sufficient. The correct answer is (B).

8. **E**   The probability of getting a red gumball is 100% − 60% = 40%. The probability of getting a lettered gumball is 100% − 45% = 55%. None of the red gumballs are lettered, so the probability of getting one that is both is 0%. Probability is represented by $\frac{want}{total}$, and to find the probability of "A *or* B," *add* the two amounts. The total options that are desired are $\frac{40}{100}$ red gumballs plus $\frac{55}{100}$ lettered gumballs, for a total of $\frac{95}{100}$ gumball options, or 95%. The correct answer is (E).

9. **A**   There are 8 possible letters and 10 possible numbers for the combination. The first character in the combination is a letter, so there are 8 possible values for the first slot. The second character can be either a letter or a number. Because the letters and numbers can be used more than once, there are 18 possible letters or numbers for the second character. There are also 18 possible letters or numbers for the third character. The fourth and fifth characters are numbers, so there are 10 possible options for both characters. Therefore, the total number of combinations is 8 × 18 × 18 × 10 × 10. Before multiplying this, work through the rest of the problem and look for ways to simplify. The problem states that one of the combinations can be coded per second and asks for the length of time to code all combinations in hours. There are 60 seconds in a minute and 60 minutes in an hour, so there are 3,600 seconds in an hour. Therefore, the final expression to solve is $\frac{8 \times 18 \times 18 \times 10 \times 10}{3,600}$. Break this down into prime factors to find that $\frac{8 \times 18 \times 18 \times 10 \times 10}{3,600} = \frac{2^3 \times (2 \times 3^2) \times (2 \times 3^2) \times (2 \times 5) \times (2 \times 5)}{2^4 \times 3^2 \times 5^2} = \frac{2^7 \times 3^4 \times 5^2}{2^4 \times 3^2 \times 5^2} = 2^3 \times 3^2 = 72$. The correct answer is (A).

10. **C** This is a value data sufficiency question, so determine what is known and what is needed in order to solve the question. The question provides four variables on a number line and states they are all evenly spaced. If the distance between each of the variables is denoted by the variable n, then $b = a + n$, $c = a + 2n$, and $d = a + 3n$. The question asks for the value of $a + d$. This can be rewritten as $a + a + 3n = 2a + 3n$. Therefore, the statements need to provide values for the variables. Consider Statement (1). This statement provides an equation containing both a and n. This provides enough information to determine that $a = 6 - 2n$. However, this is not enough information to solve for a single value of n. This statement is not sufficient. Write down BCE. Consider Statement (2). This statement gives a value of b, but does not provide any information about a or n. This statement is not sufficient. Eliminate (B). Consider the two statements combined. If $b = 2$ and $b = a + n$, then $2 = 6 - 2n + n$ and $n = 4$. With this value of n, it is possible to determine that $a = 2 - 4 = -2$ and $d = 6 + 4 = 10$. Therefore, the value of $a + d$ is $-2 + 10 = 8$. The statements combined produce one possible answer to the question, so the statements are sufficient. The correct answer is (C).

ALGEBRA

1. **A** This is a Yes/No data sufficiency question, so be prepared to Plug In more than once. The question asks if $x^6 = 64$. Break 64 down into its prime factors to reveal that $64 = 2^6$. Therefore, the question is asking if $x^6 = 2^6$. In other words, is $x = 2$. Evaluate the answer choices individually. Consider Statement (1). The term x^{-5} is equal to $\frac{1}{x^5}$, which means that $x^5 = 32$. Break 32 down into its prime factors to find that $32 = 2^5$. Statement (1) provides the information that $x = 2$, so the answer to the question is Yes. Because there is no other possible value of x according to this statement, the statement is sufficient. Write down AD. Now consider Statement (2). If x is prime, it could be equal to any of the prime numbers. Therefore, Statement (2) is insufficient. Eliminate (D). The correct answer is (A).

2. **C** This is a value data sufficiency question, so determine what is known and what is needed to answer the question. The question provides an expression and asks for the value of that expression. There is no further information given about the variables in the expression. To be sufficient, the statements need to provide information about the values of a, b, and c. Consider Statement (1). There are 3 variables and 1 equation. This means there is no way to solve for the equation, so Statement (1) is insufficient. Write down BCE. Consider Statement (2). Again, there are 3 variables and 1 equation, so Statement (2) is insufficient. Eliminate (B). Now consider Statements (1) and (2) together. There are 3 variables and 2 equations. But if Statement (2) is subtracted from Statement (1), the resulting equation is $6a + 6b + 6c = 42$. Divide by 6 to get $a + b + c = 7$. The correct answer is (C).

3. **C** This is a value data sufficiency question, so determine what is known and what is needed to answer the question. The problem provides an expression and asks for the value of the expression. There are variables in the expression, so the statements need to provide a way to solve for the variables. Consider Statement (1). This statement provides one equation with two variables. There is no way to solve for individual values of the variables in this equation, so this statement is not sufficient. Write down BCE. Consider Statement (2). This statement provides a value for h but does not provide any information about g. This statement is insufficient. Eliminate (B). Now consider both statements together. Statement (2) provides a value of h that can be substituted for h in Statement (1). This allows you to solve for a value of g. The statements combined provide a way to solve for both variables and get a single answer to the question, so the statements together are sufficient. The correct answer is (C).

4. **B** Plug In a value for Calvin's age 3 years from now. If 3 years from now Calvin is 18, then 3 years from now Jill is 6. Therefore, Calvin is currently 15 years old, so $c = 15$, and Jill is currently 3 years old. In 6 years, Jill will be 9, which is half as old as Tom in 6 years. So, in 6 years Tom will be 18, which means that Tom is currently 12. Plug In 15 for c in all the answer choices, looking for one that matches the target answer of 12. Choice (A) results in 10, which is incorrect. Eliminate (A). Choice (B) results in 12, so keep (B). Choice (C) is also 12, so keep (C). Choice (D) is $\frac{51}{2}$, which is not equal to 12, so eliminate (D). Choice (E) is $\frac{45}{2} + 2$, which is not equal to 12, so eliminate (E). Now Plug In again, looking for ways to eliminate either (B) or (C). If Calvin is currently 9, then Jill is currently 1 and Tom is currently 8. In this case, (B) is 8 so keep (B). Choice (C) is 10, so eliminate (C). The correct answer is (B).

5. **D** The question provides an equation with two exponents that have different bases, so begin by converting the bases to be equal. Because $6^2 = 36$, the equation can be rewritten as $6^{2x+2} = (6^2)^{2x-2}$. Apply the Power-Multiply rule of exponents to find that $6^{2x+2} = 6^{4x-4}$. Eliminate the bases and write the equation as the exponents equal to one another and solve for x. This equation is $2x + 2 = 4x - 4$, so $2x = 6$ and $x = 3$. The correct answer is (D).

6. **A** This question asks about the possible units digit of a number raised to a power. The units digit of a number raised to any power is the same as the units digit of the original number raised to that same power. The question states that r, s, and t are negative consecutive odd digits and that $r < s < t$. The units digits of any combination of any three negative odd consecutive integers are one of the following sets: {9, 7, 5}; {7, 5, 3}; {5, 3, 1}; {3, 1, 9}; or {1, 9, 7}. Because the question also asks about the value of s^5, rewrite all the potential sets of units digits raised to the fifth power. For instance, 9^5 results in a units digit of 9, 7^5 results in a units digit of 7, and 5^5 results in a units digit of 5, and 3^5 results in a units digit of 3 so the first set can be written as {9, 7, 5, 3}. The only value that is not possible for s^5 is 1. In order for the units digit of s^5 to be 1, s has to equal 1, which means that t is not a negative odd digit. The correct answer is (A).

7. **E** This is a Yes/No data sufficiency question, so be prepared to Plug In more than once. The question asks if m is a positive integer. The statements need to provide a way to determine if m is a positive or negative integer. Consider Statement (1). Plug In values for m that satisfy the statement. If $m = 2$, then the statement is satisfied because $-2^3 \leq -1$ can be rewritten as $-8 \leq -1$, which is true. In this case, the answer to the question is Yes, because 2 is a positive integer. Plug In again. If $m = \dfrac{5}{2}$, then the statement is satisfied because $-\dfrac{5}{2}^3 \leq -1$ can be rewritten as $-\dfrac{125}{8} \leq -1$, which is true. In this case the answer to the question is No because m is not an integer. The statement produces two different answers to the question, so it is not sufficient. Write down BCE. Consider Statement (2). Plug In values that satisfy the statement. If $m = 2$, then the statement is $4 \geq 1$, which is true. In this case, the answer to the question is Yes. Plug In again. If $m = \dfrac{5}{2}$, then the statement is satisfied because $-\dfrac{5}{2}^2 \leq -1$ can be rewritten as $-\dfrac{25}{4} \leq -1$, which is true. The answer to the question is now No. Eliminate (B). Consider both statements together. The values that satisfy Statement (1) also satisfy Statement (2). Because of this, it is possible to get an answer of Yes and an answer of No to the question. Eliminate (C). The correct answer is (E).

8. **C** This is a function problem, so substitute values into the provided equations. The problem asks for the value of $g(f(5)) - f(g(5))$. Begin with one term at a time. The term $g(f(5))$ results in $g(3(5) + w) = g(15 + w) = 4(15 + w) - w = 60 + 4w - w = 60 + 3w$. The term $f(g(5))$ results in $f(4(5) - w) = f(20 - w) = 3(20 - w) + w = 60 - 3w + w = 60 - 2w$. The expression in the question stem is now $60 + 3w - 60 - 2w = 5w$. The correct answer is (C).

READING COMPREHENSION

1. **B** The subject of the question is *how a company might become a flat organization* and the task is referenced by the phrase *described in the passage*, so this is a retrieval question. Determine what the passage says about the characteristics of flat organizations. The passage notes that flat organizations *abolish middle management structures and instead assign most workers to the same level*, use *non hierarchical committees* that *share in a decentralized decision-making process*, and limit *specialization in job titles*. Evaluate the answer choices individually, looking for one that reflects these ideas. Choice (A) is a reversal of the information in the passage. *Outsourcing middle management* is different from abolishing middle management and would not make an organization flatter. Eliminate (A). Choice (B) is a good description of a step a company could take to become flatter, so keep (B). Choice (C) is a reversal of the information in the passage. Creating *specific guidelines for approval of new ideas* is in opposition to the idea of non-hierarchical committees that share in decision-making. Eliminate (C). Choice (D) is a reversal of the information in the passage. The passage says flat organizations limit job specialization. Eliminate (D). Choice (E) can also be eliminated as it describes a hierarchical structure as opposed to a flat organization. The correct answer is (B).

2. **B** The subject of the question is the entire passage, and the task is referenced by the phrase *primary purpose*, so this is a primary purpose question. The passage begins by stating how *the preeminent organizational strategy designed to maximize efficient productivity may actually be detrimental* and then asserts the *long-term success of a corporation requires flexibility and new ideas to respond to ever-evolving political, social, and economic conditions*. The passage then suggests becoming a "*flat organization*" as the key to unlocking these needs. The remainder of the passage describes the characteristics of flat organizations and their benefits. Evaluate the answer choices individually, looking for one that reflects this content. Choice (A) is a memory trap. The passage does *compare various corporate organizational strategies*. However, the primary purpose of the passage is to advocate for one structure in comparison to another. Eliminate (A). Choice (B) is a good paraphrase of the primary purpose of the passage, so keep it. Choice (C) is a reversal of the information in the passage. The passage states that hierarchical structures are *the preeminent organizational strategy* and the passage is not primarily about hierarchical structures. Eliminate (C). Choice (D) is a reversal of the information in the passage. The passage does not *criticize a new method of conducting business*. Instead, the passage supports a new method. Eliminate (D). Choice (E) is a no-such-comparison answer, as the passage does not *acknowledge the similarities* between hierarchical and flat structures. Eliminate (E). The correct answer is (B).

3. **A** The subject of the question is *hierarchical workplaces*, and the task of the question is referenced by the word *inferred*. This is an inference question. Determine what the passage says about hierarchical workplaces. The passage says these structures *unwittingly discourage* traits such as *creative thinking, adaptability, and collaboration* and that they are *designed to maximize efficient productivity* but *may actually be detrimental*. Evaluate the answer choices individually, looking for one that reflects these descriptions. Choice (A) is a good paraphrase of the information in the passage as delayed approval processes for new ideas are not *adaptable*. Additionally, more streamlined approval processes are listed as one of the benefits of flat structures that is not present in hierarchical structures. Keep (A). Choice (B) is a no-such-comparison answer, as the passage does not compare the number of middle and upper managers. Eliminate (B). Choice (C) uses the recycled language *maximize efficiency*. This is used to describe the intention of hierarchical structures but is not related to *promoting specialization*. Eliminate (C). Choice (D) is a no-such-comparison answer, as the passage does not compare large and small companies. Eliminate (D). Choice (E) contains the extreme language *do not allow*. While the passage suggests hierarchical structures make it more difficult to have flexible roles, it does not state that flexible roles are not allowed. Eliminate (E). The correct answer is (A).

4. **D** The subject of the question is the *originators of the general equilibrium theory* and the task of the question is referenced by the word *implies*, so this is an inference question. Determine what the passage says about the originators of the general equilibrium theory. The theory is derived from *Smith's idea* about the "*invisible hand*" and states that *invisible market forces guided the interaction of supply and demand toward a natural balance*. The passage goes on to note the *ubiquity of this model in both popular and scholarly thinking* despite *the guiding influence of Smith's invisible hand in moving markets toward such a balance has not been shown*. The passage concludes that the theory *presents an optimistic view of self-correction that has not been borne out by actual economic conditions*. Evaluate the answer choices

individually, looking for one that reflects the information in the passage. Choice (A) is a reversal of the information in the passage which states the theory *has not been borne out by actual economic conditions.* Eliminate (A). Choice (B) is a memory trap. The passage mentions that Adam Smith was around in the eighteenth century, but only states that the originators of the general equilibrium theory were *subsequent theorists.* This does not give a timeframe for when they developed the theory, so eliminate (B). Choice (C) uses the extreme language *immediately.* While the passage does say the theory is ubiquitous *in both popular and scholarly thinking,* it does not state that the theory was immediately popular. Eliminate (C). Choice (D) is a good paraphrase of the information in the passage. Keep (D). Choice (E) is a memory trap. The passage mentions the theory is derived from Adam Smith but does not give any indication if any of the originators worked with Smith. Eliminate (E). The correct answer is (D).

5. **B** The subject of the question is the passage as a whole and the task of the question is referenced by the phrase *primarily concerned with,* so this is a primary purpose question. Determine why the author wrote the passage. The passage introduces Smith's theory of the *"invisible hand"* and then discusses how *subsequent theorists expanded Smith's idea* to create the general equilibrium theory. The passage then states *there is no evidence for [the theory's] truth* and spends the remainder of the passage calling into question the validity of the theory. Evaluate the answer choices individually, looking for one that reflects the primary purpose of the passage. Choice (A) uses the recycled language *economic regulation.* Discussing economic regulation is not the primary purpose of the passage. Eliminate (A). Choice (B) is a good paraphrase of the information in the passage, so keep (B). Choice (C) is a reversal of the information in the passage. The passage seeks to delegitimize Smith's beliefs, not *defend* them. Eliminate (C). Choice (D) is a memory trap. The passage does mention the idea that *market forces naturally maintain balance,* but this is not the primary purpose of the passage. Eliminate (D). Choice (E) is a no-such-comparison answer. The passage does not *compare several economic theories.* Eliminate (E). The correct answer is (B).

6. **E** The subject of the question is how *defenders of the general equilibrium theory…regard economic regulations,* and the task of the question is referenced by the word *inferred.* This is an inference question. Determine what the passage says about the subject. The passage states that the *belief that markets actively move toward an equilibrium has been used by proponents of deregulation, who insist that removing government interventions promotes economic strength.* So, defenders of the general equilibrium theory most likely regard regulation as ineffective. Evaluate the answer choices individually, looking for one that reflects this idea. Choice (A) is a reversal of the information in the passage and the opposite of "ineffective," so eliminate (A). Choice (B) is an example of extreme language, as the passage does not support the idea that defenders see regulation as *catastrophic.* Eliminate (B). Choice (C) is a reversal of the information in the passage as *salutary* means producing a good effect. Eliminate (C). Choice (D), *insufficient,* is a reversal of the information in the passage. Eliminate (D). Choice (E) is a good match for "ineffective." The correct answer is (E).

7.   **C**   The subject of the question is the *passage* as a whole and the task of the question is referenced by the phrase *primary purpose,* so this is a primary purpose question. Determine why the author wrote the passage by using the key sentences approach. The key sentence of the first paragraph is the introduction to the topic of the article, which is *a critical aspect of product advertising is the choice between positive and negative approaches.* The second paragraph discusses the benefits and risks of both positive and negative advertising and concludes *consumers may thus more readily believe negative information compared to arguments made in favor of a brand or product, and the former often makes a stronger mental impression.* The third paragraph *explains why such advertising can be more memorable: negativity bias.* The final paragraph sums up the final conclusion of the passage by stating *In spite of these benefits, negativity in advertising is not always more effective than the alternative.* Evaluate the answer choices individually, looking for one that reflects the primary purpose of the passage. Choice (A) uses the extreme language *argue the inferiority.* The passage does not argue for inferiority of one approach to another, but instead lays out the benefits and risks of each. Eliminate (A). Choice (B) is a memory trap. The passage does *explore the advantages of different forms of advertising,* but it also explores the risks, and the primary purpose is not concerned with *different audiences.* Eliminate (B). Choice (C) is a good paraphrase of the information in the passage, so keep (C). Choice (D) is a memory trap as the passage does spend some time explaining what makes negative advertising *effective,* but this is the subject of only one paragraph and not the primary purpose of the passage. Eliminate (D). Choice (E) is an appeal to outside knowledge. It is true that there is a *need for companies to advertise their products,* but the passage is unconcerned with this need. Eliminate (E). The correct answer is (C).

8.   **A**   The subject of the question is *potential risks in advertising* and the task of the question is referenced by the phrase *the following are mentioned,* so this is a retrieval question. Determine what the passage says are potential risks in advertising. The passage says that positive advertising can be perceived as *insincere or predatory due to their reliance on manipulating emotions rather than presenting factual information* and that can *lead to skepticism…as consumers assume they are still being manipulated for the goal of producing positive feelings.* Negative advertising that features a competitor *can inadvertently provide a boost to the competing brand* and *poses a risk that the audience will be alienated from both the competitor and the company criticizing it.* The passage also states that consumers who buy based on negative advertising may *not [be] as loyal as those for whom merit guides the decision.* Finally, there is a concern that *consumers may view attacks on competitors as petty and untoward.* This is an except question, so evaluate the answer choices looking for one that is not reflected by the information in the passage. Choice (A) is not mentioned as a potential risk in advertising, so keep (A). Choice (B) is listed as a risk when the passage states that negative advertising *poses a risk that the audience will be alienated from both the competitor and the company criticizing it.* Eliminate (B). Choice (C) is listed as a risk of positive advertising. The passage states positive advertising can be perceived as *insincere or predatory.* Eliminate (C). Choice (D) is not explicitly stated in the passage but is implied through statements such as *consumers assume they are still being manipulated for the goal of producing positive feelings.* Eliminate (D). Choice (E) is referenced by the statement that negative advertising *can inadvertently provide a boost to the competing brand.* Eliminate (E). The correct answer is (A).

9. **C** The subject of the passage is *an example of negative advertising* and the task of the question is referenced by the phrase *as it is described in the passage*, so this is a retrieval question. Determine how the passage describes negative advertising. The passage describes negative advertising as *not painting a rosy sheen over its own products but rather warning consumers of a competitor's flaw*. Evaluate the answer choices individually, looking for one that could serve as an example of negative advertising based on this description. Choice (A) is a memory trap as this would be an example of positive advertising. Eliminate (A). Choice (B) is also an example of positive advertising, so eliminate (B). Choice (C) is a good example of negative advertising as described in the passage. Keep (C). Choice (D) is an example of one company criticizing another but is not an example of negative advertising as the environmental group is not trying to sell its product through the negative association with a competitor. Eliminate (D). Choice (E) is not an example of negative advertising as described in the passage, so eliminate (E). The correct answer is (C).

10. **D** The subject of the question is the *highlighted sentence* and the task of the question is referenced by the phrase *describes the function*, so this is a specific purpose question. Determine the role of the highlighted sentence. The highlighted sentence follows a sentence that introduces a *contrast* between positive advertising and negative advertising. The contrast is that *negative advertising can appear more truthful* than positive advertising. This leads to the content of the highlighted sentence, which states that consumers *more readily believe negative information compared to arguments made in favor of a brand or product, and the former often makes a stronger mental impression*. The highlighted sentence closes a paragraph that leads into a conversation regarding *why such advertising can be more memorable*. Evaluate the answer choices individually, looking for one that reflects this idea. Choice (A) contains the extreme language *demonstrably superior*. The sentence does not suggest that negative advertising is demonstrably superior, so eliminate (A). Choice (B) is a memory trap. While the passage does describe *differences between the two strategies,* this sentence does not *summarize* the main differences. Eliminate (B). Choice (C) contains the extreme language *refutes the argument*. The first paragraph does not contain an argument that this sentence could refute. Eliminate (C). Choice (D) is a good description of the function of the sentence, so keep (D). Choice (E) is a memory trap. This sentence states the impact of one strategy in comparison to one from earlier in the paragraph, but evaluating what *most experts believe* is not the function of this sentence. Eliminate (E). The correct answer is (D).

CRITICAL REASONING

1. **A** The task of this question is referenced by the phrase *argument depends on*, so this is an assumption question. Find the conclusion, premise, and assumption or pattern. The conclusion is *Although the patient's health would improve with daily outdoor walks, I have advised against it in the health plan.* The premise is *an increase in walking exercise would stress the already overstressed knee joints and would therefore put the patient at increased risk of injury.* The argument assumes that *daily* walks mean an *increase* in a byproduct of walking exercise. The correct answer will confirm the assumption in the argument.

    (A) Correct. If *the patient would use her knees more than she currently does* as a result of *daily walks* then the byproduct of the movement would increase.

    (B) No. This choice is out of scope. *The amount of exercise the patient currently undertakes* is not tied to the conclusion or premise of the argument.

    (C) No. The use of the phrase *any patient* is too extreme for this argument, which is just about one patient.

    (D) No. This choice is out of scope. Whether the patient decides to follow the *recommendation of the physiotherapist* is unrelated to the conclusion and premise of the argument.

    (E) No. The use of the phrase *the patient's best well-being as the foremost concern* is out of the scope of the argument.

    The correct answer is (A).

2. **A** The question task is referenced by the phrase *provide the most support for which of the following conclusions.* This is a strengthen question. The conclusion is the answer choices. The premise for the conclusion is *the incidence of cancer in mice is many times that of humans, even though humans have over 1,000 times as many cells as mice do. Furthermore, elephants have even more cells than humans do, but the incidence of cancer in elephants is much lower.* The correct answer will be supported by the premise.

    (A) Correct. The premise in the argument supports the conclusion that cancer *is due in part to factors other than body size.*

    (B) No. This answer is not supported by the premise of the argument.

    (C) No. This answer choice uses the extreme language that *The number of cells in any organism's body is not a predictor.* This is too strong for a passage in which only three species are listed.

    (D) No. The *number of abnormal cells in an organism* is out of scope and is not a conclusion supported by the argument.

    (E) No. *Curing cancer in humans* is out of scope.

    The correct answer is (A).

3. **E** The task of the question is referenced by the phrase *assumes which of the following,* so this is an assumption question. Find the conclusion, premise, and assumption or pattern. The conclusion is *Jones or Alyers had the most motive and opportunity to commit the theft.* The premise is *Singh, the more senior employee with the higher pay grade, was supervising Jones and Alyers, who were processing the inventory* and that *Singh has already testified that both Jones and Alyers were out of his sight numerous times throughout the shift.* The shift of language in this argument is from *senior employee* and *pay grade* in the premise to *motive* in the conclusion, so the argument assumes that these are indicative of *motive.* The correct answer will confirm the missing link between *motive* and *pay grade* or will rule out an alternate cause of the theft.

    (A) No. The use of the phrase *all theft* is too extreme for this argument.

    (B) No. The relative amount of time Jones and Alyers were out of Singh's sight is out of the scope of the argument.

    (C) No. The phrase *Any testimony* is too extreme for this argument.

    (D) No. The *number of trucks with stolen items* is out of scope.

    (E) Correct. Use the Negation Test. The negated form of the answer indicates that tenure of employment and salary are not directly related to the likelihood of committing theft. This suggests that Singh's status as a senior employee with a higher paygrade does not exclude him from possibly having committed the theft.

    The correct answer is (E).

4. **C** The question task is referenced by the phrase *most logical completion of the passage,* so this is an inference question. The passage discusses a proposal to increase ads but warns about an initial loss in profits. The correct answer will provide a reason that an increase in ads would lead to a loss in profits.

    (A) No. The relationship between the *biggest competitor* and the advertisers the company *is likely to sell the new inventory* to is out of the scope of the passage.

    (B) No. This answer choice is out of scope, as it contrasts ads devoted to new versus current advertisers.

    (C) Correct. If *creating the infrastructure to host more advertisements at different locations on our website requires a large up-front investment,* then profits will decrease until the revenue surpasses the cost.

    (D) No. The use of the word *none* is an example of extreme language that is not supported by the passage.

    (E) No. The revenue from the new ads is in conjunction with the revenue from the old ads. That the rates for the new ads are *slightly lower* is not going to cause a profit loss, only a smaller increase in profits than it would if the new ads were the same price.

    The correct answer is (C).

5. **B**   The question task is referenced by the phrase *an assumption on which the…argument depends,* so this is an assumption question. Find the conclusion, premise, and assumption or pattern in the argument. The conclusion is *to keep our store profits at the same level, we will have to raise the prices of products in these categories until the nationwide truckers' strike is over.* The premise is t*he majority of the profits in our hardware store during the last quarter depended on the sales of paint and household tools.* This argument fits the Planning pattern as the conclusion of the argument is a recommended course of action, so another assumption is that there are no problems with the plan to *raise the prices of products in these categories until the nationwide truckers' strike is over.* The correct answer will contain information that rules out a problem with the plan.

   (A) No. The use of the phrase *only the actions of the truckers' union that caused the shortages* is too extreme for this argument.

   (B) Correct. Use the Negation Test. The negated form of this answer is *Raising prices of paint and household tools until the end of the truckers' strike would decrease patronage.* Because the negated form of the answer hurts the plan, this answer contains the assumption.

   (C) No. The use of the phrase *raising prices of paint and household tools is more important than diversifying the hardware* is too extreme for this argument.

   (D) No. What *other stores* do is out of scope.

   (E) No. Ending the trucker's strike is out of scope.

   The correct answer is (B).

6. **B**   The question task is referenced by the phrase *most strengthens,* so this is a strengthen question. Find the conclusion, premise, and pattern or assumption in the argument. The conclusion is *if you want your garden to thrive under any condition, use Q-Earth.* The premise is *Q-Earth's nutrient generation technology provides better support for your plants when natural nutrient formation is inhibited due to lack of sunlight, rain, or heat.* The argument assumes that the best support for plants requires the ability to support plants *under any condition.* Therefore, the correct answer will provide information that supports the assumption.

   (A) No. *Plants that tend to grow quickly* is out of the scope of the argument.

   (B) Correct. If *Q-Earth is the preferred soil of interior gardeners—those who build gardens inside homes using plants that typically thrive outside,* then people are choosing to use the soil under not ideal conditions.

   (C) No. Q-Earth's market share is out of the scope of the argument.

   (D) No. This answer uses the extreme language *all branded soil,* which is too strong for the argument.

   (E) No. Where Q-Earth is manufactured is out of the scope of the argument.

   The correct answer is (B).

7. **D** The task of the question is referenced by the phrase *vulnerable to criticism,* so this is a flaw question. Find the conclusion, premise, and assumption or pattern. The conclusion is *most students in the school earn at least some extra credit,* and the premises are *Most students in the school are honors students* and *the amount of extra credit per test earned by any student generally does not fluctuate from test to test.* The shift of language in this argument is from *honors students* in the premises to *most students in the school* in the conclusion. The argument is linking the ideas of *honors students* to *most students.* This argument is following a sampling pattern. The standard assumption of a sampling pattern is that the sample is representative. The correct answer will identify a flaw or a bad assumption about the sample of honors representativeness of most students.

(A) No. Specific *classes with honors students* is out of the scope of the passage. The passage discusses only the students as a whole.

(B) No. This answer is out of scope. It targets the premise of the argument that the *certain average score is earned on a test* and *approximately the same amount of extra credit,* instead of identifying the bad assumption or the flaw in the way the argument moves from the premise to the conclusion.

(C) No. This answer cannot be matched to the argument. The conclusion of this argument is not *about the test scores,* but rather about the students who earn the scores.

(D) Correct. The argument ignores the fact that extra credit could be earned by *some types of students.* The flaw of the argument is that many students may earn no extra credit at all, so the generalization *most students in the school earn at least some extra credit* is not warranted.

(E) No. The argument does not *overlook* the possibility that any one student may earn no extra credit. The argument acknowledges that the *amount of extra credit per test earned by any student generally does not fluctuate from test to test,* so that amount could be none.

The correct answer is (D).

8. **A** The task of the question is referenced by the phrase *roles in the argument,* so this is an identify the reasoning question. Identify the Conclusion and Premise. The conclusion is *The troubling discovery of cheating on the most common college entrance examination should not impact the reputation of the College Admissions Board.* The bolded phrase is an intermediary claim, *the revelation confirms that the system works,* which is itself supported by the premise *the students themselves were the ones who reported their peers for unethical behavior.* The answer should confirm that the bolded phrase is an intermediary claim that supports the conclusion.

(A) Correct. The argument gives evidence for the bolded claim, and the bolded claim supports the primary claim.

(B) No. This answer reverses the roles in the argument. The bolded phrase is not the argument's primary position.

(C) No. This answer does not match the structure of the argument as the argument does have *stated evidence* for the bolded phrase.

(D) No. This answer does not match the structure of the argument as the bolded phrase is not the *main conclusion* of the argument.

(E) No. While the bolded phrase does support the main conclusion of the argument, and the bolded phrase is a part of a sentence that contains a premise, the bolded phrase itself does not contain an assumption. This answer is only a partial match.

The correct answer is (A).

9. **D**   The question task is referenced by the phrase *most seriously weakens,* so this is a weaken question. Find the conclusion, premise, and pattern or assumption. The conclusion of the argument is *savory recipes invented by culinary experts with over 20 years of experience in general yield better dishes that enjoy a much broader popularity than savory dishes based on recipes by chefs with less than 20 years of experience.* The premise is *more experienced chefs are more precise and careful when designing their savory recipes than their counterparts, who may just be experimenting with trendy cuisines.* The argument has a causality pattern, assuming the cause of the *better dishes that enjoy a much broader popularity* is that the more experienced chefs are *more precise and careful.* Therefore, the correct answer will provide an alternate cause for the *dishes that enjoy a much broader popularity.*

(A) No. *Recipes for sweet dishes* is out of the scope of the argument.

(B) No. The recipes that are easier *for domestic cooks to follow* are out of the scope of the argument.

(C) No. The *range of spices* used by young and old chefs is out of the scope of the argument.

(D) Correct. This answer choice weakens the argument by giving an alternate cause of a recipe's popularity. If most popular dishes are discovered in cooking magazines and cooking magazines feature recipes by chefs with industry connections, the more experienced chefs are likely to be in magazines as they have been working in the industry for a longer period of time.

(E) No. The age of the culinary expert is out of the scope of the argument.

The correct answer is (D).

Part VII
The Princeton Review GMAT Math and Verbal Warm-Up Questions and Explanations

Chapter 22
GMAT Math and Verbal Warm-Up Questions

The purpose of this 60-minute question set is to get a rough idea of your current scoring range and rough percentiles on the Math and Verbal sections of the GMAT. Using these scores as a guide, you can then select from the bins of practice questions that follow to improve your performance.

According to the test makers, the computer-adaptive sections of the GMAT focus on your approximate scoring level after only a few questions. You then spend the rest of the test time answering questions from around that level of difficulty, chosen by the computer from bins of potential questions.

To further refine your assessment of where you are right now, we recommend that you take one of The Princeton Review's computer-adaptive tests (available for free online). See the Get More (Free) Content section at the beginning of this book for details. We also highly recommend that you take an actual computer-adaptive GMAT, downloadable for free from the GMAT website at www.mba.com.

Math Test
Time—30 Minutes
15 Questions

This test is composed of both problem solving questions and data sufficiency questions.

<u>**Problem Solving Directions**</u>: Solve each problem and choose the best of the answer choices provided.

<u>**Data Sufficiency Directions**</u>: Each <u>data sufficiency</u> problem consists of a question and two statements, labeled (1) and (2), which contain certain data. Using these data and your knowledge of mathematics and everyday facts (such as the number of days in July or the meaning of *counterclockwise*), decide whether the data given are sufficient for answering the question and then indicate one of the following answer choices:

(A)   Statement (1) ALONE is sufficient, but statement (2) alone is not sufficient.

(B)   Statement (2) ALONE is sufficient, but statement (1) alone is not sufficient.

(C)   BOTH statements TOGETHER are sufficient, but NEITHER statement ALONE is sufficient.

(D)   EACH statement ALONE is sufficient.

(E)   Statements (1) and (2) TOGETHER are not sufficient.

---

1.   If $(16)(3^2) = x(2^3)$, then $x =$

   (A)   81
   (B)   72
   (C)   18
   (D)   16
   (E)   8

2.   By how many dollars is the price of a computer reduced during a sale?

   (1)   The price of the computer is reduced by 25% during the sale.
   (2)   The sale price of the computer is $36.

   (A)   Statement (1) ALONE is sufficient, but statement (2) alone is not sufficient.
   (B)   Statement (2) ALONE is sufficient, but statement (1) alone is not sufficient.
   (C)   BOTH statements TOGETHER are sufficient, but NEITHER statement ALONE is sufficient.
   (D)   EACH statement ALONE is sufficient.
   (E)   Statements (1) and (2) TOGETHER are not sufficient.

GO ON TO THE NEXT PAGE.

Math

3. Of the 720 players who participated in a softball tournament, 65 percent traveled more than 200 miles to play. What is the difference between the number of participants who traveled more than 200 miles and the number of participants who traveled 200 miles or less?

   (A) 108
   (B) 216
   (C) 252
   (D) 468
   (E) 655

4. If $r - s = 240$, does $r = 320$?

   (1) $r = 4s$
   (2) $s = 80$

   (A) Statement (1) ALONE is sufficient, but statement (2) alone is not sufficient.
   (B) Statement (2) ALONE is sufficient, but statement (1) alone is not sufficient.
   (C) BOTH statements TOGETHER are sufficient, but NEITHER statement ALONE is sufficient.
   (D) EACH statement ALONE is sufficient.
   (E) Statements (1) and (2) TOGETHER are not sufficient.

5. If a heavy-load trailer travels 7 miles in 1 hour and 10 minutes, what is its speed in miles per hour?

   (A) 6
   (B) 6.5
   (C) 8
   (D) 8.5
   (E) 10

6. If Bob purchases 18 cans of soda, how many of the cans are diet soda?

   (1) The number of diet soda cans Bob purchases is equal to the number that are not diet soda.
   (2) Bob purchases an odd number of cans of diet soda.

   (A) Statement (1) ALONE is sufficient, but statement (2) alone is not sufficient.
   (B) Statement (2) ALONE is sufficient, but statement (1) alone is not sufficient.
   (C) BOTH statements TOGETHER are sufficient, but NEITHER statement ALONE is sufficient.
   (D) EACH statement ALONE is sufficient.
   (E) Statements (1) and (2) TOGETHER are not sufficient.

7. At Perry High School, the ratio of students who participate in either the band program or the choral program to students who participate in neither program is 3 to 8. If 220 students attend Perry High School, how many of them participate in neither program?

   (A) 40
   (B) 60
   (C) 100
   (D) 160
   (E) 180

GO ON TO THE NEXT PAGE.

8. A \$240 interest-free loan is to be paid back in equal monthly payments. If a total of $2\frac{1}{2}$ percent of the original amount of the loan is paid back every 6 months, then how many months will it take to pay back \$21.00 ?

   (A)   6
   (B)   7
   (C)   18
   (D)   21
   (E)   24

9. If x and y are positive integers, is x a factor of 12 ?

   (1) xy is a factor of 12.
   (2) $y = 3$

   (A)   Statement (1) ALONE is sufficient, but statement (2) alone is not sufficient.
   (B)   Statement (2) ALONE is sufficient, but statement (1) alone is not sufficient.
   (C)   BOTH statements TOGETHER are sufficient, but NEITHER statement ALONE is sufficient.
   (D)   EACH statement ALONE is sufficient.
   (E)   Statements (1) and (2) TOGETHER are not sufficient.

10. If a zebra can only get water from either a stream or a pond, which of the two sources of water is closer to the zebra's current position?

    (1)   Moving at a constant rate from its current position, the zebra reaches the stream in 2 hours.
    (2)   Moving at a constant rate from the stream, the zebra takes 2 hours to reach the pond.

    (A)   Statement (1) ALONE is sufficient, but statement (2) alone is not sufficient.
    (B)   Statement (2) ALONE is sufficient, but statement (1) alone is not sufficient.
    (C)   BOTH statements TOGETHER are sufficient, but NEITHER statement ALONE is sufficient.
    (D)   EACH statement ALONE is sufficient.
    (E)   Statements (1) and (2) TOGETHER are not sufficient.

11. What is the value of $x^2 - y^2$?

    (1) $x - y = 0$
    (2) $x + y = 4$

    (A)   Statement (1) ALONE is sufficient, but statement (2) alone is not sufficient.
    (B)   Statement (2) ALONE is sufficient, but statement (1) alone is not sufficient.
    (C)   BOTH statements TOGETHER are sufficient, but NEITHER statement ALONE is sufficient.
    (D)   EACH statement ALONE is sufficient.
    (E)   Statements (1) and (2) TOGETHER are not sufficient.

GO ON TO THE NEXT PAGE.

12. A mixture of ground meat consists of 2 pounds of veal that costs x dollars per pound, and 5 pounds of beef that costs y dollars per pound. What is the cost of the mixture in dollars per pound?

    (A) $2x + 5y$

    (B) $\dfrac{2x+5y}{xy}$

    (C) $5(2x + 5y)$

    (D) $x + y$

    (E) $\dfrac{2x+5y}{7}$

13. Is $0 < y < 1$?

    (1) $0 < \sqrt{y} < 1$

    (2) $y^2 = \dfrac{1}{4}$

    (A) Statement (1) ALONE is sufficient, but statement (2) alone is not sufficient.
    (B) Statement (2) ALONE is sufficient, but statement (1) alone is not sufficient.
    (C) BOTH statements TOGETHER are sufficient, but NEITHER statement ALONE is sufficient.
    (D) EACH statement ALONE is sufficient.
    (E) Statements (1) and (2) TOGETHER are not sufficient.

14. Last year, an appliance store sold an average (arithmetic mean) of 42 microwave ovens per month. In the first 10 months of this year, the store sold an average of only 20 microwaves per month. What is the average number of microwaves sold per month for the entire 22-month period?

    (A) 21
    (B) 30
    (C) 31
    (D) 32
    (E) 44

ADVANCE PURCHASE DISCOUNTS FOR AIRLINE TRAVEL	
Days Prior to Departure	Percentage Discount
0–6 days	0%
7–13 days	10%
14–29 days	25%
30 days or more	40%

15. The table above shows the discount structure for advance purchase of tickets at a particular airline. A passenger bought a ticket at this airline for $1,050. Had she purchased the ticket one day later, she would have paid $210 more. How many days before her departure did she purchase her ticket?

    (A) 6 days
    (B) 7 days
    (C) 13 days
    (D) 14 days
    (E) 29 days

GO ON TO THE NEXT PAGE.

Verbal Test
Time—30 Minutes
13 Questions

This test is made up of critical reasoning and reading comprehension questions.

Reading Comprehension Directions: Each of the <u>reading comprehension</u> questions is based on the content of a passage. After reading the passage, answer all questions pertaining to it on the basis of what is <u>stated</u> or <u>implied</u> in the passage. For each question, select the best answer of the choices given.

Critical Reasoning Directions: Each of the <u>critical reasoning</u> questions is based on a short argument, a set of statements, or a plan of action. For each question, select the best answer of the choices given.

---

16. It is posited by some scientists that the near extinction of the sap-eating gray bat of northwestern America was caused by government-sponsored logging operations in the early 1920s that greatly reduced the species' habitat.

   Which of the following, if true, most strongly weakens the scientists' claims?

   (A) Logging operations in the 1920s are widely held responsible for the near extinction of other species that lived in the same area.
   (B) A boom in new home construction in the early 1920s led congress to open federal lands to logging operations.
   (C) A 5-year drought in the early 1920s severely reduced the output of sap in trees in northwestern America.
   (D) Numbers of sightings of sap-eating gray bats fell to their lowest numbers in 1926.
   (E) Sightings of sap-eating gray bats in Europe stayed roughly the same during the same period.

17. Whenever a major airplane accident occurs, there is a dramatic increase in the number of airplane mishaps reported in the media, a phenomenon that may last for as long as a few months after the accident. Airline officials assert that the publicity given the gruesomeness of major airplane accidents focuses media attention on the airline industry, and the increase in the number of reported accidents is caused by an increase in the number of news sources covering airline accidents, not by an increase in the number of accidents.

   Which of the following, if true, would seriously weaken the assertions of the airline officials?

   (A) The publicity surrounding airline accidents is largely limited to the country in which the crash occurred.
   (B) Airline accidents tend to occur far more often during certain peak travel months.
   (C) Media organizations do not have any guidelines to help them decide how severe an accident must be for it to receive coverage.
   (D) Airplane accidents receive coverage by news sources only when the news sources find it advantageous to do so.
   (E) Studies by government regulators show that the number of airplane flight miles remains relatively constant from month to month.

GO ON TO THE NEXT PAGE.

Questions 18–21 are based on the following passage:

The function of strategic planning is to position a company for long-term growth and expansion in a variety of markets by analyzing its strengths
(Line) and weaknesses and examining current and
(5) potential opportunities. Based on this information, the company develops a strategy for itself. That strategy becomes the basis for supporting strategies for the company's various departments.
This implementation strategy is where all too
(10) many strategic plans go astray. Recent business management surveys show that most CEOs who have a strategic plan are concerned with the potential breakdown in the implementation of the plan. Unlike corporations in the 1980s that instinctively
(15) followed their 5-year plans, even when they were misguided, today's corporations tend to second-guess their long-term plans.
Outsiders can help facilitate the process, but in the final analysis, if the company does not make
(20) the plan, the company will not follow the plan. This was one of the problems with strategic planning in the 1980s. In that era, strategic planning was an abstract, top-down process involving only a few top corporate officers and hired guns. Number
(25) crunching experts came into a company and generated tome-like volumes filled with a mixture of abstruse facts and grand theories that had little to do with the day-to-day realities of the company. Key middle managers were left out of planning
(30) sessions, resulting in lost opportunities and ruffled feelings.
However, more hands-on strategic planning can produce startling results. A recent survey queried more than a thousand small- to medium-sized
(35) businesses to compare companies with a strategic plan to companies without one. The survey found that companies with strategic plans had annual revenue growth of 6.2 percent as opposed to 3.8 percent for the other companies.
(40) Perhaps most important, a strategic plan helps companies anticipate—and survive—change. New technology and the mobility of capital means that markets can shift faster than ever before. Some financial analysts wonder why companies
(45) should bother planning two years ahead when market dynamics might be transformed by next quarter. However, it is this pace of change that makes planning so crucial. Now, more than ever, companies have to stay alert to the marketplace.
(50) In an environment of continual and rapid change, long-range planning expands options and organizational flexibility.

18. The primary purpose of the passage is to
(A) refute the idea that change is bad for a corporation's long-term health
(B) describe how long-term planning, despite some potential pitfalls, can help a corporation to grow
(C) compare and contrast two styles of corporate planning
(D) evaluate the strategic planning goals of corporate America today
(E) defend a methodology that has come under sharp attack

19. It can be inferred from the passage that strategic planning during the 1980s had all of the following shortcomings EXCEPT
(A) a reliance on outside consultants who did not necessarily understand the nuts and bolts of the business
(B) a dependence on theoretical models that did not always perfectly describe the workings of the company
(C) an inherent weakness in the company's own ability to implement the strategic plan
(D) an excess of information and data that made it difficult to get to key concepts
(E) the lack of a forum for middle managers to express their ideas

GO ON TO THE NEXT PAGE.

20. The author most likely mentions the results of the survey of 1,000 companies in order to

    (A) put forth an opposing view on strategic plans which is later refuted
    (B) illustrate that when strategic planning is "hands-on," it produces uninspiring results
    (C) give a concrete example of why strategic planning did not work during the 1980s
    (D) support the contention that strategic planning can be very successful when done correctly
    (E) give supporting data to prove that many companies have implemented strategic plans

21. The passage suggests which of the following about the "financial analysts" mentioned in lines 44–47 ?

    (A) They believe that strategic planning is the key to weathering the rapid changes of the marketplace.
    (B) They are working to understand and anticipate market developments that are two years ahead.
    (C) Their study of market dynamics has led them to question the reliability of short-term planning strategies.
    (D) They might not agree with the author that one way to survive rapidly changing conditions comes from long-range planning.
    (E) They consider the mobility of capital to be a necessary condition for the growth of new technology.

22. Informed people generally assimilate information from several divergent sources before coming to an opinion. However, most popular news organizations view foreign affairs solely through the eyes of our State Department. In reporting the political crisis in a foreign country, news organizations must endeavor to find alternative sources of information.

Which of the following inferences can be drawn from the argument above?

    (A) To the degree that a news source gives an account of another country that mirrors that of our State Department, that reporting is suspect.
    (B) To protect their integrity, news media should avoid the influence of State Department releases in their coverage of foreign affairs.
    (C) Reporting that is not influenced by the State Department is usually more accurate than are other accounts.
    (D) The alternative sources of information mentioned in the passage might not share the same views as the State Department.
    (E) A report cannot be seen as influenced by the State Department if it accurately depicts the events in a foreign country.

GO ON TO THE NEXT PAGE.

23. A decade after a logging operation in India began cutting down trees in a territory that serves as a sanctuary for Bengal tigers, the incidence of tigers attacking humans in nearby villages has increased by 300 percent. Because the logging operation has reduced the number of acres of woodland per tiger on average from 15 acres to approximately 12 acres, scientists have theorized that tigers must need a minimum number of acres of woodland in order to remain content.

Which of the following statements, if true, would most strengthen the scientists' hypothesis?

(A) In other wildlife areas in India where the number of acres of woodland per tiger remains at least 15 acres, there has been no increase in the number of tiger attacks on humans.

(B) Before the logging operation began, there were many fewer humans living in the area.

(C) The largest number of acres per tiger before the logging operation began was 32 acres per tiger in one area of the sanctuary, whereas the smallest number of acres per tiger after the logging operation was 9 acres.

(D) Other species of wild animals have begun competing with the Bengal tigers for the dwindling food supply.

(E) The Bengal tiger has become completely extinct in other areas of Asia.

24. A greater number of fresh vegetables are sold in City X than in City Y. Therefore, the people in City X have better nutritional habits than those in City Y.

Each of the following, if true, weakens the conclusion above EXCEPT:

(A) City X has more people living in it than City Y.

(B) Most of the people in City Y work in City X and buy their vegetables there.

(C) The people in City X buy many of their vegetables as decorations, not to eat.

(D) The per capita consumption of junk food in City X is three times that of City Y.

(E) The average price per pound of vegetables in City Y is lower than the average price per pound of vegetables in City X.

GO ON TO THE NEXT PAGE.

Questions 25–28 are based on the following passage:

In Roman times, defeated enemies were generally put to death as criminals for having offended the emperor of Rome. In the Middle Ages, however, the practice of ransoming, or (5) returning prisoners in exchange for money, became common. Though some saw this custom as a step toward a more humane society, the primary reasons behind it were economic rather than humanitarian.

(10) In those times, rulers had only a limited ability to raise taxes. They could neither force their subjects to fight nor pay them to do so. The promise of material compensation in the form of goods and ransom was therefore the only way of inducing (15) combatants to participate in a war. In the Middle Ages, the predominant incentive for the individual soldier was the expectation of spoils. Although collecting ransom clearly brought financial gain, keeping a prisoner and arranging for his exchange (20) had its costs. Consequently, procedures were devised to reduce transaction costs.

One such device was a rule asserting that the prisoner had to assess his own value. This compelled the prisoner to establish a value without (25) too much distortion; indicating too low a value would increase the captive's chances of being killed, while indicating too high a value would either ruin him financially or create a prohibitively expensive ransom that would also result in death.

25. The primary purpose of the passage is to

(A) discuss the economic basis of the medieval practice of exchanging prisoners for ransom
(B) examine the history of the treatment of prisoners of war
(C) emphasize the importance of a warrior's code of honor during the Middle Ages
(D) explore a way of reducing the costs of ransom
(E) demonstrate why warriors of the Middle Ages looked forward to battles

26. It can be inferred from the passage that a medieval soldier

(A) was less likely to kill captured members of opposing armies than was a soldier of the Roman Empire
(B) operated on a basically independent level and was motivated solely by economic incentives
(C) had few economic options and chose to fight because it was the only way to earn an adequate living
(D) was motivated to spare prisoners' lives by humanitarian rather than economic ideals
(E) had no respect for his captured enemies since captives were typically regarded as weak

GO ON TO THE NEXT PAGE.

27. Which of the following best describes the change in policy from executing prisoners in Roman times to ransoming prisoners in the Middle Ages?

    (A) The emperors of Rome demanded more respect than did medieval rulers, and thus Roman subjects went to greater lengths to defend their nation.
    (B) It was a reflection of the lesser degree of direct control medieval rulers had over their subjects.
    (C) It became a show of strength and honor for warriors of the Middle Ages to be able to capture and return their enemies.
    (D) Medieval soldiers were not as humanitarian as their ransoming practices might have indicated.
    (E) Medieval soldiers demonstrated more concern about economic policy than did their Roman counterparts.

28. The author uses the phrase "without too much distortion" (lines 24–25) in order to

    (A) indicate that prisoners would fairly assess their worth
    (B) emphasize the important role medieval prisoners played in determining whether they should be ransomed
    (C) explain how prisoners often paid more than an appropriate ransom in order to increase their chances for survival
    (D) suggest that captors and captives often had understanding relationships
    (E) show that when in prison a soldier's view could become distorted

END OF WARM-UP TEST

Chapter 23
GMAT Math and Verbal Warm-Up Questions: Answers and Explanations

GMAT WARM-UP QUESTIONS SCORING GUIDE

Detailed explanations to these answers can be found on page 636.

ANSWER KEY

MATH		VERBAL	
1.	C	16.	C
2.	C	17.	B
3.	B	18.	B
4.	D	19.	C
5.	A	20.	D
6.	A	21.	D
7.	D	22.	D
8.	D	23.	A
9.	A	24.	E
10.	E	25.	A
11.	A	26.	A
12.	E	27.	B
13.	A	28.	A
14.	D		
15.	D		

The Math Score

If you got 6 or fewer math questions correct: Your percentile rank is in the lower one-third of the testing group, and you should begin by practicing the problems in Math Bin 1. Once you've mastered the material in Math Bin 1, you should move on to the questions in Math Bin 2.

If you got between 6 and 13 math questions correct: Your percentile rank is in the middle one-third of the testing group, and you should begin by practicing the problems in Math Bin 2. Once you've mastered the material in Math Bin 2, you should move on to the questions in Math Bin 3.

If you got 14 or more math questions correct: Your percentile rank is in the top one-third of the testing group, and you should begin by practicing the problems in Math Bins 3 and 4.

The Verbal Score

If you got 6 or fewer verbal questions correct: Your percentile rank is in the lower one-third of the testing group, and you should begin by practicing the problems in Verbal Bin 1. Once you've mastered the material in Verbal Bin 1, you should move on to the questions in Verbal Bin 2.

If you got between 6 and 13 verbal questions correct: Your percentile rank is in the middle one-third of the testing group, and you should begin by practicing the problems in Verbal Bin 2. Once you've mastered the material in Verbal Bin 2, you should move on to the questions in Verbal Bin 3.

If you got 14 or more verbal questions correct: Your percentile rank is in the top one-third of the testing group, and you should begin by practicing the problems in Verbal Bin 3.

(If you want additional practice for either the Math or the Verbal section, you may find it helpful to do the problems in a bin with a lower number than the one suggested. So if your math diagnostic score indicates that you should do the questions in Math Bin 2, you might want to do the questions in Math Bin 1 as well.)

The Combined Score

If you got 12 or fewer of the 40 total questions correct: Your combined score at the moment is less than 450.

If you got between 12 and 31 of the 40 total questions correct: Your combined score at the moment is between 450 and 550.

If you got 32 or more of the 40 total questions correct: Your combined score at the moment is more than 550.

1. If $(16)(3^2) = x(2^3)$, then $x =$

   (A) 81
   (B) 72
   (C) 18
   (D) 16
   (E) 8

2. By how many dollars is the price of a computer reduced during a sale?

   (1) The price of the computer is reduced by 25% during the sale.
   (2) The sale price of the computer is $36.

   (A) Statement (1) ALONE is sufficient, but statement (2) alone is not sufficient.
   (B) Statement (2) ALONE is sufficient, but statement (1) alone is not sufficient.
   (C) BOTH statements TOGETHER are sufficient, but NEITHER statement ALONE is sufficient.
   (D) EACH statement ALONE is sufficient.
   (E) Statements (1) and (2) TOGETHER are not sufficient.

3. Of the 720 players who participated in a softball tournament, 65 percent traveled more than 200 miles to play. What is the difference between the number of participants who traveled more than 200 miles and the number of participants who traveled 200 miles or less?

   (A) 108
   (B) 216
   (C) 252
   (D) 468
   (E) 655

1. **C** Before doing the algebra to uncover the value of x, recognize that the algebra is made easier by breaking 16 down into its prime factors. The prime factorization of 16 is 2^4, so this equation can be rewritten as $(2^4)(3^2) = x(2^3)$. Now solve for x by dividing 2^3 from each side of the equation to find that $x = 2(3^2)$. Solve to find that $x = 18$ and the correct answer is (C).

2. **C** This is a Value Data Sufficiency question, so start by determining what is known from the question and what is needed from the statements to answer the question. What is known is that a computer's price is reduced during a sale. The statements need to provide a way to determine the original price and the sale price. Evaluate each statement individually. Statement (1) gives the percent reduction in price, but the actual price or sale price is not given. Statement (1) is insufficient, so write down BCE. Statement (2) gives the sale price of the computer, but no information about the original price, so statement (2) is insufficient. Eliminate (B). The statements combined give the percent reduction and the sale price, which is enough information to determine the original price. Because the original price is lowered by 25%, the sale price is 75% of the original. Therefore, the sale price can be determined with the equation $36 = \frac{75}{100} x$ and $x = 48$. The statements combined are sufficient. The correct answer is (C).

3. **B** This is a percent problem, so start by finding the number of players who traveled more than 200 miles: 65% of 720 is 468. The number of players who traveled 200 miles or less, then, is $720 - 468 = 252$ (or, alternatively, 35% of 720 is 252). Although both 468 and 252 are answer choices, the question asks for the difference between the two types of participants: $468 - 252 = 216$. The correct answer is (B).

4. If $r - s = 240$, does $r = 320$?

(1) $r = 4s$
(2) $s = 80$

(A) Statement (1) ALONE is sufficient, but statement (2) alone is not sufficient.
(B) Statement (2) ALONE is sufficient, but statement (1) alone is not sufficient.
(C) BOTH statements TOGETHER are sufficient, but NEITHER statement ALONE is sufficient.
(D) EACH statement ALONE is sufficient.
(E) Statements (1) and (2) TOGETHER are not sufficient.

4. **D** This is a Yes/No Data Sufficiency question, so look to Plug In. The question provides variables and asks to solve for one of the variables, so look for a way to consistently answer the question "Yes" or "No." Evaluate Statement (1). If $r = 4s$, then substitute $4s$ into r in the original equation to find that $4s - s = 240$. Therefore, $3s = 240$ and $s = 80$. So, $r = 320$. Write down AD. Statement (2) provides a value for s that can be used in the original equation to solve and find that $r = 320$. The correct answer is (D).

5. If a heavy-load trailer travels 7 miles in 1 hour and 10 minutes, what is its speed in miles per hour?

(A) 6
(B) 6.5
(C) 8
(D) 8.5
(E) 10

5. **A** The question mentions distances and rates, so make a Rate Pie. The distance is 7 miles. The time is 1 hour and 10 minutes. Convert 1 hour and 10 minutes to hours. 10 minutes is $\frac{1}{6}$ of an hour. So, the time is $1\frac{1}{6}$. Divide to find time: $\frac{7}{1\frac{1}{6}} = \frac{7}{\frac{7}{6}} = 7 \times \frac{6}{7} = 6$. The correct answer is (A).

6. If Bob purchases 18 cans of soda, how many of the cans are not diet soda?

(1) The number of diet soda cans Bob purchases is equal to the number that are not diet soda.
(2) Bob purchases an odd number of cans of diet soda.

(A) Statement (1) ALONE is sufficient, but statement (2) alone is not sufficient.
(B) Statement (2) ALONE is sufficient, but statement (1) alone is not sufficient.
(C) BOTH statements TOGETHER are sufficient, but NEITHER statement ALONE is sufficient.
(D) EACH statement ALONE is sufficient.
(E) Statements (1) and (2) TOGETHER are not sufficient.

6. **A** This is a Value Data Sufficiency question, so begin by determining what is known and what is needed to answer the question. What is known is that Bob purchased 18 cans of soda. The question asks how many cans are not diet soda. The statements need to provide a way to determine the number of cans that contain diet and non-diet soda. Statement (1) states there is an equal number of diet and non-diet cans, which means that there are 9 cans of each. Statement (1) is sufficient. Write AD. Statement (2) states that Bob purchased an odd number of cans of diet soda. However, there is no way to tell if that means he purchased 5 cans of diet soda or 11 cans of diet soda. Statement (2) is insufficient. The correct answer is (A).

QUESTIONS

7. At Perry High School, the ratio of students who participate in either the band program or the choral program to students who participate in neither program is 3 to 8. If 220 students attend Perry High School, how many of them participate in neither program?

(A)   40
(B)   60
(C)   100
(D)   160
(E)   180

8. A $240 interest-free loan is to be paid back in equal monthly payments. If a total of $2\frac{1}{2}$ percent of the original amount of the loan is paid every 6 months, then how many months will it take to pay back $21.00 ?

(A)   6
(B)   7
(C)   18
(D)   21
(E)   24

9. If x and y are positive integers, then is x a factor of 12 ?

(1) xy is a factor of 12.
(2) $y = 3$

(A)   Statement (1) ALONE is sufficient, but statement (2) alone is not sufficient.
(B)   Statement (2) ALONE is sufficient, but statement (1) alone is not sufficient.
(C)   BOTH statements TOGETHER are sufficient, but NEITHER statement ALONE is sufficient.
(D)   EACH statement ALONE is sufficient.
(E)   Statements (1) and (2) TOGETHER are not sufficient.

MATH EXPLANATIONS

7. **D** The question involves ratios, so set up a Ratio Box. The ratio of the students who participate to those who don't is 3 to 8 and the total number of students is 220. Filling those into the box gives a total ratio of 11, which results in a multiplier of 20, because $11 \times 20 = 220$. Then, multiply 8 by 20 to get 160 students who don't participate in either program. The Ratio Box looks like this:

	Participate	Don't Participate	Total
Ratio	3	8	11
Multiplier	20	20	20
Actual	60	160	220

The correct answer is (D).

8. **D** Start by finding $2\frac{1}{2}$ percent of $240, which is $\frac{2.5}{100} \times 240 = 6$. So every 6 months a total of $6 is repaid. If these amounts are paid back in equal monthly payments, then each month $1 is paid toward the loan. So, to pay back $21.00 would take 21 months, and the correct answer is (D).

9. **A** This is a Yes/No Data Sufficiency question, so Plug In for the variables. Evaluate Statement (1). If the product of xy is a factor of 12, then xy is equal to 1, 2, 3, 4, 6, or 12. Plug In. If $x = 2$ and $y = 3$, then the answer to the question is "Yes." Plug In again to try to get an answer of "No." In fact, as long as the product of xy is a factor of 12, and x and y are integers, x is a factor of 12. Write down AD. Evaluate Statement (2). This statement provides no information about the value of x. Therefore, it is impossible to know if x is a factor of 12. The correct answer is (A).

10. If a zebra can only get water from either a stream or a pond, which of the two sources of water is closer to the zebra's current position?

   (1) Moving at a constant rate from its current position, the zebra reaches the stream in 2 hours.

   (2) Moving at a constant rate from the stream, the zebra takes 2 hours to reach the pond.

   (A) Statement (1) ALONE is sufficient, but statement (2) alone is not sufficient.

   (B) Statement (2) ALONE is sufficient, but statement (1) alone is not sufficient.

   (C) BOTH statements TOGETHER are sufficient, but NEITHER statement ALONE is sufficient.

   (D) EACH statement ALONE is sufficient.

   (E) Statements (1) and (2) TOGETHER are not sufficient.

10. **E** This is a Value Data Sufficiency question, so begin by determining what is known and what is needed to answer the question. The question provides that there are two locations to reach and asks which is closer. The statements must provide a way to determine the distance between the two points and the current position. Statement (1) gives the time it takes the zebra to reach the stream from its current position; however, it gives no information about the time required to reach the pond. Statement (1) is insufficient. Write down BCE.

Similarly, Statement (2) only gives the time it takes the zebra to get from the pond to the stream—and doesn't mention the zebra's current position. Statement (2) is insufficient. Eliminate (B).

Statements (1) and (2) together give how long it takes for the zebra to reach the stream and then how long it takes the zebra to reach the pond from the stream. However, no information is given about the direction. For example, the zebra, pond, and stream might be in a straight line, they could form many different triangles, or the zebra could even double back from the stream to the pond. The two statements together are insufficient. The correct answer to this question is (E).

11. What is the value of $x^2 - y^2$?

(1) $x - y = 0$
(2) $x + y = 4$

(A) Statement (1) ALONE is sufficient, but statement (2) alone is not sufficient.
(B) Statement (2) ALONE is sufficient, but statement (1) alone is not sufficient.
(C) BOTH statements TOGETHER are sufficient, but NEITHER statement ALONE is sufficient.
(D) EACH statement ALONE is sufficient.
(E) Statements (1) and (2) TOGETHER are not sufficient.

11. **A** This is a Value Data Sufficiency question, so determine what is known and what is needed. Start by noticing that $x^2 - y^2$ is the common quadratic $(x + y)(x - y)$. The question asks for the value of the expression, so the statements need to provide a way to determine the value of the variables or the expression as a whole. Statement (1) gives that $x - y = 0$. If $x - y = 0$, the value of $(x + y)(x - y)$ is also 0. Statement (1) is sufficient. Write AD.

Statement (2) says that $x + y = 4$. No information is given about $x - y$. For example, x and y could both be 2 or x could be 3 and y could be 1, both of which yield a different value for $x^2 - y^2$. Statement (2) is insufficient. The correct answer is (A).

12. A mixture of ground meat consists of 2 pounds of veal that costs x dollars per pound, and 5 pounds of beef that costs y dollars per pound. What is the cost of the mixture in dollars per pound?

(A) $2x + 5y$

(B) $\dfrac{2x + 5y}{xy}$

(C) $5(2x + 5y)$

(D) $x + y$

(E) $\dfrac{2x + 5y}{7}$

12. **E** There are variables in the answer choices, so Plug In. The question asks for the cost of the mixture in dollars per pound. Because there are 7 total pounds of meat, plug in numbers that are divisible by 7, such as $x = 14$ and $y = 7$. In that case, the total cost of the mixture is $(2)(14) + (5)(7) = 63$. Divide by 7 to get the cost per pound, which is \$9. Plug $x = 14$ and $y = 7$ into the answers, looking for one that equals 9. Only (E) equals 9, so the correct answer is (E).

QUESTIONS

13. Is $0 < y < 1$?

(1) $0 < \sqrt{y} < 1$

(2) $y^2 = \dfrac{1}{4}$

(A) Statement (1) ALONE is sufficient, but statement (2) alone is not sufficient.
(B) Statement (2) ALONE is sufficient, but statement (1) alone is not sufficient.
(C) BOTH statements TOGETHER are sufficient, but NEITHER statement ALONE is sufficient.
(D) EACH statement ALONE is sufficient.
(E) Statements (1) and (2) TOGETHER are not sufficient.

14. Last year, an appliance store sold an average (arithmetic mean) of 42 microwave ovens per month. In the first 10 months of this year, the store sold an average of only 20 microwaves per month. What is the average number of microwaves sold per month for the entire 22-month period?

(A) 21
(B) 30
(C) 31
(D) 32
(E) 44

MATH EXPLANATIONS

13. **A** This is a Yes/No Data Sufficiency question, so be prepared to Plug In more than once. Statement (1) states that $0 < \sqrt{y} < 1$, so test out possible values of y. The only values of y that will satisfy $0 < \sqrt{y} < 1$ are fractions (such as $\dfrac{1}{4}, \dfrac{1}{2}, \dfrac{4}{9}$, etc.). Therefore, the value of y is always between 0 and 1, and the answer to the question is "Yes." Statement (1) is sufficient. Write AD. Statement (2) states that $y^2 = \dfrac{1}{4}$, so y could be either $\dfrac{1}{2}$ or $-\dfrac{1}{2}$. In one case, the answer to the question is a "Yes" and in the other it is a "No." Statement (2) is insufficient. The correct answer is (A).

14. **D** If the appliance store sold an average of 42 microwaves per month last year, then the total microwaves sold for the year was $42 \times 12 = 504$. For the first 10 months of this year, the total sold was $20 \times 10 = 200$. So, the total sold for the 22-month period is 704. Divide 704 by 22 to get the average. $704 \div 22 = 32$. The correct answer is (D).

ADVANCE PURCHASE DISCOUNTS FOR AIRLINE TRAVEL	
Days Prior to Departure	**Percentage Discount**
0–6 days	0%
7–13 days	10%
14–29 days	25%
30 days or more	40%

15. The table above shows the discount structure for advanced purchase of tickets at a particular airline. A passenger bought a ticket at this airline for $1,050. Had she purchased the ticket one day later, she would have paid $210 more. How many days before her departure did she purchase her ticket?

(A)   6 days
(B)   7 days
(C)   13 days
(D)   14 days
(E)   29 days

15. **D**   The problem asks for a specific value, and that value is represented by the answer choices, so Plug In the Answers. Start with (C). If the passenger bought a ticket 13 days in advance versus 12 days in advance (one day later), then there would be no savings (discount is the same for 13 days and 12 days), so eliminate (C). Try (D). If the passenger bought a ticket 14 days in advance, then the discount is 25%. So, the cost of the ticket is 75% of the undiscounted cost. Set up an equation to find the undiscounted cost, which is $\frac{75}{100}x = 1,050$. Solving for x gives an undiscounted cost of $1,400. The discount if the ticket had been bought one day later is 10%. Since 10% of $1,400 is $140, the cost of the ticket is $1,260. The difference in cost is $1,260 − $1,050 = $210, which meets the condition of a $210 savings. The correct answer is (D).

16. It is posited by some scientists that the near extinction of the sap-eating gray bat of northwestern America was caused by government-sponsored logging operations in the early 1920s that greatly reduced the species' habitat.

Which of the following, if true, most strongly weakens the scientists' claims?

(A) Logging operations in the 1920s are widely held responsible for the near extinction of other species that lived in the same area.

(B) A boom in new home construction in the early 1920s led congress to open federal lands to logging operations.

(C) A 5-year drought in the early 1920s severely reduced the output of sap in trees in northwestern America.

(D) Numbers of sightings of sap-eating gray bats fell to their lowest numbers in 1926.

(E) Sightings of sap-eating gray bats in Europe stayed roughly the same during the same period.

16. **C**   The question asks which of the answer choices *most strongly weakens the scientists' claims*, so this is a weaken question. This is a causal argument, as the scientists' claim is that the bats' near extinction was caused by logging. The standard assumptions of a causal argument are that there are no other causes and it's not a coincidence. The argument is weakened by presenting an alternate cause or providing evidence that the argument presented is a coincidence. Evaluate each answer choice individually. Choice (A) strengthens the argument by presenting evidence that logging was responsible for the extinction of other species. Eliminate (A). Choice (B) is out of scope because the reasons for the logging are not the concern of the scientists. The scientists are concerned only about the link between the logging and the extinction of the bats. Eliminate (B). Choice (C) provides an alternate cause for the extinction of the bats. If there was no food source for the bats, then that could be the reason for their extinction. Keep (C). Choice (D) is out of scope because the *sightings* of the bats is not the concern of the scientists. Eliminate (D). Choice (E) is out of scope because it concerns the population of the bats on another continent. Eliminate (E). The correct answer is (C).

17. Whenever a major airplane accident occurs, there is a dramatic increase in the number of airplane mishaps reported in the media, a phenomenon that may last for as long as a few months after the accident. Airline officials assert that the publicity given the gruesomeness of major airplane accidents focuses media attention on the airline industry, and the increase in the number of reported accidents is caused by an increase in the number of news sources covering airline accidents, not by an increase in the number of accidents.

Which of the following, if true, would seriously weaken the assertions of the airline officials?

(A) The publicity surrounding airline accidents is largely limited to the country in which the crash occurred.

(B) Airline accidents tend to occur far more often during certain peak travel months.

(C) News organizations do not have any guidelines to help them decide how severe an accident must be for it to receive coverage.

(D) Airplane accidents receive coverage by news sources only when the news sources find it advantageous to do so.

(E) Studies by government regulators show that the number of airplane flight miles remains relatively constant from month to month.

17. **B** The question asks which of the answer choices *would seriously weaken the assertion of the airline officials,* so this is a weaken question. This argument uses a sampling reasoning pattern as the official asserts that there is no increase in mishaps during the months after an accident, but an increase in the number of news sources reporting mishaps. Therefore, the claim that *there is a dramatic increase in the number of airline mishaps* is contested by the airline officials. The standard assumption of a sampling reasoning pattern is that the sample is representative. Because the airline officials are challenging the assumption to weaken the assertion of the airline officials, the correct answer will show that the sample is representative. Choice (A) discusses the *country in which the crash occurred,* which is out of scope, so eliminate (A). Choice (B) weakens the claim of the airline officials by implying that certain months are more likely to have frequent accidents due to the high volume of flights. Keep (B). Choice (C) strengthens the argument because if there is no standard definition for what an accident is, then news organizations can use a broad definition of accident to inflate the number of accidents. Eliminate (C). Choice (D) strengthens the argument by providing evidence to suggest the sample is not representative because accidents are covered only *when the news sources find it advantageous to do so.* Eliminate (D). Choice (E) also strengthens the argument because if the *number of airplane flight miles remains relatively constant,* then the officials' commentary is correct, as the number of accidents would then be expected to be relatively constant, as well. Eliminate (E). The correct answer is (B).

Questions 18–21 are based on the following passage:

The function of strategic planning is to position a company for long-term growth and expansion in a variety of markets by analyzing its strengths
Line and weaknesses and examining current and
(5) potential opportunities. Based on this information, the company develops a strategy for itself. That strategy becomes the basis for supporting strategies for the company's various departments. This implementation stage is where all too
(10) many strategic plans go astray. Recent business management surveys show that most CEOs who have a strategic plan are concerned with the potential breakdown in the implementation of the plan. Unlike corporations in the 1980s that instinctively
(15) followed their 5-year plans, even when they were misguided, today's corporations tend to second-guess their long-term plans.

Outsiders can help facilitate the process, but in the final analysis, if the company does not make
(20) the plan, the company will not follow the plan. This was one of the problems with strategic planning in the 1980s. In that era, strategic planning was an abstract, top-down process involving only a few top corporate officers and hired guns. Number
(25) crunching experts came into a company and generated tome-like volumes filled with a mixture of abstruse facts and grand theories that had little to do with the day-to-day realities of the company. Key middle managers were left out of planning
(30) sessions, resulting in lost opportunities and ruffled feelings.

However, more hands-on strategic planning can produce startling results. A recent survey queried more than a thousand small- to medium-sized
(35) businesses to compare companies with a strategic plan to companies without one. The survey found that companies with strategic plans had annual revenue growth of 6.2 percent as opposed to 3.8 percent for the other companies.
(40) Perhaps most important, a strategic plan helps companies anticipate—and survive—change. New technology and the mobility of capital means that markets can shift faster than ever before. Some financial analysts wonder why companies
(45) should bother planning two years ahead when market dynamics might be transformed by next quarter. However, it is this pace of change that makes planning so crucial. Now, more than ever, companies have to stay alert to the marketplace.
(50) In an environment of continual and rapid change, long-range planning expands options and organizational flexibility.

18. The primary purpose of the passage is to

(A) refute the idea that change is bad for a corporation's long-term health
(B) describe how long-term planning, despite some potential pitfalls, can help a corporation to grow
(C) compare and contrast two styles of corporate planning
(D) evaluate the strategic planning goals of corporate America today
(E) defend a methodology that has come under sharp attack

18. **B** This is a primary purpose question. The subject of the question is the passage itself, and the task is to determine the primary purpose of the passage. The first paragraph of the passage states the *function of strategic planning* and that the strategy *becomes the basis for supporting strategies for the company's various departments*. The rest of the passage expands on the virtues and drawbacks of strategic planning. This is the primary purpose of the passage, so look for an answer choice that reflects this idea. Choice (A) is an example of extreme language, as the passage does not indicate that *change is bad*. Eliminate (A). Choice (B) effectively summarizes the main idea of the passage that despite some potential problems, strategic planning can allow a company to expand and grow. Keep (B). Choice (C) is a no such comparison answer, as the passage does not seek to *compare and contrast two styles of corporate planning*. Eliminate (C). Choice (D) is a memory trap as the passage does discuss the evaluation of goals, but the primary purpose is not to evaluate the *goals of corporate America*. Eliminate (D). Choice (E) is extreme language, as the passage does not seek to *defend* anything. Eliminate (E). The correct answer is (B).

19. It can be inferred from the passage that strategic planning during the 1980s had all of the following shortcomings EXCEPT

   (A) a reliance on outside consultants who did not necessarily understand the nuts and bolts of the business
   (B) a dependence on theoretical models that did not always perfectly describe the workings of the company
   (C) an inherent weakness in the company's own ability to implement the strategic plan
   (D) an excess of information and data that made it difficult to get to key concepts
   (E) the lack of a forum for middle managers to express their ideas

19. **C** The subject of the question is the *shortcomings of strategic planning during the 1980s.* This is an inference question, so the task is to determine what is true from the passage. This is an EXCEPT question, so the correct answer is the choice that is not true based on the information in the passage. Choice (A) is true because the third paragraph of the passage states that the use of outsiders was *one of the problems with strategic planning in the 1980s.* Eliminate (A). Choice (B) is also verified in the third paragraph which states that one of the problems was *abstruse facts and grand theories that had little to do with the day-to-day realities of the company.* Eliminate (B). Choice (C) is a memory trap from the second paragraph, which states that *today's corporations tend to second-guess their long-term plans* is a modern phenomenon, not one related to companies in the 1980s. Keep (C). Choice (D) is supported by the third paragraph, which states that *number crunching experts came into a company and generated tome-like volumes filled with a mixture of abstruse facts and grand theories.* Eliminate (D). Choice (E) is also supported by the third paragraph, which states *key middle managers were left out of planning sessions.* Eliminate (E). The correct answer is (C).

QUESTIONS

20. The author most likely mentions the results of the survey of 1,000 companies in order to

   (A) put forth an opposing view on strategic plans which is later refuted
   (B) illustrate that when strategic planning is "hands-on," it produces uninspiring results
   (C) give a concrete example of why strategic planning did not work during the 1980s
   (D) support the contention that strategic planning can be very successful when done correctly
   (E) give supporting data to prove that many companies have implemented strategic plans

VERBAL EXPLANATIONS

20. **D** The subject of the question is the *survey of 1,000 companies* and the task of the question is *most likely mentions,* so this is a purpose question. The passage states that the survey was to *compare companies with a strategic plan to companies without one* and that the survey *found that companies with strategic plans had annual revenue growth of 6.2 percent as opposed to 3.8 percent for the other companies.* This information bolsters the stance that strategic planning is valuable. Choice (A) is a reversal of the point of including the survey, so eliminate (A). Choice (B) contains recycled language as the passage does discuss *"hands-on"* but not in the context of the survey. Eliminate (B). Choice (C) is a memory trap, as the passage does discuss companies during the 1980s, but not in the context of the survey. Eliminate (C). Choice (D) is a good summary of the value of including the information about the survey, so keep (D). Choice (E) uses the extreme language *prove.* The survey does not prove that *many companies have implemented strategic plans,* only that companies that have a strategic plan have experienced higher annual growth. Eliminate (E). The correct answer is (D).

QUESTIONS

21. The passage suggests which of the following about the "financial analysts" mentioned in lines 44–47 ?

(A) They believe that strategic planning is the key to weathering the rapid changes of the marketplace.

(B) They are working to understand and anticipate market developments that are two years ahead.

(C) Their study of market dynamics has led them to question the reliability of short-term planning strategies.

(D) They might not agree with the author that one way to survive rapidly changing conditions comes from long-range planning.

(E) They consider the mobility of capital to be a necessary condition for the growth of new technology.

VERBAL EXPLANATIONS

21. **D** The subject of the question is the financial analysts in lines 44–47 and the task of the question is the word *suggests*, which means this is an inference question. Determine which of the answer choices is true based on the information in the passage. The passage states that *financial analysts wonder why companies should bother planning two years ahead* and then goes on to state that *it is this pace of change that makes planning so crucial. Now, more than ever, companies have to stay alert to the marketplace.* The financial analysts' argument is presented, and the author provides a reason why that argument is incorrect. Choice (A) is a reversal of the stance of the financial analysts, so eliminate (A). Choice (B) is a reversal of the stance of the financial analysts, so eliminate (B). Choice (C) is a reversal, as *short-term planning* is not the focus of the passage. Eliminate (C). Choice (D) is a good summary of the financial analysts mentioned in the passage, so keep (D). Choice (E) uses the recycled language *mobility of capital,* but this is not used in the context of the financial analysts. Eliminate (E). The correct answer is (D).

22. Informed people generally assimilate information from several divergent sources before coming to an opinion. However, most popular news organizations view foreign affairs solely through the eyes of our State Department. In reporting the political crisis in a foreign country, news organizations must endeavor to find alternative sources of information.

Which of the following inferences can be drawn from the argument above?

(A) To the degree that a news source gives an account of another country that mirrors that of our State Department, that reporting is suspect.

(B) To protect their integrity, news media should avoid the influence of State Department releases in their coverage of foreign affairs.

(C) Reporting that is not influenced by the State Department is usually more accurate than are other accounts.

(D) The alternative sources of information mentioned in the passage might not share the same views as the State Department.

(E) A report cannot be seen as influenced by the State Department if it accurately depicts the events in a foreign country.

22. **D** The question stem asks which of the answer choices is true based on the information in the passage. The question uses the word *inference* to describe the answer choices, so the correct answer has to be provable based on the passage. Choice (A) implies that the State Department's views are always likely to diverge from other news sources, which is extreme language. Eliminate (A). Choice (B) implies that the State Department should never be used as a news source, which is also extreme language that is not supported by the passage. Eliminate (B). Choice (C) is out of scope because the passage gives no information about *reporting that is not influenced by the State Department*. Eliminate (C). Choice (D) is supported by the passage because the *alternative sources* are akin to the *divergent sources* mentioned in the passage as necessary for coming to an opinion. Keep (D). Choice (E) uses the extreme language *cannot*, and the conversation about accuracy is out of scope. Eliminate (E). The correct answer is (D).

23. A decade after a logging operation in India began cutting down trees in a territory that serves as a sanctuary for Bengal tigers, the incidence of tigers attacking humans in nearby villages has increased by 300 percent. Because the logging operation has reduced the number of acres of woodland per tiger on average from 15 acres to approximately 12 acres, scientists have theorized that tigers must need a minimum number of acres of woodland in order to remain content.

Which of the following statements, if true, would most strengthen the scientists' hypothesis?

(A) In other wildlife areas in India where the number of acres of woodland per tiger remains at least 15 acres, there has been no increase in the number of tiger attacks on humans.
(B) Before the logging operation began, there were many fewer humans living in the area.
(C) The largest number of acres per tiger before the logging operation began was 32 acres per tiger in one area of the sanctuary, whereas the smallest number of acres per tiger after the logging operation was 9 acres.
(D) Other species of wild animals have begun competing with the Bengal tigers for the dwindling food supply.
(E) The Bengal tiger has become completely extinct in other areas of Asia.

23. **A** The question asks which of the answer choices *would most strengthen the scientists' hypothesis*, so this is a strengthen question. The argument uses a causal reasoning pattern, so identify the conclusion, premise, and any assumptions. The conclusion is that *tigers must need a minimum number of acres of woodland...to remain content*. The premise is that the *logging operation*, which has *reduced the number of acres of woodland per tiger*, has caused the increase in the *incidence of tigers attacking humans in nearby villages*. That standard assumption of a causal argument is that there is no other cause and it is not a coincidence. To strengthen the argument, the answer choices need to provide evidence that there is no other cause for the tiger attacks, or it is not a coincidence that the logging and the tiger attacks are not related. Choice (A) provides evidence that it is not a coincidence, so keep (A). Choice (B) gives an alternate cause for the increase in tiger attacks—in other words, it weakens the argument instead of strengthening it. Eliminate (B). Choice (C) adds details without really strengthening the argument, so (C) is out of scope. Eliminate (C). Choice (D) weakens the scientists' hypothesis by presenting a possible alternate cause for the tigers' attacks on humans. Eliminate (D). Choice (E) emphasizes the seriousness of the problem without shedding light on its cause, so (E) is out of scope. Eliminate (E). The correct answer is (A).

24. A greater number of fresh vegetables are sold in City X than in City Y. Therefore, the people in City X have better nutritional habits than those in City Y.

   Each of the following, if true, weakens the conclusion above EXCEPT:

   (A) City X has more people living in it than City Y.
   (B) Most of the people in City Y work in City X and buy their vegetables there.
   (C) The people in City X buy many of their vegetables as decorations, not to eat.
   (D) The per capita consumption of junk food in City X is three times that of City Y.
   (E) The average price per pound of vegetables in City Y is lower than the average price per pound of vegetables in City X.

24. **E** The question stem states *weakens the conclusion*, so this is a weaken question. The question stem also uses the word *EXCEPT*, so the task of the question is to determine which of the answer choices does not weaken the conclusion. The conclusion of the argument is that *the people in City X have better nutritional habits than those in City Y.* The premise of the argument is that the *greater number of fresh vegetables are sold in City X than in City Y.* Evaluate the answer choices individually, looking for one that does not weaken the conclusion. Choice (A) weakens the conclusion because if there are more people in City X than in City Y, then that explains why there are more fresh vegetables sold. Eliminate (A). Choice (B) weakens the argument because it provides another reason why more vegetables are sold in City X than in City Y. Eliminate (B). Choice (C) weakens the argument because it provides an alternate reason why more vegetables are sold in City X than are sold in City Y that is independent of *better nutritional habits.* Eliminate (C). Choice (D) also weakens the conclusion because it challenges the statement that *people in City X have better nutritional habits.* Eliminate (D). Choice (E) suggests that vegetables are cheaper in City Y, which does not weaken the argument. The correct answer is (E).

QUESTIONS

VERBAL EXPLANATIONS

Questions 25–28 are based on the following passage:

In Roman times, defeated enemies were generally put to death as criminals for having offended the emperor of Rome. In the Middle
Line Ages, however, the practice of ransoming, or
(5) returning prisoners in exchange for money, became common. Though some saw this custom as a step toward a more humane society, the primary reasons behind it were economic rather than humanitarian.

(10) In those times, rulers had only a limited ability to raise taxes. They could neither force their subjects to fight nor pay them to do so. The promise of material compensation in the form of goods and ransom was therefore the only way of inducing
(15) combatants to participate in a war. In the Middle Ages, the predominant incentive for the individual soldier was the expectation of spoils. Although collecting ransom clearly brought financial gain, keeping a prisoner and arranging for his exchange
(20) had its costs. Consequently, procedures were devised to reduce transaction costs.

One such device was a rule asserting that the prisoner had to assess his own value. This compelled the prisoner to establish a value without
(25) too much distortion; indicating too low a value would increase the captive's chances of being killed, while indicating too high a value would either ruin him financially or create a prohibitively expensive ransom that would also result in death.

25. The primary purpose of the passage is to

    (A) discuss the economic basis of the medieval practice of exchanging prisoners for ransom
    (B) examine the history of the treatment of prisoners of war
    (C) emphasize the importance of a warrior's code of honor during the Middle Ages
    (D) explore a way of reducing the costs of ransom
    (E) demonstrate why warriors of the Middle Ages looked forward to battles

25. **A** The subject of the question is the passage as a whole, and the task of the question is to determine the *primary purpose* of the passage. The passage is focused on discussing the *primary reasons* behind *ransoming* prisoners. Evaluate the answer choices individually. Choice (A) correctly summarizes the primary purpose of the passage, which is stated in the first paragraph sentence that states *the primary reasons behind* [ransoming] *were economic rather than humanitarian.* Choice (B) is a memory trap as the passage begins by discussing the historical treatment of prisoners of war, but this is not the primary purpose. Eliminate (B). Choice (C) discusses the *warrior's code of honor,* which is out of the scope of the passage. Eliminate (C). Choice (D) is a memory trap, as reducing the costs of ransom is part of the passage but not the primary purpose. Eliminate (D). Choice (E) is out of the scope of the passage. Eliminate (E). The correct answer is (A).

QUESTIONS

26. It can be inferred from the passage that a medieval soldier

    (A) was less likely to kill captured members of opposing armies than was a soldier of the Roman Empire
    (B) operated on a basically independent level and was motivated solely by economic incentives
    (C) had few economic options and chose to fight because it was the only way to earn an adequate living
    (D) was motivated to spare prisoners' lives by humanitarian rather than economic ideals
    (E) had no respect for his captured enemies since captives were typically regarded as weak

VERBAL EXPLANATIONS

26. **A** The subject of the question is the *medieval soldier*, and the task of the question is found in the word *inferred*. Determine what is true about the medieval soldier based on the information in the passage. Choice (A) is supported by the information in the first paragraph of the passage, so keep (A). Choice (B) is an example of extreme language because the soldiers are not *basically independent*. Eliminate (B). Choice (C) is a memory trap from the passage, but it is also an example of extreme language because the passage does not state that combat was the *only way to earn an adequate living*. Eliminate (C). Choice (D) is a reversal of the information in the passage from the first paragraph. Eliminate (D). Choice (E) is extreme language, as the passage does not support the idea that medieval soldiers had *no respect* for captured enemies. Eliminate (E). The correct answer is (A).

27. Which of the following best describes the change in policy from executing prisoners in Roman times to ransoming prisoners in the Middle Ages?

    (A) The emperors of Rome demanded more respect than did medieval rulers, and thus Roman subjects went to greater lengths to defend their nation.
    (B) It was a reflection of the lesser degree of direct control medieval rulers had over their subjects.
    (C) It became a show of strength and honor for warriors of the Middle Ages to be able to capture and return their enemies.
    (D) Medieval soldiers were not as humanitarian as their ransoming practices might have indicated.
    (E) Medieval soldiers demonstrated more concern about economic policy than did their Roman counterparts.

27. **B** The subject of the question is the *change in policy from executing prisoners in Roman times to ransoming prisoners in the Middle Ages,* and the task of the question is to determine which of the answer choices *best describes* the change. The passage states that *rulers…could neither force their subjects to fight nor pay them to do so* and that *the promise of material compensation in the form of goods and ransom was…the only way of inducing combatants to participate in a war.* Evaluate the answer choices individually. Choice (A) is out of scope, as the passage is not concerned with how much *respect* the rulers of the different time periods demanded. Eliminate (A). Choice (B) is a good summary of the information in the passage. Keep (B). Choice (C) is out of scope as *strength and honor of the Middle Ages* is not reflective of the reason for the change in policy. Eliminate (C). Choice (D) is a memory trap, as the passage does discuss the word *humanitarian,* but this is not a description of the change in policy. Eliminate (D). Choice (E) is also out of scope, so eliminate (E). The correct answer is (B).

QUESTIONS

28. The author uses the phrase "without too much distortion" (lines 24–25) in order to

(A) indicate that prisoners would fairly assess their worth
(B) emphasize the important role medieval prisoners played in determining whether they should be ransomed
(C) explain how prisoners often paid more than an appropriate ransom in order to increase their chances for survival
(D) suggest that captors and captives often had understanding relationships
(E) show that when in prison a soldier's view could become distorted

VERBAL EXPLANATIONS

28. **A** The subject of the question is the quoted phrase, and the task is to determine why the author uses the phrase. The phrase from the passage is mentioned in relationship with the concept that a prisoner had to *assess his own value.* The phrase is part of a description of a ransom value that was neither too low nor too high. Evaluate the answer choices individually. Choice (A) is a good summary of the reason for using the phrase, so keep (A). Choice (B) is a reversal of the information in the passage because the prisoners were not able to determine *whether they should be ransomed,* only how much they were ransomed for. Eliminate (B). Choice (C) is a reversal of the information in the passage because the prisoners did not pay more; they only set the value. Eliminate (C). Choice (D) is an example of extreme language, as captors and captives did not have an *understanding* relationship. Eliminate (D). Choice (E) is a reversal, as the information in the passage shows that prisoners do not become distorted. Eliminate (E). The correct answer is (A).

BONUS MATERIALS

Business School

INSIDER

Admissions and Financial Aid Advice

While *GMAT Focus Premium Prep* will prepare you for your exam, Business School Insider will help you navigate what comes next. The bonus materials included here contain invaluable information about what b-school is really like, wending your way through the financial aid and admissions processes, writing winning application essays, getting a job with an MBA, and more. Feel free to take advantage of this content, and we wish you the best of luck on your studies and preparation for business school.

Contents

Part 1

Is an MBA for You?

The MBA presents many opportunities but no guarantees. Whether you go to a first-tier full-time school across the country or to a less well-known, part-time school close to home, you'll acquire skills that could jumpstart a new career or take your existing career to levels that were previously unattainable. An MBA can be a ticket to power networks and recruiters, elite employers, and, of course, generous paychecks. It can transform you from low-level lackey to executive material in a mere 21 months, possibly fewer. But you could also end up with a mere piece of paper that doesn't help your career all that much, considering all your trouble—not to mention a very uncomfortable amount of debt.

The MBA is not remotely indispensable if you want to be a titan of industry, or even a vice titan. Don't let anyone tell you it is. Plenty of fabulously successful businesspeople who never bothered to get an MBA have done exceedingly well for themselves, including, just for example, Jeff Bezos, the founder of Amazon, and Steve Jobs, a co-founder of Apple. Mary Kay Ash, founder of Mary Kay Cosmetics; Bill Gates, co-founder of Microsoft; and Mark Zuckerberg, co-founder of Facebook, didn't even bother graduating from college, much less hitting b-school.

Of course, lots of really successful people in the business world do have MBAs. There's Phil Knight (Stanford, '62) who co-founded Nike. There's also George W. Bush (43rd president of the United States, Harvard, '75), Leonard A. Lauder (chairman emeritus of The Estée Lauder Companies Inc., Wharton '54), David Viniar (CFO and Executive Vice President of Goldman Sachs, Harvard '80), and banking bigwig Sallie Krawcheck (Columbia, '92). About a third of the CEOs at the biggest and best multinational firms have MBAs.

Most people who are thinking about getting an MBA aren't looking to start the most successful shoe company on the planet, or run for president, or preside over a large semiconductor chip-making company, though. Those accomplishments would be great, sure, but it would also be pretty swell just to become a fairly anonymous cog in upper management at an established company one day.

The first question you have to ask yourself if you are thinking of getting an MBA is big, basic, and blindingly obvious: Do you really want a career in business? If you are a writer or a scientist, an MBA isn't going to add much value unless, say, you want to write for the *Wall Street Journal* or you want to get into management at a big pharmaceutical conglomerate.

Provided that you can affirmatively answer that you want a business career, the next equally important question is: What exactly do you think an MBA is going to do for your career in business? In some niches of the business world (such as big consulting firms and big banks), virtually nobody is going to hire or seriously promote you unless you have this particular credential.

In other areas, though, such as trading, you can get by just fine with a bachelor's degree. So, what's an MBA going to do for you exactly? What barriers is it going to break down? Are you looking to gain credibility, accelerate your development, or move into a new job or industry? Are you simply looking to make more money? Are you looking for a promotion where you work now? How will an MBA help you reach those goals?

You Need a Plan

Don't go to business school unless you have a very firm idea about why you want to go to business school. Go to law school if you feel rudderless. (That's a joke, sort of.) We're not going to tell you that you can't go to b-school without some crazy 50-year life strategy and a laser-like industry focus, but it really will be better if you have some pretty concrete plans about your future as a businessperson, and some legitimate reasons for getting an MBA before you apply. It would be nice, for example, if you could declare that you are getting an MBA because you want to move from some technical area of expertise to, say, something finance-oriented, or even just that you want to move from a smaller firm to a larger one. Try to come up with something as defined and unambiguous as possible.

At the very least, you need to have a solid, coherent story that will impress an admissions staff. Knowing what you want doesn't just affect your decision to go, it also affects the quality of your application to various b-schools. Admissions committees favor applicants who have clear goals and objectives. They want a compelling story. Ideally, that story would even have the added benefit of being true because, obviously, you'll get more out of your education if you can find a school that offers the coursework and curriculum that fit your individual needs. Additionally, once you are actually enrolled, you'll be able to suck a lot more of the marrow out of your two years (or one year, or three, or whatever) if you have a clear objective in mind. If you're uncertain about your goals, you'll squander a lot of opportunities for career development, such as networking, mentoring, student clubs, and recruiter events.

WHY DO OTHER PEOPLE GO TO BUSINESS SCHOOL?

Networking. According to a survey by the Graduate Management Admission Council (the people who also bring you the GMAT), close to 50 percent of students enrolled in one- and two-year MBA programs say that networking opportunities most motivated them to pursue the degree. Business schools can provide an instant pedigree and amazing access. The cachet of an MBA opens doors to choice internships, blue-chip recruiters, and vast and loyal alumni networks. It's a veritable "in" for sectors such as private equity that tend to shut out the hoi polloi. There are also the professors on the faculty. They know people you want to know. The various business bigwigs who visit campus are good for even more contacts. And there are your classmates, who themselves have big ideas and vital connections.

To learn. Development of "the ability to control situations more effectively" is a very distant second in the Graduate Management Admission Council's survey of top reasons why people attend b-school. Graduate business schools teach the applied science of business. The best business schools combine the latest academic theories with pragmatic concepts and real-world solutions. They provide a very well-structured and fairly thorough grounding in operations, economics and accounting, finance, and marketing. B-schools also teach the analytical skills used to make complicated business decisions. You learn how to define the critical issues, apply analytical techniques, develop the criteria for decisions, and make decisions after evaluating their impact on other variables. Certainly, you'll get a slew of information from people who are vetted and qualified, and some of that information may even prove useful in your career. There is plenty of skills training as well. Business school stresses experiential learning. It's hands-on learning by doing, even if it's largely a sort of pseudo doing.

The prospect of interesting and exciting work. The prospect of finding better work to do motivates some b-school students. It's a remote third on the GMAC survey, just below the acquisition of management skills. Business school represents a nice, easy, fairly safe opportunity to reassess your career situation. One way or another, the job you have before you get an MBA will be among the principal factors influencing the job you get after you get your MBA. Nevertheless, the MBA route is a great way to catapult yourself into a different job or to move to a different industry altogether. An MBA is perhaps the only credential that allows you to make a lateral career move without reducing your income or your status. Many graduates use the degree to embark on entirely new career paths than those that brought them to the school; consultants become bankers, entrepreneurs become consultants, marketers become financiers, and so on. The MBA has been and will continue to be a terrific opportunity to reinvent yourself, and it's exceedingly common for people to make big professional changes once they get their degrees.

Part-time MBA and EMBA students are atypical. For part-time and executive MBA students, maintaining a marketable resume and learning how to manage more effectively are roughly tied for first place on the GMAC survey. Gaining confidence is a remote third among motivating factors for these students, and networking opportunities aren't nearly as coveted, for the obvious reasons that these students are already have positions in industry.

More money. Let's be honest here. Networking opportunities, management skills, and all the rest are great, but what a very high percentage of people ultimately want to do above all else with an MBA is make more money. There's definitely nothing wrong with that. We're talking about business, after all, not social work. And those three additional letters near your name can translate to a higher salary—sometimes a significantly higher salary—and all the trappings that come with it, particularly if you work or would like to work for a large, established company.

More prestige. Ideally, if you build a better mouse trap, the world will beat a path to your door. Actual, manifest accomplishment should be rewarded, right? Sadly, things don't always work that way. Status is a big deal and a fancy advanced degree confers status quickly and efficiently. Is that good and fitting? Maybe, maybe not, but the fact is that there's prestige attached to an MBA, particularly one from an exclusive, highly-ranked school. Your opinions are likely to carry more weight once you get the degree. Your resume might receive more attention. You might progress up the corporate ladder more quickly.

A NOTE FOR BUDDING ENTREPRENEURS

If you are a budding entrepreneur thinking about starting your own business, there are arguments both for and against getting an MBA.

The argument for b-school is that you'll be exposed to an array of different business issues and plenty of innovative management and leadership training. The greatest idea in the world is a loser if you don't know how to steer it to profitability. All of that instruction and coursework should equip you to turn your business idea into a cold, hard, cash-generating reality. Also, business school is all about networking and you are unlikely to find a better place to find capital and potential partners than an MBA program, especially if you are younger.

The argument against b-school for entrepreneurs is that the cost of getting an MBA is very high in one particularly critical aspect: time. If you go the traditional b-school route, you lose at least the better part of two precious years of working on and nurturing and growing your idea. Worse still, somebody else with pretty much the same idea might beat you to the market. The cost of getting an MBA is very high in the critical aspect of money too. You'll likely incur debt, which is a problem for any fledgling industrialist.

On top of all that, you'll probably learn to be more risk-averse—anathema to entrepreneurial gumption.

Getting a Job with an MBA

It's critically important to consider placement rates and the list of companies that typically recruit at the schools you consider. There is great variability in placement rates and starting salaries among schools. The industry you chose to work in strongly affects your job prospects, and several other factors also affect job placement and starting salary.

FACTORS THAT MATTER

Reputation. At the top programs, the lists of recruiters read like a "Who's Who" of American companies. The fancy-pants schools not only attract the greatest volume of recruiters, but they consistently get the attention of the companies where jobs tend to be most sought after. Traditionally heavy hirers such as investment banking and consulting companies continue to offer the highest starting salaries and signing bonuses, and recruiters from those firms gravitate to the name-brand schools. At the same time, there's something to be said for a homegrown MBA. Lesser-known, regional schools often have very strong relationships with local employers and industries. The business community in a given region often regards local b-schools (many of them state universities) very highly. Rutgers University in New Jersey, for instance, holds great sway at nearby, national employers such as Johnson & Johnson, providing graduates with a unique competitive advantage.

You. Your background and experiences also affect your success in securing a position. Important factors are academic standing, prior work experience, and the skills and knowledge you gained both during and before b-school. Intangibles matter too, such as your personal fit with the company. These days, prior experience is particularly important; it helps establish credibility and gives you an edge in competing for a position in a specific field. If your goal is to switch to a new industry, it's helpful if something on your resume ties your interest to the new profession. It's also smart to secure a summer job in the sector in which you want a career.

Student groups. On-campus clubs and organizations also play a big part in getting a job because they extend the recruiting efforts at many schools. Clubs host a variety of events that allow you to meet big kahunas, so that you can learn more about their industries and their specific companies. Clubs are also very effective at bringing in recruiters and other interested parties that do not recruit through traditional mainstream channels. For example, the high-tech, international, and entertainment student clubs provide career opportunities not available through the front door.

Alumni. The people who preceded you as graduates of an MBA program are also an important part of the b-school experience. While professors teach business theory and practice, alumni provide insight into the real business world. When you're ready to interview, alums can provide advice on how to get hired by the companies recruiting at your school. In some cases, they help you secure the interview and shepherd you through the hiring process. At the very least, alumni will help you get your foot in the door. A resume sent to an alum at a given company, instead of to "Sir or Madam" in the personnel department, has a much better chance of being noticed and acted on. Moreover, regional alumni clubs and alumni publications keep you plugged in after you graduate with class notes detailing who's doing what, where, and with whom. (It's that networking thing again.) Throughout your career, an active alumni relations department can give you continued support. Post-MBA executive education series, fund-raising events, and continued job placement efforts are all resources you can draw on for years to come.

Pluck. Finally, at the end of the day, getting a job once you have an MBA is pretty much the same as getting any other job. Persistence and initiative are always going to be helpful. Increasingly, even at the best schools, finding a job requires off-campus recruiting efforts and ferreting out the hidden jobs.

SOME BAD CAREER NEWS

There has been a pretty severe retrenchment of traditional MBA destinations (such as investment banks and consulting firms) in recent years. Do employers see the skill sets of today's MBAs bringing measurable value to their companies? In many cases, they don't. Companies big, small, and in-between just aren't hiring MBAs at anywhere near the level they did before the advent of the Great Recession. The business isn't there, so the revenue isn't there, so the jobs aren't available. According to a survey by the Graduate Management Admission Council, roughly 60 percent of traditional, full-time MBA students have offers by the spring of their second year. That's up nicely from the downright grim figure of 40 percent of a few years ago, but it's less than rosy.

Corporate recruitment strategy isn't what it used to be, either. Businesses are tightening their belts, fighting tooth and nail to stay competitive, and all manner of other bad clichés. Many companies in the consulting, finance, and consumer goods industries are opting to hire people with Bachelor's degrees instead of MBAs for management-track positions. Certainly, the salaries the companies must pay are lower. A typical hire out of college can expect to make a little more than $40,000 a year, while the average graduate of an MBA program can expect to make around $95,000. Younger applicants have fewer skills, but they are also less likely to have formed too many bad habits. Freshly-minted undergrads, with their minds full of mush, are more malleable. Companies get to start with a clean slate.

SOME GOOD CAREER NEWS

Check out The Princeton Review's latest rankings for "Best Career Prospects" in your Student Tools.

A recent Bloomberg *Businessweek* survey of 1,500 people who got their MBAs in 1992 found that salaries and bonuses are robust (at least for those people). A large number of the survey participants occupy executive positions in their respective companies. So that's some consolation.

It's also comforting to keep in mind the fact that hundreds of companies continue to visit and recruit from business school campuses. Job offers happen frequently and regularly. Recruiters exist in a symbiotic relationship with business schools. Employers maintain a strong presence on campus—even during an economic downturn—because doing so is in their best interests. When the good times eventually roll again, they'll want to have easy access to MBA programs. Consequently, MBA programs remain one of the most effective means to get yourself in front of recruiters and senior managers from the most desirable companies.

How many—and what kind—of offers will you receive? That's largely dependent on the appeal of your school to recruiters (which companies recruit on campus and how often they do so are statistics that will be readily available at any reputable school) and the particular industry you elect to pursue. For example, investment banks and consulting firms are always going to come to the schools for formal recruiting periods, whereas more off-the-beaten-path choices will require you to go off campus in search of opportunity.

At programs such as Chicago, Harvard, and Duke, six-figure salaries and sweet signing bonuses are still the norm for graduates. The majority of top grads receive a generous relocation package too. Indeed, if you were fortunate enough to have spent the summer between your first and second year at a consulting company, then you may also receive a "rebate" on your tuition. These companies often pick up your second-year tuition bill as well.

Types of Degree Programs

TWO-YEAR PROGRAMS

Traditional two-year MBA programs are ubiquitous, so they're the ones we've spent most of the time discussing here. They involve the same basic academic year, the same weekday classes, and the same long summer break that you've experienced since kindergarten.

ACCELERATED PROGRAMS

Accelerated MBA programs are faster versions of two-year programs. There's no summer vacation and holiday breaks are shorter. Course loads are higher; exams are frequent; and the whole experience is more rigorous and intensive. There's also no time for a summer job, which can be a big deal since many students hope summer jobs will lead to post-grad offers. Accelerated programs which typically last between 10 and 15 months are pretty standard in Europe, and they are becoming more common in the United States as well. Durations vary stateside. The accelerated program at Cornell University's Johnson School lasts a year (from May to May). Pepperdine's Graziadio School offers both 12-month and 15-month options. And finally, some full-time programs are basically accelerated programs. For example, it takes only 18 months to get an MBA at the Mays Business School at Texas A&M.

PART-TIME PROGRAMS

In conventional part-time MBA programs, you take classes on weekday nights and on the weekends. They last three years, sometimes longer. The process is essentially the same. You have access to the same professors, or at least a lot of them. It just takes longer and course loads are lighter. The obvious draw of part-time enrollment is that you get to keep your day job and the income it provides. The drawback is that networking and social opportunities are more limited. Also, part-time students aren't able to participate in on-campus recruiting events nearly as often as their full-time counterparts.

EXECUTIVE MBA PROGRAMS

EMBA programs are designed for managers and executives who already have fairly impressive full-time jobs and a higher level of professional experience. There are a few hundred EMBA programs to choose from around the world, and they tend to have a few essential features. Committing to a garden-variety EMBA program means spending every other Friday or so at school for, say, 20 months. That's important to consider because your boss will have to support your degree quest (or, at least, agree to your absence every other Friday). It's fair to say that EMBA programs have less rigorous admissions requirements as well. (Many don't even require a GMAT score.) Curricula are lighter and there are fewer course requirements. Also, EMBA programs vary a lot—and we mean a lot. Some schools are noted for finance, while others are all about entrepreneurship. At some schools, EMBA students rarely see rock-star professors; at other schools, those professors teach many classes. There's tremendous variance.

DUAL-DEGREE PROGRAMS

There's not much to say here since you probably have a solid understanding of what a dual degree entails. Dual MBA programs combine an MBA degree and another degree (typically a JD, or some additional master's degree). It's a way to cut costs and time, but the trade-off is that you'll be signing up for a ton of work. It's also worth noting that some business schools offer the opportunity to get a bachelor's degree in business as well as an MBA in five years (or perhaps four if you are ridiculously diligent). Obviously, dual-degree programs are cheaper and quicker than pursuing both degrees separately, but they still cost more in time and money than a single degree, so all the same caveats about deciding to attend apply. If you're considering a dual-degree program, make sure you know why you need both degrees to achieve your goals. While many graduates of these programs are very satisfied with their choices, anecdotally, we've also spoken with a number of grads who say that they really use only the MBA or their other degree, and that they would have been better off doing a single-degree track.

DISTANCE LEARNING PROGRAMS

The Internet is pretty awesome and many schools allow you to earn an MBA from the comfort of your own home (or wherever your computer is). It's an affordable alternative and it's nothing if not flexible. There are some drawbacks. You won't be able to take advantage of many networking opportunities from your living room, for example. On the job front, there's not going to be much at all in the way of recruitment. Also, taking classes on a campus retains a lot of snob appeal. Maybe that's sad and wrong, but it's reality. Finally, if you do decide on the distance learning route, be careful about the school you choose. Some of them are great. Others, not so much.

MBA Concentrations

Back in the day, it was enough just to earn your MBA and enter the working world a more knowledgeable and employable individual for it. Today, business represents an increasingly multifaceted and diverse world. It's much harder to be a jack of all trades. As a result, specialization is king across most MBA programs.

When you are looking at potential business schools, it's imperative to know whether they offer the concentration you're keen on. Here's an all-too-brief guide to some of the common ones.

Finance. The finance concentration is about money—how to manage it, make it, and make more of it. A specialization in finance will prepare you to make smart financial decisions for individuals, institutions, and companies.

Marketing. Marketing professionals anticipate consumer demands. They help to create products and services that consumers want, attract consumers to that product or service, and work to retain consumers over the long haul. They also have their hands in pricing and distribution, figuring out what stuff should cost and how to get it to customers.

Accounting. As an accounting specialist, you'll become an expert in the gathering and interpretation of financial data and the ways in which that data can affect a company.

Supply chain management. In a world of global suppliers and tight profit margins, effective supply chain management can mean the difference between profitability and bankruptcy. A specialization in supply chain management will prepare you to create and manage the entire selling process for any company with a good or service to vend.

International management. A concentration in international management will prepare you to succeed in today's global business environment. Many programs require students to spend a semester overseas, working at a company or studying at a partner university.

Entrepreneurship. A concentration in entrepreneurship offers you the chance to develop real business savvy, network with potential collaborators and investors, and try out new ideas with fewer risks than you'll encounter in the cold, unforgiving world outside the Ivory Tower.

Nonprofit management. Running a nonprofit requires the same skills you need to run any business: raising capital, managing an organization for maximum cost efficiency, and effectively delivering goods and services. It also requires some different skills, such as an understanding of nonprofit laws and policies, and an emphasis on fundraising, grant-writing, and campaigning, among other skills. Thus, the specialization.

Leadership. This concentration is designed to help you develop skills that are essential to success in any field: critical thinking, problem-solving, communicating, negotiating, and acting ethically in professional situations.

Healthcare administration. This specialization will teach you how the nation's very intricate and convoluted healthcare system works. It will also help you learn how to deal with the challenges facing healthcare organizations—from government agencies to hospitals to biotech, pharmaceutical, and medical technology companies.

Human resources management. In this concentration, you'll learn how to maximize human output in a business environment, from understanding individual behavior to designing effective management structures, training programs, and compensation schemes.

Part 2

Admissions

PREPARING TO BE A SUCCESSFUL APPLICANT

Get Good Grades

If you're still in school, concentrate on getting good grades. A high GPA says you've got not only brains but also discipline. It shows the admissions committee you have what you need to make it through the program. If you're applying directly from college or have limited job experience, your grades will matter even more. The admissions committee will have little else on which to evaluate you.

It's especially important that you do well in courses such as economics, statistics, and calculus. Success in these courses is more meaningful than success in classes like "Monday Night at the Movies" film appreciation. Of course, English is also important; b-schools want students who communicate well.

Strengthen Math Skills

Number-crunching is an inescapable part of b-school. If your work experience has failed to develop your quantitative skills, take an accounting or statistics course for credit at a local college or b-school. If you have a liberal arts background and did poorly in math, or got a low GMAT Quantitative score, this is especially important. Getting a decent grade will go a long way toward convincing the admissions committee you can manage the quantitative challenges of the program.

Work for a Few Years—But Not Too Many

Business schools have traditionally favored applicants who have worked full-time for several years. There are three primary reasons for this:

1. With experience comes maturity.

2. You're more likely to know what you want out of the program.

3. Your experience enables you to bring real-work perspectives to the classroom. Because business school is designed for you to learn from your classmates, each student's contribution is important.

Until recently, b-schools preferred to admit only those students with two to five years of work experience. The rationale was that at two years you have worked enough to be able to make a solid contribution, while beyond four or five, you might be too advanced in your career to appreciate the program fully. However, there is a new trend among top schools toward admitting "younger" applicants—that is, candidates with limited work experience as well as those straight from college.

Depending on the schools to which you're applying and the strength of your resume of accomplishments, you may not need full-time, professional work experience. Of course, there's a catch: The younger you are, the harder you'll have to work to supply supporting evidence for your case as a qualified applicant. Be prepared to convince admissions committees that you've already done some incredible things, especially if you're hailing straight from college.

If you've targeted top-flight schools such as Wharton, Columbia, or Stanford, applying fresh out of college is still a long shot. While your chances of gaining admission with little work experience have improved, your best shot is still to err on the conservative side and get a year or two of some professional experience under your belt.

If you're not interested in the big league or you plan on attending a local program, the number of years you should work before applying may vary. Research the admissions requirements at your target school. There's no doubt the MBA will jumpstart your career and have long-lasting effects on your business (and perhaps personal) outlook. If you're not ready to face the real world after college, plenty of solid b-schools will welcome you to another two years of academia.

There is one caveat to this advice, however. If your grades are weak, consider working at least three years before applying. The more professional success you have, the greater the likelihood that admissions committees will overlook your GPA.

Let Your Job Work for You

Many companies encourage employees to go to b-school. Some of these companies have close ties to a favored b-school and produce well-qualified applicants. If their employees are going to the kinds of schools you want to get into, these may be smart places to work.

Other companies, such as investment banks, feature training programs, at the end of which trainees go to b-school or leave the company. These programs hire undergraduates right out of school. They're known for producing solid, highly skilled applicants. Moreover, they're full of well-connected alumni who may write influential letters of recommendation.

Happily, the opposite tactic—working in an industry that generates few applicants—can be equally effective. Admissions officers look for students from underrepresented professions. Applicants from biotechnology, health care, not-for-profit, and even the Peace Corps are viewed favorably.

One way to set yourself apart is to have had two entirely different professional experiences before business school. For example, if you worked in finance, your next job might be in a different field, such as marketing. Supplementing quantitative work with qualitative experiences demonstrates versatility.

Finally, what you do in your job is important. Seek out opportunities to distinguish yourself. Even if your responsibilities are limited, exceed the expectations of the position. B-schools are looking for leaders.

March from the Military

A surprising number of b-school students hail from the military (although the armed forces probably had commanders in mind, not CEOs, when they designed their regimen). Military officers know how to be managers because they've held command positions. And they know how to lead a team under the most difficult of circumstances.

Because most have traveled all over the world, they also know how to work with people from different cultures. As a result, they're ideally suited to learn alongside students with diverse backgrounds and perspectives. B-schools with a global focus are particularly attracted to such experience.

The decision to enlist in the military is a very personal one. However, if you've thought of joining those few good men and women, this may be as effective a means of preparing for b-school as more traditional avenues.

HOW THE ADMISSIONS CRITERIA ARE WEIGHTED

Although admissions requirements vary among business schools, most rely on the following criteria: GMAT score, college GPA, work experience, your essays, letters of recommendation (academic and/or professional), an interview with an admissions representative, and your extracurriculars. The first four are generally the most heavily weighted. The more competitive the school, the less room there is for weakness in any area. Any component out of sync, such as a weak GMAT score, is potentially harmful.

Happily, the admissions process at business school is one where great emphasis is placed on getting to know you as a person. The essay component is the element that allows the schools to do just that. Your essays can refute weaknesses, fill in gaps, and in general, charmingly persuade an admissions board you've got the right stuff. They are the single most important criteria in business school admissions.

But as we've just said, they're not the only criteria. All pieces of your application must come together to form a cohesive whole. It is the entire application that determines whether you win admission.

Anticipate and Coordinate

The application process is very time consuming, so anticipating what you need to accomplish within the admissions time frame is critical. To make the best use of our advice, you should first contact each of the programs on your personal list of schools. Their standards and criteria for admission may vary, and you'll need to follow their specific guidelines. Please note that the less competitive a school is, the more easily you may be able to breeze through (or completely omit) the rigorous requirements we identify as crucial in the application process for the top programs.

In addition, business school applicants are often overwhelmed by how much they have to do to complete not only one, but several applications. Proper management of the process is essential, since there are so many factors to coordinate in each application.

You'll have to prep for the GMAT, then actually take the test, round up some writers for your recommendations, follow up with those chosen to write recommendations, make sure the recommendations are mailed in on time, have your college transcript sent, and finally, write the essays. Of course, some schools require an interview as well. What makes all of this particularly challenging is that many applicants have to do all of this while balancing the demands of a full-time job.

We know that it takes a supreme force of will to complete even one application. As grad school applications go, a top business school's is pretty daunting. So if you don't stay focused on the details and deadlines, you may drop the ball.

There are many common and incredibly embarrassing mistakes you can avoid with prudent early planning. These include allowing your recommenders to miss the deadline, submitting an application full of typos and grammatical errors, sending one school an essay intended for another, or forgetting to change the school name when using the same essay for several applications. Applicants who wind up cramming for the GMAT or squeezing their essay writing into several all-nighters end up seriously shortchanging themselves.

Apply Early

The best advice is to plan early and apply early. The former diminishes the likelihood of an accidental omission or a missed deadline. The latter increases your chances of acceptance.

The filing period ranges anywhere from six to eight months. The earlier you apply, the better your chances. There are a number of reasons for this:

First, there's plenty of space available early on. Many b-schools have rolling admissions, and as the application deadline nears, spaces fill up. The majority of applicants don't apply until the later months because of procrastination or unavoidable delays. As the deadline draws close, the greatest number of applicants competes for the fewest number of spaces.

Second, in the beginning, admissions officers have little clue about how selective they can be. They haven't reviewed enough applications to determine the competitiveness of the pool. An early application may be judged more on its own merit than on how it stacks up against others. This is in your favor if the pool turns out to be unusually competitive. Above all, admissions officers like to lock their classes in early; they can't be certain they'll get their normal supply of applicants. Admissions decisions may be more generous at this time.

Third, by getting your application in early you're showing a strong interest. The admissions committee is likely to view you as someone keen on going to their school.

To be sure, some admissions officers report that the first batch of applications tends to be from candidates with strong qualifications, confident of acceptance. In this case, you might not be the very first one on line; but being closer to the front is still better than getting lost in the heap of last-minute hopefuls.

Rounds vs. Rolling Admissions

Applications are processed in one of two ways: rounds or rolling admissions. Schools that use rounds divide the filing period into three or so timed cycles. Applications are batched into the round in which they are received and reviewed in competition with others in that round. A list of a b-school's round dates can be obtained by contacting its admissions office if it employs this method. Applications to schools with rolling admissions are reviewed on an ongoing basis as they are received.

GMAT and GPA

The GMAT and GPA are used in two ways. First, they're "success indicators" for the academic work you'll have to slog through if admitted—will you have the brainpower to succeed in the program? Second, they're used as benchmarks to compare each applicant to other applicants within the pool. At the more selective schools, you'll need a higher score and average to stay in the game.

Your college transcript is a major factor in the strength of your candidacy. Some schools focus more closely on the junior- and senior-year grades than the overall GPA, and most consider the reputation of your college and the difficulty of your course selections. A transcript loaded with offerings such as "Environmental Appreciation" and "The Child in You" won't be valued as highly as one packed with calculus and history classes.

The Essays

Admissions committees consider the essays the clincher, the swing vote on the admit/deny issue. Essays offer the most substantive information about who you really are. The GMAT and GPA reveal little about you, only that you won't crash and burn. Your work history provides a record of performance and justifies your stated desire to study business. But the essays tie all the pieces of the application together and create a summary of your experiences, skills, background, and beliefs.

The essays do more than give answers to questions. They create thumbnail psychological profiles. Depending on how you answer a question or what you present, you reveal yourself in any number of ways—creative, witty, open-minded, articulate, mature, to name a few. On the other hand, your essay can also reveal a negative side, such as arrogance, sloppiness, or an inability to think and write clearly.

For international students
If you are an international student, you may be required to submit a Test of English as a Foreign Language (TOEFL) score. For more information on the test and how The Princeton Review can help you prepare for it, visit Princetonreview.com/k12/toefl-tutoring-course. Or check out our test-prep book *TOEFL iBT Prep with Audio/Listening Tracks.*

Visit your Student Tools for additional information on business school recommendations.

Letters of Recommendation

Letters of recommendation function as a reality check. Admissions committees expect them to support and reinforce what they're seeing in the rest of your application. When the information doesn't match up with the picture you've painted, it makes you look bad. Because you won't see the recommendation (it's sent in "blind"), you won't even know there's a problem. This can mean the end of your candidacy.

That's why you need to take extreme care in selecting your references.

Scan each application for guidelines on choosing your references—business schools typically request an academic and a professional reference. The academic reference should be someone who can evaluate your performance in an academic environment. It's better to ask an instructor, teacher's aide, or mentor who knew you well than a famous professor who barely knew your name.

The same holds true for your professional reference. Seek out individuals who can evaluate your performance on many levels. The reference will be far more credible. Finding the right person to write your professional reference, however, can be trickier. You may not wish to reveal to your boss early on that you plan on leaving, and if the dynamics of your relationship are not ideal (hey, it happens once in a while), they might not make an appropriate reference. If this is the case, seek out a boss at a former job or someone who was your supervisor at your current job but has since moved to another organization. Avoid friends, colleagues, and clients as references unless the school explicitly says it's okay.

Advise your writers on themes and qualities you highlighted in your application. Suggest that they include real-life examples of your performance to illustrate their points. In other words, script the recommendation as best you can. Your boss, even if they are your biggest fan, may not know what your recommendation should include.

A great recommendation is rarely enough to save a weak application from doom. But it might push a borderline case over to the "admit" pile. Mediocre recommendations can be damaging; an application that is strong in all other areas now has a weakness, an inconsistency.

A final warning on this topic: Procrastination is common here. Micromanage your references so that each recommendation arrives on time! If need be, provide packaging for an overnight letter, have your reference, seal it up, and then ship it out yourself.

The Interview

Not all business schools attach equal value to the interview. For some, it's an essential screening tool. For others, it's used to make a final decision on those caught somewhere between "admit" and "reject." Some schools may encourage, but not require, the interview. Others make it informative, with little connection to the admissions decision.

Like the letters of recommendation, an interview may serve as a reality check to reinforce the total picture. It may also be used to fill in the blanks, particularly in borderline cases.

If an interview is offered, take it. In person, you may be a more compelling candidate. You can use the interview to further address weaknesses or bring dull essays to life. Most importantly, you can display the kinds of qualities—enthusiasm, sense of humor, maturity—that can positively sway an admissions decision.

Act quickly to schedule your interview. Admissions departments often lack the time and staff to interview every candidate who walks through their doors. You don't want your application decision delayed by several months (and placed in a more competitive round or pool) because your interview was scheduled late in the filing period.

A great interview can tip the scale in the "admit" direction. How do you know if it was great? You were calm and focused. You expressed yourself and your ideas clearly. You developed a solid rapport with the interviewer.

A mediocre interview may not have much impact, unless your application is hanging on by a thread. In such a case, the person you're talking to (harsh as it may seem) is probably looking for a reason not to admit you, rather than a reason to let you in. If you feel your application may be in that hazy, marginal area, try to be extra-inspired in your interview.

Approach this meeting as you would a job interview. Remember, you're being sized up as a person in all of your dimensions. Here are a few tips to use during the interview.

- Dress and act the part of a professional but avoid being stiff or acting like a stuffed shirt.

- Limit your use of business jargon. Interviewers often hear a lot of the same generic answers. They are more interested in you being your witty, charming, natural self.

- Be personable and talk about your passions, such as hobbies or a recent trip you've taken. The idea is to get the interviewer thinking of you as someone who will contribute greatly to the quality of campus life.

Highlight your achievements and excellence, even in something like gourmet cooking, but avoid stunts, such as pulling out a platter of peppercorn pâté sautéed in anchovy sauce.

Part 3

Quotas, Recruitment, and Diversity

B-schools don't have to operate under quotas—governmental or otherwise. However, they probably try harder than most corporations to recruit diverse groups of people. Just as the modern business world has become global and multicultural, so too have b-schools. They must not only teach diversity in the classroom but also make it a reality in their campus population and, if possible, faculty.

Schools that have a diverse student body tend to be proud of it. They tout their success in profiles that demographically slice and dice the previous year's class by gender, race, and geographic and international residency. Prospective students can review this data and compare the diversity of the schools they've applied to.

However, such diversity doesn't come naturally from the demographics of the applicant pool. Admissions committees have to work hard at it. In some cases, enrollment is encouraged with generous financial aid packages and scholarships.

While they don't have quotas per se, they do target groups for admission, seeking a demographic balance in many areas. Have they admitted enough women, minorities, foreign students, marketing strategists, and liberal arts majors? Are different parts of the country represented?

As we've said before, the best b-schools tend to attract top talent, students, and recruiters to their campus. Women and minorities are the most sought-after groups targeted for admission. So it's no surprise that programs that report higher-than-average female and minority enrollments tend to be among the very best.

AN INITIATIVE FOR MINORITIES

Some schools report higher minority enrollments than others, so our advice is consistent: You need to thoroughly research the program you've set your sights on. Consider your goals. Do you simply want to attend the most prestigious program? How will social factors impact your goals and experiences on campus?

Most business schools aspire to diversify their programs. It's the number of minorities applying to business school that has remained consistently low. An initiative of the Graduate Management Admissions Council called The Diversity Pipeline Alliance (GMAC.com/Diversity) was formed to reverse this trend and increase the number of underrepresented minorities pursuing a business career. Much like the initiative for women, this organization plans a powerful marketing campaign with a pro-business career message for minority students from middle school to graduate school. It offers information on current opportunities for mentorships, internships, and financial assistance and provides an impressive roster of member organizations, services, and educational opportunities.

Minority enrollment at business schools is still quite low, so in all likelihood, you will not experience the dramatic upward shift in b-school demographics in the near future that initiatives such as the Diversity Pipeline Alliance hope to influence. However, by recognizing the disparity between the minority presence in the United States and minority involvement in business education and practice, we are working toward a solution.

As you make up your mind about where you want to go for b-school, know that the scenario is positive and that new infrastructures exist to support your business career.

FEMALE APPLICANTS AND STUDENTS

To check out which b-schools have the "Greatest Resources for Women," visit your Student Tools for the latest Business School Ranking lists.

If you've toured the campus and classrooms of a business school, you may have noticed something: On average, roughly 65 percent of any given MBA program's students are male. It's not something business schools are happy with—far from it! In fact, it's something they are working to change as quickly as they can.

Beyond showing significantly higher application volume, MBA programs of all types are seeing female applications increase. About 64 percent of full-time MBA programs have seen applications from women rise since 2006; the figure is 40 percent for part-time-programs and 33 percent for executive programs. Flexible MBA programs, which allow students to change between full-time and part-time throughout their time in the program, see the highest percentage of applications from women at 47%. While these numbers may not match the 50 percent male-to-female ratio of other graduate programs, closing the b-school gender gap is only a matter of time.

School Initiatives

How can we be sure that female enrollment will continue to increase? One reason is that getting women enthused about a career in business is a sky-high priority at business schools across the country these days. To wit, many business schools have launched their own outreach and recruiting events geared towards closing the gender gap. Many b-schools are also making strides to support and foster connection among female students. The Foster School of Business at the University of Washington hosts programs and events to promote the advancement of women as entrepreneurs and leaders. The Buerk Center's Women's Entrepreneurial Leadership program (WE Lead) welcomes students of any gender to participate in workshops, panels, and mentoring circles.

Stanford's events, says Wendy Hansen, Director of Operations, MBA Admissions, at the Stanford Business School, "focus on the educational experience, but also on the unique types of issues women have, such as: how does getting the MBA fit in with having a family or having a spouse? How do I make this experience fit in with my life?" Julia Min, Assistant Dean of Career Management Group and Corporate Engagement at UC Berkeley's Haas School of Business, says attendees often find comfort in numbers. "Seeing such a large presence of women is empowering. They realize they're not in this alone, that there are other women around like them."

If all this sounds like good public relations, it is. Schools want to get the word out: MBAs offer women viable opportunities. But if the business schools are talking the talk, they're also walking the walk. There's nothing superficial about this campaign. Bit by bit, the MBA landscape for women is changing. Opportunities begin even before the first day of class. At Stanford, women admitted to the program are treated to one-on-one admit-lunches with female alumni. Once an admit gets to campus, she finds MBA life is chock-full of student-run women and management programs, support groups, retreats, executive conferences, mentoring programs, and other dedicated resources for women only.

For many years now, most business programs have had an on-campus Partners Club for spouses and significant others—a benefit to both female and male students. Newcomers to the business-school scene include groups like The Parents Club and Biz Kids where students can find family-oriented classmates and activities. Columbia University's Mother's Network is an initiative that provides a formal support network for new, current, and future b-school moms. Perhaps the most symbolic gesture of the increasing influence of women in business school is Stanford's provision of a private nursing room for MBA moms and their babies in its main classroom facility.

Our Advice

Look at the number of female MBA students attending your targeted school and evaluate whether you would feel comfortable there. Research the number and range of student organizations for women and speak with female MBAs about school life.

Part 4

Paying for
Business School

HOW MUCH WILL IT COST?

To say that business school is an expensive endeavor is an understatement. In fact, to really gauge how expensive business school is, you need to look not only at your tuition costs and living expenses but also at the opportunity cost of foregoing a salary for the length of your program. Think about it: You'll have a net outflow of money.

But keep in mind that, unlike law school or medical school, business school is just a two-year program. Once those two years are over, you can expect to reap the rewards of your increased market value. Unfortunately, business school differs from law school and medical school in a much less desirable way as well—there are serious limitations on the amount of money available through scholarships and grants. Most business school students seeking financial aid will be limited to loans, and lots of them.

Try not to get too upset about borrowing the money for business school; think of it as an investment in yourself. But, like all investments, it should be carefully thought out. You need a law degree to practice law, and a medical degree to practice medicine, but a business degree is not required to work in business. That said, certain professional opportunities may be tougher to pursue without an MBA on your resume.

The Cost of B-School

So get out some paper, a pencil, and a calculator, and figure out how much it will cost you to attend school. What should you include? Your opportunity cost (lost income) and your cost of attending b-school (tuition and fees). One more thing: For a more accurate assessment of your investment, you should figure taxes into the equation by dividing tuition cost by 0.65 (this assumes taxes of about 35 percent). Why? Because in order to pay tuition of $35,000, you would have to make a pre-tax income of about $54,000. If you are lucky enough to have a source of aid that does not require repayment, such as a grant, scholarship, or wealthy benefactor, subtract that amount from the cost of attending b-school.

For example, if you currently make $60,000 and plan to attend a business school that costs $35,000 per year, your investment would be approximately $228,000.

$(60,000 \times 2) + [(35,000 \times 2)/0.65] = \$227,692.31$

Now say you receive an annual grant of $5,000. Your investment would now be approximately $212,300.

$(60,000 \times 2) + [(30,000 \times 2)/0.65] = \$212,307.69$

How Long Will it Take You to Recoup Your Investment?

To estimate this figure, you first need to estimate your expected salary increase post-MBA. Check out the average starting salaries for graduates of the programs you are looking at and adjust upward/downward based on the industry you plan to enter. Subtract your current salary from your expected salary and you'll get your expected salary increase.

Once you complete the step above, divide your investment (tuition and fees plus lost income) by your expected salary increase.

Going back to the example on the previous page, if your pre-MBA salary is $60,000 and you expect to make $80,000 when you graduate, your expected salary increase is $20,000 (a 33 percent increase). Let's assume you did not receive a grant and that your investment will be about $228,000.

228,000/20,000 = 11.4

It will take you approximately 11 years from the completion of the program to earn back your investment.

Keep in mind, these are approximations and don't take into account annual raises, inflation, and so on. But it is interesting, isn't it?

While business school is an expensive proposition, the financial rewards of having your MBA can be immensely lucrative as we discussed before. You won't be forced into bankruptcy if you finance it correctly. There are tried-and-true ways to reduce your initial costs, finance the costs on the horizon, and manage the debt you'll leave school with—all without selling your soul to the highest bidder.

Comparison Shopping

While cost shouldn't be the first thing on your mind when you are choosing a school, depending on your goals in getting an MBA, it might be fairly high on your list. Private schools aren't the only business schools. Many state schools have fantastic reputations. Regional schools may be more generous with financial aid. Tuition costs will vary widely between public and private schools, especially if you qualify as an in-state student. Keep in mind, however, that salary gains tend to be less dramatic at more regional schools.

HOW DO I FUND MY MBA?

The short answer: loans. Unless your company is underwriting your MBA, or you're able to pay your way in cash, you'll be financing your two years of business school through a portfolio of loans. Loans typically come in one of two forms: federal and private. Only a few of you will be lucky enough to qualify for, and get, grants and scholarships.

Anyone with reasonably good credit, regardless of financial need, can borrow money for business school. If you have financial need, you will probably be eligible for some type of financial aid if you meet the following basic qualifications:

- You are a United States citizen or a permanent U.S. resident.

- You are registered for Selective Service if you are a male, or you have documentation to prove that you are exempt.

- You are not in default on student loans already.

- You don't have a horrendous credit history.

International applicants to business school should take note: Most U.S. business schools will require all international students to pay in full or show proof that they will be able to pay the entire cost of the MBA prior to beginning the MBA program.

Federal Loans

The federal government funds federal loan programs. Federal loans are usually the "first resort" for borrowers because many are subsidized by the federal government and offer generous interest rates. Some do not begin charging you interest until after you complete your degree. Most federal loans are need-based, but some higher interest federal loans are available regardless of financial circumstances. Your business school's Financial Aid Office will determine what your need is, if any.

Private Loans

Private loans are funded by banks, foundations, corporations, and other associations. A number of private loans are targeted to aid particular segments of the population. You may have to do some investigating to identify private loans for which you might qualify. As always, contact your business school's Financial Aid Office to learn more.

Alternative Sources of Funding

We've already mentioned these in one form or other, but they are worthy of a bit more attention.

The first alternative is sponsorship by your employer or educational reimbursement. Not all companies treat this the same way, but if you are able to get your employer to kick in a portion of the cost, you are better off than before. But beware, this benefit also comes with strings attached. Most companies that pay for your MBA will require a commitment of several years upon graduation. If you renege, you could be liable for the full cost of your education. Others will require that you attend business school part-time, which you may or may not want to do. Often, part-time students are unable to participate in on-campus recruiting and networking efforts to the same extent as full-time students.

Educational reimbursement can come in another form as well. Some companies will provide sign-on bonuses to new MBAs that will cover the cost of a year's tuition. This is a fantastic development from the years of a robust economy, but it is by no means a guarantee during tougher times. Don't assume that you will have this option open to you just because it has been a common occurrence in past years.

The other "alternative" source of funding is a financial gift from family or another source. Either you have a resource that is willing and able to fund all or part of your MBA, or you don't. If you do, be thankful.

Applying for Financial Aid

In order to become eligible for financial aid of any kind, you will need to complete the Free Application for Federal Student Aid, also known as the FAFSA. You can complete and submit this form as early as October 1st of the year prior to when you plan to enter business school. You should aim to complete and submit this form as soon as possible after the first of the year to avoid potential delays. The FAFSA is available from a school's Financial Aid Office. You can also download the form directly from the website of the U.S. Department of Education at FAFSA.ed.gov. A third option is to use the FAFSA Express software (also downloadable from the website) and transmit the application electronically. Some states may have their own deadlines for the FAFSA, so make sure you go online and double-check!

It is important to note that the form requires information from your federal income tax returns. Plan to file your taxes early that year.

In addition to the FAFSA form, most schools will have their own financial aid form that you will be required to complete and submit. These often have their own deadlines, so it is wise to keep careful track of all the forms you must complete and all their respective deadlines. Yes, it's a lot of paperwork, but get over it. You'll be much happier when the tuition bill arrives.

GUIDE TO FEDERAL LOANS

Stafford Loans

Stafford loans require you to complete the FAFSA form in order to qualify. These are very desirable loans because they offer low-interest rates and are federally guaranteed. There is a limit to how much you can borrow in this program. Graduate and professional school students may borrow up to $20,500 per year from the unsubsidized Federal Stafford Loan. The cumulative loan limits are $138,500, including undergraduate debt (and no more than $65,500 in subsidized Federal Stafford loans). The aggregate amount includes any Stafford loans you may have from your undergraduate or other graduate studies.

Stafford loans come in two types: subsidized and unsubsidized. Subsidized loans are need-based as determined by your business school. They do not accrue interest while you are in school or in an authorized deferment period (such as the first six months after graduation). This cost is picked up by the government (hence the name "subsidized"). Repayment begins at that time. Unsubsidized loans are not need-based and do charge interest from the time of disbursement to the time of full repayment. You can pay the interest while you are in school or opt for capitalization, in which case the interest is added to the principal.

You will pay more in the long run if you choose capitalization. Interest payments may be tax deductible, so be sure to check. The standard repayment period for both is 10 years.

You will pay a small origination and guarantee fee for each loan, but this is not an out-of-pocket expense. It is simply deducted from the loan amount. Some schools will allow you to borrow the money under the Stafford program directly from them, while others will require you to borrow from a bank. For more information on federal loans, call the Federal Student Aid Information Center at 800-433-3243 or visit studentaid.ed.gov.

Direct PLUS Loans

Direct PLUS loans are made available through schools, though the U.S. Department of Education is actually the lender. You may borrow up to the full cost of attendance as determined by your school, less any other financial aid received. Like other federal loans, Direct PLUS loans have a small origination fee and a fixed interest rate, which is currently 6.41 percent. These funds are paid directly to your school to cover tuition, fees, and room and board. Any remaining balance will be refunded to you to cover other expenses associated with your education—when a school determines the cost of attendance, books, travel, and other expenses are typically included.

PRIVATE/COMMERCIAL LOANS

This is expensive territory. Not only are interest rates high, but terms are also quite different from those found with federal loans. You may not be able to defer payment of interest or principal until after graduation. Origination and guarantee fees are also much higher since these loans are unsecured. After all, banks and other specialized lenders exist to loan money to folks like you, and unlike the federal government, want to make money doing it. If you go this route, shop around diligently. Think of it as good practice for your post-MBA executive career.

SCHOLARSHIPS AND GRANTS

The usual sources for this type of funding are alumni groups and civic organizations. This funding is limited, and actual awards tend to be small. Even if you benefited from generous scholarship funding as an undergraduate, it would be unwise to assume you'll have the same experience as a graduate student. But do investigate. You never know what's out there. Schools will frequently list any scholarships and grants that are available at the back of their financial aid catalog.

FOR MORE INFORMATION

Find out more about your financing options for business school education at PrincetonReview.com.

Part 5

What B-School Is Really Like

Need help deciding which business school to attend?

Explore our featured business schools to find those that both match your interests and are looking for students like you at Princetonreview. com/business-school.

AN ACADEMIC PERSPECTIVE

The objective of all MBA programs is to prepare students for a professional career in business. One business school puts it this way:

Graduates should be all of the following:

- able to think and reason independently, creatively, and analytically

- skilled in the use of quantitative techniques

- literate in the use of software applications as management tools

- knowledgeable about the world's management issues and problems

- willing to work in and successfully cope with conditions of uncertainty, risk, and change

- astute decision makers

- ethically and socially responsible

- able to manage in an increasingly global environment

- proficient in utilizing technology as a mode of doing business

Sound like a tall order? Possibly. But this level of expectation is what business school is all about.

Nearly all MBA programs feature a core curriculum that focuses on the major disciplines of business: finance, management, accounting, marketing, manufacturing, decision sciences, economics, and organizational behavior. Unless your school allows you to place out of them, these courses are mandatory. Core courses provide broad functional knowledge in one discipline. To illustrate, a core marketing course covers pricing, segmentation, communications, product-line planning, and implementation. Electives provide a narrow focus that deepen the area of study. For example, a marketing elective might be entirely devoted to pricing.

Students sometimes question the need for such a comprehensive core program, but the functional areas of a real business are not parallel lines. All departments of a business affect each other every day. For example, an MBA in a manufacturing job might be asked by a financial controller why the company's product has become unprofitable to produce. Without an understanding of how product costs are accounted for, this MBA wouldn't know how to respond to a critical and legitimate request.

At most schools, the first term or year is devoted to a rigid core curriculum. Some schools allow first-years to take core courses side by side with electives. Still others have come up with an entirely new way of covering the basics, integrating the core courses into one cross-functional learning experience, which may also include sessions on topics such as globalization, ethics, and managing diversity. Half-year to year-long courses are team-taught by professors who will see you through all disciplines.

TEACHING METHODOLOGY

Business schools employ two basic teaching methods: case study and lecture. Usually, they employ some combination of the two. The most popular is the case study approach. Students are presented with either real or hypothetical business scenarios and are asked to analyze them. This method provides concrete situations (rather than abstractions) that require mastery of a wide range of skills. Students often find case studies exciting because they can engage in spirited discussions about possible solutions to given business problems and because they get an opportunity to apply newly acquired business knowledge.

On the other hand, lecturing is a teaching method in which—you guessed it—the professor speaks to the class and the class listens. The efficacy of the lecture method depends entirely on the professor. If the professor is compelling, you'll probably get a lot out of the class. If the professor is boring, you probably won't listen, which isn't necessarily a big deal since many professors make their class notes available online.

THE CLASSROOM EXPERIENCE

Professors teaching case methodology often begin class with a "cold call." A randomly selected student opens the class with an analysis of the case and makes recommendations for solutions. The cold call forces you to be prepared and to think on your feet.

No doubt, a cold call can be intimidating. But unlike law school, b-school professors don't use the Socratic Method to torture you, testing your thinking with a pounding cross-examination. They're training managers, not trial lawyers. At worst, particularly if you're unprepared, a professor will abruptly dismiss your contribution.

Alternatively, professors ask for a volunteer to open a case, particularly someone who has had real industry experience with the issues. After the opening, the discussion is broadened to include the whole class. Everyone tries to get in a good comment, particularly if class participation counts heavily toward the grade. "Chip shots"—unenlightened, just-say-anything-to-get-credit comments—are common. So are "air hogs," students who go on and on because they like nothing more than to hear themselves pontificate.

Depending on the school, class discussions can degenerate into wars of ego rather than ideas. But for the most part, debates are kept constructive and civilized. Students are competitive, but not offensively so, and learn to make their points succinctly and persuasively.

LIFE OUTSIDE OF CLASS

Business school is more than academics and a big-bucks job. A spirited community provides ample opportunity for social interaction, extracurricular activity, and career development.

Much of campus life revolves around student-run clubs. There are groups for just about every career interest and social need—from MBAs for a Greener America to the Small Business Club. There's even a group for significant others on most campuses. The clubs are a great way to meet classmates with similar interests and to get in on the social scene. They might have a reputation for throwing the best black-tie balls, pizza-and-keg events, and professional mixers. During orientation week, these clubs aggressively market themselves to first-years.

Various socially responsible projects are also popular on campus. An emphasis on volunteer work is part of the overall trend toward good citizenship. Perhaps to counter the greed of the 1980s, "giving back" is the b-school style of the moment. There is usually a wide range of options—from tutoring in an inner-city school to working in a soup kitchen to renovating public buildings.

Still another way to get involved is to work on a school committee. Here you might serve on a task force designed to improve student quality of life, or you might work in the admissions office and interview prospective students.

For those with more creative urges there are always the old standbys: extracurriculars such as the school paper, yearbook, or school play. At some schools, the latter is a dramatization of "b-school follies" and is a highlight of the year. Like the student clubs, these are a great way to get to know your fellow students.

Finally, you can play on intramural sports teams or attend the numerous informal get-togethers, dinner parties, and group trips. There are also plenty of regularly scheduled pub nights, just in case you thought your beer-guzzling days were over.

Most former MBA students say that going to b-school was the best decision they ever made. That's primarily because of non-academic experiences. Make the most of your classes, but take the time to get involved and enjoy yourself.

Part 6

The Importance of the Essay

An essay is a school's Rorschach test when considering your candidacy. Whether you're applying to business school, law school, or medical school, what you write says more about you than your GPA or test score.

Unlike the law or med school admissions processes, b-school admissions are unique in their request for many essays and their heavy weighting of those essays. Although grades and standardized tests are considered key benchmarks for admission, they function more as a threshold. Your stories are what close the deal one way or the other.

THE REAL YOU, REVEALED AND DISSECTED

In b-school admissions, the essays tie all the pieces of your application together. They weave a narrative of who you are and why you belong in a particular program. They provide a framework for your personal and professional activities, highlighting your choices and attitudes as well as your analytical and communication skills. They also reveal your character and integrity. That's because those onerous essay questions are designed to elicit thumbnail profiles of the real you, and together they are arguably the most heavily weighted criterion in the admissions process. For these reasons, the essays are invaluable screening tools.

At the top business schools, evaluating a candidate's character, genuine accomplishments, and potential has always been pivotal. That's because b-schools operate like micro-communities, and there is an expectation that you will work well and make connections within that community. Furthermore, the curriculum is designed so that you learn from your classmates. Therefore, each student's perspective, experience, and behavior is vital. B-school learning is also team-oriented, so a cooperative spirit (or lack thereof) says a lot about whether you're a strong fit for a particular program.

But perhaps most important, b-schools are a primary source of future business leaders. So attributes like honesty (yes, that includes what you put on your resume), leadership, and ethics matter. In the wake of Enron, WorldCom, Tyco, Lehman Brothers, and other corporate scandals, they matter more than ever. You can almost hear the collective b-school groan when the latest Wall Street violator turns out to be another MBA.

Figuring out whether you'll one day prove to be a source of pride or an embarrassment to your alma mater and the business community is the gray zone in admissions. So how does a b-school attempt to get at your true character and determine your potential as a business leader?

While it may be almost impossible to make such a prediction, the essays are good indicators of character strengths and flaws. So as you compose your stories, know that you're being looked at through many different lenses. B-schools are uniquely interested in characteristics beyond test scores. High on their list is emotional maturity, self-awareness, leadership ability, creativity, teamwork potential, and morality. Even the venerable Harvard Business School has a stated mission to do no less than "educate leaders who make a difference in the world." To screen for all these qualities, the schools rely on the essays. And herein lies the problem.

An Essay Can Be an Imperfect Screener

It may be difficult for an engineer who will one day launch an industry-transforming product to craft a compelling self-narrative. How many great business leaders might be disqualified from getting their MBA at a top school because their writing or storytelling skills are poor, or because at this young age they don't know how to show or articulate self-awareness in their essays?

In this way, the essays on b-school applications can be overreaching. But they're imperfect in other areas as well. When you consider the questions posed by the most selective programs, you realize that it's genuine frontline caretakers, like social and health care workers, who may best embody the value systems b-schools are looking for. It's by virtue of their chosen profession that caretakers demonstrate such value systems. For aspiring MBAs—also by virtue of their chosen profession—such redeeming qualities are often less evident.

Caught Between a Rock and a Hard Place

Ironically, success and financial reward are part of the b-school hype. Indeed, many schools are judged each year on their career placement statistics (translation: the number of grads who secure high-paying positions, and how quickly they do so), so they work hard to ensure that their statistics are competitive. But an applicant who articulates too much interest in the very pot of gold the MBA dangles may be penalized for lacking the softer skills b-schools desire these days.

The truth is that the negative aspect of the MBA stereotype might at times be true; many pre-MBAs are ambitiously preoccupied with success and financial reward. But why should that be considered unattractive? As you can see, these essay questions don't necessarily play to a would-be MBA's strengths. The essay writers of today need an advocate.

So how does one navigate between posturing as a sincere do-gooder and an ambitious future financial officer?

It's a difficult challenge. The majority of b-school applicants are deeper than their stereotypes would suggest. As we said before, they are reflective, accountable, and morally sound. Finessing all of those qualities in a series of short stories with strict word limits is no easy task.

How to Craft Your Essays

HIDDEN AGENDAS

Now that you know that the essays are used to check applicants for a range of qualities, it makes sense that each question on the application has a reason for being there. Even seemingly straightforward essay questions, such as those in the vein of, "Why do you want the MBA? Why do you want the degree at this juncture in your life? And why here?" have an agenda.

As essay questions go, these are fairly clear-cut. Although you'd probably rather do anything (including clean the bathroom) than sit down to suss out an honest and intelligible response, the task seems doable. So why do so many applicants fail to answer the question successfully? Because even a straightforward question needs to be thought through.

Here's the inside line: Schools consider this essay the ballast to your candidacy. They want to see well-crafted goals for your education and career outlined here. When I explain this to applicants, it surprises them. After all, they argue, b-school is a journey, and part of the journey is not knowing what lies ahead. Would-be MBAs treat this essay as an opportunity to share their excitement about the discovery. But if you're not sure where you're headed or why, it's nearly impossible to answer such questions convincingly.

It is critical that you present well-defined goals and expectations in your essays. At the best schools, admissions committees want you to lay down a compelling rationale for why you need the MBA and why their program specifically meets your needs. If you can't do that, then why should they award you one of their coveted spots? They want students who will value the resources at their program, not those in need of a two-year pit stop.

Half the battle in writing a winning essay is in knowing what the essay question is attempting to draw out, and we aim to offer some guidance in that respect. We don't want you to spend hours working on one question and completely miss the mark. Later on, we'll identify and translate commonly asked essay questions. But let there be no mistake about it, equally important to the content, or the "what" of the essay, is the "how."

THE "HOW" OF AN ESSAY IS IMPORTANT

Think of your essay-writing this way: All written communication lives or dies on the "how" in its message. The way you present yourself in your essays and frame your subject is crucial to the impression you create. Ever receive an apology letter that felt warm and real (as opposed to perfunctory)? Did it have a positive impact on how you felt about the person after you read it? If it did, you saw an example of a good use of "how."

Still not sure what the "how" is? It is

- the mood and tone in your writing

- your writing style and skill and the clarity of your thinking

- your ability to follow directions

- the judgment you use in selecting your subject matter

- the impact you leave on the reader

Tone and mood can communicate that you are candid, warm, friendly, and a true leader by example. It can also betray negativity, inappropriateness, or a lack of maturity.

There are many variables to the "how" of anyone's writing. There is no one formula we can hand off to you. What might work for one essay or one applicant won't necessarily work for another. The trick is to be self-aware.

WHAT YOUR ESSAYS SHOULD SAY ABOUT YOU

Applicants tend to place great emphasis on their accomplishments and strengths. But as we said before, there is more to writing an essay than this. You'll need to weave evidence of these favorable qualities into your essay so you can appear in the best possible light without boasting, lying, or being mushy or corny. In other words, the trick is to navigate between maintaining a modest position and showcasing your accomplishments.

As you compose your essays, remember to remain aware of what the details of your stories actually reveal about you.

Your essays should suggest that you are

- a leader
- humble
- mature
- goal-oriented
- creative
- dignified
- intelligent
- hard-working
- concerned for others
- team-oriented

- positive, with a can-do attitude
- introspective
- moral and ethical
- accountable
- able to learn from failure
- wise
- self-aware
- unique
- of sound mind and perspective

Your essays should avoid communicating that you are

- arrogant
- vain
- entitled
- egotistical
- competitive
- a perfectionist
- blindly ambitious
- angry or quick to blame
- immature

- overly bookish
- mediocre
- prejudiced regarding race and/or gender
- a poor or boring writer
- one who exercises poor judgment
- one who sets unrealistic goals

Take the favorable qualities from the first list that best describe you, and jot those down. It's time for you to find a vehicle through which to convey your finest features.

Consider what compelling stories you have to tell and sketch them out. Reflect on what each story says about you and what kind of picture each paints. Then when you sit down with your application, you'll start to draw connections between your stories and the questions that are asked of you.

Common Essay Questions (and What They're Really Asking)

CREATING PERFECTION TAKES TIME

"Essays are the love letter of why a student wants to attend business school."

—Julia Min, Assistant Dean of Career Management Group and Corporate Engagement at Haas School of Business, UC Berkeley

No one ever said it was going to be easy. Depending on where you're applying and how prolific a writer you are, a b-school application will take anywhere from fifty to one hundred hours to complete. Sound excessive? Go ahead and try it. You'll probably scrap and rewrite an essay many times over. It takes time for thoughts to gestate. Indeed, it might feel like a fine wine ages faster than you write an essay.

You'll need to look at every essay question on each of your applications to determine how to optimally allocate your stories and anecdotes. One story might work well for either a leadership essay or an essay about failure. But you might have several good stories for leadership, and none for failure. Mapping out how you're going to allocate your anecdotes and stories is critical to your overall strategy.

Take a look at a recent year's essay questions from Harvard and Wharton below to get an idea of what you're up against. Keep in mind that not all schools will require you to write such exhaustive essays. The more selective a school is, the more rigid and demanding its standard for admission will be. That said, we're going to focus on the most brutal applications. They are the gold standard for essays, and their questions demand the greatest effort.

Harvard Business School

1. Discuss an experience that has had an impact on your development as a leader. (400-word limit)

2. What are your three most substantial accomplishments, and why do you view them as such? (600-word limit)

3. Recognizing that successful leaders are able to learn from failure, discuss a situation in which you failed and what you learned. (400-word limit)

4. Discuss an ethical dilemma that you experienced firsthand. How did you manage and resolve the situation? (400-word limit)

5. Provide a candid assessment of your strengths and weaknesses. (400-word limit)

6. What are your career aspirations, and how can Harvard Business School help you to reach them? (400-word limit)

7. (Optional) Is there any other information that you believe would be helpful to the Board in understanding you better and in considering your application? Please be concise.

The Wharton School, University of Pennsylvania

1. Describe how your experiences, both professional and personal, have led to your decision to pursue an MBA at the Wharton School this year. How does this decision relate to your career goals for the future? (1,000 words)

2. Describe a situation where leadership and teamwork were critical to the outcome of a project in which you were directly involved. What did you learn from the experience and how have you applied what you learned to other situations? (1,000 words)

3. Describe a personal achievement that has had a significant impact on your life. Give specific details. What did you learn from this experience? How did it help shape your understanding of yourself and the world around you? (500 words)

4. Please tell us something else about yourself that you feel will help the Admissions Committee know you better. (500 words)

READING BETWEEN THE LINES

Being a great storyteller and gifted writer can be a major advantage to the prospective b-school student. But be forewarned: A wonderful answer to a question not asked will not help you here. We can't stress enough that you must answer the question.

Each school has its own set of questions. Although posed differently, all search for the same insights. Here's a list of commonly asked questions and what's behind them.

Theme 1: Career Goals and the MBA

Describe your specific career aspirations. How will your goals be furthered by an MBA degree and by our MBA program in particular?

How do you feel the "X" school MBA degree can help you attain your specific career and personal goals for the five years after you graduate?

Discuss your career progression to date. What factors have influenced your decision to seek a general management education? Based on what you know about yourself at this time, how do you envision your career progressing after receiving the MBA degree? Please state your professional goals, and describe your plan to achieve them.

Translation: What do I want to be when I grow up, and how will the MBA get me there?

This may be the most important essay question. It lays out the reasons why you should be given one of the cherished spots in the program. Even if your post-MBA future is tough to envision, this question must be answered.

A good way to frame this essay is to discuss how the MBA makes sense in light of your background, skills, and achievements to date. Why do you need this degree? Why now? One common reason is being stymied in your work by a lack of skills that can be gained in their program. Or you may want to use the MBA as a bridge to the next step. For example, an actor who wants an MBA to prepare for a career in theater management. The more specific, the better.

It may be easier to provide specifics by breaking your plans into short-term and long-term objectives.

Don't be afraid to present modest goals. If you're in accounting and want to stay there, say so. Deepening your expertise and broadening your perspective are solid reasons for pursuing this degree. On the other hand, feel free to indicate that you'll use the MBA to change careers; 70 percent of all students at b-school are there to do just that.

If you aspire to lofty goals, like becoming a CEO or starting your own company, be especially careful that you detail a sensible, pragmatic plan. You need to show you're realistic. No one zooms to the top. Break your progress into steps.

Finally, this essay question asks how a particular program supports your goals. Admissions committees want to know why you've selected their school. That means you not only have to know, but also show, what's special about their program and how that relates specifically to your career aspirations. Hint: Many admissions officers say they can tell how much someone wants to go to their school by how well their essays are tailored to the offerings in their program.

Theme 2: Extracurriculars and Social Interaction—Our Nonwork Side

What do you do for fun?

What are your principal interests outside of your job or school?

What leisure and/or community activities do you particularly enjoy? Please describe their importance in your life.

Translation: Would we like to have you over for dinner? Do you know how to make friends? What are your special talents—the b-school Follies needs help. Are you well-balanced, or are you going to freak out when you get here?

B-school is not just about business, case studies, and careers. The best programs buzz with the energy of a student body that is talented and creative and that has personality. You won't be spending all your time in the library.

Are you interesting? Would you contribute to the school's vitality? Are you the kind of person other MBAs would be happy to meet? Describe activities you're involved in that might add something to the b-school community.

Are you sociable? B-school is a very social experience. Much of the work is done in groups. Weekends are full of social gatherings. Will you participate?

Initiate? Get along with others? Communicate that people, not just your job, are an important part of your life.

Can you perform at a high level without being a nerd?

B-school can be tough. It's important to know when to walk away and find some fun. Do you know how to play as hard as you work?

How well-rounded are you? Business leaders have wide-angle perspectives; they take in the whole picture. How deep or broad are your interests? A warning: Don't just list what you've done. Explain how what you've done has made you unique.

Theme 3: Whom You Most Admire

If you were able to choose one person from the business world, past or present, to be your personal professor throughout the MBA program, who would this person be and why?

Describe the characteristics of an exceptional manager, using an example of someone whom you have observed or with whom you have worked. Illustrate how his or her management style has influenced you.

Translation: What are your values? What character traits do you admire?

This is the curveball question. The committee isn't looking to evaluate your judgment in selecting some famous, powerful person in your firm or in the world. What they're really after, which you reveal in your selection of the person, are the qualities, attributes, and strengths you value in others, as well as in yourself. Some important qualities to address: drive, discipline, vision, ethics, and leadership. As always, provide specific examples. And avoid choosing anyone too obvious.

Since the person you select is not as important as what you say about him or her, your choices can be more humble. You might write about a current boss, business associate, or friend. Bad choices are your mother or father.

If you like, it's perfectly fine to go for a famous figure. Indeed, there may be about whose career and style you're passionate. Make sure your essay explains why you find this person so compelling.

Theme 4: Teamwork—How Do You Work with Others in a Group Setting?

At X School, a team, which consists of approximately five first-year students, is often assigned group projects and class presentations. Imagine that, one year from now, your team has a marketing class assignment due at 9:00 A.M. on Monday morning. It is now 10:00 P.M. on Sunday night—time is short, tension builds, and your team has reached an impasse. What role would you take in such a situation? How would you enable the team to meet your deadline? (Note: The specific nature of the assignment is not as important here as the team dynamic.) Feel free to draw on previous experiences, if applicable, in order to illustrate your approach.

Translation: We need cooperative, one-for-all-and-all-for-one students here. Are you cut out to be one, or are you a take-over type who has all the answers? Are you likely to help everyone get along and arrive at solutions? (We like those kinds of students.) Can you lead others to order and synergy? (We especially like leaders.) Or do you retreat or become a follower?

This, too, is a curveball question. But you can't afford to get it wrong. After the career goals question, it probably ranks as the most critical essay you write. Here the committee isn't looking to see how you save the team (so put yourself on ego alert as you sit down to write this one); they want to see how you can create an environment in which everyone contributes so that the sum is greater than its parts. Bottom line—the admissions committee is looking to see whether you have "emotional intelligence." Understand that schools today believe that emotional intelligence, the ability to navigate emotion-laden situations, is as important as strategic and analytical skills. This question is intended to illustrate this particular type of ability.

Expect to shift gears with this essay. Almost the entire application process thus far has asked you to showcase "me-me-me." Now the focus of your story needs to be on the "we" and how you made the "we" happen.

As you write your essay, consider that when you get to school, some team members will be from different countries where cultural attitudes play into team dynamics. Your sensitivity to these cultural differences, as well as to personality types, will go a long way toward demonstrating your emotional intelligence. For example, a team member hailing from a certain culture may withhold an opinion in an attempt to foster consensus. How can you help this person make a contribution? Likewise, consider differences among team members in terms of their academic and professional strengths. If the assignment is heavy on numbers, finance students may dominate teammates from softer sciences. How can you ensure that everyone feels valued? Teams are inspired to succeed when everyone is motivated and taking ownership within a context of respect.

Remember, the team in this particular essay is at an impasse, as most teams are at some point in time. Write about how you "unjammed" the jam. Ideas: A change of scene, food, twenty push-ups, a quick round-the-room confessional about why you came to b-school. Introducing some process is also useful; ground rules such as voting, speaking times, a division of labor, and a time line all create a method from the madness. Perhaps you encourage members to adopt roles—business or otherwise. Hint: The leader or CEO in this case might be your most soft-spoken team member. Whatever you do in this essay, be careful not to present yourself as the one who single-handedly gets the team dynamic going.

Theme 5: Diversity and What Makes You Unique

Our business school is a diverse environment. How will your experiences contribute to this?

During your years of study in the X program, you will be part of a diverse multicultural, multiethnic community within both the Business School and the larger university. What rewards and challenges do you anticipate in this environment, and how do you expect this experience to prepare you for a culturally diverse business world?

Translation: What about you is different in terms of your background, your experience, or your cultural or geographic heritage? Can we count on your unique voice and perspective in our wide-ranging classroom discussions? How will you support the diverse cultural climate we are fostering here?

This essay gets at two concerns for the admissions committee: How will you enrich the student body at this school? And what is your attitude toward others' diverse backgrounds? Today's business leaders must be able to make decisions in situations that cut across geographic and cultural boundaries. If your essay reveals that you have dinosaur-era, only-white-males-rule thinking, you're going to close the door on your candidacy.

So what if you are a white male? Or you have no immediate point of distinction? Maybe a grandparent or relative is an immigrant to this country and you can discuss the impact of his or her values on your life. Perhaps you are the first individual in your family to attend college or to attend graduate school. What does that mean to you? Perhaps you are involved in a meaningful or unusual extracurricular activity. How has this changed your perspective? Perhaps you did a business deal with a foreign country. What did you observe about that culture, and how did it affect your decisions?

Whatever you write about need not be dramatic—maybe you take art classes, coach a little league team, or race a motorcycle. Sound goofy? It's all in the framing. Racing a motorcycle might be about the physical and mental stamina, the ability to take risks, the commitment to learning something new.

This question can be relatively easy to answer if, of course, you have diversity or some unique element in your background. If you don't have something obvious, then you're going to have to dig a bit and find something you can amplify to suggest you bring a unique voice to the school.

Theme 6: Your Greatest Personal Achievement/Accomplishment

Describe a personal achievement that has had a significant impact on your life. In addition to recounting this achievement, please analyze how the event has changed your understanding of yourself, and how you perceive the world around you.

In reviewing the last five years, describe one or two accomplishments in which you demonstrated leadership.

Translation: Do you know what an achievement is? Have you done anything remarkable? What made it remarkable to you? Bonus points if you showed leadership or inspired others in some way.

This is one of those maddening essay questions because on the one hand, b-schools seek out applicants whose average age is twenty-seven (a relatively young age to have achieved much of anything). On the other hand, the schools want to know what miracles you've performed. Don't pull your hair out yet. There is a way out. Like all the others, this essay is just one more prove-to-us-you-have-some-character hoop you'll have to jump through. It's less about the achievement and more about who you are and how you see yourself.

Again, this question can be easy to answer if you have some clear accomplishment or event in your background. But if you're like the rest of us—you guessed it—you'll have to rely on framing.

Let's cover bad essay topics for achievements. Getting straight A's in college is not an achievement because everyone else at b-school has probably done the same. Surviving a divorce or breakup is a bad accomplishment topic. Personal stories are acceptable, but one taboo area is romance and marriage. If this is all you can come up with, you're going to look like you're as deep as a doughnut.

The accomplishment you choose might show some of the following qualities: character, sacrifice, humility, dedication, high personal stakes, perseverance over obstacles, insight, and learning. You need not have published a business article or won an award to answer this question. This essay is not about excellence of outcome, but what it took for you to reach some personal worthy objective. Maybe you didn't lead a sports team to a victory. The victory may be just that you made it onto the team.

Theme 7: Failure/What Mistakes Have You Made?

Discuss a non-academic personal failure. In what way were you disappointed in yourself? What did you learn from the experience?

Translation: Can you admit to a genuine failure? Do you have enough self-awareness to know what kind of failure is real? Can you learn from your mistakes? Do they lead to greater maturity and self-awareness? Do you take responsibility when the fault is yours?

Many applicants make the mistake of answering this question with a failure that is really a positive, such as "I'm a perfectionist and so therefore I was too demanding on a friend when she was in a crisis." Or they never really answer the question, fearful that any admission of failure will throw their whole candidacy into jeopardy. The truth is, if you don't answer this question with a genuine failure or mistake, one that the committee will recognize as authentic, you may have jinxed your application.

In this essay, you want to write about a failure that had some high stakes for you. Demonstrate what you learned from your mistake and how it helped you mature. What's the relevance to b-school here? Your ability to be honest, show accountability, and face your failures head-on reflects what kinds of decisions and judgments you will make as a business professional.

Can't think of a time you failed? Discuss the essay question with a friend or family member. An outsider's perspective may jog your memory. Remember, if your whole application has been about work, work, work, this is a great place to convince the committee you're a real person.

Theme 8: Ethics

Describe an ethical issue you have faced in your professional life and how you dealt with it. What was the outcome?

Translation: Do you even know what an ethical dilemma looks like? Are you tomorrow's corporate miscreant? What kinds of decisions and judgments might you make in your future practices as a business leader?

The last few years have brought attention to the ethical issues of the business world and the failure of corporate self-governance. In the aftermath of many high-profile scandals, b-schools don't want to turn out graduates who are fast into their suspenders, fast into a deal, and fast to swindle their clients and shareholders.

The above question tests your judgment, integrity, and perspective. It's most important to present a legitimate ethical dilemma here, one that has consequences. Applicants often write about the dilemma of not obeying a supervisor's orders because they wanted to do things their way, a known better way. But this is not an ethics problem (unless the order was improper or illegal); it's a management problem. Likewise, handing in a report to your boss that you know is full of errors is also not an ethical problem; it's a trivial, single-impact, easy-to-fix problem.

If you were thinking of telling a story like one of those mentioned above, it may be because you wanted to play it safe. This is one of those uncomfortable, hot-seat essays after all. But playing it safe here would only make you appear clueless or morally bereft.

This essay requires you to roll up your ethical shirtsleeves and get down in the dirt. True ethical issues are neither clean nor pretty. Don't shrink away from a discussion of failure here or present an overly optimistic, no-loose-ends solution.

It's key that you write about an ethical dilemma in which there was no easy course—one that entailed costs either way. For example, let's say you sold a product to a client and later discovered the product was faulty; your employer wanted you to keep mum. You'd built your sales relationships on trust and personal attention, so you wanted to be forthcoming. What did you do?

This essay must show that you can work through a complex ethical impasse, and it must highlight your sense of honor and conduct. This essay screams relevance. Make sure you shout back that you know right from wrong.

GMAT Insider comprises excerpts from the following titles:

Do I Need an MBA? Figuring Out if Business School Really Fits Your Future Needs, by Kal Chany and the Staff of The Princeton Review (Random House/Princeton Review Books)

The Best 296 Business Schools, 2015 Edition, by the Staff of The Princeton Review (Random House/Princeton Review Books)

Business School Essays That Made a Difference, 5th Edition, by Nedda Gilbert and the Staff of The Princeton Review (Random House/Princeton Review Books)

NOTES

NOTES

NOTES

NOTES

NOTES

NOTES

NOTES

NOTES

NOTES

NOTES